Madam Secretary

MADELEINE ALBRIGHT

Madam Secretary

WITH BILL WOODWARD

MIRAMAX BOOKS

A LEATHER-BOUND, SIGNED EDITION OF THIS BOOK HAS BEEN PUBLISHED BY THE EASTON PRESS.

FOR INFORMATION ADDRESS:

Hyperion, 77 West 66th Street
New York, New York 10023-6298

ISBN 0-7868-6843-0

10 9 8 7 6 5 4 3 2 1

TO MY FAMILY

PAST AND PRESENT

WHOM I HONOR AND LOVE

Contents

CONTENTS

PART TWO

FOURTEEN SUITS AND A SKIRT

PART THREE

MADAM SECRETARY

CONTENTS

PART FOUR

WAGING WAR, PURSUING PEACE

Preface

WE ALL HAVE OUR STORIES. This is mine. It reflects the turbulence of the past century, the expanding and changing roles of women, and the clash between those around the world with faith in freedom and those who place power above human values.

Before sitting down to write, I read memoirs by other former Secretaries of State. The books were excellent but the approach their authors took did not seem right for me. I wanted to combine the personal with policy and describe not just what happened but also why and how events were influenced by human relationships. I also wanted to be sure the main character didn't bore people to death.

Many lives progress in a more or less predictable path, like water through a well-marked channel. My journey has been different. The idea that a daughter of Czechoslovakia, born shortly before the outbreak of global war, would one day become America's first woman Secretary of State once could not have been imagined. It was almost as inconceivable that someone who had not held a government job until she was thirty-nine years old and the mother of three would become the highest-ranking woman in American history. Well into adulthood, I was never supposed to be what I became.

But if I had a late start, I also hurried to catch up. I began as a public-spirited volunteer, raising money for political candidates and various good causes, meeting new people, and steadily expanding my personal horizons while also obtaining a Ph.D. With my family's support, I crossed the threshold into professional life, working in the Senate and White House, advising Democratic candidates for national office, heading a think tank, and teaching international relations. Year by year, I acquired essential knowledge, experience, and skills. Relatively few people had heard of me when President Clinton asked if I would serve as U.S. ambassador to the United Nations in 1992. By Washington standards I had had a stealth career, but I was ready. As Senator Barbara Mikulski, a trailblazer herself, said about the two of us, "We were twenty-five-year overnight successes."

Once in government, I had to deal with the problem of operating in a predominantly man's world. The challenge was not new to me, but the level was higher and the pressures more intense. I am often asked whether I was condescended to by men as I traveled around the world to Arab countries and other places with highly traditional cultures. I replied, "No, because when I arrived somewhere, it was in a large plane with 'United States of America' emblazoned on the side." Foreign officials respected that. I had more problems with some of the men in my own government.

Having completed college at the end of the 1950s, I was part of a generation of women who were still uncertain about whether they could be good wives and mothers and also achieve success in the workplace. From my graduation day until the graduation of my last child, I had to deal with the age-old problem of balancing the demands of family with academic and professional interests. As I began to climb the ladder, I had to cope with the different vocabularies used to describe similar qualities in men (confident, take-charge, committed) and women (bossy, aggressive, emotional). It took years, but over time I developed enough faith in my judgment to do my job in my own way and style, worrying at least a little less about what others thought.

I do think I was lucky to serve a President, Bill Clinton, who saw clearly America's role as a unifying force in a world moving at warp speed from one era to another. The President believed, as did I, that our country's purpose was not just to bear witness to history but rather to shape it in ways that served our interests and ideals. He also gave me the opportunity that no other individual, male or female, has had to serve full terms both as U.S. ambassador to the United Nations and as U.S. Secretary of State. These were the most exciting jobs, and I had the chance to perform them at a time when the UN was newly empowered and, in fact, virtually every foreign policy institution, relationship, assumption, and doctrine was being reevaluated in light of the fall of the Berlin Wall.

I loved being Secretary of State and could have written happily about everything that took place during my years of service. While in office, I was regularly criticized after a speech or congressional testimony for not discussing this or that issue or part of the globe. The problem is that there is not enough space—whether in a speech or in a book—to do justice to everything. I found in writing this memoir that literally hundreds of pages had to be chopped to keep the full text at a manageable size. So in covering my years in government, I have had to be extremely selective.

I regret what has been left out and mean no disrespect to the people and nations whose names do not appear within these pages. I will continue to write, telling other parts of the story along the way.

This volume, then, is a personal account, not a history of the Clinton administration foreign policy or even a remotely comprehensive chronicle of world affairs at the end of the last century. It does, however, deal with the highlights, some involving issues that have continued to dominate the headlines since I left office, including terrorism, Iraq, the Middle East, and North Korea. The danger in writing such a book is that the world continues to change while the text has to be copy edited, printed, bound, and distributed—a process requiring months. The text of this volume was completed during the tumultuous spring of 2003. What has happened since is known to you—the reader—but not to me as I write. You have that advantage, and it will, I am sure, influence your reading of some of the key chapters that follow.

Lives are necessarily untidy and uneven, but there is a certain symmetry to the tale of my own. While for some people diplomacy and foreign policy are acquired interests, I had them in my blood. My father had been a diplomat and also a professor, and from childhood I was his most avid student.

Historical forces similar to those that shaped my personal destiny resurfaced during my years as a decision maker in government. When I was still a little girl, my family was driven from its home twice, first by Fascists, then by Communists. While in office I was able to fight against ethnic cleansing in Yugoslavia, a country where I had lived as a child. For most of my life Communism divided Europe. I spent my academic life studying its effects. Once in office I was able to help the newly democratic nations of Central and East Europe, including the land of my birth, Czechoslovakia, become full partners of the free world.

I could apply the lessons of my own experience to support the aspirations of women at work, at school, and in the home. I also strove to reform and revitalize the United Nations, an institution my father had served at a pivotal moment in our lives.

Most of all, having been witness at a very young age to what happens when America plays only a passive role in world affairs, I used my position to work closely with allies and friends on every continent to build a united front in support of liberty and in opposition to the forces of intolerance, unbridled ambition, and hate.

I have read many autobiographies and found the best to be the most honest. So, honest I have tried to be, even when it has been hard. My most joyful experience was marriage and raising a family. My most painful was divorce and finding a way to move on and up. The most riveting was learning about my Jewish heritage. The saddest was discovering that three of my grandparents had died in concentration camps. An important part of this book deals with the shock of that discovery and the complexity of coping with revelations so deeply personal at the very moment I was starting out as Secretary of State.

As I move in these pages from private to public life, the phases may seem disconnected, but they are not. Each phase prepared me in some way for the next and influenced what I became. In talking to young women, I have often said that women's lives come in segments, dictated in part by biology. I have also said that this is actually an advantage because it allows women to explore different paths. It is important, however, to have some guiding star. For me that star has always been faith in the democratic promise that each person should be able to go as far as her or his talents will allow.

This is a faith I derived from my parents and developed throughout the varied experiences of my life: it is the same faith that inspires the heroes I have met, the causes I have supported, and the millions of people I have seen, directly or indirectly, struggling each day to open the door of opportunity to others. Faith in the democratic promise reflects America at its best and the world at its most hopeful. I will always be grateful for the chance I had to serve that promise and to pay back, as best I could, the gift of freedom given to me and to my family by the United States.

PART ONE

From Madlenka to Madeleine Albright

ONE

Heroes and Villains

I DIDN'T WANT IT TO END.

Hoping to freeze time, I thought back to the phone ringing one December morning and the words, "I want you to be my Secretary of State," and to the swearing-in ceremony where my eagle pin came unstuck. I thought of little girls seeking autographs on a triumphant train trip from Washington to the United Nations in New York; of Václav Havel's face, warm and wise, as he placed a red sash on my shoulder and a kiss on my cheek; and of names enshrined on the wall of a synagogue in Prague. I thought of buildings in Kenya and Tanzania reduced to rubble; of coffins draped with the American flag; and of President Clinton in a rumpled shirt, with glasses perched on his nose, pleading the cause of Middle East peace.

I thought of the countless meetings, some in grand palaces in the middle of the night, others in remote villages where nothing grew except the appetites of young children yet people still laughed and lived in hope. I thought of the cheering of crowds, joyous in Kosovo and Central Europe but robotic in North Korea, and of women and girls sharing their fears in a refugee camp a few miles from the Afghanistan border.

The sound of tape being pulled away from giant rolls broke my reverie. We had been so busy, we hadn't started packing until well after dark. Now boxes and bubble wrap were everywhere, sitting amid stacks of books, discarded bags of pretzels, and mementos gathered during a million miles of travel and almost three thousand days of government service. Staff members were scurrying about, preoccupied with sorting, wrapping, sealing, and labeling. Silently I withdrew into the small inner office of the secretary of state, *my* office for a few hours more, and went instinctively to the window.

It was the view I would miss almost as much as anything else. Circles of light on the National Mall surrounded the Lincoln Memorial and Washington Monument. Between them, obscured by the January night, were the haunting bronze figures commemorating America's engagement in the Korean War, and the silent yet eloquent black marble of the Vietnam wall. Across the Tidal Basin I saw the dome marking our nation's memorial to Thomas Jefferson, America's first Secretary of State, and across the river the more distant glow of the eternal flame at John Kennedy's grave in Arlington National Cemetery. I felt intense gratitude for each day I had been given to build on the tradition of honor and sacrifice celebrated in front of me.

I may not have wished it to end, but the clock was ticking and there was much to do. I went to my desk for the last time, focusing on a piece of stationery I had centered there. "Dear Colin," I wrote. "We have been working hard and hope when you arrive in the office it is clean. It will, however, still be filled with the spirit of our predecessors, all of whom felt representing the United States to be the greatest honor. So I turn over to you the best job in the world. Good luck and best wishes. Madeleine."

MADELEINE WASN'T MY ORIGINAL NAME. I was born in Prague on May 15, 1937, in a hospital in the city's Smíchov district. In Czech, *smíchov* means laughter but there was little of that in Czechoslovakia during the year of my birth. It was an ominous time. I was christened Marie Jana, the first child of Josef and Anna Körbel, but I wasn't called that. My grandmother nicknamed me Madla after a character in a popular show, *Madla in the Brick Factory*. My mother, with her special way of pronouncing things, modified it to Madlen. Most of the time I was called Madlenka. It took me years to figure out what my actual name was. Not until I was ten, and learning French, did I find the version that pleased me: Madeleine. However, despite all the language and country changes of my youth, I never altered my original name, and my naturalization certificate and marriage license both read "Marie Jana Korbel."[1]

To UNDERSTAND ME, you must understand my father. To understand him, you must understand that my parents grew up in what they thought was a golden place. Czechoslovakia was the only functioning democracy

---

1. My family stopped using the umlaut in Körbel while in England during World War II.

in Central Europe during the period between the two world wars and was blessed with a wise leader, peacefully competing political parties, and a sound economy.

The new democratic republic had been born at the end of World War I, when my father was nine years old and the entire map of Europe was reshaped. Germany and its allies had been defeated. Among those allies was the Austro-Hungarian empire, which had dominated Central Europe for three centuries and was now dismantled. Fifty-one million people of diverse nationalities suddenly found themselves in new or rearranged countries in accordance with President Woodrow Wilson's principle of self-determination.

From its beginning the new country of Czechoslovakia was linked to the United States. Its creation was actually announced in Pittsburgh in 1918. Its president and the author of its Declaration of Independence was Tomáš Garrigue Masaryk, an intellectual born of a Slovak coachman and a Moravian mother, who enthusiastically embraced the principles upon which America's political system was based. Masaryk had also married an American, Charlotte Garrigue, and taken the unusually progressive step of adopting her maiden name as his middle name.

The birth of any country presents challenges. In Czechoslovakia there were many economic and social problems, including sensitivities between the more industrially advanced Czechs and the predominantly agrarian Slovaks. There were also tensions that would steadily worsen involving the ethnic German minority in what was known as the Sudetenland, a region that curls along Czechoslovakia's lengthy border with Germany. But Masaryk was not an ordinary president. He was a leader of strong humanist and religious convictions, and under his guidance Czechoslovakia truly did become a golden place, with a free press, quality public education, and a flourishing intellectual life. Although Masaryk died when I was four months old, in every other sense I grew up with him. My family spoke about him often, and my father was deeply influenced by Masaryk's profound faith in democracy, his belief that small countries were entitled to the same rights as larger ones, and his respect and affection for the United States.[2]

My father's recollections of the 1920s and early 1930s show the pride

2. In 2000, when I visited Prague to join in celebrations commemorating the 150th anniversary of Masaryk's birth, an old Czech man I had never met left a present and a message at my hotel. The present was an album of news articles from Masaryk's death and funeral. The message was that he was giving the album to me because he thought I stood for the same ideals that Masaryk had. I was very touched.

and exuberance he felt. "As other European countries went through polit-ical and social upheavals, unstable finances, and one by one succumbed to fascism," he was to write, "Czechoslovakia was a fortress of peace, democ-racy, and progress. We university students gulped the elixir of liberty. We read avidly national and foreign literature and newspapers, we attended every opening night in the National Theatre and National Opera; we wouldn't miss a single concert of the Prague Philharmonic Orchestra."

Prague had been a cultural mecca for centuries, and for young intel-lectuals like my parents it was an irresistible magnet. My father, growing up in the small town of Kyšperk, had dreamed of moving to the great city, of going to the places where Mozart had performed and sitting in cafés where Franz Kafka had conceived his ideas. He wanted to be avant-garde—to read Karel Čapek's utopian fiction[3] and buy paintings by Čapek's brother, Josef.

There was not even a high school in Kyšperk, so at the age of twelve my father had to go to school in the larger Kostelec nad Orlicí nearby. He was a hardworking student, and always active in political and cultural life. He knew at an early age that he wanted to be a diplomat, newspaperman, or politician and planned accordingly. What he had not planned for was falling in love.

They met in high school. My mother was a little younger and quite pretty. She was petite, with short brown hair worn flapper style, and dim-pled cheeks. My father had a strong, serious face and wavy hair; my mother used to say he got more handsome as he grew older. According to my father, when they met he introduced himself by saying that she was the most talkative girl in Bohemia, so she slapped him. Her name was Anna, a nickname for which was Andula, but from the time she was in high school she was known as Mandula, a contraction of my father's name for her, Ma (My) Andula. She called him Jožka. Her parents, apparently not thrilled with the relationship, sent her away to a finishing school in Geneva. If this was a move to break them up, it almost worked. My mother wrote much later in a short essay on a yellow pad that I found at the time of her death, "Jožka was certainly a man worthwhile waiting for for seven years, before he was ready to get married." She then added—and crossed out—"but I was not always so passioned. Couple times I was thinking of leaving this." (Even after more than four decades in England and America, my mother's English was heavily accented and she had her own version of grammar and idiom.)

3. In his 1920 play, *R.U.R.*, Čapek introduced the concept of robots, derived from the Czech word *robota*, meaning labor or drudgery.

She continued, "Very often I was wondering what was I admiring most in his personality. Was it his perseverance which he probably inherited from his father, who from a little shopkeeper became a shareholder and director of a big building company, or did I loved him because of his good heart, gentleness, unselfishness and loyalty to his family, which he inherited from his lovely mother?" Whatever it was, she never stopped adoring him.

My father completed his education as rapidly as possible, studying German and French with tutors during school vacations, then spending a year at the Sorbonne in Paris, perfecting his French and getting a sense of the world beyond Czechoslovakia. At the age of twenty-three, he received a doctorate of law from Charles University in Prague, the oldest in Central Europe. Following fourteen months of obligatory military service, he was accepted by the Foreign Office and, in my mother's account, "after few months when he had to work without pay we could get married."

The wedding took place on April 20, 1935. My mother, as was typical of the women of that era, did not have the university degrees my father had. However, she shared his cultural interests and was delighted to join in any adventure that led her out of the countryside and into Prague. They moved into an art deco apartment done up in black and white, and were soon part of the city's café society. The following year my father was appointed press attaché to the Czechoslovak legation in Yugoslavia, and my parents were on the move again, this time to Belgrade. Yugoslavia was still a kingdom, and the fact that my father was an ardent democrat prompted him to befriend leaders of the democratic opposition, with whom he met frequently but discreetly.

"Maybe because we were young and happy," my mother wrote of the time in Belgrade, "we have sometimes ignored the dark clouds which were forming on the political sky around us. We all were aware of it, but were hoping that somehow it will pass without catastrophy." The young couple was optimistic enough to start a family—which brought me into the picture—but "catastrophy" was not far off. "The time of our personnel happiness was far too short," recalled my mother. "Hitler was too strong and too aggressive and the Western Democracies at that time too weak and so the little Democratic Republic of Czechoslovakia was the first to suffer, and with it the millions of innocent people."

Czechoslovak diplomats had long counted on alliances with France and the Soviet Union for protection, coupled with their faith that the lofty principles of the League of Nations would be observed. Tragically, they had not counted on the rise of Hitler. Taking office in 1937, the country's new President, Edvard Beneš, while sharing Masaryk's humanist philosophy, lacked his charisma and ability to inspire people. He was, in my father's

7

words, "a mathematician of politics." Still, Beneš did his best to warn Western Europe that Hitler's ambition could not be appeased. In March 1938, Hitler successfully forced Austria into a union. In September, he demanded that Beneš yield control over the Sudetenland. Instead of siding with Prague, the Western powers hoped to avoid war by pressing Beneš to yield. In Munich, on September 29, the United Kingdom, France, Italy, and Germany signed an agreement demanding that Czechoslovakia capitulate. Two days later, the Nazis began occupying the Sudetenland. Beneš resigned. England's Prime Minister Neville Chamberlain notoriously declared that the Munich Agreement would "ensure peace in our time." Those five words, along with the black umbrella Chamberlain carried, have stood ever since as shameful symbols of appeasement.

Applying pressure from Berlin, the Germans installed a puppet regime in Prague that purged the government and moved to erase all vestiges of the philosophy of Masaryk and Beneš. My father's contacts with the democratic opposition in Yugoslavia had made him objectionable to Belgrade, and the new Czechoslovak Foreign Office complied quickly with a request that he be withdrawn. So in December 1938, we moved back to Prague. According to my mother, my father was given a routine desk job in the foreign ministry, but with the Nazis about to take over the rest of the country, he, like other loyal and prominent supporters of Beneš, faced a grim and uncertain future.

Since Beneš and several of his ministers had already fled, my father began looking for a way out as well. "To leave Czechoslovakia immediately was technically impossible," my mother recorded. "There was complete chaos in Prague. Communication was stopped for a little while, banks were closed, friends were arrested. We learned from competent sources that Jožka's name is also on some list of people who should be arrested." For a short time I was sent away to the country to stay with my maternal grandmother, while my parents left their apartment and spent each night with different friends and the days on the streets and in restaurants, planning our escape. "It was mostly during the nights when Gestapo arrested the people," my mother recalled. "With all the possible and impossible planning and with the help of some good friends and lots of luck and little bribes the last plan worked and we managed to get the necessary Gestapo permission to leave the country." Speed was essential. On March 15, 1939, the German army had marched into the Czechoslovak capital. Ten days later, on March 25, my grandmother brought me to Prague. By 11 P.M. that evening my parents and I were on a train out of the country with two small suitcases—all they were able to pack in our hurry. Simply and chillingly my mother wrote, "That was the last time we saw our parents alive. It took us six years before we could return."

We went first to Belgrade and then onward to London, arriving in May, around my second birthday. The city was flooded with foreigners looking for work, so my father was relieved when, not long after we arrived, Jan Masaryk, son of the former president and foreign minister of what was to become the Czechoslovak government in exile, came to London. Masaryk rented a small office and hired young former employees of the Foreign Office—among them my father. In July, Beneš arrived. The goal of the exiles was to work through British radio and newspapers to publicize the facts about Hitler's occupation and to rally fellow Czechoslovaks.

I had always thought that my parents had acclimatized to life in England, but when I read my mother's recollections, I saw differently. "We were surrounded only by Czech people, without making friends with English people with only a very few exceptions....I have always admired their honesty, fairness in time of shortages, their courage in time of bombing, their determination to fight Hitler under very unfavorable conditions, but it took me longtime before I could understand some of their way of life and was feeling comfortable in their midst....But just as we were waiting for our time to be able to return home they were waiting for the time when all the foreigners will be able to leave them."

MY EARLIEST MEMORIES are of an apartment on Kensington Park Road in Notting Hill Gate. My parents slept on a bed pulled out from the wall, and we had a green telephone. When I heard my father broadcasting over the BBC, I thought he was *in* the radio. He had been put in charge of information for the government in exile, and his speeches were also beamed into our homeland for several hours every day. Other Czechoslovak families lived in our apartment house, which had been built especially for refugees. The neighbors sometimes fed me brown bread with pork grease and salt. We joined them in the basement at night when the air raid sirens sounded. I sang songs like "One Hundred Green Bottles Hanging on the Wall" and we all slept on makeshift bunks. My parents said it was good to be in a cellar, but there were pipes filled with gas and hot water running through it, and I realize now that we would not have survived had the building been hit.

This was when I had my first taste of fame. The émigré community—with the help of the Red Cross—wanted to make a film about the plight of refugee children, and I was chosen to play the starring role. The filming was done at a shelter not unlike the one in which we stayed. I took the assignment seriously and as payment received a pink stuffed rabbit that comforted me throughout the war.

We were not the only family members in England. My father's older brother, John, his wife, Ola, and their children, Alena and George, had settled into a Howards End–like country house in Berkhampstead. We lived with them for a short period before moving to London, but the brothers had vastly different personalities and squabbled constantly. When they finally stopped arguing, they stopped speaking. Dáša, the eleven-year-old daughter of my father's sister Greta, came from Czechoslovakia to live with us. Occasionally during the first couple of years, we received letters from my three surviving grandparents,[4] which my parents read aloud. "We love you, and we'll see one another after the war." Later we received word my mother's sister Máňa had died from kidney disease. I remember because my mother was inconsolable.

Although the worst of the Blitz was over, my parents wanted to move out of London. We stayed briefly in Beaconsfield, the hometown of Queen Victoria's influential Prime Minister Benjamin Disraeli. It was there on October 7, 1942, that my sister Kathy was born. Then it was on to Walton-on-Thames, about an hour's ride from London, where we lived in a brick house with a strange prickly plant out front called a monkey puzzle tree. I went to Ingomar School, donning its brown and white uniform, including a tie and a straw hat with a striped hatband. For lunch every day I ate cold meat and bubble and squeak (a mixture of leftover potatoes and cabbage, all fried up, so named because of the sound it made in your stomach after you ate). I was busy becoming a proper little English girl. Because I spoke English better than my mother, I was often dispatched with ration books four long blocks and across a bustling street, pushing Kathy in her pram, to the greengrocer's. I received generally good grades but embarrassingly—given my future career—received a D minus in geography.

Even though Walton-on-Thames was in the countryside, the war was still very much a part of our lives, providing both the drama and the routine. My father was an air raid warden. We acquired a steel table, known as a Morrison shelter, after Churchill's Home Secretary Herbert Morrison. It was the latest thing, advertised as able to save a family hiding under it when a house was bombed. The table became the center of our life. We ate on it, played around and on top of it, and when the sirens sounded, pulled down the blackout shades and slept under it. From my perspective then, all this was normal life: war didn't keep me from enjoying my days or learning how to share high tea with our English friends.

4. My mother's father had died in 1938, before we left Prague.

As difficult or frightening as any situation might be, my parents smoothed the edges. They wanted to make sure my sister and I felt safe and comfortable, and we did. They had the love and ability to make the abnormal seem normal—such as conversing in one language at home and another at school, and going as a family to swim at Lyme Regis, in Dorset, even though there were huge black steel barricades on many beaches to keep the Germans from invading. I also found nothing unsettling about the Sunday gatherings of their Czechoslovak friends. After everyone had eaten, the men walked up and down our small garden in twos and threes in earnest discussion. They paced with their hands clasped behind their backs as European men do, my father always with a pipe in his mouth and a puff of smoke around his head. It was not until I was in college and wrote my honors thesis on the postwar period in Czechoslovakia that I came to understand what my father's job had been during the war, how the government in exile had functioned, and how vital the issues were that had been debated so heatedly in our backyard those Sunday afternoons.

I don't remember the moment I learned the war had ended and we would be going back home. I do know there were joyous celebrations. We talked about nothing else. The table in our dining room was now just a table, not a civil defense shelter. We were about to begin, we thought, a truly normal life.

My father was on the first plane to liberated Czechoslovakia, along with President Beneš and his team. My mother, sister, cousin Dáša, and I followed some weeks later in the belly of a bomber, an experience so terrifying it took me several years to overcome an intense fear of flying.

Since the Czechoslovak leadership had been forced to capitulate after Munich, the Germans had not bombed the capital, so Prague remained intact and to my eight-year-old eyes magical. The country as a whole, however, had suffered irredeemable loss. The economy was crippled. The people had experienced six years of demoralizing occupation. The Jewish population had been all but destroyed.

Because of my father's service in London and his position in the new government, we were given a beautiful apartment on Hradčanské Náměstí (or Square), not far from Prague Castle, where President Beneš lived and worked. The apartment was large and bright, with leaded windows, and came with surprisingly splendid furnishings. My parents told us they had learned that my grandparents had died during the war. They said their parents had been old, and that's what happened when you got old. My mother cried often but, when I asked, would only say, "It's just that I am so glad to be back home." My cousin Dáša continued to live with us. Her parents too had died, a reality I simply accepted.

Soviet soldiers roamed the streets. My parents were fearful of them, while privately mocking their boorishness. I was told an American plane had accidentally dropped the only bomb that had fallen on Prague. Given that I had grown up learning that the Germans were bad and the Americans and Russians good, I found this totally confusing. My father worked a few blocks away, at the foreign ministry, and walked me to school. I had loved school in England but hated it in Prague; my teachers seemed equally unimpressed by me. I spent most of my time being sent to stand in the corner. When my parents asked what I had done wrong, my teacher told them I had been arrogant. "How so?" they asked. The teacher replied that I had told her she had a pretty dress. In England this would have been a pleasantry, but on the continent it was unacceptable for a child to speak so informally to a teacher.

Before the war, Czechoslovak freedom had been crushed by Fascists; now it was endangered by Communists. The Czechoslovak Communist Party had been founded in 1921, four years after the Bolshevik Revolution had transformed Russia. It survived because Czechoslovakia was an egalitarian country and many of its citizens were taken in by the Communist claim to be protectors of the working class. There were also many Czechs and Slovaks who identified with "Mother Russia" as a nation of fellow Slavs. After the war, the party gained strength because the Western powers, not Moscow, were held responsible for the betrayal at Munich. The Soviet Union had also been an ally in fighting the Nazis, and General Dwight Eisenhower had agreed to let the Red Army liberate Prague. As a result the Communists became the single largest political party and even achieved a plurality of the vote in the 1946 elections. Given the desire for national unity, and the country's parliamentary system, Beneš agreed to a coalition government headed by a Communist prime minister and composed of both Communists and a variety of democratic parties along with Jan Masaryk, an independent, as foreign minister.

Beneš and those who supported him, such as my father, wanted Czechoslovakia to return to the democratic values of the prewar era. The president made the mistake of believing Czechoslovak Communists had the same goal. Communists were put in charge of the police and ministry of defense, and a Slovak Communist was appointed Masaryk's deputy. With direction and assistance from Moscow, the Communists penetrated key institutions, including the trade unions, large industries, and the media. The democratic parties, on the other hand, were neither united nor coordinated.

Elsewhere in Europe, the great Cold War between East and West had begun. The Soviets were systematically taking over Eastern Europe. After their 1946 success, Moscow believed the Czechoslovak Communists could win power legally through elections, creating a model for success in

Western Europe, where France and Italy also had large Communist parties. Once again Czechoslovakia was caught in the middle. Beneš tried to put the best face on this by calling his country a bridge between East and West, partly belonging to both. Masaryk thought little of this image, saying to England's King George VI, "Horses walk over bridges and often litter them with droppings." I remember Masaryk as a kind man, with a strong sense of fun and dry sense of humor. When I saw him at official occasions, he usually had his right arm in a sling. I asked my father, "Does the foreign minister have a broken arm?" "No," my father replied. "He wears the sling because he refuses to shake hands with Communists."

My father had a brief stint as Masaryk's chief of staff and then, in the autumn of 1945, he was named Czechoslovakia's representative to Yugoslavia and neighboring Albania, attaining the rank of ambassador at the unusually young age of thirty-six. So after only a few months in Prague, we returned to Belgrade.

My father found a Yugoslav nation that was, in his words, "worn out." More than one-tenth of the population had died during the war fighting the Germans or one another. My father had looked forward to seeing old friends, but now many had become devout Communists and avoided him. He spoke to Serbs who complained bitterly of massacres committed by Croats during the war, and about the steady erosion of their national identity under the dictatorial Communist government of Josip Broz, better known as Marshal Tito. He met Croats who opposed the very existence of Yugoslavia and desired a separate, ethnically distinct nation. By coincidence I would later spend a large portion of my years in government dealing with the same problems my father encountered in 1945 and about which he wrote in his first book, *Tito's Communism*. His affection for the country was deep; he even dedicated his book "To the Yugoslav people, who often in their tormented history have shed blood for the common cause of freedom and democracy, which have been denied to them."

The Czechoslovak embassy in Belgrade was on a main thoroughfare, across from the central post office, a block or two down from the Parliament building. It seemed very grand to me, and indeed it was. On the side of the building fronting the main street was a long balcony, where we stood for official parades. The entrance was guarded by Tito's Partisans in fatigues, and the ambassador's residence was off the large courtyard. We had a butler, a chauffeur, a cook, and maids. Because my father did not want me to go to school with Communists, I had a governess. While the building had not been bombed during the war, it had been occupied by the regional high command of the German army, and pictures, rugs, furniture, and a tapestry had disappeared with the command. Only office equipment had been left behind, so my parents had to use many of the furnishings given to them from our apartment in Prague.

Although life was completely different from what we had known in London, or even during the short period back in Czechoslovakia, my parents seemed to adjust easily. When he was not at an official lunch, my father ate with us in the family dining room, after which the chauffeur often drove us in our black Tatra, a Czechoslovak car with a fin on the back like a Batmobile, to the woods outside the city, where we took long walks.[5]

Despite the political confusion and terrible poverty around them, my parents seemed to me much happier than they had been in England. After all, the diplomatic life was what they had been preparing themselves for, and we were all together. We were also excited by the arrival of my baby brother, John, on January 15, 1947. My mother managed the embassy staff and made sure we all had food. Sometimes she sent to the country for live lambs, which we played with in the kitchen until they became dinners my sister and I declined to eat.

In her inimitable way, my mother refused to do things according to protocol. After formal dinners, she liked to invite a small group back to the family dining room and serve Czechoslovak sausages, known as *párky*. On one occasion she did this with Tito. Apparently the president's tasters opposed the whole idea—until my mother took one sausage, cut it in half, ate hers, and presented the Communist dictator with the other. The formidable leader gobbled it down.

My mother renewed acquaintance with some of her old friends and drank Turkish coffee with them, not so much because she enjoyed the coffee but because she loved turning the cups over and telling fortunes from the coffee grounds. I always thought this one of her principal eccentricities but later found that many Czechs believed both in fortune-telling and astrology.

As the daughter of the ambassador, I became the "official child." Bearing bouquets of flowers and wearing my national costume—a white blouse with large puffy sleeves embroidered in yellowy orange, a pink patterned pleated skirt, navy blue embroidered apron, and lots of ribbons—I accompanied my father to the airport to greet arriving officials. My "duties" allowed me to meet some historic figures at an early age; I even had my own encounter with Tito, presenting him with white roses when he came for a National Day reception.

5. The Czechoslovak government gave a Tatra to Tito, who passed it on to his son, who had lost an arm during the war. The son drove the vehicle around Belgrade at terrifying speed, and I recall my father saying it would be a huge diplomatic mess if Tito's offspring were killed driving a Czechoslovak car.

I was ten years old when my parents concluded that academically I had gone as far as I could go being taught by a governess. I was too young to enroll at the Gymnasium in Prague, so they announced they would send me to boarding school in Chexbres, Switzerland, to learn French. I reacted as most ten-year-olds would. I did not want to leave home. When we stopped in Prague en route to Switzerland, I became literally sick from anxiety and was late for the start of school. My mother, totally out of character, insisted I was well enough to go. I cried during the entire plane ride to Zurich, where we spent the night. I had heard that Zurich was the center for treating polio, so the next morning when I woke up, I said my legs hurt so much I could not move. My mother didn't buy it and found a doctor who pronounced me well. Ther was nothing left but to go on to school.

I arrived at Prealpina Institut pour Jeunes Filles in September 1947. The school was housed in a large building on beautiful grounds overlooking Lake Geneva. My room had a view of the lake—and three roommates. I was given to believe I could not get anything unless I asked for it in French, of which I then knew nothing. For a while I was miserable. Eventually I figured out the language and, ever the diligent student, ended up doing quite well. I soon developed the habit of taking my assignments too seriously. I was made responsible for room inspections, an apple polisher's duty to be sure, but I took matters even further. The room inspection turned into a personal inspection, and I insisted the girls show me whether they had clean hands and nails before they could go to meals. It didn't take long before they made their feelings plain, and I had to work my way back into my friends' good graces. I made my first American friend in Prealpina, a girl with blond hair, a bright smile, and a gray Parker pen, all of which I coveted.

The headmaster of the school was supposed to give us two francs allowance every week and let us go into the village. He did it only sporadically, but when we did go, I always bought the triangular Toblerone chocolate, which I still love. We walked a couple of miles to church every Sunday, no matter how cold, and it was in Switzerland that I learned to ice-skate and ski—with the same boots. Much later my well-equipped American children doubled over in laughter when I told them I had once attached my ice skates to my ski boots with a key.

BACK HOME the Czechoslovak experiment with a coalition government consisting of democrats and Communists was falling apart. The struggle for political control was relentless. The Communists had been on the upswing, but now there was a backlash against their heavy-handed effort to expand influence throughout society. As their electoral prospects receded, they turned to more openly coercive techniques. Moscow also became more direct in pressuring Prague.

In the summer of 1947, the United States announced a massive program of assistance—the Marshall Plan—to help European nations recover from the devastation of war. Every country in Europe, including the Soviet Union and Czechoslovakia, was invited to participate. The Soviets were distrustful, seeing the plan more as an American Trojan Horse than as a means for economic recovery. In Prague Beneš, who wanted Czechoslovakia to participate, formally accepted the American invitation. Jan Masaryk, in Moscow on official business, was summoned by Stalin and informed that his country would not be permitted to take part in the plan. Back in Prague a bitter and sarcastic Masaryk told colleagues, "It's a new Munich. I left for Moscow as minister of foreign affairs of a sovereign state. I am returning as Stalin's stooge."

Despite this setback Beneš remained hopeful, placing his faith in elections scheduled for May 1948. When my father visited the president in January of that year, he tried to warn Beneš that the Communists would use every means to take over. As they discussed who was trustworthy and who wasn't, Beneš said, "Don't worry. The danger of a Communist putsch has passed. Return to Belgrade and carry on." My father wrote, "Those were President Beneš' last words to me. I saw him no more."

Beneš was wrong. Determined not to wait for elections, the Communists branded democratic leaders as reactionaries, distributed arms to militants, demanded the immediate and radical socialization of the economy, and sent packages with explosives in an unsuccessful attempt to kill three government ministers, including Masaryk. Weakened by two strokes, Beneš couldn't compete against a determined foe not playing by the rules. In February, a dozen democratic cabinet ministers submitted their resignations in an attempt to force immediate elections. Instead the Communists used mobs, the media, and militias to coerce Beneš into agreeing to a new government of national unity. The coup of February 25 put real control in the hands of Communists, where it would remain for more than four decades. On March 10, 1948, Masaryk's body was found beneath the broken window of his apartment in the Czechoslovak foreign ministry. The authorities declared it suicide. My parents—and most Czechoslovak democrats—believed it was murder. On June 7, President Beneš resigned. The Soviet bloc was complete. To prevent Communism from making further inroads in Europe, the Truman administration joined Canada and friends across the ocean in forging the North Atlantic Treaty Organization—NATO.

For my parents, the coup meant the end of their dream of a free Czechoslovakia. I did not see them until later that spring when they came to Switzerland to inform me that my father had a new assignment, this time with the UN. Shortly before the coup, he had offered to resign as ambassador to Yugoslavia on the grounds that only a Communist could possess the confidence of the regime in Belgrade. There was some discussion at the time about his becoming ambassador to France, but he was instead offered a position representing Czechoslovakia on a new UN commission dealing with the disputed status of Kashmir, a province claimed by both the newly independent countries of India and Pakistan. My mother, sister, and brother would be moving to London while my father was in South Asia. My parents presented this calmly, as if it were a routine course of events.

When school finished, I joined my family in London, where we lived in a dark basement apartment with the bathtub in the kitchen. My father wrote us cheery letters extolling the beauties of Srinagar in Kashmir, and telling us about the monkeys in New Delhi he swore came into his hotel room. I can't imagine what he wrote to my mother, but I do know he was looking for, and found, a way for us to go to America, where he would join us as soon as he could.

Thus began a new chapter in Europe's history and my life. For the second time in less than a decade, my parents were forced to leave their homeland behind. I, at eleven years old, together with my mother and siblings, prepared to cross the Atlantic. We had booked passage on a giant ocean liner, the SS *America*, and I was looking forward eagerly to the five-day voyage. We boarded in Southampton at night. When we awoke, we had a huge breakfast of bacon and eggs, and only later noticed that it was so calm because we were docked in Le Havre. That breakfast was our last full meal for a long time. Once we started moving, we were all seasick. My mother took to her bed for the entire journey, while we children subsisted on baked potatoes.

Our ship passed through a November sea. The winds were strong and the waves high. Enormous black clouds gathered overhead, bringing pelting rain and freezing cold. We peered through the portholes and only rarely ventured out on deck. I thought the trip I had anticipated so much would never end. Only when we neared our destination did the skies clear. Finally, on November 11, 1948, Armistice Day, we steamed into New York Harbor. There was the Statue of Liberty. Holding my sister's hand, I stared in awe at the welcoming figure.

TWO

Becoming an American

My MOTHER, Kathy, John, and I settled into a rented cottage on a fairly large estate in Great Neck, Long Island, not far from the UN's temporary headquarters at Lake Success. Looking back on that period, I realize what an amazing job my mother did in coping with change. For most of her life she had been a pampered daughter and most recently an ambassador's wife. Now she was trying for the second time as a refugee to create a home for her children in a strange country, at this point without her husband. She was only thirty-seven, but terribly old in my young eyes. I don't recall her having American friends yet, but I do know she got hooked on radio soap operas, not realizing the stories never ended.

For me the desire to adjust and make new friends was already second nature. I felt "foreign" of course, but I was used to that. I had even felt foreign in the Czechoslovak school I attended because it was so strict. Even so, it was in Great Neck that I first became aware of a dilemma I would face throughout my life: given my personal experiences and drive to do well, how could I overcome my inherent seriousness and fit in?

The first step was to sound like an American. My mother enrolled Kathy and me in a school near our cottage called Arrandale School. I had already gone to two schools in England and one in Czechoslovakia, studied two years with a governess in Belgrade, had a year at boarding school in Switzerland, and spent three months at the Lycée Français in London. I spoke four languages—Czech, Serbo-Croatian, French, and English— but I didn't yet speak American. As quickly as possible, I got rid of my English accent.

My father arrived in time to join us for our first Christmas in the United States. To my father, America meant freedom and security. He did, however, see the amusing side of adjusting to a new culture. When not working at the UN, he took time to write a short story entitled "Mr. DP [displaced person] Discovers America." According to the tale, it was the little things that made the difference. Like my father, Mr. DP loved to walk, but on Long Island in the late 1940s everyone drove. Soon Mr. DP found he couldn't go anywhere without someone pulling alongside, asking if he were all right and insisting he accept a ride. When Mr. DP gave in, he became an American. Mr. DP had never heard about allergies. When Mrs. DP developed an allergy to soap powder, she became an American. When the DP children found they couldn't live without Howdy Doody and bubblegum, they became Americans. Pretty soon the DP family felt quite at home.

In reality it wasn't that easy to persuade official America to see us as its own, but I didn't know that at the time. I am still described as a "refugee," which is accurate, but in contrast to many who came to America before and after us, my family wasn't a hardship case. We did not have to escape through barbed wire. We didn't have much money, but we did come on diplomatic passports.

This is not to say that my parents didn't face serious troubles. They did, both financial and political. But there never seemed any reason for us children to worry: as my mother would say, "Your father has everything under control."

It was not until my first day as UN ambassador in 1993 that I learned how precarious our family's status had been. One of the researchers from the UN mission library handed me a stack of documents that traced the difficult path my father had had to follow. His main interest was to arrange for political asylum, and he tried to determine whether it was better to resign the Kashmir Commission post—or be fired from it. In either case timing was critical, because he needed asylum before he lost his Czechoslovak diplomatic status and was forced to leave the United States. In requesting asylum he was in a particularly tough spot, because he also had to show that even though he technically represented a Communist government, he had not been a sympathizer and hadn't reported to the Communists. In the UN files I found memos and correspondence testifying that my father had always supported democratic causes and been helpful to his British and American counterparts. The files were deeply moving for me to read, especially the letter my father sent on February 12, 1949, to Warren Austin, then U.S. ambassador to the UN, asking Secretary of State Dean Acheson to let us all stay:

> May I be allowed to say the following, I was selected to be a Member of this Commission before the Communist putch [sic] took place in Prague on 25th

February 1948. In agreement with my political friends in exile, I decided to stay on the Commission because I was of the opinion that I was helping the common cause of democracy and peace in preventing a Czechoslovak Communist to take my place. About this decision I informed Mr. Lewis Douglas, the United States Ambassador in London, in June 1948.

While on the Commission I refused to follow the policy of the Soviet bloc, the representatives of which obstructed any positive work in the United Nations, its Commissions and other agencies. I did not send a single report to the Czechoslovak Communist Government about the Commission's activities, considering myself to be a representative of the democratic and peace-loving Czechoslovak nation. Having this in mind I tried to contribute to the common cause of democracy and peace by working with other Members of the Commission in a spirit of mutual confidence. I worked in close and friendly contact with the United States Representative on the Commission.

I participated in the Commission's activities until its return to the Indian Subcontinent, February 1st, 1949.... I learned about my dismissal which was caused by my democratic conviction and work on the Commission.

The final paragraph summarized his problem clearly:

I cannot, of course, return to the Communist Czechoslovakia as I would be arrested for my faithful adherence to the ideals of democracy. I would be most obliged to you if you could kindly convey to his Excellency the Secretary of State that I beg of him to be granted the right to stay in the United States, the same right to be given to my wife and three children.

Four months after my father sent this letter, we were granted political asylum.

FOR MANY the 1950s in America was a time of normalcy, even complacency. Others found it an unsettling period, made dangerous by the Cold War and roiled internally by its domestic aberration, McCarthyism. All these currents were reflected in the life our family was to find in its new home in Colorado.

We wound up in Denver thanks to Dr. Philip Mosely, director of the Russian Institute at Columbia University, who also had an association with the Rockefeller Foundation. Through his assistance my father received a grant from the foundation and an offer to teach at the University of Denver with a stipend of five thousand dollars the first year. He promptly bought a green Ford coupe, loaded the family into it, and we headed west. Our few belongings followed in a Mayflower Company moving van, allowing my father to joke forever after that we had arrived on the *Mayflower*.

Denver at the time was a medium-sized western city, with a small downtown and few suburbs. It was quiet and friendly, and perfect for us, because for all its isolation there was also a segment of the university that was internationally minded. The Social Science Foundation of the University of Denver, founded in 1926, developed the first international relations department in the United States. Its director, Benjamin Cherrington, one of its founders, not only looked like an angel but indeed was one to my father in every way. Cherrington, who had worked at the State Department, hired my father. When I was in high school, this gentle man took an interest in me. We went to lunch and talked about international relations and the Democratic Party. He is also the reason behind the unlikely friendship I later developed with a very Republican Senator, Alaska's Ted Stevens, who married Cherrington's daughter, Ann. Tragically, Ann was killed in a plane crash in 1978. While I was Secretary of State, Stevens was chairman of the all-important Appropriations Committee. I met regularly with this wise but curmudgeonly Senator to seek a State Department budget reflecting our foreign policy needs, but always, before we got down to business, we got down to the serious exchange of family stories.

Looking back on my time in Denver, I am amazed at how brief it was—just over six years from when we arrived to when I left for college. During that stage I put my own twist on becoming a bona fide American teenager, trying not to put off classmates as I competed to be top of my class, and coping with my hopelessly strict and uptight European parents. It was hard to be popular when you had an overly protective mother who worried about you all the time and who found the concept of slumber parties completely alien. Even after years in Denver, when the memories of war were receding, my mother continually feared that something would happen to us, and when I went out at night, she stayed up, wandering round the house in her nightgown until I got home.

Sometimes it seemed that the harder I worked to become a plain vanilla American, the more my parents insisted on being their spicy selves. My mother often wore an embroidered leather jacket, lined in sheepskin, that she had bought in Yugoslavia. In recent years, when "ethnic" clothing became chic, that jacket would have been to die for; in the 1950s its appearance practically killed me. I never wanted to invite anyone over for a meal or to spend the night at our house, for fear my parents would embarrass me by doing something European. They, on the other hand, cheerfully held parties in our scruffy garden and served *sarma* (Yugoslav cabbage rolls filled with ground meat and covered in a hot tomato sauce) and *knedlíky* (Czechoslovak fruit dumplings swimming in melted butter, covered with sugar and ground nuts). Then to top it off my father sang Czech, Slovak, and Serbian songs, and my mother read guests' palms and unhesitatingly told middle-aged women that they would have more children and the men that they would have affairs. The Denver friends they made loved the atmosphere. And my parents grew to love Denver. My mother would say, "There are two great cities in the world, Prague and Denver," while my father never tired of repeating the slogan of the *Denver Post*: "'Tis a Privilege to Live in Colorado."

We moved around a lot when we first came, living in furnished, rented houses. That first summer of 1949 we lived in a small house in south Denver. It all seemed wonderfully calm. My father mowed the lawn, something I had never seen him do before. We were befriended by the Spencleys, nice, conservative neighbors who welcomed these strangers from a country of which they had never heard. I worked meticulously on my stamp collection, encouraged by my father because it might help my geography. We swam in the lake at Washington Park until frightened off by the polio epidemic. At the end of the summer, we rented another house, this one separated by a wrought-iron fence from a cemetery and owned by two elderly sisters.

Even though we had all acquired varying degrees of English, we continued to speak and eat Czech at home, and my "adult" responsibilities as the older sister involved walking Kathy to school and to church (John was too young). I had just made my First Communion, and I enjoyed catechism class and loved the church services even more after I started learning Latin. When we were in England, I used to play at being a priest and soon became the most religious person in my family. My mother occasionally came to church; my father went only at Easter and Christmas. They told me they could do just as well thinking about God at home and made a point of objecting to the way the money-collecting envelopes were numbered so the priests could check to see if we'd actually gone to mass.

In the fall of 1949, I started junior high at Morey, a school that drew students from both wealthy and less-than-wealthy sections of Denver. I envied my classmates' lives whichever neighborhoods they came from. They seemed so happy. Everything and everyone appeared, on the surface, to be innocent and uncomplicated. This was especially true of Marilyn Van Derbur, the most beautiful of my classmates, later crowned Miss America 1958. I was shocked when she bravely acknowledged publicly in 1991 that during those years at Morey—when she had seemed the perfect all-American girl—she was being molested by her father, a pillar of Denver society.

It was hard for both my parents and me to understand that school could and should be fun. They couldn't believe I had a class like home economics, where I was taught the order of washing dishes (glassware, silverware, small china, large china, pots and pans) and where I learned to sew, a pastime that enabled me to make my own clothes and run up curtains for every new house into which we moved.

My attempt not to stand out was thwarted on a number of occasions. I remember two vividly—and painfully. The first was when we had to have tuberculosis patch tests. Mine was positive. The only other class member to have that result was a boy who often came to school unkempt. The explanation for my result turned out to be scar tissue—I clearly had come into contact with tuberculosis during the war—but as far as I was concerned the reason did not matter. I was stigmatized along with this boy.

Then came Valentine's Day, a holiday about which I had never heard. The girls were to bring in box lunches to be auctioned off to the highest boy bidder. The bidding had nothing to do with what was inside the box: it was presentation that counted. I didn't know this, so I brought delicious food in a shoebox, wrapped in newspaper. The other girls had theirs adorned with glorious bows. Mine was the last to be sold—bought by the boy with the positive tuberculosis test. I of course had a crush on the tallest, handsomest boy in class, who, while sharing my passion for international relations, had no interest in me—or in badly packaged Valentine lunches.

When I was in eighth grade, the elderly sisters reclaimed the house next to the cemetery, so we moved into faculty housing in downtown Denver, two blocks from the Colorado Capitol, long before urban gentrification. This definitely put me into the category of Morey students from the marginal neighborhoods. We lived in a two-bedroom walk-up. My sister and I shared a bedroom. My parents shared the other bedroom with my brother, which may help explain why I had no more siblings.

When university housing became available closer to the campus, we moved once again, this time to a small bungalow near the University of Denver's football stadium, between two parking lots that were filled on fall Saturdays. We remained there for most of the fifties. The house was one story high, with a semifinished basement where my father had his study. Whenever the basement flooded, which happened frequently, he sat with his feet on bricks in order to continue working. My parents taught English to Czechoslovak newcomers on Friday evenings, when it was my job to stay home and cook for Kathy and John, who fortunately loved cold baked beans on toast. On Saturdays I took them to the movies, where we watched newsreels, serials, and double features, including westerns such as *The Lone Ranger.*

I was looking forward to being a ninth grader, because they were the oldest class in junior high and got to tell everyone else what to do. But then my father came up with the idea that I should go to Kent, a small private girls' school in Denver that was offering scholarships to daughters of professors. I yelled and fumed, but as in all the arguments I had with my father, my protests were useless. I came to appreciate the education I got during my years at Kent, but as a relatively poor, foreign Catholic, I did feel as if I were part of some program to diversify a school for rich Protestants. I was saved from daily embarrassment only by the rule that we had to wear uniforms. On one occasion, when I arrived out of uniform, I wore a plaid skirt with a print top and was upset when one of my teachers said that was never done. What would she have thought years later, when it became quite the rage of the best designers?

As I grew older, I fit in better, but my serious streak dogged me. I went all out in class, field hockey, glee club, and the school play (in which I played Mr. Bennet in *Pride and Prejudice*). By tenth grade, I was popular enough to be elected to the student council, but (alas) became overzealous once more and turned someone in for talking during study hall. I was never elected to anything again. Perhaps to compensate, I started an international relations club and named myself president: we met over lunch once a week. When I became UN ambassador, I often got laughs from audiences by saying that one of my qualifications for the job was winning the Rocky Mountain Empire United Nations Contest as the student who knew the most about the UN. I had memorized the names, in alphabetical order, of the sixty countries that were members in 1953.

Even though I increasingly saw myself as an average American girl, my father was never at ease with the social life of American teenagers. I remember my first dance with horror. First there was the issue of whether I would be allowed to go at all. I can't remember the name of the poor boy who asked me there, but I do remember that he was sixteen and therefore had a driver's license, which, it seemed to me, answered the question of how I would get to the dance and back. But no; driving with "the boy" was out of the question. Finally, after prolonged discussion, my parents and I struck a compromise. I could drive with "the boy," but my father would follow us to the dance in his car, then follow us back home afterward. For all I know, he sat outside peering through the windows for the whole dance. When our little motorcade arrived back home, my father asked "the boy" in for milk and cookies. There was no second date.

Given all this, and the fact I was more apple-cheeked and round than tall and blond, I couldn't compete with the more sophisticated, all-American-type girls. I clearly was not Denver Country Club material. However, because I went to Kent, I got to go to the parties. Or more accurately, I was invited to the torture of being a permanent wallflower.

I was known as a serious girl with a good-enough personality but not someone with whom the boys lined up to dance. The whole experience was painful, but there was one incident that was particularly cruel. Much to my surprise, at one of these dances a young man—not a boy—asked me to dance. He, like me, was a sophomore—except in college, not high school. Even more to my surprise, after the dance he asked me out on a series of dates. He seemed genuinely interested in me, even putting up with my maddening 10 P.M. curfew. Then all of a sudden he disappeared and started dating a certain upper-class girl. Through the school chatter I learned the truth: his dating me first had been a test she had given him as the price he'd had to pay to date her. For weeks, thinking everyone was talking about my humiliation, I dreaded even showing my face. Is there any group meaner to one another than girls in high school?

I had one party dress. It did offer two wearing options, however. It was navy blue taffeta, with white rickrack on the top and a detachable tulle skirt I could wear over the taffeta for a change. Neither option served for a "formal," so when I was invited to one, a faculty member from the university, a Miss Elizabeth Fackt, took pity on me and offered to lend me something suitable. It too was tafetta, only in white, off the shoulder, with two rows of flounces at the hem. It may have been attractive on Miss Fackt, but she was in her late fifties. I was sixteen, and on me it looked like a lampshade. I tried desperately to fix it. As the daughter of a former diplomat, I had seen fancy dress balls, so I went out, bought a four-inch-wide velvet scarlet ribbon, and draped it over one shoulder like a royal sash. Unfortunately that looked ridiculous too, so I was persuaded to wear the ribbon around my waist.

Miss Fackt, her dress, and the sash are all now part of my personal lore, Miss Fackt because of how my parents pronounced her name: for them a short *a* came out as a short *u*. As for the dress and the sash, almost half a century later I was awarded the highest honor a foreigner can receive from the Czech government, the Order of the White Lion. We were in Prague Castle, surrounded by dignitaries, and as President Havel placed a red and white ribbon around my shoulders, I was profoundly honored. Still, as I walked around Prague that day, wearing my scarlet sash, I couldn't stop thinking about that old dress and the woman my parents had called "Miss F*ckt."

My social life was further curtailed by my parents' insistence on staging family outings every Sunday. We drove into the mountains and picnicked. My father, dressed in suit and tie, took up fishing, while my mother gathered mushrooms, which we children were afraid to eat because we were sure she didn't know which were poisonous and which weren't. We always had the same meal: some Czech version of hamburgers called *karbenátky* (more like cold meat loaf) and my mother's version of potato salad, which consisted of potatoes, a thawed bag of mixed vegetables, and tablespoons of mayonnaise. On the way home we stopped in restaurants where, because of our limited finances, Kathy, John, and I were taught to order the cheapest items on the menu—a habit that sticks with me still.

Over the years the three of us developed a family mythology about how strict our father was, but in truth he was more loving than strict. He did demand respect, and sometimes problems with language got in our way. My sister once disobeyed, and my father refused to speak to her. My sister asked him, "Are you mad?" My father exploded. "How dare you call me that!" He was thinking in British English, taking "mad" to mean "crazy."

My mother was definitely not the family disciplinarian. In fact her totally subjective view of us convinced her that one of my brother's bad report cards must have belonged to somebody else: it couldn't be his, and if it was, it was because his teachers were stupid. In her case language was also an issue, but usually good for a laugh—as when she failed to grasp the difference between "passed away" and "passed out" in describing the condition of an ailing elderly neighbor, or when my parents had to lower the asking price for their first house to twenty-nine thousand dollars because prospective buyers couldn't understand that "serty" was actually a number.

We had to have what my father called "family solidarity," because we had come to America with most of our family left behind. My father's brother and his wife and children remained in England, and the brothers were still not on speaking terms. My cousin Dáša, who had been with us in England and who had visited us in Belgrade, had chosen not to leave Czechoslovakia when my father asked her to come with us.

While the Korbels were creating a new life in Denver, Stalin's rule was being set in cement in Central and East Europe. Whatever distinctions had existed among countries of the bloc were systematically obliterated as national leaders, even Communist "deviationists," were sentenced to death in show trials. Terror ruled. After Stalin's death in 1953, the Soviet bloc consolidated further, as Czechoslovakia and the other satellites joined the Warsaw Pact—a warped mirror image of NATO.

As a refugee from Communism, my father was prepared—eager, in fact—to talk and write about its horrors. His book on Yugoslavia, *Tito's Communism*, was published in 1951 and made him much in demand for interviews. I always imagine that other people's fathers talk about less serious subjects, like sports. My father talked to me about history and foreign policy whenever he got the chance, and his convictions became mine.

He could make whatever period in history I was studying come alive with stories and place any battle or conference in context. When he spoke of World War II, he never strayed far from the lessons of Munich: unspeakable tragedies ensue when great countries appease evil, make decisions over the heads of smaller powers, and do not pay attention to what is happening in faraway places. He said that smaller countries must fight for themselves and that the Czechoslovak people had been ready to fight. In fact, as a member of the reserves, he had been mobilized briefly himself and along with many Czechoslovaks was disappointed in Beneš' decision to accede to the major powers.

My father told me a lot about the Holocaust. It was not a subject that was discussed as much publicly in the fifties as it has been since. I knew from him about the trains filled with people going to concentration camps and that millions had died in ovens. And that anti-Semitism was unacceptable and tolerance essential. My mother echoed his words, except added that we were supposed to hate Germans and all whom she termed "collaborants." We talked about so much, there was no reason to think there were things I did not know. I thought I knew too much about sadness, given I was only a teenager; it seemed to me I had been born an adult.

Inside the bungalow, the anomaly of our life was evident to all. Our furniture was either borrowed or bought at cheap stores, and we ate at a kitchen table covered with an oilcloth. On our walls, though, was an unusual collection of splendid oil paintings—the result of an extraordinary mistake. When in 1948 my parents were about to flee Yugoslavia, they pretended they were packing for a routine change in diplomatic assignments. My mother, they told people, would be taking Kathy and John to meet me for a vacation in Switzerland before going back to Prague, while my father would leave for India and Pakistan. Only my father's secretary knew they did not plan to return to Czechoslovakia.

Our furnishings from the ambassador's residence were to be shipped to Prague, while, secretly, crates filled with family photographs and my parents' personal library were to follow us into exile. But there was a mix-up, and after we arrived in Denver we received crates packed with Czech glass, a huge carpet from one of the embassy's ceremonial rooms—and the paintings. The crates containing our personal belongings never arrived and have never been found. The fact that our family photographs vanished meant I had no pictures of myself as a baby. I can now reveal that the baby picture labeled as mine in my high school yearbook was actually of my brother, John, who as a small child had blond curls that were kept much longer than he likes to remember.

Despite the fact that our European art works were totally out of place in our house, we were pleased to have so many familiar objects around us. The paintings included two Josef Čapeks, purchased before the war, of children playing. I love the paintings, which now hang in my bedroom. We also had some Yugoslav oils bought while we were in Belgrade, as well as those we had been given along with the apartment in Prague following the war. As for the carpet, it was so big it had to be folded in quarters to fit into our living room.[1]

In order to make ends meet, my mother worked as a secretary in the Denver public schools. As a young woman she had taken a secretarial course, so she knew how to type and could figure out filing, and her English, while idiosyncratic, was good enough for her to manage. My mother's full-time job and my father's professorial schedule meant that it was he who was home when we came back from school. Together, the former ambassador and I did the dishes every night and cleaned the house on Friday afternoons, with Kathy responsible for the bathroom and John for taking out the garbage, all to the accompaniment of operas such as *Aida* and *Eugen Onegin*. My father plunged into work on his second book, *Danger in Kashmir*, still described as the best history of that painful conflict. For a time, the whole family went around the house bowing beatifically to each other, in imitation of Mahatma Gandhi. Ever the dutiful daughter, I produced a long history paper on the great Indian leader. Kathy and John later did the same.

Life was not, however, all family. I did end up having a wonderful high school romance with a boy a year ahead of me. I met Elston Mayhew at a party. He had light blue eyes, which matched his blue V-neck sweater.

---

1. Shortly after becoming Secretary of State in 1997, I was contacted by an heir to the family that had previously lived in the apartment given to us during our stay in Prague in 1945 and whose property had been confiscated by the Czechoslovak government under the so-called Beneš decrees. The Nebrich family were Germans who fled Prague in 1945. They moved to Austria, claimed Austrian citizenship, and subsequently and unsuccessfully tried to reclaim their property from the Czechoslovak government. In their request to me, they sought the return of any property that was possibly in the Korbel family's possession. I turned the matter over to my brother, John, to handle on behalf of our family. He and his attorneys investigated the matter and ultimately sought guidance from the Czech government. On May 20, 1999, my brother received a response from the Czech ambassador to the United States, Alexandr Vondra, confirming that "members of the Nebrich family resided in Czechoslovakia before and during World War II, and were citizens of the German Reich." Their property, wrote Vondra, had been confiscated properly under the Beneš decrees, and "there is no basis for any claim against the Korbel family in respect to any such property." The next day John's attorney communicated the Czech government's position to the Nebrich family heirs, and with this we considered the matter concluded.

I really liked him and he liked me. Elston was a science whiz and not part of the country club crowd. The adopted son of a nice middle-class family, he was allowed to drive his father's green Oldsmobile. We started double-dating with a girl who had come to Kent as a sophomore and who lived out in one of the less fashionable suburbs. Val Blum became my best friend, if an unlikely one: she was a daredevil, smoked, and had a car. She was also great fun, and with her boyfriend, Robert Dupont, who was Elston's best friend, we were inseparable for two years until Elston headed off for Princeton. We certainly did things my parents would have disapproved of—had they known what we were up to. I often spent the night at Val's, where there was no curfew. We sometimes told her parents we were going to the movies, but instead the four of us drove thirty miles to Boulder, speeding along on a new highway to visit Val's brother at the University of Colorado. Either that or we went to watch the airplanes land at Stapleton Airport and steamed up the windows in the roomy Oldsmobile.

While perhaps not quite as high-pressured as today, getting into college was nevertheless a big deal. For me the question was not so much whether I would be accepted but whether I would get a scholarship, because there was no way my parents could afford to send me without one. My college advisor was a wonderful, patient woman named Aileen Nelson; she taught history, my favorite subject. I had already decided to apply to Wellesley, but because I was terrified that I wouldn't get a scholarship, I also applied to a spectrum of other colleges—Stanford, Mount Holyoke, the University of Pennsylvania (because it was near Princeton and thus Elston), and the University of Colorado. The headmistress of Kent, Miss Mary Bogue, objected: I was applying to too many schools, she said. Mrs. Nelson disagreed, so I stood my ground, applied—and waited.

Stanford sent out its acceptances a month earlier than the other colleges. I remember coming home and finding the letter: I had been accepted, but with no scholarship. For me this was tantamount to being turned down. I ran out of the house and across one of the parking lots, in tears. My father came to find me and calmed me down, saying over and over again that there must have been some mistake. The next day at school, when Miss Bogue called me in, she was not interested in consoling me. "This is most unfortunate," she said, "because these schools all tend to assess students the same way."

I was hysterical. A couple of weeks later, I came home to find a second envelope, very much like the first. Inside was a letter informing me that I had received the Colorado Stanford Club scholarship. The process worked separately from admissions, I was told, which is why I hadn't been notified earlier. Further letters started to arrive, each with offers. In the end I received a scholarship offer from every one of the colleges to which I had applied including Wellesley, my first choice.

Miss Bogue called me into her office again. "This is most unfortunate," she intoned. "By applying to so many schools and then turning them down, you have not helped the reputation of the school."

I left her office not feeling unfortunate at all. I felt ready for college. Despite traumatic moments—some normal for a teenage girl, some attributable to my "foreignness"—I had enjoyed high school. I had studied hard, had a boyfriend, and found girlfriends too. I had babysat for twenty-five cents an hour. I had all my swimming certificates. Thanks to my parents, sister, and brother, I also had a great sense of belonging and optimism. My father used to say, "There is such a difference between the United States and every other country. Elsewhere, when you arrive as a refugee, they say, 'We are sorry you had to leave your country. What can we do to help you? And by the way, when are you going home?' In America they say, 'We're sorry you had to leave your country. What can we do to help you? And by the way, when will you become a citizen?'"

Ironically, it was taking longer than the normal five years for us to get our citizenship. McCarthyism was taking its toll, and presumably because my father had worked for a Czechoslovak coalition government that included Communists, there were more questions than usual to be asked. If they were worried, my parents didn't let on.

In the fall of 1955, equipped with charcoal gray and charcoal brown wool Bermuda shorts, matching crew neck sweaters, and a camel hair polo coat (with the requisite number of bone buttons), I boarded the Denver Zephyr for the train trip to college. At Wellesley, in contrast to Kent, no one would care that I was on scholarship, but I would be listed as a foreign student. I was from Denver and felt like a thoroughly American Maddy, only I wasn't an American citizen. Yet.

THREE

Best of All Possible Worlds

"I T'S ALL FOR THE BEST in this best of all possible worlds." That line of Voltaire's from the 1956 Leonard Bernstein musical *Candide* captured my excitement about my college years. I was surrounded by new friends, great professors, stimulating courses, and freedom—not just in the American sense, but in the sense that I was expected to make my own decisions. My Denver years had marked my transition from a war-experienced European diplomat's child into an American teenager, but I had been inhibited by my parents' close monitoring. Now I was away from them, if not yet fully on my own. The process of growing up accelerated, and from the moment I arrived at Wellesley's spectacular campus, set in five hundred acres of meadows and woodlands about a dozen miles west of Boston, I enjoyed every minute.

The young women who entered Wellesley in the fall of 1955 (the class of '59) were either the last of the silent generation with its contingent of bright, dutiful daughters prepared to join the ranks of well-educated, bright, dutiful wives or the first class of women eager to be taken seriously in the workforce and recognized as independent individuals, not just appendages to their much sought-after husbands. Actually, they were both; in any case, I was both. I was preparing myself for a career in journalism or diplomacy, while I wanted to get married as soon as possible to the perfect partner. The notion that there might be a contradiction between these two aspirations didn't occur to me. So I concentrated on my studies and worried about my social life.

The transitional nature of my generation was reflected in the contrast between the modern education we received and Wellesley's traditions. These were the product of a much earlier age, and we didn't question them. Almost as soon as we arrived, we were sent to the physical education department to pose for what was called a "posture picture." This was to see whether we had "an understanding of good body alignment and the ability to stand well." We were not allowed to wear any clothing above the waist. School authorities scrutinized the pictures, and if we flunked they made us do exercises. To my relief, I passed.[1]

At the time of graduation, senior girls (we were not uncomfortable calling each other that in those pre–politically correct days) held a hoop-rolling race, which required using a stick to roll a wooden hoop about the size of hula-hoop down a path. The contestants wore their graduation gowns hiked up and their mortarboard caps tied down with scarves knotted under the chin. It was all very nineteenth-century. The winner would supposedly be the first in the class to get married, although the victor my year, Amalya "Mal" Kearse, instead became the first African-American woman to serve on the U.S. Court of Appeals for the Second Circuit (as well as a world-class bridge player).

Wellesley in the 1950s also reflected the contemporary idea of diversity, or lack thereof. Mal was one of only two black girls in my class (the other, Shirlee Taylor, became an accomplished author and journalist.)[2] Roommates were assigned according to religion. Mine was a fellow Roman Catholic, Mary Jane Durnford of Windsor, Connecticut. She was blond and pretty, and we got along immediately, even though we were quite different. She intended to major in math; I in political science. Whenever we ate Howard Johnson's ice cream, I put on weight; she did not. She had a boyfriend at Harvard whom she saw constantly. I was in love with Elston, whom I saw not enough. Mary Jane and I often complemented each other, for example in French. I, the student who had wowed her high school teachers with fluent spoken French, got my comeuppance in college. On my first paper Monsieur François wrote, "*Vos idées sont très bonnes, mais vous avez massacré la grammaire.*" Your ideas are very good, but you have massacred the grammar. Mary Jane knew her grammar perfectly. She took to correcting my papers, while I helped her speak more confidently.

Down the hall from us in the Victorian house that served as our dorm lived two Jewish girls. Susan Dubinsky, on her way to becoming a successful writer, was one of those people who could comprehend every image in Shakespeare's sonnets and Faulkner at his most obscure. Emily Cohen, a sparkling graduate of the Bronx High School of Science and already an

1. I wondered for a long time what happened to the pictures. Then a few years ago they were discovered in a vault. At Yale.

2. Among Shirlee Taylor Haizlip's works is the classic *The Sweeter the Juice: A Family Memoir in Black and White*, published in 1994.

outspoken feminist, questioned all our assumptions and became for me a lifelong friend. Later we shared a passion for journalism and politics, but first we shared shopping. Emily, a true New Yorker, took me to her family apartment on the Grand Concourse in the Bronx for spring vacation and allowed me to follow her around as she rushed from sale to sale. She loved bargains so much that she would even buy the wrong size bra if it were marked down. As a Catholic I had to eat fish on Fridays. When I stayed with Emily, that meant trying gefilte fish for the first time.

In a political science class the first week after arriving, I sat down next to a girl named Wini Shore. Within minutes we discovered that we had been classmates before, in sixth grade at Arrandale School in Great Neck. That made her my oldest friend in the United States. Over the years our friendship grew and deepened as we passed through life's stages, and it now encompasses our children and grandchildren as well.

Mary McCarthy's novel *The Group* describes the lives of a circle of young women who met at Vassar in the 1930s. With some allowance for updating, there are marked similarities to my years at Wellesley. I made my best friends there, and it was there I developed my enduring need for a group within which to operate.

In Denver my struggle had been to fit in. At Wellesley I had a much easier time—mostly. Not yet a citizen, I was technically an "alien," required to register with the government every January, for which I received much good-natured kidding. In one instance my friends decorated my bedroom with official post office posters stating "Aliens Must Register." I was also startled early that first semester to be summoned to the front desk of our dorm. Waiting there was a group of alumnae who had come to help the foreign student—me—adjust to the American way of life. They had intended to take me to town to show me what an American girl wears. As I appeared quite appropriately attired in Bermuda shorts, matching Shetland sweater, and ubiquitous circle pin, I could see their faces fall.

My "group" was naturally interested in men and having relationships, only we were far more circumspect and dressed a good deal more modestly than young women today. Our underclothing was designed to conceal, not reveal, and our hemlines showed nothing above our knees. We had to be in from dates by 11 P.M., and boys were allowed in our rooms only on Sunday afternoons, with the door open and their—and our—feet on the floor.

We were also somewhat naïve. When my English class was analyzing William Blake's "The Sick Rose," in which the invisible worm finds the rose's bed of crimson joy, the professor, David Ferry, called on me to explain the symbolism. I responded gamely about flowers being a symbol of renewal and gardens representing the cycle of life. This did not impress Ferry, who harrumphed, "Yes, quite right, but what about the sexual connotations, Miss Korbel?"

Today a college classroom is filled with the clicking of mouses as students take notes on their laptops. In my classes the clicking came from our knitting needles as we made sweaters and socks for our boyfriends. I knitted my way through many a class on behalf of Elston and his successors. On one occasion the professor became so annoyed by the collective racket that he announced that he would henceforth consider knitting an admission of pregnancy.

The fact that Wellesley was a women's college made a big difference, because women (or girls) held all the leadership positions. We were the student council presidents, newspaper editors, athletic team captains, and valedictorians. No one had to pretend to be dumb in class in order not to show up the boys, although the tactic remained common on dates. All through high school I had wanted to be smart but not to stick out too much. Now I was surrounded by girls who had been first in their high schools, many of whom more than matched my seriousness.

A women's college was also different because of the recognition accorded women professors. Although we didn't call them role models at that time, the professors at Wellesley challenged us to excel. I had four outstanding women mentors: Professor Margaret Ball, who taught international relations, Professor Alona Evans (international law), Professor Louise Overacker (politics and interest groups), and Professor Barbara Green (honors thesis advisor). The lessons they taught me about how the international system functions, and about the role played by America as a primary organizer of that system, have stayed with me ever since.

Despite all the fitting in, I was still part of one minority. Wellesley students were mostly Republican. I was in the College Democrats. A small group, we thought we were brave and outspoken. In later years I participated at high levels in presidential campaigns, but in 1956 I was a foot soldier among those "madly for Adlai" Stevenson as he ran without much hope against President Eisenhower. Filled with enthusiasm, I signed up to collect Dollars for Democrats. I was walking around Boston carrying my sign when one salty old man snapped, "Not one dollar for Democrats, but how about five dollars for you?"

At the end of my sophomore year, I went home feeling pretty good. I was twenty years old. I loved my professors. I was getting my journalistic feet wet as a reporter for the school paper, the *Wellesley News*. I even had a respectable social life. My friends and I decided Elston looked a bit like Elvis Presley, except for the hair, and I loved having him at least reasonably close by. We did have a temporary falling-out, and I briefly replaced his orange-and-black Princeton scarf with a gray-and-maroon one from a boy at MIT. I also dated Roger Cipriani from Chicago, who went to Harvard and whom I had met on the train to Boston. Our short friendship was to influence my fate in a fortuitous way. By the summer, however, Elston and I were back together.

My life seemed on an upward trajectory. I had started working for the *Denver Post* (much better than my previous summer job, selling lingerie at a department store) and was scheduled to become an American citizen. Everything did indeed seem for the best in this best of all possible worlds.

MY FAMILY HAD BECOME U.S. citizens in March of 1957, while I was away at school. So I had my own moment that summer. Having been in college for two years, I felt I knew everything and was a bit full of myself when I sat down for the examination. The interviewer wanted to be sure that I understood the responsibilities of citizenship and that I was not a Communist. I wanted the interviewer to know my opinion of the McCarran Act, a federal law that I felt unduly restricted immigration. Fortunately I managed to refrain from pressing my arguments too far, and the examiner was tolerant enough to overlook them. So, along with a group of other eager candidates, I swore allegiance to the United States. After being instructed on the privileges and duties that came with that oath, I received my naturalization certificate. At last I was an American.

I was happy to have this proof of belonging, but I was young and the full meaning of citizenship would take time to sink in. In the years since, I have often thought about that distant Denver day. On July 4, 2000, I spoke at a naturalization ceremony at Monticello, the home of America's first Secretary of State. I gave remarks about the responsibilities of citizenship and later stood under the portico studying the crowd, waiting for the oath taking to begin.

Beneath the hot summer sun there were hundreds of faces, brown and white, Asian and black, young and old, refugees, immigrants, and adoptees. By the time the ceremony concluded, each of these people would be an American. They were asked to stand on the steps in front of us and pledge allegiance. I joined them and with them repeated the patriotic oath. As each new citizen came forward for the certificate, I shook his or her hand and said, "I have a certificate just like this. Keep it safe. It's the most important piece of paper you'll ever have." At home that night I checked my filing cabinet and found the document I had received in Denver just where it should have been—tucked in beside those of my mother and father.

MY HOPED-FOR CAREER as a journalist began at the bottom. My responsibilities at the *Denver Post* were to read and clip stories in the "morgue," the paper's library, answer phone queries, and take packages of clips to reporters in the city room. It wasn't long before I noticed an appealingly tweedy young reporter who regularly climbed the stairs to our office to research the stories he was writing. We smiled, the way people who are noticing each other do, but because he wore a gold ring on his left hand, I thought he was married and so didn't smile in quite *that* way. Then one morning I accidentally happened to get a closer look, and found to my pleasure that it was a class ring he was wearing.

Having just been a sophomore, I dared to pose a rather sophomoric question to this young man with the open face and boyish appearance: "Where do you go to school?"

"Williams in Williamstown, Massachusetts."

"I go to Wellesley in Wellesley, Massachusetts. Where're you from?"

"Chicago."

"Really? I used to date a boy from Chicago—Roger Cipriani. Know him?"

"Know him? He's my best friend. Oh my God," the young reporter said, "you must be Miss Wellesley."

And with those few words I started my relationship with Joe Albright. Since Roger and I had not had the calmest parting, Joe and I didn't pursue that conversation, but I did tell him about Elston, and Joe told me about his girlfriend at Bennington. He said that he was living near the University of Denver in a frat house. I said it was two blocks from mine. He offered me a ride home. I invited him to dinner.

My parents were prone to testing my boyfriends, as if I were some princess and suitors had to solve riddles or slay dragons to get through the door. The problem was there was no parade to my door, we were not in Central Europe, and my tests were different from those of my parents. Besides, Joe was hardly a friend yet, much less a boyfriend.

One of the tests that would immediately disqualify anyone arriving at the Korbels was a challenge no young man could possibly anticipate. Our house was full of those eclectic paintings from the apartment in Prague. No one who knew the first thing about art would think they had been painted by the same person, yet I had had several potential beaus assume just that. "Gee," they would say, "You have a lot of paintings. Does your father paint?" At which point my mother would say, in Czech, "This one is an idiot." My father, in Czech, would agree.

When Joe walked into the house, his first words were, "You have some wonderful paintings. My father is a painter."

My father rolled his eyes and said, in Czech, "So this time she has brought home a boy whose father paints houses."

My mother was more charitable. In Czech, she told me, "He does look nice." Over dinner we discussed Harry Truman, whom my father greatly admired. Joe admitted he had grown up in a household that despised Truman. Perhaps because he had complimented her cooking, my mother overlooked this gaffe and without consulting me invited Joe to return for dinner the next night, and the next. Joe, without consulting me, accepted.

He and I also began having lunch. On the weekends he worked nights while I continued going out with Elston. Adding to the fun, a young man from the Harvard Business School whom I had met at the end of the school year was in Denver, so we went out a few times. I felt, most unusually, like the belle of the ball. Naturally my father was appalled. He expressed his disapproval with a Serbian word, *zaglavíćeš*, which with his intonation meant "You are heading down the wrong road and will end up in the gutter as a whore." When it came to my "morals" my father didn't mince words, even foreign ones.

He needn't have worried. Elston and I were headed for a breakup. An aspiring engineer, he had complained for some time that I was a "pseudo-intellectual," because I had talked so much about history and politics. Now I told him about Joe. He accused me of two-timing him, which was true enough, but he'd done the same to me many times. In any case, Elston—though not happily—went on his way.

Joe and I, meanwhile, never ran out of things to say to each other. Joe made it clear that he was interested in what I thought, and he was also full of surprises. In July, when he asked if I wanted to go to the Cheyenne Frontier Days rodeo, I thought it would be a great way to introduce him to the West. But when this city boy picked me up in worn-out jeans, scuffed cowboy boots, and a battered Stetson, I was impressed. It turned out that his family had a ranch in Wyoming, where he had spent the summers since he was small, even roping calves in rodeos. That day we talked, we walked, we held hands, we kissed, and we fell—and those are the right words—deeply in love.

As the days passed, Joe heard a lot about my family and I began to learn more about his. My transplanted diplomatic family was unusual; his family was extraordinary. Joe's great-great grandfather was Joseph Medill, who built up the *Chicago Tribune*. His grandfather, Joseph Medill Patterson, founded the *New York Daily News*. His great aunt Cissy Patterson owned the *Washington Times-Herald*, which was later sold to Katharine Graham's father, Eugene Meyer, and merged with the *Washington Post*.

The person in Joe's family who hated Harry Truman had been his grand-father's cousin, Colonel Bertie McCormick, the former publisher of the *Chicago Tribune*, who had waged a bitter editorial battle against the President. Further family revelations came slowly—"on a need to know basis." When my father won a Guggenheim Fellowship, Joe was at our house, and we all celebrated. At the end of the evening Joe took me aside and said, "Madeleine, I don't know if I should tell you, but my uncle is Harry Guggenheim."

My father got a similar shock when a friend who was knowledgeable about art happened to meet Joe at our house. "Young man," the friend said, "did you know that you bear the name of a famous American artist, Ivan Albright?"

"Yes, sir," Joe replied. "He's my father."

I still remember my father's face, which combined in equal measure astonishment and relief that Joe could not possibly have understood what he had said to my mother that first day in Czech.

Actually Ivan Albright was not Joe's real father. He was the second husband of Joe's mother, Josephine Patterson. Josephine was smart, beautiful with a face well-mapped from all her rugged adventures, but sadly insecure. She had earlier been married to a trial lawyer named Fred Reeve. Reeve and Josephine had two children—Joe and his sister, Alice—then Reeve decided to go back to his first wife. The way Joe explained it to me, Reeve felt that he could return to his wife as if he had never left because the Catholic Church hadn't recognized Reeve's first divorce or his second marriage. To Josephine, Joe said, this seemed like hypocrisy, making her bitter not only against Reeve but also against the Church. As for Reeve, he visited the children but never developed a close relationship with them. Joe always spoke of his birth father with a mixture of admiration and sadness.

Six weeks from the time we met, Joe asked me to marry him. I accepted, understanding that the wedding wouldn't take place until after my graduation. Clearly we didn't know each other well, but who cared? We were head over heels and Joe seemed a prince arriving completely out of the blue. He gave me his Theta Delta Xi pin to wear and left for Wyoming to tell his parents about me. When he returned, he said he had run into problems. His mother definitely did not like my being Catholic and not so subtly asked Joe if I were marrying him for his money. I had fallen in love with Joe very quickly, before I knew about his family, let alone its money, and in fact had thought that his frequent visits to our house for dinner helped out his finances. I was insulted—on my behalf and on his. How could his family think so little of him? It seemed disingenuous to complain about wealth and prominence, but for many years Joe was under constant pressure to prove that his status was merited, not simply inherited. I believe he found the responsibility that came with his genealogy uncomfortable and the burden heavy.

I returned to Wellesley for my junior year. My friends shrieked when they saw a fraternity pin over my left breast. I had departed for the summer with no special beau and now I was to be engaged. I was proud to say that the pin and I belonged to a spectacular senior at Williams College. Joe was the managing editor of his paper, junior Phi Beta Kappa, and willing to drive down to Wellesley every weekend or have me come to Williams. Everything seemed perfect. I was doing well in school and was going to marry a fascinating man who thought I could have a career that complemented his.

I wore Joe's fraternity pin constantly and draped myself in a Williams scarf, as well as a black sweater of Joe's with purple numerals, 1958, on the back. When I visited him at Williams, his fraternity brothers serenaded me.

It was considerably harder winning over his family. Shortly after Joe broke the news to his mother, she asked her sister, Alicia, to check me out. So on our way to college, Joe and I went to visit Alicia Patterson and Harry Guggenheim at their grand estate overlooking Long Island Sound. Joe explained it was called Falaise after a town in Normandy and that some of the bricks had been brought over from Europe. The manor house was surrounded by immense iron gates and grounds that looked as large as the entire Wellesley campus. Charles Lindbergh was among the many famous people who had stayed there; years later I was astonished to realize when I went to see *The Godfather* that Francis Ford Coppola had used one of the rooms at Falaise and also the house's stables for his movie. Look hard enough in one scene, and you can see a portrait of Alicia Patterson on the wall.

For the first time I flew east rather than take the train. Joe picked me up in New York and we drove to Long Island. I had been fully briefed. Harry Guggenheim was Alicia's third husband. Like Joe's mother, she had brains—and a face reflecting her strong character, with high cheekbones and deep-set eyes. She looked like Katharine Hepburn in *The Lion in Winter* and dressed like the Duchess of Windsor. She was also just plain gutsy. She smoked, drank, hunted big game and quail, played tennis and bridge, all with elegant style. Having no children, she saw Joe and his sister, Alice, as her heirs.

The day was hot but I, expecting fall weather, had on a baby blue lambswool sweater set and a tweed skirt. Alicia met us and we went for a walk. Even though "Aunt Alicia," as she asked me to call her, tried to make me feel comfortable, I wasn't good at playing Cinderella and felt ill at ease. After our walk, she announced we would dress for dinner. I had brought my entire college wardrobe with me, so I was adequately prepared, or so I thought, but when I emerged from my bath, wrapped in a towel, there was not a stitch of clothing in my room.

After some moments of panic, I saw a maid entering with all my clothes freshly ironed. I now know that this is the upper-class way of dealing with houseguests, but at the time I feared that they thought I needed cleaning up. At dinner I began my life as a member of the Patterson clan, for that was what they always were, even though they had different married names. During the toasts—very much a part of family gatherings—there was one to my mother and father, "distinguished diplomats and representatives of a free Czechoslovakia." I loved that.

My parents met Joe's parents before I did. On their way back from Wyoming to Chicago, the Albrights stopped to meet the Korbels in Denver. In our naïveté Joe and I had thought this would be a good idea, but it's hard to imagine two more different couples. They shared one thing: the mission of finding out if the others' child was good enough for theirs. My father, the diplomat intellectual, thought he could make every encounter work. My mother, the spontaneous extrovert with a sharp tongue, wanted everyone to like her. Ivan Albright, who could capture the minutest detail of character on canvas, was uncomfortable communicating via words. And Joe's mother, a mixture of rebel and socialite, was alternately charming and blunt. Not wanting to upset us, both sets of parents reported that the meeting had gone well; details of its awkwardness only emerged years later.

I first met Joe's mother and father in New York over Thanksgiving. Although there was more tension than with Aunt Alicia, we seemed to get along fine. We stayed in Alicia and Harry Guggenheim's house on Seventy-fourth Street, and with their help and the fun of going as a group to dinners and the theater, I thought I was able to answer satisfactorily all the questions the Albrights had about me.

During Christmas vacation, I stopped in Chicago on the way back from Denver and visited the Albrights again, this time in their spacious brownstone on Division Street. Ivan Albright's lavish, meticulously detailed canvases hung everywhere. My prospective father-in-law was one of the most original American artists of the twentieth century, best known for his *Picture of Dorian Gray*. I have come to admire his work tremendously. At the time, however, I struggled with his macabre realism; I never got used to his depiction of the *Temptations of Saint Anthony*, with drowning corpses being devoured by half-eaten fish while slavering wolves looked on. This spectacle hung above the dining room table.

One feature of the Christmas stop was the opportunity to meet Joe's grandmother, Alice Higinbotham Patterson, a natural matriarch. The family called her Gaga, which she certainly wasn't. She was old Chicago, the daughter of the cofounder of Marshall Field's department store. Gaga was less than five feet tall, frail, and beautiful. A divorcée, she lived alone in an elegant apartment filled with paintings and ancient Chinese statues, overlooking Lake Shore Drive. At lunch we were presented with a cheese soufflé. I'd never eaten such a thing before. As I plunged the serving spoon into the delicate creation, it collapsed, and so with it did my heart. I was convinced I had committed a major faux pas.

To say that I was overwhelmed by Joe's family would be an understatement. In their defense, once they saw that the two of us were determined to get married, they tried to make things work, but that realization took time. It was a shock to them that Joe, once a regular at Chicago debutante parties, escorting Misses Roosevelt and Coolidge, had chosen me. In the past when family members had married foreigners, they had at least acquired titles in the process. I was no countess.

I returned to Wellesley after Christmas thinking not only that I had survived the in-law tests, but that I was actually managing to balance a full-time boyfriend with my studies. As it turned out, neither was true.

I had always been an organized student. Very organized. I took notes in class in a spiral notebook and while reading on looseleaf notebook paper. Then I put the reading notes together with the matching class notes and bound them with large metal rings. Each page of notes corresponded precisely to each particular assignment. I used different color pens, thinking of all the time I would save when referring to the notes later. I summarized the notes for exams on carefully organized index cards, then summarized the summaries. But now Joe's visits and my trips to Williamstown were impinging on my study habits. I had no time to color-code notes or summarize summaries.

Exams were upon us, and I felt underprepared and convinced I was going to flunk everything. Adding to my turmoil, Joe was having second thoughts. During a winter weekend in Williamstown, he sat me down in Baxter Hall, the student center, and told me he felt we had moved too quickly. He could never be "great," he said, if he married so young. I was dumbfounded.

I started to take off my pin slowly, hoping he would stop me. When he did not, I dropped it in his lap. He got up and threw it out the window. Drama demanded that I stomp out, but there was no way out of Williamstown at night in the winter without a car, and I didn't have one, so I went back to my rented room. I couldn't sleep as I tried to figure out what had happened and whether there was any chance that Joe would change his mind. My conclusion wasn't particularly encouraging: Joe's mother had worked her magic on him.

Joe must have done some thinking of his own. He arrived to take me to breakfast and returned the pin he had retrieved. I thought it was a miracle that he had found it. We agreed to keep the relationship going but to slow down. I returned to Wellesley completely deflated. I did not want to believe that my prince had turned into a frog, but I couldn't help thinking back to the college boy who had dated and dropped me in high school. Maybe I was doomed to keep getting my hopes dashed by starting relationships that were too exciting to be true. Perhaps Joe was not the problem; perhaps the problem was me.

Over the next months Joe continued to write to me every day. The difference was that the letters were signed "Sincerely yours" instead of "Love." When we met, we found we still had more to say to each other than to anyone else. What sealed our relationship, though, was the Library of Congress. We both realized we needed to do research there for final papers we were writing, so we traveled to Washington over spring vacation. This time there were no doubts, no question of "sincerely yours." We had a glorious time and managed somehow to agree that getting married would not stand in the way of Joe's "greatness." From then on "going to Washington" became our secret code for having a good time together.

Joe's mother, however, remained unconvinced—a fact that became painfully evident at her son's graduation. As we gathered in his room before the ceremony, Joe showed his finished thesis to his parents. He had received the highest honors for it and was to be singled out at the ceremonies, but his mother took one look at the dedication—"TO MADELEINE WITH WHOM...."—and she and Ivan walked out, not to return to see Joe graduate. The thesis was about Joseph Medill Patterson, Joe's mother's father, whom she revered and had held out as a role model to him, so Joe probably should not have dedicated it to me, but there it was.

Still, what may have worked for Josephine at Christmas didn't work over the summer. When Joe returned that fall from a bus tour through the Soviet Union, he gave me an antique emerald and diamond engagement ring he had bought in London. Our engagement was officially announced a few months later. The story ran in the *Chicago Sun-Times* under a six-column headline—"Joseph Albright Will Marry in June"—and featured a photo not of the prospective bride, as was customary, but of the groom. My name did make it into the second sentence, the first one being, "Joseph Medill Patterson Albright will take a bride in Denver next June."

That fall Joe started his full-time first job, on the *Chicago Sun-Times*.

We spoke on the phone every night, and aside from my work as news editor of the college paper and manager of the snack store, there were no distractions. I concentrated on my studies, particularly my senior honors thesis.

It would have been uncharacteristic for me not to follow a suggestion made by my father on any subject, much less the culmination of my undergraduate work. He proposed that I write about a man who, in post–World War II Czechoslovakia, had played the role of villain. Zdeněk Fierlinger was a Social Democrat who eagerly led his party into partnership with the Communists. The result ultimately was the death of Masaryk, the resignation of Beneš, and the end of democracy.

In my father's circle Fierlinger was referred to as Quislinger, after Vidkun Quisling, the Norwegian politician whose cooperation with the Nazis before and during World War II made his name synonymous with a flaccid spine and a treasonous heart. The term "fellow traveler" had become well-known to Americans, thanks to Senator Joseph McCarthy, who made a career out of accusing people, regardless of their guilt or innocence, of going along with Communists. Fierlinger was a true fellow traveler. I suspect he would have been surprised to find that, in the spring of 1959, a whole dorm of American college women knew his name. For months I talked almost as much about him as about Joe; certainly I spent more time with him.

My thesis kept me focused on my birthplace. Although I had become an American, I couldn't separate myself from the struggles in Europe. As much as I wanted to be like my American contemporaries, I was not. I had spent nights in a bomb shelter. I had felt in my own life some of the disruption war could cause. My family had been driven from its homeland by the admirers of Stalin. These experiences made me a person with strong opinions, and I had been born with a tendency to express them.

The Cold War struggle was very real to me, and I followed events closely––Khrushchev denouncing Stalin; the launching of the Soviet satellite Sputnik, which shocked our scientists and marked the beginning of the space age; the Communist revolution in Cuba only ninety miles from our shores; the collapse of colonialism and the competition among America, the Soviets, and Mao's China for influence among the newly independent states of Asia and Africa. This was an era of anxiety but also—for me—stark moral clarity. We were good; the Communists were bad. Half of Europe was free; the other half imprisoned. People everywhere who believed in the kind of democratic humanism that had been preached by Tomáš Masaryk had to stand together.

Out in Denver my father was removed from Czechoslovak-American political circles, but his thoughts still dwelt on our native land. He started working on his third book, *The Communist Subversion of Czechoslovakia*, which was essentially a warning about the fragility of democracy and the dangers of coexistence with Communists. In his conclusion he wrote that Lenin had urged his followers "to use any ruse, dodges, tricks, cunning, unlawful methods, concealment, veiling of truth" to achieve their ends. He urged democratic leaders not to be taken in by their own faith in democratic practices and their desire to trust. Communists could not be trusted, because they did not desire coexistence; they desired conquest. As for the possibility that the Soviet Union would one day renounce Communism voluntarily, Khrushchev himself scoffed that it wouldn't happen "until shrimp learn to whistle."

Writing an honors thesis was daunting, but it taught me how to stick with a single project over an extended period. Many of the materials I found were in Czech, and I quickly discovered that I didn't really have a full grasp of written Czech, which I had stopped learning at age nine. For me it was an oral language, so I started reading out loud to myself. My parents had given me a small Olivetti typewriter when I went to college, on the condition I write in Czech and never type a letter home. My father thought it rude to compose personal letters on typewriters and that this would be a good opportunity for me to practice my Czech. When he sent me my letters back corrected in red ink, I rebelled and said that if he ever expected to hear from me again, it would have to be in English. Even though my spoken Czech is good, when I write to Czech friends to this day, I do so in English because I am embarrassed by my childlike written Czech.

For all my efforts I don't think anyone other than my father, Joe, and my advisor ever read my thesis. On the other hand, my father's book was read not only in the West but, as I learned later, in Czechoslovakia. In 1990, after the Berlin Wall fell, I attended a conference in Germany where I had a conversation with Jaroslav Šedivý, who would later become Czech foreign minister. He told me that while he was working in the archives of the Czechoslovak foreign ministry during the Cold War years, he had argued with those who had been instructed to remove all information about my father, whom the Communists considered a traitor. He had then gone to work in an institute where he managed somehow to obtain a bootleg copy of *The Communist Subversion of Czechoslovakia*. When he read it, he said, he understood for the first time what had really happened to his country between the end of the war and the Communist takeover in 1948. Šedivý became a dissident and was arrested. After serving time in jail, he labored as a window washer until Czechoslovakia once again became free.

I DID ENJOY the occasional break from school. During my senior year, Joe asked me to come to Chicago for Easter vacation to spend more time with him and his family. Joe's grandmother—the formidable Gaga— took me under her wing. This development had both pluses and minuses. She was wonderfully entertaining, but frankly I was afraid of her. Early in the visit she took me to lunch at the exclusive Casino Club on Lake Shore Drive. In those days proper young women wore hats and white gloves. It hadn't occurred to me that lunch was such an occasion, but I looked around, and the others there had on hats, as did Gaga. I should have just kept quiet, but in my embarrassment I started down a treacherous path.

"I always love having a new hat for Easter, but I wasn't able to find one that I liked in the village of Wellesley. I thought I would buy one here."

"Wonderful idea," said Gaga. "We will go to my milliners right after lunch and get you a hat."

"Milliners?" I thought—right, a special store for hats. I had always bought my hats in department stores.

All we had to do was cross Michigan Avenue to arrive at Bes-Ben. The shop was filled with mirrors and chairs in front of them, so that one could spend hours sitting and trying on hats. There were a few on stands scattered around, but Gaga told me to sit and directed the salespeople, who were obviously used to her, to bring out their Easter creations for her "grandson's fiancée"—or maybe it was for his "intended." (It was important to use the right word with the Pattersons. I was told early in my relationship with the family that one said "evening gown," not "for-mal," "curtain," not "drape," "sofa," not "couch," "present," not "gift," and "rich," not "wealthy.")

As the milliners brought out their wares, the price tag on one flitted in front of my eyes. When I put on the hat and looked in the mirror, I saw Minnie Pearl at the Grand Ole Opry, but what terrified me was the price. The hat cost two hundred dollars—well over a thousand in today's currency. This was not an option.

"It's lovely, but the color is all wrong," I said.

"Don't worry, dear, we can do it in whatever color you want," the salesperson assured me.

"I'm really not sure these particular flowers look right."

"We can put any type of flowers or berries on you want."

"You know, I really don't need a new hat."

At that point Gaga chimed in and said, "But dear, at lunch you said you did."

That settled the matter. Before I knew it, they had a tape measure around my head; we were choosing colors, hatbands, berries, and flowers. The saleslady said this would all be mine in time for Easter.

I was paralyzed. Was I paying for the hat, or was it a present? If Gaga was paying and I didn't thank her, she would think I was impossibly rude. If I thanked her and it *wasn't* a present, I would be considered impossibly presumptuous. We went back to her apartment for tea. My mind was empty. I had just about decided that the money I was saving for Joe's wedding present would have to go for the hat, when Gaga said, "I hope you like your little Easter present." I was saved. The hat is natural straw, with fuschia flowers, berries of various kinds, and a raspberry-colored velvet hatband. I wore it that Easter and months later to our wedding rehearsal. It sits now in my closet, still in its original blue box.

With the wedding approaching, Joe broached a sensitive subject: would I would mind becoming an Episcopalian? I talked the subject over with my parents, who responded that the decision was entirely up to me. I had always attended church more regularly than they, and they simply did not have strong feelings. I was reminded that although Tomáš Masaryk had been deeply religious, many Czechoslovaks were more secular. That was the case with my parents. What concerned them more than my conversion was the fact that everyone in Joe's family seemed to have been divorced at least once. My father had a blunt talk with Joe about the unacceptability of divorce. As my mother would have reason to tell me many times later, "But Joe told your father he didn't believe in divorce."

As for my own feelings, I didn't mind converting except for one thing: I believed in the Catholic tenet that the Virgin Mary could carry one's prayers to God. I said the rosary and every year celebrated my name day, which as Marie Jana was on August 15, Feast of the Assumption of the Blessed Virgin. Once I agreed to become an Episcopalian, Joe's mother asked me to meet with the Episcopal bishop of Chicago, and this is what we discussed. Where faith is concerned, my own view is you can add to your beliefs, but it's hard to subtract. The mother of Jesus has an honored place in every Christian church, but I was most comfortable with the Catholic perspective. I did not think I could give Mary up, and I never have.

My leaving the Catholic Church also affected where we would get married. Since the church I had attended in Denver was inappropriate, we decided on Saint Andrew's, a beautiful little Episcopal church in Wellesley. Even under normal circumstances I could not have seen my mother planning an American-style wedding. Given the location and the issues with the Albrights, it worked out best that it was in my hands. In between writing my honors thesis, I selected bridesmaids' dresses, handwrote the invitations, picked a place for the reception, and chose the menu. The challenge was to ensure that the choices met Patterson standards without breaking the Korbel bank.

I graduated on June 8. If I hadn't been getting married, I would have hated the thought of leaving Wellesley. During the three days between commencement and matrimony, I stayed in the dormitory with Mary Jane, whose own wedding was set for two days after mine.

On June 11, 1959, a lovely spring day, I married Joe. My parents and Kathy and John drove out from Colorado. The Albrights hosted a rehearsal dinner at Joseph's restaurant in Boston. The next day I got up, washed my hair, and put on my wedding dress and a veil with a somewhat quaint small crown with pearls made by a Czech friend of my mother's. My father, of course, gave me away. Kathy was maid of honor. She was so nervous during the ceremony, her flowers shook. Joe was so intent on answering the priest's questions correctly that when asked, "Wilt thou...," he responded, "I wilt." His parents seemed perfectly happy with our perfectly Episcopal ceremony. The only disruption was caused by Joe's ultrasophisticated sister, Alice, a freshman at Radcliffe. She hated her pale green bridesmaid's dress; after the wedding and the picture taking she ripped it in two and left it in the trash basket in the bathroom. But that one fit of pique couldn't diminish my joy. I had become Mrs. Joseph Albright—with all kinds of monogrammed stationery to prove it.

Twelve years after coming to the United States, as a refugee, I was an American citizen. I had acquired a precious circle of friends. I had graduated with honors from a top-notch college that specialized in equipping women with leadership skills. I had married an American prince whom I adored and who loved me. I had tried the glass slipper, and it fit. In the fairy tale that is where the story ends. In life it's merely the beginning of a new chapter.

FOUR

Family Values

MY YOUNGEST DAUGHTER, Katie, was born in 1967, and by the time she reached college there was a course on the sixties. She took it. The decade had become synonymous with countercultural experiments—hippies, drugs, sexual freedom, Woodstock, antiwar demonstrations. In many ways those of us who graduated at the end of the fifties missed the sixties. While our younger brothers and sisters were doing their own thing, we were doing our parents' thing, starting careers and raising families.

Even among our more buttoned-down colleagues, Joe and I were exceptional in our earnestness. We did, however, begin with a not-so-earnest six-week island-hopping honeymoon in the Caribbean. Immediately after that, at the end of July, Joe was required to report to Fort Leonard Wood, Missouri, for six months of military service. When he went off for basic training, I headed back to Denver to be with my parents, and took the only short-term job I could find, selling tours for the Gray Line Bus Company, while I prepared to join Joe.

I got to Missouri as soon as I could. Joe had to stay on base, so I found a converted motel room in which to live. I considered but turned down "positions" as a carhop and a tattoo parlor come-on girl before landing a perfect job for an aspiring journalist. I worked on the *Rolla Daily News*— "Serving the Greater Rolla Area"—doing a bit of everything. I wrote obituaries and articles for the society page, took ads,[1] reported the occasional sports story, and interviewed folks who had spotted UFOs. I drove thirty miles to work each day in Joe's old blue-and-white Ford, often

---

1. One ad I still remember: "Cemetery plot: owner must move; will sell at sacrifice."

stopping on the way back for a date with my new husband. Before joining the military Joe had been tanned, with a full head of dark brown hair: I'd thought him very handsome. Now he was still handsome, but his head was shaved and I thought he was too thin. I did, however, receive a letter from the army telling me how proud I should be that Joe received the highest grade in his training course.

The peacetime Pentagon, declaring Operation Santa Claus, clipped a month off Joe's military service so he and many of his colleagues could spend Christmas with their families. After the holidays in Denver we went to Chicago in January 1960 for a fresh start. Joe's parents took their younger children, Adam and Dina, out of school and went on a world tour, giving us space. We settled into their house until we found our own apartment, a third-floor walk-up with a roof garden on North Pine Grove Avenue.

We furnished the flat with stuff we bought at auction. Later I did all my graduate work studying in a huge armchair that we bought by mistake because up on the stage it looked normal size. (It's now at the farm I have in Virginia, and all my grandchildren can sit in it at once.) We found a great group of young friends and became regulars at Chicago's Second City, the improvisational theater. We also spent time with Joe's grandmother. I tried to figure out how to socialize with local debutante types, some of them former girlfriends of Joe. It took me weeks to sew a garnet-colored, long-sleeved velvet ball gown to wear to the biggest social event of the season. The dress matched an antique garnet necklace my parents had given me as a wedding present. Rather than being proud I had made the dress myself, when asked where I had bought it, I only smiled.

Joe returned to the *Sun-Times* and I started looking for a job. Since there were four papers in Chicago at the time, I thought I had a good chance of finding a spot at one of the other three, but it wasn't to be. One night during a social dinner Joe's managing editor asked, "So, what're you going to do, honey?"

"Get a job on a newspaper," I replied.

"Well," he said, "you can't work at the same paper as your husband because it's against newspaper guild policy. And of course it really wouldn't be helpful to your husband's career if his wife were working for a competing paper. So I'm afraid you'll have to consider doing something else." Decades later I can think of many answers I might have given that evening. Instead I said nothing and went along.

The something else I ended up doing was to become assistant to the picture editor at the *Encyclopaedia Britannica*. During the job interview I was asked when I planned to get pregnant. I can't remember being offended; I just said I wasn't in a hurry. I was amazed when they hired me, because I had no particular experience with photographs. I guess it was enough that I could read. *EB*, as we called it, had a policy of revising one type of article a year. In 1960, they were updating their geographical articles, and it was my job to select photographs, write captions, and prepare picture layouts. Later I moved to the public relations department, where my job was to scan *EB* carefully for "fillers" that could be dropped in at the end of newspaper columns. I selected such gems as, "Ostriches are voiceless, according to the *Encyclopaedia Britannica*."

The 1960 election was to be our first presidential vote; Joe and I followed the campaigns closely. Like many women, I was besotted with John F. Kennedy. In 1958, I had had the opportunity to interview the future President for the Wellesley paper during his Senate reelection campaign. Not only did I ask him questions for my story, I also asked for his autograph. Joe told me I had acted very unprofessionally. He was right, but I still ended up with the autograph.

The 1960 campaign led to Joe's first big scoop. The Republican Convention was being held in Chicago, where he hid in the bathroom attached to the Sheraton-Blackstone hotel room in which Richard Nixon was holding a conference with top party leaders to choose his running mate. As Joe crouched in a bathtub, furiously scribbling notes (some even on toilet paper), Nixon said he needed Henry Cabot Lodge because Lodge would provide an anchor in foreign affairs while he could concentrate on domestic issues. The story snared Joe a front-page byline.

It was around this time that another young reporter, James Hoge, was hired by the *Sun-Times*. Hoge had it all—golden hair, square jaw, social grace, and a Yale education. Not surprisingly, he went on to a long and distinguished journalistic career in Chicago and New York, but at the time competition and hard feelings between Joe and Jim were inevitable. Although the two men had managed to stay out of each other's way professionally, it soon became impossible not to interact. Amid much clenching of Patterson teeth, Jim married Joe's sister, Alice. After Joe and I were divorced, and Jim got more involved in foreign policy, I found I had much to talk about with my former brother-in-law.

I may have been the dutiful daughter, but Joe was expected to be—and tried to be—the dutiful grandson, son, and nephew. He was raised to join the family business. In addition to the family's other papers, Joe's Aunt Alicia and Harry Guggenheim had started Long Island's very successful *Newsday*. By the time I joined the family, it had long been anticipated that Joe would someday take it over.

In the spring of 1961, he received a letter from his aunt saying that the time had indeed come for him to move to Long Island and go through the *Newsday* training program. The thought of moving did not scare me. I had just discovered I was pregnant, so our life was bound to change anyway. Still, we both had mixed feelings. We had loved our sense of independence in Chicago, but we were also ready to take the next step.

I never doubted that Joe and I would have an exhilarating life once he took over the paper, and I remained fascinated by his family, but what I loved most about my husband was that he wasn't like them. He didn't spend a lot of time talking about the family tree, thinking about where to take the next thrilling vacation, or pondering what property to buy. Nor did he participate in the most irritating of all Patterson conversations, which concerned who was leaving what to whom.

One reason there was so much discussion about wills was that the ownership of *Newsday* was at stake. When the newspaper was founded, Alicia became editor and publisher, with an ownership share of 49 percent. Harry kept his eye on the business side and controlled the other 51 percent. Because Harry was more than a decade older than Alicia, it was generally assumed that she would survive him, at which point an additional two percent of the stock would go to her, and she and ultimately her heirs would control the paper.

Although the union between Alicia and Harry had grown uneasy, it was clear why Alicia had found him fascinating. A graduate of Cambridge, he had been distinguished in war and diplomacy, had run a major mining company, and had been a pioneer in backing the new aviation industry. He was also a philanthropist with a marvelous family art museum, a man who could tell stories about Charles Lindbergh and Jimmy Doolittle and had owned a Kentucky Derby winner.

They wrote each other long letters when they were apart, letters addressed D.D. (Dearest Darling), but Alicia and Harry had bitter disagreements about how she ran the newspaper and about politics. Harry was a Republican, Alicia more of a Democrat. In 1956, that meant that Harry backed President Eisenhower's reelection. Alicia was for Adlai Stevenson.

Alicia and Adlai had known each other for many years. In the fifties they were linked romantically and Alicia even contemplated leaving Harry to marry Stevenson. In the end she stayed put, mainly because the critical two percent was at stake. She and Adlai did however remain great friends. Even in the early 1960s, Stevenson used to come out to Long Island quite openly when Harry was away. I was somewhat disillusioned listening to the great Adlai engage in petty gossip about his yachting sojourns on the Riviera. On the other hand, it was fascinating to hear his anecdotes about President Kennedy and his description of life as America's ambassador to the UN.

After driving from Chicago to Long Island, Joe and I settled into a small apartment in Garden City, about a mile away from the main office of the newspaper. My job, per the instructions of my obstetrician, was to walk. So I did, at least five miles a day. In an era before sonograms and health foods, I drank only Metrecal, the diet drink of the time, and black coffee. Still I kept getting fatter. Finally, at six months the doctor told me I was having "at least twins."

On June 17, Joe was delivering newspapers out of the trunk of our car (part of his apprenticeship in the circulation department) when I sent word to him to come quickly. Our identical twin daughters were arriving six weeks early. After their birth I was not allowed even to touch them. The infants were tiny and not breathing properly: they were rushed into incubators and we were told they might not live. When I was younger, my parents had shielded me from danger and sadness. They could not shield me now. I had never felt so helpless. We didn't even want to name the children until we knew they would live. But our babies were fighters and soon "baby A" became Anne Korbel Albright and "baby B" Alice Patterson Albright.

I was sent home, but Anne and Alice were kept in the hospital for another six weeks. It was painful—and, I felt, unnatural—to have two babies and not go near them. According to the practice then, I could tap on the window and "view" the girls—and even that only for limited periods.

I was going out of my mind trying to figure out how to occupy myself. On one of my long prenatal walks I had seen a sign offering an eight-week intensive Russian language course at Hofstra College (now University). I decided to enroll. For six hours a day I studied, then went off to the hospital for my daily peering at my daughters. Knowing Czech was a help in learning Russian, and by the end of the course I was speaking comfortably.

Finally we brought the children home (in a laundry basket) with only one instruction: feed them. They still did not weigh enough, and they had to eat every three hours, night and day. If they slept, they had to be woken up to eat, which took each of them an hour. So began a new segment in my life, one defined by formula, diapers, rattles, burps, teething, hugs, frequent weight checks, visits to the doctor, and shrieking, splashing baths. I was so proud of my beautiful and good daughters; I was also growing frustrated because I wanted to make full use of my education.

Aunt Alicia, who stopped by frequently, was aware of my quandary and that of many of the young women in my age group. When asked by Radcliffe College to participate in a session analyzing social factors that work for and against women's careers, she contacted me. She wrote, "I thought you might have some ideas on the subject in view of your great urge to continue working despite the babies." In an attempt to give her a picture, I contacted various women's colleges to get some statistics, then wrote an essay about myself which was factual and depressing. When I found it recently among my papers, I was surprised how relevant it still is to the classic women's dilemma: juggling marriage, motherhood, and a profession. I had written:

> Twice in two years, I have had to leave good jobs with good futures to follow my husband's path. And that was even before I had children. Now, even to get a job, I would have to find and hire a dependable nurse and pay her perhaps more than I could make myself. Perhaps I am being overly pessimistic. Perhaps I could go out tomorrow and get a job as a typist. The next question is, why bother? Do I want a job merely to have a job, or do I want to work in order to be doing something worthwhile?

This sounded more downbeat than I was, and so I concluded with a slightly rosier view:

> I must admit though that I feel somewhat like a pioneer. I am not satisfied to sit back for the rest of my life and contemplate in which order to clean the rooms. I want to find a solution and still feel that somehow it must be possible to be a responsible mother, a good wife and have an intellectually satisfying job.

Joe was my ally in all this and actually edited my work. He was even sensitive enough in 1961 to cross out the word "girl" where I had written it and insert "woman."

Despite my questioning, our life was very pleasant. We went into New York City every weekend for shows or shopping or elegant dinners at Alicia and Harry's with celebrity guests. Alicia also invited us down to her place in Georgia, where I worked hard to become a sportswoman. Tennis was my game, but I also learned to play killer croquet and took up quail hunting. I had a harder time learning to water ski on the Saint Mary's River, which was filled with snakes, even though Aunt Alicia assured me that snakes don't bite in water. Fine, I thought, but do the snakes know that?

After a year on Long Island it became time for Joe's training to expand, so he was sent to *Newsday*'s Washington bureau. Arriving in the spring of 1962, we rented a small red clapboard house shaded by a huge crape myrtle tree. The house was located in Georgetown at 3421 R Street, on the less fashionable side of Wisconsin Avenue. We were delighted to be part of Kennedy's Washington. This was pre-Vietnam, pre-Watergate, pre-every-other-gate. Camelot was at its peak. The public was more trusting, and we watched White House press conferences not only for information but because the President was brilliant, debonair, and witty.

We were only twenty-five years old, but because Joe was a journalist, albeit low on the totem pole, we had quick entrée into the Washington social and political scene. We became part of a crowd of seemingly inter-changeable young couples. Our own circle included Ward and Jean Just, Eric and Muffie Wentworth, and Worth and Joan Bingham. When Joe's sister, Alice, and Jim Hoge came to Washington, they joined the group. All the husbands were journalists who competed to get the best stories. The wives competed to see who could make hollandaise sauce that didn't curdle. We ladled it on top of virtually everything before bringing out the dessert of green grapes in sour cream and brown sugar that was all the rage. We played tennis at St. Albans, courts everyone coveted. We talked endlessly about the "three p's"—policy, politics, and personalities.

It is a trait of Washington parties that the first question after "What's your name?" is always "What do you do?" or, back then, "What does your husband do?" The answer often determines whether the conversation continues, so we were terribly impressed that our next-door neighbor, Richard Gardner, had the lofty title of Deputy Assistant Secretary of State for International Organizations. His wife, Danielle, became my closest Washington friend.

Aunt Alicia often visited for a dinner at the White House or to partic-ipate in newspaper-related meetings. When in town she took time out to see the babies and play bridge. I first met the legendary Washington pow-erhouse Kay Graham during these bridge games at a time when, accord-ing to her own account, she still saw herself primarily as her husband's wife and children's mother.

Even though I participated in these activities, I did so part-time because I had begun graduate work at the Johns Hopkins School of Advanced International Studies. I had given up hope of a career in jour-nalism but thought I might follow my father's lead and become a college professor. I was taking the full load of five courses, plus Russian. The twins were a year old and I had good help, but other young mothers were not exactly supportive; they questioned me constantly about how I felt leaving my children with a housekeeper. It was the first, but certainly not the last time the dichotomy between mothers who stay at home and those who don't was made clear to me. I thought then and think now that women should be able to make their own judgments based on their par-ticular circumstances, and those who disagree should mind their own business.

It was now mid 1963. We had completed a year in Washington. Joe was doing well at work. I had brought home A's. Anne and Alice, jabbering away and trying to climb out of their double stroller as we walked around Georgetown, were striking, with huge eyes and blond curls. When our pediatrician warned that the girls would not stay so beautiful for long, because their looks were due to the fact that they had been born prematurely, we got a new pediatrician. Over the years he was proven completely wrong.

We were getting ready for a pleasant summer when the news arrived that Aunt Alicia had been taken to the hospital with a bleeding ulcer. The hard-driving, hard-living newspaper editor was told she had a choice: switch to a bland diet and no alcohol or have an operation. She chose the latter, ignoring advice to put off the operation until she had regained her strength. Sometimes it is dangerous to be rich and powerful enough to override the judgment of others, even doctors. Alicia died on the operating table on July 2, 1963, at the age of fifty-six. Her death would mark another pivotal point in Joe's life—and mine.

In accordance with Alicia's plans eventually to turn the paper over to her nephew, Uncle Harry immediately summoned Joe to Long Island. Not long after, we attended a cocktail party where a woman who didn't know Joe said to him, "I hear her nephew is coming up to take over, and everyone's worried about him."

"I don't know about *everybody*, but *I* certainly am," Joe responded.

He was only twenty-six years old and his discomfort in difficult social situations was evident. While later in life he loved the fact that he always appeared younger than his age, in 1963 it was a huge disadvantage. His hair was close-cropped; he wore black horn-rimmed glasses and Brooks Brothers suits. He looked twenty. It did not help that many at *Newsday* knew him as "Joey," as Alicia had referred to him for years.

No one, least of all Joe, expected that he would become editor and publisher right away, so it wasn't disturbing when Uncle Harry asked Mark Ethridge, the highly respected retired editor and publisher of the *Louisville Courier-Journal*, to run the paper in the interim. Joe was named assistant to the publisher and given a series of short-term jobs, ostensibly to gain experience. Even so, Joe had to demonstrate the confidence and sophistication required to run a major newspaper, while at the same time being modest and unpretentious, to show that he had no delusions of grandeur. He needed to impress Uncle Harry but not irritate him. It was, in the end, an impossible balance to maintain.

In retrospect I see our years on Long Island as a key transitional period in Joe's career, my evolution and aspirations, and ultimately our marriage. At the time, however, I had a sense that the path we would follow had already been set. We were anxious, but we were also confident that *Newsday* was our future.

AFTER BEING SHOWN MANSIONS as Mrs. Joseph Medill Patterson Albright, I went out with agents as Madeleine Korbel and found an enchanted eighteenth-century Long Island farmhouse, covered with wisteria and surrounded by long-neglected but astonishingly elaborate gardens. I don't think I will ever love another house as much. When I first saw the twins climb the steps to the front door, I had visions of them coming out of the house in their wedding dresses. Joe loved it too. A patient father, he taught his daughters how to ski on the mini hill near the house in winter and to swim and dive in the pool when the weather grew warm.

Our move there also proved beneficial to my academic career. I was able to continue my graduate work at Columbia University. In addition to working toward my Ph.D., I decided to try to obtain a certificate from the university's Russian Institute, considered the finest in the country. This meant I had to take even more courses, so I drove into town three days a week. The rest of the time I spent being a Long Island wife, mother, and tamer of an overgrown garden. With help I made it work.

On November 22, I was in a Manhattan taxicab on the way to meet Danielle Gardner at the University Club before going up to Columbia. I was thinking about the fragmented nature of my life when I heard on the car radio that President Kennedy had been shot. I got out of the cab and ran to the club, where I met Danny and retreated with her to the ladies' room. As we consoled each other, we heard a woman in one of the stalls say, "He deserved it." We were so appalled, we didn't even want to see who had made such a statement. Later we joined the huge crowds gathered in shock, staring at a wall of Walter Cronkites on a bank of televisions stacked in an electronics store window. I took the train home in a stupor.

Joe and I had regretted leaving Washington during the height of the Kennedy era, but with the President gone we were glad not to be there. We were however under a constant microscope. Joe was always being observed and rated. When we hosted a Christmas party, I found people in the upstairs hall feeling the carpet. "It's not wool," a guest sniped. As Joe moved from one position to another, scrutiny and gossip intensified. Certainly there were positive indications. Uncle Harry regularly took us to the horse races and staked us to generous bets, and we routinely shared with him a Sunday lunch of rare roast beef and Yorkshire pudding. But he was not one to give praise easily; Joe never knew where he stood. Ever the extrovert, I tried hard to make the relationship run smoothly. Ever the optimist, I kept rationalizing that all Joe's job moves were a good sign.

My work at Columbia was demanding, and I often wondered why I had set such a hard course for myself. The answer was that I found it exhilarating. There couldn't have been a better time to be doing Soviet studies. The 1962 Cuban missile crisis had demonstrated the life-and-death stakes involved in trying to understand the mysteries of the Soviet system, and I had the best professors from whom to learn. The faculty was a *Who's Who* in Communist studies—Seweryn Bialer, Alexander Dallin, John Hazard, Donald Zagoria, and Zbigniew Brzezinski, who would later become President Jimmy Carter's National Security Advisor, and my boss.

I first met Brzezinski when, as a young Harvard professor, he had come to give a lecture at Wellesley. In the interim he had published *The Soviet Bloc*, a perceptive analysis of how Stalin had put together his empire. He was still only in his mid-thirties but was already being quoted everywhere and was increasingly visible in policy circles. I thought it essential to get into a seminar he was offering on comparative Communism, itself a novel idea. With all respect to my other former professors, I judged it the best course I took in graduate school. The professor was challenging, the material totally new, and the students all thought they were the best. Brzezinski assigned lengthy readings in Russian without questioning our ability to understand them. Because he was a good friend of my friends the Gardners and I was older than most students, I was able to see his human side. To most of his students, however, he seemed unapproachable. He was brilliant, did not put up with blather, and while he spoke with a Polish accent, he did so in perfect, clear paragraphs. Even at this time there was little doubt he was going to play an important role in U.S. foreign policy.[2]

On the first day Brzezinski asked for a volunteer to be the first to deliver an oral report. Silence. We all knew that whoever was first would have less time to prepare and no examples from which to profit. More silence. The smart thing was to wait, even if Brzezinski grew impatient. My hand shot up. Whether father or professor, I had to please. I'm not sure Brzezinski appreciated my "sacrifice," but I never forgot it, and today there is a special place in my heart for any student of mine willing to do that first report.

---

2. Among our small group of students was Joseph Starobin, the former editor of America's Communist newspaper, the *Daily Worker*. Joe was even older than I, slightly balding with large glasses, and able to talk with intimacy about changes in Communist thinking and his meetings with Mao and Ho Chi Minh. Another in our group was William Taubman, whose definitive biography of Nikita Khrushchev was published in 2003.

At semester's end I turned in my paper comparing how nationalism and Communism had developed in Yugoslavia and Vietnam, slipping it under Brzezinski's locked office door with a note asking him to send me my grade. Dread hit me the moment the note was out of sight—the same dread that would strike many times in subsequent years when I worked for him in the White House: How had I spelled his name? "B-r-z-e-z..." or, God forbid, "B-r-e-z"? I've still got the note, which remained attached to my paper when I got it back. Brzezinski had given me an A minus, and I had spelled his name correctly.

I was always afraid I would run out of time to complete my Ph.D. There was a seven-year deadline for taking the courses and writing a dissertation. I wanted to finish, but I also wanted to have more children. I was grateful to learn that I could get a leave of absence for a pregnancy. Alice and Anne were four and a half years old and enrolled at what we loved to call Miss Stoddard's School for Very Little People, when I got pregnant again. I was looking forward to being able to spend more time with the twins. However, things did not evolve as I had planned. While I was in my first trimester, the girls caught the measles. I had had measles as a child in Prague, but neither my mother nor I could remember whether I had had what the twins had contracted— what we called "three-day measles," also known as German measles. The obstetrician gave me gamma globulin, the standard treatment back then. But by the time I was six months pregnant, I was once more as big as a house, and the doctor, thinking I might be having twins again, decided to X-ray me.

I was not having twins. In fact my baby was very small. I was suffering from a condition called hydramnios, in which too much amniotic fluid is produced and presses on the baby's skull.

"What are the chances this baby will be brain-damaged?" I asked.

"Very good," the doctor answered calmly.

I thought from his tone that I had asked the question backwards, so I asked again. The answer was the same. Joe and I were flattened. I saw a specialist in New York City for a second opinion. He gave the same diagnosis. When I asked with great difficulty about an abortion, the doctor said it was not only illegal but much too late, guidance which I accepted.

These months were silent, scary, crushing, horrible. We told only our immediate families, and I tried to keep my mind off what was happening by knitting the world's most complicated Irish sweater. At eight months, the doctor failed to detect the baby's heartbeat, but that, he said, could be because of all the water. I became allergic to my own body and itched constantly. When I went into labor at full term, the doctors told me the baby would be stillborn. They put me out completely. When I came to, I did not itch anymore and my stomach was relatively flat, but my arm looked like a balloon. The IV had slipped the vein and all the solution had gone into my arm. Because Joe looked so young and I so awful, the nurse asked if Joe were my son. There should have been a baby there to cry. Instead, I did.

We were so confused. We were dealing with a tragedy; a baby we had wanted had died. Yet when we were ready to think about it, we also felt relief. We had spent weeks trying to figure out how the birth of a child who could have been severely mentally retarded would affect the twins. Our friends were shocked and sympathetic about the baby's death, but because we had not told them what the doctors had said, we couldn't explain fully that, along with the pain, we were consoled that this heartrending experience was over. At the time it is happening, you think you're the only woman in the world experiencing such agony, but as the years have passed, I have met others who have endured similar tragedies.

I know what I have written about my thoughts and emotions during this time will cause some who have children with a mental incapacity to criticize me. I know these families love their children, and had the baby lived, I would have loved my child without limit. I also know that the experience made it clear to me that a woman should have the right to choose, especially in difficult cases, and that a decision to terminate cannot possibly ever be made without much pain—whether the reason relates to the health of the fetus, or the woman's own health, or other sad circumstances.

I BECAME PREGNANT again in 1966, and Katharine Medill Albright—Katie—was born on March 5, 1967. Thank God, this time the pregnancy was smooth and the baby healthy and gloriously full of life. Joe and I enjoyed a pleasant summer with our trio of girls. When Alice and Anne went back to school in the fall, so did I.

My Ph.D. program didn't require a master's thesis, but I decided to write one to have something tangible to show for all my work in case I proved unable to get my Ph.D. There was increasing emphasis in academic and policy circles on trying to understand how Soviet society operated. I chose to study one elite group, the Soviet diplomatic service. I concluded that even though the majority of Soviet ambassadors serving in 1964 had an engineering background, they had actually been recruited by the NKVD, or secret police, the predecessor of the KGB. In other words, their main job was to spy. When I was at the UN and later as Secretary of State, my conclusions made for interesting conversations with

Russian Foreign Minister Yevgeny Primakov and his successor, Igor Ivanov, both of whom had been briefed about my research work. They often made a point of telling me about how different the contemporary Russian foreign service was from its predecessor.

Adding a thesis to a heavy course load was an academic challenge that carried over to my personal life. I wanted good grades, but I also wanted to spend more time with the children. I wanted to be a good wife and help Joe with some of his public obligations. I wanted to be a good hostess to the lively group of friends we had developed and for whom I cooked semi-gourmet dinners. Joe was wonderfully supportive, but the feeling that had started to haunt me in Washington was with me all the time: no matter what I was doing, I thought I should be doing something else. Along with other women, I had a common middle name: guilt.

I remember one occasion particularly well. Anne was dreadfully sick the night before I had a final exam. I was up with her all night, and while she felt better in the morning, I was a wreck. I put on an olive green wool dress and jacket, one of a batch of designer clothes I had inherited from Aunt Alicia's closet, and drove into New York for the exam. I was stunned when I got an A. I decided the dress, despite its sad provenance, was good luck. I wore it to most exams after that, including when I defended my Ph.D. dissertation many years later.

There was no magic dress, however, to help me with the guilt issue, and for as long as my children were at home, I worried I was not getting my priorities straight. Without Joe telling me I was doing the right thing, I am not sure I would have continued doing it.

Joe was having an even harder time. He was striving to please Uncle Harry, but it is questionable whether he ever had a chance. Looking back, I don't think Harry ever intended to turn the paper over to his wife's nephew. He had children, grandchildren, nephews, and grandnephews of his own. Besides, at various times before Alicia died, he had questioned her direction of the paper. If Alicia had lived, I'm sure she would have nurtured Joe's editorial and managerial skills, but the situation was so murky now that no one came forward to mentor him. Aside from a few exceptions at work and some extremely good friends our own age, it seemed there were two kinds of people around Joe at the time—both insincere. Some were trying to ingratiate themselves, on the off chance he would win the sweepstakes. Others were waiting for him to fail. In reading a book about *Newsday*[3] published years later, I was interested to

3. Robert F. Keeler, *Newsday: A Candid History of the Respectable Tabloid*, New York, William Morrow, 1990.

see how many of his former colleagues spoke about Joe as an extremely nice, unpretentious guy, a good reporter who, most felt, had been placed in an extremely difficult situation.

In 1966, Harry Guggenheim hired Bill Moyers to run *Newsday*, a man who was only three years older than Joe but who had been Lyndon Johnson's press secretary. From the perspective of Harry and *Newsday*'s reputation, getting Moyers was a big deal. He was highly respected, politically sophisticated, and full of lofty ideas about the duty of journalists.

Some saw Moyers' arrival as a way to make *Newsday* more than a family newspaper. Obviously we saw the choice more personally. Joe was happy for the paper to grow, but he wanted to be the one to take it to new heights. Mark Ethridge had been a stopgap, but Moyers was a threat. The relationship between Joe and Bill was cordial personally but difficult professionally. Joe became day editor of the paper's Suffolk edition, which meant he had to drive to the eastern end of Long Island each day—leaving him out of the main decision-making loop. Then Moyers allowed Joe to move to Washington as the paper's bureau chief. Although we were pleased by the prospect, we were also beginning to reassess our future. The publisher's desk at *Newsday* now seemed unattainable. We figured Joe might get more involved with the *Tribune* company or in time step into some executive job at another major paper.

It was 1968, and we were getting ready to move back to Washington. I had passed my written and oral comprehensives, turned in my master's thesis, and received a certificate from the Russian Institute. A substantial part of my graduate work had been completed, and the field of study I had chosen was fascinating. I had met Stalin's daughter, Svetlana, who had come to Long Island denouncing her late father's methods. A Soviet fishing vessel had come too close to our beaches, and as a Russian speaker I was asked by *Newsday* to talk to the officers. In Czechoslovakia a group of reformers was arising, trying to humanize the Communist system.

Meanwhile the country I had adopted and which had adopted me was involved in its own philosophical struggle. Initially I wasn't engaged in it at all, though the growing protests against the Vietnam War surrounded me. I was strongly anti-Communist both by heredity and conviction, and my instinct was to support the U.S. government. For a long time it didn't occur to me to question the war. That started to change in early 1968 after the Tet offensive, during which North Vietnamese forces attacked and breached our embassy compound in Saigon before being beaten back. Whatever our intentions, it seemed increasingly unlikely that we would prevail.

Even when I turned against the war, the student protestors drove me crazy. I had set aside certain days to come into Columbia, and when I found the library blocked by protestors, I not only didn't join them, I saw them as a major irritation. I was afraid I wouldn't be able to get into the building where my oral exams were being held. As a young mother with three children, I did not see myself getting involved in demonstrations.

The sixties, which for Joe and me had started so predictably, didn't end that way. The road Mr. and Mrs. Joseph Medill Patterson Albright were supposed to travel was blocked. That did not bother me too much; my whole life had taught me to make adjustments. It would be harder for Joe. Where that difficulty would lead I couldn't imagine.

For now we were heading back to Washington, where the action was. Joe could put his formidable writing and investigative skills to work. Alice and Anne were in school; Katie was a babbling baby. I could continue my graduate studies—and more. I was no longer the putative publisher's wife who had to be above it all, like Caesar's wife. I could, for the first time, become involved in politics myself.

FIVE

Mrs. Albright
Goes to Washington

W HEN I WAS NAMED Secretary of State, some people said I had
been plotting to get the job all my adult life. That's not so. For
most of that time I could not even have imagined it. What is true
is that as it became increasingly evident that Joe would never become publisher of *Newsday*, I began to think about the possibilities for combining my
dual passion for foreign policy and politics. But what were the possibilities?

The women I most admired were exceptional in all senses of the
word; I couldn't expect to follow them. Eleanor Roosevelt had done spectacular work drafting the Universal Declaration of Human Rights, but
she had been the wife of a President. Indira Gandhi had become India's
first woman prime minister, but she had been a prime minister's daughter.
Golda Meir—a schoolteacher in the United States—had to move to
Israel before she was seen as a potential leader. Of course I was not aiming to be a president or prime minister, I just wanted an interesting job,
ideally in foreign policy. But there were not many women in foreign
policy–related positions. There were a few women ambassadors, but
most of those had started early and were career foreign service officers.

So I didn't have any particular path in mind, but I did want to do
something. To get started I needed proper credentials and the backing of
someone with enough faith to help me, not out of charity but because he
(that's how it was) would recognize my value, either to him or to some
project. So I continued working on my Ph.D. and took whatever opportunities came along to develop both credentials and contacts.

I began by becoming a class A volunteer, fund-raising and starting a newsletter for a small school. I served on a variety of boards offering advice on everything from education to administration. I helped organize auctions. I stood in front of polling stations, urging people to vote, and provided bed and breakfast to the occasional Czechoslovak visitor. I put on dinner parties and picnics at the forty-six-acre farm we acquired in Virginia, with its two-hundred-year-old stone house, pasture, and cows. I also did a lot of mother things, sewing the occasional dress or costume, poring over homework, arranging car pools, and maneuvering through the not always child-friendly streets of Georgetown selling Girl Scout cookies. These activities had many satisfactions but were hardly focused. My life felt like a jigsaw, only I was working with pieces from several puzzles simultaneously and there was no finished picture to tell me how it should all end up.

WHEN JOE AND I returned to Washington in 1968, it was easy to fit back in because Joe was still part of that lionized group, the journalists. But we had grown less dreamy about our future, and the city was less dreamy too. This was no longer Camelot. Vietnam and civil rights protests disrupted the capital. In the wake of Martin Luther King, Jr.'s assassination, Resurrection City had been erected on the Mall to remind politicians of the Poor People's Campaign. When Joe and other journalists covered unrest in the streets, they wore hard hats. Joe's visiting mother and younger brother Adam returned from marches and candlelight vigils to wash tear gas out of their eyes. During one of the more tumultuous demonstrations, Alice and Anne watched from their bedroom as students pried bricks from the sidewalk to use as missiles. Once I had to go searching for our car, which protestors had moved with their bare hands, for reasons I still cannot fathom. Starting in 1969, when we turned on the TV, instead of JFK's graceful presence we saw the glowering faces of Richard Nixon and Spiro Agnew.

Many of our friends from the earlier days had left, but we did our best to plunge back into the life of the city. As a liberal with a social conscience, I wanted to do what I could to bridge the economic, social, and racial divides that fragmented Washington even more sharply then than they do today. I tried to get involved in local political races and participated in campaigns aimed at increasing funding for public schools. At the same time I somewhat guiltily enrolled our daughters in Beauvoir, a private school that began at the nursery level and went through third grade. Beauvoir was the school of choice for many politicians' children, as well as those of Washington's most prominent families. It was one of three schools associated with Washington's National Cathedral, superb but hardly diverse.

My way of compensating—or rationalizing—was to lead a campaign to recruit African-American teachers and students and to increase scholarship funds. This was a whole new outlet for my energy, and I discovered I had a talent for it. I had never raised a penny before, but I saw fund-raising as primarily a question of organization, and—with my history of note taking, color-coded pens, and index cards—I was organized.

It may sound crazy, but no one would be reading this book had I not been asked to be on the Beauvoir board of trustees and run the annual fund drive beginning in the fall of 1969. In life one thing leads to another, and in Washington one personal recommendation does too. Of course a recommendation counts only if it is favorable. I was determined that, no matter what kind of job I was given, I would do it well.

My fund-raising partner one year turned out to be a fellow parent, Harry McPherson—in that era a political legend. Harry had been an advisor to Lyndon Johnson in both the Senate and White House. He was blessed with Texas-style charm, and we laughed, told stories, and sang country-western songs while addressing fund-raising solicitations, which Harry—in a playful mood—sometimes signed with LBJ's name.

My success at fund-raising was noticed and I was asked to become chairman of the Beauvoir board, where Harry joined me as a member.[1] At one point we had a problem with another board member who was well regarded in our community but was alleged to have cheated people out of money in a pyramid scheme. It was a nasty situation, but we had no choice: the person involved had to be told to resign. Harry was with me when I delivered the bad news. I had to be tough and diplomatic. "Madeleine," Harry declared when it was over, "to use an old Texas expression, you are the kind of person to go to the well with." Never before had I received such a compliment from a man. For years afterward when I was asked for a reference, I would send people to Harry. He came through every time.

However, it was another Beauvoir breakthrough that truly changed my life. People who had watched me work at the school asked if I would help organize a fund-raising dinner for Maine Senator Edmund Muskie's 1972 presidential campaign. I said I would be delighted, for two reasons. I wanted a Democrat to reclaim the White House and I loved being active.

Four years earlier, Muskie had impressed voters with his integrity and intelligence as Hubert Humphrey's running mate, despite their loss. His

---

1. As board chairman, I devoted so many hours to Beauvoir that my mother exclaimed, "What is it with you and this school? You act like it is Harvard, but it's only nursery school through the third grade!"

craggy face and lanky six-foot-four frame earned frequent comparisons to Lincoln. On the eve of the midterm election in 1970, Muskie had delivered an eloquent television address calling for civility in politics, dramatically boosting his popularity. As the large field of Democratic candidates gathered in 1972, Muskie stood out both in experience and name recognition. The Vietnam War was still the big issue, and his position of thoughtful opposition earned him support from a broad array of party leaders. Then, two weeks before the New Hampshire primary, the arch-conservative *Manchester Union Leader* published a letter claiming—falsely—that Muskie had condoned use of the word "Canuck" to refer to French-Canadians, who in New Hampshire are plentiful.[2] The paper also ran an editorial slamming Muskie's wife, Jane, for acting in an "unladylike" way—allegedly chewing gum and swearing.

Furious, Muskie climbed aboard the back of a flatbed truck parked in front of the *Union Leader* to defend himself and berate the paper's publisher for attacking his wife. The scene was emotional, and as snow fell journalists reported that the Senator had tears on his cheeks. Today a male politician who cried while defending his wife would probably go up in the polls. In 1972 men were not supposed to shed tears in public, especially when running for president. Muskie insisted that what reporters had seen were melting snowflakes. He still won the primary, but by a smaller margin than predicted. Suddenly his campaign was in trouble.

This setback added to the pressures I felt. There were six weeks between the New Hampshire primary and the fund-raising dinner I had been asked to organize. At first the dinner mattered because of the money. Now it would also be scrutinized to see if Democrats in official Washington were still enthusiastic about a Muskie candidacy.

Working feverishly and with plenty of help from friends, I solicited contributors at the then-record cost of $125 a ticket. I decided on decorations and ordered more than a thousand meals—and learned personally about the complications involved in designing invitations that had to be on recycled paper with proof they had been printed by union workers. As the big day approached, I was excited: the dinner had sold out. We were going to raise a huge amount of money and perhaps give the Muskie campaign the spark it needed.

Early on the day itself I received a strange phone call from the Embassy of Chad. The chargé d'affaires told me he had been invited to

---

2. In later years it was revealed that the "Canuck" letter had been written by Kenneth Clawson, President Nixon's deputy director of communications.

the dinner by our campaign. "When are you sending the limousine to pick me up?" I put the chargé on hold and called campaign officials,[3] who recalled no such invitation. "Let him come, anyway," they said, "but tell him we don't have any limousines." I conveyed the message and put the call out of my mind.

The dinner was in the ballroom of the Washington Hilton. Muskie was to be feted by almost every big-name Democrat. I wore what I thought was a smashing evening dress, with lots of gold in it, which I had purchased at Bergdorf's for the daunting price of three hundred dollars. On my head was a blond pageboy wig (I had lost a lot of hair after the twins were born, and not all of it had grown back) that I had bought just before our reentry to Washington. Somehow I convinced myself that people would think all the hair was mine and I would be what I had always wanted to be—a sophisticated blonde. From the photo I still have of myself in that wig, it's clear I could not have fooled anyone.

Since I was responsible for the dinner, I couldn't relax: I had to make sure everything went smoothly. Preparations in the hours immediately preceding the event went well, but then a florist showed up saying he had the fifty "floral arrangements" we had ordered outside in his truck. Where was our payment? We were baffled. We hadn't ordered any. In fact, in honor of the Maine Senator's environmental leadership, we had decorated the Hilton with live fir trees in pots.

Our people had just finished rebuffing the flowers when a man showed up with a dozen cases of liquor—also C.O.D. No, thank you, we said, we already had our liquor. Then several men staggered in with two hundred pizzas, large, with toppings—again, C.O.D. We sent everything back, enduring vigorous protests from the delivery people who—to our further distress—had order slips with our names on them. At this point we had no idea what was going on.

Then it was time for the predinner VIP reception. I spotted a couple dressed in African robes and went up to them. "You must be from the Embassy of Chad."

"Oh, no," the man responded, "I am the ambassador of Kenya." I looked up. At the entrance was another African couple, then another, many also in their national robes. Behind them, I soon discovered, were limousine drivers demanding to be paid. Within half an hour no fewer than twenty African ambassadors had shown up. We found ourselves

---

3. Muskie's campaign manager in 1972 was Berl Bernhard, a renowned lawyer and public servant. His deputy was George Mitchell, who replaced Muskie in the Senate in 1980 and went on to become majority leader.

scrambling to seat them at a dinner where the tables were full. We didn't want to set up a table just for the Africans: that would seem insulting. We were saved by Gretchen Poston, who scrunched people together here and prevailed on friends there, and each ambassador and spouse got a seat. Gretchen later became social secretary for the Carter White House.

Finally everyone was seated. The meal had begun. I breathed a sigh of relief. Then in walked two more people I didn't recognize. I thought, "Oh God, what next?" and put up a hand to halt them. "We're the magicians hired to entertain the children," they announced. I informed them this was a political dinner, not a children's party. After several minutes of back and forth, they said, "We truly are magicians, and good ones. We learned in the Virgin Islands. If you don't let us in, we'll turn you into something terrible." I couldn't help smiling. "Oh heck, what can it hurt? Come on in."

The next day, I had lunch with my team. We had raised more money than any previous Muskie fund-raiser, but we had an array of outraged, unpaid vendors with whom to deal. "What in heaven's name happened?" We didn't know but suspected we had been sabotaged by a rival Democratic campaign. Most likely, we thought, the phony invitations and deliveries had been arranged by Dick Tuck, a famed political prankster then working for George McGovern, one of Muskie's chief Democratic rivals. Two years later, during hearings on the Watergate scandal, we finally learned the truth. Donald Segretti, the lawyer who headed the "dirty tricks" campaign for Nixon's reelection committee, had planned it all. The Republicans, thinking Muskie would be the strongest Democratic candidate, wanted to derail his campaign. Segretti told the Watergate committee the only trick he had decided against was sending elephants into the ballroom.

Since 1972, I have often returned to the Hilton for events, most recently as a cabinet member, and every time I walk along the hall to the grand ballroom I think about entering that room, in my gold dress and blond wig, next to Senator Muskie. I had hoped to find a leader whom I could believe in and who would have faith in me, and I did. Although Muskie did not win the presidential nomination, for me the dinner that night marked the beginning of a greatly valued, decades-long friendship with the Senator and his family.

AFTER THE HUSTLE of the campaign, I found it hard to concentrate on my dissertation. It wasn't that the work was so difficult, it was all the other demands. Writing a dissertation is lonely. What's more, as most mothers discover, older children often take up more time than babies. They have homework and extracurricular activities and have to be driven all over. Of course being with the children was much more fun than writing a dissertation. I especially loved Friday afternoons when they got off school early and we ran errands, or I took them horseback riding or to guitar lessons. I loved our "ladies' teas," as my daughters titled them.

But even when the girls were at school, the phone never seemed to stop. With every success at one activity came an invitation to another. I raised money for the senatorial campaigns of Walter Mondale and Adlai Stevenson's son. I was asked to join the boards of the Negro Student Fund (soon renamed the Black Student Fund) and D.C. Citizens for Better Public Education. I was on the board of the National Cathedral's College of Preachers, and as chairman of the Beauvoir board was automatically on the board of the National Cathedral, or "the Chapter," as it was called.

The cathedral is the locus for many of the Washington area's largest Episcopal and ecumenical gatherings, as well as funerals and holiday celebrations. While I served on the Chapter, the cathedral was undergoing a major expansion program, which meant I got to vote on the design of the new rose window and debate what precisely the next set of gargoyles should look like. When the cornerstone was laid for the expanded nave, I gave a reading from the pulpit. As I stood there, I tasted a bit of my childhood dream of becoming a priest, although even the Episcopalians had yet to permit women to be ordained. As anyone who has served in a similar position at a church or foundation will recognize, there are always conflicts of personality and policy to be worked out. Although the Chapter started every meeting with a prayer, I learned as much about politics there as I did working in campaigns.

When it came time to write my resumé, I always had a hard time describing this period, which I took to calling "my time of good works." I may not have had a "real" job, but I was constantly occupied. I learned to organize, manage, network, motivate, and ensure that I always delivered what I promised. Yet all this activity didn't seem to register in the regular world, and I wished there were some rating system for volunteer work that could be equated with government or business titles. "Senior vice-president for communications" sounds so much more important than "put out school newsletter." Many a Washington insider's impressions of me were formed during this period, and those impressions were far from uniform. Some people saw me as an energetic, bright woman who could deliver. But no matter how high in government I rose, there were others who would forever see me as their wife's friend or the cooperative mother who arranged car pools.

And there was still that dissertation. I felt like the white rabbit in *Alice in Wonderland*, constantly checking the clock to see if I would run out of time. I finally found the solution: get up before the daily chaos in the household started. For the better part of three years I rose every morning at 4:30 A.M., made myself a cup of coffee, climbed up to the third floor of our house, and wrote.

A good dissertation topic needs to be more than original and researchable. It also has to keep your attention through the protracted time it takes to write. I had settled on a topic several years before, in August 1968, when I'd been packing up the house on Long Island in preparation for the return to Washington.

With the radio blaring through the house, I had listened anxiously as Soviet tanks rolled into Czechoslovakia, crushing what was called "Prague Spring." This was a dramatic experiment started under the leadership of First Secretary Alexander Dubček, a reform-minded Slovak, who had tried to institute what he called "socialism with a human face." Under Dubček, press censorship stopped, political prisoners were released, economic reforms were begun, and prior government abuses were exposed. The cloud of fear that had enshrouded the country for two decades began to lift.

Although Dubček insisted his reform program was an internal matter, it was too much for the totalitarian regime in Moscow and the other satellites. Tanks rolled in. Dubček was arrested, expelled from the Party, and prohibited from speaking in public without permission. The heavy Soviet boot would succeed in crushing dissent for a while, but the behavior of the Czechoslovak people during the first eight months of 1968 would ultimately prove to them that they were not Soviet clones; the stranglehold of Communist ideology could be broken.

At the risk of sounding self-involved, I must say that Prague Spring was a gift from heaven for someone seeking a dissertation subject. I decided to write about the role played by the Czechoslovak press, combining my knowledge of the country's history and language, my study of change in Communist systems, and my abiding interest in journalism.[4]

No one actually enjoys writing a dissertation. Even professors who have written other books look back upon the experience with horror. It does not stop them, however, from subjecting their students to the same rigors. Your work is the culmination of years of striving, into which you place your whole ego; you are judged by people who are not only passing sentence on you but also being judged by their colleagues as to how tough they are on students.

Just as our earlier move to New York had been fortuitous because I

---

4. I was grateful when Professor Seweryn Bialer, a Polish émigré who had lived through the worst Communist period in his own country and who had been my master's thesis advisor, agreed to be my advisor on the dissertation as well.

was able to join Columbia's Russian studies program, I was lucky to return to Washington now. The Library of Congress boasts a superb Slavic section, where I could pore over major Czechoslovak newspapers to try to determine when journalists felt they could begin to diverge from the party line. I scribbled notes on index cards, as I had at Wellesley, except the cards were now four by six instead of three by five. It sounds today like a primitive technique, but it was satisfying to watch my files fill up.

The material I was reading was fascinating but lacked spark. Far more compelling were insights from the people I met through a prominent Czechoslovak couple, Jan and Meda Mladek, who lived down the street. The Mladeks' house was a welcome place for Czechoslovak visitors and refugees, and I tried to talk to every one. Two journalists were of prodigious help, spending hours with me, providing information and color. In my dissertation I had to list them as anonymous sources to protect them. A quarter-century later, I have no such qualms. They were Olga Králová, a prominent broadcast correspondent, and Jiří Dienstbier.

Dienstbier had been an outspoken radio commentator for the eight months of Prague Spring. Throughout the Soviet invasion he had managed to keep Radio Prague on the air and reporting honestly. With help from colleagues he was then flown to Washington on an assignment. I was stunned when he decided to return to Czechoslovakia. He faced certain arrest but felt he owed it to his country to go back. When he did, he was barred from journalism and forced into menial jobs. Ultimately he was indeed arrested. When Dienstbier disappeared back behind the Iron Curtain, I didn't think I would ever see him again.

Getting my Ph.D. was the hardest task I have ever faced on my own. It took thirteen years. I began when Anne and Alice were barely out of their cribs. When I finished, they were in high school. In between they taunted me, saying they shouldn't have to finish their homework if I couldn't finish mine.

On the morning of May 1, 1975, in a hotel room in New York on a particularly hot day, I put on my lucky woolen olive green dress and headed up to Columbia to defend my dissertation. Characteristically, I was nervous. My examiners looked like Central Europe. There was a Hungarian professor, a Yugoslav, a Pole, and an expert on Bulgaria. Given my own background, I stressed the uniqueness of the role played by journalists in Bohemia and interwar Czechoslovakia. The professors acted as though I had insulted their own country's journalists; each clearly felt his nation's history was unique. So I sweated, both from the heat and the probing questions. Nevertheless I received their top grade. Feeling triumphant, I immediately called my parents. Typically, I had been the only one with doubts that I would succeed. Joe was so confident he had already organized the surprise party with which I was greeted upon my return.

WHEN THE 1976 election cycle began, those of us who worked for Muskie had begun to think he should run for president again. Although he had lost in the 1972 primaries, as chairman of the new Senate Budget Committee he was making a name for himself trying to get the unwieldy legislative appropriations process under control. He had sponsored historic environmental legislation aimed at cleaning our nation's polluted waterways and air, and he chaired an oversight subcommittee that exposed wasteful government spending. Muskie was a liberal Democrat, but he was also from tightfisted Maine. "There's nothing liberal," he declared, "about squandering taxpayer money." Muskie had a reputation—richly earned—for a ferocious temper, but Democrats and Republicans alike admired him for his strength and principles.

We thought we had an opportunity to launch Muskie's candidacy when he was asked to deliver the Democratic response to President Ford's 1976 State of the Union message. The Senator's speech before the 1970 mid-term elections had been a huge success. Hoping to duplicate that effort now, we called upon some of the Democratic Party's most respected gurus to prepare the presentation. These included Bob Squier, a longtime political consultant who had played a key role in orchestrating the 1970 speech; Richard Goodwin, who had written for President Kennedy and his brothers; and the famed pollster Patrick Cadell. My job was to raise the funds to pay these men. We thought it would be worth it.

It was a bad sign when Bob Squier was quoted in the *New York Times* in connection with a possible Muskie presidential bid: "I'm taking the position that I'm Dr. Frankenstein: We invented Muskie in 1970 and we can invent him again in 1976." Then endless meetings of the three outsiders failed to produce an acceptable draft.[5] Next the telecast began with a shot of Muskie sitting in a chair too small for him, rolling his eyes because the wrong text was on the monitor. The people I had invited to my house to watch started laughing, while I tried to distract them with trays of hors d'ouevres. In the end the Senator did a credible job, but the spark didn't ignite, and he did not run.

Muskie did make it, however, to the short-list of vice-presidential candidates being considered by Jimmy Carter. As the Muskies flew to Georgia

---

5. Ultimately much of the speech had to be written by two Senate staffers, John McEvoy and Al From.

to be interviewed, I was sent to New York, where the Democratic Convention was to be held, to make arrangements for the Muskie delegates and to oversee the installation of a private line to Muskie's room. Carter wanted to be able to call each vice-presidential contender without being overheard. After Carter was nominated, we waited. The phone call came on the morning of July 15, on the hotel phone—not the private line I had so laboriously installed. Muskie picked up. In about three seconds he had put the receiver down. All Carter had said was, "It's not you. Thank you." The curtness rankled for some time.

Shortly after we returned to Washington, Muskie's chief legislative assistant signed on to the Carter-Mondale campaign. It was unclear who would replace him. Never having worked in the Senate, I wasn't sure I was qualified, but Joe urged me to apply. For the first time, my Ph.D. made a difference. It was possible for Muskie to say, "I have hired Dr. Albright for this top job," rather than, "I have hired Joe Albright's wife, who happens to have raised a lot of money for me." So in 1976, aged thirty-nine, with three children, I had landed my first full-time paying job since the *Encyclopaedia Britannica* fifteen years before.

The United States was busy celebrating its bicentennial. There were festivals, parades, tall ships, breathtaking fireworks, and a presidential election. My parents, as was their custom, called to make sure the children were singing patriotic songs and to remind them how lucky they were to live in the United States. I was feeling that way too. As chief legislative assistant to Muskie, I was finally at the inner table, with the men, where the decisions were being made, and where my education could continue.

I studied with the best. Ed Muskie was a great teacher in the sense that I could learn much merely by observing him as he worked both publicly and behind the scenes. The Senator knew when to be conciliatory as he elicited information and forged coalitions and when to use his famous temper to hold officials accountable and stop opponents cold. Working for Muskie, one had to learn quickly because it was unacceptable that the senior Senator from Maine should have a staffer who couldn't keep up.

I had to become instantly knowledgeable about industries vital to Maine, such as shoes, fishing, and paper. I shared responsibility for writing a memo before every vote, on every subject. I helped develop arguments in support of the controversial treaty to give Panama control over its canal. And I learned about the many ways Congress can influence foreign policy—lessons that proved invaluable later.

Most Senate staffers were five to ten years younger than I, the majority either still single or just married. In the evenings they fanned out among Capitol Hill's many watering holes to talk politics and flirt. I went straight home. Alice and Anne were fifteen years old, but Katie was only nine. Feeling guilty, I asked her if she minded my taking a full-time job. She answered "No" because she would at least know where I was: all my volunteer activities had made it difficult for her to keep track of me. So from my first day in government until my last, I had a rule that any call from one of my daughters was, if at all possible, to be put through immediately.

One night when I walked in, Katie could hardly wait to find out what had been going on. "Mom, when I called your office, I was told you were on the floor with Senator Muskie. What were you two doing?" I explained about how legislative business is conducted on the Senate floor. The next day I told the story to Muskie, who had always liked Katie, whom he called Katydid. When she had first met him, she was only five and had looked up at his six-foot-four-inch frame and asked, "Senator Muskie, are you a giant?"

Anyone who has followed life in Washington knows about the struggle between the executive and legislative branches. Each is jealous of its prerogatives; each believes it better represents the people; each cites the Constitution to substantiate its claims. When the two branches are controlled by different political parties, as was the case at the end of the Ford years, the struggle is exacerbated.

When Jimmy Carter defeated President Ford in November 1976, we looked forward to having a Democrat in the White House, but the reality was not without complications. The Muskie camp had close ties to incoming Vice-President Mondale, but the vice-presidential selection process had left raw feelings. Not knowing it was Jimmy Carter's style, we were quite put off by the President's first letter to our Senator, addressed not to "Dear Ed" but "To Ed Muskie." Nor did our early meetings with the top Carter people go well. They had run for office "against Washington" and seemed determined to maintain that attitude. There was a lot of grumbling within our staff about what we saw as newcomer arrogance.

One day we were busy grousing that our Senator was not being treated with the proper respect when Muskie walked into the room, asked us what our problem was, and pronounced, "Let's keep one thing straight here. I know who I am and I also know we have only one President at a time, and this one also happens to be a Democrat. To the best of our ability we are going to cooperate." We had our orders. There were many times while President Clinton was in office that I would think back to that moment and wish, wistfully, that other Democratic members of Congress had been there to learn that lesson.

As I was beginning to put my life together, Joe's plans seemed gradually to be falling apart. In the spring of 1970, while recovering from hepatitis contracted by eating raw oysters abroad, he got a call from Uncle Harry. I was there and heard Joe protest, "What do you mean, you're selling *Newsday*? You can't do that. You can't. My family owns forty-nine percent." Convinced that *Newsday* was becoming a liberal mouthpiece under Bill Moyers' management, Harry told Joe he planned to sell the paper to Norman Chandler, conservative owner of the *Times Mirror* Company.

Joe and Bill Moyers had never been close, but now they scrambled to put together enough money to bid on the 51 percent Harry Guggenheim owned. They succeeded, but Harry would not sell to them. Joe and his family ended up with more cash for their minority share than Harry received for the majority, but money was beside the point.

Although Joe was deeply disappointed, he recovered quickly. He wrote a book, *What Makes Spiro Run*, telling for the first time the full story behind the sordid events leading to Spiro Agnew's forced resignation as Nixon's Vice-President. He also continued his career as an investigative journalist, working for the *San Francisco Chronicle* and other papers, then with the Cox newspaper chain.

Through research, he learned about a number of nuclear weapons installations that the U.S. government had concluded were in need of security upgrades. Posing as a contractor, he was given maps of weapons plants and permitted to tour them, finding himself in close proximity to nuclear arms. He wrote a series of compelling articles about the lack of security at such installations. The series won numerous prizes and was nominated for a Pulitzer—every journalist's dream. Joe allowed his hopes to rise and was depressed when his series failed to win. I tried to rationalize the loss for him, reporting that I had heard that the committee, settling on new ethics rules, had decided not to award prizes to reporters who went undercover in pursuit of a story. I suggested that perhaps some of the judges resented his family for some reason. But nothing I could say did much to ease the hurt.

Still, we agreed we had a pretty wonderful life. Joe may not have become a publisher, but he was working in his chosen profession and was respected by his colleagues.

A portrait of the Albright family in the mid-seventies would have shown a happily married couple with three smart and beautiful daughters. We continued to go to Georgia to play and hunt. We skied in Colorado. We had our farm in Virginia, where we added land whenever we could and worked on and around the old stone house. We had so many projects going at the farm—gardening, painting, building—that we started calling it Gulag Albright, but we also took long walks, read, played tennis, went to the local racetrack, had parties, and watched the cows crisscross the pasture with our daughters galloping around them. Joe was never shy when it came to auctions, and his bidding skills filled the farm with great buys. In contrast to my childhood, we had lots of family around. Both Joe's and my parents visited regularly. My brother, John, an economist, had moved to Washington, and he and his wife, Pamela, came to the farm every weekend and shared in the work and fun.

We had a pleasant and varied group of friends, but our best times were when we were together. Joe and I were not only husband and wife but also best friends.

Wini Shore from Wellesley was now Wini Shore Freund, and still a person in whom I confided constantly. Wini was also happily married, with wonderful daughters. "Aren't we lucky?" I said to her.

"Don't say that," she shuddered, "I'm superstitious."

SIX

From Pole to Pole

C HRISTMAS VACATION 1976 I was home with pneumonia. The phone rang; it was my former professor, Zbigniew Brzezinski. Over the years we had become friendly, and I had even dressed up as the rear end of a horse at a costume party at his family's New Jersey home. More recently he had phoned me in Maine, where I was with Muskie on election night, concerned by the tight finish and anxious to find out how the state's four electoral votes were leaning. Now, in that slight Polish accent I knew so well, Zbig said, "President-elect Carter has asked me to be his National Security Advisor."

"I know," I said. "Congratulations, it's great news."

"Can you find me a place to live?"

I said jokingly, "Sure, but I thought you were calling to offer me a job."

"No," he said. "Just calling to find a place to live."

He later moved permanently to McLean, Virginia; our families became even closer. It helped that Zbig's wife, Muska, was also Czechoslovak-American and an alumna of Wellesley. Early in 1978 she called to ask about our annual skating party and if we had any venison from the deer at our farm. She asked, as a throwaway I thought, whether I had ever considered working in the executive branch. I gave her the location of the party, said that we actually never killed the deer, and answered that I liked being on the Hill with Muskie.

Later that day, one of the assistants in our office said Dr. Brzezinski was on the phone. "About that conversation you had with Muska...," Zbig began. I was wondering why he cared about skating or venison. Then: "Would you like to work at the White House?"

I was sitting in a typical Senate office, which is to say we all sat virtually on top of each other. In a low voice I told him, "No, I love what I'm doing." As soon as I hung up, I decided I had been insane to say no so quickly, ran to a phone booth in the hall, and called back anxiously. "I was too hasty," I said, and we made a date to meet.

I really didn't know if I wanted to accept the offer. I had never met President Carter and had spent a year being critical of the new administration's dealings with Congress. On the other hand, at the White House I could work exclusively on foreign policy issues and directly for Brzezinski. Besides, Joe was urging me on. "Why would you ever turn down an opportunity like this?" he kept saying. "This is what you always wanted to do. Go for it."

The job was to handle congressional relations for the National Security Council (NSC). I would be working with the NSC staff to present our foreign policy priorities to Congress, coordinating the administration's legislative strategy, sitting in on presidential meetings with members of Congress, and responding to questions from the Hill.

I had never expected to leave Ed Muskie. We had a great relationship and I was learning more every day. But as much as I loved him, Muskie managed to make me furious by casting doubts on whether I was up to the move. He wasn't sure, he said, that a woman could succeed in a congressional relations job, in part because virtually all Senators and U.S. Representatives were men. Even though three of his five children were daughters and he had a gutsy, outspoken wife, Muskie was unsure how to deal with professional women, a fact he proved again at my going-away party. He stood up in front of everyone and said, "I now have many women on my staff, but I will always treasure Madeleine, because she was the first one to bring sex to the office." We all stared at him and started laughing.

"Senator," I said, "I think you mean 'gender.'" Referring to his own ethnicity and that of my new boss, he then said, "I'm very sorry to see Madeleine go, but this means she will always be known for being the first woman in the world to go from Pole to Pole."

My FATHER CAME to Washington fairly frequently on business, and he and my mother had been present for my fund-raising dinner for Ed Muskie. I think I surprised him with my fund-raising; certainly he surprised me with his. The year I got married he had become dean of the Graduate School for International Studies at the University of Denver. In love with the idea of developing what he called "the Harvard of the West," he raised a lot of money for that purpose. I was glad he got to see me join Muskie's staff and only wished he had lived long enough to see me at the White House.

My father died relatively young. He was not yet sixty-eight and hadn't been ill long. Although over the years he had had stomach problems, he was in pretty good health, and we actually spent more time worrying about my mother. In her fifties she was diagnosed with an incurable disease, scleroderma. After, my father fretted all the time about her symptoms—blue fingers, hardening skin, difficulty breathing.

My mother's health didn't prevent my parents from traveling. In the spring of 1977, my father finished his book *Twentieth-Century Czechoslovakia* and was in the midst of a new project on the Czechoslovak Legionnaires, troops who had found themselves abandoned in Russia at the end of World War I. He was off to see what he could uncover in the British archives. When they stopped in Washington on the way, we went to the farm and, for an outing, began climbing the hill behind our house. For the first time I could remember, my father announced he was too tired to go on; he had to return for a nap.

All the same, my parents enjoyed themselves in Europe; they even had the opportunity to see my father's brother, with whom, after so many years, he had made peace. Then, shortly after they came back in April, my mother called to say my father had turned yellow. I guessed it might be hepatitis and flew out to Denver. In the hospital, waiting for test results, my father insisted he felt well. He had been swimming two days before. We were optimistic, but the test results soon revealed he had cancer of the pancreas. After the operation, we were optimistic again because the surgeons said they had removed it all. My father started regaining his strength and resumed swimming.

A few weeks later, my mother called again, panicked. He was getting worse. He had high fevers and was hallucinating. I returned to Denver, where the doctors told Kathy, John, and me that the cancer had reached his liver and was spreading through his body. Nothing could be done. Even after all her years in the United States, my mother was used to European doctors who never told you exactly what was wrong. When she heard the news, she fainted.

Walking into my father's room, we were shocked to see how quickly he had deteriorated. A man who had been totally cerebral was now reduced by the disease to incoherence. The doctors were unsure how much time he had. We agreed we would take shifts to be with him. Kathy, an educator who had the summer off, took the first shift. It turned out to be the last. John and I have said to each other that we don't think we could ever have said good-bye to our father, but we have forever wished we had been there with our mother and Kathy when, on July 18, 1977, he died. Our mother seemed swallowed up by grief, and all three of us children wondered if she would survive. They had been each other's lives since their teenage years. For the rest of her life she made it a point to call us on the eighteenth of every month to share memories.

I was forty years old, clearly someone who could think for herself, but my father had been my greatest friend and advisor. In a strange way, while I grieved, I never had that feeling of "If only I had...." I had been a dutiful, loving daughter. I didn't feel burdened by sins either of commission or omission. As I sought to emulate him, I felt that he never left my side because I never completely stopped thinking about him. Even today, though I need no special reminders, the smell or sight of a man with a pipe always brings him back to me.

At the funeral in Denver, the tributes were bountiful. John, Kathy, and I were moved to see how deeply our father's colleagues and former students respected him and how warmly they spoke of him. It was as if he had an entire other family. Our house was filled with flowers, among them an unusual planter in the shape of a piano filled with philodendrons. When my mother saw me examining it, she said, "That came from your father's favorite student." "Who?" I asked. "A young woman," said my mother, "Condoleezza Rice."[1]

My father had loved teaching. He was voted best university lecturer more than once and, after he stepped down as dean, continued to teach. He was highly respected in academic circles, in part because of his books[2] and numerous scholarly articles. Whenever a major international event occurred, Dr. Korbel was asked to comment.

We sometimes talked about what would have happened had the Communists not taken over Czechoslovakia. Some of those who knew him felt he would eventually have become foreign minister, but my father was uncomfortable with that sort of speculation. He obviously gave up any hope of achieving that post when he became an American citizen. He traded in his suit and tie for a turtleneck and sport coat, and grew a beard.

---

1. Condoleezza Rice had been a music major, hence the piano, but had switched to international relations after taking a course from my father and had worked on her Ph.D. dissertation with him. Ten years later I was Michael Dukakis' foreign policy advisor, rounding up experts to serve as a brain trust for his presidential campaign. I called Condi, thinking she would be perfect. She was a Soviet expert, lived outside Washington, and was an African-American woman. But after I went through my spiel, she responded, "Madeleine, I don't know how to tell you this, but I'm a Republican." "Condi," I said in amazement, "how could that be? We had the same father."

2. In addition to his first book on Tito, my father wrote *Danger in Kashmir, The Communist Subversion of Czechoslovakia, Poland between East and West, Détente in Europe: Real or Imaginary?*, and *Twentieth-Century Czechoslovakia*.

I know he mourned for his people suffering under Communism, but he didn't second-guess his decision to bring our family to America. As my mother wrote, "He used to say often, I was in many glorious jobs, but to be a college teacher in a free country is what I am enjoying best."

While my father was the one who kept the family on an even keel, he could not have made it without my mother. She was street-smart and charming, able to get away with saying and doing the most outrageous things—even to him. According to her, my father had quite a temper when he was young. On the occasions when it returned, she put him in his place. Once he lost it over some "arrogant" comment one of us children made and set down his breakfast plate with such force it broke. That night at dinner the rest of us had china plates, but she served his dinner on a paper plate. "What's the meaning of this?" he thundered. "We don't have enough plates for all of us," she replied sweetly. My father glowered, then started laughing, got up, and gave her a kiss.

My parents were never happier than while living in Colorado. Even when money was no longer an issue, my mother continued as a secretary, in an office dealing with financial services, because she enjoyed her friends. Whenever new Czechoslovak immigrants arrived, she adopted them. Students came over for her meals and my father's animated dinner table conversation. He disapproved of her trips to fortune-tellers and séances, so she waited until he went out of town, then found a friend to accompany her.

My parents were to my children all that my grandparents were denied the chance to be to me. They had a huge influence on my daughters' lives. My mother baked cookies with the girls and taught them Czechoslovak songs they never understood. More important, she taught them the value of family. My father taught them to fish and love history. Every summer we sent all three out to Colorado for a visit. When the girls went to camp near Colorado Springs, my parents were there on parents' weekend. At Christmas the whole clan, including John and Kathy, their spouses, and assorted kids, gathered in Aspen. My children adored their Grandma and "Bumpa," and now compare me with my mother when I worry and with my father when I start lecturing on the latest news item.

As I entered the next stage of my professional life, I missed my father terribly. My mother, with her extrasensory powers, used to tell me, "Don't worry: he sees everything you're doing and loves it." He would have delighted in how I followed his own passions, just as he had been thrilled when I got my Ph.D. When he wrote his last book, my dissertation was listed in the bibliography, after the primary sources. I have never been one to carry on imaginary conversations, but during my years in the Carter administration I often reflected on what my father might be thinking. I expect he would have applauded Carter's boldness in making human rights an important factor in our relations with other countries, although I doubt he could have brought himself to say, as Carter did, that in so doing we should rid ourselves of our "inordinate fear of Communism."

IN MARCH 1978, I settled into what was literally a closet in the basement of the West Wing of the White House. I could have had a larger office, with a marble fireplace, but it would have been in the Old Executive Office Building, where most members of the NSC staff were located. In White House office politics, as in real estate, location is everything.

It's not unusual for people who have an avid interest in politics to move from one end of Pennsylvania Avenue to the other and back again. The experience of working on the Hill enriches the executive branch experience and vice versa. What is amazing, though, is how quickly one becomes irritated with the other branch's point of view. I had my "where you sit is where you stand" revelation on my very first day.

Ed Muskie was one of the Senate advisors to the negotiations taking place on the Law of the Sea Treaty to revise international rules governing the use of the oceans. He respected international agreements, but he also represented a state with a long coastline and an economically vital fishing industry. One of my final acts as his chief legislative assistant had been to write a letter to President Carter explaining our support for the treaty generally but complaining that the administration failed to understand the problems it would create for our constituents. The letter was signed and sent to the White House on a Friday.

I arrived at my job at the White House the following Monday ready to take on my new responsibilities—one of which was to answer mail from the Hill. There on my desk was the letter I had written. I sat down and drafted a response, explaining that, although we certainly understood the concerns of the Senator's constituents, the overall impact of the Law of the Sea Treaty was more important for U.S. national interests. The letter was typed on the light green paper the President used, the appropriate people autopenned it, and off it went. What a Washington moment.

I spent three years working at the NSC absorbing everything around me. I learned how the national security decision-making apparatus worked, refined my skills in dealing with Congress, and sank my teeth into an array of real-life, real-time foreign policy issues.

I was thrilled to be working in the White House, where every room and corridor suggests history, drama, and intrigue. The actual working space, however, is cramped and small. As I climbed the stairs from my basement office to my first meeting in the Cabinet Room, I wondered how it had been possible for anyone in the Nixon White House not to have known about the Watergate scandal. Officials of various ranks had to pass each other all the time. Facial expressions must have revealed something.

Then I was in the Cabinet Room for the first time. Around the large oval table sat the President, Vice-President Walter Mondale, Secretary of State Cyrus Vance, Defense Secretary Harold Brown, CIA Director Admiral Stansfield Turner, Chairman of the Joint Chiefs of Staff General George Brown, Brzezinski, and some Senators who had come to listen to the President. I sat on a chair at the side.

The group had been summoned to discuss a Middle East arms sales package. President Carter had made it clear he was committed to Israel's security but at the same time felt it was crucial to strengthen relations with moderate, pro-Western Arab nations. To this end, in the middle of February, the administration had announced plans to provide F-16s and F-15s to Israel and Saudi Arabia, and less sophisticated F-5Es to Egypt. The Israelis objected to the Arab transfers and the American Jewish community was arguing against the plan.

I listened intently to the President as he explained why it was essential to make the sales, and I took notes when the Senators started asking questions, because it would be my responsibility to provide the answers later. As a newcomer, I soaked it all in—studying the portraits lining the room, staring out the window, and wondering how the Rose Garden would look in the summer when it actually had roses.

The meeting ended and I returned to my office, full of myself and my new job. The phone rang immediately. It was my direct line with Brzezinski. "Madeleine, please come up." Zbig was still conferring with officials who had attended the meeting. "Would you please consult your notes and tell Secretary Vance and Secretary Brown how the President phrased a particular point on the sale?"

Staring down at the barely legible scratches on my pad, I felt as I had the day of my Ph.D. exam. I hadn't taken notes on that part of the discussion, so I had to say, "I can't." Dismissed, I slunk back to my basement hideout, convinced I would be fired.

In thinking what next, I figured the best defense was a good offense, so I returned to Brzezinski's office as soon as he was free. This venture reflected the fact that I had been put in a relatively high position without the training that comes from going through the ranks. Exhibiting more than a little attitude, I said, "I was not aware I had been hired as a secretary."

Without raising his voice, Brzezinski said he didn't know what I was talking about. "Did you look around at who was in the Cabinet Room?'

"Of course."

"Were you not the most junior person there?"

"Without a doubt."

"Well, there's your answer. You're not a secretary, just the most junior person in a high-level meeting, and that's your job." I had been justly chastened without being chastised.

As I grew more comfortable, and my friendship with Brzezinski grew, I dared chasten him. He had hired me to work with Congress but didn't fully appreciate what that meant. He resisted going to the Hill, not because he didn't want to be seen there, but because he thought it too time-consuming to meet with one senator at a time, especially as they often kept him waiting. When he complained, I had to remind him that they were elected officials and he wasn't. Later in my career, when I myself was summoned to appear on Capitol Hill to be yelled at for something I did not do, I had to remind myself of what I had told Zbig.

One of the best parts about my work was our weekly staff meeting, which was like a first-class seminar. It was a very smart group. Brzezinski said he would always tell us about his meetings with the President as long as there were no leaks. There weren't, and he did. After his comments, he would choose a relevant subject for discussion—ranging from the pros and cons of arms control to exploring new relations with China, or to analyzing what he saw happening in the Middle East—and expected us all to contribute, whether it was our area of expertise or not.

For those who only saw Brzezinski on television, he seemed an austere figure, with sharp features that cartoonists gleefully transformed into those of a hawk. He had frightened me as a professor, but as a boss he was warm. He didn't just talk about collegiality, he practiced it. He never introduced us as "staff"; we were his colleagues. Often, at the end of the day, those of us who were in the West Wing would meet in his office to listen to the news or talk over the day. He got teased for his accent, and his short haircut was the subject of debate. Hamilton Jordan said he looked like Woody Woodpecker. We couldn't hold back our laughter the day Brzezinski came in with his hair blow-dried in an attempt by the press spokesman to alter his image.

Although most of the NSC's senior-level directors were men, there were exceptions. The brilliant young Jessica Matthews was in charge of "global issues"—a new foreign policy category that included some of President Carter's favorite subjects: human rights, the environment, and other resource issues. Christine Dodson, whom I had first met at Columbia, served as Zbig's chief of staff and confidante. Christine and I became and remain close. She is a woman of uncommon common sense, that rare person who never varnishes the truth.

As time passed, I began to work closely with members of the White House staff. They thought I had a pretty good grasp of politics for a foreign policy specialist, and I was a loyal Democrat. I attended the daily staff meeting in the Roosevelt Room, which began every day at 7:30 A.M., often followed by breakfast at the round staff table in the White House mess. Each morning, I summarized the international news and concerns of the day, highlighting those that might affect the President or Vice-President.

The death of an important leader fell in that category. For many weeks I tracked the deteriorating condition of Yugoslav President Tito,[3] reporting finally on May 4, 1980, that he had died. Tito had been wooed by both superpowers, while also gaining respect from the developing world. As a result, his funeral would be well attended. Vice-President Mondale was chosen to head the American delegation, joined by a number of cabinet officials and a large assortment of other dignitaries. Because of my previous association with Yugoslavia, I was invited. In the end, we had so many VIPs there wasn't enough room for former Governor and Mrs. Averell Harriman, the famously enchanting Pamela, to sit in the front of the plane.

One VIP who did rate a front seat was the President's mother, known to all as "Miz Lillian." Miz Lillian differed in style but not in strength of conviction from her famous son. While he was understandably careful in his public comments, she was beloved for her frankness and high spirits. The staff knew a trip with her would be an adventure. She didn't sleep well on planes and needed to be entertained. We took turns. My shift came in the middle of the night; it started when Miz Lillian emerged from the bathroom just after Pamela Harriman had been there. Holding a fistful of rings, the President's mother told us in salty language that Mrs. Harriman had left them on the sink. She added, "And did you see her sitting on the arm of that attractive Walter Mondale's seat? Close up like that? She has to do that, married to that old coot."

Our plane had bunk beds that were pulled down from the ceiling overnight and retracted in the morning. The night passed, and after we had all been up for a while, getting ready to land, Pamela started walking

---

3. In 1978, before his final illness, I had the chance—thirty years after presenting flowers to Tito in Belgrade—to welcome him again, this time at a ceremony on the White House lawn. I was struck by how well-preserved the Yugoslav strongman was, although it was impossible to overlook his orange hair.

up and down the aisle with an anxious look on her face. "Has anyone seen Averell?" she asked. Seats and bathrooms were checked. There was no sign of the eighty-eight-year-old statesman. We looked about in bewilderment. How could we have misplaced Averell Harriman? Pamela was frantic. Then a crew member thought to unlatch the bed above Averell's seat. Evidently the governor, being hard of hearing, had been unaware of the morning bustle and failed to rise with the rest of us. The crew had closed him back up into the ceiling, from which he now emerged, quite unruffled.

MY LEARNING CURVE was steep, but it was an exhilarating climb. When he hired me, Brzezinski urged me not to seek a clear definition of what I would be doing, because that would also make it clear what I was *not* supposed to do. "Be careful," he said, "not to define yourself out of an interesting job." In the end he gave me carte blanche to sit in on the foreign policy meetings the President had with members of Congress and to coordinate legislative strategy on every issue the NSC was considering. As a result I had to study events in all regions, learn about the Defense Department and CIA, and keep track of where each of our foreign policy dollars was supposed to go. Above all, I had to master the complicated details of arms control. President Carter was preparing to seek the Senate's consent to the SALT II Treaty, designed to restrain the nuclear arms race with the Soviet Union. It would clearly be a difficult fight. Many Senators felt the treaty would give the Soviets an advantage and could not be adequately verified, while others simply did not want to hand a Democratic President a major foreign policy victory. Approval of the treaty was so important, the administration set up a special task force headed by Washington lawyer Lloyd Cutler to coordinate strategy. My job was to keep close to the Senators and report where they stood.

The SALT II agreement was finally signed in Vienna on June 18, 1979. One of the last issues to be resolved had to do with a Soviet bomber known as the Backfire. Concerned that the medium-range bomber could be modified to strike the United States, we wanted to set limits on its capabilities and its rate of production.

A special letter of assurances and understandings about the plane was made part of the formal negotiating record. A few days later the blue leather-bound treaty, two inches thick, turned up on my desk for transmittal to the Senate. I looked for the signatures. Carter's I knew well—strong strokes. Beside it was Leonid Brezhnev's, surprisingly weak and feathery. But where was the Backfire letter? It had to be submitted with the treaty. I called the NSC's arms control expert, who wasn't sure: they had left Vienna in a hurry. Then someone remembered seeing what he had assumed was a copy of the letter in a wastepaper basket. An alarm went up. By some miracle, the letter was retrieved. It was delivered to my office, totally wrinkled. My housewifely instincts took over. I ironed it out, but it still didn't look very official, so I went to the White House mess and "borrowed" a blue leather menu cover, then to a dime store and found some red, white, and blue ribbon to lay across the letter. I put it all together, enclosed the letter with the rest of the treaty, and sent it to the Senate.

Toward the end of 1979, the debate over SALT II was in full force and the vote count was beginning to go our way. We probably would have gained Senate consent to the treaty, if on Christmas Day Soviet troops had not invaded Afghanistan. By crossing that high mountain border, the Soviets crossed another line as well. They used military force to expand their sphere of influence beyond what they claimed after World War II. It was an act of pure imperialism, and although the SALT treaty was still in our national interests, the Senate was obviously not going to approve it.

The invasion opened a new front in the Cold War. The administration responded economically by halting grain shipments, banning the transfer of advanced technology, and restricting fishing rights. We responded politically by boycotting the 1980 Moscow Olympics and reinstating draft registration, and militarily by initiating an arms supply and training relationship with the Afghan resistance, the Mujahedeen, using Pakistan as a base. The unintended consequences of this relationship, which expanded through the next decade, would be felt during and even after my years as Secretary of State.

The Afghanistan crisis united Vance and Brzezinski—at least temporarily. Although the two had worked together to help get President Carter elected, they took very different approaches to major foreign policy questions, including how to deal with the Soviet Union. Vance, an astute lawyer, believed negotiations could moderate U.S.-Soviet tensions and so serve both sides. For Brzezinski, U.S.-Soviet relations were virtually a zero-sum game. While not opposed to negotiations on such matters as arms control, he doubted that the Soviets would be content with "peaceful coexistence." He had been warning about Moscow's intentions in Afghanistan for some time and believed the Soviets had to be dealt with firmly, on all fronts.

Vance and Brzezinski competed constantly—if discreetly—for influence over President Carter's head and heart. The result was some often unpleasant infighting. In theory the secretary of state's job is to formulate and carry out U.S. foreign policy. The mandate of the national security advisor is to make sure all the elements of our national security policies, including defense, diplomacy, and intelligence, move in the same direction. He (or she) is supposed to coordinate policy, not make or carry it out. In practice, however, these lines blur. It is a standard observation in Washington that the only time the NSC and State Department worked together well was when Henry Kissinger was in charge of both.

Disagreements between State and the NSC, suppressed in responding to the invasion of Afghanistan, erupted over the nearly simultaneous crisis in Iran, where militants backed by the revolutionary regime of Ayatollah Khomeini were holding fifty-three Americans hostage. State and NSC agreed it was worth trying a diplomatic route to get the hostages released but disagreed on everything else. Should we retaliate and risk the lives of the hostages? What should be done about Iran's deposed Shah, whose admission to the United States for cancer treatment had triggered the crisis? Should we try to rescue the hostages ourselves or wait for the UN or some other mediator to arrange for their release? The President was consumed with saving the lives of the captured Americans. The press meanwhile was brutal. ABC news journalist Ted Koppel rode to prominence with a nightly program called *America Held Hostage* (later changed to *Nightline*). Each night, when signing off the evening news, the grandfatherly Walter Cronkite reminded America how many days the hostages had been held. Republicans lambasted the President for his alleged naïveté in dealing with the Soviets and apparent helplessness in responding to Iran.

On April 24, carrying huge maps of the Middle East, I had accompanied Brzezinski as he briefed some of Colorado Senator Gary Hart's constituents about the Israeli-Palestinian situation. No sooner had he started when he was interrupted by a message and abruptly excused himself. Later I attended a meeting in the Situation Room that lasted much longer than expected, and as I left the White House around 9 P.M., I passed a line of cabinet members' limousines on West Executive Drive. Something big was up, I thought. But what?

At 3 A.M. the next morning, our home phone rang. I heard Joe say, "What do you mean, a rescue mission failed?" He began getting dressed. "Why don't you leave it alone?" I said, thinking the phone call must have been for me. "That was my bureau," he said. "It's public. It failed." The awkward thing was that there would have been a conflict of interest for us to discuss what he had heard or what I knew or did not know.

That morning first Joe, then all America, woke to the news that three marines and five airmen had died when a helicopter and a C-130 collided in the Iranian desert. The planned rescue mission had already been aborted due to a sandstorm and to mechanical problems. It was an incredibly daring attempt that ended in tragedy. Cy Vance had objected, because he didn't think it would work. Out of principle, he resigned.

"Your friend Ed Muskie has been chosen to succeed Cy," Zbig told me a day before it was announced. The administration needed someone of Muskie's stature to quiet the clamor caused by the failed mission and Vance's resignation. I went to the Cabinet Room to hear the announcement, and President Carter winked at me and later asked me if I were pleased. I responded with an enthusiastic yes, adding, "Perhaps you don't remember where I came from?"

"Of course I do," he replied.

As Muskie fielded questions from the press, we watched him on the monitor from the Cabinet Room. Initially the mood was good. Then there began to be muttering that he was speaking so authoritatively, he was eclipsing the President. I got the feeling some staffers were wondering if they would regret the selection.

The Muskie-Brzezinski relationship began well, then deteriorated. Muskie brought aides with him to the State Department who were totally loyal to him, had a predisposition to dislike Zbig, and—with a couple of exceptions—had never worked in the executive branch. Further, the Carter national security team—having been together for more than three years—spoke in a shorthand that Muskie had no way of understanding. I was in a strange position, since both men hoped I could mitigate problems between them. Muskie, a former governor, presidential candidate, and the chairman of the Senate Budget Committee, felt patronized. He called me up and said, "What's with Zbig? Why does he have to show off all the time, telling us things like the names of all the tribes in Nigeria?"

"It's natural," I said. "Zbig's a professor and has spent his life studying these things."

Then Brzezinski called me up. "What is with your friend Muskie? All he does is ask questions, but he never tells us what he thinks."

"It's natural," I said. "He's a Senator and they ask questions."

Muskie, whose father was Polish, complained, "Brzezinski acts like he's more Polish than I am."

What could I say? "He is. Both his parents are Polish and he speaks the language perfectly."

The two Poles did, however, work in concert in the fall of 1980 when there was intelligence that the Soviets were going to move troops into Poland to crush the rising Solidarity movement. They apparently agreed it was wise to alert a third leader of Polish descent, Pope John Paul II, but the White House operator had trouble finding the number. After it was found, Brzezinski said, "Put it in my address book under P for Pope."[4]

When he hired me, Zbig told me we were the President's praetorian guard, the inner circle, and supposed to be on call at all times. He knew I had three children, as did he, but he worked hard and expected everyone else on his staff to do the same. Hours on the Hill had been long, but there were frequent breaks when senators returned to their constituencies. At the NSC the pace never slowed.

Joe was great. He took over homework supervision and eating meals with the kids, prepared by our parade of housekeepers. I tried to get home by dinner every night but didn't always succeed. Of course Alice and Anne, being teenagers, wanted out of family meals as much as possible, while Katie, always amenable, went along. Sometimes they joined me for Saturday lunch in the White House mess, or at welcoming ceremonies for foreign dignitaries, or for the Fourth of July fireworks on the South Lawn. The girls were less enthusiastic about leaving their friends every weekend to go to the farm. Joe and I were not keen about leaving them with their friends. Our farm weekends turned into Sunday day trips to keep up with our fix-up, paint-up projects and our prized tomato crop.

Not surprisingly, I continued to feel guilty about not spending more time with the family, but as far as I could tell, no one was suffering. Joe was an involved father and much more skilled at teaching our daughters to write splendid sentences than I was. He tried to absolve me by saying that they were all proud of me and that I was just the kind of mother daughters should have. He loved telling everyone about the time in Colorado when Katie reported on a conversation she had had more than once on the ski lift. It was customary to write your phone number on your skis, and when people spotted the area code for Washington, D.C., on Katie's, they'd ask, "Does your father work for the government?" She would answer promptly, "No, my mother does."

I, in turn, was filled with admiration for Joe. He had put *Newsday* behind him and was using his journalistic talents to ferret out good stories on everything from government leasing of western land to grain sales to Russia. As far as I could see there was no subject he couldn't master.

---

4. We actually used that number a few months later. In May 1981, I was in Zbig's personal office when we heard that an assassination attempt had been made against the Pope. I called and ended up talking to a nun. Then Brzezinski took the phone to express his affection and concern.

I USED TO TELL MYSELF that, much as I liked Muskie and Brzezinski, I was not sure I could survive a second term with the two of them. This turned out to be moot. President Carter was one of our most intelligent chief executives and one who showed a fierce dedication to conflict prevention and individual human dignity both during and after his term in office. He was a proactive President who achieved much in foreign policy, including the historic Middle East Peace Accords at Camp David.

Politically, however, he was unlucky. Rising oil prices wrecked the economy. The Soviet invasion of Afghanistan undermined our foreign policy. The hostage crisis created a sense of national helplessness. And the Republican candidate, Ronald Reagan, proved a far more formidable adversary than many Democrats had predicted. I, in my eternal optimism, still thought we could pull it out. I was wrong.

Inevitably, January 20, 1981, and the inauguration of a new President arrived. Christine and I stayed in the White House until an hour before the noon ceremony. In the Situation Room people were still struggling with the hostage crisis. As a final insult to President Carter, the Iranians would release the hostages as Reagan was sworn in. Out on the street we ran into laughing Reaganites, ready to take our offices and our jobs. We climbed into my car and drove to Andrews Air Force Base in Maryland where Carter, pale and cold, was bidding farewell to grim-faced staff out on the tarmac. He boarded the plane, destined for Georgia. Joe Albright, assigned to cover the departure, climbed aboard another one. Christine and I went off to eat crabcakes and lots of French fries.

AFTER A SHORT VACATION I went to work for Zbig, helping him research his memoirs, *Power and Principle*. I enjoyed it but at the same time realized I needed a project of my own. It was time to think about yet another Pole. In August 1980, Lech Wałęsa, an electrician, illuminated the injustices of a workers' state when he climbed the fence at the Lenin Shipyards in Gdańsk and demanded a free trade union. As the Czechoslovaks had tried in 1968, the Poles were attempting to free themselves from Communist domination, and once more I was interested in the role the press would play. I applied for a fellowship to the Woodrow Wilson International Center for Scholars and was accepted.

In early September 1981, I began a new routine. As always, I needed to lose weight, so three mornings a week I walked across Key Bridge into Virginia and went to a Diet Center for a weigh-in and vitamin supplement. I then continued on for a one-hour class in Polish that, in a moment of exuberance, I had promised to learn so that I could interview

Polish journalists. From there I took the Metro to the Smithsonian Institution castle where the Wilson Center was housed.

The rapid evolution of events in Poland did not permit my orderly plan. As the Solidarity movement picked up momentum, it seemed likely the Soviet Union, remembering Czechoslovakia's Prague Spring, would step in and block further liberalization. My project would be much less interesting if I couldn't get into Poland. Although the Wilson Center wanted its scholars in Washington, James Billington, a great historian who was the director, understood I needed to go.

At the end of October, I packed my suitcases with gifts—Nescafé, Marlboros, chocolate, and, of all things, tins of Polish ham—and headed for Poland, where I spent two intensive weeks. I began with the names of a few journalists given me by a scholar named Jane Curry, who was willing to share her contacts. By the end of my visit, as one journalist passed me to another, I had been able to meet most major writers in Gdańsk, Kraków, and Warsaw. I spoke with them in their editorial offices, in their apartments, in noisy restaurants, over drinks, early in the morning, and late at night. I was amazed that they had no qualms about being taped. They were only too eager to tell the story of how they had begun with typed news sheets and complicated delivery routes, how they had decided to distribute cassettes with news of their activities to workers in factories, how they had carefully pushed to publish the truth in their newspapers, and how they had acquired newsprint. Even though it had been much harder for me to learn Polish than Russian, I conducted most interviews in Polish—with a few Czech words sprinkled in.

I was interviewing the outspoken editor of *Gazeta Krakowska* in his office when he got a call saying Wałęsa was going to be speaking at Nowa Huta, one of the largest steel works. Did I want to go along? I grabbed my tape recorder and managed to be present when Wałęsa gave one of the most impressive speeches I have ever heard. He was heading a workers' movement, yet at that time he was trying to talk them out of a strike, because he wanted to make sure the Solidarity movement wouldn't be shut down. Wałęsa had long hair and a dark, flowing mustache; he was wearing a blue denim jacket. Every inch a worker, he spoke with power and emotion. I love to compare the picture I took of him then with one taken of us years later, showing him in a three-piece gray suit, hair neatly cropped. The responsibilities of office had tamed his style but not reduced his charisma.

I was in Gdańsk when the city decided to rename one of its shipyards in honor of Poland's first President, Józef Piłsudski. Priests and dignitaries were there, and the crowds roared when one speaker reminded them that Piłsudski had sent his forces towards the east. He didn't have to add that Piłsudski had been fighting the Bolsheviks.

In Warsaw I stayed with my Polish teacher's mother. The apartment had obviously been comfortable at one time. It had a beautiful parquet floor, and I quickly learned to take off my shoes and walk around on soft wool squares from some old blanket, so as to polish rather than damage it. Mrs. Stypułkowska shared her food with me and allowed me to use her tub, which I dared fill with only a couple of inches of hot water. I read by a forty-watt bulb to conserve electricity. When I tried to offer her some of my provisions, she refused. I actually had quite an interesting time giving away what I had brought. The Nescafé went over well, as did the chocolate for the children. I gave the ham to a school. The cigarettes were another matter. I did not smoke, but because I didn't want to embarrass people by just giving them cigarettes, I would take one and leave the packet on the table. Later I learned that by opening the package I had undermined the whole scheme: full packs could be traded for practically anything.

I kept the same cab driver throughout, and we talked a great deal about my project. I asked several times if he knew anyone who might have a full set of the Solidarity paper, *Tygodnik Solidarność*, a publication that had come into existence in April 1981. It had chronicled the aims and ideas of the trade union movement until it was shut down eight months later, by which time it had the largest circulation of any Polish weekly. After a few days, the cab driver trusted me enough to admit that he owned a set. I paid him several hundred dollars for it, making him very happy and giving me a goldmine of research.

Soon it was time for me to go home. When the customs people threw open my suitcases, they were immediately suspicious. There were piles of newspapers and some ceramics, but I had given most of my clothes to my hostess and some women journalists. I had more than a dozen micro tapes hidden in various places, including a beer mug. Always trying to save money, I had been recording over a bunch of Joe's old tapes. When the border policeman asked me about them, I said they were from my husband, who had sent me some messages. By some miracle the tape the policeman asked me to play I hadn't yet used, and Joe's very American voice satisfied him.

The two weeks I was gone was the longest time I had ever been away from my family. I was concerned they would worry. During the first week, I braved a fiercely cold wind to go to a telegraph office to let Joe know all was well. When I got to Kraków, I checked for messages. When I got to Gdańsk, I checked for messages. In Warsaw I checked again. All in vain. There were none.

SEVEN

'Til Death Do Us Part

O N WEDNESDAY, JANUARY 13, 1982, a blizzard paralyzed
Washington. At National Airport a line of aircraft formed, awaiting clearance to take off. At 4:01 P.M. Air Florida Flight 90 rose
hesitantly from the runway, fighting the ice on its wings, before losing
altitude and crashing into the northbound span of the Fourteenth Street
Bridge. The stricken plane crushed cars then snapped apart and sank
beneath the frozen crust of the Potomac. The city watched helplessly as a
handful of survivors struggled to stay afloat long enough for rescuers to
pull them from the ice-cold waters. Even as that chaotic scene was unfolding, a Metrorail subway train cannoned into a concrete pillar between the
Federal Triangle and Smithsonian stops, killing three passengers and
injuring twenty-five. No one in the city that afternoon could ever forget
that day. Washington was in shock.

So was I. But my shock had begun hours earlier, with my own devastating crash. There were no deaths, but there was mayhem and numbness,
and a total disruption of normal life. Joe and I had sat, sipping coffee, in
the comfortable armchairs of our living room a thousand times. That
morning was different. For some weeks, ever since my trip to Poland and
the subsequent Christmas vacation, Joe had been distant and moody, but
there are less-than-great moments in any marriage, especially one that had
lasted twenty-three years. Joe, just back from an overseas assignment, said
we had to talk. Then without warning he said, "This marriage is dead and
I am in love with someone else."

My husband told me he was moving out that afternoon to live in
Atlanta, where the woman he loved was a reporter. Beyond saying that
she was considerably younger, and beautiful, Joe didn't volunteer more
information. He said he had been unhappy for some time. I tried to

think back to signals I might have missed. Nothing made sense. I had kept long hours while working at the White House, but that had ended more than a year ago. Recently, aside from my Polish trip, Joe had been the one on the road. I couldn't believe this was happening; I groped for an alternative explanation. As Joe talked on, I thought ridiculously that maybe he was being noble and brave. Perhaps he had been diagnosed with a brain tumor and was trying to spare his family the pain of watching him suffer. Or perhaps he did not really mean what he was saying. Maybe my remarkable husband was having a very ordinary midlife crisis and would take back tomorrow everything he was saying today. Maybe it would prove a false alarm like that night in Williamstown almost a quarter of a century earlier.

I didn't know what upset me the most—that Joe had presented me with a done deed and was not prepared to discuss how we could stay together, or that he said that I had become too old-looking, or that he couldn't see why I was so upset. After all, he said, "Other people get divorced."

While Joe's announcement was a thunderbolt to me, he obviously had taken the time to do some research. Under the District of Columbia's no-fault law, he said, he could get a divorce automatically after one year, or in six months if I cooperated. Listening to him, I thought of dramas where the heroine screams defiantly, "You will get a divorce over my dead body!" I had never sympathized with the character because I could never envision myself in the role. Now I didn't scream, but I did identify. There was more. Joe wanted me to tell the children that the decision was mutual. I said, "Absolutely not." We agreed that for the time being we would keep this all a secret and tell our daughters and friends that Joe was on assignment out of the city. Then Joe went upstairs to pack.

I had a lunch date with Brzezinski which, incredibly, I kept. It was snowing so hard, the only way to get downtown was to walk, so I hauled on my boots, put my shoes in a big bag, and headed out into the snow. Zbig and I presumably talked about people and policies, though I do not remember a word. I went back out into the snow, feeling lost, emotionally a bag lady, just wandering.

Joe left later that afternoon. The next months were a unique brand of torture. Obviously Joe had meant to be decisive, but once he got to Atlanta he evidently felt either less certain about what he was doing or more uncomfortable about the way he had done it. So he called me— daily. He loved me, he loved me not. He actually described his feelings in percentages. "I love you sixty percent and her forty percent," or the next day, "I love her seventy percent and you thirty percent." I alternated between feeling sorry for myself and sorry for him. He clearly was a good man agonizing. I told only the smallest circle of friends—Danny Gardner, Christine Dodson, and a friend from the Beauvoir and Muskie period, Dale Loy. For years she had shared things with me, from children to political work, from Chinese cooking classes to yoga. Now she bucked me up after Joe's calls.

I don't think my daughters suspected. Why would they? There had been no overt signs of unhappiness. Alice was a junior at Williams. Anne was at home on a Dartmouth's work semester, but she had two college friends living with us and was busier than ever. Katie was also absorbed with her studies and friends. Over the years Joe had had assignments take him out of town, so it was perfectly conceivable that another had taken him away. Whenever he was out of touch for what seemed a long time, he called the girls, told them what he was doing and that he missed them. Unsuspectingly, Katie had volunteered Joe and me to be chaperones on a school skiing trip. Not wanting to let her down, Joe came back for that. Still hoping perhaps that he would change his mind, I welcomed it.

After the ski trip he went back to Atlanta until March, when he apparently decided to see if we could put our life back together. We had always gone to Aspen for spring skiing, so why not go now? Joe noticed that I had lost weight and complimented me. It's amazing what the Diet Center plus the threat of divorce can do. I skied better than I ever had, perhaps because I did not particularly care if I broke my neck. We returned to Washington, uneasily. From moment to moment Joe was either the man I knew or a stranger whose thoughts I couldn't fathom. To avoid holding discussions in the house, we took long walks in the evening around Georgetown.

A friend who didn't know what was going on stopped me one day when I was out shopping. "I've seen you two on your walks," she said. "How nice. I wish my husband and I would do that." I smiled and thought, "No, you don't."

We went to see a marriage counselor whose only value was that the two of us agreed he was useless. By now it was April, time for the Pulitzer Prizes to be announced again. Joe had won many prizes for his reporting, but ever since his dream of becoming a publisher had evaporated, he had coveted the Pulitzer. He had been a finalist before, but this year he thought a series of articles he had written (on snub-nosed revolvers), which had been honored by the White House Correspondents' Association, had a serious chance of success.

As we approached the date, Joe grew fixated on winning. One day he came up with a startling proposition: If he got the Pulitzer, he would stay with me. If not, he would leave and we would get a divorce. I did not know how to react. I certainly didn't see how getting or not getting the prize should affect his feelings toward me. All I could think was that my husband had lost his confidence and if he were not validated somehow, he would have to find a new life.

Late on the afternoon of April 12, the phone rang. It was Joe. "I didn't get it," he said, "so I'm going back to Atlanta." That was that. At least the uncertainty was over. I could never make sense of the possibility that my marriage might have been saved if only the Pulitzer Committee had made a different decision.

Joe had told his mother about our breakup, and she wrote me a very kind letter. Over the years we had come to like each other, and she obviously knew the pain of divorce herself. I could not bear to tell my mother. She was feeling less and less well, and frankly, I was not strong enough emotionally to make her feel better about anything. I did tell my sister, Kathy, who had also been divorced. If there was some good that came out of my pain, it was that she and I became very close. I was grateful that John and his wife, Pam, were living in Washington and did everything they could. One of the people I found hardest to tell was my friend Wini Freund because she had warned me so many times that it was tempting fate to say out loud that I was lucky.

With a divorce formally in the works, we couldn't put off telling the girls any longer. When Alice came back from college for the summer, Joe flew in from Atlanta and we sat the three down in the living room. Joe told them he had been unhappy for many years, was in love with someone else, and was leaving. I could barely look at the girls. First they just stared, tears streaming down their faces. Then, between sobs, they started asking questions. Amazingly, they were quite systematic, working backward to try to determine when Joe's unhappiness had started. You mean you weren't happy when we went hunting in Georgia last year? What about when we were in Puerto Rico for Thanksgiving? What about when we were traveling in Europe? They were stunned, confused, and angry. I sat silent. What could I say? That everything was going to be okay? That it was wrong to be angry? That our expectations of living together forever as a family could be thrown away without regret? No.

Katie left for camp, Anne for Dartmouth, and later Alice to Nantucket for a summer job as a waitress. I was relieved to be alone, not to have to pretend to be functional. I did a lot of thinking. The tumor theory about Joe obviously had to be abandoned, but the genuinely nice, thoughtful, and supportive Joe I had known for so long couldn't simply disappear. The hurtful things he had said must have been the product of his personal pain. And certainly, when it came to saying hurtful things, I had contributed some gems of my own when talking about what he had done and about the "other woman."

Meanwhile the world had not stopped. I had to make an oral presentation of my work at the Woodrow Wilson Center. Once back from Poland, I had been looking forward to continuing my research, hoping to produce a book by the time I left the center that summer. I hadn't, however, factored into my plans the possibility of becoming unhinged, not to mention receiving phone calls every day from a husband undecided about whether to leave me or not. I tried to pretend everything was fine; with a mind unable to concentrate in any language, I struggled to make sense of Polish newspapers. Day after day I stared out the windows of my office at the Smithsonian and took walks on the Mall.

Inexorably, the date of my presentation came—a sweltering day in August. I entered the wood-paneled conference room and took my seat at a long table covered in green baize. Before me sat an audience of one hundred or so academics and journalists, people who would definitely be able to tell if I were babbling or providing insights. I started talking but had to keep studying the audience to see if I was making any sense. No one looked puzzled, so I kept going. All the same, it took me another year to pull the material I had into a book.

The divorce became final on January 31, 1983. I was forty-five years old, having spent more than half my life with Joe. I had never lived by myself: even the three days between graduation from Wellesley and marriage I had spent with Mary Jane in the dormitory. Under the terms of the settlement, I would keep the Georgetown house and the farm. Financially, I couldn't complain. Psychologically, I had to start over.

I was an adult unmarried woman. I had never been that before, had never thought of myself that way. I did have three children, and Katie was still at home. I have been described as a single mother, and to all intents and purposes I was, but not in the classic sense. My children didn't depend on me for their economic well-being; Joe was generous. And if anyone depended on anyone else during this time, it was I who depended on the girls: they provided my grounding. All I had to do was look at them or talk to them on the phone to know that I—we— must have done something right. Each was loving, had an ingrained work ethic, was considerate of all around them, and had the right values. We developed a special bond as we Albright girls faced the world as a group.

I began to work my way through the fog, but slowly. I found that it was hard to make decisions about anything as an "I" instead of a "we." I was incapable of saying no to any invitation: my decision-making mechanism had been geared largely to whether Joe wanted to go somewhere. I could not even make up my mind about what groceries to buy: Joe's tastes had become mine. I stood in the cereal aisle, struggling to choose between Cheerios and Shredded Wheat. I rediscovered the fact that I really didn't like beef, even though for years that is what we had eaten nearly every night.

I don't think anyone who had known me up to that time would have described me as indecisive or vulnerable, but they were wrong. Perhaps without realizing it, I had always needed someone to reaffirm my worth, whether it was my father, Joe, or a boss. As I began to take care of myself, I remember thinking that I didn't want to become the person I thought I might have to in order to survive. I did not want to become cynical or stoical or hard-bitten, or to stop wondering whether what I was doing would please somebody else. The next ten years would test whether I could remain myself, and make it.

ULTIMATELY I FOUND refuge in two places, one as a professor, and one as a participant in politics. During that awful spring, after Joe's declaration but before the Pulitzer announcement, I was faced with a job decision. Walter Mondale was already planning to run for President and I had been asked to sign on as a deputy campaign manager. I also had an opportunity to teach at Georgetown University.

Although the choice between academia and politics was difficult, I chose Georgetown. The idea of following in my father's footsteps appealed to me. That was, after all, why I had worked so hard for a doctorate. I also had some personal calculations to make. If Joe were leaving because my White House stint had given me a status he resented—whether consciously or not—my joining a high-profile presidential campaign would make matters worse. I still hoped he would come back. On the other hand, if he really did leave, I would need the stability of a long-term job.

At the time I thought I had to choose one path or the other, but this wasn't so. In Washington the opportunity to participate politically is always there, whether part-time or full-time. In the end I was able to experience the best of both worlds.

My charge at Georgetown was threefold: teach, create the Donner women's program,[1] and serve as a role model for the young women there. I believed that if women were to compete with men in the international

---

1. Alian E. Goodman, dean of the graduate program of the School of Foreign Service, had raised money from the Donner Foundation to establish a program to encourage women to enter international relations.

arena, they needed to receive an education that prepared them for every challenge, including those no woman had faced before.

I taught classes on international affairs to women and men, drawing on what I had learned in the Carter White House. I was a great believer in role-playing, so I had my students renegotiate the Panama Canal Treaty and argue the merits of arms control from the perspective of senior government officials. Often I was able to provide them with newly declassified documents to help them bolster their arguments. I had female students play roles they wouldn't have had at that time in government, and I had male students report to them. I invited women professionals to discuss their varied and jagged career patterns to illustrate that the shortest distance between two points might not be a straight line.

And I used my own experiences. I said I had often hesitated to make a a point during meetings for fear that it, and I, would be dismissed as stupid, only to have some man make the same point—and be considered clever. "Speak up!" I told students. "Interrupt!" My classes may have been a little boisterous, but the women learned and the men got used to it. I still remember, however, one case where my planning backfired. Assigning roles to handle an imagined international crisis, I chose a woman as Chairman of the Joint Chiefs of Staff. To the lesser position of Air Force Secretary, I assigned a reserved young male student named David Hale. Hale was extraordinarily bright and unfortunately within minutes, without malice, had reduced the Chairman of the Joint Chiefs of Staff of the world's mightiest military to tears.[2]

I had sometimes made fun of my father when he was a professor, saying that he had a cushy job: several hours of teaching, some student meetings, then off for the summer. How wrong I was. Every hour of lecturing had to be preceded by dozens of hours of preparation. What's more, the work is done alone. There is no staff to help, and nothing can be more terrifying than a roomful of bright young people eager to learn, yet skeptical that there are things they don't already know. You have to be on top of everything. If you are caught short once, you have had it.

Still, as hard as teaching was, it was even more difficult for me to feel I qualified as a role model. I discussed the difficult choices women face and implored my students not to let others see the chips that might have settled on their shoulders—especially during job interviews. I spoke with passion about how women must make sure not to push the ladder of success away from the building after they have climbed to the top but must

2. Years later, when I was Secretary of State and Hale a career Foreign Service officer, he became my executive assistant.

help each other succeed. I was confident about the logic of all this, but my shift in marital status had in my own mind made me lose credibility. When my students asked how I had managed to be married and have children and work at the same time, I felt like a phony because I hadn't succeeded.

I was excited to be at Georgetown with a stellar faculty. We had great seminars, we arranged and went to conferences, and we just plain liked each other. At the same time I must say that much that is written about the jealousies and pettiness of faculty politics is true. Even though my classes bulged with students, a few of my colleagues acted as if I should be grateful to be among them. I was labeled a "political" professor. When I was selected for the tenure track, a couple of those not chosen griped that I had won only because of connections. After I was voted best professor at the School of Foreign Service for the fourth year in a row, I almost slugged one of my colleagues for telling me, "You know, the only reason this happened is because your classes are so large."

I took great pleasure in working with students but had no intention of giving up politics. I liked the issues and figuring out how they affected people, and I certainly did not share the popular distaste for politicians. People in politics have to compromise, spend too much time raising money, and often overpromise, but they also put their egos on the line, work hard, take risks, and the best of them accomplish things of real and lasting value.

While teaching, I also found time to serve as a foreign policy advisor to the Mondale campaign. Having clinched the 1984 Democratic nomination, the former Vice-President came to the party's convention in San Francisco with some choices to make. One was to announce in his acceptance speech that he planned to raise taxes to reduce the gargantuan budget deficit that Reagan's economic policies had produced. Mondale's honesty proved, tactically, a bad move. His second choice was to make history by selecting a woman as his vice-presidential candidate. U.S. Representative Geraldine Ferraro was a rising star in the party. I had first met her in 1978 when, newly elected, smart and spunky, she had come to meet with President Carter. We got to know each other during the writing of the Democratic platform, when she was chair of the platform committee and I was serving as Mondale's foreign policy representative. I was pleased when the campaign asked me to go to Lake Tahoe, where she and Mondale were waiting, to review our foreign policy positions with her.

As I walked into the room, the candidate ran up and threw her arms around me. It was a surprise to be singled out in front of all the political heavyweights, mostly male, who were present. "Great to see you, Madeleine," she whispered. "Do you have a half slip I could borrow?"

The men on the campaign quickly got a taste of what it would be like to have a woman candidate as a partner. Gerry was quizzing the campaign experts on a series of issues when her three children walked in. Without taking a breath, Gerry shifted the direction of her questions. "Have you had your orange juice?" she demanded. "You don't think I'm going to let you go to church in that wrinkled dress, do you?" In the van on the way back to the hotel, a few men grumbled. "How're we going to get through this if she worries about what her children are wearing?"

Chills ran down my back and that of many other women when Gerry Ferraro appeared on the convention podium to accept her nomination for the vice-presidency. Her smile was luminous and she gleamed in a white suit. She was beautiful but all business. "My name is Geraldine Ferraro." That's all it took for the convention to explode in applause. Her candidacy was a landmark, another first in the history of women's participation in American politics.

My assignment was to travel with Ferraro and advise her on foreign policy. I loved being part of the political road show, but I did not love the logistics. I hadn't had time to arrange for a leave of absence from teaching, so I had to return to Washington two days each week. Although we spent time on the East Coast and in the Midwest, on Tuesdays, when I had to get back, the campaign travel gods somehow managed always to have us on the West Coast or in some small town. Wherever I happened to be, I had to leave the campaign's cocoon, where all the basics of food, travel, and luggage were taken care of, for the trials of commercial travel, scurrying to make connections through odd places at odd times. I was not the best passenger, as I stuffed my briefing books and carry-on bags into overhead compartments and collapsed into the confinement of a seat in which—unlike on the campaign plane—you were actually expected to sit.

As would prove typical with my experience on campaigns, I was among the oldest people around. I wanted to be one of the gang, however, and never admitted to being tired. It was fun having to be ready to answer any national security question, working on speeches, and seeing virtually every one of the continental United States.

All candidates are tested during a campaign, but as the first woman candidate on a national ticket, Ferraro was subjected to especially probing questions. On *Meet the Press* Marvin Kalb asked her whether she was strong enough to push the nuclear button. He never asked that of her opponent, George Bush. And on *Nightline* Ted Koppel marched her through the most detailed set of questions about arms control any of us had ever heard on television.

Some time after the election Koppel came to speak at Georgetown.

Not knowing I was in the audience, he recalled the episode and noted that his performance had been described as prosecutorial, pedantic, and professorial. "Yes!" I exclaimed from where I was seated. "All three." I then asked, "Do you believe that you, as well as other commentators, were harder on Congresswoman Ferraro on foreign policy than you were on her opponent because she was a woman?"

"Yes," Koppel admitted. "We were."

In spite of it all, Gerry was indomitable. No matter how tough things were, she got on the plane every morning and led the cheers. It worked on me. Every political pro in the country thought we were going to get trounced. I thought we were going to win. As election day neared, the crowds grew larger and more enthusiastic. The issues, I thought, were clearly on our side. Gerry did well in her debate with Bush, and Mondale had done well in the first of his debates with Reagan.

It did not, of course, turn out that way. The Democratic ticket was obliterated. I hated losing, but the campaign did help me begin a new life. I made new friends and proved able to hold my own within the highest circles of the Democratic party. Much to my amusement, the very professors and deans who had once put me down as "political" began to spotlight my background and views when they wanted to add a little spice to the conferences they were organizing. They enjoyed watching me argue with other "political" professors like Chester Crocker, who had just spent eight years as assistant secretary of state for African affairs under President Reagan. They also accepted when I invited them to my house for the regular discussions I began to have about foreign policy.

I started these evening meetings in an effort to avoid the kind of divisive fight over national security policy that Mondale and Gary Hart had waged during the primaries in 1984. I thought that if Democratic experts on foreign policy knew each other and hashed out the issues ahead of time, the party would avoid debilitating disagreements during the campaign. So I began inviting people from Congress, think tanks, and law firms to dinners at which one expert presented ideas the rest of us would then discuss. Later people would say I had hosted "salons" in my "elegant" Georgetown house. The truth is my house is comfortable, not elegant, and my dinners were simple buffet affairs—salad, roll, and a slice of something. As one participant told a reporter, anonymously, "We certainly didn't go there for the food."

ONE OF THE MORE difficult calculations in presidential politics is to figure out the right moment to commit yourself to a specific candidate. Decide early and you are more likely to be part of the inner circle if your candidate wins. Decide late and you're more likely to pick the candidate who is nominated, but you may find it hard to breach that inner circle. In 1987, I decided early. I had seen Massachusetts Governor Michael Dukakis in action at the 1976 platform hearings and been impressed with his command of the issues and his ability to get people to agree. He had since developed a reputation as one of the nation's best governors, and I knew him to be a genuinely decent and thoroughly honest man. I also admired the people around him. His campaign manager, John Sasso, had also managed the Ferraro campaign. Susan Estrich, whom I had met when she was staff director for the platform committee in 1984, was Sasso's deputy and later his successor. Dukakis' speechwriter, Bill Woodward, would years later become mine, as well as one of my closest advisors.

I joined the relatively small Dukakis team in March 1987. There were many who felt I was crazy to sign up so soon, but as the campaign progressed and other candidates fell away, the experts changed their minds. Suddenly I was the top foreign policy advisor to the likely Democratic nominee. My phone was especially busy on Wednesday mornings after a victorious Tuesday primary. By the time Dukakis accepted his nomination at the 1988 convention in Atlanta, I was taking dozens of calls a day.

That convention is remembered best for Texas governor Ann Richards' speech poking fun at then–Vice-President Bush ("Poor George, he was born with a silver foot in his mouth"), Bill Clinton's overlong nominating speech, and the triumphant entrance of Dukakis, a child of immigrants, to the sound of Neil Diamond's "America." My own memory is more high-tech. My job was to roam the convention floor and make sure we won the platform fights over foreign policy. Convention floors are always chaotic and communications there difficult. Every rumor has to be checked out, so my movements were directed via walkie-talkie by Susan Brophy, a senior campaign aide, from a trailer just outside the convention floor. For some reason I had chosen to wear a blue silk dress with my yellow and turquoise sneakers. I also had on a blue nylon vest and headphones. The staff gave me a *Star Wars* nickname: R2D2. As I moved about, I got knocked in the head repeatedly by roving cameras, and I tripped more times than I could count on legs, ankles, feet, cables, and pizza boxes. It was wild, but I was in my element, doing battle over foreign policy and feeling as if I owned the convention floor. What is more, we won all our fights.

Returning to Washington, I found my association with Dukakis had transformed my status. This is what I called my "Brooke Shields" phase. An article in the *National Journal* described a cocktail party at which a woman was immediately surrounded by men: "It must be Brooke Shields," an onlooker thought. Not quite, but in Washington's terms, it was someone more alluring—Madeleine K. Albright, the Dukakis campaign's top foreign policy advisor." Even people who had never shown any sign of liking me now thought I was charming. They also seemed to think I had gotten smarter. Before, even at my own dinner discussions, I had barely been able to get a word in. Now every syllable I uttered was met with nodding heads. I was being quoted every day in the newspapers, while the usual big boys were not. It got so ridiculous that at one meeting at my house I excused myself, went to the bathroom, looked in the mirror, and lectured my reflection: "You're no smarter than you were last month, and if we lose no one will listen to you again."

How right I was. Soon after Dukakis' defeat, I went to the Kennedy Center to see a play. At intermission I wandered into the foyer. No one even looked at me. Finally a Washington lawyer, who had been positioning himself for an administration job if we had won, bumped into me by mistake. "You certainly f——ed that up," he said.

Although the Democrats lost again, the Dukakis campaign was another educational experience for me and a bridge to other opportunities. I was especially grateful for the new friends in my life, because—perhaps unfairly—I was disappointed in some of the old ones. I thought somehow they should have helped talk Joe out of what he was doing after we had gone public. Later, when more and more people I knew got divorced, I realized I had been asking the impossible.

As with most newly divorced people, I had to figure out my social life—difficult, given that I hadn't looked at another man since I was twenty, I had no confidence thanks to Joe's departing comments about my looks, and I was a prude. My last date had been in the 1950s. This was the 1980s. With no idea what the new rules were, I felt like a forty-five-year-old virgin. When you meet someone in your teens or twenties, there is not that much past to talk about. In your forties and fifties, the people you meet have a lot of history, complicated family stories, special interests, and personal habits that may be both idiosyncratic and inflexible.

In the 1960s, if Joe and I had friends for dinner, the children would be introduced and sent to their rooms or given something out of the way to do. Now if I went with a date to the home of a modern couple, the children would be the center of attention all night. If I were out with someone younger, I had to remember to offer to split the check. If out with an older foreign man, such as my dashing new friend Ricardo Dell'Orto of Argentina, I had to remember to allow him to order, never to sit with my back to the restaurant door, and to act offended if other men failed to stand when I left the table. If I were "involved" with someone, I had to deal with the specter of herpes and later AIDS. I felt renewed anger at Joe for forcing me to deal with these kinds of issues at my age. When I had lectured my daughters about safe sex, I had had trouble putting myself into those conversations.

Despite all this, I did try to fill the void left by Joe. I had met Barry Carter during the Mondale campaign. He was a law professor at Georgetown who had worked at the NSC under Kissinger, but he was also an expert on arms control and a Democrat who loved politics. We had a lot in common and spent so much time together, he finally moved in. I am not sure this was the best example for Katie, but he was so kind to all three of my children that we felt like a family for a while. After a couple of years Barry and I parted amicably. He was younger than I and wanted to have his own children; I had already done that. He had been a great friend at a difficult time. I finally realized I could not fill the huge hole in my life. When I gave up that search, I became more content.

I still didn't enjoy being single, but with help from women friends I made a start. After several years of being one of the few women in academe, I had begun to meet wonderful professional women in the course of my political work. Most were in their thirties, a decade younger than I. Campaign friendships and conversations can be superficial, but sometimes they are the opposite. It's late at night and you are exhausted and you just talk on a darkened bus between stops. You get together for a good meal, first complain about something that went wrong during the day, then switch quickly to more interesting and often personal issues.

One evening, close to the end of the Dukakis campaign, six of us met for dinner. Most of the conversation was about the fact that, although there had been many women in high positions during the campaign, at crunch times they had been pushed aside. For me, however, the conversation about what came next was what mattered. Each of us was in a way typical. One was in her late thirties, had dated a lot, but had never found the right person to marry. Another was living with an older man and wanted to have children, but he had some from his first marriage and didn't want to go through parenting a second time. A third woman was about to give up her established life on the East Coast to move west and start a family with her new husband. A fourth was happily married with children but lived in Oklahoma, far away from national political action. She took a leave of absence from her normal life every four years to get her political fix. Yet another already had one child and wanted more, but was unsure whether she should or could.

As I listened, I was fascinated by these women's problems and a bit jealous—especially of those who were married. Then one of my friends turned to me and said, "Madeleine, you're the one who has it all. You've been married, you have three fabulous daughters, a great job. How did you do it?" I was stunned. I realized then that I had fallen into self-pity, focusing not on what I had, but on what I had lost. I have never forgotten that evening. Before that episode I felt I had no advice to offer younger women because I had failed. This discussion banished those thoughts.

In 1989, I was going to my thirtieth reunion at Wellesley. One of my classmates asked me if I would give a talk on whether my career had caused my divorce. Curtly, I declined. I also decided that if that was what people wanted to know from me, I wouldn't go to the reunion at all. It took the joint efforts of Emily, Wini, and Mary Jane to persuade me to make the trip. The reunion organizer had pushed a real button.

Did my career cause my divorce? I have always resented the question; I consider it insulting to women who want a career, and I reject the implication that I was selfish. I also resent the question because I don't know the answer. There are many contradictions in the way I feel. When I became Secretary of State, I realized that, though others might, I would never have climbed that high had I still been married. Yet I am deeply saddened to have been divorced. I know that at the time I would have given up any thought of a career if it would have made Joe change his mind.

It took me a long time to figure out what I was doing. Since I had begun my volunteer work in those first years after returning to Washington, I had been proceeding a stepping stone at a time. It didn't matter that they had been placed at random and were sometimes slippery. I was determined not to fall in the river. I concentrated on doing every job well. And when the crossing became hardest, there were friends there to help me retain my balance.

Slowly and steadily, as the 1980s progressed, I exchanged my feelings of loneliness for a sense of freedom. My capacity for decision making returned. I could use the house the way I wanted. When I had an early morning class, I invited the students to breakfast in my living room. I had my political dinners. As various Eastern Europeans came through Washington, they stayed with me, at what we started calling the Albright Inn.

I traveled for weeks during the summers, to Georgetown conferences, or as part of a U.S. program that sponsored American experts on their specialties abroad, or as vice-chair of the National Democratic Institute for International Affairs (NDI), an organization aimed at promoting democracy around the globe.[3] I went to the Middle East and the Far East, to Africa and Europe.

I learned to rely on myself. I had never been a loner, but now I could spend a whole Saturday without talking to anyone. I was able to spend the night at the farm alone. I went to concerts and operas alone. I was able to go to a restaurant accompanied only by a book, although I still found this easier to do abroad than in Washington. I no longer felt like an egg without a shell.

I also was ready for new opportunities. When Ed Muskie asked me to become president of the Center for National Policy (CNP), a think tank, I accepted, even though it meant I could teach only part time. I had enough money and didn't need tenure; I could keep teaching at Georgetown without it. I didn't need to jump through hoops anymore. And while I was getting myself together, the Communist world was disintegrating. There was so much new to explore and learn. I wanted to be ready, when the time came, to leap to the next stone.

3. NDI is one of the world's most effective nonprofit groups working to promote and strengthen democracy. Led first by Brian Atwood and then Kenneth Wollack and Vice-President Jean Dunn, NDI's programs have helped millions across the globe to develop durable and successful democratic institutions. I was honored to become chairman of its board when I left office.

EIGHT

The Velvet Revolution

M Y TELEVISION WAS ALIVE with images. In Prague's historic Wenceslas Square the crowds were chanting slogans and waving signs reading "Poslední Zvonění," "the last bell." Demonstrators rattled the keys in their pockets, emulating the sound of a bell tolling the end of four decades of Communist rule. On a balcony that overlooked the vast and ebullient gathering stood Alexander Dubček, hero of 1968's short-lived Prague Spring, and Václav Havel, a dissident playwright about to become one of the world's most respected figures. A month earlier Havel had been arrested. A month later, he would be inaugurated president of a new Czechoslovakia. The date was November 24, 1989. "This is it," I said out loud to myself, in amazement, joy, and relief. "Thank God."

East Germany had abandoned the Berlin Wall's checkpoints on November 9. On November 10, the supposedly stolid Bulgarians ousted their longtime Communist dictator. By then Hungary was already preparing for elections and Poland was ruled by Solidarity. What about Prague? A few days later, in an op-ed in the *Washington Post*, I wrote sadly, "Czechoslovakia, the country that provided much of the intellectual underpinning [for overthrowing Communism]…is [still] hiding behind a self-imposed iron curtain and criticizing those who dare to practice the freedoms that Czechs and Slovaks themselves enjoyed briefly 21 years ago."

Within a week my gloom was dispelled. On November 17, marching students veered from their approved route and strode boldly into the center of Prague. Police descended upon them, beating them brutally. Instead of dispersing, the students rallied. Then their parents—appalled by the viciousness of the authorities and amazed by the bravery of their children—joined them in the streets. The spirit of dissent surged. The entire Czech Philharmonic Orchestra turned up to play for the protestors, whose numbers grew daily until three hundred thousand Czechoslovaks were crammed into the square. Exuberant demonstrators pointed out that when "68" is turned upside down, the number reads "89." Prodemocracy coalitions were rapidly assembled by Czechs (The Civic Forum) and Slovaks (Public Against Violence), calling for the resignation of President Gustáv Husák and other party officials. Finally, two days before the end of 1989, Dubček was elected Chairman of the Federal Assembly and Havel President. Communism was dead in Czechoslovakia. The Velvet Revolution—so called because of its peaceful character— had triumphed.

Although I was thousands of miles away in Washington, I subscribed to a press service that provided detailed descriptions of daily events throughout Central and East Europe, events I followed avidly. I also led discussions in my classes at Georgetown. I knew all the personalities and felt I was there in spirit.

THE IRON CURTAIN had descended upon Central and East Europe in the late 1940s. In most places the voices of dissent were stifled and, to the West, unheard; but once or twice a decade a wind arose that caused the Curtain to part just long enough to sustain hope that freedom would one day be restored. In 1948, Tito broke with Stalin. In 1953, there were riots in East Germany. In 1956 first the Poles, then the Hungarians tried to rebel. In 1968, it was the Czechoslovaks' turn. In the late 1970s, Polish dockworkers launched the Solidarity movement, prompting the imposition of martial law in 1981. Then there was Nicolae Ceauşescu in Romania, whose rule began in 1965 and spanned almost a quarter-century. At the outset he was a breath of fresh air, defying the Soviets and proposing reforms, before he turned into a destructive tornado.

The cement holding the Soviet empire together had been stressed, but it didn't crack until 1985, when Mikhail Gorbachev became general secretary of the Soviet Communist Party. Gorbachev engineered a program of economic restructuring (*perestroika*), coupled with a new social and intellectual approach (*glasnost*) that challenged the assumptions upon which the Soviet system had been built. He made clear that the satellite states no longer had to take orders from Moscow. Suddenly the emperor was more liberal than his princes. The aging, backward-looking leaders of the satellites were exposed as inept hacks; the shift in Soviet attitudes reinforced changes throughout East Europe. Dissident movements bloomed. The Hungarians implemented economic and political reforms, developing their unique brand of "goulash Communism." In Poland authorities were pressured into lifting martial law, giving Solidarity a second life.[1] East German officials thought they had everything under control until Gorbachev, on hand to help celebrate their regime's forty-second anniversary, warned that without change there would be massive popular resistance.

Relatively little attention was paid to Czechoslovakia, and I understood the reasons for that. The Soviet invasion of 1968 had broken the spirit of many. People turned inward and spent as little time as possible at their jobs. Instead they put their energy into building weekend countryside retreats, or *chatas*, to which they disappeared as early on Fridays as they could. But the shoots of Prague Spring, not altogether destroyed, began slowly to push back above ground.

Oddly, American rock music provided one source of nourishment. A group called the Plastic People of the Universe, named after a Frank Zappa song, was formed one month after the Soviet invasion. Its concerts attracted such large crowds that the authorities prohibited the group from playing in public. Planning in secret, the band continued to perform, until its members were arrested and charged with disturbing the peace and playing music with an "antisocialist and antisocial impact." The group's trial was viewed as a key test by intellectual dissidents. Shortly after its conviction, on January 1, 1977, more than 250 writers, professors, and human rights activists signed a manifesto—Charter 77— calling upon the Czechoslovak government to respect the civil and political rights embodied in the Helsinki Final Act, which Soviet bloc members had signed sixteen months previously. One of the leaders of Charter 77 was Václav Havel, who was arrested on several occasions and spent more than four years in jail.

Religion also played a role. Even to young people raised as atheists, defrocked Catholic clerics became heroes. The priests, forced to take menial jobs such as cleaning latrines, officiated at clandestine church services. But until 1989, these and other moments of rebellion seemed no match for the crushing weight of the Communist state.

I was naturally curious about events in my native land, and in 1986 seized the chance to visit as part of a U.S. Information Agency educational program. For protection I stayed with the American chargé Carl

---

1. For many years I had a running discussion with Zbig Brzezinski about the differing characteristics of Czechoslovaks and Poles. Despite his marriage to a Czech, he would regularly point a finger at my countrymen, saying they were not as courageous as his. The only time I had a comeback was when the Polish generals imposed martial law. "Zbig," I said, "at least the Czechoslovaks didn't invade themselves."

Schmidt and his wife, Rika, both great sources of information about what was going on. I knew I had to be discreet, because Czechoslovak authorities, nervous about the continued activism of Charter 77, were cracking down, but I hoped nevertheless to talk with some dissidents. A U.S. official had quietly arranged an evening meeting. By chance, U.S. Senator Larry Pressler of South Dakota was also in Prague at the time and had been told of the rendezvous—about which he was a little too enthusiastic. Sharing a car earlier in the day, he had asked, "Will there really be dissidents at this meeting?"

Since the car was almost certainly bugged, I signaled him to be silent.

"Which dissidents will be there?"

I signaled again.

"Why won't you tell me about the dissidents?"

I put my hand over my mouth, shook my head, and pointed to imaginary bugs.

That evening we were told the people we were supposed to see couldn't come because they were being watched, so Pressler stayed away. But one leader of Charter 77, Martin Palouš, showed up anyway because he hadn't yet gone home to where the police were staked out. The two of us talked for almost four hours. About midway we received a call from Pressler. "Hello, Madeleine," he said over the open phone line, "I heard some dissidents did show up. Are they still there?" I said quickly, "You must have the wrong number," and hung up. A little later there was a knock on the door. It was Pressler. He strode straight over to Palouš and poked him repeatedly in the chest with his finger. "Are you really a dissident?" he asked. I wasn't sure whether to laugh or cry.

In those days U.S. embassies in Communist countries marked the Fourth of July with celebrations that often included leading local dissidents among the guests. I attended that year's party in Prague, but because of the crackdown, few dissidents showed. As I surveyed the sparse crowd, a young woman approached and held out her hand. "Hello," she said, "I'm the wife of Jiří Dienstbier."

Dienstbier was the Czechoslovak journalist who more than a decade earlier had helped me with my doctorate. I had never expected to see him again. His wife explained that Jiří had not been able to attend the party but nevertheless wanted to meet me the following day at the Savarin Café, a popular spot just off Wenceslas Square. I agreed without hesitation, but when I told embassy officials, they said, "Are you out of your mind? Don't you realize what's going on? They're watching him, and—as Josef Korbel's daughter—they're watching you too. You can't just meet up in public. Besides, you're here under the auspices of the U.S. government, and we don't want any problems." So I did not go. Dienstbier was indeed picked up as he sat at the restaurant waiting for me.

I returned to Prague the following year, and this time both the embassy and I were more adventuresome. A public affairs officer arranged for me to meet another dissident, but this time it was all very cloak-and-dagger. I was told to wait for a man in a raincoat at a precise time, in front of a certain building, near a church on a well-known square with a monument. I showed up, and as much as I tried to act completely casual, I couldn't help looking around nervously. From exactly which direction I don't know, but suddenly a man in a raincoat appeared. "Follow me," he said in Czech. "We're going on the metro to a stop several minutes away. Don't ask me where."

When we got on the train, he said, "Get close to me. We'll pretend we are lovers and no one will notice." I then received a nice kiss on the lips from a man I didn't know en route to a destination about which I could only guess. We arrived, walked a few blocks to a nondescript building, and headed down into the basement. There, on simply built shelves, were the prized possessions of the group the man represented: copies of *Rolling Stone* magazine. He was a member of the Jazz Section, a group that formed in 1971 just to play music but had evolved into an important gathering of dissidents. We talked for hours about their problems, the strategies dissidents used, and the hopes they had. Before leaving I gave him the cash I had with me and offered to send them two hundred dollars, then more if that got through. He told me where to send a money order, which I did as soon as I was back in Washington. When I told my mother what I had done, she was furious, sure the funds would be traced. I told her not to worry. My beneficiary wrote and thanked me for the two hundred kisses, but when he was arrested for other reasons, my mother insisted she had been right.

On subsequent visits to Prague, I felt more comfortable and wandered the streets and rode the metro alone. Although my clothes were of better quality, I blended in physically, since many of the local people were also short and round. I ordered my favorite fattening foods in restaurants, attended movies and plays, and understood the language without any problems. But my American passport made all the difference. I was able to meet with dissidents, then board a plane and leave. I didn't have to make the choices they had to make each day of their lives.

As I walked around Prague, a city both beautiful and sad, I asked myself some hard questions. What would have happened had my parents decided not to leave when the Communists took over? I was sure I would have been a dissident politically, but I didn't know whether or how I might have acted. Would I have had the courage to protest? Or would I have kept quiet in order to get a university education? How would I have behaved if I had been subjected to interrogation? What would it have been like in jail? As I pondered, I thought of the story about the dissident leader who meets an old friend and asks for help. "I would help you," his friend said, "but you see I cannot, because I have children." The dissident replies, "I would remain silent like you, but you see I cannot, because I have children."

My NEXT TRIP to Prague was in March 1989. I went to a dinner at the embassy, and this time Jiří Dienstbier did indeed show up. He had shaggy gray hair now and a luxuriant mustache, very handsome. We embraced as long lost friends. He had to leave dinner early to report for his job as a night furnace stoker, and the next time I heard of him was in January 1990. By then Havel was President, and Dienstbier his foreign minister.

When I called the foreign ministry, Jiří was on the line in a matter of seconds. I asked what I could do. He said, "Help the students. They're the ones who did this."

I was delighted, in the middle of that historic January, to lead a NDI delegation to Czechoslovakia. When I arrived, I called Jiři, who invited me to accompany him to a play, *Audience*, written by Havel. The new president's dramatic works had long been banned in his native country, although productions had been staged in New York and elsewhere. *Audience* depicts the refusal of a brewery worker to become a Communist stool pigeon despite the bullying entreaties of his drunken boss. It was based on Havel's own experiences, coupled with his conviction that effective resistance to totalitarianism is possible through self-discipline and faith. When the curtain came down, the audience exploded in applause for Havel and, I think, for Czechoslovakia.

The following day Jiři received me in his office. It was incredible to see my old friend ensconced as foreign minister. As I walked in, I had goose bumps. Forty-three years earlier, my father had walked into this same room as *chef de cabinet* (chief of staff) to Jan Masaryk. I shivered when Jiří took me back to his private apartment in the ministry and showed me the white-tiled bathroom out of which Masaryk jumped—or was thrown—to his death on March 10, 1948. To "prove" Masaryk had jumped, the Communists had preserved the simple wooden chair to show how the foreign minister might have used it to hoist himself onto the window ledge. The new government would preserve it also for a time, so that they would not forget how freedom was lost.

Christmas Eve 1943, with my father in our brick house in Walton-on-Thames. Although war raged, my parents made everything seem as safe and normal as possible.

My parents, Josef and Mandula Korbel during WWII. She slapped him for calling her the most talkative girl in Bohemia, but my mother never regretted waiting seven years to marry her Jožka.

Jan Masaryk, later Czechoslovak foreign minister, with his father, Tomáš Masaryk, founder of modern Czechoslovakia. The contrast between two eras is reflected in their clothing and footwear and in the elder Masaryk's luxuriant mustache. Commenting on the photo, Jan Masaryk recalled the pleasure of sitting quietly with his father, greatly preferring it to the unnecessary chatter of official meetings.

Arnošt Körbel, my grandfather, flanked by my father (l) and his older brother John (r).

I love this early picture of my parents. My mother looks like a flapper; my father had already begun smoking a pipe.

In Berkhampstead, England, with my cousins George and Alena (front row), Aunt Ola, my cousin Dáša, and my parents.

This was taken by my father in May 1948 when my parents came to Switzerland to tell me we would not be going back to Communist-controlled Prague. Lake Geneva is in the background.

As a nine-year-old, I earned my keep as the flower girl at the Czechoslovak embassy in Belgrade. Blanka, my governess, supervises; I am assisted by my sister, Kathy, and a family friend.

Presiding over the International Relations Club at the Kent School in Denver. I founded the club and named myself president.

High school photo, 1955.

Posing in the white dress with the red sash I borrowed from Miss Fackt. I thought it looked like a lampshade.

Mr. and Mrs.
Joseph Medill
Patterson Albright,
June 11, 1959.

Arms full with Anne and Alice, or is it Alice
and Anne?

Daughter Katie, just after her christening.

Joe, buttoned-down and eager, with the man who alternately charmed and intimidated us, Harry Guggenheim, majority owner of *Newsday*.

Joe's uncle and aunt. Both Harry Guggenheim and his wife, Alicia Patterson, rated cover treatment by *Time* magazine.

Three generations of Pattersons. Joe's sister, Alice (l), mother, Josephine, and grandmother, Alice Higinbotham Patterson, the lovely and formidable "Gaga." Peering over my shoulder is Dina, Joe's younger sister.

Senator Edmund Muskie at the fund-raising dinner I organized on behalf of his 1972 presidential campaign. Republicans sabotaged the dinner but I was responsible for my wig, which I somehow thought would transform me into a tall, sophisticated blonde. Also helping the Muskie campaign were (from l to r) Enud McGiffert, Dale Loy, Jane Muskie, June Isaacson, and Madzy Beveridge.

Sandwiched between two of the men I most admired, Senator Muskie and President Jimmy Carter, at a party celebrating the Senator's sixty-fifth birthday.

Enjoying a moment with my boss, National Security Advisor Zbigniew Brzezinski, in his office in the West Wing of the White House.

President Václav Havel, relaxing in Bermuda. Note the Rolling Stones tee shirt and Havel's characteristic way of signing his name.

Campaigns are all about planes. The first woman nominated for a place on the ticket of a major party, Geraldine Ferraro blazed a trail others may soon follow.

Former Vice-President Walter Mondale was the Democratic nominee in 1984. He was courageous in selecting a woman running mate, honest on taxes, widely respected for his intellect and decency—and trounced at the polls.

En route to another stop during the 1988 election, Governor Michael Dukakis looks over the work of Bill Woodward, then his speechwriter, now mine.

Jiří arranged for my NDI delegation to meet Havel at Prague Castle. The furniture in the presidential office was still "bulky Communist," but the new president was neither. A relatively small man with a strikingly large presence, he had on black jeans and a black turtleneck. I had brought with me as a present a copy of my father's last book, *Twentieth-Century Czechoslovakia*. Havel was prepared to meet an American delegation and hadn't focused on any Czechoslovak connections, so when I handed him the book he seemed nonplussed. "Oh, yes," he said, "Mrs. Fulbright." "No," I said, "I am Mrs. Albright. Josef Korbel was my father." So began one of the most precious friendships of my life.

Havel had been in power only a few weeks. Our delegation offered help in drafting a new electoral law, which he accepted immediately. Soon we had a team of experts that included not only Americans but also people from countries such as Portugal that had undergone relatively recent transitions to democracy. As I was leaving, I mentioned to some of Havel's advisors that I had worked in the White House and would be delighted to help design a structure for their new presidency. They invited me to a restaurant just behind the dark towers of Saint Vitus Cathedral within the castle walls, and we sat there for hours, drawing up personnel flowcharts and work diagrams with arrows pointing this way and that, analyzing how the new government would function. They also told me that Havel would soon visit the United States, and they needed help making the arrangements. Once again I volunteered.

There was snow on the ground when I came out of the restaurant that evening, but the moon was strong and full. I descended the steep steps that led from the castle, down the winding Nerudová Street, past the old baroque church of Saint Nicholas, into the smaller, narrower streets that lead to the fourteenth-century Charles Bridge, with its black statues of the saints. I thought about how my father had told me that the reason the bridge had survived so long was that the mortar had been mixed with eggs. As I looked out at the Vltava River, I had the uncanny sensation that I had never left Czechoslovakia. Crazy. How could I have helped the Czechoslovaks organize their presidency if I had not learned firsthand about the American one?

Back at my hotel there was a note from a woman named Rita Klímová. "We don't know each other yet," she wrote, "but we will—soon and well." She had just been named ambassador to the United States and was inviting me to meet a few of her friends that same evening. When I arrived, her apartment was filled with members of the new government, while she was busy cooking. As she and I talked, both in the kitchen and out, it became clear that our personal stories were mirror images of each other.

Both our families had spent World War II outside Czechoslovakia, mine in London, Rita's in New York. Both returned to Prague after the Nazis' defeat. In contrast to my father, Rita's was a Communist, so her family stayed after the Iron Curtain came down. She lectured on economic thought at Charles University and ultimately concluded that Marxism made no sense. In the purge that followed the crushing of Prague Spring, she lost her job. She had had to answer for real the questions I had posed to myself rhetorically. For years she struggled to earn money as a translator, usually for Americans meeting with dissidents. During the Velvet Revolution she was Havel's English-language voice, albeit in perfect Brooklyn American. From our first meeting we became allies. Afterwards, in Washington, we got together often to talk and laugh as she ordered pastrami on white because she liked the American bread she could not get in Prague, while I always looked forward to the sour rye taste of Czechoslovak bread I could get only at her embassy.

PRESIDENT HAVEL'S VISIT to America in February 1990 was part celebration and part circus. History's accelerator had hit the floor and the world had suddenly turned right side up. There had been no master script. Havel was as shocked as anyone to find himself a head of state and worldwide democratic hero about to address a joint session of the U.S. Congress. I turned my house into Havel's advance headquarters, mobilized friends from previous political campaigns, and recruited some of my Georgetown students to help.

I went to Rita's residence to prepare Havel for the days to come. After my Senate and White House experiences and the Ferraro and Dukakis campaigns, I was in my element. The only challenge was breathing. Havel was a chain-coughing chain smoker, surrounded by aides with similar habits. I just held my breath and gave Havel the memos I had prepared, along with pages of potential questions and answers for the press. I was delighted when he turned to his staff and said in Czech, "Now *that* is an advisor."

Havel had written his speech out on a long yellow pad that he gave to Rita, asking her to translate the text into English. She didn't need any help, but I enjoyed making suggestions anyway. I had also arranged for the media consultant Frank Greer to coach Havel on his delivery. Some people are naturally gifted performers on television or in front of a crowd, but most of us are pretty wretched at first. Havel's own people said he was not a success on television because he didn't look into the camera. He read his texts slowly and didn't use a teleprompter because he thought it looked phony. Even with reporters he avoided eye contact, a habit developed to foil repeated cross-examinations in prison. For all the rehearsals and coaching, Havel's delivery during his big speech on Capitol Hill was still flat.[2] However, no one cared: the message was what counted.

At the core of that message was a paradox. "You can help us most," Havel told a surprised Congress, "if you help the Soviet Union on its irreversible, but immensely complicated, road to democracy....The sooner, the more quickly, and the more peacefully the Soviet Union begins to move along the road toward genuine pluralism," Havel continued, "the better it will be not just for Czechs and Slovaks, but for the whole world."

In this and other speeches, Havel also worried that the same human tendencies that had made possible the Holocaust and the Soviet empire—including complacency in the West—were likely to reassert themselves in some new form. That is why, while others talked about politics as "the art of the possible," Havel urged his audiences to pursue "the impossible." In some ways he is not a practical man. He is an inconvenient man, an idealist with a knowledge of society's frailties and of the faults of human character, but one who insists that cynicism is fatal. Unless political behavior is guided by conscience, he argues, we'll not simply have bad government, we will be doomed.

Naturally, I was delighted to show Havel around Washington and to accompany him to meet students at Georgetown and elsewhere. When he invited me to go with him to the White House to meet President George Bush, I knew enough—as a well-known Democrat—to decline. Havel was pleased with his visit, showing me a fountain pen he had received from the President, for which I later sent him refills.

I then accompanied Havel to New York, where he was able to indulge his artistic side. At the Actors Studio, he met with Paul Newman, who talked about his mother's Slovak origins. There was a star-filled gala at the Cathedral of Saint John the Divine. And Robert Silvers of the *New York Review of Books*, who had published Havel during the Cold War days, organized a party on the stage of the Vivian Beaumont Theater, during which I translated for the informally assembled quartet of William Styron, Edward Albee, Norman Mailer, and Václav Havel. Unbelievable.

Later that spring when I visited Czechoslovakia again, Havel asked

---

2. Havel was helped, however, by the animated interpretation provided by Michael Žantovský, later Czech ambassador to the United States.

me to stay in Prague Castle.[3] I was given a gigantic iron key to an immense wooden door and told I had to be in by 11:00 P.M., when the iron gates closed. My bedroom faced Hradčanské Náměstí, and so I saw, from a different angle, the same square, park, and cobblestones I had seen as a child. Perched in my window, I watched the changing of the palace guard, newly attired in uniforms designed by Theodor Pištěk, the Oscar-winning costumer for the movie *Amadeus*. I craned my neck to find the trumpeters who from a high balcony accompanied the marching honor guard.

The whole scene was deeply moving especially since my brother, John, happened to be in Prague and was able to share it with me. The castle is where Tomáš Masaryk had lived during Czechoslovakia's first golden era, when my parents had met and begun dreaming of the life they would live together. Here Hitler shattered the dreams of their entire generation by marching through the castle's doors and proclaiming the country his. During the Cold War, Communist potentates such as Brezhnev, Ceauşescu, and East Germany's Honecker had stayed in these same rooms, resting their backsides on the hideous socialist realist furniture that was still there.

I returned to Prague yet again in June, as co-chair of the NDI international election observer team. The euphoria was palpable. The election law we had helped to shape in January was about to be implemented. Polling stations were decorated with red, white, and blue bunting. When the votes were counted, the prodemocracy Civic Forum and Public Against Violence were victorious. I joined a party of former dissidents at the Magic Lantern Theatre. Together we wept in joy as we sang the American civil rights anthem, "We Shall Overcome." In the evening the Old Town Square filled with people, packed in around the huge monument to the Czech martyr, Jan Hus. The celebrations were enhanced by the presence of Paul Simon, whose music and lyrics—language differences or not—were understood by all.

MY ENCOUNTERS WITH Czechs and Slovaks were both more frequent and more complicated in the years immediately after the Revolution than they had been before. In living rooms in Washington and Prague, over dinner, in academic settings and television interviews, I had intense dis-

---

3. The foundation for Prague Castle was laid during the ninth century. Unlike other presidents, Havel worked in the castle but didn't live there. He had an apartment across the river and later built his own home.

cussions with acquaintances old and new about what democracy really meant. We debated the value of political parties, the role of the press, the importance of foreign investment, and ways to make the economy work for the people. The Czechoslovaks loved their new freedom and were great admirers of the United States, but they also had some classic criticisms about America's role in Vietnam, our supposed lack of culture, our materialism. So I was amused when I took some of my friends to a mall or department store around Washington and they found it hard to restrain themselves from buying everything in sight. For Americans the liberty to choose from a dozen different brands of nearly everything is taken for granted. To someone accustomed to staring forlornly at the shelves of government-run stores in Communist Central Europe, it was like Christmas every day.

My new friends were surprised at my Czech, and I was especially pleased when they said I had no discernible foreign accent. I had to learn a new vocabulary, however. First, I had never really had political discussions in Czech; some of the words I used made my listeners laugh. But language was not the main issue. My way of thinking had been shaped by my coming of age as a free American. As I explained how a democratic government should function, what it meant to own your own business, how important individual rights were, and why there must be no restrictions on the media, I tried not to sound patronizing. I didn't always succeed, and occasionally one of my friends would say tartly, "You know, we didn't just come down from the trees."

The increased openness in Czechoslovakia also allowed me to look up my cousin, Dáša. I had seen her only once since my family had left in 1948. In the summer of 1967, Joe and I had made a tour of Central Europe and stopped in Prague. Then, even though I was in the country with an American name, passport, and husband, I was nervous. Some of my parents' friends told me my father had been tried in absentia and sentenced to death. I didn't want to get Dáša in trouble with the authorities, so she and I met only for about an hour in a rather tense visit in a Prague café.

In 1990, we could talk without worrying about the government. However, it was still not easy. To be a relative is not necessarily to be similar. She had had a much harder life than I, made worse by the fact that she was my father's niece. She was more resigned than bitter. Although Dáša wanted to hear about my family, I felt uncomfortable telling her the details of all we enjoyed. I was actually relieved to be able to tell her that everything wasn't perfect; my husband had left me.

During one of my visits I also saw Josef Marek, who had been my father's press attaché in Belgrade. He was also my brother's godfather. He told me that because of this family connection, he had been thrown into jail. The contrast between the joy I felt at the liberation of my native land clashed continually with the sadness I felt at learning in such a personal way about the suffering its people had experienced—some of it in retaliation for my father's democratic activism.

The most intellectual conversations I had were with Václav Havel. We were approximately the same age, and his life experiences and his creative mind gave us plenty to talk about. In the summer of 1990, I joined him and his first wife, Olga, in Bermuda. We visited the NASA tracking station and that evening sat under the stars, talking about how Czechoslovaks, perhaps because they are landlocked, spend a lot of time looking at the heavens and imagining what it would be like to navigate by them.

All the while a more serious question nagged at me. I wanted to know if Havel was critical of the Czechoslovaks who had left after the Communists had taken over. Although his answer was phrased diplomatically, I believe he thought they had been wrong to go. Havel had had a number of opportunities to live in the West; he could have gone to Hollywood to write and live a good life. I asked him why he had not. He said simply that he felt an obligation to stay. I wondered again whether I could have survived all he had.

In 1991 and '92, as democracy took hold, the old Prague revived. As in my parents' youth, there were concerts everywhere. Galleries opened, filled with wild modern art. Long-forbidden photos of the Masaryks and Edvard Beneš appeared in government buildings. Tourists thronged the cobblestone streets. Havel became an icon in his own country and abroad. Although he started dressing and walking like a president, U.S. magazines preferred to photograph him in a Rolling Stones tee shirt or a black leather jacket, which made him look like a Czech version of Bob Dylan. He was a serious world leader, and also a moral and intellectual force—and playful in a way that let you know he didn't take his own fame too seriously. When he gave an autograph, he customarily used a green pen to sign and a red one to draw a heart beneath his name.

But then Czechoslovakia, like a prisoner held in jail for decades without sunlight, burned too quickly. The euphoria began to fizzle. Even in his inaugural address, Havel had wondered whether the ideals that had sustained the Velvet Revolution would long survive it. He worried especially that long-suppressed ethnic grievances—"a feeling history has done us wrong"—would resurface. In 1992, in connection with Andrew Kohut and the Times Mirror Center for the People and the Press, I helped conduct a survey on post–Cold War attitudes in Europe. The good news was that Czechoslovaks wanted to be part of Western Europe and favored a free market. The bad news was that the spirit of interethnic cooperation Masaryk had championed and Havel preached was breaking down. Of all the people in the region, Czechoslovaks were the most negative in their opinion of the Roma, or gypsies. Even more seriously, many Slovaks wanted to go their own way. We asked members of a Slovak group whether they would prefer to see Slovaks reach number one in the world as part of a Czechoslovak hockey team or number eight as a purely Slovak team. They preferred the Slovak option.

The nationalist debate sharpened. There were those in the Slovak capital of Bratislava who did not like the economic plans coming out of Prague. Slovaks were also disadvantaged by privatization because many huge Soviet-era factories were located in their region and no one wanted to invest in them. Nationalist politicians exploited the sense that Slovaks were being discriminated against, while memories of past differences between Czechs and Slovaks were recalled. At midnight on December 31, 1992, the union dissolved. In contrast to the breakup of Yugoslavia, the end of the Czechoslovak state was peaceful. It was called the Velvet Divorce. The breakup saddened me, because I had always thought of myself as a Czechoslovak, as had my parents. I believed then that the two nations were stronger together, and still do, though I am pleased that relations since the breakup have improved.

Even before the breakup, political life in both republics had been complicated by another ghost from the past. When secret police files from the Cold War era were opened, many people discovered that friends had been reporting on them for decades. Others with a reputation for dissent were in fact double agents. In 1991, a process had begun called "lustration," the careful examination of people's backgrounds to determine exactly who was doing what when. I had often wondered how dissidents had known whom to trust during the Communist period. Now I had my answer: they never had.

SADLY, MY MOTHER did not live to see a free Czechoslovakia. She died on October 4, 1989, six weeks before the students marched. In the years preceding, her scleroderma had progressively worsened and she was always hooked up to oxygen. The mile-high altitude of Denver, which had nourished her for so long, was now making it more difficult for her. We tried to persuade her to move to Washington to be near John and Pam, their children Josef and Peter, and my family, but she resisted. She wanted to stay where she had been so happy with my father, saying, "There is more to life than breathing. Jožka and my friends are here. Come and see me."

Finally, in 1987, she consented, and for the time she had left she was part of our Washington lives, settling into a lovely apartment. We spent a lot of time together, going to the farm, seeing movies, playing with the children. It made me wish even more that she had moved near us sooner. Joe, learning from our daughters about their grandmother's condition, called to ask if he could visit, which he considerately did.

My mother became an inveterate newspaper clipper ("I need to do this, because someday you might want to write a book," she'd say) and was fascinated by what was going on in Central and East Europe. I think that following events there kept her closer to my father. As much as she tried, my mother never really recovered from his death. Whenever I saw her, she said, "Your father predicted there would be a united Europe. He told me that again last night." She was frustrated with the Czechoslovaks for their slowness but said shortly before she died, "Your father told me Czechoslovakia would be free. He's always right."

THROUGH MOST OF the 1980s, I taught a course on U.S.-Soviet relations. When Gorbachev came to power, I had to throw out my notes. After that, there was not a semester when I could teach the same material as the semester before. I started a course on Central European politics but had to change that every semester as well. Once I had been an expert on the Communist system. Now I felt more like an archeologist delving into the past.

I told my classes we had reached a rare moment, when all the old assumptions had to be revisited and existing institutions either adapted or abolished. The superpower rivalry appeared over, but that was hardly the end of history. New challenges were already rising. The Soviet empire would be replaced, but it was not clear by what. As Havel prophesied, resurgent nationalism created fertile ground for conflict. Traditional foreign policy approaches would be diluted for better or worse by the growing power of nonstate actors, including multinational corporations, public interest groups, organized crime, and terrorists. The Cold War was over, and some were saying the West had won a permanent victory, but I worried that the widespread triumphalism would lead to complacency and a dangerous withdrawal by America from its responsibilities. I surprised my students by predicting that the new world might be even more perilous than the old.

On a personal front, the path had zigzagged, but I had learned much since my first professional job in 1976. In addition to my dealings with Czech and Slovak leaders, I had traveled and met with officials and citizens throughout Central and East Europe and the former Soviet Union. I had gone to conferences in China, Africa, and Latin America. I was teaching, writing articles, giving speeches appearing on television, and testifying before Congress. I was head of a progressive think tank, and one of a group of former Carter administration officials still active and visible in Washington, contributing regularly to foreign policy debates.

I was also deeply interested in the outcome of the 1992 presidential election. Democrats had been out of power for a dozen years. I was fifty-five. If I were ever to have a chance to shape foreign policy instead of just talk about it, this was it. Because of my association with the nonprofit Center for National Policy, I could not play the same full-time role in the presidential campaign I had previously, but I did what I could. When the ballots were counted, I felt a strong sense of anticipation. Displeased by our slumping economy, the voters had given the Democrats a chance. There would be a new President, and one of his first tasks would be to select his foreign policy team.

PART TWO

Fourteen Suits and a Skirt

NINE

A Sign Saying Simply "United States"

T HE GUARD at the White House North Gate studied my driver's license. "I know you," he said. "Worked here before, didn't you?" "Yes, and we're back," I said happily.

Almost twelve years had passed, but the walk up the driveway to the West Wing entrance was wonderfully familiar. It was mid November, two weeks after the 1992 election, and I was among the first members of the Clinton team to enter the White House. My job was to help coordinate the handover of responsibilities at the National Security Council.

I was supposed to meet my Bush NSC contact near the cyberlock doors guarding the entrance to the fabled Situation Room—the precise spot from which I had departed the White House on January 20, 1981. I headed down the small staircase to the NSC offices. Everywhere I looked there were Bush-Quayle photos. When I had last seen the area just outside the Situation Room, it was a rabbit warren of offices with mismatched desks and large iron filing cabinets. Now many of the smaller rooms had been converted into larger ones, with built-in mahogany cabinets and matching desks. I felt as if I had rented my house to strangers and was returning to find it redecorated and adorned with portraits of unfamiliar children and pets.

Soon, I knew, the portraits would be replaced by Clinton-Gore pictures. I felt exhilarated but also anxious. I was to serve as the contact point between the President-elect and the outgoing NSC staff, which meant I had to identify issues likely to require early decisions, sift through piles of resumés, and prepare briefing books for the incoming President and National Security Advisor.

As coordinator I made recommendations for organizing the national security operations of the new administration, one of which would later affect me, though I had no reason to think so at the time. I proposed that the U.S. permanent representative to the UN should be a member of the Principals Committee, the President's senior foreign policy team.[1]

I wanted to handle my temporary assignment capably for its own sake, but also knew I was being evaluated for a position in the administration. I hadn't played the same role advising Bill Clinton that I had with Democratic candidates in previous elections. However, I had run into him several times during the campaign and had written papers at his staff's request. I first met him in 1988, when he came to Boston to help Dukakis prepare for a debate. A group of us had gone to dinner, and I stayed in touch with him after that, even recommending him for membership in the Council on Foreign Relations.

After the 1992 election victory, Nancy Soderberg, a Clinton staffer and former student of mine, prepared a memo for the President-elect about candidates for jobs. She sent me a copy of his reply. My name had been the only one underlined and the word "good" written in the margin. That made me think I would be offered something, but I didn't know what.

Given my Carter administration experience, I had expected if I returned to government to do so at the NSC, hopefully in one of the top two positions. That now was unlikely. Two of my friends—Anthony Lake and Samuel ("Sandy") Berger—were clearly slated for the jobs. Tony had been in charge of State Department policy planning in the Carter administration, with Sandy his deputy. Both participated in the foreign policy dinners I later hosted in Georgetown. In 1988, I had been the foreign policy advisor closest to the Democratic presidential candidate. In 1992, Berger and Lake were. Sandy was a prominent trade lawyer, with muscular shoulders, a somewhat cherubic face, and an unpretentious manner. A first-rate thinker, writer, and strategist, he was occasionally brusque but more often patient. As a longtime friend of the President-elect, he could have had the job of National Security Advisor. Instead he did the unheard-of in Washington and deferred to Lake. Tony had begun his career as a Foreign Service officer but had resigned in protest over the Nixon administration's invasion of Cambodia during the Vietnam War

1. In the Clinton administration, the Principals Committee considered major foreign policy questions and formulated recommendations that were then passed on to the President. Other members of the committee, which was chaired by the President's National Security Advisor, included the Secretaries of State and Defense, the CIA Director, the Chairman of the Joint Chiefs, and the National Security Advisor to the Vice-President.

and become a professor at Mount Holyoke College. He was extremely bright, with strong humanitarian instincts and particular expertise on Africa. Now the Lake-Berger team would be reunited at the NSC—with Tony in the top job and Sandy again his deputy.

I turned my attention to the State Department. There my most ambitious hope was to become the first woman to serve as deputy secretary. I wasn't interested in an overseas embassy post and didn't give a thought to the UN. Richard Gardner had wanted the job of UN ambassador since we had first met during the Kennedy administration. Dick was superbly qualified and had been an early supporter of Clinton-Gore. He seemed a sure thing.

Shortly after Thanksgiving, Sandy asked me to his office to talk about jobs. I was caught short when he inquired, "How would you like to be ambassador to the UN?" Instead of the appropriate response, "I would be thrilled," I said, "Dick Gardner will kill me." Sandy replied, "Don't worry, that's not your problem." He repeated the question, and this time I said, "Of course, but my secret aspiration is to be deputy secretary of state." Sandy didn't react to that, and soon the interview was over.

For days nothing happened. I thought I had blown it. Of course I didn't want anyone to know how nervous I was, so I just stewed, telling myself they would certainly name me to *something*. As the days went by, I started polishing all my shoes at night and reorganizing my office at home, shuffling papers from one place to another, then back again. On December 20, a Sunday, I decided I couldn't sit waiting any longer for the phone to ring, so I went to my transition office and worked on memos, checking my answering machine every few minutes. When I returned home around 6 P.M., the phone rang. It was Warren Christopher, the former deputy secretary of state who was in charge of the entire transition process. He was calling from Little Rock to tell me that the President-elect intended to offer me the UN job but wanted to talk to me first. Christopher instructed me to join him the following afternoon and to tell no one about the conversation or that I was going to Arkansas. "As you know, Madeleine," he said, "there's many a slip between cup and lip. Take your tax returns and other papers over to the lawyers to start the vetting process, then come see me when you arrive. And bring a toothbrush in case things run late." Thanks to all the organizing I'd done, I had all the paperwork, including proof the Albrights had made the appropriate Social Security withholdings for our children's nannies.

I got on the plane to Little Rock excited, exhausted, and worried about being seen. Then I saw Richard Riley's wife, Tunky. Riley was close to the President-elect and thought to be slated for a cabinet post. Tunky told me Dick had also been summoned and had spent the entire day before sitting in a hotel room waiting for a call, wondering what had gone wrong. In the end all was well; she was flying down for the official announcement of her husband's selection as Secretary of Education.

When no one met me at the airport I became nervous again, the more so when I arrived at Christopher's office and someone asked, "What're you doing here?" Eventually I was told to go to the Excelsior Hotel, check in, and avoid being seen. I slipped into my room and swiftly locked the door, feeling confident I had escaped detection. Within seconds the phone rang. "This is CNN and we know you are there." I threw down the receiver as if it were a snake.

It was still only midmorning, and I was afraid to answer any other call, go out, or even send down for room service. So I sat and waited and watched television, with all the commercials seemingly about food. Finally, around 5 P.M., I broke my vow of silence and called Nancy Soderberg. "What's going on?" I inquired. "Everything's fine," she said, before adding the words I would hear repeatedly over the next eight years. "He's just behind schedule."

Nancy asked if I had arranged to bring my daughters down. I told her I hadn't been sure I would be part of any announcement and was sworn to secrecy. I mentioned the CNN call and swore I had not uttered a word to anyone. "Well, sit tight," said Nancy. "We'll be in touch."

Christopher's office soon called to say my appointment with the President-elect would not be until ten that night and to invite me to have dinner with Mr. Christopher before that. I leapt at the invitation, thinking I might finally find out what was going on.

I made my way to the restaurant and was shown to a table in the far corner of a vast, empty, dimly lit room. Warren Christopher arrived a few minutes later. I had known Christopher, or Chris as he was called, during the Carter administration. We were comfortable with each other, if not close. Now we had just started to chat when Christopher interrupted himself to say very quietly, "Madeleine, I want to tell you something. I'm going to be Secretary of State."

I put my hand on his arm and said, "Chris, that's fabulous—and much deserved." Although we were the only ones there, he continued with a straight face, "Now, don't show any emotion." When a moment later a waitress appeared, he started talking about the weather. As soon as she left, he looked around to left and right before saying, "I've asked Clifton Wharton to be my deputy, and the President-elect is going to ask you to be ambassador to the UN. But remember—not a word to anyone."

I showed up at the Arkansas governor's mansion a few minutes before ten. Asked to wait, I sat on a semi-enclosed porch as people rushed about inside, preparing simultaneously for Christmas, staffing the new administration, and the Clinton family's move to Washington. Cardboard boxes were everywhere. Suddenly a girl with long blond curly hair darted out from a side-room and started to peer into the boxes. This was Chelsea. A few minutes later James Woolsey, who would be selected to head the CIA, walked by and said he had just concluded his meeting; Bill Clinton was waiting for me in his study.

As soon as I entered, the President-elect offered and I accepted the UN job. We proceeded to talk until almost midnight. Although both our lives were about to change dramatically, our conversation was relaxed and open. Bill Clinton sat in an armchair with his feet up, and we roamed around the world talking about his plans for foreign policy. He shared with me his enthusiasm for making the UN more effective, a comment I would often recall later as I sought his support for various initiatives. He told me about the other national security team appointments, to be announced along with mine the following morning. He said he was putting the UN position back at the cabinet level, where it had not been under President Bush. He also commented, "I sure am impressed you won the best teacher award at the School of Foreign Service four years in a row." Obviously it didn't hurt that Georgetown was his alma mater. Finally we were done and I returned, weary but excited, to my hotel. Nancy—bless her—had left a message saying she had been in touch with my daughters, who were on their way down. It was only then that I had the confidence to take out a pad and write what I would say the next day.

The following morning the new national security team assembled at the governor's mansion.[2] Despite the mildly sentimental tone of my statement, I had pledged to myself that I wouldn't cry. Then I looked at the audience. Anne, Alice, and Katie were already in tears, and some of the tough women journalists sitting in front of me were wiping their eyes. As I finished, I turned and hugged the President-elect, and saw that even he was teary.

When my daughters congratulated me, they said, "Mom, we know most of these people. They've been to our house to dinner." It was true. The members of our team knew each other well and were eager to work together. That evening, as we all started to go our separate ways, we were told the Little Rock airport was so fogged in that we would have to spend

---

2. The gathering included prospective officials Warren Christopher (who would become Secretary of State), Clifton Wharton (Deputy Secretary of State), Les Aspin (Secretary of Defense), Tony Lake (National Security Advisor), Sandy Berger (Deputy National Security Advisor), Jim Woolsey (Director of Central Intelligence), and me.

the night. I went out with the other prospective appointees for a celebratory dinner; I was so wired after, I had trouble falling asleep. Then, in the middle of the night, the phone rang. "Ambassador Albright?"

I had never been called that before. "Yes?" I answered cautiously.

"This is the ambassador from Bangladesh. I am across the street and want to be the first to congratulate you."

"But it's one o'clock," I protested.

He said, "I just wanted to make sure that you would never forget me."

I never have.

I NOW HAD A NEW BOSS. The selection of Warren Christopher as Secretary of State was logical and well received. During the Carter administration he had personally handled the negotiations that led to the freeing of U.S. hostages in Iran. He had also mediated hard-edged, racially tinged urban disputes, including the aftermath of the notorious beating of Rodney King in Los Angeles in 1991.

Christopher was a lawyer's lawyer, who emphasized preparation, precision, and persistence. Both his body and his statements were spare. Observing him, I came to identify a raised eyebrow as evidence of high emotion. He was dapper and perhaps a trifle fastidious, although his perfectly tailored navy pinstriped suits were lined in red paisley. On his first overseas trip as Secretary, his plane stopped for refueling in Shannon, Ireland—an enormously popular destination for press and staff, partly because the bar featured potent Irish coffees, laced with homemade whiskey. Christopher wanted to maintain his faculties without appearing standoffish, so he ordered a decaffeinated Irish coffee with no alcohol, a compromise that rapidly became legend. President Clinton later joked that Chris was the only man in the world who ate M&Ms with a knife and fork.

I was soon to learn how fortunate I was to work with Christopher. His experience and many accomplishments had left him seemingly incapable of pettiness or jealousy. We didn't always agree, and our temperaments were quite different, but he was the consummate team player. I often met with him, prior to meetings of the Principals Committee, to resolve any disparity between our views. When I didn't fully agree with the State Department position, he urged me to say what I thought, a generous act on his part since I did, after all, work for him. On the whole he was very supportive, and perhaps fairer to me than his successor would be to mine during the following presidential term.

There was still a month until the Senate would vote on whether to approve my nomination. I went away on Christmas vacation, energized by my new job, bringing along huge binders to study for my confirmation hearings. The binders bulged with facts about UN peacekeeping operations, proposals for UN reform, the budget, and the incoming administration's position on everything from the Middle East to human rights in China. My new portfolio was global, and I had to know what to say and also what *not* to say on each topic—taking care to avoid answers that would come back later to haunt me.

Then there was the Inaugural Ball, no small matter. What to wear? I certainly couldn't repeat the gold brocade number I still had in my closet from the Muskie days. I went out shopping at one of Washington's fancier stores, and I must admit I was looking awful: all in black and no makeup. It was little wonder the perfectly turned out saleslady gazed on condescendingly as I examined the few dresses on the racks. I have never been good at the butcher's where you have to ask for specific cuts of meat or at dress stores where they keep the good stuff in the back.

"I'm looking for something to wear to the Inaugural Ball," I told her.

"And why," she inquired pointedly, "would *we* be doing that?"

By happenstance the famed reporter Helen Thomas walked by at that very moment and greeted me, "Hello, Madam Ambassador."

The effect on the saleslady was almost comical. In fact the whole place swung into action. I was whisked off into a large room, and the better dresses were brought out.

As I was trying on one of the new creations, another saleslady came in to say that Dr. Hanan Ashrawi, the renowned Palestinian spokeswoman, was in the next dressing room and wanted to say hello. One of my predecessors, Andrew Young, had been forced to resign for meeting with a Palestinian representative, and besides, I was in my slip. So I demurred—but too late. In Ashrawi walked, and we were soon chatting away.

I was pleased with my dress and greatly enjoyed the Inaugural festivities but didn't stay out too late, because my confirmation hearing was the next day. I was proud to be introduced to members of the Senate Foreign Relations Committee by my former boss, Senator Muskie, who was then invited by the panel's chairman, Claiborne Pell, to join him on his side of the witness table. Pell was the Senate's foremost champion of the UN and always carried with him a dog-eared copy of the UN Charter. I had prepared myself to answer many more questions than the committee could ever have found time to ask, so the hearing went smoothly. I remember it primarily for my first official experience with Senator Jesse Helms, the inimitable right-wing Senator from North Carolina.

Helms had been in the Senate at the time I worked for Muskie, but I had steered well clear because he seemed to be against everything I believed in, from effective arms control to active American leadership at the UN. Despite that, he was also known for his southern courtliness, especially toward women.

Before I testified, Helms asked me to introduce my family. Alice, Anne, and Katie dutifully stood up. Helms focused in on Katie, who was twenty-six years old but looked far younger. "What a lovely young girl you are," he said, adding he also had a granddaughter called Katie. I saw Katie clench her fist at being mistaken for a child and prayed she wouldn't say anything out of place. Luckily she kept her counsel. Later I took her to a White House dinner, where she again caught the Senator's eye. He told Katie he remembered her and asked how school was. Katie replied that she was an attorney. He responded, "Oh, a lady lawyer." Again Katie held her tongue, but on the way home we laughed at what Helms' reaction might have been if she had said, "a lawyer, but no lady."

ON FEBRUARY 1, I flew up to New York. I was going to represent America at the institution my father had served when our family first came to America. At the Security Council I would sit behind a sign saying simply "United States." And I would be arriving at the UN at a turning point in its history.

The organization had emerged from the ruins of World War II, reviving hopes for global peace that had earlier been embodied and then embalmed by the League of Nations. Tragically, the Korean War and the extension of Soviet influence rapidly destroyed any illusion that the UN alone could guarantee peace. Many in the United States and around the world continued to value the world body for its high ideals, as well as for the unique forum it provided and its work through such bodies as the World Health Organization and UNICEF. Only rarely during the Cold War, however, did the UN act to preserve international security. With the Soviet Union and China among the veto-wielding permanent members of the Security Council, the UN couldn't take action unless East and West agreed, which did not happen very often or about very much.

Now the Cold War was over, the Soviet Union had ceased to exist, and the barrier to coordinated Security Council action had come down. This was illustrated most dramatically by the council's authorization of "all necessary means" to roll back Iraq's 1990 invasion of Kuwait, a resolution that helped the Bush administration assemble a broad coalition for Operation Desert Storm.

Unfortunately, the post–Cold War world was born with a split personality. Millions of people had been liberated from authoritarian rule.

Opportunities arose to resolve "proxy wars" that had been fueled by East-West tensions in places such as Cambodia, Mozambique, Angola, and Central America. But the Soviet empire also unleashed a new round of "ethnic wars" caused by unresolved nationalist and territorial grievances in Central Africa, the Balkans, and the Caucasus.

In the past, UN peacekeepers had only rarely become involved in "hot" wars. By tradition, the UN waited until cease-fires were achieved, then sent in lightly armed forces to separate opposing factions with their consent and give diplomats time to forge a comprehensive peace—a process that might take weeks or decades. These were known informally as "cook and look" missions; the UN presence was stabilizing, but the troops themselves were only occasionally at risk.

Now, with the explosion in the need for international peacekeeping, coupled with the end of the Security Council's paralysis, the UN's role was expanding. During the four years of the Bush presidency and the first of Bill Clinton's, the council authorized more new peacekeeping operations than the UN had attempted in its previous forty-five years. In 1990, there were less than fourteen thousand UN peacekeepers. In 1993, the number would peak at more than seventy-eight thousand. For decades in the past the Security Council had rarely met. During my four years we convened almost daily.

For me, and for my UN colleagues, all this activity created a kind of trial by fire. We were excited to find ourselves at the center of action on so many issues, but at the same time we had to strive to keep the newly popular organization from collapsing beneath its added burdens. The UN, the ultimate committee, had never been a model of efficiency. Underutilized during the Cold War, it had grown overweight and out of shape. In my speeches I joked that the UN bureaucracy had grown to elephantine proportions, and all of a sudden the world was asking it to do gymnastics. "Let the UN do it" had become the operative phrase in Washington and other capitals. This shift was partly due to the hope that the UN would finally fulfill the dreams of its founders. But it was due as well to the desire of many national governments, including the United States, not to take on the hard tasks themselves.

My job was further complicated by the ambivalent attitudes many in the United States had toward the UN. For every Senator Pell who cherished the institution, there was a Senator Helms who derided it. Because of its makeup, the UN was vulnerable to allegations it was a semi-useless talk shop filled with diplomats accumulating New York City parking tickets they never paid. Over the years, congressional skepticism and micromanagement had caused the United States to fall several hundred million dollars behind in paying what we owed to the UN. This fact proved a constant headache. Every time I demanded that other countries meet their international obligations, I was reminded that my country was violating its own commitments. Even the normally sympathetic British took to using a line they must have been waiting two hundred years to deliver—accusing the United States of seeking "representation without taxation."

The U.S. Mission to the UN (USUN) is right across First Avenue from UN headquarters. The location is prime, but the building is an ugly rectangle of unadorned concrete a dozen stories high. My office was on the eleventh floor, with what would have been a fine view of the river and Queens if it hadn't been interrupted by concrete lattice work. I had brought with me a picture of my father that showed him and members of the UN Commission on Kashmir in the summer of 1948. I also asked to have a bust of my illustrious predecessor Adlai Stevenson placed in my office. Later, when I was given a UN blue helmet, I put it on Adlai's bald head. The picture and bust were like having friends from my past with me at all times.

My first official day as ambassador, Warren Christopher had accompanied me to New York, where I presented my credentials to Secretary General Boutros-Ghali, whom I was predisposed to like. Because he too was a former professor, we talked about the transition from academic to diplomatic life. I had met him in Africa in 1986, when he had represented Egypt at a conference on democracy sponsored by NDI. He had struck me then as impressive, blessed with brains, confidence, and style. On the way back to the United States, I had met his wife, Leia, and visited their beautiful apartment in Cairo overlooking the Nile.

Boutros-Ghali was a born diplomat. His grandfather had been Egypt's prime minister, and one of his uncles foreign minister. Boutros-Ghali himself served for fourteen years in the number-two position in the foreign ministry, denied the top post, it was rumored, only because he was a member of Egypt's Coptic Christian minority and because his wife was Jewish. Eventually he was appointed deputy prime minister for foreign affairs and emerged as a compromise candidate for secretary general, prevailing because of his diplomatic experience and his promise to serve only a single five-year term.

In our early dinners and meetings, the two of us discussed how to improve America's image of the UN; we went down a long list of specific issues. He was unfailingly polite. I was eager and friendly. It was months before I realized that our relationship had begun on a high point and would only slide downhill thereafter.

I had expected my first Security Council meeting to be in the huge room with the horseshoe-shaped table that is always shown on television, but that chamber is used only for formal sessions. The room used for informal meetings—where much of the real work is done—was no bigger than the Georgetown seminar rooms I had just left. When I entered, the cramped space was already filled with assorted ambassadors and their staffs. I squeezed my way in and sat down. The other fourteen permanent representatives, all men, also sat and folded their arms in front of them. I thought immediately that if I lived to write my memoirs, I would call the book *Fourteen Suits and a Skirt.* I found myself struggling between instinct and duty. As a woman, I wanted to get a sense of who was who and what the dynamics among the players were before speaking. As the American delegate, I knew I had to speak up if I wanted my country's views to be heard. After a few minutes I took a deep breath and raised my hand.

SHORTLY AFTER BECOMING Permanent Representative, I ran into Helen Thomas once again while shopping, and she asked me to address the annual white tie dinner of the Gridiron Club. The club has nothing to do with football; it exists solely to host the dinner, at which members of the Washington press corps satirize the newsmakers they cover through a program of songs and skits. Each year the President and one person representing the Democrats and another the Republicans are invited to speak, with the expectation that they will either be funny (which is good) or publicly humiliate themselves while trying to be funny (even better).

Helen, the Gridiron Club's first woman president, was determined to line up a female speaker. Hillary Clinton and Elizabeth Dole had already declined, so she asked me. Many presidents have found it impossible to put Helen off; I did no better. Having accepted, I was petrified because although such events are theoretically "off the record," the *Washington Post* informs everyone the next day who flopped and who flew. I knew I could tell stories, but I had never been adept at telling jokes, and didn't think I needed to embarrass myself voluntarily.

Helen told me, "Don't worry. The speakers don't write their own material. I'll find someone to help." I'm sure she did her best, but I wasn't reassured by the writer who called. He began by asking me what kind of sense of humor I had, continued by informing me that his fee was ten thousand dollars, and concluded by saying he had no idea who I was.[3]

This put-down gave me an idea. Like third party presidential candidate

---

3. I did end up paying a token amount to Mark Katz, a young comic writer I had met during the Dukakis campaign. I was also grateful to Robert Shrum for his valuable—and free—advice.

Ross Perot's 1992 running mate, Admiral James Stockdale, I decided to walk to the podium and ask the audience, "Who am I, and what am I doing here?" Soliciting other suggestions from staff and friends, I tried to develop a routine that poked fun at myself without overdoing it, and at others without truly skewering them. At the Gridiron Club, this is known as the "singe, not burn" principle.

The night of the event, Senator Robert Dole warmed up the audience of 650 by saying, "The lovely dress Helen Thomas is wearing tonight is from the new J. Edgar Hoover collection." There followed an eclectic mix of songs and sketches about Nannygate, Albert Gore, the Supreme Court, and book-writing presidential pets. A number of the funnier bits were performed by Washington's most hirsute journalists in drag. No wonder photographers weren't allowed.

When my turn came, I looked out at an audience that included half the President's cabinet, the President's mother, and virtually the entire *Who's Who* of Washington from Ethel Kennedy and Pamela Harriman to Chief Justice William Rehnquist and Sam Donaldson. There's nothing scarier than having to be funny. I didn't know whether the audience would respond or sit on their hands while I fell on my face.

As I spoke, the laughs came and—to my relief—in the right places. I thanked Helen Thomas for elevating the status of women within the Gridiron Club, saying I had congratulated her personally while she was serving hors d'oeuvres in the lobby. I took a chance with a friend by comparing Warren Christopher to the Egyptian Sphinx he had recently visited, and described him as "certainly statesmanlike, practically sagelike, and almost lifelike." I said Bob Dole's wit had drawn blood so often his wife had had no choice but to become head of the Red Cross. And I said I had known George Stephanopoulos during the Dukakis campaign, when he was better known as George Stuffingenvelopes.

After telling your jokes, you are expected to have a serious ending. I closed with a reference to President Clinton's Arkansas hometown, invoked during his campaign as "a place called Hope." I said, "I was eleven years old when I arrived in America from a neighborhood in Prague called *Smíchov*, which happens to be the Czech word for laughter. No matter how serious the world becomes, I still believe in a place called *Smíchov*."

Washington humor is extremely topical and, as the "highlights" above reflect, doesn't wear especially well. One joke that went over well that night but which I came to regret was the following: "I am very happy at the UN; the only problem is that we seem to do the same thing over and over again. It can be very, very repetitive—or so Boutros Boutros-

Ghali tells me." The audience laughed, but my attempt at humor may have contributed to Republican efforts later to bash the UN by making fun of the Secretary General's name.

The next morning I turned nervously to the *Washington Post* Style section. I found there an extensive account of the Gridiron's history, the atmospherics, the clothes, the skits, the President, and the songs. I thought, "Who cares about that stuff? What about me?" I was about to give up when I came across the magic sentence: the speakers "finished with a home run. Ambassador Albright, not known as a laff riot, wowed the crowd with a batch of deadpan one-liners."

Longtime Washington powerhouse Vernon Jordan told me later that my appearance had made a huge difference in how I was perceived. I thought it ironic that, to be taken seriously in a policy role, you first had to be funny.

WITH THE COLD WAR OVER, the game of global diplomacy was no longer—as it had been for nearly all my adult life—a matter of two sides, one the good guys, the other the bad, in direct competition. Now there were far more than two teams; the uniforms were mixed, while the scoreboard had gone haywire. And the spectators—civil society—had come pouring down onto the field. I thought, as I settled into my job as ambassador, that if we were going to understand this new world, we'd have to begin by finding a new way to talk about it. Sitting in New York, among representatives from nearly every nation, was an ideal vantage point. Soon I began to formulate what my staff came to call the "four food groups," my way of explaining the world in the absence of Cold War divisions.

The first group of nations, according to this analysis, consisted of those who were full members of the international system. They had governments that signed treaties and forged alliances with each other, official institutions that functioned, private sectors that traded, citizens whose rights were respected, and legal systems that generally succeeded in upholding the law.

The second group was in many ways a product of post–Cold War democratic trends. These were nations trying to make the difficult transition from autocratic to democratic rule. Their focus was on building institutions at home that worked and joining institutions abroad that would help them prosper and keep them safe.

The third group comprised countries with weak or nonexistent governments, often held back by poverty or mired in conflict. They needed help in holding their heads above water.

The fourth group was represented by governments that, for one reason or another, were hostile to the rules of the international system and sought to circumvent or subvert them. Saddam Hussein's Iraq and Kim Il Sung's North Korea were prime examples.

This was hardly a scientific way of looking at the globe, and many nations did not fit convincingly into any one of the categories, while others fit into more than one. It also failed to account for the rising influence of nonstate actors, which range from international terrorists to multinational corporations to global public interest organizations. All the same, I found the model useful, because the four groups led directly to four foreign policy tasks for the United States and its allies. Together we had to forge the strongest possible ties among the first group, so that there was a solid foundation upon which to build; we should help the second group succeed, so that democratic trends would continue; we should aid those in the third group who were most willing to help themselves, so that areas of conflict and lawlessness diminished; and, finally, we should strive to protect ourselves by reforming, isolating, or defeating those in the fourth group.

The concept underlying all these policies was "integration"—not an exciting term but one that embodied a process of bringing nations together around basic principles of democracy and open markets, the rule of law and a commitment to peace. Ultimately we wanted all countries to be in the first group. Inevitably, perhaps, my staff and I had our shorthand for the various categories we had identified, and—abandoning political correctness—took to calling the third group the "basket cases." Soon I would be dealing with several such cases almost full-time.

Throughout my years at the UN, I had two contradictory feelings. At optimistic moments I thought, "Isn't it remarkable that the Security Council is actively striving to ease suffering and end conflicts, including some not even international, but rather inside countries, in remote corners of the globe?" On bad days I would think, "Why are we sitting around here arguing about commas when people are dying?" As events would prove, both feelings had a basis in reality.

TEN

New World (Dis)Order

PRESIDENTS DO NOT INHERIT A CLEAN SLATE. Early critics of the Clinton administration's foreign policy questioned the President's wisdom in focusing so much attention on parts of the world that were not central to America's strategic interests, but this was both unfair and hardly his choice. The new administration was deeply involved in strengthening ties to our European and Asian allies, fashioning a new relationship with Russia, seeking peace in the Middle East, winning support for a free trade agreement with Canada and Mexico, and dealing with other "big-ticket" items. But the Clinton team could hardly overlook the fact that, early in its term, a civil war was under way in Bosnia, more than twenty thousand U.S. troops were busy saving lives in Somalia, ethnic tensions would explode in the Central African nation of Rwanda, and thousands of desperate migrants were fleeing a cruel and illegitimate regime in Haiti.

Sitting at my desk in New York or at the State Department, I read each morning of new clashes, murders, outrages, and threats. I did so knowing that people everywhere looked to the United States and the Security Council to find solutions. We had no chance to catch our breath. Everything was urgent, and so we made our decisions based on the best information available each day, inevitably influenced by the effect of decisions reached the previous day, week, or year. We felt our way step by step, sometimes stepping wrong and having to retrace. In Somalia we tried to do too much. In Rwanda we did too little. In Haiti and Bosnia, after false starts, we eventually got it right.

SAY "SOMALIA" to an American today, and the images most likely to be conjured up are those of a helicopter going down, a courageous crew under fire, and a U.S. soldier's body being dragged through the streets by a mob. But in the years immediately prior to President Clinton's election, Americans and the world were assaulted by a different image: Somali children with stick-thin arms, hollow eyes, and empty, distended stomachs. The country had long been poor, but in the early 1990s it was shattered by rival factions, including one led by a flamboyant former general, Mohammed Farah Aidid. International efforts to provide humanitarian relief were thwarted by armed gangs. A UN peace operation, established to smooth the delivery of aid, failed to do so. The Bush administration airdropped packages of food, which were stolen. Starvation spread and an estimated 350,000 Somalis died.

Around Thanksgiving 1992, acting Secretary of State Lawrence Eagleburger told Boutros-Ghali that the United States was willing to lead a multinational effort to bring relief to Somalia, after which it would hand responsibility back to the UN. The Secretary General accepted but asked that, in the process, the United States disarm warlords such as Aidid. Otherwise, he argued, secure conditions would not last. Eagleburger rejected this, saying the United States wanted to get in and out of Somalia as quickly as possible.

The U.S.-led Operation Restore Hope deployed in December and met virtually no resistance as it reopened supply lines and saved many lives. As planned, the U.S. forces made no effort to disarm the warlords, instead brokering meetings at which Aidid and other leaders promised to observe a cease-fire.

When I arrived in New York early in 1993, my instructions were to negotiate the rapid handover of principal responsibility from the United States to the UN. The Pentagon was eager to call its mission a success and bring our soldiers home. Boutros-Ghali resisted, arguing that the world body was neither staffed nor equipped to take on another major new operation.

The NSC was relentless, calling me nearly every day to ask, "What's taking so long?" New on the job and eager to earn my place as a full member of our foreign policy team, I told the Secretary General he had no choice, U.S. troops would leave whether the UN was prepared to take their place or not. Toward the end of March, we arrived at a compromise. The UN would recruit a force of 28,000 peacekeepers. The United States would keep roughly 4,000 troops in the area, including a 1,300-member Quick Reaction Force, under U.S. command, as insurance against emergencies. The UN would be expected to disarm warlords, provide security, set up regional councils, and create a long-term political process based on cooperation among local leaders. This was an ambitious mandate, requiring the UN to do more than the United States had accomplished but with fewer and far less potent forces. The compromise also created confusion about the relative roles of the UN and United States, especially since the UN's special representative in Somalia was an American—retired Navy admiral Jonathan Howe.

As soon as U.S. troop levels went down in Somalia, tensions heated up. General Aidid began broadcasting virulently anti-U.S. and anti-UN propaganda and sabotaged efforts to foster reconciliation. On June 5, Aidid's gunmen ambushed Pakistani peacekeepers, killing and mutilating more than two dozen. Spurred by Pakistan's Permanent Representative Jamsheed Marker, the Security Council reacted with fury, feeling that if UN peacekeepers could be killed with impunity in Somalia, they would become targets everywhere. Aidid's attack was a test of whether UN peacekeeping had indeed entered a new era.

So, with little debate and no dissent, the council condemned the assault and called for the apprehension of those responsible. The American Quick Reaction Force soon led several raids on Aidid's weapons caches. UN forces were also active—but with tragic results. Pakistani peacekeepers, apparently fearing a repeat of the June 5 attack, fired into a crowd of unarmed Somali civilians. The result was a popular backlash Aidid was quick to exploit.

I followed events closely through cables, reports from my staff, and the media but was not satisfied I was getting the full picture. I had always tried to make the best of every job. Now I was determined to be a hands-on ambassador.

In July 1993, I traveled with a team of advisors to Somalia, beginning in the southern port city of Kismayo. As we drove in from the airport, we saw the results of the bitter fighting that had occurred only months previously. Few buildings were still standing. On either side of the road was a sea of turquoise—not water, but plastic sheeting used to create huts for the displaced. The local clan leaders with whom I met were eager to organize themselves and resume normal economic activity. They fully backed measures to eliminate or marginalize Aidid. Here, as in most other parts of Somalia, the handoff of responsibility from the United States to the UN was working.

It was not, however, working well in Mogadishu, our next stop. The capital was less a city than a war zone. The roads were so dangerous we took a Blackhawk helicopter from the airport to UN headquarters. As the helicopter took off, I didn't know whether to be assured or alarmed by the machine guns deployed around the tarmac and protruding from the aircraft to ward off attacks. Aloft I looked in vain for even one building that still had a roof and all four walls. Virtually every apartment, store, and business had been gutted. Power lines had been torn down, plumbing fixtures ripped out, and shops shuttered. Once on the ground, we saw that the American embassy had been trashed, with marble facing pried from the outside stairs and wires dangling forlornly from the walls. UN troops moved about the city in heavily armed convoys.

When I had last seen Admiral Howe, he had been the deputy National Security Advisor to President Bush, working in a spotless White House office with direct phone lines to important officials around the globe. In Mogadishu, as the UN representative, he sat on a folding chair at a plain wooden table surrounded by cartons. He was frustrated because the UN operation was not functioning as a coherent military force. National contingents insisted on operating in their own way. He said apprehending Aidid was essential but didn't feel he had the necessary firepower. He had asked the Pentagon for tanks, antipersonnel carriers, attack helicopters, and a U.S. Special Forces unit, and he urged me to press Washington to act—which I did. The Defense Department initially rejected his requests because it didn't want to "Americanize" the situation further. Near the beginning of August, however, it relented and dispatched a 400-man team of Rangers, plus a contingent of Special Forces and some additional equipment.

Returning to New York, I was more optimistic than I should have been. At the President's request I drafted an op-ed piece for the *New York Times* urging the international community to "stay the course" in Somalia. In a speech on August 27, Secretary of Defense Les Aspin expressed the same sentiment in even stronger terms. We wanted to believe that our efforts would pay off and were being told by those on the ground that Aidid was all that prevented success. We were also getting reports that Aidid's own clan would cooperate in persuading the renegade general to leave Somalia. Certainly Aidid's capture would have lent momentum to the political process and restored cohesion to the UN force.

However, despite increased military pressure, Aidid continued to elude capture. By mid September congressional support for our policy was declining. We had fallen into the trap of personalizing the fight with Aidid, then failing to nab him. U.S. forces had suffered casualties in several incidents and pressure was building to get out. African leaders were also urging a diplomatic, rather than a military, solution to the problem of Aidid. The time had come to modify our approach. On September 22, at U.S. urging, the Security Council approved a resolution stressing the importance of going forward with a political and economic strategy. In line with our desire to depersonalize the conflict, I didn't even mention Aidid in my statement.

Security Council resolutions are not self-executing, and this one was no exception. We had decided on a new strategy, but coordination among officials in New York, Washington, and Somalia was not the best. No diplomatic solution was found and there was no letup in Aidid's attacks. The standing orders to the U.S. Ranger force in Mogadishu remained the same—snatch him. On Sunday afternoon, October 3, U.S. forces stormed a building near Mogadishu's Olympic Hotel. Aidid wasn't there, but the Americans took prisoner more than two dozen of his aides and were preparing to bring them back when a Blackhawk helicopter was shot down.

The Americans came under heavy fire as they tried to extricate the fallen crew. Somali fighters put up barricades to block their retreat. A rescue helicopter was hit by small arms fire and forced to return to base, while the larger and more heavily armed Blackhawks couldn't land in the narrow streets near the crash site. Troops and a medical team were trapped at the first crash site. A convoy of Humvees and trucks tried to reach the encircled troops but failed. Another Blackhawk was shot down. Other forces were bombarded as they drove through the city with the wounded and prisoners. A third contingent was trying to reach the site of the second crash. It was after midnight before a U.S. infantry company, assisted by Malaysian and Pakistani troops, reached the largest group of embattled men. The rescued American soldiers didn't reach their base until dawn. By the time rescuers arrived at the second crash site, the bodies had been removed. The only survivor was pilot Michael Durant, who was taken hostage for eleven days. Evening television broadcasts showed the body of one member of Durant's crew being dragged through the streets as Somalis kicked and jeered. In the course of this violent outbreak, eighteen Americans died and seventy-three were injured. I was appalled. In our meetings we talked about what had happened and why. At home, at night, I questioned every aspect of what we had done. I had been a part of the decisions that had led to this. What had we done wrong? It was a nightmare.

Shocked and deeply saddened, I called some of the family members of the soldiers who had been killed. I also helped represent the administration on *Nightline* and other shows. I thought I had learned how to handle difficult television moments, but this was a human tragedy; mere words were not enough. The interviewers showed the horrifying film footage, then asked, "What do you tell the parents of those who died? For what, exactly, did they sacrifice their lives?"

There were answers, but none good enough to help the families. Certainly with more time we might have found the formula to defuse the Somalia crisis, but the truth was we had not provided the means to achieve the goals we had set, and some brave Americans died.

During the next six months, the United States handled the endgame in Somalia responsibly and professionally. The President took heat by resisting pressure to pull out immediately, while the Pentagon organized or provided security not only for our troops but also for those of other contributing nations, many of whom had gone there at our request. Congress supported our plans, and the U.S. withdrawal was completed around the end of March 1994.

Overall, American involvement in Somalia had elements of both success and failure. Operation Restore Hope succeeded in establishing the short-term conditions for the resumption of humanitarian relief. It ended the famine and saved lives. However, the U.S.-led force explicitly refused to undertake the harder job of disarming the militias, a task left to the UN, which it was not equipped to do.

In Congress, the press, even in the White House, much was made of the "UN's failure" but that was not the whole story. The Secretary General's representative in Somalia was an American, and so was the deputy military commander. The United States had supported every Security Council resolution on Somalia, and there had been little internal debate about my instructions. The Army Rangers had run into disaster under U.S. command.

Furthermore, other nations contributing peacekeepers had followed their own agendas instead of functioning as a team. The Italians had openly disagreed with the UN strategy and were suspected of bribing Aidid's forces in order to protect their own. The Saudis had said their unique status within Islam prohibited them from engaging in offensive operations. The French had cooperated sometimes, sometimes not. India had provided a brigade but then refused to deploy it to Mogadishu. The Pakistanis had grown understandably gun-shy.

Somalia was a test of whether the UN could carry out a peace operation involving the use of force against an adversary determined to sabotage that operation. The UN is only as strong as its members, and UN members did not pass the test. The original humanitarian mission had been broadened for good reasons but without sufficient preparation or resources. The relationship between the United States and the UN was never clearly straightened out. The UN's firepower was insufficient to overcome a wily opponent acting on his home turf. Under the circumstances, the mission had needed luck to succeed, and lucky it most certainly was not.

THE UNITED STATES REALIZED, well before Somalia, that if we were going to turn to UN peacekeeping more often, we needed to make it work better. At the UN General Assembly in September 1992, the first President Bush had outlined proposals for improving UN capabilities. By the time I took office, planners from the Pentagon, NSC, and State Department were hard at work on a detailed policy. The proposal, ultimately known as Presidential Decision Directive 25 (PDD-25), endorsed UN peacekeeping as an option, while establishing criteria to make it more successful abroad and supportable at home.

Both Presidents Bush and Clinton understood that the UN was not equipped to handle its expanding responsibilities. When I first arrived in New York, there were only about a dozen people in UN Headquarters assigned to manage peacekeeping. There was no twenty-four-hour operations center and virtually no control over logistics. Every new operation had to start from scratch, recruiting commanders and troops, and procuring everything from blue helmets to pencils and trucks. I told audiences that the global 911 number was either busy or open only from nine to five, and that the Secretary General had to devote much of his time to begging for participants and money.

Although the UN steadily improved its capabilities with help from the United States and other major powers, it had much ground to make up. As the experience in Somalia reflected, there was an urgent need for discipline in establishing mandates for peacekeeping operations, especially in situations where armed opposition might be anticipated. This discipline had to come from the Security Council.

The development of PDD-25 was complicated by press leaks, partisan politics, and the turbulence of day-to-day events. The main shape of the document, however, changed little during the drawn-out deliberations. Its purpose was to put America squarely on the side of strengthening UN peacekeeping operations, with the understanding that we would henceforth make the chain of command clearer and insist that such missions be carefully planned, with a precise mandate, efficiently implemented, and preceded by a significant period of consultations with Congress. We were determined not to have another Somalia.

The PDD, the product of more than a year and a half's work, was issued formally on May 3, 1994. By then its central thesis was already being put to an excruciating test in another part of Africa.

I WAS NOT AMONG the very few who saw early that the decade's most shocking crimes would engulf the small country of Rwanda. My deepest regret from my years in public service is the failure of the United States and the international community to act sooner to halt those crimes. President

Clinton later apologized for our lack of action, as did I. Much has been written about those events. Some accounts are fair, others simplistic and at best half true. I cannot hope to recount the complete history; rather I will attempt to describe concisely how it appeared from my perspective.

The Rwandan crisis grew out of a rivalry between ethnic Hutus and Tutsis in Central Africa. Most recent histories blame colonial Belgium for fostering the tension by creating a caste system, in which the Tutsi minority held a favored position. After the Belgians departed in the early 1960s and Rwanda became independent, extremist violence was common, both in Rwanda and neighboring Burundi. The Security Council was encouraged, therefore, when in August 1993 a peace agreement was signed between Rwanda's ethnic Hutu President Juvénal Habyarimana and leaders of the Tutsi-controlled opposition Rwandan Popular Front.

On October 5, 1993, just two days after the Army Rangers were killed in Somalia, the Security Council established a UN peacekeeping mission for Rwanda (UNAMIR), with a mandate to monitor the cease-fire and prepare for elections. Unlike the UN force in Somalia, this was designed as a traditional mission, dependent on the willingness of the Hutus and Tutsis to abide by their agreement. A force of 2,500 was authorized, under the command of Brigadier General Roméo Dallaire of Canada, and told not to take sides or engage in fighting. The best-armed and most capable troops would be Belgians, still suspected by the Hutus of having a pro-Tutsi bias.

The UN force, arriving in November, found little peace to keep. Ethnic violence flared, while government-influenced radio broadcasts exhorted Hutu peasants to decapitate Tutsis. Efforts to achieve political reconciliation seemed to be going nowhere.

On January 11, 1994, Dallaire sent a cable to UN Headquarters relaying allegations from an informant that extremist Hutu militias were being secretly armed. The informant also revealed plans to attack Belgian peacekeepers, murder opposition politicians, and kill Tutsis.

UN officials in New York instructed Dallaire to inform the Rwandan president of the allegations and urge him to investigate. The American, French, and Belgian embassies were also asked to caution the government about the dangers posed by the extremists. The U.S. ambassador to Rwanda, David Rawson, reported to Washington that President Habyarimana had seemed "to get the message." On February 23, Dallaire warned UN headquarters that Hutu militias were preparing for massive violence. A representative of the UN high commissioner for refugees also raised concerns. Unfortunately, these alarms had to compete for attention against an avalanche of other information from crisis spots around the globe. At the time, there were clashes or extreme tensions in Bosnia, Somalia, Haiti, Georgia, Azerbaijan, Armenia, Angola, Liberia, Mozambique, Sudan, Cambodia, Afghanistan, and Tajikistan, as well as ongoing defiance of Security Council resolutions by Saddam Hussein's Iraq. Throughout this period, I read intelligence summaries of events in countries where UN peacekeepers or humanitarian agencies were engaged. Rwanda was not cited either prominently or frequently.

On March 24, I began a two-week trip to Europe, Africa, the Balkans, and South America. While I was away, my deputy, Ambassador Edward Walker, met with the incoming Security Council president to discuss the council's April agenda. No fewer than a dozen topics were reviewed, including four dealing with Africa. Rwanda didn't make the list.

The day before I arrived back, on April 5, the council approved a short-term extension of the UN mission, while expressing grave concern at the lack of progress. The next day President Habyarimana's plane was shot down while approaching Kigali, Rwanda's capital. All aboard died. Few if any outsiders realized in the confusion of the moment that the president's death had triggered a plan by Hutu radicals to slaughter Hutu moderates and all Tutsis. In a matter of hours, roadblocks had been set up and leading moderate politicians tracked down and killed.

It would be weeks before most of us understood the nature and scale of the violence. At the beginning we saw only that the Rwandan president had been killed and that Hutu security forces were launching a coup against civilian authority. On April 7, we learned that the prime minister had been murdered and ten Belgian peacekeepers—assigned to guard her—had been hacked to death. The same day, the local UN commander sought permission to use arms. Fearing another Somalia, UN Headquarters didn't want to be viewed as taking sides, so it turned the request down. Moreover, the military capabilities of Dallaire's forces were limited. Its contingents from Tunisia and Ghana didn't even have flak jackets. Reserves of water, rations, fuel, ammunition, and medical supplies were low.

As I look back at records of the meetings held that first week, I am struck by the lack of information about the killing that had begun against unarmed Rwandan civilians, as opposed to the fighting between Hutu and Tutsi militias. Many Western embassies had been evacuated, including our own, so official reporting was curtailed. Dallaire was making dire reports to UN Headquarters, but the oral summaries provided to the Security Council lacked detail and failed to convey the full dimensions of the disaster. As a result, the council hoped unrealistically that each new day would bring a cease-fire.

There was also confusion about who was to blame. The French, historically favorable to the Hutus, supposed initially that Tutsi extremists had shot down the president's plane to provoke Hutu attacks and justify Tutsi counterassaults. American analysts unhelpfully narrowed the culprits to radical Hutus, moderate Hutus, and Tutsis—just about everybody. Meanwhile, those actually directing the killing put forward a steady stream of lies about what they were doing and why.

To complicate matters further, as in Somalia, the UN commander did not have full control over his forces. Belgium, shocked by the murder of its peacekeepers, announced its intention to withdraw, thereby depriving Dallaire of his best-equipped troops. Authorities in Brussels had appealed to the United States, as a NATO ally, to support the termination of the entire UN mission, but I cabled Washington that most Security Council members wanted to retain at least some elements. Nevertheless, on April 15, I was instructed to inform the UN that the United States favored "full, orderly withdrawal of all UNAMIR personnel as soon as possible." "Our opposition to retaining a UNAMIR presence in Rwanda is firm," read my orders. "It is based on our conviction that the Security Council has an obligation to ensure that peacekeeping operations are viable...and that UN peacekeeping personnel are not placed or retained, knowingly, in an untenable situation."

Like others, I had become both defensive and cautious about UN peacekeeping in general and didn't see any practical way for the UN to restore order in Rwanda at this point. Mindful of my conversations with the parents of Americans killed in Somalia, I worried that more of the lightly armed UN peacekeepers might be victimized. At the same time, I agreed with my Security Council colleagues that the UN should not withdraw completely. As I listened to the informal debate led by Nigerian Permanent Representative Ibrahim Gambari I became increasingly convinced we were on the wrong side of the issue. I asked my deputy to take my seat and went to one of the phone booths in the hall. Even though my instructions came from the State Department, I thought I might be able to get faster action from the NSC, which on peacekeeping played a critical coordinating role and where Tony Lake's knowledge of Africa was crucial. Speaking to one of his top aides, I described what was going on in the council and reported that the American position was being viewed as obstructionist. I first asked for more flexible instructions, then yelled into the phone, demanding them. I was told to calm down. The NSC would look again at what to do.

During council discussions that week, New Zealand Ambassador Colin Keating cited a report by the medical relief group Doctors Without Borders describing Hutu militia entering a hospital and killing all the local staff, then returning the next day to kill the patients. This stark account prompted me to glance at the ambassador from Rwanda, whose turn to serve on the council had come by coincidence this fateful year. I raised my hand and suggested we ask the Rwandan to explain: it was, after all, customary for the council to call upon the permanent representatives of countries involved in a conflict. This led to a prolonged uncomfortable silence. Finally the Rwandan found his tongue, responding only to say that his government's willingness to participate in peace talks was not being reciprocated by the Tutsis. I thought it disgraceful that Rwanda's lawless regime was still permitted to sit in the council.

On April 20, I met with the Secretary General, who described his dilemma. African members of the council wanted UNAMIR to be rein-forced. The Belgians wanted a full UN pullout to cover their own with-drawal. African leaders were trying to arrange peace talks. If a cease-fire were reached, troops would be needed to monitor it. The decision on Rwanda would be critical to the image of the UN, so Boutros-Ghali wanted the UN mission to remain.

That day he submitted a report to the council with three options. The first was immediate and massive reinforcement of UNAMIR. The second was downsizing the force from roughly 2,500 to 270, with a mandate to seek a cease-fire. The third was complete withdrawal. Of these, the second was the only one seriously discussed. The reinforcement option seemed illusory, since there were no adequately equipped troops prepared to go.

The instructions that had angered me were to support option three— total withdrawal. Now I received new instructions with the flexibility I had sought. On April 21, the council unanimously adopted the second option. Ironically, the planned further "downsizing" of the UN mission never happened. The Belgian and Bangladeshi contingents had already left, but the remaining 540 troops from Ghana and Tunisia would stay for months, until the fighting finally stopped.

During the last ten days of April, I realized along with most of the world that what was occurring was not just terrible violence but genocide. Press accounts had become more comprehensive, and I learned much from a meeting with Monique Mujawamariya, a Rwandan human rights activist, who argued forcefully that the goal of the Hutu extremists was to wipe out the Tutsis forever. Meanwhile the International Committee of the Red Cross told our UN mission in Geneva that it had raised its esti-mates of the death toll to 300,000–500,000 people.

Belatedly, the priority in Washington and New York shifted to what it should have been all along—to stop further killing. Secretary Christo-pher cabled major European and African capitals urging a concerted effort to persuade Rwandan authorities to halt the violence. Prudence

Bushnell, deputy assistant secretary of state for African affairs, called Rwandan leaders directly and warned they would be held personally responsible if the killings continued.

On April 29, the Security Council approved a presidential statement blaming Rwanda's interim government for most of the atrocities; the statement used language from the Genocide Convention to warn that such acts were punishable under international law. But strong words were not enough. What mattered was whether and how the international community could save lives. Through a grim coincidence of timing, the shadow of Somalia hung over both questions.

On May 3, the White House released America's new policy toward UN peace operations, based on PDD-25. That same day the Security Council adopted a parallel set of principles, adding that before starting a mission the council should consider "whether reasonable guarantees can be obtained from the principal parties or factions regarding the safety and security of UN personnel." The UN Commission of Inquiry on Somalia had also completed its work, declaring that "the UN should refrain from undertaking further peace enforcement actions within the internal conflicts of states." Meanwhile, in Washington, the prestigious Stimson Center reported: "When the Security Council approves a peace operation with an ambiguous or impossible mandate simply as a political 'gesture' . . . it damages the UN as an institution and reduces its ability to act."

The experts had concluded, then, that the UN should refrain from intervening in circumstances precisely like those in Rwanda, where there were no security guarantees, no cooperation between the parties, and no readily achievable mandates. Perhaps the only solution would have been a large and heavily armed coalition led by a major power, but because of Somalia, the U.S. military wasn't going to undertake that. The French would have been strongly opposed by the Tutsis. The Belgians weren't about to go back. The British had thousands of troops tied down in Bosnia. That left the possibility of a mix and match force organized either by the UN or the Organization of African Unity (OAU), both of which hoped the other would go first. To spur a decision, the Security Council asked Boutros-Ghali to devise a concept of operations. Unfortunately the plan he came up with didn't make sense to U.S. military planners, who would have been asked to help transport and supply such a mission. They developed their own proposal.

For days I had to sit in my chair at the Security Council and ask for more time as U.S. and UN experts argued over tactics and strategy. UN officials wanted a force based in Kigali that would somehow "ensure safe conditions," while using force only in self-defense but without waiting for a cease-fire. The Pentagon did not think the UN could get countries to participate in such a plan, which was billed as a humanitarian operation but would take place in the midst of a still-raging civil war. The U.S. military also objected to the logistical difficulty and risk of airlifting heavy equipment and troops into the embattled Rwandan capital and said bluntly they were not prepared to do it. Instead the Pentagon proposed establishing a secure zone just inside the Rwandan border to protect endangered civilian populations and provide security for the delivery of supplies.

After prolonged haggling, on May 17 we agreed to a resolution that provided for an expanded UN mission, with a mandate to create secure humanitarian areas "where feasible."

Sadly, our doubts about the willingness of nations to serve in such a mission proved justified, showing once again that council resolutions meant little unless implemented. For weeks Boutros-Ghali cajoled countries to come forward. Some made commitments only to take them back. Several, such as Canada, requested clarification about the relationship between the operation's mandate and its limited resources. Australia's Foreign Minister Gareth Evans said his country was willing to do its part but would not commit troops until the UN solved its basic problem. "You can only mount a peacekeeping operation if there is a peace to keep. You can only mount a peace enforcement operation if you have got the resources to enable you to do the job properly." Australia thought an international force of 30,000 to 40,000 would be needed to restore order. In fairness, the United States—unenthusiastic about the prospects of the mission as designed by the UN—didn't exert itself trying to get other countries to sign up.

As the search for a larger UN force dragged on, so did the killing. In mid June, the French finally offered to send in 1,500 troops, joined by 500 from Senegal. The plan was presented to the council by France's persuasive Permanent Representative Jean Bernard Mérimée. Although the Tutsis objected and five council members abstained, Mérimée prevailed. Operation Turquoise established a security zone in southwestern Rwanda that was credited with saving more than 15,000 lives.

In late July, America also sent troops to care for the refugees fleeing Rwanda. By stemming cholera outbreaks, this deployment too would save thousands. When measured against the scale of a genocide in which an estimated 800,000 people perished, however, the French and U.S. interventions were much too little and far too late. The refugee camps, moreover, served as a temporary safe haven for many of the Hutu extremists who had participated in the butchery before fleeing as the Tutsi militia advanced.

Some commentators have held America primarily responsible for the failure to respond effectively to Rwandan genocide. Their argument is that we should have backed the reinforcement of UNAMIR in April, instead of voting to reduce it, but the council view on that point was unanimous and the prospect of significant reinforcement a mirage. Another argument is that in May we should have immediately supported Boutros-Ghali's design for a peacekeeping mission, even though our military leaders did not think it would work.

Certainly much criticism is valid, but the circumstances were far more complicated than those writing with the benefit of hindsight admit. History is written backwards but lived forwards. During the critical days between April 15 and April 22, State Department spokesman Michael McCurry received only one question about Rwanda at his daily press briefing, and that concerned the safety of UN peacekeepers. The killings were happening in real time, but the madness in the method did not stand out until later against the background of other world events.

For weeks we thought we were looking at another Burundi, where vicious killings had occurred the previous fall—terrible violence, but which had stopped without reaching the same proportions. We had just spent a year learning the lessons of Somalia. We had fought for and gained Security Council consensus, and something close to agreement with Congress, on a cautious and deliberate approach to UN peace operations.

When the violence exploded, we tried to fit the situation in Rwanda into the framework we had created. We talked with UN officials and African colleagues about how to get the peace process back on track. We tried to stay neutral and condemned the violence on all sides. From the beginning to the end of this crisis, no country offered to send troops to Rwanda for the purpose of actually fighting.[1]

Tragically, the lessons we thought we had just learned in Somalia simply did not apply in Rwanda. Somalia was something close to anarchy. Rwanda was planned mass murder. Somalia counseled caution; Rwanda demanded action. Reinforcing UNAMIR would have been far better than nothing, if we could have found the right troops. Truly effective action would have required a heavily armed, almost certainly U.S.-led coalition

1. "The failure by the United Nations to prevent and, subsequently, to stop the genocide in Rwanda was a failure by the United Nations system as a whole. The fundamental failure was a lack of resources and political commitment devoted to developments in Rwanda, and to the United Nations presence there. There was a persistent lack of political will by member states to act, or to act with enough assertiveness."

Report of the Independent Inquiry into the Actions of the United Nations during the 1994 Genocide in Rwanda, included as an enclosure in a letter from Secretary General Annan to the president of the Security Council S/1999/1257, 1999. 15 December 1999, p. 1.

able to deploy quickly, intimidate extremists, arrest leaders, and establish security. I deeply regret not advocating this course. Many people would have thought I was crazy and we would never have won support from Congress, but I would have been right, and possibly my voice would have been heard.

I cannot close this discussion without paying tribute to those who *were* right, not later, when it was easy to see, but at the time when their warnings—if heeded—could have made a difference. These include UNAMIR commander Roméo Dallaire and representatives from NGOs (nongovernmental organizations) such as the Red Cross, Doctors Without Borders, and Human Rights Watch. Next time, I pray the world will listen and act, but I am far from confident it will.

With the possible exception of ancient Rome, no society has ever auditioned for the role of world policeman. Certainly the United States— at least through the end of the twentieth century—never desired that part. As for the UN, it has shown the ability to play world night watchman. It can monitor and raise the alarm, but it cannot guarantee that the alarm, once sounded, will be answered.

The world would probably respond if another scenario clearly recognizable as Rwanda-like started to unfold, but genocides each have their own shape, and every day crushing amounts of information pour across the desks of world leaders. Since 1994, new and frightening dangers have arisen that also compete for their attention. There are no grounds for confidence that the next intimations of genocide will be detected in time or that there would be volunteers for the job of preventing wide-scale killing once it got under way.

The world has taken a number of steps to make future Rwandas less likely, but added together they do not equal in importance the fundamental question of political will. If the alarm does sound again, will the lessons of Rwanda loom largest in the minds of our leaders—or those of Somalia?

THE ABORTED MISSION in Somalia also cast a shadow over events closer to American shores. On October 11, 1993, less than a week after Army Rangers had been killed in Mogadishu, U.S. and Canadian army engineers and trainers on board the USS *Harlan County* prepared to land in Haiti's capital, Port-au-Prince. Their mission was to assist construction projects and help reform Haiti's decrepit military. Instead of the expected cordial welcome, the ship was denied permission to dock and confronted by a stick-wielding, fist-shaking mob waving signs marked "Remember Mogadishu." After two days the *Harlan County* turned back. Especially after Somalia, the sight of the U.S. military retreating in the face of an unfriendly mob was a low point in Clinton administration foreign policy.

The *Harlan County* had been sent to Haiti as part of an agreement with its military leaders, reached the previous July on Governors Island, New York. The pact laid out a road map for restoring to power the democratically elected President, Father Jean-Bertrand Aristide, who had been ousted by a military junta headed by Lieutenant General Raoul Cedras.

I had first become familiar with the terror and poverty of Haiti in the early 1960s, when Joe Albright reported from there about conditions under the harsh rule of François "Papa Doc" Duvalier, a dictator later succeeded by his equally venal son, Jean-Claude or "Baby Doc." At the time of Joe's visit, Haiti was the poorest country in the Western Hemisphere. It still is. Perhaps 75 percent of its people are ill-fed, ill-housed, ill-clad, or just plain ill. Its population is seven million and rising; experts say its land can support a population of three million. Most of its trees were long ago burned for charcoal.

Haiti is as divided as it is poor. The end of Duvalierism in 1986 brought a new constitution, popular elections, and the superficial trappings of democracy, but it didn't resolve the island's tensions. Two percent of the population controlled almost half the country's wealth, and members of the elite were famed for corruption and greed. Politically, however, they met their match in the wiry and intense Father Aristide, a brilliant orator who emerged in the late 1980s as leader of a populist alternative to the regular Catholic Church. Aristide argued political power should be used to serve, not exploit, the people—a novel concept in Haiti. He became a hero to the poor and in December 1990 was elected president with nearly 68 percent of the vote.

Aristide's commitment to radical change led to his overthrow by the military less than a year after he took office; the coup was accompanied by widespread repression. In July 1993, the UN brokered the Governors Island Agreement, under which General Cedras promised to "avail himself of the right of early retirement" and allow Aristide to return. The agreement also lifted economic sanctions imposed at the time of the coup. Unfortunately, as the *Harlan County* incident illustrated, the military leaders had no intention of keeping their word. If they were going to go, they would have to be pushed.

That push began in the Security Council with a resolution reimposing economic sanctions and dispatching a joint team of monitors from the UN and the Organization of American States (OAS) to report on violations of human rights. Through the early months of 1994, pressure built relentlessly. The embargo on fuel damaged Haiti's already feeble economy, requiring the UN to feed a million people a day. Our efforts to find a diplomatic solution were stymied. Human rights monitors reported regularly on the torture and murder of Haitians thought to be loyal to Aristide. Meanwhile thousands of islanders tried to flee across the Caribbean to the United States.

Our policy—inherited from the previous administration—was to block the boat people despite the cruel conditions in Haiti. By discouraging migrants from taking to sea in leaky rafts and overcrowded boats, we saved lives, but the policy was denounced by Aristide as racist and opposed vigorously by the Congressional Black Caucus, usually a presidential ally. The administration was divided. Many in the White House, the Vice-President's office, and the NSC did not believe the status quo—of sanctions, suffering, and Cedras—could or should be sustained. However, neither the Defense Department nor many State Department professionals favored a change in policy. The military and intelligence communities distrusted the radical Aristide and didn't want to risk American lives returning him to power. Our special envoy to Haiti, Ambassador Lawrence Pezzullo, believed that the diplomatic approach would ultimately succeed and that the alternative—U.S. military intervention—would be opposed throughout the hemisphere.

I favored action. Both the UN and OAS had called for Aristide's return. Caribbean representatives in New York told me that their governments would support a multinational military operation. I was convinced that, if we did the diplomacy right, we could subdue the military and dislodge the junta in a short period of time, without being viewed as Yankee interventionists. We had to turn the lesson of Somalia into a positive one. Our defeat there didn't mean we should never get involved; it meant we needed to be better prepared.

On May 8, 1994, the President announced a new policy. To squeeze Haiti's elite, we barred top military, police, and civilian officials from traveling abroad. To defuse criticism at home, we ended the direct return of Haitian migrants. In response, the Haitian military dug in even harder, then made a fatal mistake by kicking the UN/OAS human rights monitors out of the country. This was a direct challenge to the international community and, for the Haitian authorities, the beginning of the end.

I spent most of July 1994 persuading the Security Council to authorize the use of "all necessary means"—code for force—to restore Haitian democracy by moving Cedras out and Aristide back in.

The first challenge was coming to agreement with Boutros-Ghali. He did not like our initial proposal for a large UN force because the world body was broke (in part because Congress was refusing to pay our bills) and having trouble finding troops for other missions. Also, the operation we had in mind would have been under U.S. command, near U.S. borders, and with a high proportion of U.S. troops. As the Secretary General pointed out, Russia had sent peacekeepers to Georgia and now wanted the council to designate them as an official UN force, thus relieving Moscow of 90 percent of the costs. Having said no to Moscow, Boutros-Ghali didn't feel he could say yes to us.

In mid July, I returned with a revised plan. Instead of beginning with a UN mission, we would ask the council to authorize a U.S.-led coalition to oust the illegitimate leaders, establish stability, and lay the groundwork for new elections. A smaller UN force would then take over. Boutros-Ghali liked this better but wanted my assurance that the UN would not be asked to do the hard work of disarming militia groups. "I don't want another Somalia."

"Do you think we do?" I asked him, then added, "Don't worry, this time, together, we'll do it right." Cautiously, the Secretary General came on board.

My next challenge was to obtain the strongest possible mandate from the Security Council. Although a number of countries raised concerns, our principal problems were Brazil and Russia. There is no harder diplomatic challenge than persuading a Latin American leader to consent publicly to a United States military initiative in our hemisphere. As Argentina's supportive Ambassador Emilio Cárdenas reminded me, the U.S. had intervened south of the border dozens of times over the decades, sometimes with dismal and undemocratic results. The Brazilians had no use for Haiti's junta but were reluctant to endorse military intervention. As a compromise, we agreed to emphasize how unique the current circumstances were, so that if force were used, it would not be seen as a precedent.

The Russians didn't much care about what we did in Haiti, but they were determined to play a little diplomatic poker. Moscow's ambassador, Yuli Vorontsov, presented me with a series of questions about our mission, hinting that Russia's backing on Haiti would depend on U.S. support for Russian proposals in Georgia. Vorontsov and I got on well. Our exchanges during council deliberations on Haiti, however, made it seem as if the Cold War had never ended.

Another obstacle was Father Aristide. In exile in Washington, he had access to the otherwise frozen funds of the Haitian government. A victim of repression, he basked in the international sympathy he received. He also seemed to be developing a taste for the physical comforts of life in America. There were cynics who felt that he didn't want to go back to

Port-au-Prince. Moreover, to Aristide, the idea of riding back to power on the shoulders of the "imperialist" United States was galling.

If Aristide, the rightful president, did not back our plan, we had no legal basis on which to proceed. Yet the exiled leader's position was muddy. In June he said he would "never, never, and never again" agree to be restored by U.S. invasion. On other days he called upon America to "surgically remove the thugs."

At last we obtained a letter from Aristide expressing support for the resolution we'd drafted. Vorontsov, after making my life as miserable as possible, grudgingly indicated that Russia would not block our plans. On July 30, with the formal council session scheduled for that evening, we worked all day tying up loose ends. I had spoken to every permanent representative personally and gotten a fix on everyone's position. This was retail diplomacy. If everyone kept his word, we would win. I was exhausted and looked awful, so during a break I went back to my apartment, washed my hair, applied new makeup, put on a blue linen dress, and strode back into the council chamber to face my haggard and unshaven counterparts.

The session lasted through the night. Several Latin American ambassadors spoke against the proposed intervention on the traditional grounds of protecting national sovereignty. Aristide's representative spoke in support. Every council permanent representative made a speech. I argued:

> The status quo in Haiti is neither tenable nor acceptable. Choices must be made...Today, the Council is making the right choice—in favor of democracy, law, dignity and relief from suffering long endured and never deserved. And the Council's message to General Cedras...is a simple one. You, too, have a choice. You can depart voluntarily and soon; or you can depart involuntarily and soon.

When the vote was called, I held my breath. The council voted 12–0–2 for our resolution. Even Russia voted yes, while Brazil and China abstained.[2] For the first time in history, the council had specifically authorized the United States to use force to intervene in another country in our hemisphere. We had our mandate; the question now was whether we could finish the job.

---

2. China has a strong dislike for any UN action that it regards, from its glass house, as interference in the internal affairs of others. During one council meeting on a different issue, I saw the Chinese chargé exercising his muscles by squeezing a hard rubber ball. I sent him a note asking, "What's with the little ball?" He replied that he was building up his strength because that day he was actually going to raise his arm and vote yes.

As Labor Day came and went, our military planning intensified but we hoped the threat of force would be sufficient to dishearten the junta and cause it to step down. In a final attempt at diplomacy, President Clinton asked former President Jimmy Carter, U.S. Senator Sam Nunn, and retired General Colin Powell to meet with the Haitian military leaders and urge them to resign. To prevent drawn-out negotiations, he established a firm timetable for military action. It was not until the planes the President had ordered from the Eighty-second Airborne Division were in the air headed for Port-au-Prince that Cedras conceded that early retirement might not be such a bad idea. The U.S. military would still go to Haiti as the dominating presence in a coalition that would include representatives of twenty-eight countries, but it was to be an invasion without resistance—the best kind. By mid October, Aristide was back in office.

That Thanksgiving I traveled to Haiti with General Jack Sheehan, head of the U.S. Atlantic Command, and shared a dinner of turkey, potatoes, and pie with some of our troops. The soldiers talked about the delirious reception they had received from a population worn down by deprivation and fear. They said they were proud to have been sent to Haiti and thanked me by giving me my own green beret, which I later placed on top of the blue helmet on the bust of Adlai Stevenson in my office.

Few countries have been as unfortunate in their leaders as Haiti. In the past, this was because honest, democratic figures couldn't survive. In the years since our intervention, Haiti has continued to be plagued by leaders who are either weak or, in the case of President Aristide, divisive. Today, the framework exists within which sound leadership can begin to lift Haiti up, while attracting ample outside assistance and investment. We know the capacity for such leadership exists, because we see it within the Haitian-American community. I only hope the day will come when Haiti finally has a government that will bring the country together.

The early 1990s were a time of experimenting and learning hard lessons about the potential and limits of multilateral peacekeeping. One of the most basic lessons taught by our experience in Somalia, Rwanda, and Haiti was that an arbitrarily rigid or cookie cutter approach would not work. Each situation was different, with a unique blend of history, personality, culture, and politics. To me, however, the overriding lesson was clear. The international community, through the UN or other means, had a responsibility to help societies endangered by natural or human-caused catastrophe. It was in America's interest to ensure that this responsibility was fulfilled because it would make the world more stable and peaceful, and because it was right.

ELEVEN

Frequent Flyer

URING THE 1960s, when I had lived on Long Island and com-
muted to classes at Columbia, I thought I would love to live in New
York City under the right circumstances. Now I was doing just that.
The residence of the U.S. permanent representative to the UN is a pent-
house in the Waldorf Astoria Towers, on the forty-second floor. There is a
gold eagle over the apartment's front door, the interior is spacious, and
there are postcard views of Manhattan, including my favorite—the huge
Saint Patrick's Cathedral looking almost toylike between the skyscrapers.

After I had been in the apartment just a few months, I decided what I
needed most was a "wife" of my own, so I was grateful when my sister
Kathy took a lengthy leave of absence from her position in the Los Angeles
public schools to help me. The demands of coping with Somalia, Rwanda,
and other crises, running a diplomatic mission, flying back and forth to
Washington, and maintaining two households made my life a daily blur.
Mostly it worked, though I never was quite sure which clothes were where.
When something couldn't be found, it was always at the other place. I
sometimes even forgot where I was. One night in New York, I actually fell
out of bed, thinking I was in Washington, where I slept on a different side.

According to the old saying, an ambassador is someone sent abroad
to lie for his country. I sometimes felt I had been sent to New York to eat
for mine. Whether as host or guest, I was constantly attending dinners,
lunches, and power breakfasts. I relished meeting people and mixing
small talk with business, but my status as a single woman created a protocol problem. Before my divorce, I had been through the experience
countless times of being identified in social gatherings primarily by the
position of my husband. As ambassador I didn't want the spouses of
other prominent guests to think that I was snubbing them or trying to

act in a superior way. At the same time, men tend to separate from women when conversing before and after dinner—not for brandy and cigars, as in the old days, but to talk business. And the business they discussed was diplomacy. It was my job to participate in these conversations, which I could not do without leaving the women. As a result I shuttled between the two groups, sometimes awkwardly, sometimes smoothly, trying to please everybody.

There were many hard—even traumatic—days, but still I loved my job. For the first time, I felt I could use "glamorous" and "my life" in the same sentence without being ironic. That first May, the President happened to be in New York and came to my birthday party. My daughter Alice was also there, very pregnant, and in response to his question told him, "any time now." The President said, "Don't worry, I'm a Lamaze father." Alice's expression made me think that she had immediately processed the possibility that the President of the United States was going to deliver her baby and had concluded, "No way." Fortunately she made it through the party and didn't give birth to David—my irrepressible first grandchild—until the following day.

Living in New York and having my very visible job put me at risk of becoming something I never could stand—a name-dropper. But there is truth in the notion that people in public life and the arts are attracted to each other. There is envy on both sides. Many artists want to have an impact on policy, and politicians can be as starstruck as anyone else.

It took me a while to adjust, but I found I could invite famous people to dinner parties and they would accept. Part of my strategy was to mix foreign dignitaries with heavyweight journalists such as Tom Brokaw, Dan Rather, and Peter Jennings. I also invited movie stars who had shown an interest in world affairs, such as Richard Dreyfuss, who was knowledgeable about the Middle East, and Michael Douglas, to whom I said I liked my job because it allowed me to follow my "basic instincts." Douglas and many other performers were sympathetic to the work the UN was doing and wanted to help increase American support. When the extraordinary singer Judy Collins became the official goodwill ambassador for UNICEF, I became a good friend of both her and her sculptor husband, Louis Nelson. On one occasion Judy sang "Amazing Grace" as everyone around my dinner table tried to hold back tears.

Sometimes I was simply selfish and invited people for no other reason than I wanted to meet them. Opera diva Jessye Norman came and also sang, reminding me of the saying, "Music is the sound of God breathing in and out." I had been overwhelmed by Frank McCourt's *Angela's Ashes*, so when I found he lived in New York, I reached out immediately. The same was true with Walter Mosley, the witty and modest author of *Devil in a Blue Dress* and other Easy Rawlins mysteries—favorites of both mine and President Clinton's.

Of all the famous people I met, I spent the most time with Barbra Streisand. Early in 1993, I was in the middle of a speech to the Hollywood Women's Political Caucus when a petite woman with a black beret half covering her face walked in and sat down. When she took the beret off, I was so surprised I almost stopped speaking. When we talked afterwards, she told me she was often in New York, so at the first opportunity I invited Streisand to lunch. She said that one of the plays she had been in early in her career was by Karel Čapek, the Czechoslovak playwright my father admired so many years before. I like Barbra because she is passionate and scrappy and says what she believes. We got together many times after that for meals, shopping, movies, and shows. One advantage of accompanying Streisand is that when you go to see a Stephen Sondheim musical, you end up at dinner later chatting with Mr. Sondheim himself.

I loved Barbra's company, and I think she enjoyed the chance to grill me about world events, seeking to back her socially conscious instincts with solid information. At one of her final concerts, at Madison Square Garden, Barbra gave me a front-row ticket and graciously shared the spotlight by introducing me to the audience as her good friend.

BECAUSE WASHINGTON WAS just a couple of hours away and I was often called to meetings of the foreign policy Principals Committee, I was frequently away from New York. This grated on some of the other UN ambassadors. They were also irritated because the combination of being a cabinet member and an American usually entitled me to a meeting with their foreign ministers when I traveled to their countries. When I returned to New York, some of them let it be known that they didn't appreciate my going over their heads. I argued back that my participation in policy deliberations in Washington helped us all by ensuring that the United States took the Security Council's perspective into account. And I told them, perfectly truthfully, that every time I met a foreign minister, my first action was to praise his country's permanent representative to the UN.

The fact is that most countries send their most capable and experienced diplomats to New York. These are people who have either proven their mettle in other diplomatic posts or exhibited exceptional promise. Many have been or will become foreign ministers. As a result there is more informed, wide-ranging, and sophisticated discussion about international issues at the UN than anywhere else. In the beginning, however, I was a diplomatic neophyte, which some of my colleagues didn't hesitate to point out. My response was to keep my eyes and ears open and learn.

Because the Security Council is a legislative body, knowing how to draft resolutions is an essential skill. Although our staffs prepared the first drafts, the "perm reps," as we were known, did the final wording—in sometimes fierce verbal combat. My predecessor-but-one, Thomas Pickering, had been a master of the language of diplomacy. A Foreign Service all-star, he had played the lead role in writing resolutions before, during, and after the Gulf War. Now, without Tom around, much of the drafting fell to Sir David Hannay, the experienced and dry-witted British ambassador. Hannay was the keeper of all Latin phrases, such as *inter alia*, and knew where all the commas should go. He also had a habit of beginning every sentence with "Sorry, but this is the correct way to put it...." At one point, when he was correcting everyone's grammar, I told him, "*Sorry*, but English is not my native tongue."

As a diplomatic wordsmith, I was no Tom Pickering. I did, however, have my experience in the Senate to draw upon, skilled advisors on my staff, and the example of my colleagues to consider. I learned rapidly how much could be done with punctuation, or the substitution of "and" for "or." I picked up the UN trick of subtly adding substance to one resolution by reference to another. As I began to know my colleagues better, I discovered ways to achieve consensus without yielding on principle, and I started to see clearly what I came to call "the billiard-ball effect"—how one decision knocks into others. I also learned when to be direct and when to persuade others to make my point while I stayed behind the scenes. By the time the contentious Haiti Resolution was debated in mid 1994, I felt I knew not only how the Security Council worked but also how to work *it*.

Part of my approach was occasionally to use the element of surprise by being self-deprecating in a world where that tactic was rarely practiced. During one debate, I told the council it would have to delay action until I had received my instructions from Washington. "The issue will not be decided," I pronounced solemnly, "until the fat lady sings." No one could believe I had actually said that, given the fact that I was not exactly thin, but neither could they say anything. After all, they were diplomats.

BECAUSE THE UN was embroiled in so many issues, I was involved in shaping and implementing U.S. foreign policy to a greater extent than many of my predecessors. This was challenging—and frustrating. As a member of the Principals Committee, I had a seat at the table where decisions were made, but I was also at a disadvantage in two ways. First, as a cabinet member I answered to the President, but as an ambassador I reported to the Secretary of State. In the State Department's official organizational chart, I was shown at the end of a dotted line growing out of Warren Christopher's ear. So my status was not quite equal to that of the other committee members. Fortunately my day-to-day link with the State Department was primarily through Under Secretary for Political Affairs Peter Tarnoff—always a sympathetic listener.

Second, while huge bureaucracies supported the other members of the Principals Committee, I was backed by a single diplomatic mission and a tiny Washington-based staff. My team labored mightily to prepare me for meetings, but on some issues we lacked the resources to provide independent input.

Especially at the outset, I had to work hard to make an impact. Some of this was my fault. Wanting acceptance, I often forgot the advice I had given to young people—speak up early and interrupt if necessary. I was too restrained. When I did speak up, I was unnerved by the manner of Tony Lake, who chaired the meetings. The pressures of the job had made Tony less easygoing and patient than the clever friend whom I had long known. I resented it when he drummed his fingers on the table while I spoke or looked at his watch. This puzzled me, because I certainly did not monopolize the meetings, and more often than not my views accorded with his. I often thought we should arrange to talk prior to meetings, but that was not Tony's style. I wasn't sure whether gender played any role, but I did resent being treated as though I were one of his students.

I soon concluded that I couldn't influence decisions simply by repeating talking points that had been prepared. On many subjects Christopher had the same words in front of him as I did. My contributions had a greater impact when based upon firsthand information, so I welcomed the chance to represent the United States on missions abroad. I visited UN peacekeeping operations because they were an integral part of my job, but I was especially pleased when asked by the President to undertake a non-UN mission to some very familiar ground.

In the early 1990s, Central Europe was still seen by many Americans as a mysterious collective entity characterized by medieval castles, spicy sausages, and an insufficient supply of vowels. In truth, each of these countries has its own history, culture, and language; each its own pantheon of heroes and adversaries; and each its own sense of having, at one time or another, been betrayed. For centuries these nations were fought over, carved up, and subjugated by powerful neighbors. After World War I, Woodrow Wilson's Fourteen Points gave them their independence. After World War II, Soviet imperialism snatched it away. Between the 1940s and 1980s, the Iron Curtain blotted out the light so that nothing grew.

Now the light was back and freedom could flourish, but so could the roots of past grievance. There was a danger that old fault lines would reopen throughout the region, tempting demagogues, inflaming fears, and prompting efforts to achieve security by force. When the Berlin Wall crumbled, expectations soared. The newly free nations, wanting to rejoin the West quickly, soon became disappointed with the pace of progress.

Some nations had expected to be welcomed almost immediately into the European Community (today's European Union) and NATO. Some had hoped for a new Marshall Plan to ease their economic transitions. America and its allies had provided assistance, but not enough to keep unemployment from rising and living standards from plummeting. Central Europeans felt let down and complained that only East Germany—reunited with its other half—had truly been admitted to the West while the rest of the region had been asked to sit in various institutional waiting rooms.

In June 1993, the Clinton administration approved a new policy toward Central and East Europe designed to bolster democracy, reduce trade barriers, and reward nations undertaking economic reform. We also developed four principles to guide our policy toward NATO—the institution countries in the region most desired to join.

First, we believed NATO had to remain at the center of the European security system. No other institution had comparable clout.

Second, it was only fair that NATO should open its doors to the new democracies, provided they met the same political and military standards as other members.

Third, we should use the prospect of joining NATO as an incentive for countries in the region to ensure civilian command of their armed forces, liberalize their economies, and respect the rights of minorities.

Finally, NATO enlargement should occur gradually. The new democracies wouldn't be prepared to meet Alliance responsibilities overnight, and not all would make progress at the same pace. An open and deliberate process would help reassure Moscow that NATO's enlargement to the east would be a step toward Russia, not against it.

To put these principles into practice, President Clinton approved an idea put forward by General John Shalikashvili, Colin Powell's successor as Chairman of the Joint Chiefs. General "Shali," as we called him, had been born in Poland, which he fled in a cattle car in 1944 just ahead of advancing Soviet troops. He told us he had learned English by watching John Wayne movies in Peoria. Shali brought a positive attitude to our foreign policy team, along with a sharp mind, a quick wit, and a lifetime's knowledge of Europe. When I learned of his nomination, I immediately called to welcome him—a fellow Slav and native of Central Europe—to the Principals Committee.

Shali's idea was to invite the emerging democracies of Europe and the former Soviet Union to enlist in a new entity, the Partnership for Peace (PFP), whose members would participate in military training exercises with NATO countries. This meant that former enemies of the Alliance would learn how to operate with it, while old rivals such as Romania and Hungary would now work together. The countries that did the most to upgrade their militaries, develop peaceful relations with their neighbors, and solidify their democratic institutions would become eligible for full Alliance membership.

The plan promised to create a new European security structure that would preserve and strengthen NATO, while creating a meaningful role for all, including Russia and Ukraine. Initially, however, Central Europeans weren't impressed. Lech Wałęsa denounced the PFP as "blackmail" and "too little." Leaders in Lithuania pressed for immediate admission to NATO. To gain support, the President decided to send a diplomatic mission to Central and East Europe immediately prior to the January 1994 NATO summit, which he would attend, and at which the PFP would be considered. I was pleased when President Clinton asked General Shalikashvili and me to head the mission.

Arriving the first week of January, we found that nations in the region were highly receptive to a little personal attention. Our first stop was Poland, where Wałęsa greeted us with much skepticism. Painstakingly we persuaded him that PFP was the path to NATO, not the detour he suspected; he agreed to say in our press conference that although he would prefer to "leap" into NATO, he was willing to settle for "small steps." On our next stop, the Hungarians were the first to embrace the PFP fully. In Prague, the Czechs said they were willing to run a budget deficit to pay for upgrading their military.

At each port of call we counseled patience, emphasizing that NATO was a military alliance, not a social club. It had high standards, which is why countries wanted to join. If a government was serious about its candidacy, it should get serious about meeting those standards. The leaders we met appreciated my assurances that the PFP provided a road map to NATO membership. They were less impressed by my sports analogies. I told them "PFP is like a football game. The ball may not be exactly where you would like it, but it's in play. Your job is to pick it up and run"—an appropriate image in Dallas or Detroit, but in Warsaw when you say "football," they think "soccer." Pick up the ball in soccer and the other team gets a free kick.

At first Shali's team and mine were uncertain how to relate to one another. I had never made a trip with the Chairman of the Joint Chiefs. The military was not accustomed to traveling with high-ranking civilian women. Although our cultures sometimes clashed, our teams ended up working well together and had some fun along the way. Shali and I each considered it an accident of history that we would hold the jobs we did at the time our native lands were seeking acceptance by the West. We were living proof to Central Europeans that there were people high in the U.S. government who understood their past problems and future hopes.

The leaders we met wanted the protection of NATO security guarantees because they worried that the Russian bear might not remain gentle for long. Guarantees of American military action, however, can't be given lightly. I was authorized to say only that the security of each country was of "direct and material interest" to the United States. This reassured without locking us into anything specific. After I explained "direct and material interest," Shali outlined what PFP participants could expect. "You will come to Brussels," he said, "and we'll give you a desk, a filing cabinet, and a phone. We'll have people there with whom you can consult and plan. We'll learn how to operate together as a military team. And we'll develop communications and other equipment that are interoperable."

Given the jealousies that existed from capital to capital, as we moved from one to the next we didn't dare vary our presentation or diplomatic routine. If we ate a meal or attended a dinner in country A, we had to do the same in countries B, C, and D. The trip was a unique opportunity for me to meet the leading officials of Poland, Hungary, the Czech Republic, Slovakia, Romania, Slovenia, Bulgaria, and Albania—all in a matter of a few days. But by the middle of the trip I was so unsure of where I was when I first got off the plane that I was reduced to saying, "It's so wonderful to be in your country." Before long we were overtired and overfed. I expressed my "direct and material interest" in moving to the next stop. Shali promised me "a desk, a filing cabinet, and a phone" for my office. And we both fell prey to the Pentagon's penchant for acronyms, referring to our journey no longer as an "accident of history" but as an "AOH."

NATO LEADERS FORMALLY approved the PFP in Brussels on January 10, 1994, after which President Clinton was to fly on to Prague. I joined him in Belgium, which allowed me to brief him on my meetings but also to carry out an assignment given to me by President Havel during my visit to the Czech capital. Thinking about how to entertain the American chief executive during his visit, Havel had decided to give him a Czech-made saxophone and take him to a jazz club. However, the President's mother had died of complications from breast cancer the previous week, and the advance people were unsure of his mood. My job was to ask the President directly what he wanted to do and, once we landed, whisper the response into Havel's ear when I saw him in the receiving line at the airport.

As we touched down in Prague and were preparing to disembark, the protocol people lined us up. Secretary Christopher was behind the President and I was to follow. Chris, considerate as always, invited me to go ahead of him. Arriving on Air Force One anywhere is exciting. Descending the steps with the leader of the free world, to be greeted by Havel, a friend and a democratic hero in the country of my birth, was high drama. Halfway down, I turned to the President and said, "This is as good as it gets." He gave my hand a squeeze. I reached the tarmac, kissed Havel, and reported the President's answer: the jazz club was a go.

We went from the airport to Prague Castle for the arrival ceremony. The honor guard passed, then the band played the Czech national anthem, "Where Is My Home?" and "The Star Spangled Banner," ending with that wonderful phrase, "the land of the free and the home of the brave." Two anthems, two homes, one me. An incredible start, and soon the day got even better.

We went up to Havel's private office, which had changed markedly since I had been there four years earlier. The ugly furniture was gone; Havel's whimsical modern art adorned the room, including a huge painting of two nudes. President Clinton took one astonished look and said to Havel, "Can you imagine what people would say if I had that painting in my office?" We then proceeded to the formal meeting, with the two delegations facing each other across a long table. I don't think it matters what job one has; it always feels good when someone praises your work to your boss. When President Havel informed President Clinton that he supported the PFP thanks in large part to my diplomacy and added, "You must be proud she is an American," I smiled. When President Clinton responded, "You must be proud she was born a Czech," I grinned from ear to ear.

The next few hours were a made-for-television extravaganza starring two charismatic leaders and an elegant lady of a certain age—Prague. After meeting in Havel's office, the Presidents went down to the Vltava River and strolled across Charles Bridge, which had been emptied of the usual vendors. The thirty baroque statues lining the bridge were lit up, creating circles of light against the gathering dusk. The sound of thousands of Czechs roaring "Clin-ton, Clin-ton" echoed off the buildings and through the narrow streets.

I rejoined the two leaders at a pub called the Golden Tiger. While enjoying schnitzel and beer, we were joined by an elderly Czech couple who had hosted Bill Clinton during a visit to Prague many years previously, while he was a student at Oxford. The President said, "Get some food for those people," in a language that the *Washington Post*'s Daniel Williams described as "fluent Arkanslovak."

We went next to the Reduta Jazz Club, where the President was presented with his new sax and invited to try it out. As he played "My Funny Valentine" and "Summertime," I thought he sounded pretty good. When he came back to the table, he said, "You have no idea how hard it is to play a brand-new instrument." Later he played a duet with a wonderful Czech sax musician, while Havel, who has no rhythm at all, accompanied them—more or less—on maracas and the tambourine. By then the room was so filled with Czech politicians and smoke I could barely see. As we were leaving, we heard what may have been a firecracker pop in the street, and the Secret Service hustled the President away to his hotel. All in all, a memorable day.

THE NATURE OF the UN's agenda was such that most journeys I made were to the world's most troubled regions. During the fall of 1994, I took a weeklong trip to the Caucasus, home to four small, rugged republics, each possessing a distinct identity, tucked between the Black and Caspian Seas. My purpose was to show American support for the sovereignty of the newly freed nations and caution Russia against unwarranted meddling or treating the area as a "sphere of interest."

I began in the tiny nation of Moldova, arriving with humanitarian supplies in response to recent floods. My comments in support of Moldovan sovereignty generated angry comments from the Russian military, whose Fourteenth Army remained in the country long after it should have left. Moldovan authorities hosted our delegation at a multi-hour, multicourse dinner in a huge wine cellar, during which we toasted U.S.-Moldovan relations, our ambassadors, the future, democracy, the food, the drink, the brave Moldovan people, and the noble American people. During a toast to me, I was compared to Margaret Thatcher ("the Iron Lady") and dubbed "the Titanium Lady."

The next stop was the Georgian capital of Tbilisi, where we boarded an aged Russian plane en route to the northern city of Zugdidi. The Russian notion of separate smoking and nonsmoking sections is to use the aisle as a dividing line. I could get used to that, but the sight of machine guns strewn around and grenades dangling from the belts of the soldiers who accompanied us made me wish we had never taken off.

Once we arrived, things only got worse. In the early 1990s, a separatist movement had uprooted many Georgians and left them in makeshift camps not far from a UN-negotiated cease-fire line. Finding a large gathering of angry people, I told them that we were working to find a way for them to return home but that I couldn't report any concrete progress. In an effort to warm the atmosphere, I entered the crowded building where the displaced families were being housed. As an ambassador I did not rate a large traveling staff. Two Diplomatic Security agents and my chief of staff Elaine Shocas accompanied me, but soon Elaine and I got separated from the agents and were overwhelmed by people shouting and pushing. The local guards did nothing to hold anyone back. Elaine's ribs were badly bruised in a collision with a rifle butt. I used my elbows to open a path back down the stairs and outside, where our courageous male "protectors," press spokesman James Rubin and speechwriter Bill Woodward, were standing around smoking cigarettes. It was one of the few times I have felt unsafe.[1]

The president of Georgia was Eduard Shevardnadze, who had previously served as foreign minister to Gorbachev, during which time he played an important role in ending the Cold War. Shevardnadze was seen as a capable and sophisticated man, which was just as well, because the challenge of bringing democratic government to Georgia is daunting. During my visit we discussed the range of problems he faced, including crime, corruption, terrorism, and ethnic conflict. Later we had a long dinner—punctuated, once again, by frequent toasts.

As the evening wore on, I couldn't resist telling the Georgian leader a story that had been going around at the end of the first Bush administration. According to the joke, President Bush asked Gorbachev how he had been smart enough to find Shevardnadze. Gorbachev responded that he had chosen "Shevvie," as he was nicknamed, because he had correctly answered the riddle, "Who is the son of your father who is not your brother?" Shevardnadze had said, "Of course, I am," so he was hired. Bush decided to call in Vice-President Quayle and ask him the same question. Quayle said he would have to think about it and went to ask Richard Cheney, who was then Secretary of Defense. Cheney said, "Well, I am." Quayle went back to Bush and said, "Ask me the riddle again." Bush did so and Quayle replied, "Dick Cheney." Bush said, "No, you

---

1. Shocas, Rubin, and Woodward were close advisors throughout my years as ambassador and Secretary of State. I met Elaine in the 1980s through NDI; she had served as an attorney in the Justice Department and counsel to Senator Edward Kennedy on the Senate Judiciary Committee. I met Jamie in 1988 when he was employed by the Arms Control Association; he was later a top foreign policy aide to Senator Joseph Biden. As noted earlier, I had met Bill during the Dukakis campaign, after which he worked for U.S. Representative Gerry Studds and Senator John Kerry.

idiot, it's Shevardnadze." Shevvie loved the joke and proceeded to propose several more toasts.

Armenia and Azerbaijan are both ancient lands, neighbors divided by history and culture. Largely Christian Armenia harbors the traumatic memory of its persecution by Turkey before and during World War I. Azerbaijan's population is largely of Turkic stock. One of Stalin's tricks had been to place the predominantly Armenian region of Nagorno-Karabakh inside Azerbaijan. As soon as the Cold War ended, fighting broke out. The Armenians soon seized control of Nagorno-Karabakh and opened a land corridor to it. During my trip I tried to advance our effort to broker a negotiated resolution to Nagorno-Karabakh's status. Unfortunately this initiative was to continue without success throughout my years in government. Every time we got close, hard-liners on one side or the other provoked a crisis.

Baku, the picturesque port and capital of Azerbaijan, is dotted with oil wells, reflecting the country's historic role as a source of petroleum. When I visited, the city was alive with deal makers talking in Southwest American accents and wearing cowboy boots. Restaurants had signs urging patrons to check their guns at the door. I stayed in the official presidential guest house, which proved another monument to the aesthetics of Soviet-era Communist rule. Hanging from the lobby ceiling was a fifteen-foot-long chandelier of purple and green blown glass in the shape of a bunch of grapes. President Heydar Aliyev told me proudly that his son had purchased it. After our formal meetings, the loquacious president invited me to go down to the cellar, where we sat on white bearskin-covered stools in a nightclub called the Cave, which featured faux stalactites and stalagmites, a movie screening room, a swimming pool, a sauna, and loud bad music. Although in official meetings Aliyev spoke Azeri, at other times he spoke Russian, a reminder that he had once been a KGB official. I was told the Cave had been a favorite cavorting ground for Leonid Brezhnev and invited friends.

THREE TIMES AS UN ambassador I visited Africa. There are many bright spots on that continent, but those were not on my itinerary. I went instead to countries scarred by wars the world body was trying to stop. As I bore witness, the stakes were enormous. In Burundi I stressed the importance of lessons learned in neighboring Rwanda about the terrors of ethnic violence and met with a group of Hutu and Tutsi women who were working to prevent a repeat of that genocide.

In Angola I walked through deserted fields with British workers who were painstakingly removing land mines. Families who lived nearby had to keep their children tethered to sticks. I went to a hospital run by Doctors

Without Borders, where they were caring for children who had lost limbs. The experience made the removal of land mines a passion for me. I gained UN approval of resolutions calling initially for a ban on the transfer or sale of mines to any country. Later, with support from the President and Vermont Senator Patrick Leahy, among others, I launched a campaign aimed at eliminating the danger posed to civilians by land mines anywhere on earth by the year 2010. I was fortunate to have a deputy, Ambassador Karl "Rick" Inderfurth, who spearheaded our initiative.[2] Among his many projects, Rick worked with DC Comics to develop special editions of *Superman, Wonder Woman,* and *Batman* warning children in their own languages about mines.

During my visits to Africa I was appalled by the young age of the soldiers, many of whom were not yet in their teens. I was also frustrated that when the UN arranged for soldiers to disarm voluntarily, all they were given was a "rehabilitation package" containing a few dollars, some clothes, and a toothbrush—hardly enough to begin building a normal life. Possession of a gun had given a man—or boy—his identity. A toothbrush hardly had the same effect. They needed an education and a job. Where were they going to find those?

Throughout my time at the UN, I was a firsthand witness to two seemingly contradictory trends. Some areas of the world were coming together as never before; others were falling apart. Europe was engaged in an historic movement toward economic union and closer political cooperation. Latin America and East Asia were forging new trade pacts and exploring the means for greater collaboration on security matters. Yet the Balkans, the Caucasus, and parts of Africa were splintering, beset by strife, and in some cases almost completely lacking the institutions of government.

Seeing the misery these conditions caused made me think of politicians back home who belittled public service and ran down our own government institutions. I thought to myself: Let them come here to the cracked edges of the world and experience life without "big government." After all, there was no federal income tax in Liberia, no ban on assault weapons in Angola, no bleeding heart judges in Rwanda, no welfare system in Sudan, and no burdensome environmental controls in the Caucasus.

---

2. I first met Rick during our days together at Brzezinski's NSC. He later served as my deputy during the transition, then as our ambassador for special political affairs at the UN. With Rick's dedication and skills in mind, I broadened that position to include Security Council and peacekeeping responsibilities. In 1997, as Secretary of State, I asked Rick to serve as assistant secretary of state for South Asian affairs.

EARLY IN 1995, the political uprising led by Speaker of the House of Representatives Newton Gingrich ended four decades of Democratic control of that body and brought to Washington a flock of new members. In an effort to reach out, the White House scheduled a foreign policy briefing for the Speaker and freshman class. One afternoon in February, Secretary Christopher, Tony Lake, General Shalikashvili, the Secretary of Defense, and I trooped up to the Rayburn House Office Building. In all my years with Senator Muskie and later at the NSC, I couldn't recall a visit to Capitol Hill by the President's entire foreign policy team for a general exchange of views. We were greeted by an empty room. Gingrich and the House Republicans were elsewhere, having a caucus on other subjects. We were asked to wait, which we did, for forty minutes. By then I was frustrated, Shali was turning colors, steam was pouring out of Lake's ears, and Christopher's left eyebrow seemed about to twitch. After three quarters of an hour we were told that the Speaker's other meeting might go on indefinitely, so we headed back downtown.

The President didn't give up: he decided to host a small dinner for congressional leaders and the national security team. That evening brought out a different side of the Speaker, who on this occasion arrived on time, sat with a few of us in the Blue Room before dinner, and chatted for more than half an hour about history, the architecture of the White House, and defense issues. When the President arrived, the range of conversation expanded further to cover essentially everything. Seeing the President and Gingrich together in a social setting was like watching two opposing generals thumbwrestling before heading out to the battlefield to pound each other's brains. Both were natural commanders, and commanders need their own armies. Gingrich could be courteous, flattering, stimulating, learned, and provocative, but he wasn't about to wheel his artillery onto our side of the field. We were the enemy he had been put on earth to oppose.[3]

Although Gingrich was complimentary to me in person, he was also a master of the political cheap shot, and UN-bashing had become the right wing's favorite sport. Spurred by its politically inspired "Contract with America," the new majority seemed determined to destroy the UN. Legislation was introduced that would have eliminated UN peacekeeping as an option. Appropriators attached more and more onerous conditions to the payment of our UN bills. Some freshmen Representatives called upon the United States

---

3. Gingrich's rise to power was accompanied by much exaggerated rhetoric about the supposed "irrelevance" of President Clinton and the Speaker himself as a "transitional figure." I couldn't help thinking of a 1936 novel by the Czechoslovak writer Karel Čapek. *War with the Newts* is about a race of overgrown salamanders who take over the world.

to withdraw from the organization entirely, and in one congressional hearing I was asked what I at first thought was a rhetorical question, "What does the UN actually do?" Then I realized the inquirer truly had no clue.

My efforts to work with Congress were complicated by two self-inflicted wounds. First, in testifying about the need for the United States to pay its UN bills, I said, "It isn't easy to represent a deadbeat." Kentucky Congressman Harold Rogers (chairman of the appropriations subcommittee in charge of my budget) immediately pounced: "How can you insult our country?" "I shouldn't have put it that way," I said sincerely. "I am so proud to be an American. I apologize." After the hearing I called the Congressman and made up, but thenceforth watched my words.

Several months later I made a second mistake, this time testifying before the Senate. In trying to explain why it was important to have partners in dealing with regional conflicts, I said, "U.S. leadership within collective bodies requires what I would term 'assertive multilateralism.'" By this I meant that when America acted with others, we should lead in establishing goals and ensuring success. I didn't in any way rule out the possibility that we would have to act on our own in self-defense or to protect other vital interests. Unfortunately, "assertive multilateralism" became the sound bite that bit me. Partisan critics distorted both my intentions and the meaning of the words to suggest that I wanted to subcontract U.S. foreign policy to the UN. Multilateralism certainly has its place as a foreign policy tool, but the term itself is without appeal—especially to Americans. The word has six syllables, includes some Latin, and ends with an "ism." For anyone wanting to criticize the administration, I had provided a perfect opportunity.

The larger problem we faced was that we were trying to sharpen a foreign policy tool—UN peacekeeping—that many in Congress didn't value. After all, we had the American military. What more did we need? If societies blew apart, that was their problem. The point I tried to make was that the President could do most for our country with a full range of tools—including our armed forces, vigorous alliances, economic leverage, and the ability, when appropriate, to work through the UN and other international organizations. I acknowledged the UN's flaws but argued that many were correctable and in the process of being corrected—a process it was in America's interests to encourage. The more effective the UN was, the more it could help us by sharing the costs, risks, and responsibilities of promoting peace. If we did not back the UN sufficiently, it would not succeed. And when the UN didn't succeed, we all paid a price. We had seen that in Somalia and Rwanda. And from my first days in New York, we had seen it in Bosnia as well.

TWELVE

Horror in the Balkans

ARLY IN MY TENURE as UN ambassador, I visited a mass grave near the Croatian city of Vukovar. What I saw was a garbage dump, a field of rusted refrigerators and scraps of farm equipment, ringed by razor wire and patrolled by Russian peacekeepers. Just beneath the soil lay more than two hundred bodies. The victims had not been combatants in any war but rather hospital patients who had been led away into the night by Serb forces. The local Serb authorities didn't deny the existence of the mass grave but wondered at my concern. They said I failed to understand the history of the region.

I thought during the visit of pictures I had seen of refugees expelled from homes in places throughout the Balkans, places such as Bihać, Brčko, and Mostar. To most Americans these are unfamiliar names, difficult to remember and hard to spell. I was reminded then of other faces, photographed on their way to other unfamiliar, hard-to-spell places, such as Auschwitz, Treblinka, and Dachau.

The horror of the Holocaust was not repeated in the conflict that raged in Bosnia during the early 1990s, but there were parallels. In 1939, when Nazi Field Marshal Wilhelm Keitel ordered the purge of Poland, he called it "political housecleaning." In the 1990s, we called it "ethnic cleansing." The context and scale were different, but the choice for the world community was essentially the same. In one of his books, my father had quoted the Czechoslovak patriarch, Tomáš Masaryk: "Love of one's neighbor, of the nation, and of humanity imposes upon everyone the obligation to defend oneself and to resist evil constantly, at all times, and in all things." For me that obligation was triggered by the campaigns of brutality launched by Serb President Slobodan Milošević.

As a Carter administration official in 1980, I had attended the funeral of longtime Yugoslav strongman Marshal Tito. In the years immediately following, the Yugoslav federation started to come unglued. There were deep economic problems and much restiveness among the country's constituent ethnic groups. When it became clear that the Cold War was ending and Communist regimes had become obsolete, opportunities arose for new kinds of leaders. Tragically, those new kinds were not necessarily better.

Milošević was a Yugoslav businessman who had risen through Communist Party ranks after Tito's death. He was elected president by the Serb Parliament in 1989 and gained popularity by appealing to ethnic fears and resentments. A ruthless opportunist, he adopted Tito's heavy-handed style while exploiting conflicts between Serbs and much of the rest of Yugoslavia. With his broad, unlined face, hearty manner, and stylish wardrobe, he did not look like a villain. His speeches, although vividly nationalist, were not laced with hatred. His cruelty was manifested in his manipulative actions, which spurred Serb forces to employ terror, rape, and indiscriminate violence against his Balkan foes.

The varying challenges I had confronted in Somalia, Rwanda, and Haiti were new to me, but Yugoslavia was familiar. Aside from Czechoslovakia and the United States, my family ties to that country were the closest. I had lived there, my brother had been born there, and my father had served there twice. As an academic who had tracked changes in Communism, I had also spent considerable time studying the nation.

In New York, at meetings of our foreign policy team in Washington, in confidential memoranda to the President, and in speeches around the world, I used the strongest language I could to support forceful action to stop Milošević. As a result I was often accused by ethnic Serbs of betraying my family legacy. I replied, "Yes, it's true my father dedicated his book about Tito to the Yugoslav people, and he loved the Serbs. He even said if he weren't Czechoslovak, he would want to be Serb. But my father's core commitment was to the ideals of freedom and tolerance. If he were alive today, he would be speaking out against Milošević and in favor of those ideals at least as vigorously as I am."

THE BITTER STRIFE that occurred during the two years before I became UN ambassador ripped Yugoslavia to pieces. First Slovenia gained its independence after a brief spell of fighting. Then Croatia broke free—though after a savage war to which the mass grave near Vukovar bore witness. Macedonia split off without violence, but Bosnia and Herzegovina became engulfed in conflict, with the Bosnian Serbs, backed by Milošević, gaining the upper hand. Day after day the world witnessed the murder of civilians, the burning of villages, the shelling of apartments, the destruction of churches and mosques, and reports of mass rape.

Initially the crisis was viewed by Europeans and the senior Bush administration alike as a European problem that should and could be settled by Europeans. Diplomats from the continent anxiously shuttled back and forth arranging cease-fires that did not stick and predicting an end to the violence that did not come. These efforts were undercut by the theory—widespread in Europe—that Serbs, Croats, and Bosniaks[1] were so intent on killing each other that it was pointless trying to stop them. This patronizing and callous attitude was grounded in the region's history of ethnic rivalries, but it ignored the centuries during which these same populations had lived together in peace and the intermarriages that had long diluted the pretensions of many to ethnic purity. There was also an historic tendency in much of Europe to identify first with the Catholics (including Croats), second with the Orthodox (including Serbs), and third, if at all, with the "Turkish" Muslims. It was not hard to read between the lines of those taking the "philosophical" view toward Balkan violence that, although the current round of score settling might be messy, the disappearance of Bosnia and Herzegovina might not be such a bad thing.

To complement their diplomacy, President Bush and his trans-Atlantic counterparts sent lightly armed UN peacekeepers to Bosnia with mandates to enforce cease-fires, deprive combatants of heavy weapons, and ensure the provision of aid. It was like sending David against Goliath, only without the slingshot or any sign of divine help. Bound by the traditional peacekeepers' neutrality, the UN forces had to ask, "Mother, may I?" before they could act. They quickly became passive witnesses to grotesque crimes. Before I even arrived in New York, the Security Council had approved more than two dozen statements vainly demanding an end to the fighting. The real failure, here again, was not that of the UN as an institution but that of council members to back their sentiments with the right actions.

One of the council's first steps had been to approve an embargo on weapons deliveries to Yugoslavia. This was supposed to reduce the violence, but its application to Bosnia after Yugoslavia broke up made no sense. Unlike Belgrade, the government in newly independent Sarajevo had done nothing to warrant UN sanctions. Moreover, the impact of the embargo was uneven. The Serbs in Bosnia had ample arms and could be resupplied when necessary from Belgrade. The Croats had help from Zagreb in circumventing the embargo. The Muslims were relatively defenseless.

---

1. "Bosniak" is the term used for a citizen of Bosnia and Herzegovina who is a Muslim.

During the first months of the Clinton presidency, our foreign policy team held numerous rambling and inconclusive meetings about the crisis we had inherited, without achieving consensus. Defense Secretary Les Aspin seemed torn between his interventionist instincts and the military's reluctance to get involved. Secretary Christopher had trouble identifying any option he could recommend. Tony Lake, who had come in charged up by the robust rhetoric of the Clinton campaign, soon had the Vietnam bug humming in his ear. Quite understandably, he didn't want to send U.S. forces to fight an unwinnable war. At the same time, he shared my view that violence in Bosnia affected European security and therefore our own interests. My convictions were reinforced by my perch at the UN, where I saw more foreign officials on a daily basis than any other member of our team. Bosnia was a constant preoccupation, and I felt I needed a good answer to representatives from Islamic nations who pressed me hard to halt the slaughter of their brethren.

Another important participant in our discussions was Vice-President Al Gore. I had known him previously as a rival of Mike Dukakis for the Democratic presidential nomination in 1988 and as an arms control expert and environmentally minded Senator from Tennessee. After I became ambassador, I often sat next to him during meetings and we exchanged notes both about policy and personalities. Notwithstanding his "stiff" image, I found Gore both at ease with himself and funny. The President treated him like a full partner in policy discussions, so there was little sense of hierarchy. In the early days especially, Gore had a steadying influence on the rest of our team. Like his National Security Advisor Leon Fuerth, he also cared passionately about issues of justice and human rights. Both were advocates of forceful action.

In our meetings the Vice-President, Tony, Leon, and I pushed for an approach called "lift and strike." Under this plan we would end the embargo on arms shipments to Sarajevo, while threatening air strikes. We would thereby create an opportunity for the Bosniaks to defend themselves and send a message to the Serbs that they should refrain from further aggression.

The President agreed to this proposal and sent Christopher to Europe to consult. The Secretary reported back on May 8, 1993; his news was not good. "Our central concept of lifting the arms embargo ran into stiff resistance," Christopher told us, in part because the allies were worried about the safety of their peacekeepers if we appeared to take sides. We could probably get them to acquiesce, he added, if we simply told them we intended to go ahead, but this course wouldn't persuade them of the merits of our approach. Christopher said that such a decision would require an all-out diplomatic campaign, about which he wasn't particularly enthusiastic and in which the credibility of the administration would be on the line. He warned that failure would be damaging both internationally and at home. On the other hand, the "consultative approach" he had used on the trip meant that the President wasn't publicly committed. "You're free to consider other options," he told the President, "though none seems attractive."

It was not a particularly helpful briefing, but it did provide a lesson. Consultations with allies are essential, but they can't be open-ended debates about what to do next. We couldn't hope to persuade others if we had not at least persuaded ourselves. At this stage, with a new President, a wary Secretary of State, a negative Pentagon, nervous allies, and crises in Somalia, then Rwanda and Haiti blowing up, we weren't prepared to run the risks of leadership on Bosnia. And thereby invited even greater risks.

Throughout the next two years our goal was a negotiated solution, but we never applied the credible threat of force necessary to achieve it. Instead we employed a combination of half-measures and bluster that didn't work. We brokered cease-fire agreements that were violated within days. We proposed a resolution in the Security Council to lift the arms embargo but were blocked when nine members, including Britain, France, and Russia, abstained. We vowed to strengthen six Muslim "safe areas," but reinforcements couldn't travel to those areas without Bosnian Serb consent. We vowed to cut off arms shipments to the Bosnian Serbs from Belgrade, but Milošević refused to allow UN border monitors on Yugoslav territory. We voted to enforce no-fly zones, but the Serbs violated them hundreds of times without paying a significant price.

From the outset we asked Colin Powell, who was then Chairman of the Joint Chiefs, to present us with military options. The sight of Powell walking into meetings with his charts and briefing papers was impressive. During the Gulf War Powell had seemed a larger-than-life hero, expressing American determination in a period of widely celebrated, if incomplete, triumph. Powell's good looks, humor, and obvious decency combined with his military bearing to make him an immensely attractive figure. While the rest of President Clinton's foreign policy team was new, Powell was a holdover from the previous administration, with nine months to serve under the new President until his term as Chairman of the Joint Chiefs expired.

During our meetings in the White House Situation Room, Powell used a red laser pointer and maps of the difficult Balkans terrain to show where bombing could take place and troops could move if we pursued a military option. When we asked what it would take to free Sarajevo airport from the surrounding Serb artillery, he replied consistent with his commitment to the doctrine of overwhelming force, saying it would take tens of thousands of troops, cost billions of dollars, probably result in numerous casualties, and require a long and open-ended commitment of U.S. forces. Time and again he led us up the hill of possibilities and dropped us off on the other side with the practical equivalent of "No can do." After hearing this for the umpteenth time, I asked in exasperation, "What are you saving this superb military for, Colin, if we can't use it?" Powell wrote in his memoirs that my question nearly gave him an "aneurysm" and that he had had to explain "patiently" to me the role of America's military.[2]

In the face of all his medals and prestige, I found it hard to argue with Powell about the proper way to employ American force. Even though I was a member of the Principals Committee, I was still a mere female civilian. I did, however, think then as now that the lessons of Vietnam could be learned too well. It was understandable that Powell would want clarity about mission and certainty about success before committing our forces, but "no more quagmires" was not a sufficient strategy in a messy and complex world. With careful planning, limited force could be used effectively to achieve limited objectives. There was an urgent need to do that in Bosnia, but Powell did not want the American military to take on that job.

DURING MY FIRST YEAR in New York, the Security Council authorized the creation of the International Criminal Tribunal for the Former Yugoslavia (war crimes tribunal). Based at The Hague, the court was the first of its kind since the panels established after World War II. The obstacles facing it and its first chief prosecutor, the fearless Richard Goldstone of South Africa, were formidable. Unlike the accused at Nuremberg, those suspected of war crimes in the Balkans were not the surrendered leaders of a broken power. On the contrary, many were still exercising authority. This hindered the court in gaining access to witnesses and gravesites in places controlled by hostile forces, which is where most of the crimes had taken place. The tribunal could hold no trials without suspects in custody, and for a long time it had none. More-

2. In late 1995, after NATO air strikes had helped end the Bosnia war, a reporter asked me about the Powell quote and I answered frankly that we had disagreed. I called Powell to give him a heads-up about the interview and teased him about his use of the word "patiently." Powell promptly sent me a copy of his book inscribed "with admiration and friendship, patiently yours, Colin Powell." I sent him a thank-you note ending "with admiration and friendship, forcefully yours, Madeleine Albright."

over, with no independent military or police, it was wholly dependent on the cooperation of governments.[3]

There seemed a real possibility that the tribunal would flop and that, once again, the world community would be accused of promising much while delivering little. But the Clinton administration, the leading financial contributor, didn't waver. We shared our technical expertise, while our volunteers helped interview witnesses and refugees. We made cooperation with the tribunal a top issue in all our bilateral relationships with governments both in and outside the region. I was proud of the role my office played, especially my counsel, David Scheffer, who devoted hundreds of hours to the project and later served as America's ambassador-at-large for war crimes issues, a position created when I became Secretary of State.

Our faith proved crucial. Over the years the tribunal built a strong body of case law upon which future prosecutions for crimes against humanity, war crimes, and genocide may be built. For example, it established that rape and sexual enslavement could be considered crimes of war. To date more than four dozen suspects have been tried, including ethnic Serbs, Croats, and Bosniaks. As I will describe later, the tribunal would eventually land the biggest fish of all.

In March 1994, I had the privilege of dedicating the future site of the U.S. embassy in Sarajevo. The event symbolized America's commitment—in words, if not yet in actions—to an undivided and sovereign Bosnia. I hadn't been to Sarajevo before, but as I drove down the broad boulevard leading into the city, I felt my emotions rising. There were destroyed buildings and shattered glass everywhere. The mountains a global audience had enjoyed during the 1984 Winter Olympics were crawling with Serb artillery. Snipers and shortages of fuel had halted public transport. Apartment buildings were gutted, with massive holes where windows should have been. Every day, Sarajevans were being killed in their apartments, shopping, sledding, or simply crossing the street. In the countryside conditions were even worse. Villages were dependent for food on hit-or-miss airdrops or unreliable convoys. People were starving and many babies died. Doctors operated without anesthetics, by candlelight.

---

3. Further complicating the tribunal's work was the fact that rape victims were often reluctant to come forward to testify. The women who were victimized in Bosnia, many of whom were poor Muslims displaced from their homes, had to face the pressure of social taboos as well as economic and physical hardships. It is amazing that the prosecutors eventually persuaded as many to testify as they did.

Years earlier I had traveled through the region and been deeply impressed by Yugoslavia's relative modernity. Haris Silajdžić, Bosnia's prime minister, told me with pride how as a child he could see from the same window the steeple of a Catholic church, the cross of an Orthodox one, and the minaret of a Muslim mosque. Now such holy places were damaged and the National Library burned and trashed.

The future embassy, which I had come to dedicate, was dilapidated. It looked out on what had been a park but was now a cemetery. In my remarks I expressed pleasure at being in "the undivided capital of the independent and sovereign state of Bosnia-Herzegovina." I also drew applause by declaring, "I am a Sarajevan," which I thought a dramatic statement then but which I find pretentious in retrospect. It did, however, reflect the way I felt.

AS TIME AND THE FIGHTING WORE ON, we labored to escape the basic dilemmas in our policy. We couldn't lift the arms embargo because we didn't have the votes on the Security Council, and we could not achieve a permanent cease-fire because that was unacceptable to the Bosniaks and would reward ethnic cleansing. Nor could we use significant force to punish the Bosnian Serbs because UN peacekeepers might be taken hostage and the humanitarian mission derailed.

Our economic sanctions, however, did provide some leverage. Milošević wanted them lifted, and we in turn wanted him to pressure the Bosnian Serbs, headquartered in the town of Pale, to come to the bargaining table. Our goal was to negotiate an agreement recognizing Bosnia and Herzegovina's independence, while dividing its territory between the Muslim-Croat Federation and a semi-autonomous Bosnian Serb entity. If Milošević would agree to recognize Bosnia and persuade the Pale Serbs to accept the map we had drawn up, we would agree to suspend sanctions.

In the fall of 1994, new momentum was added to our efforts when the veteran diplomat Richard Holbrooke assumed the job of assistant secretary of state for European affairs and chief negotiator for the Balkan conflict. His arrival added much energy; I finally felt I had real support. We used to say we were joined at the hip on Bosnia policy.

At year's end negotiators agreed on a four-month cease-fire. This seemed a great accomplishment. On the other hand, it was snowing, and offensive military actions naturally slowed. In the Balkans the time of greatest danger is the spring. Sure enough, there followed weeks of bureaucratic wheel spinning as negotiators sought the right combination of sanctions relief, map adjustments, and terms of mutual recognition that would lure the Pale Serbs onto one side of the bench without the Bosnian Federation falling off the other.

Then came May, and the return of hell.

The Bosnian Serbs celebrated the end of the cease-fire by unleashing the worst shelling Sarajevo had received in months. General Rupert Smith, the decisive new commander of the UN peacekeeping force, requested air strikes, which were turned down by Yasushi Akashi, the Secretary General's obsessively neutral civilian representative.

NATO couldn't conduct air strikes on its own because of the so-called "dual key" system, under which UN and Alliance leaders had to agree before military actions were taken. Akashi feared that air strikes would prompt Serb reprisals against UN peacekeepers. I had one of my least pleasant conversations with Boutros-Ghali as I protested this inaction, saying it would only invite more Bosnian Serb attacks. My arguments had an impact. As the shelling continued, Smith again requested air strikes; this time Akashi relented.

On May 26, NATO planes twice bombed ammunition dumps near Pale. As Akashi feared, the Serbs went on a rampage, shelling five of the six Muslim safe havens in Bosnia, and taking hostage more than 340 UN personnel. Finding my soft spot, the sharp-witted new Russian Permanent Representative Sergei Lavrov began talking about the lessons of Somalia. The following week, a U.S. Air Force F-16 patrolling the Bosnia no-fly zone was shot down. Notified that the pilot, Captain Scott O'Grady, was missing, I felt terrible. I *am* right about the bombing, I thought to myself, but what else can go wrong?

As I walked out of a Security Council meeting past the ever-present press pool, a reporter yelled out, "How do you feel now, Madam Ambassador? Are you happy with the air strikes?" I replied with apparent confidence, but I was shaken. The air strikes had happened, and now the UN—on the eve of its fiftieth anniversary—looked ridiculous. The Bosnian Serbs had chained peacekeepers to bridges, air defense sites, and other potential targets and invited the world's media to watch. And for days prior to his rescue, we thought O'Grady was dead or taken prisoner. We needed a better strategy.

The basic question was what to do about the UN peacekeeping force. Boutros-Ghali was ready to pull the plug. General Smith argued that we had to make a decision to fight or not to fight; we couldn't go on pretending there was a middle ground. I agreed, but there were also strong reasons not to abandon the UN presence. The peacekeepers played an essential humanitarian role. If nothing else, they served as witnesses who might restrain the worst instincts of the fighters. And withdrawal promised to be messy. NATO planners anticipated that UN troops trying to leave would be vulnerable to attack from all sides. They estimated a force of sixty thousand, including twenty thousand Americans, would be required to pull them out safely. In a NATO planning meeting the year before, the United States had agreed to participate in such an effort.

This meant, in effect, that we were pledged to help our allies retreat, but not to win—an absurd position. At a meeting of our foreign policy team in late June 1995, I argued, "When U.S. leadership is questioned in one area, it affects our leadership in others. French President Chirac's recent statement that 'the position of leader of the Free World is vacant' has been chilling my heart for weeks. The strategy we have now makes the President look weak. We need to get ahead of the game."

While recognizing the difficulty of the choice, I recommended that we accept the inevitability of the UN's withdrawal. With the peacekeepers no longer in danger, our allies couldn't object to arming the Bosnians and allowing them to fight for themselves. NATO could launch air strikes to shield them while they prepared. We should insist that Milošević recognize Bosnia and cut ties to the Pale Serbs in return for sanctions relief. At the same time we would make clear to Pale that a deal was still available and to the other Bosnians that they had to accept a reasonable negotiated outcome or lose Western aid.

The President said that he "liked the thrust" of my proposal and that it was the "right direction to go." Lake agreed, which pleased me, and encouraged us to engage in blue-sky thinking about how to bring the Bosnian conflict to a conclusion. In subsequent days the elements of a new strategy did indeed come together, but not before a whole town died.

ONE MORNING IN JULY 1995, Stuart Seldowitz, a political officer on my UN mission staff, walked into the office of UN Under Secretary General Shashi Tharoor. Tharoor was the ultimate diplomat, articulate, analytical, and suave. I had never heard him raise his voice or betray emotion, but that morning, Stu recalled, the diplomat's face was filled with shock and grief. Seldowitz asked him what was up. Tharoor answered, "I think we're facing a humanitarian disaster of historic proportions. There are reports of mass killings in Srebrenica."

Seldowitz raced across the street to report to me. I picked up the phone to call Washington. Another phone rang and my political counselor Cameron Hume answered it. As I talked to D.C., I could hear Cameron saying, "I understand, Mo, I understand." I put down my receiver. Hume handed me his. "It's Sacirbey," he said, referring to Bosnia's UN ambassador, "and he's crying."

Srebrenica was one of three remaining Muslim enclaves in eastern Bosnia. Each had been designated a UN safe area and was swollen with refugees. Each was coveted by the Bosnian Serbs and highly vulnerable to attack.

Buoyed by the hostage fiasco, Bosnian Serb General Ratko Mladić felt the time was right to strike. On July 6, his forces began shelling Srebrenica, which, located in a valley, became like a shooting gallery. Five days later they took the town, expelled most of the women and children, and detained the men, whom they slaughtered. According to figures later compiled by the International Red Cross, between July 12 and July 16, more than seven thousand Bosnian Muslims were murdered. Most of the bodies were dumped in mass graves.[4]

During an emotional meeting at the White House, the Vice-President made an impassioned plea that we not "acquiesce in genocide." I argued the need to be firm with our allies. Thinking of our earlier failures, I insisted, "We need to tell them this is it." The President nodded. "We need to press the French and British to go our way." That meant no more dual key nonsense from the UN and no more hesitancy about using NATO airpower to deter future Serb attacks. In subsequent weeks a secret NATO-UN memorandum was drafted constituting a joint commitment to respond forcefully to a Serb assault on any of the remaining safe areas.

As in Rwanda, we didn't know the scale of the killing immediately. Early intelligence was sketchy, and those responsible for the atrocities were lying. We had strong suspicions but lacked hard evidence. The Bosnian Serbs said no massacre had taken place. In Belgrade, Milošević suggested that the missing men had panicked and would slowly emerge from the woods. Perhaps, he speculated, they were already back with their families and the Bosniaks were refusing to admit it, just to embarrass the Serbs.

Determined to find the truth, I asked the CIA for help. If the missing were being held prisoner, where? If killed, could we prove it? It was possible

---

4. The Dutch peacekeeping contingent in Srebrenica lacked the firepower to stop the Serbs. Thirty of the peacekeepers were taken hostage during the Serb attack. Commanders accepted at face value General Mladić's promise not to harm the men of Srebrenica. By the time the killings took place, the peacekeepers had been withdrawn. In April 2002, an independent inquiry commissioned by the Dutch found their government responsible for committing Dutch peacekeepers to an "ill-conceived and virtually impossible mission" of protecting Srebrenica without adequate preparation and support.

that lives could still be saved and essential that those responsible for murder—if murders had taken place—should be held accountable.

The intelligence community began searching but for two weeks found nothing. Then a dedicated analyst came across images appearing to show detainees standing in a field. In pictures of the same field taken two weeks later he found large areas of disturbed earth and multiple vehicle tracks. We began a process of declassifying the photos and matching the information to data from other sources. Within days, we had a story to tell the world.

The morning of August 10, the Security Council gathered in informal session. Drawing on a combination of intelligence, aerial photos, and interviews with survivors, I proceeded to describe two incidents. A refugee from Srebrenica reported that he and other Muslim men had been brought to a field in the town of Nova Kasaba. The men were lined up in groups and machine-gunned. The refugee survived by falling beneath other bodies and later escaping. I passed around a photo dated July 13, showing the Nova Kasaba soccer field. Arrows pointed to two dark clumps, which analysts said consisted of approximately six hundred people standing together. I then distributed a photo dated July 27, showing terrain visible in the first picture but a little down the road, with white arrows pointing to three areas where the grass had been upturned and the light-colored dirt beneath exposed. Tracks could be seen.

A second refugee, a teenage boy, told how he had been among four hundred males from Srebrenica forced onto trucks and taken to a school near Bratunac. Once assembled, small groups were taken outside. Those inside heard shots. When the boy's turn came, he was transported by truck to a nearby field littered with corpses. Although wounded, he was also able to feign death and then escape.

As the photographs circulated, the council room—scene of so many noisy debates—grew still. I could hear fingers brushing the stiff photographs as they passed from hand to hand. American intelligence imagery is ordinarily highly classified, and it takes an expert to decipher what is being depicted. But the basic message conveyed by these pictures was clear. The refugees were telling the truth.[5]

That afternoon the council reassembled in formal session to demand that the Pale Serbs grant immediate access to Srebrenica and the sur-

---

5. Not long after, I visited another site of the massacre, almost stepping on a bone sticking out of the ground. In a hedgerow I saw bloody clothes. I asked a local Serb farmer for an explanation and he said dismissively, "They're left over from World War II." The killings there had taken place near a heavily traveled road, with a row of houses close by. According to the residents, no one had heard the screams of the people being executed. More likely, they did hear and did nothing.

rounding towns to the Red Cross. As with most council demands, the Bosnian Serb response was accusatory, belligerent, obstructive, and slow.

THREE FACTORS ENDED the Bosnian war. The first was overreaching on the part of the Bosnian Serbs. For years they had bet successfully on the fecklessness of the West, but they didn't know when to fold their hands. The second was the changing military situation. In early August, Croatia launched an offensive to reclaim territory seized by ethnic Serbs. The offensive quickly succeeded, sending a message to the Bosnian Serbs that they weren't invincible and could not, in a crisis, count on help from Milošević. The third factor was Bill Clinton's willingness to lead.

After Srebrenica, the President's frustration had boiled over, and Tony Lake had asked for endgame papers focusing on the kind of post-conflict Bosnia we wanted to see. The papers were discussed at a key meeting in the White House Cabinet Room the same week as my presentation at the Security Council on Srebrenica. As we had been from the beginning, the President's advisors were divided.

I argued that U.S. troops were going to be in Bosnia sooner or later, so it made sense to send them on our terms and timetable. Europe had failed to resolve the crisis and, in the process, had diminished both NATO and the UN. Our reluctance to take charge had weakened our own claim to leadership. The Bosnian Serbs must be forced to agree on reasonable terms or face a rollback of their military gains. If a negotiated settlement were not forthcoming, we should urge withdrawal of the UN mission and train and equip the Bosnian military behind a shield of NATO airpower.

Recommending a similar approach, Tony proposed sending a high-level team to Europe to gain allied backing for the new hard line. Neither the State Department nor the Defense Department suggested doing anything different from what we had been doing, with the Pentagon recommending a "realistic" approach under which we would accept the reality of Serb military power and seek a permanent cease-fire based on the status quo.

Lake summed up: "Madeleine feels the stakes are so high, they affect the administration's leadership at home and abroad, and that we have no choice but to accept a considerable risk. The biggest fear of State and Defense is that we will become entangled in a quagmire. They favor a more limited approach."

While Tony spoke, I couldn't help looking at the President. Bill Clinton was a very good listener. His habit was to sit doodling or writing notes with his other fist clenched against his face or when he had a headache, with a cold can of Diet Coke pressed against his temple. At times I thought he was disengaged, only to realize later that he hadn't missed a thing. During my years as UN ambassador, I felt I got more respect from the President than I did from most members of the foreign policy team. Where others were sometimes dismissive, he was uniformly attentive and heard me out. I have always found it easier to deal with people who have self-confidence, which Bill Clinton certainly did.

I now waited tensely as Tony completed his summation and we all turned to the President to see his reaction. For me, it was a moment of truth. I had presented my best arguments on the issue that mattered to me most. The President normally began his response to a presentation with a series of questions. This time it was obvious from the moment he started to speak that he had his mind made up. "I agree with Tony and Madeleine," he said. "We should bust our ass to get a settlement within the next few months. We must commit to a unified Bosnia. And if we can't get that at the bargaining table, we have to help the Bosnians on the battlefield."

During the next days, Lake headed for Europe to explain the plan to our allies and Russia. Another team, led by Dick Holbrooke, traveled to the Balkans to begin shuttle-style negotiations among the parties. The European response was favorable, and I felt encouraged, but talks in the region had barely begun when, on August 19, three members of Holbrooke's negotiating team were killed in Bosnia in an accident on a treacherous mountain road. The dead were Ambassador Robert Frasure, Lieutenant Colonel Nelson Drew of the National Security Council, and Joseph Kruzel of the Department of Defense. I admired them all but knew Bob Frasure best. I was relieved that Holbrooke and my former liaison with the Joint Chiefs, General Wesley Clark, who were both in the ill-fated convoy, were safe. I will not forget the sadness of their homecoming, accompanying the bodies of our colleagues.

Our negotiators did not return to Europe until August 28. The Bosnian Serbs chose that moment to overreach again. At 11:10 A.M. on a sunny Monday morning, five mortar shells came flying out of the hills around Sarajevo to land in the bustling Markale market, killing thirty-seven and wounding eighty-five. I conferred with UN Under Secretary General for Peacekeeping Kofi Annan, who agreed that the joint UN-NATO understanding drafted after the Srebrenica massacre should be applied. On August 30, more than sixty aircraft, flying from bases in Italy and the aircraft carrier USS *Theodore Roosevelt* in the Adriatic, pounded Bosnian Serb positions around Sarajevo. French and British artillery joined in. At the time it was the largest NATO military action ever.

The psychological balance had changed. The Bosnian Serbs could no longer act with impunity, while NATO was no longer barred from using its power. American diplomatic leadership was fully engaged. Belgrade was desperate for sanctions relief, while Milošević received explicit authority to negotiate on behalf of the Pale Serbs.

On September 8, the foreign ministers of Bosnia, Croatia, and Yugoslavia agreed that Bosnia would continue as a single state, but with Bosniak-Croat and Serb entities sharing territory on roughly a 51–49 percent basis. By the end of the month our negotiating team had gained an agreement on general principles, including the recognition of Bosnia and Herzegovina as a sovereign and democratic state.

On October 5, the parties agreed to a countrywide cease-fire. At the start of November, they were scheduled to arrive in Dayton, Ohio, for talks that would lead to a final settlement. As the countdown entered its final days, Milošević demanded that sanctions against Belgrade be suspended as soon as negotiations began, and lifted entirely when an agreement was signed. Our position had always been to suspend sanctions only when agreement was reached and lift them only after implementation.

Holbrooke warned that Milošević might refuse to show if he didn't get his way and argued strongly that we give in. At a Principals Committee meeting on October 27, I argued that sanctions relief was too valuable a tool to fritter away: we would need all our leverage to get Milošević to meet his commitments. I knew this was the President's position too, because weeks earlier, during a special session of the General Assembly, I had found him alone and talked with him about it. I said there were proposals circulating at the UN to lift sanctions prior to an agreement. He was incredulous and said "No way"—or rather something more colorful. We decided to hold firm.

I was in Chicago when I got a call from Holbrooke. He knew I opposed lifting sanctions. While diplomacy may be practiced between diplomats of different countries, the rules are different between diplomats of the same country. We had a most undiplomatic conversation. As Holbrooke predicted, Milošević then threatened not to come. As the rest of us expected, he came anyway.[6]

After three weeks of contentious talks, featuring a tireless negotiating

6. UN sanctions against Yugoslavia (Serbia and Montenegro) were lifted when elections in Bosnia were held a year after the Dayton Accords were signed. The Clinton administration, however, maintained bilateral sanctions as a source of pressure against Milošević to comply with Dayton, cooperate with the war crimes tribunal, and refrain from initiating violence in Kosovo. Milošević never met these standards, and U.S. sanctions were not lifted until he was forced from power by the Serb people in 2000.

effort by Holbrooke and essential deal-closing by Christopher, the Dayton Accords were initialed at Wright-Patterson Air Force Base on November 21, 1995. It was Thanksgiving week. The war in Bosnia was over.

To me, the outcome vindicated several principles. It showed that the limited use of force—even airpower alone—could make a decisive difference. It showed the importance of allied unity and of American leadership. It showed the possibilities of this new era, in that Russian forces would end up side by side with NATO troops in implementing the accords. And it showed the importance of standing up to the likes of Milošević and Mladić.

In 1938, Neville Chamberlain revealed the thinking behind the Munich Agreement, which gave Hitler a green light to take over Czechoslovakia. "How horrible, fantastic, incredible it is," he said, "that we should be digging trenches and trying on gas masks here because of a quarrel in a faraway country between people of whom we know nothing." A year later Chamberlain's own nation was at war, in part because he had done nothing to help that "faraway country" and its little-known people. America and its allies may be proud that, belatedly or not, we did come to the aid of the people of Bosnia—to their benefit, and ours.

ON NEW YEAR'S DAY, 1996, only a few weeks after the Dayton Accords were signed, I came across a story[7] in the *New York Times* that illustrated much of what our efforts had been about. It was an illustration of what I call "the Bosnia idea," the simple premise that every person has value and that neighbor must look upon neighbor not as Serb, Croat, and Muslim, but as one individual to another.

It told of a Bosniak farmer named Fadil Fejzic, who lived in the mostly Muslim town of Goražde during the years it was under siege, and a Serb family, Mr. and Mrs. Drago Sorak, who also lived in Goražde and refused for a long time to leave despite the heightening tensions.

In June 1992, Muslim police had taken the Soraks' eldest son, Zoran, who never returned. Their second son who had fought against the Bosniaks was dead. Not long after, Zoran's widow gave birth to a girl, but food was scarce and the mother unable to nurse. The family gave the child tea, but it was clear the infant would soon die. It happened that Mr. Fejzic owned a brown-and-white cow, which he kept outside of town to avoid Serb snipers.

On the fifth day after the Sorak child's birth, the family heard foot-

---

7. By award-winning journalist Christopher Hedges.

steps on the stairs. A half-liter of milk was handed up to their small apartment by a man they barely knew. On the sixth day the same thing happened, and on the seventh, and so on for 442 consecutive days, until the Soraks left for Serbia. Notwithstanding cold and snow and shortages of food, Mr. Fejzic never missed a day and never accepted anything in return. When the war ended, the *Times* reporter found Fejzic, huddled in a room with other Bosniak refugees, his home destroyed and cow long since dead. Told by his visitor that he had seen Mr. and Mrs. Sorak, Fejzic's eyes brightened. "And the baby?" he asked. "How is she?"

THIRTEEN

The Strength of My Own Voice

M Y ROLE IN THE DEBATE over Bosnia and the success of the policies I had advocated, coupled with Security Council wins on Haiti and other issues, gave me increased confidence. I felt more and more comfortable defending our positions before Congress, drafting council resolutions, and speaking up in the Principals Committee. I had grown accustomed to the job of ambassador and welcomed the chance to represent America in situations where I could bring my own personal experiences and convictions to the table—whether at the UN or in forums around the globe. One such opportunity involved the ultimate personal attribute—gender. My role as chair of the U.S. delegation to the Fourth World Conference on Women enabled me to contribute to an historic event, while forging a friendship with a woman whose place in history continues to grow.

HILLARY CLINTON WAS well known long before her husband was elected President. There was the fuss, while he was governor of Arkansas, about her wanting to keep her maiden name, and stories about how smart she was. She came to Washington with some frequency to speak at civic and political events. I met her at a benefit for one of my favorite organizations, the Children's Defense Fund, on whose board she served and at one point chaired. I introduced myself as a fellow graduate of Wellesley and told her I had been impressed by her speech. She responded warmly and the seeds of friendship were sown.

I saw her a few times during the 1992 campaign and again at a retreat for the cabinet held at Camp David after the inauguration. This was a bizarre event, with barely acquainted people crowded into cabins and force-fed a dose of New Age relationship building. In the closed atmosphere, the First Lady was pure oxygen. Excited by the promise of what lay ahead, she was on top of all the issues and a persuasive participant in discussions. In the following months I learned how informed she was and how interested in foreign policy.

Americans were fascinated by Hillary Clinton, but also of two minds about her. Many admired her passion, compassion, and intelligence; others disagreed with her outspoken views. Those who didn't like her thought she was cold. Those who did saw her commitment. Like another remarkable First Lady, Eleanor Roosevelt, she was both lionized and vilified. The comparison deepened late in the President's first term when Hillary joked about having conversations with her long-dead predecessor.

The relationship I had with the First Lady evolved gradually. Because she often had reason to visit New York, my office worked with hers to arrange meetings where I could brief her on UN issues. I invited her to meet officially with some of the foreign delegates, whom she invariably impressed. One year I lent my apartment to her, her mother, and Chelsea in New York around the Christmas holiday; another time she came and spent the night and we chatted in our nightgowns. When the President hosted a foreign leader at the White House, the visiting head of state sat next to the First Lady; Hillary often put me on the guest of honor's other side, figuring that with my UN portfolio there would be no problem finding topics to discuss. Our collaboration blossomed in the summer and fall of 1995, as we prepared for the Fourth World Conference on Women, to be held in Beijing, China.

The status of women was obviously something I cared about. When I had first arrived in New York, I wanted to develop a network with the other women permanent representatives. There were more than 180 countries in the UN at the time, so I assumed there would be a couple of dozen women I could invite to an organizing lunch. I was wrong. When I entered my apartment for the meal, there was only one table set up and just six other countries represented: Canada, Jamaica, Kazakhstan, Liechtenstein, Philippines, and Trinidad-Tobago.

Being American, I naturally proposed we form a caucus, which we did, and suggested that we pledge always to take each other's phone calls. The agreement on instant access upset some male representatives, who didn't think it logical that the ambassador of Liechtenstein could get through to the U.S. ambassador more readily than they could. I told them the solution was for them to give up their posts to women, which stopped them cold. Our group—which we dubbed the G-7—met once a month. We shared stories and talked about how the UN was probably the only building in New York where there was no line in the ladies' room, but we also developed important projects. When the international war crimes tribunal was created, we pushed for the selection of women justices because many of the victims had been women. We succeeded in gaining the appointment of two women judges, including the outstanding American jurist Gabrielle Kirk McDonald, who later became president of the court.[1] We visited the Secretary General and urged that more women be appointed to high-level positions within the organization. We also prepared our respective countries for the Beijing Conference. In the United States, this was no simple task.

To the administration's opponents in Congress during those politicized days, the Women's Conference was a juicy target. It was, after all, sponsored by Boutros Boutros-Ghali's UN, dedicated to women's rights, to be held in China, and with the First Lady possibly in attendance. This led to a lot of hyper-ventilating. Conservative activists argued that U.S. participation would constitute an endorsement of China's human rights policies. Columnists suggested that the U.S. delegation was intent on redefining motherhood, fatherhood, family, and gender. Talk show hosts claimed that the First Lady sought absolute statistical parity between men and women in every workplace in every field of endeavor. A rumor even spread that I was plotting to gain legal recognition for five sexes, to which I replied that I had always lost count after two.

China had been chosen to host the event before President Clinton even took office. The leaders in Beijing must have been interested in the prestige, because they clearly underestimated the headaches. They didn't realize, until they began planning, that freedom is practiced at such gatherings. Nongovernmental organizations (NGOs) show up in the thousands, each with its own issues and style. Their representatives mix freely with official delegates, often influencing the outcome of negotiations and sometimes driving the entire agenda. Inevitably, there are efforts to attract attention through demonstrations, marches, and provocative placards. Independent newspapers spring up like grasshoppers.

As is typical at a UN conference, an NGO Forum in Beijing was slated to accompany the official women's gathering. More than forty thousand NGO representatives were expected. However, a few months

---

1. The second was Elizabeth Odio Benito of Costa Rica. In November 1999, Justice McDonald was succeeded by another fine U.S. justice, Patricia Wald. The tribunal's second chief prosecutor was also a woman, the tenacious Louise Arbour of Canada, who was succeeded by the equally tough Carla del Ponte of Switzerland.

before the event, China declared the stadium designated for the NGO Forum "structurally unsafe" and announced that the event would have to be held in Huairou, a city an hour's drive from Beijing. NGOs were furious, in part because the "structurally unsafe" stadium continued to be used for sporting events, and also because Huairou lacked adequate facilities. Months of negotiations resulted in some concessions by the Chinese, but the basic battle lines were drawn. The NGOs intended to act like NGOs. The Chinese intended to prevent "embarrassing incidents." They even equipped cab drivers with sheets to throw over the naked females they expected to find streaking through the streets.

Members of Congress from both parties urged the administration to boycott the conference. I countered that it was possible to attend without embracing every policy of the host government. China could only benefit from the presence of forty thousand delegates dedicated to improving the status of women. In making this case, I was helped by my anti-Communist credentials, which carried more weight with Congress than my feminist ones.

The controversy created a dilemma for the First Lady. She wanted to go to Beijing, but White House advisors questioned whether it was worth the political risk. The spotlight would be intense, and if she said or did the wrong thing, the President's political opponents would pounce. For weeks pundits played a game of "Will she, won't she?" The situation was complicated by China's detention of Harry Wu, a Chinese-American activist who was laboring heroically on behalf of human rights. In the end, the First Lady's determination coupled with Wu's release settled the matter. She would go.

Meanwhile I had my own dilemma. My daughter Katie was getting married to a law school classmate, Jake Schatz, but none of us had thought, in setting the date, to check the international calendar. The wedding was scheduled two days before the women's conference was to begin half the world away. I had to figure something out. Normal flight changes and time zones conspired against me. As soon as the dancing was over—at midnight—I rushed home and grabbed a couple of hours of sleep before packing and catching an early morning flight for Hawaii. I missed the "day after" wedding gossip and festivities, including a party at the farm, but reduced the travel time by hitching a ride from Honolulu to Beijing with the First Lady. Hillary and I used the time aloft to coordinate our speeches and sleep.

We arrived about four in the morning. It was pouring rain, which would continue almost throughout the conference. Each day platoons of young Chinese women were deployed at hotel entrances, handing out plastic bags to enclose dripping umbrellas. Among the prettiest sights in Beijing were the ubiquitous bicyclists, wearing ponchos of yellow, purple, light green, navy blue, and red, a whole rainbow set against the splashy streets and gray sky, creating the fleeting feeling of an impressionist painting. Indulging my artistic side, I bought a dozen ponchos in different colors for my family. The effect on rural Virginia roads was obviously not the same, but they have kept us dry in the rain at less than a dollar apiece.

We stayed at the China World Hotel, whose lobby became a stage for a swirling spectacle of saris, scarves, robes, burkhas, and dresses, along with more conventional business attire. As women strode busily about, Chinese men loitered in the corners, whispering into tiny microphones concealed in their cuffs. In the evening a trio from Thailand crooned such traditional oriental ballads as "Moon River" and "New York, New York."

The first day after our arrival featured Hillary's speech. Having done my fair share of public speaking, I know how hard it is to excite a crowd. It is especially difficult at a conference showcasing a long procession of accomplished orators. I didn't think it possible to arouse the audience in Beijing, which was made up of people from every culture listening to translators mangle the First Lady's grammar in a monotone.

But Hillary's speech was a stunner. It was beautifully written and forcefully delivered; it expressed strong support for family values, rapped China for its failure to allow freedom of expression, and highlighted the sentence that would become the hallmark of the whole conference—"Human rights are women's rights, and women's rights are human rights." As the First Lady spoke, the multilingual chatter in the hall quieted. When she finished, the applause came in waves. At the press conference later, I noted that our most persistent media gadfly, George Archibald of the *Washington Times*, had described the First Lady's speech as "an out of the ball park home run." No wonder the Chinese excluded it from their coverage.

The next day, I gave my speech outlining the commitments the United States would make to improve women's lives in America and the world. Although much was made of our being in China, the message conveyed in both the First Lady's speech and mine would have been the same wherever the conference was held. That message was simple and universal: violence against women must stop; girls should be valued equally with boys; and women should have full access to education, health care, and the levers of economic and political power.

Throughout the week, delegates and participants felt the presence of Chinese security in ways that were generally oppressive but occasionally amusing. For example, one member of the U.S. delegation had trouble with the picture on her TV. She fiddled with the dials until the image cleared; and what she saw then, plain as day, was herself attempting to adjust her TV. Another delegate tried to iron a dress—against hotel rules. No sooner had she begun than hotel staff burst in and scooped up her clothes, leaving her there in her slip. Hours later they returned with her clothing, freshly pressed and neatly folded. At the NGO Forum, there were demonstrations on behalf of women's rights in virtually every part of the world, from Afghanistan to the United States. Watching one group march past with its signs held high, a puzzled Chinese official asked a nearby American, "Please, can you tell me? Where is this place called Lesbia?"

Early on I received a phone call from Marie Wilson of the Ms. Foundation. Her group had enabled hundreds of women with disabilities to attend the NGO Forum. Only now she had a problem. Incredibly, the Chinese organizers had scheduled a workshop for the disabled on the third floor of a building with no elevator, then had become upset when the women started chanting for access. They had also placed the disabilities tent far from the road. Since it was impossible to maneuver wheelchairs through the mud, many of the delegates had to be carried to the site. Their trip was turning into a disaster.

At Marie's request I agreed to make my speech to NGOs at the Women with Disabilities Tent. When we arrived, I saw firsthand how hard it must have been for those women who had difficulty getting around. We trekked up and down hills, through gates, along a narrow path, and into a field. In my remarks I faulted the organizers for their failure to ensure full access for persons with disabilities. Then I said that, despite recent gains, women around the world remained an undervalued and underdeveloped human resource. This was not to say that women had trouble finding work. In many societies, they did the vast majority of work, but they didn't own land, weren't taught to read, couldn't obtain credit, and didn't get paid. This mattered, I said, because when women had the power to make economic and social choices, the chains of poverty could be broken, families strengthened, the spread of sexually transmitted disease slowed, and socially constructive values more readily passed on to the young.

After visiting the women, we headed back to Beijing via a side trip to the Great Wall of China. No one has ever topped President Nixon's initial reaction ("This is a great wall"). I had seen the wall before, during the Carter administration, and was amazed this time by the thousands of vendors lined up in front of the entrance selling identical tee shirts, towels, and knickknacks. Each was willing to barter, but all had exactly the same bottom line for every item. This was free enterprise at its most competitive, only without the freedom.

The First Lady's speech was the high point of the conference, but outside the spotlight much hard work was done, including adoption of a Platform for Action to improve women's lives on every continent. In the years since, I have met many women from many places who tell me they were at Beijing, or had friends who were, or who were inspired by the conference to launch initiatives. In each case, they are strengthened by the knowledge that, in Beijing, their government promised before the world to respect the rights of women and girls.

EVERYONE HAS HEROES. Some of mine, such as Eleanor Roosevelt and Mahatma Gandhi, I never met. Some, such as my father and Ed Muskie, have passed away. But one—Aung San Suu Kyi—is very much alive, leading the democratic forces of the Southeast Asian nation of Burma. Burma is both breathtakingly scenic and—under the current leadership—desperately poor, a country still powered primarily by oxen.

George Orwell wrote an early book, *Burmese Days*, but Burma reminded me of another Orwell novel—*1984*. The military junta that ran the nation had co-opted or crushed every free institution, engaged in forced labor practices, stifled political opposition, and closed universities. Aung San Suu Kyi headed the National League for Democracy, whose candidates attracted more than 80 percent of the vote in Burma's 1990 parliamentary elections. The junta had pledged to respect the balloting but lied. Many legislators were arrested for the "crime" of having been elected. Others were forced into exile. Refusing to acquiesce in this repression, Aung San Suu Kyi was placed under house arrest for more than five years. In 1991, she was awarded the Nobel Prize for Peace.

I had never met Aung San Suu Kyi but was acquainted with her husband, Michael Aris, who was British. In 1992, Aris asked if I could arrange for Václav Havel to draft a short introduction to a volume of his wife's writings. I called Havel, who was pleased to help. So I felt a link.

Stopping in Rangoon on the way home from Beijing, I became the first cabinet-level official to visit Burma since the political upheaval began, and the first from any country to see Aung San Suu Kyi since her release from house arrest. I began by meeting the leading member of the junta, known then as the SLORC (State Law and Order Restoration Council). General Khin Nyunt assured me that the military was saving Burma by imposing peace upon an ethnically diverse population. He insisted that the government was not only respected by the people but also loved. "After all," he said, "our people have happy faces."

Anxious to rebut this double-talk, I replied that I had spent a lifetime studying repressive regimes and knew that dictators often deluded themselves. People sometimes smile not out of happiness but out of fear. I urged the general to open a dialogue with Aung San Suu Kyi about how to return the country to democratic rule. He replied, patronizingly, that the junta saw Aung San Suu Kyi as a younger sister they needed to protect. As for movement toward democracy, he would only say, "These things take time."

The next morning Aung San Suu Kyi welcomed me to her house, set in the middle of a garden surrounded by a high fence. She stood under the little portico wearing traditional Burmese clothes in shades of purple and lavender, a flower in her hair. As we embraced, she told me that she had been so excited by my visit, she had personally washed the walls and washed and ironed the curtains. She led me inside where, on the wall, there hung a huge portrait of Aung San Suu Kyi's father, General Aung San, founder of an independent Burma, assassinated by political rivals in 1947.

During our discussion, Aung San Suu Kyi told me she had met her husband while studying in England and had returned to Burma in 1988 for what she thought would be only a brief time caring for her dying mother. Instead she found herself involved in a nascent democratic movement that soon became the country's most popular political force. She was now fifty years old but seemed ageless: her suffering could only be seen in her eyes. I marveled at her discipline in coping with house arrest, saying that I couldn't imagine being locked up in my own house month after month. She told me that she had derived strength from reading and meditation and from the occasional visits of colleagues and her sons that had been allowed.

Asking me to call her Suu, she emphasized that the world community had not pushed for her release just so she could have guests for breakfast, as pleasant as that might be. She intended to press relentlessly for democracy.

As we talked, I was struck by the contrast between her ethereal beauty and steely resolve. Abroad, she could be leading an easy life. Silent, she could have a secure one. Instead she had chosen the hard road of principled and nonviolent opposition to an unprincipled and brutal regime. After breakfast we stood together on the steps of her house, held up a poster from the Beijing conference, said a few words to the press, and— behind our backs—clasped hands.

Before departing Rangoon, I held a press conference during which I didn't bother with diplomatic niceties. I said Burmese leaders could begin to move down the democratic path, and thereby reduce their isolation, or continue on the path of repression and ultimately ruin both themselves and their country. As I spoke, some of my fellow U.S. diplomats looked pained. Our chargé, the highest ranking member of our embassy, thought my statement too strong and she told me frankly, "Now we will have to clean up the mess you have left." I was unapologetic, and my executive assistant

Stuart Jones pointed out that she had cleared the statement herself. The difference, I think, was not in my words but in the force with which I had delivered them. I was beginning to discover the strength of my own voice.

In the years since, I have found ways to let Suu know she is never far from my thoughts. In 1999, Michael Aris was stricken with cancer. We appealed to the Burmese authorities to let him visit his wife before his death. The request was denied. Aung San Suu Kyi still doesn't dare leave her country, because she knows she wouldn't be allowed to return. She relies on videos to carry her message to the world. I have seen many of them over the years and always study them for clues. As time has passed, it is evident that the stress is taking its toll as the pressure on her continues to increase, but her voice and message are as strong as ever.

It is unusual to think someone you have met in person only once is a real friend. I know she is mine and have reason to trust that she feels the same way.

A FEW MINUTES before 3 P.M. on February 24, 1996, a pilot informed Cuba's control center of his intention to continue flying an unarmed U.S. civilian aircraft, accompanied by two others, south of the twenty-fourth parallel, about halfway between Florida and Cuba. The control center warned the pilot not to do so because the area below the parallel was "active and dangerous." The pilot, José Basulto, retorted proudly, "We know we're in danger each time we cross the area to the south of the twenty-fourth, but we're willing to do it as free Cubans." The three aircraft maintained their course.

At about 3:10, the U.S. Customs radar detected two Cuban MiG fighters airborne north of Havana. Ten minutes later, one of the MiG pilots reported to Havana Ground Control (GRC): "Okay, the target is in sight. It's a small aircraft... white and blue." After a few seconds he added, "We have it on lock-on. Give us authorization... it is a Cessna 337."

> GRC: Authorized to destroy.
> MiG 29: I'm going to fire at it.
> GRC: Authorized.
> MiG 29. First launch. We hit him! Cojones! We hit him! Cojones! We busted his cojones!
> MiG 23: This one won't mess around anymore.
> GRC : Congratulations.

A few minutes passed.

> MiG 29: I have another aircraft in sight.

GRC: You are authorized to destroy it.

MiG 29: The other is destroyed! The other is destroyed! Fatherland or
death! The other is down also!

Thousands of feet below, in international waters, the passengers of a
Norwegian cruise ship and the crew of a U.S. fishing boat bore shocked
witness to the killings in the sky.

It was a Saturday; I was in New York when the State Department
operations center reached me. I was told two American planes belonging
to a Miami-based Cuban exile group had been shot down by Castro's
armed forces. Four men, including three U.S. citizens and a legal resident, were dead.[2] A third plane had returned safely.

The next morning's newspapers told a fuller story. On board the
doomed Cessnas had been four members of Brothers to the Rescue.
Founded in 1991, the Brothers flew light aircraft between the U.S. and
Cuba in search of Cuban rafters fleeing the island. It was a humanitarian
group with a political agenda. At least twice prior to February 1996, its
pilots had flown over Havana to drop anti-Castro leaflets. José Basulto,
the group's leader and pilot of the plane that returned, was being investigated by the FAA in connection with an illegal overflight of Cuban territory the previous July. Notwithstanding this history, the State Department
said the shoot-downs had occurred in international airspace. Officials in
Havana disagreed. The world was waiting to see how we would respond.

Even before finishing the papers, I was on the phone to Washington. It
was my turn to be president of the Security Council and I decided to call an
emergency session. We needed to establish the truth before Castro could
cloud the facts. Quickly we arranged for technical experts to fly to New
York and brief the council on exactly where, when, and how the shoot-
downs had occurred. The preliminary evidence from radar, witnesses, and
wreckage buttressed the U.S. position. I provided my colleagues with a
timeline of events and circulated a draft presidential statement condemning the killings and calling for an investigation by the International Civil
Aviation Organization (ICAO).

During our informal session the next day, the Chinese ambassador
suggested we wait until the Cuban foreign minister arrived to present his
government's side of the case. I said no. The foreign minister had been in
Europe when the killings occurred and later flew to Mexico City. It was
his fault he wasn't there. The Chinese diplomat then said he couldn't

2. The victims were Pablo Morales, Carlos Costa, Mario de la Peña, and Armando
Alejandre Jr.

agree to the statement—which had to be cleared by everyone—because he hadn't received instructions from Beijing.

The Chinese and their instructions were a perennial frustration. It is true they had to cope with a twelve-hour time difference, and that given their system, their UN delegation was tightly controlled, but sometimes they just wanted to delay. I said we would take a recess and return at 11 P.M., allowing plenty of time for instructions to arrive. When we returned, the Chinese ambassador said he still had not received word, evidently hoping other ambassadors, irritated and tired, would support a postponement. I wasn't about to allow that. Instead I said, "Perhaps we should turn this statement into a resolution and have an official vote." Miraculously and instantaneously, the Chinese instructions materialized, agreeing to the presidential statement. The Chinese asked only that I permit Cuba's UN ambassador to make a statement of his own. I had no trouble with that. Feeling I had kept my colleagues up too long, I was also willing to forgo my statement as the American representative and only read out the presidential statement of condemnation.

It was 3:30 A.M. by the time the Cuban had finished a wildly anti-American diatribe. I heard myself denounced as a scheming imperialist liar but couldn't respond because I had given up my right to speak in my national capacity. In the end UN protocol gave me an opportunity to strike back, albeit with honey, not vinegar. The first time a council president is addressed with words of congratulations by another ambassador, a script prepared by UN staff directs the appropriate response. When my accuser finished, the room grew silent. I looked down at the scripted reply and said, "I thank the Cuban representative for his statement, and for his kind words addressed to me." Council members who were not asleep laughed at this bizarre bit of theater, and we all headed home to bed.

The presidential statement mattered because it put the council on record as saying that the Cuban action had been a crime. The blatancy of that crime became more vivid the following day. From Washington we received Customs Service radar charts showing that the two planes had been shot down well north of the Cuban territorial limit. We also received transcripts of the conversations between the two MiG pilots and Havana Ground Control before and after the shoot-downs. As I reviewed the transcripts, my anger grew. The MiG pilots clearly knew they were destroying civilian planes, yet they had made no effort to warn the Brothers by establishing voice contact, dipping their wings, or trying to escort them in a different direction. They had simply—and sadistically—shot the aircraft out of the sky.

I didn't think it took much testosterone to shoot down unarmed aircraft

"MADELEINE ALBRIGHT KICKED BUTT IN THAT SUIT."

with missiles. I said to Jamie Rubin, "I don't think they have *cojones*; I think they're cowards." After running the language past Elaine Shocas, my arbiter of "over the top," I delivered a statement that would never in a thousand years have been cleared by the State Department if submitted in advance. After outlining the facts, I referred to the recorded conversations and said, "I was struck by the joy of these pilots in committing cold-blooded murder. Frankly, this is not *cojones*. This is cowardice."

In the pressroom, jaws dropped. CNN had broadcast the press conference, but reporter Richard Roth's summary lost something in translation: "Ambassador Albright said, noting the use of a common vulgarity, that 'this is not that vulgarity, this is cowardice.'"

My lack of diplomacy ran into a hornet's nest of criticism from experts on Latin America, including my friend Diego Arria, the permanent representative from Venezuela. Arria told the press, "I wouldn't say that word, not even on my farm." Later Arria relented, perhaps with a nudge from his wife. By contrast, my comment generated broad support from U.S. citizens, including the Miami exile community. As a result I was asked to represent the administration at a memorial service in Miami to be held for the deceased Brothers. White House officials advised me to dress conservatively and maintain a somber mien. "This is a community in mourning," I was told.

I suspected that it was not to be a routine event when we became snarled in traffic on the way in from the Miami airport. We had seen many Cuban and American flags sticking out of car windows and were told that the Orange Bowl was already packed. As I sat looking at people in the other cars, I noticed they were looking back. Then they were getting out of their cars, coming over, smiling, waving, and banging their hands on the hood, yelling, "Señora Cojones!" "Madam Cojones!"

Eventually we reached the Orange Bowl and went into the stadium offices to meet the families of the victims. They were desolate, saying that the Brothers were only trying to help their fellow Cubans. My security team wanted to drive me into the stadium, but the father of one of the victims asked if I would walk with him. I readily agreed. I took the dignified gentleman's arm and stepped through the tunnel ordinarily used by the Miami Dolphins and out onto the field.

We were met by a wall of sound. I strained at first to hear what the crowd was chanting. Then I got it. "Libertad, Madeleine," "Libertad, Madeleine," over and over again. The program began and I listened to the testimonies and tributes of those who had loved the men who had died. I approached the microphones. My goals were twofold. I wanted to assure the audience that we wouldn't allow Castro to escape responsibility, but I also wanted to put a damper on any actions that might provoke further violence.

Never having spoken in a stadium, I wasn't prepared for the echo. The words that left my lips came back to me several seconds later. This made me slow down, which only meant the words took longer bouncing back. Jamie Rubin, standing just below the platform, kept signaling me to speak faster. I did my best to deliver what I thought was an important message. Somehow I must have been heard, because practically every sentence was greeted by applause and foot stomping, including my conclusion: "The mistake tyrants make is to confuse the power to control armies with the power to sway the human soul. Castro couldn't sway the souls of the four brave men we honor today. He cannot still the trend towards democracy that is building across the globe. [And] he cannot stand against the power of love and the love of freedom that exist in this stadium right now."

In subsequent weeks the war of words between Cuba and the United States continued. The Cubans accused the Brothers of being terrorists. They conjured up memories of the 1961 Bay of Pigs invasion and talked about thirty-seven years of Yankee aggression. They continued to cite "facts"—already discredited—about where and when the tragedies had taken place. To this day, Cuban officials have never expressed regret about the loss of life or acknowledged making a mistake or violating the law.

In July, the ICAO completed its investigation, endorsing the U.S. position. Undeterred by the tragedy, Brothers to the Rescue continued to fly for the next seven years. Meanwhile the *"cojones"* quote developed a life of its own. In Miami it appeared on bumper stickers. Tony Lake said that every time he heard a reference to it, he wanted to cross his legs. President Clinton observed publicly that it was "probably the most effective one-liner in the whole administration's foreign policy."

As MY SENSE of surefootedness at the UN grew, so did my willingness to take the initiative. In 1996, I did just that in trying to prevent the election of Boutros Boutros-Ghali to a second five-year term as Secretary General. Month by month, our differences with the Secretary General had grown. In Somalia Boutros-Ghali had been the first to embrace and the last to relinquish the unsuccessful strategy of confrontation with Aidid. In Rwanda he had been disengaged during the period leading up to the genocide, a neglect he never acknowledged. In Bosnia his insistence on the dual key system and his dismissal of the conflict as "a rich man's war" were indefensible. He was also hyper status-conscious and seemed to believe that administrative tasks were beneath him.[3] As time passed, he became more and more critical of America, which may have earned points for him elsewhere but made it even harder for me to garner support for the UN on Capitol Hill.

This mattered, because with Republicans in full control of Congress, every UN issue was a struggle and the Secretary General himself had become radioactive. He insisted he could convert legislators by talking to them directly but made matters worse every time he tried. His imperial manner didn't go over well, and our more partisan opponents had no desire to listen because they enjoyed bashing the UN too much. Republican presidential candidate Bob Dole's most reliable applause lines made fun of the UN leader, whose name he pronounced slowly and disdainfully.

I regretted all this because, on a personal level, I admired both the Secretary General and his wife, Leia—a strong personality who once walked into a room full of high-level officials and quipped, "Oh! A harem of men." Boutros-Ghali and I often had lively dinner discussions, including one in 1995 when he told me a story about a Nigerian seer who had

3. Before I even arrived in New York, my immediate predecessor at the UN, Ambassador Edward Perkins, described the Egyptian diplomat in a memo as "vain, petulant and impulsive," with "work habits and demeanor that have driven morale within the Secretariat to an all-time low."

come to visit and said, "I see a woman, and she will double-cross you. Her name is Madeleine." We both laughed.

When the Secretary General had been elected in 1991, he pledged to serve a single term. Now, like some U.S. politicians who embrace term limits in order to be elected, only to abandon them after, he was preparing to run again, traveling everywhere and doling out job appointments with the care and skill of a ward heeler in New York's old Tammany Hall. His activism meant I had to decide whether to do nothing and allow him to be nominated for another term or to take the drastic step of trying to block him.

I concluded that if UN-U.S. relations were going to improve, the Secretary General would have to go. That meant a fight. We began with one big advantage. If we didn't vote for him, he could not win. A secretary general had to receive the votes of each of the five permanent members of the Security Council. Even so, there were risks. France, also a permanent member, would fight us; we would be accused of being high-handed; and the debts we still owed the UN would be thrown in our face. Boutros-Ghali was unlikely to withdraw voluntarily, and it was always possible that, when the smoke cleared, we would be stuck with someone even worse.

During trips to Washington, I explained my thinking to Christopher and Lake. Both had questions, but they also had even more complaints about the Secretary General than I had. During a flight to Bosnia in January 1996, I raised the issue with the President, who told me he agreed.

Christopher asked me to put my arguments in writing. The resulting memo set out the rationale for forcing a change and discussed possible replacements, including my preferred candidate, Ghana's Kofi Annan—a career UN employee with broad experience in the toughest jobs.[4] Annan had been on the front lines of the struggle to make UN peacekeeping more professional and—unlike his bureaucratic brethren—hadn't tried to duck responsibility for failures. The son of a tribal chief, he seemed born for leadership. Although not a big man physically, he carried himself in a way that commanded respect. He was soft-spoken, with a lilt in his voice and an engaging manner—a welcome change from the austere Boutros-Ghali. It

4. "The rationale for opposing BBG is compelling on substantive, legislative and political grounds. He is not committed to, or capable of achieving, our urgent reform goals. Blocking his second term will significantly improve our chances to obtain funds from Congress, to pay our arrearages and sustain our obligations in the future. Finally, the chances of ensuring a domestic consensus that supports UN actions in the future will be greatly improved if he departs from the scene." Memo from the author to the President, March 1996.

helped that Annan was African because Boutros-Ghali had been elected as an African representative and would argue that our effort to displace him was an affront to the entire continent. Kofi Annan could also speak the language of Molière well enough to avoid immediate disqualification by the French. I cautioned, however, that we shouldn't express a public preference for any candidate until late in the game. We knew people were likely to be mad at us and didn't want them taking their anger out on Annan.

For months we kept our decision secret while Christopher tried to persuade the Secretary General to bow out gracefully and accept a one-year extension, until his seventy-fifth birthday. Boutros-Ghali insisted on at least another half-term—two and a half years. Egypt's President Mubarak tried to bridge our differences but couldn't. Meanwhile the Secretary General continued campaigning.

In mid June, Warren Christopher decided to leak the news of our position to the *New York Times*. Going public made sense for a number of reasons, but we failed to get the diplomatic coordination right. I heard about the decision while journeying by car from San Diego to Los Angeles. I knew I had to reach my Security Council colleagues in New York, who would be furious about not being consulted. My mobile had started to malfunction, so we found a pay phone in front of a dining establishment called Bubba's Hundred Sandwiches. Feeding in the quarters, I spread the word. As I had anticipated, the other ambassadors weren't happy.

Our campaign, having begun poorly, soon stumbled again. We had hoped to persuade the Organization of African Unity (OAU) not to endorse a candidate, but we had waited too long. With France and Egypt pushing, the fifty-three countries of Africa went on record at their annual meeting in support of the man we had vowed to veto.

We intensified our diplomacy, emphasizing our belief that a change in leadership would make the UN more effective. We distributed talking points for use in official meetings. We stressed our desire to find qualified alternatives, especially from Africa. Although few governments were enthusiastic supporters of the Secretary General, even fewer wanted to join us in openly challenging him. Most were cautious, choosing to wait and see. Boutros-Ghali, meanwhile, wasn't giving up. Advisors assured him that our motives were political and our position would change after the November election. Ever stubborn, he refused to consider the various plans we put forward to ease him out in a dignified fashion. At various points I proposed that the Secretary General be appointed to the International Court of Justice, become head of the worldwide Francophone Group (a post he ultimately did assume), or be given a new role as "Secretary General Emeritus," with an office and ceremonial duties. I very much wanted to avoid a personal confrontation, but this wasn't a fight I intended to lose.

In October, Boutros-Ghali and I had another working dinner at his residence. He began by telling me that he had no hard feelings. "I've been in politics a long time," he said, "and know one can be up or down without ever knowing the real reason." He predicted bad things for the UN and said the next secretary general would have a difficult time. I talked again about our desire to arrange a graceful exit, and he asked if I were offering him baksheesh, a bribe. I said obviously not.

After about forty-five minutes, we moved to the dining room. The butler brought out steaming bowls of split pea soup. I took one spoonful and began feeling very hot. As we discussed Iraq and Burundi, I didn't say anything about the temperature because it didn't seem to be bothering the Secretary General. In any case I had long ago decided not to comment on the temperature of a room, given the possibility I was having a hot flash.

Around dessert, the butler brought me a note on a silver tray. It said, in French, "John Whitehead says everything will be okay." I was puzzled. Why was the note in French? Why would Whitehead—a friend who was head of the UN Association and lived a few doors down—write me a note? How did he know I was with Boutros? My host had his own questions. "Is that a note from your staff? Are they afraid I have poisoned you?" At that moment Leia burst into the dining room, exclaiming, "What are you two doing here in this heat, you must be boiling!"

Her husband said, "Thank goodness, I've been sweating, but Madeleine didn't say anything, so I thought I was having a heart attack and didn't want her to know." Then I told them why I hadn't mentioned the heat. We all laughed—amused and embarrassed that after all this time we would be too shy to be honest about something so simple. Right to the end, the Secretary General and I had failed to communicate. Later I ran into Whitehead and asked him about the note. He said he had seen Leia at a cocktail party and she had misinterpreted what he'd said. The note must have been from her to her husband and given to me by the butler by mistake. I wondered what Leia and Boutros said to each other afterwards.

Although we insisted to the world that Boutros-Ghali wouldn't prevail, alternative candidates were reluctant to surface. Meanwhile the public relations battle was not going well. At the UN the embattled Secretary General was playing the role of underdog against a bully who was well behind in paying its dues. The international press was hammering us, and so were critics at home. We were prevented by the logic of our own strategy from defining the choice in more appealing terms, the charismatic Kofi Annan against the aristocratic Boutros-Ghali.

May 1993, in the Oval Office with President Clinton and Secretary of State Warren Christopher. The President's inscription reads, "To Madeleine—Here we are with an 1801 copy of Thomas Jefferson's book—You are a worthy successor to him in diplomacy—and so much younger even on your birthday."

Casting my vote on behalf of the United States. The sign reading "President" indicates it was my turn to chair the UN Security Council. On my right is Secretary General Boutros-Ghali, whom I respected as a diplomat, but whose re-election I felt compelled to oppose.

When I first met Kofi Annan, his hair was black. By the time he was elected the UN's seventh Secretary General, there were—I teased him —streaks of gray. The Secretary General's hair has since become entirely silver, but the warmth and dedication of this Nobel Prize winning public servant have never changed.

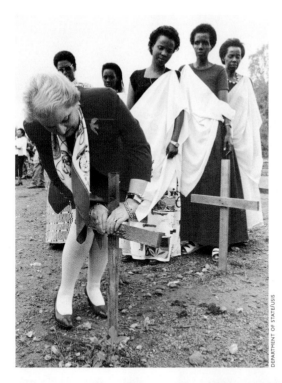

Straightening a cross marking the grave of a victim of genocide in Rwanda. My biggest regret in public life was that we did not do more, sooner, to halt the killing.

In 1996, First Lady Hillary Clinton and I toured the hallowed grounds of the Jewish cemetery outside the Pinkas Synagogue in Prague. A year later I would return to the Synagogue, my mind filled with startling new information about my family's past. Behind me is Jenonne Walker, U.S. ambassador to the Czech Republic.

To Madeleine—who leads fearlessly where others may fear to tread—with great pride and affection from your friend in the "Girls Room"—Hillary 1996

Walking through Wenceslas Square with the First Lady and President Havel, who is pointing to the balcony from which he addressed crowds during the Velvet Revolution. I am pointing to a restaurant that serves my favorite Czech foods.

Pope John Paul II was a hero to me for his role in sparking the pro-democracy movement in Poland. I hoped his visit to Cuba in 1998 would give similar hope to Cuban opponents of Communist rule.

L'OSSERVATORE ROMANO

I took every opportunity to voice my support for policies that would respect the religious and cultural heritage of the people of Tibet. One way of doing that was to ignore China's objections and meet personally with the Dalai Lama.

DEPARTMENT OF STATE

Nelson Mandela brought freedom to his country and new hope to the world. He also achieved the most complete kind of victory over his jailers—not by punishing them, but by forgiving them.

DEPARTMENT OF STATE/USIS

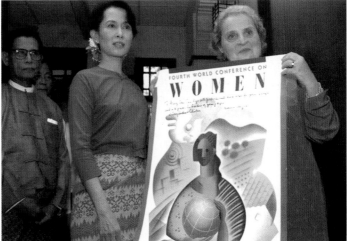

I was pleased to present a signed poster from the Beijing Women's Conference to the leader of Burma's oppressed democratic forces, Aung San Suu Kyi. Beneath Suu's fragile beauty, there exists a determined heart, a fine mind, and a fierce commitment to the rights of her people.

At Hillsboro Elementary School near my farm in Virginia, Professor Albright addresses a somewhat younger than usual class. Whenever I went to a school, I brought a globe and told students it was important to care about people on the other side of the world.

Disembarking in Moscow with my tireless and astute Deputy Secretary of State Strobe Talbott. I often wore my black Stetson, especially on days when I couldn't do anything with my hair.

In Bosnia surrounded by Diplomatic Security and U.S. military. Over my right shoulder, wearing dark glasses, is my invaluable chief of staff, Elaine Shocas.

Walking through the UN accompanied by the thousand-megawatt smile of my deputy chief of staff, Suzy George.

Announcing my designation as the sixty-fourth Secretary of State. The President said later that he had been advised by the First Lady, "Only if you pick Madeleine will you get a person who shares your values, who is an eloquent defender of your foreign policy, and who will make every girl proud."

Introducing my daughters (l to r) Katie, Alice, and Anne prior to my confirmation hearing as Secretary of State. Seated across the aisle from them in the front row (also l to r) are White House official Jeffrey Liss and some of my top advisors: David Scheffer, Bill Woodward, Meg Donovan, Elaine Shocas, Jamie Rubin, and Barbara Larkin. The display board in the back was prepared by the staff of committee Chairman Jesse Helms, reflecting his anti-UN bias.

The brood gathers at Katie's wedding. From l to r: Greg Bowes (holding David), Alice, Katie, Jake Schatz, the proud mother, Anne (pregnant with Jack), Geoff Watson.

My brother, John Korbel, with an ever-protective arm around me.

Kathy Silva, my sister and best friend, who helped me in a thousand different ways.

My group from Wellesley, in the process of aging beautifully: to my right is Susan Dubinsky Terris; to my left Wini Shore Freund and Emily Cohen MacFarquhar.

Soon I began to hear grumbling within our own government about "the mess we had gotten into." One day in New York I had a screaming match with Tony Lake as we sat in the den of my residence at the Waldorf. Tony said he'd never been sure it was the right decision to oppose Boutros-Ghali and that I was on my own. I countered that we had made the right choice, even though a hard one, and we should switch to another business if we weren't prepared to take some criticism. The argument was so heated, Richard Clarke and Michael Sheehan from the NSC and Elaine Shocas from my staff—none of them exactly shrinking violets—left the room to let us exchange unpleasantries in private. Later that night, to calm down, I knitted two red hats shaped like tomatoes for my grandsons David and newly born Jack.

The fall of 1996 was consumed by our campaigns to reelect Bill Clinton and to unelect Boutros-Ghali. To ease the tension surrounding both, I made a bet with my Security Council neighbor, Joseph Legwaila, the permanent representative from Botswana. During the Democratic Convention, Vice-President Gore had joked about doing the macarena, a mildly physical Latin dance. So I bet Legwaila that if the Democrats won the election, I would dance the macarena with him in the Council Chamber. The first chance we had after the Clinton-Gore ticket prevailed, Joe and I did our dance. Since I had been spending a lot of time twisting their arms, I think the ambassadors got a kick out of seeing me try—at least briefly—to twist parts of my own body.

As the showdown neared, my team in New York was going flat out, meeting with other delegations, making phone calls, strategizing, and counting votes. Unfortunately, counting the ballots of those on the Security Council who would be with us did not prove a very challenging test.

On November 19, I vetoed a resolution that would have given the Secretary General a second term. The vote was 14–1 against us. The confrontation we had wanted to avoid was out in the open, and it appeared we were isolated. I wasn't happy, but I saw the seeming defeat as a turning point. Yes, we had taken a punch, but we were still standing—and had shown that the President's reelection hadn't softened our determination to elect a new secretary general. If Boutros-Ghali thought we would flinch at the last minute, he was wrong. Moreover, much of the international support he seemed to have was only ankle deep. Our veto provided diplomatic cover for many countries that had seen merit in our arguments and were now willing to switch openly to a less tired horse.

Ethiopian President Meles Zenawi wrote to Cameroon's President Paul Biya, who was also serving as head of the OAU, urging him to find African alternatives. Biya himself had always been tepid in his backing for the incumbent. His priority was to ensure that the job went to an African. Soon it seemed all New York was involved in informal discussions with various African delegations, trying to identify candidates capable of running a massive organization and who met the particular requirements of the United States (in favor of reform), the French (fluent in their language), and the Chinese (no relations with Taiwan). Finally, on the day after Thanksgiving, Biya issued a letter releasing OAU members from their obligation to support the Secretary General.

With Boutros-Ghali defeated, I was in meetings almost constantly, discouraging support for candidates about whom we had doubts while quietly promoting Kofi Annan. This was helped by the fact that Annan was clearly the most qualified person. No one, from any continent, was more knowledgeable or better prepared. The French held out to the last minute, both to make us sweat and to gain our support for filling Annan's position as head of UN peacekeeping with a Frenchman. Finally, on December 13, the Security Council unanimously nominated Annan as the UN's seventh secretary general.[5]

The administration's judgment in seeking to replace Boutros-Ghali was borne out in subsequent years. In 1998, Congress agreed to pay U.S. arrears, while encouraging additional UN reforms. Although I wouldn't agree with Annan on everything, he proved a popular, creative, and hardworking Secretary General, who in 2001 was unopposed when standing for reelection and subsequently awarded—jointly with the UN—the Nobel Peace Prize.

In his memoir, *Unvanquished*, Boutros-Ghali reveals much of the attitude his colleagues found grating. He admits in five years at the UN's helm to exactly one mistake (allowing Italy to send peacekeepers to Somalia). Everything else that went wrong is blamed on the United States or the West. He gets in plenty of swings at me, which is fine. I haven't seen the Egyptian diplomat, but one day in New York I did run into Leia on the street. I wasn't sure what to do, but she immediately threw her arms around me and said, "Darling, we so miss seeing you." During my years in New York I learned a lot about diplomacy from Secretary General Boutros-Ghali. I think I could have learned even more from his wife.

---

5. Boutros-Ghali had alleged that I had started all this because I was campaigning to be secretary of state. That is untrue. It wasn't until near the end that the two issues got tangled. I knew if I failed in this most important diplomatic battle it would be said, "She can't get things done." Of course, once I was designated, it all became easier. Who was going to oppose the next secretary of state?

PART THREE

Madam Secretary

FOURTEEN

"I Want You to Be My Secretary of State"

"**T**HE BOYS ARE CATATONIC," reported Tom Oliphant. "They never thought it would happen. Half of Washington is in a state of shock." It was the afternoon of December 5, 1996, and I was receiving many messages of congratulations from colleagues and close friends like Tom, a columnist for the *Boston Globe*. The "shock" was caused by President Clinton's decision earlier that day to nominate me for the job of secretary of state.

The events leading up to that moment were shaped by a peculiar Washington tradition. Unlike candidates for election who are expected to vie fiercely for their positions, flaunting their own virtues while deriding their opponents, cabinet hopefuls are assigned the equivalent of a passive role in an old-fashioned courtship. It is considered inappropriate to brag, denigrate others, or openly display your interest. Subtlety is required. Campaigning is simply not done—or at least not admitted.

Through most of my life, I would not have considered heading the Department of State a realistic possibility. During the 1988 Dukakis campaign, the press speculated that I might head the NSC if we won. I could picture myself as a behind-the-scenes policy coordinator, but not in a post as visible as secretary of state. After that election, whenever I was introduced as someone who could have been national security advisor, I responded by using my favorite phrase for truly hypothetical situations by saying, "Yes, and if my mother had wheels, she would have been a bicycle."

However, my years at the UN had given me much on-the-job experience and a hefty dose of public exposure. Late in 1994, when Secretary

Christopher briefly contemplated resignation, his deputy Strobe Talbott told me I might be a logical successor. This planted the idea in my mind in a serious way for the first time. Christopher didn't resign then, but it was widely anticipated that he would step down at the end of the President's first term two years later.

As that date approached, Senator Patrick Leahy of Vermont spent an evening in New York trying to convince me I had a realistic chance of being chosen. Melanne Verveer, the First Lady's deputy chief of staff, assured me my prospects were as good as anybody's. Judith Lichtman and Marcia Greenberger, respected leaders of national women's groups, urged me to "go for it." Television and newspaper reporters advised me confidentially to give it a shot, as did former presidential press secretary and *Newsday* publisher Bill Moyers. I thought it would be the most incredible honor and challenge to help the President find the right way to exercise American influence in a world in flux. So when White House Chief of Staff Leon Panetta surveyed cabinet members about our future plans, I said what I didn't know until that moment I would have the courage to say, "I would love to continue serving at the UN, but I would also be interested in becoming Secretary of State."

On the day of the President's reelection, Christopher confirmed his intention to leave. By then speculation about his replacement was already heated. Predicting the identity of presidential appointees is a pastime all Washington loves. The capital's phone lines and dinner parties come alive with the latest take on who's up and who's down. Each news cycle brings a fresh supply of names, commentary, and gossip. Everyone plays the game, which is both irresistible and largely pointless, since the only players who really count are the Chief Executive and a small circle of advisors.

That November, the buzz about who would be named secretary centered on five names. The front-runner was former Senate Majority Leader George Mitchell, whose success as special envoy to the Northern Ireland peace process had lent foreign policy luster to his formidable political credentials. I received what I considered a reality check when some of my best friends told me directly what a great secretary Mitchell would be. More importantly, Tony Lake and perhaps Christopher as well were among those backing Mitchell's nomination.

Richard Holbrooke was thought to be Mitchell's chief rival. He had been assistant secretary of state for East Asian affairs during the Carter administration and had feuded with the NSC and my boss, Zbig Brzezinski, over China policy. During the 1988 presidential campaign, while I was advising Dukakis, Holbrooke advised Al Gore. I had always respected his brains, so clearly evident during the Dayton negotiations, and tried on numerous occasions to forge a good relationship. He could be extremely charming when he wanted to be and, from Bosnia onwards, we were usually allies on policy questions. I found that he was a good person to have on your side in a fight. We didn't, however, tend to go about things the same way. Holbrooke was known for being very aggressive, a quality that sometimes got in the way of both effective diplomacy and personal relationships.

Two other contenders were Senator Sam Nunn of Georgia and Ambassador Tom Pickering. Nunn was widely respected for his integrity and knowledge of defense policy but wasn't personally close to President Clinton and had opposed him on key issues. Pickering was rightly regarded as one of America's best professional diplomats but was at a disadvantage because he lacked political connections. Only one career Foreign Service officer (Larry Eagleburger) had ever been named secretary of state, and that was to complete James Baker's term. It was not fair, but Pickering's chances were contingent on the more strongly backed candidates being eliminated.

The final name on most lists was mine, usually preceded by the words "another possibility" or "an outside chance." Although I was happy to be mentioned, I had no real way to gauge my prospects. I knew the President agreed with me on core issues and had confidence in my ability to deliver our foreign policy message either diplomatically or bluntly. I felt he viewed me as a good team player, but I didn't know whether he would even think about me for the top cabinet job. I was encouraged when *New York Times* reporter Elaine Sciolino asked the White House if I was under consideration and spokesman Mike McCurry conveyed a positive response, reportedly from the President himself.

Some of the Democratic Party's most influential "wise men" advised me early on not to "campaign" for the job. I thought, *hmmm*. Obviously I wasn't going to manufacture campaign buttons, but I doubted that George Mitchell and Dick Holbrooke were sitting demurely at home waiting for the phone to ring. I was sure they would do everything they could to activate the network of supporters and friends each had developed.

For men in official Washington, reliance on such networks is second nature. Ties are forged as early as prep school or college, or later in entry-level positions in law firms or on Capitol Hill. As careers progress, these networks broaden. Friendships are cultivated over drinks, cigars, steaks, Redskins games, and rounds of golf. Favors are exchanged for friends and relatives. Problems are solved and deals arranged through quiet phone calls and conversations, with outsiders none the wiser.

Washington women also have networks, but until recently these networks were primarily social or philanthropic. Men focused on power. Women focused on everything except power. In the 1960s this began— very slowly—to change. Kay Graham, late publisher of the *Washington Post*, was the pioneer. Leading journalists such as Meg Greenfield, Helen Thomas, and Mary McGrory became influential. Pamela Harriman also emerged on the scene, first alongside the men in her life, then in her own right as a political fund-raiser and strategist and later ambassador to France. More and more women were elected to Congress or appointed to positions in the executive and judicial branches. Outside government, determined women formed organizations to influence public policy and enlarge the scope of intellectual and political debate.

As the non-campaign for secretary began, my own network was small compared to those of Mitchell and Holbrooke, but it did include some smart and determined people. Geraldine Ferraro, Senators Leahy and Mikulski, Representative Barbara Kennelly and Wendy Sherman (former assistant secretary of state for legislative affairs) conveyed to all who would listen a positive message about my ability to work with Capitol Hill. Jamie Rubin, who had temporarily left my staff for the presidential campaign, continued to look out for my interests. In addition, each day Elaine Shocas sorted through information provided by well-placed allies who gathered intelligence, provided suggestions, and put out fires.[1] They had excellent sources and so we were often able to stay a step ahead. For example, we learned that one rival camp was about to tell reporters that a female secretary of state would be unable to work effectively with conservative Arab leaders. We immediately directed reporters to Arab diplomats at the UN, who said the allegation was an insult and gender was not an issue in their diplomacy.

I knew that most of the Washington and New York foreign policy community was split between Mitchell and Holbrooke. I thought, however, that I probably had some backing. Then two members of my net-

---

1. These included Judith Lichtman, Marcia Greenberger, Sally Painter, Anne Reingold, Susan Brophy, Elaine Kamarck, Lula Rodriguez, Barbara Larkin, Meg Donovan, Ertharin Cousin, Jean Dunn, Rachelle Horowitz, and Tom Oliphant. Also, many people provided advice and contacted key officials on my behalf, including John Cooke, Ellen Malcolm, Marylouise Oates, Bob Shrum, Elaine Jones, Irene Natividad, Kate Michelman, Eleanor Smeal, Patricia Ireland, Pat Reuss, Nikki Heidepriem, Carol Foreman, Sammie Moshenberg, Audrey Tayse Haynes, Carmen Delgado Votaw, Nancy Zirkin, Elizabeth Bagley, Harriet Babbitt, Anne Wexler, and Michael Berman. I also learned later of efforts to keep my name in play by several members of the staffs of the President, Vice-President, and First Lady. Many Senate and House members were also helpful. I thank them all and regret not being able to acknowledge everyone by name.

work reported that one of the President's closest advisors was against me and saying I had no chance of getting the job.

In fairness, I understood that Mitchell and Holbrooke had been on the scene for a long time, were qualified, and had many friends who wanted them to be secretary. I was disturbed, however, by the extent to which women seemed to be for me and—with rare exceptions—the men for someone else. Many of my supporters were convinced that the opposition from males was a kind of discrimination, but I did not want to use that word. I thought it was a combination of factors including the historic male monopoly on the post, a feeling of men being more comfortable with men, and concerns I hoped were misplaced about my qualifications. These issues were not unique to me: every "first" woman or minority has confronted them. The excuse was always made that there were never enough "qualified" candidates. Until you do the job, no one thinks you can. Whatever the cause, the result unsettled me.

I didn't want the President to reject me because his advisors couldn't envision a female secretary of state. At the same time, if he did select me, I wanted it to be on the basis of merit, not gender. I believed, in any case, that if my appointment were made a litmus test of the President's commitment to women's rights, I almost certainly would not be chosen. Bill Clinton had already shown his commitment to that cause many times and wouldn't respond well to those suggesting that he still had something to prove. As a result, my allies urged women's groups to act with restraint and stopped plans to circulate a letter on my behalf among women members of Congress.

Of course there were those who questioned whether I was up to the job. Some said my background was too Eurocentric, despite the global portfolio I had handled at the UN. Others expressed doubts about my intellect. In the end there was no one tougher on me than me. I often internalized criticisms, especially when I found what I thought to be a grain of truth in some or parts of them. I was truly furious with myself for telling the reporter Elaine Sciolino, "I'm not that smart, [but] I work very hard," a quotation displayed in large print in the New York Times. Friends lectured me that a man would never have said such a thing, although one reason I said it was that I had often heard my father say exactly that about himself. I wondered if the men being considered had their own quiet fears or were questioning themselves as I was. I recalled these feelings years later when I saw Supreme Court Justice Sandra Day O'Connor being interviewed by NBC's Katie Couric. When asked if she had been scared about becoming the Court's first woman, O'Connor said, "Yes, I was concerned about whether I could do the job well enough to deserve saying yes" to President Reagan's offer.

There has been much speculation about the First Lady's role in my selection. After the Beijing Conference, our friendship had continued to deepen. When we met, we always began by discussing policy issues, then found more personal subjects. I enjoyed talking about my daughters and she about Chelsea.

In the summer of 1996, while on separate official trips, we met in Prague. Hillary had developed a friendship with Havel during his visits to America, and so we were a compatible trio. The Czech president, who had just moved to his new residence, entertained us there. I offered to show Hillary around the city. We strolled through Wenceslas Square with Havel, who pointed out the balcony where he had stood during the Velvet Revolution. We visited the Old Jewish Cemetery, took a Fourth of July boat ride up the Vltava River, and browsed through shops full of carved crystal, fantastic glass animals, and antique jewelry.

Some of the sights and smells were more successful than others. I took her to the restaurant within the castle walls where I had earlier sat with Havel's inner circle. I decided that Hillary needed a taste of typical Czech food, particularly my personal favorite—*zelí*—a kind of hot sauerkraut that could be made in red or white versions. When the waiters brought it out, I took one look and said, "These portions are too small to get any real sense of what the dish is about. Could we please have some more?" The chef went wild and soon huge mounds of the stuff were piled in front of us, even though it was evident from the first bite that this was not Hillary's dish. After that I am convinced she lost confidence in my judgment about food.

It wasn't easy moving along a sidewalk with Hillary because people kept stopping her, but we persisted, even to the point of walking in a crazy rainstorm, with our umbrellas turned inside out and Secret Service agents trying to herd us back into cars. During our walks, we discussed professors we had had at Wellesley and talked about the dynamics of the White House and especially the foreign policy team. Although my name had surfaced by then as a potential successor to Christopher, we never dealt with that directly.

The only real knowledge I gained on the question of Hillary's influence over the selection of secretary of state came months after my designation, at a U.S. embassy event in Barbados. The First Lady was there, and so was the President. In his remarks, the President said flattering things about me and quoted Hillary's advice about my selection: "Only if you pick Madeleine will you get a person who shares your values, who is an eloquent defender of your foreign policy, and who will make every girl proud."

ONE MORNING IN NOVEMBER, Elaine Shocas phoned me at 6 A.M., telling me to open that day's *Washington Post*. "They've done it," she said, "they've done it to themselves." Buried in a story speculating on cabinet appointments was the sentence, "UN Ambassador Madeleine K. Albright, widely believed to be among the top contenders for the job, in fact belongs in the 'second tier' of likely candidates, one Clinton advisor said yesterday, a judgment confirmed by two administration officials." Although the sentence was well down in the story, it stood out like ketchup on white linen. Obviously, some of those around the President were trying to block me and doing so in a clumsy, patronizing way. Despite my credentials, I was being both dismissed and dissed.

The quote galvanized my supporters and prompted requests by women's groups that the White House disavow it. It had clearly hit a nerve. A previously scheduled meeting between the Vice-President and women leaders took place the following week, during which Gore assured everyone that I was being considered seriously. The "second tier" remark may not have decided anything in the end, but it made it far harder for those in the President's circle who opposed my selection to bury me quietly. If I were not chosen, someone would have to explain why.

During this period, the President and Vice-President summoned me to separate job interviews. The conversations reflected the very different styles of the two men. Gore was earnest and specific, grilling me first about big issues, then about smaller ones. What did I think should be done in the Maghreb? What was my view about the problems in the Sakhalin Islands?

My interview with the President would be more easygoing, but I didn't know that in advance. I thought that if I were nervous, I would blow it. When I arrived at the Oval Office, I was told the President wanted to see me in his upstairs study in the residence. I was ushered in and offered tea and, as I waited, looked around the room at the various memorabilia and at a massive painting of a group of men huddled around a paper. When the President came in, he explained that we were in the Treaty Room; the painting showed the Spanish-American armistice, signed there in 1898. The table the President used for his desk had been used for signing that treaty and subsequent ones, including the Camp David Accords.

After he shared this history, we sat down across from each other in wing chairs with a coffee table between us. He said I was the first person he was seeing and that we didn't have to go through my qualifications—I had done my job extremely well under difficult circumstances—so we should just talk about ideas. There followed a far-reaching discussion of the President's vision for his second term, a vision laced with a contagious excitement, and of his desire to break through on hard cases such as China, Iran, the Middle East, and relations with the Islamic world. The President didn't so much ask questions as invite my thoughts. With the Vice-President, I had felt as if I were taking my SATs. My session with the President was comparable to the essay parts of an exam—which for me were always the most comfortable. I relaxed and felt the interview went well. On my way out, I passed George Mitchell—obviously next in line. We just said hello, both aware of what was going on. I was also instructed to meet with White House lawyers, who questioned me about my past. At the end they asked if there was anything about me that might surprise them. I said I had been receiving some letters lately that made me think my parents might have been of Jewish ancestry. The lawyers shrugged, "So what?"

On the afternoon of December 3, I was at my Georgetown home with Elaine and Suzanne George, a bright and tireless young lawyer who did a million different jobs on my small Washington staff.[2] Together we were rummaging through boxes, looking for articles I had written during my academic career. In my meeting with them, the President's vetters had asked for a copy of everything I had ever written.

The phone rang. It was the White House operator asking if I would take a call from the President. For seven minutes I was on hold. As I stood there listening intently but hearing nothing, my stomach felt as if it were riding upside down on a roller coaster. I told Elaine and Suzy, "I'm going to throw up. He's calling the rejectees. It's all over. I'm toast."

Finally the President came on the line. He said hello and apologized for his voice, husky due to allergies. Then he asked about Václav Havel's recent health problems, discussed the Boutros-Ghali situation, and made some general comments about Europe. I responded appropriately and the President hung up. "He was calling to say no," I speculated, "and chickened out. Just wait, he'll get Panetta or Erskine Bowles [Panetta's deputy] to play the heavy."

Elaine, as always, was reassuring. Whether because of psychic powers or political instinct, she had been saying for months that I would be selected. I knew all her arguments. At the UN, I had received the best possible training. I could work with Congress. I had shown toughness. I did well in speeches and on TV. I knew the issues and was right on many of those the President cared about. He also liked drama, and appointing a woman would be dramatic. Even so, deep down I couldn't be objective. I

2. Suzy served subsequently as my deputy chief of staff and trip director. I will always be grateful for her loyalty, energy, humor, and creativity in performing the most demanding jobs.

was thrilled about being considered for the job, knew the chance would only come once, and wanted to give it my best shot. But neither in my heart nor in my head did I ever believe the President would select me.

The next day, back in New York, Bowles did call. With resignation I took the line and waited for the bad news. He then asked two questions. "If the President asked you to be Secretary of State, would you say yes?" And "Will you be available to take a call from the President at nine o'clock tomorrow morning?" While listening intently and trying to stay calm, I silently thought, "Do you expect anyone to say no to these questions?" Aloud I said, "Yes, of course, absolutely, yes."

Elaine, Jamie, and I took the last shuttle back to Washington. Also flying were rumors that I would be named, so Jamie went off to deal with a bevy of press calls as soon as we landed. I asked Elaine to spend the night with me in Georgetown and gave her one of my flannel nightgowns so she would not have to go home. In the morning we sat in my living room wearing matching pink terrycloth bathrobes, afraid to take showers because we might miss the call. Nine o'clock came, then quarter after. The phone rang. It was Wendy Sherman wanting to know if we had heard from the White House. We said hurriedly, "No, not yet, good-bye." At 9:30 the phone rang again. It was another friend, Susan Berger, Sandy's wife, wanting to know if we had heard from the White House. We said more hurriedly, "No, not yet, good-bye."

It was quarter to ten. I was sipping coffee, but by then my body was manufacturing its own caffeine. I still couldn't allow myself to believe. I told Elaine, "The President has changed his mind. He stays up so late, someone talked him out of it in the middle of the night. He might not even let me stay at the UN." Finally, at 9:47, the call came. Elaine answered, listened for a second, then silently handed me the receiver.

"I want you to be my Secretary of State." These were his first words. I finally believed it. My own words came slowly: "I am honored and grateful. Of course I accept, and I will give it all the energy I have." The President congratulated me warmly and began to say good-bye, but I interrupted. "Thank you again, Mr. President. I wish my parents were alive. I will never let you down."

I hung up, hugged Elaine, and sat down for several minutes trying to absorb the fact that my life had just been transformed. It had really happened. I wondered if I had thanked the President properly, then thought there would be ample time for that. I picked up the phone and called my daughters, sister, brother, and as many friends as I could. Then I took a bath, got my hair done, put on a red dress and jacket and a pearl necklace with an eagle pendant and headed for the White House, where the public announcement was to be made. Standing next to the President and my new colleagues,[3] I said in reference to Secretary Christopher, "I only hope my heels can fill his shoes."

THE FOLLOWING DAY I woke up, put on my pink bathrobe once again, and went out to retrieve the morning newspapers—to find my picture on the front page of both the *Washington Post* and the *New York Times*. After breakfast I headed for Union Station to take the 9 A.M. AMTRAK train to New York. I often did this when the weather was bad and planes were delayed. Usually I was frazzled, because the decision to travel by train had been made at the last minute and I was worried I would be late for something. On the morning of December 6, I may still have been frazzled, but also felt elated.

My mind was filled with what lay ahead, but I still had a ton of work to do at the UN, so I settled into my seat intent on reading as much as possible during the three-hour trip. As soon as the train started to move, the conductor came to take our tickets. He apologized for also bringing over a young girl who asked me to autograph her copy of the *Post*. I wrote, "You can be anything you want to be. Good luck and best wishes," then went back to my reading.

A minute or so later, the conductor returned. "Madam Secretary, that girl showed off her autograph for folks in the next car, and now they all want to say hello. If we let them back here, we'd have a mess on our hands. Would you mind walking up there instead?"

Entering the next car, I saw the commuters sitting with their backs to me, each with their *Post*, and I was confronted with a sea of images of a smiling President with a smiling me. I made my way up the aisle, to be hugged and kissed as papers were folded and thrust at me to sign. It took me so long to make my way through the train that *Washington Posts* gave way to *Baltimore Suns*, and *Philadelphia Enquirers*, and *New York Times*, but the picture and the enthusiasm remained the same. I may not have known anyone on the train personally, but that morning I felt I knew them all. Someone shouted, "Go for it, Madeleine!" and it began to sink in how extraordinary the President's decision had been and how momentous the next years would be.

3. National Security Advisor–designate Sandy Berger, Defense Secretary–designate William Cohen, and Tony Lake, who was supposed to become CIA Director but whose nomination was subsequently withdrawn due to partisan opposition from a handful of Republican Senators.

As we rolled across the New Jersey flatlands, past New York Harbor and into the city, I returned to my seat and stared out the window. For all my awareness of how unexpected events can be, I had to marvel. I had arrived in that harbor half a century before, an eleven-year-old immigrant from Prague staring up at the Statue of Liberty. How astonishing that that girl was about to become the sixty-fourth secretary of state and the highest-ranking woman in U.S. history.

IN THE DAYS FOLLOWING, our offices were swamped with bouquets of flowers, congratulatory telegrams, phone messages, and resumés.[4] I called many people for advice, including every living former secretary of state. Henry Kissinger chided me for taking away the one thing that had made him unique, his foreign birth. I chided him back by saying he would still be the only secretary who spoke with an accent.

Another nomination meant another confirmation hearing before the Senate Foreign Relations Committee and another encounter with Jesse Helms. It was hard to defend a man who took pride in *not* traveling overseas and was so often unfair in criticizing the U.S. Foreign Service. If I had known Helms only through television and newspapers, I probably would not have had a high opinion of him. In person, however, Helms had important redeeming qualities. He was what used to be called a square. Most politicians would willingly yield their Sunday mornings for a spot on one of the weekly news shows. Helms refused, because appearing on television would prevent him from appearing in church. His patriotism, faith, and family commitments were genuine. Helms also placed a high priority on honor in personal relationships, and he told me many times that although we disagreed on key issues, we didn't have to be disagreeable in our own discussions. "Madam Secretary, we're going to surprise everyone and make some history together."

Joining us in that effort would be the committee's respected senior Democrats, led by Delaware's Joseph Biden—a fiery orator whose passionate opposition to ethnic cleansing in Bosnia had mirrored and reinforced my own—and including Paul Sarbanes, John Kerry, Christopher Dodd, Dianne Feinstein, and later Barbara Boxer.

Although I had many friends on the committee, and every reason to

---

4. Among the notes I received, a particularly classy one stands out. Robert Strauss, a Washington institution, longtime Democratic leader, and former ambassador to Russia, congratulated me while admitting that he had not favored my designation. Few others were that direct—or honest.

expect my nomination to be approved, that didn't mean I intended to relax. The same work habits that got me through Wellesley and graduate school came into play. I sat at home with makeup off and pens in my hair, reading memos, taking notes, and scrawling questions on yellow Post-its. In the mornings, I arrived in my transition office with the collection of Post-its and asked my staff to find answers. Then I sat through hours of questions from State Department officials pretending to be senators. These "murder boards" were organized by Barbara Larkin, assistant secretary for legislative affairs, and her deputy Meg Donovan. They advised me on the specific policy interests of each Senator and which questions I would most likely get. The sessions were great practice for me, while giving my colleagues a chance to compete in seeing who could put their future boss on the spot by asking the hardest questions possible.

As I had for the UN job four years previously, I went off to Colorado over the holidays with huge notebooks and spent the time between family events doing homework. Every night I dreamt I was preparing for a confirmation hearing to become Secretary. Every day I got up and did it for real. There was no escape. The only break was on Christmas itself, a day spent cross-country skiing with security agents hot on my trail.

My hearing was held on January 8 in the spacious but charmless Hart Senate Office Building. Traditionally a nominee is introduced by the senators from his or her home state. Sadly, as a resident of Washington, D.C., I could not uphold that tradition. Secretary Christopher kindly agreed to establish a new precedent and introduce me himself. With grace and wit, he summarized my career and expressed confidence in my abilities. Then, after leaning over and giving me a kiss, he departed to appreciative applause from everyone in the room.

In my statement I outlined the themes I intended to pursue as Secretary. We had reached a point, I told the Senators, halfway between the disintegration of the Soviet Union and the start of a new century. The world was freer than ever before, but continued progress couldn't be taken for granted. American leadership was essential. Half a century earlier, it hadn't been enough to defeat the Nazis. The generation of Truman and Marshall had worked with allies to forge a set of institutions designed to ensure lasting peace.

"Today," I testified, "it is not enough to say that Communism has failed. We must build a new framework—adapted to the demands of a new century"—to control the threats posed by weapons of mass destruction and terror; settle dangerous regional conflicts; maintain America as the hub of an expanding global economy; and defend cherished principles of democracy and law. At the center of that framework "are our key alliances and relationships. These are the bonds that hold together not only our own foreign policy but the entire international system. When we are able to act cooperatively with the other leading nations, we create a dynamic web of principle, power, and purpose that elevates standards and propels progress around the globe." To seize the opportunities and defeat the perils we would face, I concluded, "we must be more than audience, more even than actors, we must be the authors of the history of our age."

After all my feverish preparation, the hearing seemed a downhill glide. Chairman Helms was at his most courtly. The Senators offered encouragement. The questions asked were probing but fair. All this delighted me and bored the press, which much prefers bloodiness to courtliness. As each Senator took a turn, the hearing stretched into late afternoon. Indiana Senator Richard Lugar, who is both thoughtful and thorough, concluded with a series of questions about environmental degradation in Africa, population growth in the Middle East, regional peacekeeping initiatives, international financial crises, the dangers of Islamic extremism, a possible Free Trade Agreement with Chile, the prospects for democracy in Serbia, U.S. policy toward Ukraine, arms control, American diplomatic representation in Moscow, the Philippines as a model for Asian democracy, and the economic implications of rising energy consumption in China. By the time I finished answering, even my daughters had stopped listening, but it was worth it when Helms promised to hold a special committee meeting on Inauguration Day to consider my nomination. He was as good as his word.

On January 22, the full Senate voted 99–0 to confirm me.[5] It had been twenty years since I had taken my first government job, fourteen since my divorce, and four since I had first become a grandmother. I had been entrusted with a position that, for virtually all that time, had exceeded even my most ambitious hopes. In my classes I had taught students to role-play, to imagine what they would do at times of crisis in the very top jobs. Now I would have that opportunity for real, knowing that the grades would come not from some professor but from history, the hardest but fairest judge.

GETTING SWORN IN as Secretary of State is something I would be pleased to do every day of my life. I only wish I could have frozen the

---

5. Senator Jay Rockefeller of West Virginia was out of the country and missed the vote. We go back a long ways, but as this footnote reflects, I have still not let him hear the last of it.

moment to savor over and over again. I had been in the Oval Office before but never as the subject of the meeting. The room is surprisingly small, and so attendance is limited. The chairs ordinarily used by the President when greeting foreign dignitaries had been moved to accommodate spectators. In addition to my family, I was pleased that Senators Helms and Mikulski were there, along with my top staff. The President stood in front of his desk. His introduction was eloquent and generous. Next to him was the Vice-President, who asked me to put my hand on the Bible and repeat the oath of office. Together, my daughters held the Bible while I repeated the historic words.

It was a few minutes before noon on January 23, 1997. Now, after 207 years, a woman would be running the Department of State. Ever since that moment people have asked how I felt. The answer is that part of my mind was stunned by the notion of inheriting a job first held by Thomas Jefferson, part was trying to concentrate on not making a mistake while reciting the oath, and part was worried about my pin falling off. Months earlier I had come across a beautiful and very expensive antique eagle pin. I promised myself I would buy it if President Clinton selected me, thinking how unlikely it would be I would ever have to write that particular check. So I did buy it, and wore it to the ceremony, but the clasp had come loose. I did not want to stick anyone or get stuck or have it drop onto the Bible. Fortunately it held, but the eagle was turned around and after all that trouble it didn't even show in the pictures.

In my remarks, I thanked the President warmly and expressed my gratitude for the opportunity he had given me. Then I thanked the others who had helped make the moment possible:

> As I stand here today in this office, which symbolizes the power and purpose of the United States, I think especially of...my mother and father who taught me to love freedom; President Václav Havel, who helped me to understand the responsibilities of freedom; and Edmund Muskie, who gave me the confidence to know that no barrier or ceiling should stop me from serving freedom in my own life.

By coincidence, my first meeting as Secretary of State was with the President and Kofi Annan. The new Secretary General congratulated me on my promotion, and I congratulated him on his. We noted that never before had there been such a close professional and personal relationship between those in our two positions. We talked about the importance of further UN reform and prospects for working out a deal with Congress that would pay our UN bills. I then returned to the State Department for a meeting on China and a look at my new office.

From the outside, the State Department looks like a box some other building might have arrived in. It is a pair of massive concrete rectangles utterly devoid of distinction. Novelist Ward Just compared it to a penitentiary. Inside there are white ceilings, endless white linoleum hallways, and white walls marked with color-coded stripes to prevent visitors from getting lost. I often thought that, if not for gravity, you could find yourself walking on the ceiling and not know the difference.

The Secretary's office is in a secure corridor on the south side of the seventh floor. The corridor is distinguished from the rest of the building by its mahogany walls lined with portraits of former Secretaries. As I walked along, my pace slowed. This was an experience never to forget. I looked again at the portraits. Many of the former Secretaries had whiskers and all wore suits.

I walked beneath the archway marked "Secretary of State" and turned left into the Secretary's large outer office, which had a fireplace and was sometimes used to receive foreign dignitaries. I continued through to the adjacent inner office, my home for the next four years. Like the Oval Office, I had been in that handsome room before, but I now saw it with new eyes. As I sat for the first time in the Secretary's chair, I was floating. According to legend, it is possible to fly on a magic carpet only if no doubts enter your mind about the carpet's ability to stay aloft. At that moment I was so excited by the challenges to come, my doubts vanished. I soon decorated the office with a lithograph showing a woman riding a chariot through the streets of Washington during the Lincoln era, with a sash labeled "Emancipation" across her chest.

At the center of the secretarial suite when I moved in was the desk of Liz Lineberry, a consummate professional who would be my personal secretary as she had been Christopher's, Larry Eagleburger's, and Jim Baker's before that. The suite's right half was home to the offices and desks of the Secretary's professional staff, both foreign and civil service, who were directed by four superb officers: Executive Secretary William Burns, later succeeded by Kristie Kenney,[6] and Executive Assistant David Hale, later succeeded by Alex Wolff. It would weary the most patient reader if I tried to list all who would contribute to the State Department's accomplishments during my years as Secretary. Every agreement, initiative, trip, hearing, statement, and task reflected the efforts of a team, often exhausted but always professional, from the most experienced ambassador to the most recent hire. Our nation is justly proud of our armed forces, the finest in the world. But the men and women who support and staff our diplomatic missions are equally vital to our security and equally deserving of our gratitude and support.

My first Monday on the job, I went to the Dean Acheson Auditorium to greet State Department employees and thank them for the hard work they were doing and were about to do. I pledged to fight for the resources they would need to serve our nation and do their jobs. I stressed plans to update our training and modernize our technology and urged everyone to join in communicating the importance of our diplomacy to the American people.

I emphasized this last point, because I intended to focus on reconnecting the American people to our foreign policy. During the Cold War, most Americans paid attention to world events because they knew Soviet missiles were targeted on their homes. One mistake and it was curtains for us all. After the Soviet Union broke apart (and before September 11, 2001), the rationale for caring about international affairs seemed less dramatic, although to my mind no less compelling. I hoped to use the bully

---

6. I had been proud to appoint Kenney as the first woman executive secretary. My front office team also included Confidential Assistant John Crowley, who had worked with every Secretary since Kissinger; Suzanne McPartland, my secretary at the UN whom I lured to Washington; scheduler Linda Dewan; computer genius Lynn Sweeney; and Nichole Tucker, Elaine's assistant and my trip scheduler. Officers in the Operations Center kept me up-to-date, and those on the "Line" provided briefing materials and trip advance. Executive Director Richard Shinnick, George Rowland, and their colleagues kept my office—and me—running at full speed. White House Liaison Charles Duncan, a maestro of advance, ensured successful events on the road. I thank them all for their dedication and service.

pulpit of the secretary of state's office to get Americans—especially young people—excited about foreign policy again.

I also wanted to encourage a revival of the bipartisan tradition in foreign affairs. I was optimistic because, with the Cold War's end, there was no longer any natural dividing line between Democratic and Republican positions on most foreign policy issues. The labels of the past—hawk, dove, conservative, liberal—no longer seemed to mean much. Reaching out to Republicans was also pragmatic, because we needed their votes. The GOP controlled both houses of Congress and all the key committees. So I joked about how, when I entered government, I had had my partisan instincts surgically removed. And I concentrated on building good working relationships. I testified early before the House Committee on International Relations and its chairman, Representative Benjamin Gilman of New York. I made home state appearances with each of the four subcommittee chairmen who controlled parts of our budget. In Alabama, Representative Sonny Callahan referred to me as "a flamingo in the barnyard of politics," which I interpreted as a compliment to me, if not to politics.

I also traveled to North Carolina with Senator Helms. Before his hometown fans, we were photographed holding hands, and I gave him a nightshirt with the inscription "Someone at the State Department Loves You." All this made for good theater, but more important from my perspective was the policy payoff. Helms assured me during this visit that he wouldn't seek to block a vote on U.S. participation in the Chemical Weapons Convention. Senate approval of the convention was among my earliest priorities, and with Helms declining to interfere, we scored an important victory.

The most visible change in my existence during this period was the virtual football team of Diplomatic Security agents now accompanying me almost everywhere I went. The Diplomatic Security Service (DS) is to the Secretary of State what the Secret Service is to the President.[7] While at the UN, I had had a small detail of agents. They had traveled with me to peacekeeping operations around the world, not to mention the lingerie departments of various stores.

Soon after I was nominated for my new job, DS officials informed me

---

7. I remain very grateful to the head of my DS detail, Larry Hartnett, and to the men and women on his team for the thousands of hours they devoted to keeping me (call sign "FIREBALL") safe and the constant professionalism they exhibited. During periods of tension over issues such as Iraq and Kosovo, there were many threats. Because of DS, I never worried and could concentrate on my job. Although there were times I wished for greater privacy, I accepted their presence and, as I got to know them better, considered them not only my protectors but also my friends.

that they had to set up shop in my house. I have a detached garage at the end of my garden that was perfect for them, except that it was filled with my daughters' high school notebooks, old trunks, backpacks, skis, my parents' papers, and a lot of dirt. We put all this in storage, including some of the dirt, then the agents decided they had to dig up my backyard to lay telephone cables (despite my giant magnolia trees). They parked their vans in an alley across the street. My neighbors went through several phases. At first they were excited about the spectacle. Then they told themselves they were pleased to be living in a safer neighborhood. Finally the thrill wore off and they began counting the days until I left office.

One of my first challenges was to assemble an effective team. The gossip in Washington was that I would not dare hire strong men because I would feel threatened. The truth is I would have grabbed George Marshall himself had he been available.

The President and I both wanted Strobe Talbott to stay as deputy secretary and he agreed. I had worked with Strobe often during my years as UN ambassador. When I was in Washington, I would sometimes end up in his office talking about peacekeeping operations or picking his brain about Russia. I knew he would be the best of partners and I was right.

My choice for the key position of under secretary of state for political affairs was Tom Pickering. It is the custom of U.S. embassies to display the pictures of former ambassadors. I sometimes felt that Pickering's image was on *every* wall. His resumé included ambassadorial service to Russia, India, the UN, Israel, El Salvador, and Nigeria. Despite this stellar record, Pickering was unpretentious and affable. I looked up to him, in part because he was about a foot and a half taller, but mostly because of his expertise both on policy and management.

For under secretary of state for international economic affairs I turned to Stuart Eizenstat, who had served as ambassador to the EU and under secretary of commerce during the first Clinton term. I had known Stu since the Carter years and admired his work ethic, fine brain, and warm heart. There was no one better qualified for hard jobs. He was succeeded in 1999 by a highly talented Foreign Service officer, Alan Larson.

One of the major accomplishments of my term would be the reorganization of the foreign policy bureaucracy to reflect the Cold War's end. In anticipation of that, I asked John Holum, director of the Arms Control and Disarmament Agency (ACDA), to "double-hat" as under secretary of state for arms control and international security affairs. John was a master of the details of his complex portfolio, able to discuss calmly and clearly the most frightening scenarios related to the potential spread and use of weapons of mass destruction.

At Strobe's suggestion, I turned to Bonnie Cohen as my under secretary for management. In her years at the Interior Department, Bonnie had developed a reputation for cutting through bureaucracy and getting results. She would do precisely that during her years at State, bringing in fresh ideas, improving efficiency, and enhancing security.

The under secretary for global affairs was Timothy Wirth, a dedicated and energetic former Senator from Colorado and a holdover from the first term. Frank Loy, an environmentalist and former head of the German Marshall Fund, succeeded Wirth in 1998. He had perfect credentials for the job.

The position of State Department counselor is of special importance because it has no formal place in the bureaucratic hierarchy and has little staff. To be useful, the incumbent must give the Secretary better advice than he or she receives anywhere else, then have the drive to make sure that advice is implemented should it become policy. My choice was Wendy Sherman, a shrewd and resilient veteran of numerous Washington wars who could learn any subject faster than anyone I knew. I had been friends with Wendy for a long time and knew I could count on her loyalty and her gift for separating meat from bull.

For director of the policy planning office, I chose Gregory Craig, a resourceful and strong-minded Washington attorney full of creative ideas about the proper shape of U.S. leadership. He served simultaneously as U.S. special coordinator for Tibet. My legal advisor was also a very smart and experienced attorney, David Andrews, ready and able to tackle the toughest assignments. For director-general of the Foreign Service, I turned to Ambassador Edward "Skip" Gnehm, who had served as my deputy in New York and would prove a steady hand in an often thankless job.[8]

There were two people on my team who were particularly indispensible. They were there to celebrate the good times and offer support during the difficult ones. There was never any doubt that my confidante, Elaine Shocas, would remain my chief of staff. She seemed able to keep a thousand projects in her head simultaneously, possessed perfect political pitch, and knew how to exercise authority. Jamie Rubin, who had handled all press relations for me at the UN, was the best choice to be assistant

---

8. In 1999, as a result of reorganization, the U.S. Information Agency merged with the State Department. I was successful in recruiting Evelyn Lieberman, a wise and ebullient leader, to serve as under secretary of state for public diplomacy and public affairs. Evelyn managed the merger magnificently and succeeded in placing public diplomacy at the heart of our foreign policy.

secretary for public affairs and because of his clear thinking would continue serving in a crucial advisory role. When Nicholas Burns, the department's official spokesman, left to become U.S. ambassador to Greece, Jamie also assumed that role and performed superbly.

As my team came together, I went to work. My first trip as Secretary had been to Capitol Hill. My second was not to some overseas capital, but rather intentionally domestic—to Houston, where I gave a speech entitled "Building a Bipartisan Foreign Policy" at Rice University in an event hosted by former Secretary James Baker. The following day I had bacon and eggs at the home of George Bush and his wife, the incomparable Barbara. We had a press conference in which the former President strongly endorsed the Chemical Weapons Convention, which his administration had originally negotiated. As a girl in Denver, I had loved Stetson hats. Being in Texas rekindled the flame. So I went out shopping and bought three, one each in red, black, and brown.

Mike Dukakis used to try to enliven his image by joking, "The future's so bright I've got to wear shades." Raring to go, I had hoped to feel the same way during these early days as Secretary of State. But I did not, and the reason had nothing to do with the future. Instead I found myself mentally and emotionally shredded by sudden, fuller knowledge of the past.

FIFTEEN

Names on the Synagogue Wall

O N THE MORNING OF FEBRUARY 4, 1997, the front-page headline of the *Washington Post* read: "Albright's Family Tragedy Comes to Light." It went on, in somewhat smaller letters: "Secretary Says She Didn't Know That 3 Grandparents Were Jewish Victims of Holocaust." That evening, a few minutes before Bill Clinton was to deliver the first State of the Union Address of his second term, the sergeant at arms strode through the doors of the House of Representatives and said in a booming voice, "Mr. Speaker, the President's cabinet." For the first time, a woman led the cabinet down the aisle between the applauding Congressmen and Senators, shaking hands and exchanging kisses with Democrats and Republicans alike. It should have been a moment of unmitigated joy. It wasn't. I had achieved what no other woman had, but at that moment I believed I would lose it ail because I had failed to discover earlier in life that I was of Jewish ancestry, and that three of my grandparents had died in concentration camps.

My ignorance had been made to seem like a crime. People could not believe that I didn't know my family's past. Instead of being allowed to take in, privately, the tragic facts I had only recently learned, I was made to feel as if I were a liar and my father, whom I adored, was portrayed as a heartless fraud.

I had on a navy blue suit, my eagle pin—this time fastened—and a forced smile. As the cabinet's senior member, I stood in front of my chair while my colleagues filed in. The next moment the President began his speech. I struggled to listen, knowing I would be the one expected to rise first to lead the applause. I also had to look back to make sure to stand if those behind me got up first. I was reminded briefly of Alice and Greg's wedding, throughout which all those present stood, because the mother of the bride—me—forgot to sit down. I told myself I needed to find a way to cope with my feelings and all the publicity about my family, because I had plenty to do and much to prove.

I remember clearly how I felt that particular night, with the President in full flow and my emotions perched on a precipice. It is much harder to describe my thoughts in the days leading up to those headlines and over the weeks that followed. The story of my Jewish ancestry, and of the fate of my grandparents and other family members, was a deeply personal matter, though I had learned about it in an unusually public way. Like much of what happens to us in life, the story does not have a distinct beginning, middle, and end. Some pieces remain unknown; some are unknowable. To this day, I ponder what about me would have been different had I uncovered the story earlier. How do you deal with such a seminal truth in the sixth decade of your life?

WHEN I BECAME UN ambassador, I began receiving letters from people around the world. This overseas correspondence, which was delivered to the State Department, to my house in Washington, and to my UN office in New York, comprised a very large mixed bag. Amid the thousands of missives, there were handwritten letters in Czech and other Slavic languages that no one on my staff knew how to decipher, and I unfortunately did not have time to sort through them all personally. Official-looking letters were normally sent to the State Department for translation and reply. Many of the hard-to-read ones simply sat there probably until someone stuck them in a drawer, where they were forgotten. Of course there were also many letters in English. Generally, the letters conveyed requests, compliments, insults, and the occasional threat.

A tiny fraction of the mail did offer information about my family, including some saying my ancestors were Jewish. It was hard to take most of these at face value because they were accompanied by ethnic slurs. For example, I was accused of being a "Jew bitch" for defending U.S. policies in the Middle East and the Balkans. In other cases, people claimed to know about my family but the details in their letters were not right. A person might say that he or she had known my father in high school, but at a time my father would have been only six. Or someone would claim to have known my mother but was wrong about the names of her parents or her hometown. I received jewelry that had supposedly belonged to a relative, but I couldn't think of a relative with that name. A few letters said my family owed the writers money and specified where a check should be sent. I had not received any letters compelling enough to make me doubt my understanding of my family history.

In addition to the mail, there had been stories here and there, especially in the Arab press, offering anti-Semitic arguments why I shouldn't be appointed Secretary. The stories prompted a few reporters to ask Jamie whether my family was Jewish. Since he knew no more than I did at the time, he said no. This continued until November 1996. By then the press was full of speculation about who would replace Warren Christopher and I was receiving general correspondence from almost everywhere.

On one of our many shuttle flights between New York and Washington, Elaine handed me a letter in Czech, not knowing whether it was important or not. As I studied it, I realized that the letter wasn't the same as the others. It was from a woman who really did seem to know my family and had most—but not all—of the details right, including where and when my parents were born. She also wrote that my family was Jewish. For the first time, I felt I had to really consider the possibility. However, it was still difficult, because to believe such a letter was to disbelieve my own parents.

I made plans in December to dig a little deeper, thinking naïvely that there was no rush. I had already shared my thoughts with lawyers at the White House; I mentioned them now to Sandy Berger, who said, "What of it? Our President isn't anti-Semitic."

I decided to tell my daughters during our annual Christmas gathering in Aspen about the information I had received. Even there it was not easy to find a good time. I said I had something to tell them. They looked at me with dread, as if I were about to reveal I had some fatal disease. I told them I had been sent some letters suggesting that our family was of Jewish heritage. I said I wasn't yet sure but thought it might be true. After the drama of my bringing them together, their reaction was relief mixed with surprise. "This is amazing," they said. "Why didn't your parents tell you?" "Do our cousins know?" "We have to figure this all out."

My sister, Kathy, had been with me in Aspen, and we had also talked to our brother, John, and his wife, Pam. We were intrigued by the prospect of confronting a family mystery. At the same time we were troubled by how much we apparently didn't know. In 1990, John and Pam had vacationed in Czechoslovakia and visited my parents' hometowns. They searched for my father's birth registration at the local Catholic church without success, but church officials nevertheless helped them locate the house where my father had been born. They also talked to people who had known my parents' families. No one had said anything about either of the families being Jewish and John of course had no reason to ask.

Kathy, John, and Pam all had full-time jobs but were better able to find a chance for personal travel than I. We decided they would go to the Czech Republic, perhaps in the summer of 1997, to see what they could discover. It turned out, however, that we didn't have that long to wait. During the transition period Jamie told me a reporter from the *Washington Post* was preparing a story about my personal history and wanted help. I had never hesitated to talk about myself, so I called the reporter, Michael Dobbs. Although I was barred by custom from offering him a formal interview prior to my confirmation, we chatted informally for some time and I said I would be pleased to meet with him after I was officially sworn in. I was also happy to give him the addresses of people he might want to talk to in Belgrade and the Czech Republic, including my cousin Dáša. I knew Dobbs by reputation to be a solid reporter, but I had never met him personally.

The weeks of transition soon passed and were, for me, a whirlwind of preparation, mixed with Inaugural festivities, parades, parties, and my own swearing in. Friday, January 24, was my first full day as Secretary. My mind felt as though it were in a hundred places simultaneously. I held a press conference and prepared for some interviews, considered job candidates, and hosted two huge receptions. In the middle of all this, I received a phone call from my daughter Anne. She was crying. She said Michael Dobbs had called to ask, "Did you know that three of your great-grandparents died in Nazi concentration camps?" While I tried to soothe her, I felt incredulous. Anne said in anguish, "Now I understand why Grandma was so protective and worried about us so much. Poor Grandma and Bumpa, this is terrible."

I was shocked, furious at Dobbs for calling my daughter, and bewildered by his information. I knew, of course, that one of my grandparents had died prior to the war and the other three while we were in England, but no one had ever said anything about concentration camps. If there were anything to this grim account, I should have been the one to break the news to my children. In outrage, I called Jamie. "Why is Dobbs calling Anne with this kind of information? Why doesn't he talk to me? And where are these so-called facts coming from?" Jamie reminded me that we had promised Dobbs an interview and suggested we get together with him as soon as possible to sort things out.

I wished I could have set everything aside to investigate this stunning news myself, but there was no time. Interviewers from CNN and *Meet the Press* queried me about our long policy agenda. I met with my new colleagues, Sandy Berger and Defense Secretary Bill Cohen, to set priorities, compare notes, and lay out plans. I talked to Secretary of the Treasury Robert Rubin about working together on economic issues. Congratulatory phone calls arrived from foreign ministers. I made courtesy calls on Capitol Hill and had lunch with acting CIA Director George Tenet. There were also social events—the annual Alfalfa Club dinner, the Washington Press Club's Salute to Congress, and a reception for the State Department press corps. Beneath all this music was an insistent drumbeat. I was frequently on the phone to my daughters, my sister, and my brother. A reporter claimed to have information that would dramatically alter our understanding of our family's past. In the preceding weeks, we had begun to examine the possibility of a Jewish heritage. Now we were confronted with the full implications of that possibility. It was one thing for my grandparents to be Jewish, quite another for them to be Jewish in a time and place where the power of life and death had been held by Adolf Hitler.

On January 30, at 5:45 P.M., Dobbs and his colleague Steven Coll came to my office. They were up against a deadline for their piece, to appear in the *Washington Post* magazine. Elaine and Jamie were also there. The interview began well. The reporters set up their tape recorder and we exchanged greetings. Then they got down to the subject at hand. Because of Dobbs' call to Anne and a phone conversation he had had with Jamie,[1] I knew something of what to expect, but I was unprepared for how hard the session would turn out to be.

After thanking me for cooperating, Dobbs told me about the people he had met who had knowledge of my family. He pulled out lists of people who had died in Nazi camps, either Theresienstadt (Terezín) or Auschwitz, including my paternal grandparents, Arnošt and Olga Körbel, and my mother's mother, Růžena Spieglová.[2] He asked me a series of questions about what I knew and when I knew it. Then he put a photograph in front of me of three girls of varying ages. "I recognize everybody in it," I said: the older one was my cousin Dáša, I was the little girl standing next to her, and my sister was the baby in the stroller. Dobbs corrected me, saying that I was the baby and the middle-sized girl was Dáša's sister, Milena. "Milena," he said, "was also taken to... Auschwitz."

---

1. There is a long discussion about this sequence in Dobbs' book, *Madeleine Albright, A Twentieth-Century Odyssey*. The only area of disagreement we have is that the reporter says he told Jamie Rubin about the circumstances surrounding the death of my grandparents on January 21, three days before the call to Anne. Jamie confirms they talked, but says the conversation was very vague and that he would certainly have passed on information concerning the fate of my grandparents to me immediately. In any event, I believe the pain caused by Dobbs was inadvertent. Although I was angry at the time, I have long since been grateful for the extensive research Dobbs did into my ancestry.

2. Dobbs did not get my grandmother's first name right in his article, believing it to be Anna, instead of Růžena.

Trying to absorb this horrendous information and stay calm, I was simultaneously crushed by what I was hearing and wondering what else there might be to come. I was also uncomfortable because the tone of the interview had shifted from its amiable start to something more adversarial. Obviously, it was the reporters' job to ask questions, but I felt like a courtroom witness being cross-examined by a lawyer who had all the facts while I had none. At one point Dobbs' colleague even said, "That's our case." What case? The *Washington Post* knew more about my family than I did, and because of that it seemed I was being accused either of trying to hide something or of being a fool. I was also sickened by Dobbs' revelations about the horrible fate of my grandparents, the people who had raised and nurtured my parents and indirectly given life to me. Because it was an interview, I had to speak—not easy when one feels speechless.

I TOOK ADVANTAGE of a moment following a meeting at the White House to share the news about my grandparents with the President and Vice-President. We were in the Oval Office and Bill Clinton put his arms around me and said, "I'm so sorry. You've got to find out more." That evening Hillary called me at home. "I know this must be really tough news to absorb," she said. "I'll do anything to help. Stay strong. We love you."

The initial public reaction when the news broke was a mixture of sympathy and fascination. I received letters and phone calls from supporters in Congress and consulted with leaders of the Jewish community, including New York Rabbi Arthur Schneier and Elie Wiesel. A number of people came forward to recount experiences not dissimilar to my own, including author and journalist Kati Marton, who had also been raised a Roman Catholic and hadn't learned of her Jewish heritage until visiting her native Hungary at the age of twenty-nine. "It makes you feel slightly bewildered and exposed," she wrote, "also a little vulnerable." Abraham Foxman, national director of the Anti-Defamation League, told the *New York Times*, "In Poland, every single day, Jews surface who thought they were Catholic all their lives." There were articles quoting eminent psychologists who had seen repeated instances of the same story and had said that many who had escaped or survived the Holocaust didn't discuss their past because they were focused on building a new life in a new country.

Although by then I did not doubt the basic truth of the *Post* story, this wasn't a matter I wanted to continue learning about through the media. Our family needed to do its own research. John and Kathy felt the same way. I called my friend Mark Talisman, who put us in touch with Tomáš Kraus, executive director of the Federation of Jewish Communities in the Czech Republic. In February, my sister, brother, and sister-in-law left for Prague.

The fact that I had a job to do and my family was trying to assemble a fuller story did not quell the furor. On the contrary, articles, commentaries, and letters flooded the media. If I had felt inundated before, I now felt I was drowning. I didn't object to the press treating my family history as news: that was part of the price of becoming a public figure. I gave scores of interviews and most reporters asked straightforward questions and wrote straightforward articles. But it did not stop there.

Some observers went beyond the tragedy of my grandparents and other family members to question both my honesty and my father's character. Professors and self-appointed experts who had never met me said it was "impossible" for me not to have known about my heritage. Others, including columnists I knew well, said it was "peculiar" I didn't know or "odd" that the secret had not been passed from mother to child, or that it seemed that I had "not wanted to know" or shown a "lack of curiosity." One writer wondered why I hadn't asked to see the graves when informed as an eight-year-old that my grandparents were dead. The clear insinuation was that I was a liar.

Among my closest friends from Wellesley, two were Jewish, Wini Shore Freund and Emily Cohen MacFarquhar. They told questioners that they had known me for almost forty years and were certain that I had not known the truth. Sadly, to skeptics the testimony of friends didn't mean much.

I was exasperated because it wasn't possible to prove a negative. I did not know what I did not know, and it hadn't entered my mind that my parents would keep something like this from me. It was easy for others to say I should have asked more questions, but I had thought I already possessed a complete family story. Neither I nor John nor Kathy felt any lack of a clear identity or sense of who we were or from where we had come. It was always obvious to us that our mother missed her own mother terribly, but the loss appeared to cause her such pain that we never probed for details. As for our father, he simply was not the kind of person you questioned. We considered him the source and definer of truth.

I had learned of my grandparents' deaths when I was eight years old, upon my family's return to Prague after World War II. I felt sorry for my parents but did not grieve myself, because I didn't really know what grandparents were. I couldn't picture their faces or remember their smiles or imagine their arms around me. I was less than two years old when I had last seen them, so I had little curiosity about them. I knew old people die.

Later I had no reason to doubt my parents' account of the past, because they were never mysterious or hesitant about it. On the contrary, we talked about those years all the time. The document I found after my mother's death reflected the way they had always spoken to us. She hinted at intrigue surrounding our journey from Prague via Belgrade to London in March 1939 but wrote nothing about being Jewish. As the family of a government official, we had ample reason to flee the Gestapo on political grounds. Once in the United States, my parents loved to discuss their high school friends, their courtship, their families, and their lives in interwar Czechoslovakia. My brother, sister, and I were told stories about past family celebrations of Christmas and Easter. Especially when I studied European history in high school, we spent a lot of time talking about the rise of Hitler, the dismemberment of Czechoslovakia, and the horror of the Holocaust. My parents were passionate in stressing the need for tolerance and the importance of opposing evil, but I never sensed the personal loss and sorrow that must have prompted that passion.

Do I wish I had learned the truth earlier? Yes. The circumstances of the loss of my grandparents would have been a terrible shock, but I would have been spurred sooner to learn more about their lives, a blessing I would have appreciated, and it would have allowed me to honor them as they deserved.

The truth is that although I was upset about some of the things written concerning me, I was furious at the criticism of my parents. A few writers questioned my parents' decision to bring our family out of Czechoslovakia. Others implied that my parents' subsequent decision not to reveal our Jewish heritage was the result either of my father's career ambitions or some kind of snobbishness or shame. These allegations simply did not square with my memory of the parents I admired and cherished.

Hindsight is a wonderful gift, especially when employed by those who haven't had comparable experiences. I have no way of knowing my parents' decision-making process. Although in early 1939 the madness of the Holocaust was still unimaginable, repression and occupation were at hand. With the Nazis in charge and my father a supporter of President Beneš, his diplomatic career was blocked and he could no longer work effectively and openly in Prague for the country he loved. But he did have the chance to join Beneš and other Czechoslovak leaders in London to rally international support for his nation's cause. He and my mother also had an infant daughter to protect.

I can only imagine the conversations my parents must have had with their parents immediately prior to their separation. My mother had been extremely close both to her mother and her older sister Marie, known as Máňa. I shudder when I think about the choice she had to make between being with her husband and her new child, or with her mother and sister. I suspect my maternal grandmother, recently widowed, did not want to leave because Máňa, sick with kidney disease, was too ill to travel. I don't know why my paternal grandparents didn't go or even if they had an opportunity before it was too late. My father's brother had set off for London before him, but their sister and family stayed, with only Dáša joining us later.[3]

As for my parents' decision not to reveal our Jewish heritage, again I can only speculate. My guess is that they associated our heritage with suffering and wanted to protect us. They had come to America to start a new life. The onset of McCarthyism in the 1950s might have made them uncertain about what to expect. They may have considered telling me but never found the right time.

I WANTED TO respond personally to every article, allegation, and comment about my family, but my days were so busy in my new job that I didn't even have time to read many of them, let alone respond. It was as if I had finally made it to the Olympics, representing my country in a race, but just as I was about to start I was handed a heavy package I had to unwrap as I ran.

While all this was going on, I felt I was not only under scrutiny personally but had to show that I could function successfully as Secretary of State. I was angered when some Arab papers said that the revelations about my ancestry would make Tel Aviv rather than Washington the capital of American foreign policy. Our press office quickly batted that allegation down, while more sympathetic writers recalled pointedly that Henry Kissinger, who was Jewish, had been a highly accomplished Secretary.

WITHIN WEEKS, Kathy, John, and Pam returned from the Czech Republic bearing videos, tapes, and information. In addition to Prague, they had visited Kostelec nad Orlicí, my mother's birthplace; Letohrad, my father's

---

3. Dáša was able to leave through the Kindertransport (children's transport), a volunteer rescue effort that enabled nine to ten thousand children from Germany and German-occupied lands to enter Great Britain between 1938 and 1940. The children, who had to be under the age of seventeen and couldn't be accompanied by parents or guardians, traveled by train and plane to England and were allowed into the country on simple travel visas.

hometown;[4] Poděbrady, a small town where my maternal grandmother had lived; and Terezín, the concentration camp north of Prague.

At the Jewish Town Hall in Prague, they had found the original Nazi war records, including cards bearing the names of my grandparents.

Arnošt and Olga Körbel had arrived at the transfer camp in Terezín on a freight train from Prague on July 30, 1942, along with 936 other Jews. Arnošt died there two months later of bronchial pneumonia, probably brought on by typhoid. Olga was sent to Auschwitz on October 23, 1944, where she soon perished. The transport card for my maternal grandmother, Růžena Spieglová, indicated that she also went through Terezín. There is no record she survived, but when and where she died is unknown. There were other relatives, an aunt and uncle, one of my cousins, and various great-uncles and great-aunts who also died in Auschwitz, Treblinka, and Terezín. My brother said, "It was like peeling back an onion. Each layer brought more tears and tragedy." Altogether, more than a dozen members of our family were among the victims of the Holocaust.

John and Kathy were welcomed warmly as they visited the birthplaces of our parents. Older townspeople corroborated some of the stories with which we had grown up. Grandfather Körbel had founded a match factory that provided jobs for many in his town of three thousand people. Our maternal grandfather had run a wholesale food business. My father had always made fun of my mother for buying too many groceries, saying she had been brought up in "a wholesale family."

When my brother played football in high school, my father had used it as an opportunity to recount his own exploits on the athletic field. "We confirmed with one of Daddy's friends that he was indeed the captain of the town's soccer team," John said, before adding dryly, "Of course, it was partly because he owned the only ball."

They had been accompanied by Tomáš Kraus, the ideal companion to introduce them to local Jewish communities. As they had driven around the country, they had discussed the importance of tradition and shared childhood memories. After one meal, John said, "I told Tomáš how, following a holiday dinner, we would compete to be the first the next morning to spread congealed turkey grease from the saucepan bottom onto a fresh piece of rye bread." As soon as he said this, John recalled, "Kraus gasped and exclaimed 'Why, that's so typically Jewish.' So Madeleine, the key to the mystery had been right in front of us all the time, and it was grease."

Of course the purpose of the trip went beyond specific facts to the

4. At the time of my father's birth, Letohrad was known as Kyšperk.

more general question of my parents' attitude toward religion. Why, if they were Jewish, had we been told of past celebrations of Christian holidays? Why had their marriage certificate indicated that they were "bez vyznání" or "without confession"—without any particular faith?

Tomáš Kraus provided some important clues. He explained that the Czech Jewish community was historically more secular than its counterparts elsewhere. During the interwar period, most families liked to think of themselves as Czech or Czechoslovak first and Jewish second. Some of the more assimilated simply stopped observing Jewish religious traditions. Others observed Passover and the high holy days Rosh Hashanah and Yom Kippur, but also Christmas and Easter. Kraus said his own family, which included survivors of Terezín, used to pick out its Christmas tree on the last day of Hanukkah. And John recalled, "One of the children's paintings in the museum at Terezín is of a Christmas tree."

John and Kathy theorized that our mother's family may have been more observant than our father's, in part because her town had a synagogue while his didn't. In any case, it seemed fair for us to conclude that the stories we had been told about past family holidays were true and hadn't been concocted to fool us. However, my parents were never rigid in their thinking, nor devout. That explained the statement of "without confession" when they married. I also learned from our cousin Dáša that many members of our immediate families have been baptized. My parents were, in short, relatively typical of their place, community, and time.

A key purpose of Kathy, John, and Pam's trip was to meet with our cousin Dáša. The article that had appeared in the *Washington Post* magazine had tried to draw a dramatic comparison between Dáša's life and my own. While I had had a good life, she had suffered. That was true, but the article also made it seem that my father was responsible for Dáša's decision not to come to the United States with the rest of our family. "I think he [Josef Korbel] did me wrong," Dáša is quoted as saying. "He should not have left me here. If he had suggested I go with them, I would have gone. He should have been aware of the dangers of staying here."

These accusatory words chilled me when I first saw them, because I knew they were wrong but would be taken for truth by thousands of readers. We had always believed that when my father had returned to Prague in 1948 for Jan Masaryk's funeral, he had asked Dáša, who was then twenty years old but still legally his ward, to come live with us. She had refused because she was in love with the man she later married and wanted to attend university in Czechoslovakia. Now she was reportedly saying that my father had abandoned her and he, of course, had no way to respond. I couldn't believe Dáša would say such a thing.

John told me that when they went to see Dáša, they had had to make their way past television cameras waiting for the "private" visit. Kathy recalled that at first everyone was uncomfortable. When they discussed my father's last visit to Prague, Dáša tellingly said, "He should've just slapped me and told me I had to go. I couldn't have imagined what living under Communism would mean." She added that my mother had written to her regularly, sending pictures of all of us, and had also transferred the title to some family property to Dáša, which she later sold, using the proceeds to buy a weekend home. John said Dáša had been shocked and upset at the furor her interview had caused.

The damage, however, had been done. Added to allegations that my father had denied our heritage were assertions forever in the public domain that he had abandoned his "ward."

IN 1997, I MYSELF MADE TWO TRIPS to the Czech Republic, the first official, the second private. In July, following the Madrid NATO Summit, I went to Prague to receive an award and to celebrate the invitation my homeland had just received to join the Alliance.

The schedule permitted only a few hours of free time, and I couldn't go to all the places my brother and sister had visited, but I did want to go to the Pinkas Synagogue—a holy and melancholy place. Entering, you observe what appears to be a fine wallpaper covering the walls, but as you get closer, you can see that the pattern is actually made up of neat black writing listing the 77,297 Czechoslovak Jews who died in the Holocaust. There is a touch of red at various intervals, denoting the towns from which the victims came and their last names and the initial letters of their first. Separated from the next listing by a small orange star, each name is followed by the dates of birth and death. A year earlier I had visited the synagogue with Hillary Clinton. It looked the same now as it had then. It was I who had changed.

The Jewish officials accompanying me pointed out the names of Arnošt and Olga Körbel on the first column I came to. We had to go up two sets of stairs to find Růžena Spieglová's name. I closed and opened and closed my eyes, imprinting the image in my mind. I had expected to feel overwhelmed and sad. I had been to many Holocaust memorials, including Yad Vashem in Israel and the Holocaust Museum in Washington. Each time I had been reminded that, in all of history, there had been nothing comparable, nothing so beyond comprehension, nothing so horrible to contemplate, and nothing so vital to remember.

I was prepared for such feelings now but unsure what else I would feel. One of the things that had been nagging at me was that my grandparents had never been real to me while I was growing up. It was only now that I was a grandparent myself that I could imagine how we might have been together. I looked at my grandchildren with love that overflowed, and I thought, "This is how my parents' parents must have looked at me all those years ago."

Whatever my expectations, I had not foreseen that I would start visualizing my grandparents in striped concentration camp uniforms, seeing their hollow faces staring back at me. I realized as I did so that I had no clear idea of what my grandparents had looked like during the war, since the few photographs we had were taken years earlier. I thought about how they must have suffered, their struggle to survive, the torture of their last hours. I thought also of the anguish experienced by my parents that had been so well hidden from me: the pain of leave-taking, the agony of not knowing, the sorrow of learning, and the unshakable determination to protect.

As I turned away from the names on the walls, I felt both profoundly sorrowful and grateful. My family's presence on those walls had added a direct personal element but not fundamentally changed my view of the Holocaust and its horror. However, I now knew that if not for my parents' decision to leave Prague, their names and mine would also be on the synagogue wall and my sister and brother would not have existed. My parents had given me life not once, but twice.

In late August, I returned to the Czech Republic, this time on vacation. My daughters and their husbands and Kathy came with me. Their company and the relaxed schedule made it impossible to feel gloomy. This was the first time I had been in the Czech Republic with my daughters. I had hoped they would be entranced, and they were. So much of what they had loved about their grandparents was evident in the places we visited and the things we did. In Prague I played the role of tour guide as we walked the route my father and I had followed when he took me to school. I showed them the windows to the apartment, and they imagined me as Madlenka playing out front in the square. We ate all the spicy foods my parents had fed them during the summers in Denver; retraced Kathy, John, and Pam's route, visiting the towns where my parents had grown up; went to the high school they had attended and saw the classrooms in which they had sat. We also went to Terezín.

ONE LEGACY OF World War II is a list of names synonymous with unutterable horror: Auschwitz, Buchenwald, Treblinka, Mauthausen, Bergen-Belsen, Majdanek, and others. Terezín is slightly less notorious because it was designed not as a death camp but as a holding area for Czechoslovak and other Jews. Nevertheless, over 33,000 Jews died there and almost 87,000 more were deported to death camps and ghettos further east. Between 1942 and 1944, more than 10,000 children entered Terezín; 8,000 were sent onward to extermination camps; fewer than 150 survived.

The town of Terezín is in the northwest part of the Czech Republic, conveniently near the German border. It was built in the 1780s as a fortress, where soldiers of the Austro-Hungarian empire could live in safety with their families. There were moats and thick walls, which later made it a natural choice for a prison. By the 1880s political and military prisoners were being sent there. In November 1941, the star-shaped fortress became an enclosed settlement for Jews. Today it is a museum dedicated to remembrance and resolve.

We drove through the green countryside to Terezín and arrived in a huge parking lot. There were not many visitors that day, but we were told that people came to visit the museum from all over the world. Although the camp had played a significant role in Hitler's plan to exterminate all Jews, at the time that mission was concealed. Nazi propagandists referred to it as a "spa town" where Jews could govern themselves, receive medical care, and "retire." Some were even fooled into paying for their admittance.

This alleged "paradise," however, was in fact a hell. In the summer of 1942, when Arnošt and Olga Körbel and Růžena Spieglová arrived, the number of inmates had risen from around 20,000 to almost 60,000. Men slept in three-tiered bunks, while women crowded together on straw-covered floors. People were starving. Able-bodied inmates were employed laying tracks for a rail extension that would make transportation to death camps to the east faster and more efficient. Sanitary conditions were poor, which led to outbreaks of typhoid. The daily number of fatalities rose and many, including my grandfather, died of the disease. During our visit, we were shown the ovens the Nazis used to cremate the bodies of those who died as a result of the inhuman conditions.

I NOW KNEW at least the outlines of the whole horrible story. Not only my grandparents but many of my relatives had died during the Holocaust. The facts had been there all along—not even buried deep or hard to find. I just had not looked. It was like a painting with no discernible pattern or images until someone says, "Can't you see a man's face in the middle?" Then you look again and see it clearly, and wonder why you didn't before.

It is crushing to know that three of my grandparents died in concentration camps and that my parents lived with that sorrow. I am proud now to know my full background. I always thought it was quite a story, but I feel further enriched by the knowledge that I am part of a valiant people that has survived and flourished despite centuries of persecution.

Since 1997, I have been asked whether I will practice Judaism. I do not think that will happen. I grew up and grow old as a Christian, and as I said earlier, it's hard to unlearn faith. I don't attend church as regularly as I did, but I do go occasionally and almost always at Christmas and Easter. That first Easter after I knew the truth, I felt uncomfortable visiting the cathedral. It is not easy to get older and be unsure about your religion.

After the news about my family broke, I was asked repeatedly how I felt about being Jewish. I knew some people, including longtime acquaintances, felt I must have known about my heritage much earlier and had tried to deny it or cover it up. That is not true. As an adult, I have always viewed myself first as an American and second as a Czechoslovak, but for me, as for my parents, identity is primarily a question of nationality and values, not blood. I realize full well, however, that blood did matter to Hitler and that fact must matter to us all, because it is why six million Jews died.

Of all the words written about my family, I was moved most by the *New York Times'* A.M. Rosenthal. "Arnost Korbel, Olga Korbel, Anna [Růžena] Spieglova," he wrote, "were murdered almost half a century ago. Now at last they are receiving what the living owe the dead of the Holocaust—to remember their names and never to forget they were put in the gas chambers because they were Jewish. There is no lesson to be learned in the Holocaust except this: Evil beyond evil was done and can be done again, unless the living remember."

SIXTEEN

Building a Europe
Whole and Free

AT THE HEIGHT OF THE FUROR over my family's past, a cartoon appeared in a newspaper showing a room full of psychiatrists sitting next to an empty sofa. On the sofa was a note that read, "Gone to work, M.A." The cartoonist couldn't have known my mental state, but she caught the truth that, despite the distractions, I had plunged headfirst into my job as Secretary. I was determined to show the American flag wherever we had interests at stake, and I had goals in mind on every continent. In Europe I had three priorities: to manage the process of NATO enlargement successfully, so there would be no question about the continued value of the world's most effective military alliance; to promote the integration of Russia into the West, to minimize the risk of returning to the divisions of the Cold War past; and to ensure that the Dayton Accords were fully implemented, to eliminate any danger of Bosnia erupting once again into flames. I began my term by taking action on all three fronts.

AFTER CZECHOSLOVAK FOREIGN MINISTER Jan Masaryk jumped (or was pushed) to his death in 1948, it was clear that Stalin was intent on dominating Central and East Europe. This challenge prompted Washington to forge a trans-Atlantic military alliance called the North Atlantic Treaty Organization (NATO) to defend against further Communist inroads and provide war-shattered economies in the West a shield behind which they could rebuild. The Alliance helped bring the former Fascist nations, first Italy, then Germany and Spain, into the family of European

PSYCHOANALYZING MADELEINE ALBRIGHT

democracies; it stabilized relations between Greece and Turkey, and it helped tear down the Berlin Wall. All without firing a shot.

By the time President Clinton took office, an obvious question had arisen. With no superpower enemy, why NATO? The President's answer was that it remained the cornerstone of European security. Although the Soviet threat had vanished, other threats such as terrorism, the proliferation of weapons of mass destruction, and ethnic cleansing had taken its place.

A second question was how to fill the security vacuum left by the dissolution of the Warsaw Pact. The area between Germany and Russia had been a flashpoint for centuries. The major powers had exploited it as a battleground to define the limits of their imperial reach, dividing and redividing the region into spheres of interest. President Clinton and his allied counterparts were determined to create a different model.

Together they set out to do for Europe's East what NATO and the Marshall Plan had done for Europe's West. Their goal was to create a sphere of common interest in which every nation could live in security. To this end, they established linkages through the Partnership for Peace between NATO and other European democracies. They transformed the Organization for Security and Cooperation in Europe (OSCE) from a mind-numbing talk shop into an arena for supporting democracy and human rights in its fifty-three member countries. In Brussels in 1994, President Clinton announced U.S. backing for a gradual process of enlarging NATO. In 1997, invitations were to be issued at the Alliance's summit in July.

While I was in favor of NATO expansion, I had kept my counsel when the proposal was first raised; I didn't want anyone to suspect me of special pleading on behalf of the Czech Republic, Slovakia, or other potential NATO candidates. As the debate gathered momentum, however, I became a vigorous advocate, and with the decision to expand now made, I was excited by the prospect of helping to implement it as Secretary of State.

One didn't have to be a native of the region to see the logic of what was planned. After four decades of Communist subjugation, the nations of Central and East Europe were eager to join an enlarged NATO. I felt we should welcome them, because if they were denied NATO protection, they would be in political limbo and might well seek security through other means, resulting in unpredictable alliances, efforts at rearmament, and the possible use of force to settle disputes.

To me all this seemed obvious, but many in the foreign policy establishment took a different view. One can easily forget how strong the opposition was. George Kennan, for instance, the ageless icon of U.S. diplomacy, denounced NATO enlargement as "the greatest mistake in Western policy in the entire post–Cold War era." The usually insightful *New York Times* columnist Thomas Friedman termed it "reckless," and former Senator Sam Nunn organized a letter signed by fifty prominent political and academic figures accusing the administration of "making an error of historic proportions." An informal Council on Foreign Relations poll showed experts opposing NATO expansion two to one.

These were serious people with a legitimate concern. Russian President Boris Yeltsin and his countrymen were strongly opposed to enlargement, seeing it as a strategy for exploiting their vulnerability and moving Europe's dividing line to the east, leaving them isolated. Moscow's anxiety mattered because Russia had become something the world had never before seen: a weak and potentially unstable country with thousands of nuclear arms. Yeltsin understood Russia's need for good relations with the West, but if resentment at NATO enlargement caused control in Moscow to shift to extreme nationalist forces, an even more dangerous Cold War might ensue.

We had to walk a tightrope to keep faith with Europe's new democracies while not recreating our old enemy. Our critics didn't think we would be able to keep our balance. I thought we could.

In February 1997, only weeks after taking office, I traveled to Moscow as part of a ten-nation around-the-world trip. My reputation preceded me. Ever since my appointment, the Russian press had portrayed me, based on my Central European birth and strong support for NATO enlargement, as an unreconstructed cold warrior. The media dubbed me *Gospozha Stal* or "Madam Steel." U.S. journalists had raised parallel questions about the new Russian foreign minister, Yevgeny Primakov, former head of Russia's foreign intelligence service, a successor to the KGB. Since taking office, Primakov had been striving to reassert Russia's global influence, often at the expense of Moscow-Washington ties. It was anticipated that as soon as the two of us met, sparks would fly.

When I arrived at the foreign ministry guesthouse in Moscow, Primakov took me into a comfortable sitting room before our formal meeting. After an exchange of pleasantries, he confided, "Because of my earlier career, I know all about you but I would like to hear directly whether you are like your old professor Brzezinski, anti-Russian." "I am close to Dr. Brzezinski," I responded, "and I respect him very much. But I have my own opinions and you shouldn't judge me based on my past association with anyone. I know you are a fierce defender of Russian interests. You should understand that I intend to be equally fierce in defending American interests. If we both acknowledge that, we should get along fine."

After agreeing to call each other by our first names, we launched into a discussion of NATO enlargement. Yevgeny, who is burly, with impressive eyebrows and a crooked smile, said that Russia couldn't agree to enlargement and didn't take seriously the possibility that Russia might one day be invited to join. I replied, "The U.S. and Russia have missed many opportunities in the past. We both have to think in new and creative ways. You should regard NATO enlargement as a way to assure stability in Central Europe. That is in Russia's interests."

Primakov responded that Russia needed a guarantee there would be no nuclear weapons on the territory of new allies and no increase in military infrastructure. Without making commitments, I said those were the kinds of issues I had come to discuss. That evening we joined our respective teams for a working dinner of borscht, sturgeon, and some truly interesting jellied prunes. Before departing, I presented Primakov with a picture of President Clinton and me as a gift to his granddaughter, who had entered the world the previous day. On the photo, I inscribed in Russian, "Little Mary, when you were born, your grandfather and I were trying to do something to make the world a better place for you to live."

The next morning I met with Boris Yeltsin, who was still recovering from a rigorous reelection campaign, heart surgery, and double pneumonia, and who was scheduled to meet with President Clinton in Helsinki the next month. Despite his occasional resemblance to W. C. Fields, the Russian president played a pivotal role in putting his nation on a democratic path. He was a major transformational figure. That morning, however, he was like a figure made of wax, his complexion pasty and his body startlingly thin. To shake hands with him, I had to cross a large expanse of highly polished wooden floor while cameras filmed my approach. I concentrated on not falling down, thinking that high heels were no help in diplomatic tightrope walking.

Notwithstanding his infirmities, Yeltsin's voice was strong and his blue eyes sparkled. I was flattered when he dismissed his interpreter, saying that I didn't need help understanding Russian.[1] He then warned that NATO enlargement would result in the redivision of Europe into two camps, and that the West had nothing to fear from the "New Russia." I replied, "Mr. President, if as you say there is a new Russia, there is also a new NATO, not one of we versus you or you versus us, but one where we are on the same side." Yeltsin then introduced what I found to be his recurring theme. "Russia and the U.S. have problems to discuss that can only be resolved by the Presidents. If we are to come to closure on NATO, Bill Clinton and I are the ones who will decide." To Yeltsin, anything was possible if only he could talk one on one with his friend, whose name he pronounced "Beeel."

The administration's goal was to proceed with enlargement while minimizing Russian heartburn. Our plan was to develop a NATO-Russia charter that would give Moscow a voice but not a veto in European security discussions. Negotiating the charter was a tedious process. The Russians wanted a permanent ban on the deployment of NATO forces and military infrastructure on the territory of our prospective new allies. However, this would have relegated these allies to second-class status, left us unable to cope with emergencies, and required us to reach an agreement affecting the security of other countries without their consent.

At one stormy meeting in Washington, I told Primakov, "Neither the President nor I are going to negotiate over the heads of the Central Europeans about their security arrangements. That's been done in the past, and it's not going to happen again, not on my watch."

"Madeleine," Primakov replied, "why aren't you willing to meet us halfway?"

"Halfway? Halfway?" I remonstrated. "You keep going back to square one."

Primakov sighed. "I don't really think we can have an agreement."

---

1. Interpreters play a vital but overlooked part in diplomacy. The best ones are able to translate not only words but also points of emphasis and tone, and are careful to ensure that idiomatic expressions are not misunderstood. I grew very fond of those who interpreted regularly for me and also of some of the foreign interpreters, whose voices I came to know intimately.

I said, "Fine, we don't need one."

Part of our strategy, of course, was to convince the Russians that enlargement would go forward with or without their agreement. We hoped Kremlin leaders would realize that they had as much to gain from a charter as we did. We didn't know, however, if Yeltsin realized that or saw more benefit in venting outrage at American "arrogance."

One test came in mid March 1997, when the U.S. and Russian leaders met in Finland for what was jokingly called the Summit of the Invalids. Yeltsin was still recovering from his surgery. President Clinton had ripped a tendon in his leg by tripping on the front steps of golfer Greg Norman's Florida home. Upon arriving at the airport in Helsinki, the newly immobilized Chief Executive was lowered to the tarmac on a catering truck, from which he was transferred to Wheelchair One. When discussions later got tough, the President said, "Hey, go easy on me, I have a bum knee," at which point Yeltsin pretended to open his shirt to show the scars from his surgery.

Both leaders had just been elected to second terms, and doubtless each had an eye on history. They had several issues on their agenda but began with NATO. Yeltsin reiterated his claim that it was both illogical and dangerous to bring new members into the Alliance, yet he also expressed his willingness to join the United States in trying to alleviate what he called "the negative consequences." He then asked for a private assurance that NATO would not bring in former captive Soviet republics (Estonia, Lithuania, and Latvia). The President refused, arguing that such an agreement would make Russia look weak, redivide Europe, demoralize the Partnership for Peace, and infuriate the Baltic states.

When Yeltsin pressed his request, Clinton got irritated and raised his voice. "Come on, Boris, even if I went into a closet with you and told you what you want to hear, Congress would find out and pass a resolution invalidating the NATO-Russia Charter. I just can't do it. I can't make commitments on behalf of NATO, and I'm not going to be in the position of vetoing any country's eligibility, much less letting you or anyone else do so."

Yeltsin retreated but would not give up. He asked our assurance that former Soviet republics wouldn't be admitted "in the first rounds." The President said he wouldn't do anything to revive old stereotypes or make it seem as if Russia and NATO hadn't changed. After what appeared to be a heated exchange between Yeltsin and his own team, the Russian leader turned to Clinton and shrugged, "Okay, Bill, but I tried."

In the run-up to the dinner, officials from both countries voiced their concern about how much Yeltsin would drink. Clinton promised to keep an eye out and could be relied upon to set a good example. The President did a good job as chaperone and was delighted with the main course—

reindeer steak. "We should serve this at the White House," he said, digging in. "It has very little cholesterol." Listening to this, and looking at what was on my plate, I had to respond. "Mr. President, with all respect, you should stick to your day job. Do you want the whole world to know you're eating Donner and Blitzen?"

The Helsinki Summit moved us forward, but for two more months we wrangled over the details of a NATO-Russia Charter. Strobe Talbott compared the Russian negotiating strategy to a dental root canal, saying Moscow wanted the ordeal to be so painful that we would forget about further rounds of NATO enlargement. For our part, we went at the Russians in waves. First Strobe searched for the smallest changes in Moscow's positions, often suggesting how compromises could be justified to the Russian people. Next I would have blunt sessions with Primakov, who always waited till the last minute to budge. Then NATO Secretary General Javier Solana would build on our progress and achieve more on his own, making clear to the Russians that they could not have what they most wanted, a formal role in Allied decision making.

Solana's efforts were critical because negotiations over the charter were officially between Russia and all sixteen NATO Allies, not just the United States. I had first met Solana when he was Spain's foreign minister and I was at the UN. Bearded and brainy, he was a master diplomat. Although he was also a physicist, our relationship had chemistry. Ironically, NATO's chief was also a Spanish Socialist, who had opposed his own country's entry into the Alliance fifteen years previously.

Our challenge, as the negotiations continued, was to bridge the divide between our approach and Russia's. We saw European security in post–Cold War terms. Our model was Bosnia, where NATO allies, the Partnership for Peace, and other countries were already working together with Russia by our side. Russia's model was the old strategic arms control process, where each side was accorded a certain number of missiles, warheads, and launchers, thereby preserving a careful balance between East and West blocs. As a result, the Russians pressed for limits on what would be permissible on the territory of new allies. We refused to negotiate on that basis but said we had "no need, no plan, and no intention" of deploying nuclear weapons or substantial new forces to the East.[2]

In early May, I traveled to Moscow again to see Primakov. Earlier,

---

2. We also pointed out that negotiations were under way in Vienna to adapt the Treaty on Conventional Forces in Europe, thereby limiting the size of national forces, including those of NATO's current and prospective European members. That was the right forum for Moscow to achieve the limits it sought.

when he had visited Washington, I had wanted to invite him to my home for dinner but couldn't because termites had devoured parts of my dining room floor. Instead we had both been hosted by Strobe Talbott and his wife, Brooke Shearer. Now Primakov invited us to his apartment to meet his wife and share a family-style dinner. The food was good and the conversation lively. We talked about the tendency of our respective bureaucracies to whittle away understandings we were able to reach when talking directly. Bureaucracies operated, we agreed during the vodka course, a lot like termites. From then on, whenever we had a misunderstanding, we would blame it on "termites."

Eventually we wore the Russians down. It had become obvious from the pattern of our meetings—hard talk followed by retreat—that Yeltsin wanted an agreement. Sure enough, on May 13, President Clinton and Secretary General Solana were able to announce that we had one—the NATO-Russia Founding Act. This document provided an institutional means for Russia to participate in trans-Atlantic security deliberations without violating any of the conditions we had set. We had succeeded in walking the tightrope.

On May 27, we assembled in Paris for the signing ceremony. Feeling celebratory, I had put on a lavender suit, and thought I looked my very best. During a lunch for foreign ministers, I was chatting happily with Germany's Klaus Kinkel until I happened to glance down at my skirt. There was salad dressing all over it. My first thought was, "Darn it, all those men in dark suits—if they spilled anything, no one would know." For me this was a disaster. Worse, French Foreign Minister Hervé de Charette announced that we were all to gather for a photograph immediately after lunch, with me, as the only woman, right in the middle.

I lost track of my discussion with Kinkel as I tried to figure out what to do. I had given up carrying a purse because I kept leaving it behind. I considered stealing the menu and holding it over the stains. Then I had an inspiration: When I got up, I would turn my skirt around. I tested to make sure the waist band was loose enough. Luckily the skirt was not one of those chic ones that had a high slit up the back. So I did it, and everything worked out fine. Not a move with which Henry Kissinger could have gotten away.

Two days following the ceremony in Paris, NATO foreign ministers met again in Sintra, Portugal, to discuss how many nations should be invited to join NATO during the first round of enlargement. The United States hadn't yet taken a formal position, but we were leaning strongly toward a group of three, rather than the four or five that some had proposed. Our hope, however, was to make this particular omelet without breaking any eggs. We were trying to unite Europe, not divide it, and didn't want NATO invitations to be seen as report cards separating Europe's new democracies into winners and losers.

A small first round seemed the best option because we expected that every problem associated with enlargement would be made more difficult if we invited five members instead of three. The costs would be higher, the risks of diluting NATO's strength greater, and the challenge of gaining Senate approval harder.

We didn't expect opposition to the three candidates we intended to support—Poland, Hungary, and the Czech Republic—but we knew there would be unhappiness about our failure to back others. One was Romania, whose candidacy was being pushed by France's President Jacques Chirac. Romania had new leaders who were initiating economic reforms and reaching out to the nation's historic regional rivals. The Romanian people were more openly enthusiastic about NATO membership than, I am sorry to say, the Czechs. Unfortunately, Romania had spent seven years at the post–Cold War starting line. From 1989 until 1996, its economy had stagnated. By 1997 Romania was doing all the right things, but it hadn't been doing them long enough.

If Romania were a late-blooming candidate, Slovakia was a wilting one. Prime Minister Vladimír Mečiar had dragged his country down with extreme nationalism, economic mismanagement, and an authoritarian style. Among his less than brilliant schemes was a call for the voluntary repatriation of Slovakia's ethnic Hungarian minority. This was not the kind of thinking likely to find favor in the new Europe. During the NATO summit in Madrid, I would tell Mečiar to his face that he had personally cost Slovakia its chance.

On May 30, at an informal lunch with NATO foreign ministers in Sintra, I explained the American position. To avoid argument, I didn't mention the names of specific countries we were for or against. My colleagues, however, were not so restrained. Apparently Chirac had been particularly active in his lobbying. The majority of the sixteen foreign ministers said they favored the inclusion of more than three countries. The headlines from Sintra implied that the United States was isolated, which on the surface seemed true. Only Great Britain and Iceland had staked out a position similar to ours.

We suspected, however, that a number of allies—while not wanting to displease France—were actually counting on the United States to impose discipline. Solana told me privately that the Alliance seemed to be divided equally. He said he would go quietly to each capital to hear what he called "confessions" and try to achieve a consensus.

In mid June, we gave the consensus-building process a nudge by going public with our position. This move reflected the importance of timing in U.S. diplomacy. We had waited so that supporters of the other candidates would feel they had been given fair consideration, but now we had to make a decision. As long as we continued saying maybe, others would continue saying *oui*.

Since NATO acts by consensus, our declaration essentially settled the matter. However, Chirac, who would never lose an opportunity to distinguish French policy from that of the United States, was determined to play his losing hand to the end. When the summit convened in Madrid, Chirac and Italian Prime Minister Romano Prodi made the case for admitting five new members. President Clinton outlined our reasons for limiting the initial round. The battle lines were drawn, until Germany's Chancellor Helmut Kohl persuaded everyone to put the heavy artillery away.

Previously the Germans had been careful not to offend France or anyone else. Now Kohl made an eloquent plea for consensus. He said it was "a miracle" that NATO had agreed to invite Poland, Hungary, and the Czech Republic. "Two or three years ago such an agreement wouldn't have been a simple matter," but clearly, "there won't be agreement on more than three countries." The Alliance should focus instead on the public message it would convey. Romanians should know that, if they continued to reform, they would be considered seriously for membership, as would the Baltics, Slovenia, and other candidates. Following Kohl's lead, the Madrid communiqué limited invitations to three countries but established the "open door"—a process for the consideration of future applicants.

The summit was also the occasion of the first meeting of the NATO-Ukraine Council and an inaugural lunch for leaders of the Euro-Atlantic Partnership Council. The creation of these new groups was just part of the institutional rejiggering that characterized the entire decade. The end of the Cold War had been like a gigantic mix-up at the European laundry. All the old labels fell off, and every nation had the chance to try on clothes with a different brand. "Satellites" had become emerging democracies, old adversaries had become allies and partners, and dull old institutions had begun to pull on bright new socks. The effect, we hoped, would be to create a twenty-first-century look that, for all the national differences, would be characterized by a common commitment to democracy, mutual security, shared prosperity, and peace.

AFTER MADRID, the President went to Warsaw to congratulate Poland on its invitation, then to Bucharest to reassure Romania. These were amazing stops. Working with our Polish hosts, the White House advance team produced an American campaign–style event in Warsaw's Castle Square. Thirty thousand jubilant "mourners" attended what was advertised as "Yalta's Funeral." There were marching bands, red carpets, balloons, and banners. The sun even broke through just as the President began to speak of the opportunities and obligations of NATO membership.

If Poland was wonderful, Romania was incredible. The President's decision to go there was a risk. The Romanians could have reacted bitterly to NATO's decision. Instead the crowds were larger and even more enthusiastic than in Poland. They made us all feel guilty. I knew we had made the right judgment for the moment but hoped fervently that Romania would join the Alliance at an early date.[3]

As the President returned home, I went to touch base with Primakov in Saint Petersburg. Our official meeting was as cantankerous as ever, with Primakov warning about how the world would end if the Baltics ever entered NATO. Later he and I went to an elegant restaurant in a park for a private dinner, at least as private as one can get with a translator sitting there. Both officially and socially, Primakov and I had an interpreter present but didn't use him unless we were stumped. Yevgeny would speak Russian and I would speak English. The time we saved by talking directly allowed us to cover a lot of subjects. I mentioned that although I had been Secretary for only six months, we had already met eight times. He said we should tell the press that we had already had eight "public" meetings, and let them guess what we were leaving out.

After we ate, he escorted our entire delegation on a private tour of the Hermitage, the quarter-millennium-old Winter Palace made famous by Catherine the Great. We were in the season of the white nights, when a blue twilight enfolds the old capital, darkness never completely comes, and dusk blends gently into dawn. It was a unique experience to see the palace's magnificent art collection under such conditions. Primakov and his staff were generous in allowing us all—including the press, administrative staff, and plane crew—to join the tour. The next morning we visited Catherine's Summer Palace, where we were greeted by a twelve-piece oompah band in period uniforms, including epaulets. The only touch missing was Marlene Dietrich on a white horse.[4]

---

3. In November 2002 NATO issued its second round of invitations, t· Romania, Slovakia, Slovenia, Bulgaria, and the three Baltic states. Naturally, I was pleased that summit was held in Prague.

4. To actually see Marlene Dietrich on a white horse, you have to watch Josef von Sternberg's classic 1934 film about Catherine, *The Scarlet Empress.*

SINCE FIRST ARRIVING in America, I had been back to Czechoslovakia, or the Czech Republic, as a tourist, goodwill ambassador, pollster, promoter of democracy, and UN permanent representative. Now President Clinton brought word of NATO's invitation to Poland; Defense Secretary Cohen had gone to Budapest; my assignment was Prague. It was, to understate the case, a somewhat emotional trip, beginning with my visit to Pinkas Synagogue, followed by Havel's presentation to me of the Order of the White Lion. As he placed a red and white sash over my head, I was reminded of the lampshade party dress I had worn way back in Denver.

My official focus, however, was the speech I was to deliver in Smetana Hall of the Municipal House, where the first Czechoslovak Republic was announced in 1918, in parallel with Tomáš Masaryk's declaration in America. The structure was designed by the art nouveau master Alphonse Mucha, with the intent of countering German influence by celebrating Slav culture. Each room is different and dedicated to a place where Slavs live. I had never been inside because the building had long been in the process of being restored. Every light fixture, mural, sculpture, and stained glass window had been returned to its original beauty.

On the stage where I would speak were the Czech and American flags. I walked down the aisle with Foreign Minister Josef Zieleniec, then on stage to wait for the presidential fanfare. Finally Havel arrived and the gathering was complete.

Zieleniec gave me an eloquent introduction, and I got up to speak. Before me were rows of familiar faces—with my cousin Dáša in the first. After four and a half years in public office, I had delivered many speeches, but never one in which the personal and the professional were so intertwined. My words were evidence of the pride I felt in the people of my native land.

"The Communist authorities kept from you the truth and still you spoke the truth," I said, thinking of Prague Spring and Charter 77. "They fed you a vacuous culture and still you gave us works of art that fill our lives with intelligence, humor, and warmth. They tried to smother your allegiances, your faith, and your initiative, and still you taught the world the meaning of solidarity and civil society. They banished your finest leaders, and still you gave us Václav Havel."

Prime Minister Václav Klaus told me later that no Czech leader could have given such a speech, because it was so optimistic and so American. After I finished, I had to deal once more with the emotions of hearing the Czech and American national anthems played in sequence. Much later I walked along the streets, tears in my eyes, waving at little old Czech ladies with tears in their eyes, seeing in each the reflection of my mother.

On NATO ENLARGEMENT, we had made the right deal with Russia and achieved the right outcome in Madrid. Now we had to win in the Senate. Later, after we had prevailed, people suggested that the outcome had been inevitable. It certainly didn't seem so at the time. We needed to convince two-thirds of the Senate to extend Alliance protection to the three new candidates. Although our case was strong, we were wary that a coalition would form between liberal and conservative Senators. We knew that some on the left would oppose enlargement because it risked radicalizing Russia; some on the right believed that we were taking Russian concerns too much into account.[5]

Our strategy was to consolidate support among knowledgeable Senators with mainstream views and work hard to convince every member with an open mind about why our policy made sense.

Before the full Senate considered the treaty, it had to be approved by the Foreign Relations Committee. This meant Jesse Helms. He had placed himself on our side initially, but the NATO-Russia Founding Act prompted him to show me the cartoons in his office that described him as "Senator NO." He didn't like cutting deals with Moscow. As a former Senate staffer, I understood well the value of legislative theater. Simple agreement in politics is boring. As a result, even friendly Senators often make demands and establish conditions they declare must be met in return for their support. This enables them to claim credit for stopping the administration from doing something foolish, even if the administration had never intended to do it in the first place.

In the case of NATO enlargement, Helms set three conditions. First, he wanted us to specify the military threats NATO might face in the new century. This was his way of getting us to say in public that we still considered Russia a danger. Second, he wanted agreement in advance on the costs of enlargement and who would pay those costs. This was to protect Helms' standing as a fiscal conservative who couldn't abide the waste of taxpayers' money on things that didn't directly benefit North Carolina. Third, he wanted us to detail Russia's nonrole in NATO decision making.

---

5. Preparing for the debate, I read James Chace's excellent biography of Dean Acheson, including an account of the Truman administration's complex fight to gain Senate consent to the original NATO Treaty. I was impressed by the administration's success in gaining the support of veterans, business, and labor groups, and by its exhaustive consultations with Congress, and felt we should undertake a similar campaign. We had recruited Ronald Asmus, the Rand Corporation's leading expert on NATO, as a deputy assistant secretary of state for European affairs, and charged him with coordinating our efforts. We also brought in Jeremy Rosner, former director of legislative affairs at the NSC, to mobilize public and congressional backing.

This was to dispel the fear raised by Kissinger and others that we had given Boris Yeltsin the keys to NATO's aircraft and tanks.[6]

Helms' conditions were precisely the type a senator would lay out if he intended, at the end of the day, to say yes. Since I knew he was more than capable of establishing conditions that were impossible to meet, I was relieved to give the chairman his assurances during a meticulously scripted exchange before his committee.

Although we were gaining converts and winning the debate, our job wasn't done. In Congress, the final vote is often not the most important. We had to avoid crippling amendments. Several surfaced during the endgame, including one offered by Missouri's John Ashcroft to limit NATO's role to collective defense and prevent any future "out of area" missions. The amendment was prompted by the myth, popular among the administration's right-wing critics, that we wanted to turn NATO into a globe-trotting peacekeeping force. Ashcroft would have had us go in the other direction by making NATO power available only where it was least needed and preventing it from responding to global terrorism and other emerging threats. The Senator claimed to be preserving the intent of NATO's founders, but Secretary Acheson had made it known half a century earlier that the Alliance could band together to defend common interests outside the geographic scope of its members—as NATO was already doing in Bosnia and would do in Kosovo.

On April 30, 1998, they finally voted. As other amendments were considered, Ashcroft insisted that Senate Majority Leader Trent Lott schedule four hours in prime time on his proposal to limit NATO missions. Instead, Lott moved to dispose of the Ashcroft amendment without any debate at all, a motion that was carried by a wide margin. The Senate then approved NATO enlargement 80–19, with healthy majorities in both parties voting in favor.

A little less than a year after that vote, I had the honor of watching Foreign Ministers Jan Kavan of the Czech Republic, János Martonyi of Hungary, and Bronisław Geremek of Poland sign the NATO Treaty. The scene was the Truman Presidential Library in Independence, Missouri. The master of ceremonies was Larry Hackman, the library's director, who endeared himself to me by mentioning that Katie Albright had spent weeks at the library researching her senior thesis on Truman and Acheson's policy in Korea.

The ceremony, with the world watching and fireworks going off

6. With uncharacteristic inaccuracy, Kissinger had accused us of doing exactly what we had not done, which was give Russia the right to veto Alliance decisions.

simultaneously in Warsaw, Prague, and Budapest, reminded me of my years as a professor. I had taught Central European politics and history at a time when most assumed that history is all the region's people would ever have, because their future would be forever frozen in Cold War ice. Now, with the United States, NATO, and Central Europe together as allies and friends, the boundaries of possibility had been pushed back to a new and seemingly limitless horizon.

When it came time for me to speak, I noted the turnaround in the prospects of Central Europe, while admitting that Americans had not always given the region sufficient attention. To illustrate this, I recounted a story that Jan Masaryk had told about a long-ago visit to the States. Asked by a U.S. Senator, "How is your father and does he still play the violin?" Jan had replied, "Sir, I fear that you are making a small mistake. You are perhaps thinking of Paderewski and not Masaryk. Paderewski plays the piano, not the violin, and was president not of Czechoslovakia but of Poland. Of our presidents, Beneš was the only one who played, but he played neither the violin nor the piano, but football. In all other respects, your information is correct."

BY BRINGING Central and East Europe closer to the West, the process of adapting NATO was a vital part of our effort to build a Europe whole and free. The urgent question I faced was whether the Balkans could also be brought closer to the West. The answer, I was convinced, would depend on the success or failure of the Dayton Accords. That agreement had ended the hot war in Bosnia by opening the door to a NATO-led peacekeeping force. As guns were holstered and tanks mothballed, water and power were hooked up, trolleys began to run, children reclaimed the streets from snipers, and reconstruction began. However, serious problems remained. Dayton had affirmed the principle of a unified Bosnia, but it would take far more than a piece of paper to make that goal a reality.

I saw evidence of the unrelieved tensions when I visited the region a few months after the agreement was signed. As UN ambassador at the time, I wanted to lend support to efforts at repatriating refugees. In this case the UN was trying to help Croats return to an area conquered during the war by ethnic Serbs, a goal not popular with the latter. As our delegation toured the marketplace in Vukovar, no one wanted to shake hands with me: then all of a sudden there were smashed eggs on the ground and shouts of "*kurva*" and "*kučka*." My Serbian served me well. While my colleagues wondered what was happening, I knew I was being called a whore and a bitch. I quickly told my security detail, "Let's get out of here." As our cars pulled up, first mud, then stones were thrown, and a rock shattered the window of the staff van.

A few hours later I received a phone call from a nervous but stern daughter. "Mom," said Anne, "CNN just carried a story that you were surrounded by a mob throwing rocks at you. What were you thinking? Why don't you show more sense? You could have been killed." The role reversal was now complete. In addition to balancing my checkbook and questioning why I was spending so much money on clothes, my children were now taking over the job of worrying. Later I gave them tee shirts made up by one of my traveling companions.[7] They read, "I got stoned with Madeleine Albright in Vukovar."

The Dayton Accords set ambitious goals for holding elections, returning refugees, and uniting the country. Unfortunately, anti-Dayton extremists were influential within each of the three ethnic communities, and the first round of elections legitimized their control. Local leaders, especially among the Serbs, were openly hostile to the accords. As my reception in Vukovar illustrated, the hatreds unleashed during the years of war were still raw.

Prospects were further clouded by the first Clinton administration's pledge that the peacekeeping force would complete its mission in one year. Warren Christopher emphasized this deadline in his post-Dayton remarks. Tony Lake elevated the "exit strategy" to the status of policy doctrine in a March 1996 speech. These statements were designed to reassure Congress and the Pentagon that Bosnia would not become another Vietnam, but it was soon evident they were utterly unrealistic. Of Bosnia's prewar population, one in ten had been wounded or killed during the conflict. Of the survivors, five in ten had lost homes; eight in ten were relying on the UN for food; nine in ten were unemployed. It would obviously take more than a year to recover.

In November 1996, the administration abandoned one premature deadline and immediately established another. A follow-on NATO-led military Stabilization Force, or SFOR, would be created. The President pledged that the new force would complete its mission by June 1998. Unfortunately, by the time I moved from the UN to the Secretary of State's office, implementation of Dayton was lagging. SFOR was engaged in what I called reverse mission creep, taking no risks and doing little to help achieve civilian-related goals. Neither Yugoslavia nor Croatia were meeting their obligations. Our European allies lacked any urgency. More and more pundits said the only realistic option was to partition Bosnia, with one segment joining Serbia, another Croatia, and the third becoming an international protectorate.

7. Jacques Klein, an American who served as the UN's transitional administrator for the region.

Partition, as far as I could see, wouldn't create stability, only a new fight over borders. We had to insist that the new Europe be built on principles of democracy and respect for human rights, not ethnic cleansing and brute force. The United States, NATO, Russia, the PFP, the OSCE, the EU, and the UN had all committed themselves to help Dayton succeed. This was hardly a trivial test.

I first needed support from my administration colleagues. The biggest question mark was the new Secretary of Defense, Bill Cohen, who had opposed the President's Bosnia policy while in the Senate and who in public statements was now suggesting that SFOR must withdraw on schedule, even if this led to a resumption of war. It took weeks of discussion, but we finally agreed that our emphasis in public should not be on when SFOR would leave but on what the entire international community, including SFOR, could help Bosnians achieve.

On May 22, 1997, I unveiled our reenergized approach in a speech at the *Intrepid* Sea-Air-Space Museum in New York City. My remarks were addressed to four audiences. I wanted administration colleagues to know I would fight to extend the U.S. military presence if that proved necessary. I explained to Congress why we should care whether Bosnia held together in peace or fell apart in renewed conflict. I sent a message that Europe's full partnership was both anticipated and required. And I presented Bosnians and their neighbors in Croatia and Yugoslavia with a choice: they could reject Dayton and be subject to sanctions or they could strive to implement Dayton, receive our aid, and begin to participate in Western institutions.

To dramatize the choice, I followed the speech by going directly to the region, starting with Croatia. I viewed houses that had been burned when ethnic Serb refugees sought to reclaim them, and met with families of mixed heritage who had been beaten up by local thugs. These families didn't see themselves as belonging to any particular ethnic group. They were Yugoslavs and proud of it; yet they were being brutalized because their blood was not "pure" enough. Among them was a white-haired grandmother who had been physically abused. "How could you let this kind of thing happen?" I berated the Croat minister of reconstruction. "You should be ashamed."

What I was asking Croatia to do wasn't easy. The series of wars in the region had scrambled populations. It seemed to me a grotesque game of musical chairs, except it was musical houses; everyone was in somebody else's house, and there weren't enough to go around. It was messy and difficult, but if we didn't enforce the right of refugees to reclaim their homes, we would acquiesce in ethnic cleansing and reinforce pressure for partition.

In Zagreb, Croatia's capital, I met with Franjo Tudjman, the silver-maned, self-styled father of his country. Years earlier, while at the UN, I had reminisced pleasantly with him about a childhood summer visit of mine to Brioni Island, off the Dalmatian coast. Now, however, I confronted in Tudjman an extreme nationalist. Politically shrewd, he had gained control over every Croat institution that mattered, while losing control over his ego. He peddled the image of Croatia as a stable Western democracy but ruled it with an iron fist and a corrupt soul.

I told him that the United States felt warmly toward the Croat people and wanted to have a good relationship but that we needed cooperation. He replied that Croatia deeply valued its relations with us and "fully supported" the Dayton Accords. Then came the "buts": Croatia couldn't accept more than a small percentage of the ethnic Serb refugees who had a right to return. Croatia couldn't promise to cooperate with the war crimes tribunal unless Serbia did, nor support the concept of a united Bosnia, because it would become a base for Islamic fundamentalism. Further, Croatia was being ignored by the West.

I reminded Tudjman that I had had stones thrown at me for defending the rights of Croat refugees in Vukovar. I said there would be no place in the West for countries that practiced or condoned ethnic cleansing, and I cautioned him that American support for international loans would depend on his cooperation.

In the children's game, paper enfolds rock. In our meeting, Tudjman, evidently hoping that a filibuster could foil reasoned discussion, launched into a long, jingoistic account of Balkan history. He spoke about the need for a Roman Catholic Croatia to break the "green crescent" of Muslims extending from the Balkans to the Middle East and the "Orthodox cross" of Slavs extending throughout the region. Traditional European values, he said, meant that we should stand with him in creating an ethnically pure "Western" state.

There was no point in responding: he was not listening. I did, however, insert a final request. "Bosnia," I said, "needs trade routes to the north. I will visit the town of Brčko tomorrow and would like to announce your agreement to open the bridge there. Is that possible?" Tudjman agreed—a positive step.

That afternoon, I traveled to Belgrade to meet with Slobodan Milošević. This was to be our only face-to-face encounter. Despite his record, Milošević had been able to persuade some diplomats that his word was credible. It helped that he spoke English and condemned with enthusiasm his counterparts among the Bosnian Serbs. While a good con man, he did not have a sophisticated understanding of the West: he certainly underestimated the Clinton administration's resolve.

I told him I had just come from a momentous week in Europe, during which the NATO-Russia Founding Act had been signed, the Euro-Atlantic Partnership created, and the fiftieth anniversary of the Marshall Plan observed. I pointed out that Yugoslavia had not been a party to any of this, but that that could change if Belgrade complied with its obligations. Milošević responded by telling me—as hostile Serbs habitually did—that I wasn't well informed about the history or present situation in the region. He said that Yugoslavia should be part of Europe but that the international community was blocking its path.

Politely, but firmly, I cut him off: "I am very well informed about the region: my father wrote a book about it, and I have followed events carefully since. I do not need your lecture on its history." I agreed that his country should be treated fairly and pointed out that I had been in Croatia earlier in the day protesting the treatment of ethnic Serb refugees. Emphasizing that we were prepared to have a good relationship but needed to see concrete deeds, I asked him to hand over to The Hague three suspected war criminals whom we believed were serving in the Yugoslav armed forces. Grimacing, Milošević said he would study the indictments that I had given him, and if the evidence were strong, he would recommend prosecuting the suspects locally. He would not agree to extraditions.

Finally, I pressed him to meet with leaders of the Albanian ethnic community in Kosovo. I said that the United States or some other country could send representatives to such a meeting if that would help. Milošević said that he did not want to internationalize the problem of Kosovo and that his government needed no outside aid. Before concluding, we had a one-on-one meeting, during which the Serb president tried to charm me and I tried to resist his charm. I had by far the easier task. As we walked out together through some ornate doors, the press was waiting. I felt set up, because we had agreed there would be no pictures, but I couldn't think of a way not to shake hands. So I did, while keeping my face rigid and expressionless—harder to do than it sounds.

While in Belgrade I found time to visit the residence of the Czech ambassador. This is where I had lived with my family half a century before. It was, of course, far smaller than I remembered, and a portion had been turned into offices. As I walked through my old bedroom, I reflected that if the Fates had chosen differently, I might conceivably have followed in my father's footsteps and moved with my own family into this house as ambassador to Yugoslavia from Czechoslovakia.

The next day, in Sarajevo, I met with members of Bosnia's joint presidency to inaugurate a committee to ensure military coordination among the ethnic groups. This was an important step and a clear break with the wartime mentality of the past. After the meeting, I walked down the street once known as Sniper Alley, stopping at a playground repaired with USAID funds, when I came across a little girl who thanked America for fixing her swings. I placed flowers on Grbavica Bridge in memory of Suada Dilberović, a medical student and sniper victim, the first of more than 150,000 Bosnians to die in the war. I also met with a contingent of the new police force. Then I became the first U.S. cabinet member to travel to the Serb-controlled entity within Bosnia and Herzegovina, the Republika Srpska (RS).

I started in the northern town of Brčko, where I meant to capitalize on Tudjman's promise of the previous day and announce the reopening of the bridge across the Sava River into Croatia. The bridge connected Bosnia to a highway leading toward the heart of Europe. The restoration of a normal border would be a sign of healing. Brčko itself was a bell-wether city still disputed by Serbs and Muslims. Its opening to the West would benefit all.

In the spirit of reconciliation, the three members of Bosnia's Joint Council of Ministers were due to join me in a short ceremony. The daunting logistics of making this happen set the stage for a virtuoso performance by Kitty Bartels, a young assistant to Jamie Rubin. Kitty is about five-four, with an angelic face, round midwestern eyes, and a bottomless reserve of creativity. Her assignment was to ensure that everyone was in the right place when I arrived.

That afternoon she confronted a mob of mutually antagonistic Bosnian politicians milling around the bridge entrance where only the three prime ministers and I were supposed to stand. Since no one was wearing name tags, Kitty couldn't distinguish the prime ministers from the rest. Bosnia is a chauvinistic place, and few showed interest in her pleas. As the sirens of my motorcade approached, Kitty feverishly began nudging people off the platform, but as I drew into sight there were still about two dozen suits standing around. In desperation, she screamed for silence, then said, "If you are a prime minister, please raise your hand. I repeat. If you are one of the three prime ministers, please raise your hand. Everyone else leave the platform now." Miraculously, first one, then two, then three hands rose skyward. When my car pulled up, the prime ministers were in their assigned positions.

Afterwards we breathed a sigh of relief not only because of Kitty's quick thinking but also because there had been no incidents. The previous night one of our team had walked out onto the bridge to survey possible angles for photographs. None of the local residents would accompany her for fear of snipers. Traveling to and from the ceremony I had been surrounded by U.S. Army troops and my own security detail openly carrying arms. I was also required to wear a bulletproof raincoat, which was hot, uncomfortable, and so big, the material stuck out above my shoulders. I eyed the photographers warily, fearing the caption, "Madeleine Albright, the Hunchbacked Dame."

The last stop was in Banja Luka, where I met with RS President Biljana Plavšić, a fierce Serb nationalist known as the Iron Lady of the Balkans. The meeting was risky for both of us. My approval rating among Plavšić's constituents was subzero, and I didn't want to imply U.S. support for her extreme views. I did, however, hope to encourage her to break with past Bosnian Serb policy by supporting compliance with the Dayton Accords.

Sitting with our two delegations in the Banja Luka Town Hall, Plavšić was stiff and unyielding, so I asked to meet with her separately. In her back office we talked at length and I found her views both complex and promising. Serb nationalism was a major part of Plavšić's identity, and she was not about to apologize for it. At the same time, she had become a bitter rival of Radovan Karadžić, a virulent hard-liner who had led the Bosnian Serbs during the war and whose corruption was among the many factors strangling the local economy. Plavšić wanted her people to have the benefit of sound governing institutions, and she acknowledged to me privately then, and publicly later, that cooperation with the Dayton process was the only practical way to move forward and attract outside help. Her pragmatism made a huge difference.[8]

For more than a year, Karadžić had been a principal target of efforts to apprehend persons indicted by the war crimes tribunal. We believed he was responsible for many of the worst atrocities during the war, including the massacre at Srebrenica. Not long after my trip in the summer of 1997, we planned a major operation. Working with four other nations, we had in mind a Bosnia-wide sweep designed to net Karadžić and fifteen to twenty other suspected war criminals in a single day. I was angered when, at the last minute, a key country—whose identity remains secret—opted out. We ended up with a far smaller action that resulted in the arrest of one suspect and the shooting of another. Karadžić remained at large.

During the fall of 1997, our State Department Balkans team concentrated on two goals in the Balkans. First, we did all we could to strengthen

8. In 2001, it was announced that Plavšić had been indicted by the war crimes tribunal in connection with her role as a Bosnian Serb leader during the 1992–1995 war. Plavšić surrendered voluntarily to The Hague and subsequently pled guilty to "persecutions on political, racial and religious grounds." In December 2002, at the request of both the prosecution and defense, I testified before the Tribunal at Plavšić's sentencing hearing. At age 72, she was given eleven years, but as of this writing remains the highest-ranking official to take responsibility for crimes against humanity and the first to do so while calling for reconciliation.

the pro-Dayton forces, especially among the Bosnian Serbs. In October, SFOR seized four Bosnian Serb radio transmitters that were being used by Karadžić to broadcast anti-Dayton propaganda. This bold stroke was orchestrated by General Wes Clark, the new NATO supreme commander. Clark had played a major role in the Dayton negotiations and knew how the military could effectively support the agreement's implementation, including the civilian aspects. As I told the President, Clark was the best partner we could have had.

Second, we persuaded the White House and the rest of the administration that SFOR should remain in Bosnia after the June 1998 deadline. By then we had shown that a determined campaign to implement Dayton had the potential to transform the political dynamics of the region. In mid December, I sent a personal note to the President urging him to support a continued deployment to Bosnia at the highest of the three levels then being considered. A strong U.S. commitment would leverage involvement by Europe, while sustaining our own leadership. This was, I told my boss, "one of the most important decisions of your second term."

In a press conference on December 18, the President announced his decision to support another follow-on military deployment, this time without any deadline. The new force would measure its progress by tasks accomplished, not months elapsed. The following week he traveled to Sarajevo, bringing with him a message of sustained commitment, and by year's end Bosnia was regarded by most observers as on the right track.

I am convinced that if the State Department had not pushed so hard to reinvigorate the Dayton Accords, the administration would have drifted and the peacekeeping force would have left prematurely. After a period of testing, hostilities would have resumed and the nightmares of earlier years might well have been repeated. Ultimately we could have been forced to go back into the region with a far larger number of troops, in far more hazardous conditions.

Over the years I developed my own benchmark for determining progress in Sarajevo—the Holiday Inn. The first time I visited the Bosnian capital, in 1994, the Inn was a wreck and no one was staying there. In 1996, I was permitted to stay at the hotel, but there was a big hole in the middle of the building, half of which couldn't be used. By 1997, the hotel had been repainted a bright yellow and all the rooms repaired. When I returned in 2000, the facility was the thriving center of a bustling metropolis. Sarajevo, the Olympic City, was coming back to life.

SEVENTEEN

Migraine Hussein

O N SEPTEMBER 12, 2002, President George W. Bush appeared before the UN General Assembly to make the case for international action to disarm Saddam Hussein's Iraq. As I listened to his words, I had to nod in agreement. It was, after all, similar to speeches I had made time and again during my years as UN ambassador and Secretary of State. The story of America's confrontation with Saddam Hussein stretched across three presidencies and reflected continuity of basic policy but sharp contrasts of circumstances and approach brought about primarily by the tragic terrorist attacks of September 11, 2001. The impact of this confrontation will be felt in the Gulf and worldwide for decades to come. There were many actors in the drama. This is what happened during my time on the stage.

OF ALL THE HEADACHES inherited by the Clinton administration, Saddam Hussein was the most persistent. We would spend eight full years grappling with issues left unresolved at the end of the 1991 Persian Gulf War. When that conflict ended, U.S. officials assumed that Saddam's career would be short-lived.[1] Even if he were not toppled by his battered military or by factions opposed to his rule, the first Bush administration

1. "It was our expectation at that point that in the aftermath of the war, Saddam Hussein would not be able to survive politically, that, more than anything else, the returning Iraqi forces would overwhelm him and overthrow him, and that one way or another he was going to be made to pay a price for this strategic fiasco." Former Bush administration official Richard Haass, interview by *Frontline*, *Spying on Saddam*, Public Broadcasting System, April 27, 1999.

expected Iraq to be rendered harmless through UN Security Council resolutions requiring the declaration and destruction of the country's weapons of mass destruction (nuclear, chemical, and biological) and missiles. In any case, the United States did not think at the time that Iraq's experiments in these areas had been extensive. The whole process of inspection and disarmament, it was felt, should be over in a few months.

As the world knows, this was not to be. Instead of capitulating, Saddam terrorized potential domestic rivals and stonewalled the UN. Iraq's weapons programs proved more substantial than originally estimated. When I arrived at the UN in 1993, we were already beginning to realize how intractable a problem Iraq would be.

I had been in office less than three months when authorities in Kuwait thwarted an assassination attempt against former President Bush during his visit there to commemorate the second anniversary of the Gulf War. After investigating, the FBI concluded that Iraqi intelligence agents were responsible. We laid plans to retaliate by bombing Saddam's intelligence headquarters in Baghdad. This led to a tricky diplomatic assignment for me on the day of the strike. I had to inform the Iraqi permanent representative that we were in the process of launching cruise missiles at a target in his capital.

Because it was a weekend, and UN buildings were locked, I visited Iraqi Ambassador Nizar Hamdun at his residence on Manhattan's Upper East Side. When I arrived, I was escorted into a spacious wood-paneled room and seated on a sofa beneath a jumbo-sized portrait of Saddam Hussein. The Iraqi ambassador came in, we exchanged pleasantries, and he offered me tea. "So what brings you here today?" he asked with a slight smile. He was clearly surprised by my visit, and even more by my message. I said, "Well, I'm here to tell you we are bombing your country because you tried to assassinate former President Bush."

So much for tea. Hamdun spluttered, "That is an outrageous lie."

"It is not a lie, and if you come to the Security Council, I will lay out the evidence for all the world to see."

He glared at me, and I thought for a moment, "He's not going to let me out of here." I rose quickly, thanked him for receiving me, and departed. The next afternoon I went to the Security Council and made a full presentation, complete with photographs, proving that Iraq was indeed behind the assassination attempt.

The confrontation with Baghdad continued with varying degrees of intensity throughout the Clinton years. During my time in New York my instructions were to do everything I could to maintain UN sanctions in order to pressure Baghdad to come clean about the full extent of its weapons programs. To ease the impact on innocent Iraqis, we gained approval of a plan allowing Baghdad to sell limited amounts of oil in order to buy food and medicine—commodities not forbidden by the sanctions regime. For years Saddam rejected this program entirely and even later never allowed his citizens to take full advantage of it. In the Kurdish sectors of northern Iraq, where the program was administered by the UN, child nutrition was better after the Gulf War under sanctions than it had been before the war. Had Saddam spent Iraq's money on humanitarian goods, his people's suffering would have been far less. Instead he squandered the country's assets rebuilding weapons factories and constructing lavish palaces for himself, his family, and cronies.

To illustrate Saddam's arrogance, we declassified aerial photography showing postwar construction of palaces, man-made lakes, and weapons factories. In 1995, I made a trip to various Security Council capitals to display the photos, which were dramatic. Some depicted a palatial multi-tiered complex about five times the size of the White House. When I showed the pictures to one Arab monarch, he exclaimed, "Why, that palace is bigger than mine!"

At the conclusion of the Gulf War, the UN had been given the job of doing something never before done—disarming a country without militarily occupying it. The mission had been assigned jointly to the International Atomic Energy Agency (IAEA) and the UN Special Commission (UNSCOM), a multinational group of experts. Although lied to, intimidated, and harassed, the inspectors accomplished much, dismantling biological and chemical warfare facilities, removing nuclear materials, and establishing an extensive weapons monitoring regime.

Saddam's goal was to foil the inspectors by gaining relief from sanctions without giving up his remaining weapons. His strategy was to publicize the hardships of Iraqi civilians in order to gain sympathy among Arabs and the West, and to an extent he succeeded. Anti-Americanism will always find a receptive audience in some circles.

I regret to say that I aggravated our public relations problems during a 1996 interview on the CBS program *60 Minutes*. The segment included a visual tour of Iraqi health care facilities, with pictures of starving children and denunciations of UN policy by Iraqi officials. Little effort was made to explain Saddam's culpability, his misuse of Iraqi resources, or the fact that we were not embargoing medicine or food. I was exasperated that our TV was showing what amounted to Iraqi propaganda. Near the program's end, Lesley Stahl asked me, "We have heard that half a million children have died [as a result of sanctions]. I mean, that is more children than died in Hiroshima. And, you know, is the price worth it?"

I must have been crazy; I should have answered the question by reframing it and pointing out the inherent flaws in the premise behind it. Saddam Hussein could have prevented any child from suffering simply by meeting his obligations. Instead, I said the following: 'I think that is a very hard choice, but the price, we think, the price is worth it.' As soon as I had spoken, I wished for the power to freeze time and take back those words. My reply had been a terrible mistake, hasty, clumsy and wrong. Nothing matters more than the lives of innocent people. I had fallen into a trap and said something that I simply did not mean. That was no one's fault but my own. There are many times in everyone's life when the mouth works faster than the brain; there was no more regrettable example in my own career than this ill-considered response to Leslie Stahl.

When I became Secretary, the White House asked me to deliver a major address on Iraq. I agreed, convinced that our policy of pressuring Iraq to disarm while containing its military was apt: each time Saddam had tested us, we had tightened his leash. Allied troops enforced no-fly zones over 40 percent of the country. A multinational Maritime Interception Force was striving to prevent illicit shipments from reaching Iraq through the Persian Gulf. UN weapons inspectors had by then destroyed more weapons of mass destruction capacity than had been eliminated during the Gulf War. The Iraqi armed forces were less well equipped and modern with each passing year.

Future progress, however, was in jeopardy. Iraq owed Russia and France money from past transactions and those countries wanted to collect. Yevgeny Primakov told me, "Without sanctions, the Iraqis would sell oil and pay us; with sanctions, they sell oil and use the sanctions as an excuse not to pay us." There was also a general sense of "sanctions fatigue" and the feeling in some quarters that Baghdad no longer posed a serious threat.

I wanted to issue a wake-up call. Saddam was not just another dictator. He had invaded both Iran and Kuwait, and yearned to develop a nuclear bomb to impress an Arab world that despised him.

The resulting speech, delivered at Georgetown University, was later mischaracterized as a change in U.S. policy. In fact, it reaffirmed it. The senior President Bush had vowed that sanctions would never be lifted as long as Saddam remained in power. The problem with that formulation was that it appeared to eliminate any incentive for Iraq to comply with Security Council resolutions. The first Clinton administration had taken a slightly different approach, saying that we would oppose lifting sanctions until Iraq met its obligations under all applicable Security Council resolutions. We didn't say it was impossible that this could happen under Saddam, but we expressed our doubts. I personally didn't believe Saddam had any intention of complying, but the combination of sanctions, inspections, military pressure, and possible air strikes had placed him in a box.

During my years at the UN, I worked continuously and successfully to maintain a coalition that kept him there. The question I faced as Secretary was whether we could sustain that solidarity despite the passage of time, the economic and human costs of sanctions, and Saddam's propaganda.

The first major test came in October 1997, when the Iraqi leader decided to test our resolve by blocking UN weapons inspections and demanding American inspectors be fired. Security Council members unanimously rejected these moves but were sharply divided on what to do if Iraq did not allow inspections to resume. Primakov publicly opposed any discussion of military force. I countered that every option must be on the table.

Saddam's strategy was to exploit the council's division by shifting blame from himself to the UN inspection team. The Iraqis argued UNSCOM was dominated by the United States and Great Britain and that sanctions would never be lifted, no matter what Baghdad did. UNSCOM's chairman, Richard Butler, a blunt-speaking Australian with little tolerance for Saddam's bluster, countered with the truth. His team was composed of staff from more than three dozen nations, and its mandate came from the entire Security Council. If Baghdad cooperated, the inspectors could be done in a year. The idea that Iraq was being treated unfairly was nonsense; it reminded me of the story about a schoolboy who returned home with his nose bloody and his shirt torn. When his mother asked how the fight had started, he replied, "It started when the other guy hit me back."

President Clinton's position was firm. UNSCOM had to be allowed to resume work with unfettered access. To underline the point, the President ordered a buildup of U.S. military strength in the Gulf. On television, Defense Secretary Cohen held up a five-pound bag of sugar and urged viewers to imagine that it was filled with anthrax—a bacterium Iraq had admitted producing prior to the Gulf War. "This amount of anthrax," he said, "if it's spread over a city, let's say the size of Washington, would destroy at least half the population." He then held up a test tube and said, "VX is a nerve agent. One drop from this particular thimble, one single drop, will kill you within a few minutes." Weapons inspectors had found almost four tons of VX in Iraq.

This was scary stuff. All of a sudden we had the public's attention. People were worried about Saddam's weapons and asking what we were going to do. The problem was, we didn't have a fully satisfactory answer. We were threatening to use U.S. airpower to attack military targets, but air strikes, no matter how punishing, would not guarantee the return of inspectors to Iraq, nor permanently destroy Baghdad's capacity to produce weapons of mass destruction. No serious consideration was given to actually invading Iraq. The senior President Bush had not invaded when given the chance with hundreds of thousands of troops already in the region during the Gulf War. If President Clinton had proposed doing so in 1998, he would have been accused of being reckless and opposed by friends in the Gulf, our allies, most senior officers in our own military, and leading Republicans.[2]

Our preference, therefore, was a diplomatic solution. We expected Russia would try to broker such a deal but were skeptical on what terms. During his years with the KGB, Primakov had developed close ties to Saddam Hussein. This relationship gave Primakov unique access to Baghdad, but it also colored Russia's view. When I asked Primakov about the Iraqi dictator, he said we were guilty of exaggerating the threat Saddam posed. Moscow wanted to establish comparatively loose inspection standards that Iraq would be able to meet, enabling sanctions to be lifted. We believed the worst possible outcome would be a clean slate for a still-menacing Saddam Hussein. We insisted, therefore, on inspection standards tough enough to ensure that Iraq would be required to account for and eliminate every element of its prohibited weapons programs.

In mid November 1997, I left for a long trip to Europe, the Gulf states, and South Asia, with Iraq topping my agenda. (I was to find throughout my years as Secretary that travel was an efficient use of time because face-to-face meetings were action-forcing and also made it easier to do business later by phone.) At my first stop I was hosted by Robin Cook in his native Scotland. In years to come I would work closely with Cook and share many tense and dramatic moments. The British foreign secretary had red hair, expressive eyebrows, a well-trimmed beard, and a well-deserved reputation as a brilliant debater and wit. During our joint tenure, Cook helped ensure Great Britain's position as a stalwart ally in backing an appropriately tough line toward Iraq. We were both determined to keep the pressure on until Iraq met its obligations to disarm. I left Edinburgh confident the United States and United Kingdom would stand together in pressing Baghdad to

---

2. Obviously, many perspectives were altered by September 11, 2001. When asked during the 2000 presidential campaign about forcibly replacing Saddam Hussein, Republican vice-presidential candidate Dick Cheney said, "I think we want to maintain our current posture vis-à-vis Iraq." He added a moment later that the first Bush administration had refrained from overthrowing the Iraqi dictator because it did not want the United States perceived as "an imperial power, willy-nilly moving into capitals in that part of the world, taking down governments." *Meet the Press*, National Broadcasting Company, 27 August 2000.

permit UN inspectors to return without restrictions. What I wasn't sure of was whether we would stand together alone.

Hopscotching from one capital to another, I stayed in constant touch with Cook and French Foreign Minister Hubert Védrine. It was vital that the allies be united in responding to whatever proposal was cobbled together by the Russians. We also needed support from Arab states, although these governments tended to be ambivalent. Many were privately contemptuous of Saddam and would have been pleased to see him gone, but they worried that our threat to use air strikes was inflaming Arab public opinion. As a result, most were hard to pin down, especially in public.

In Qatar, the Amir expressed deep concern about the impact UN sanctions were having on the Iraqi people, saying, "We are losing the next generation" of that country "to bitter radicalism." I also met with Bahrain's Amir, a gentle old man who repeatedly proclaimed his desire for peace. At the press conference, reporters asked whether I had convinced Bahrain to support military strikes. I didn't want to answer that question, so I told them instead that Bahrain fully supported our demand that Iraq allow inspections to resume. When we returned to the plane, we were given two large shopping bags filled with gifts from the Amir. Opening them, we were stunned to find Rolex watches for everyone on board, including a diamond-encrusted gold one for me. Under State Department rules, we couldn't accept them. Under the rules of Arab diplomacy, we couldn't reject them. So we brought them back to the States to be auctioned off for the benefit of the U.S. taxpayer.

Next was Kuwait, where I was supposed to stay just long enough for a joint press conference. Unfortunately, earlier in the day, in Cairo, the Kuwaiti foreign minister had said he opposed military action against Iraq. This wasn't what Kuwait had told us previously, so I wanted to use the press conference to obtain an official correction. Ultimately the Kuwaitis wrote a statement in Arabic that we had translated into English. When the Kuwaiti defense minister proclaimed it to the press, it sounded as if he were reading from some ancient text: "Iraq's insistence on escalations opens the door for all options which might not be in the interest of Iraq." Was that an endorsement of U.S. policy? Sort of, I thought. "Absolutely," I told the press.

While on the Arabian Peninsula I also had a chance to meet with the ousted UNSCOM inspectors, who were angry, disheartened, and eager to return. They told me that, in their judgment, Saddam's ability to produce weapons-grade uranium had been all but destroyed, which would severely limit Iraq's ability to build a nuclear bomb unless materials were procured abroad. Chemical and biological arms, however, were easier to build—and hide.

From the Gulf I flew to South Asia, arriving on November 17. I knew that thousands of miles to the north, top Iraqi officials had been huddling in Moscow with Primakov and Yeltsin. What were they up to? In India the next night, instead of sleeping, I placed or received twenty-six phone calls. Hubert Védrine told me Primakov had delayed a planned trip to Latin America. Yevgeny wanted to set up a meeting of key foreign ministers in Geneva on the evening of the 19th to discuss a deal with Iraq. I said I couldn't be in Geneva until the morning after that and we shouldn't schedule anything until we knew whether Iraq had agreed to resumed inspections.

I called Primakov and so began a classic game of telephonic one-upsmanship. He said he was sorry I couldn't be in Geneva because he thought there would be progress to report. I said I had already cut short my South Asia trip and couldn't leave without meeting Indian leaders; he should be willing to chop another twelve hours off his own visit to Brazil. He said that was impossible and I should send a deputy. I said that wasn't an acceptable way to do business and I would be in Geneva at two A.M. Yevgeny said, "Fine, but I will be gone."

A few hours later, Primakov called back to say that Iraq was willing to allow UNSCOM to return to Baghdad without any change in its composition. He said he could brief me on the details at midnight in Geneva. I replied, "I will be there at two A.M."

"No way. I cannot stay past midnight."

"Yevgeny," I replied, "it will look pretty strange for the Russian foreign minister to exclude the American Secretary of State from a meeting on Iraq over a scheduling difference involving only a couple of hours. Especially after President Clinton has been so supportive of your country's admission to the G8."

Primakov sighed loudly. "I will see you in Geneva at two A.M."

"Thank you," I said, and hung up.

I found it interesting that I was in India, a Cold War friend of the Soviet Union, while Primakov was eager to begin his visit to Brazil, a long-time friend of the United States. The superpower game of the old days was clearly over, but we were both out there trying to score points in the new game, even if the rules were still being written.

As I flew to Geneva, I worried about what kind of arrangement Primakov might have reached. I knew Yevgeny would tell us Baghdad had decided to be reasonable, but I didn't know under what conditions the inspectors would be allowed to operate or what promises Moscow had made to gain Baghdad's consent.

Geneva is beautiful, but when it's two A.M. and drizzling, every city looks the same. Our motorcade pulled up to the Palais des Nations, which had been built in 1936 to house the League of Nations shortly before that organization collapsed. I had visited the palace as a child when my father worked for the UN and remembered peacocks strutting across the grounds. It was too dark for peacocks now.

Wearily and warily I greeted my colleagues and seated myself, ready for Yevgeny's show. He began by announcing that Iraq had indeed agreed to allow UNSCOM to return without conditions. He then applied the soft soap, congratulating us all for working so well together and hinting at "positive steps" that might be taken after the inspections resumed. He also said he had prepared a draft statement for us to sign that would show Iraq a little light at the end of the sanctions tunnel.

Robin Cook asked if the Iraqis truly understood the return of UNSCOM would be unconditional and the composition of its inspection teams unaltered. Primakov said, "Yes, but there are issues that should be addressed after UNSCOM is back."

I complimented Primakov while probing for hooks beneath the bait. Where was the draft statement? Was it understood that UNSCOM was to remain independent? Did Iraq think it had some sort of deal on lifting sanctions? Did Moscow make any secret promises? "This is not a Russian trap," Primakov assured me, which made me suspect it was. I knew he wouldn't tell me the full truth about his discussions, but I made it clear that no promise, commitment, or understanding between Moscow and Baghdad would be remotely binding on the Security Council. Primakov said he understood.

Meanwhile most of the discussion centered on the wording of the joint statement. I insisted the text refer to Iraq's decision to allow inspections as "unconditional" and that we include a mention of the Security Council resolution spelling out UNSCOM's right to be as intrusive as necessary. I also insisted we make clear that any decision to change UNSCOM's composition or procedures had to be approved by the council.

As I got up from the table, I felt we had won a victory, if only a temporary one. We had used the threat of force effectively and kept Saddam from exploiting differences among our allies, Russia, and us. UNSCOM would be given another chance to test Iraq's intentions. We had given away nothing, but we were also pretty much back where we had been, and we had not erased Saddam's power to provoke a new crisis.

THE GENEVA AGREEMENT worked for about two months. First there were disagreements about UNSCOM's access to so-called "presidential sites," which consisted of palaces and other government complexes suspected of harboring secrets. The Iraqis said these should be off-limits, while UNSCOM insisted on the unconditional access mandated in Geneva. In mid January, Baghdad blocked a series of surprise inspections, then demanded a three-month moratorium on all such activities and a six-month deadline for lifting sanctions, regardless of Iraq's disarmament status. The result was a reprise of the previous fall.

Once again the continued viability of UNSCOM was in doubt. Once again the President was firm in demanding that Iraq be held to account and ordered an increase in U.S. military capabilities in the Gulf. Once again I crossed the Atlantic to engage in face-to-face consultations with allies and friends, describing my task in words that would have their echo in later years, "Over the next few days, I will be explaining the American position to leaders in the countries I visit, while making it clear that, in confronting the clear and present danger posed by Iraqi lawlessness, the diplomatic string is running out." Arriving in Europe, I found the British fully supportive and the French unusually so. In Paris, Védrine told the press, "All options are open," his toughest statement yet.

My top priority in returning to the Gulf was to obtain the backing of Saudi Arabia, the region's most influential state. Its head of government was the old and ailing King Fahd. Real power resided in the hands of the King's younger half-brother Crown Prince Abdullah—one of thirty-seven sons by sixteen wives sired by his father, King Ibn Saud, founder of modern Saudi Arabia. The Crown Prince, who had been raised in the desert in traditional Bedouin fashion, received me at an elaborate campsite where he occasionally stayed outside the Saudi capital city of Riyadh. We had driven out in a motorcade of luxury buses and recreational vehicles, arriving at what seemed a small city of tents and air-conditioned trailers. Upon arrival, our delegation was presented with large boxes of desert truffles which, because the gifts were perishable, we were allowed under State Department rules to keep. After a group lunch, I adjourned with the Crown Prince into one of the trailers for a more private discussion.

Although physically imposing in his white robes, the Crown Prince, like most other Arab leaders with whom I met, was unfailingly gracious. Notwithstanding the stereotypes, I never had the sense of being patronized or taken less than seriously. His good words about me to other Arab leaders would later make my path easier. On the subject of Iraq, the Crown Prince shared the mixed feelings of those leaders. He had no use for Saddam Hussein but was concerned about the reaction of Arab populations to any attack on a brother Arab state. The matter was particularly sensitive for the Saudis, he said, because of their special position within Islam. I argued that it is "precisely for that reason of having a unique role in the Islamic world that Saudi Arabia also has a unique responsibility to protect that honorable religion. You and the entire world know Saddam Hussein is an evil man who represents a slap on the face of Islam." The Crown Prince drew some clear lines about what could and could not be revealed publicly about the outcome of our talk, but I returned home pleased with what we had been able to accomplish. All told, I was able to report to the President that we had at least fifteen nations willing to contribute military resources, plus a dozen more that would allow us to use their territory or airspace in connection with military action.

Having secured backing abroad, we needed to do a better job of making our case at home. The NSC's Office of Communications came up with the idea of an internationally televised open meeting featuring the National Security Advisor and the Secretaries of State and Defense. The site chosen was Ohio State, the date February 18, 1998.

There are many ways to express protest during a public event without impinging upon the rights of others. You can hold up a sign, turn your back, make impolite gestures, or dress in a weird costume. You are more likely to be noticed, however, if you shout. There were a lot of shouters at Ohio State. The protestors, dispersed throughout the audience, interrupted in sequence. Every time a heckler was removed or silenced, another started up. The event's host, CNN, did little to help. In ninety minutes, Bill Cohen, Sandy Berger, and I were interrupted twenty-nine times, making it hard to present our arguments. Each of us was miked, so we couldn't talk to one another, but we exchanged looks asking, "What the hell are we doing here?"

Unfortunately, I hadn't yet learned how to deal with protestors. Still more professor than politician, I always hoped sweet reason would prevail. Besides, I never put up with shouting in class. I tended to take things personally and got indignant when people said, for example, that I was responsible for murdering millions of people. At Ohio State one professorial-looking gentleman questioned whether America had the moral right to threaten military action against Iraq. It seemed to me obvious that, under the circumstances, it would have been immoral *not* to confront Saddam Hussein.

The intentions of the protestors were lofty but their information was not as good as their lungs. Wanting to shield Iraqis from suffering, they thought the way to do that was to oppose us. But most hadn't seen the video footage of Saddam's attack on the Kurdish village of Halabja in 1988, where five thousand died; nor the pictures of fathers trying to protect their children from the poison falling from the sky or of women dying while trying to get water down their throats. They had not talked to the Kuwaitis whose family members had disappeared during Iraq's occupation and about whose fate Baghdad refused all answers, or to Iraqi dissidents tortured in Saddam's prisons, or to Iraqi defectors who detailed Saddam's manic pursuit of ever-more-lethal arms. They accused us of not caring but seemed to have no conception of the suffering that appeasing a ruthless dictator might cause. And they insisted, facts notwithstanding, that our embargo included medicine and food.

Because the protestors succeeded in stealing the story, our appearance at Ohio State was a fiasco, my roughest day in office to that point. I was unhappy with the NSC, the protestors, and myself. It didn't help when I received a cheerful note from CNN informing me that the broadcast had reached a potential audience of 800 million people in more than two hundred countries. A cartoon showed the three of us stumbling into the Oval Office to report to the President looking as if we had just returned from a war. From then on, whenever anyone had what seemed like a harebrained scheme for communicating our message, just saying "Ohio State" was enough.

The previous November, Yevgeny Primakov had taken the lead in preventing a confrontation with Iraq. Now Kofi Annan stepped in. In mid February he traveled to Baghdad and negotiated an agreement designed to assuage Iraqi sensibilities while also meeting UNSCOM's bottom-line requirements. The agreement included yet another last-minute commitment from Iraq to comply with Security Council resolutions and cooperate with UNSCOM. In return, the Secretary General would appoint diplomats to accompany IAEA and UNSCOM personnel when visiting presidential sites, presumably to ensure that the inspectors were polite.

There was much muttering about this agreement in Washington. I had helped the Secretary General get his job; now I was being held accountable for his performance. Annan for his part was doing what he thought best to preserve peace, but I was troubled by his propensity to equate procedural promises with real progress. I also cringed when, at a press conference, he called Saddam "a man with whom I can do business." The agreement did, however, require the resumption of inspections, and we gained approval of a new Security Council resolution promising the "severest consequences" if Iraq failed yet again to provide unconditional access.

For several months, the UN-brokered arrangement worked. UNSCOM returned and inspections resumed. Then in early August 1998, the troubles began once more. Angry that UNSCOM was not ready to give Iraq a clean bill of health, Saddam threw another tantrum. Baghdad ceased cooperating with inspections, although it did allow important monitoring activities to continue.

Almost simultaneously, one of UNSCOM's most aggressive American inspectors resigned, claiming that I was personally obstructing the UN agency's work. He said I had stopped more inspections than Saddam. This was raw meat for the administration's partisan detractors on Capitol Hill, who thought I had been caught red-handed trying to undercut America's own policy goals.

Republican Senate Leader Trent Lott gleefully escorted the disgruntled inspector down the aisle at a congressional hearing, during which I was accused in absentia of virtual treason. A second Senate grilling was planned with me as the main course and Bill Cohen as roughage. It never happened, because Senators soon realized that the inspector's "revelations" were the result of his narrow perspective and that we had done nothing wrong.

What we had done was quietly adjust our strategy to have a better chance of maintaining pressure on Baghdad. We had learned from earlier confrontations that Saddam's goal was to divide the Security Council. His tactic was to charge UNSCOM or the United States, or both, with being arrogant and unreasonable. This was a good plan, because the Russians and French were already critical of UNSCOM, as were some of the more credulous members of Kofi Annan's staff.

We expected a new confrontation would come and wanted to be sure when it did that the blame would fall on Iraq, not on UNSCOM. We therefore consulted with Chairman Butler about inspection plans and recommended brief postponements in a small number of cases. In some instances Butler had already decided to delay. In others he readily agreed. In every case, the final decision was his. In all our discussions, our joint purpose was to make it more likely that UNSCOM would ultimately be able to fulfill its mandate.[3]

Russia and France continued to argue that the Iraqis would cooperate if only they were given a clear understanding of what was required to lift sanctions. The UN responded by preparing to offer Iraq a "comprehensive review" of its obligations, provided it allowed UNSCOM inspections to resume. If Saddam had any intention of ever complying, this was the opportunity for which he should have been waiting. Instead, on October 31, 1998, Iraq abruptly shut down international inspection and monitoring activities completely.

3. "Senior U.S. officials never crossed the clear line between saying what they thought would be best, on the one hand, and seeking to give me directions on the other. They accepted my sole responsibility as the chief executive of UNSCOM for its directions, policy decisions and actions." Richard Butler, in his memoir *The Greatest Threat*, Public Affairs, New York, 2000, pp. 179–80.

Yet another confrontation was at hand. Our earlier restraint improved our ability to respond. Saddam's actions were now in stark violation of the agreement he had reached with the UN. This meant that Kofi Annan's own credibility was on the line. The Russians and French were publicly distressed and privately astounded. "His logic is not ours," Védrine told me. "Saddam has given up any effort to work his way out of sanctions." President Clinton's active engagement in Middle East peacemaking, plus my own visits to the Gulf, also paid off diplomatically. Eight Arab states—among them Egypt and Syria—declared, "Iraq must heed UN Security Council resolutions and abide by them all to avoid military confrontation."

The President secretly approved a substantial bombing campaign to begin on November 14, while ordering military maneuvers designed to create the impression that we wouldn't strike until later in the month. To complicate matters, I was due in Malaysia on the same day for the annual meeting of the Asia Pacific Economic Cooperation forum. Canceling the trip would have caused problems in Asia, which was in the midst of a traumatic financial crisis. It would also have revealed our plans. At the same time, I would be needed in Washington to manage our diplomacy during and after the anticipated bombing campaign.

In order to get to Asia and back quickly, I was able to obtain use of what was once known as a Doomsday plane. The vintage 747 was one of those designed to serve as an airborne command and control center in the event of nuclear war. By refueling in mid-air, it would allow me to save time. We departed the afternoon of the fourteenth and headed away from the sun across the Atlantic and over northern Africa and the Middle East. Ordinarily the huge plane had excellent communications, but as I discovered once we were aloft, the military had stripped much of the equipment out to use in the Gulf. Although I couldn't begrudge that, the intermittent loss of contact with Washington tested my nerves.

During the long night, Tom Pickering called to say a repeat of earlier episodes in the Iraq story was unfolding. Leaders in Baghdad had once again written to the Secretary General promising to resume cooperation with UNSCOM and the IAEA.

"We're supposed to provide an answer within three or four hours," Tom said.

"How long 'til we have to launch?"

"Two hours and forty minutes."

"Too bad we don't have more time."

Before I could say that I thought we should go ahead with air strikes because Saddam was clearly up to his old tricks, the call was cut off and we were unable to restore the connection. Lacking further guidance,

Pickering and Strobe Talbott informed the White House that the State Department favored holding off.

By the time we landed in Kuala Lumpur, the strikes had been delayed, but only for a few hours. I was furious when I found out my position had not been reported correctly, although I blamed the communications, not the messengers. I went immediately to the hotel, where I could participate in a conference call with the President and the rest of the foreign policy team. I felt we had been through this drill too many times already and if we didn't use force now, we would be back in the same position within a matter of weeks.

The meeting ended inconclusively. Still sleepless in Kuala Lumpur, I proceeded with my schedule, speaking on the financial crisis and pressing local authorities on human rights. Between meetings, I talked repeatedly to the President and others in Washington. I learned that the Iraqi letter had indeed undercut diplomatic support for military action, changing minds in the White House as well. The President did not believe we could run the risk of killing hundreds of Iraqi civilians if their government was publicly agreeing to our demands—even if we thought Baghdad was lying. So military strikes were postponed yet again.

In the days that followed, UN inspectors returned to Iraq, knowing that the next blocked inspection would be the last. On December 15, Richard Butler reported to the Security Council that Iraq had failed to turn over documents related to its chemical and biological weapons programs and had indeed obstructed another inspection. This time there would be a price to pay.

On the morning of December 16, 1998, we met in the Situation Room. The UN report was clear: Iraq was not complying. The foreign policy team was unanimous in supporting air strikes. The timing mattered because we wanted to finish before the anticipated start of the Islamic holy month of Ramadan four days later. Operation Desert Fox, with the British participating, was launched that afternoon. Lasting seventy hours, it consisted of 650 bomber or missile sorties against a variety of security-related targets. As we had hoped, the attacks did significant damage to Iraq's military command infrastructure. Saddam's Republican Guard dispersed and began camping out in tents, fearing another attack. Iraqi missile production programs were set back, according to U.S. military estimates, by two years. Thanks to the precision of our armed forces, there were few civilian casualties.

Operation Desert Fox marked a turning point in what had become an international soap opera with the United States, the Security Council, and Saddam Hussein in lead roles. With UNSCOM and the IAEA no longer in Iraq, we shifted our policy toward Baghdad from containment with inspections to an approach we called containment plus. We counted upon allied military forces in the region to keep Saddam in his box, while we took other steps to weaken him. In practice, this meant stricter enforcement of the no-fly zones over northern and southern Iraq. When provoked, we did not hesitate to hit Saddam's radar and antiaircraft facilities. To maintain Arab support, we backed further expansion of the oil-for-food program and began developing plans for "smarter" sanctions that would cause Saddam more harm and his people less. We took steps to unite and strengthen the Iraqi opposition. And we adopted "regime change" as an explicit goal of U.S. policy. None of this was dramatic, but it did succeed in limiting Saddam's options, extending his isolation, and encouraging his Iraqi opponents—whether outside or inside the country—to work together to loosen his hold on power. It also significantly weakened his military, making him progressively less able to survive for long an attack by a superior force.

I remain convinced that ours was the right approach to Iraq for its place and time. When President Clinton left and President Bush took office, some voices in the new administration pushed for radical change, but the basic elements of U.S. policy were not altered until after September 11. Nevertheless, President Clinton recognized, as did I, that the mixture of sanctions, containment, Iraqi defiance, and our own uncertainty about Saddam's weapons couldn't go on indefinitely. Although I expressed many doubts about the Bush administration's diplomatic timing, tactics, rationales, and postwar plans in the months before and after the 2003 war, I could not question the goal of ousting Saddam Hussein. As President Clinton said in 1998, the Iraqi leader threatens "the security of the world," and the "best way to end that threat once and for all is with a new Iraqi government."

EIGHTEEN

Welcome to the Middle East

THE AFTERNOON OF SEPTEMBER 13, 1993, seemed a true moment of miracle and wonder. From a front row seat on the White House lawn, I watched as President Clinton spread his arms and gently nudged Israeli Prime Minister Yitzhak Rabin and Yasser Arafat, chairman of the Palestine Liberation Organization (PLO), toward each other. After a moment's hesitation on Rabin's part, the two men clasped hands, creating an image that would appear on the front page of virtually every newspaper in the world. The ceremony marked the signing of the Oslo Declaration of Principles, outlining a plan to reconcile the security of Israel with the territorial hopes of the Palestinian people. Noting the presence of young Israelis, Palestinians, and Egyptians sponsored by the organization Seeds of Peace, President Clinton called the declaration a "brave gamble that the future can be made better than the past." During the next seven years, the United States devoted immeasurable amounts of time, energy, resources, and prestige to helping Israelis and Palestinians win that gamble. The effort was noble and will, I expect, be judged by history as worthwhile. But neither the President nor I would leave office with the promised land of a peaceful Middle East in view.

I LEARNED ABOUT the Middle East the way I learned Russian, first listening, then speaking, then tackling the grammar and reading the literature. Sparring with colleagues during my years at the UN, I learned the vocabulary of the peace process and was exposed to the standard litany of arguments on all sides. When I became Secretary, I had to learn more about the history, the record of past negotiations, and the personalities of those whose decisions would determine the region's direction.

Personally, I did not approach the Middle East inflexibly except for one point. I had always believed that Israel was America's special ally and that we should do all we could to guarantee its security. I thought President Truman's decision to recognize Israel immediately upon its birth in 1948 one of his most courageous. I also admired Israel's commitment to democracy. The enduring nature of our interests had made U.S. policy toward the Middle East relatively constant through Republican and Democratic administrations. Since Israel's victory in the 1967 Six-Day War, we had helped Israel preserve regional military superiority so that its enemies couldn't destroy it. We provided generous help to Israel's partners in peace and endorsed the principle of land for peace embodied in UN Security Council Resolutions 242 and 338.

Arabs often protest that the United States hasn't done enough over the years to force Israel to comply with those resolutions. They forget their own history. At the time it was approved, Resolution 242 was angrily rejected by the PLO. In 1967, the Arab League declared that there could be no recognition, negotiation, or peace with the Jewish state. Until the Israeli-Egyptian peace treaty in 1979, virtually every Arab country was committed to Israel's extinction. When Anwar Sadat, the leader who had made peace with Israel, was assassinated, few Arabs outside Egypt shed tears. It would have been much easier to persuade Israel to withdraw from the lands occupied in 1967 if a return to the prewar borders seemed likely to result in security. Because of continuing Arab hostility and extremism, even the smallest Israeli concession had to be weighed with great care.

Softening Arab hostility, on the other hand, would have been simpler had some Israeli leaders not asserted the right to govern the West Bank and Gaza completely and permanently. During the 1970s and '80s, Israeli prime ministers encouraged the proliferation of settlements for security reasons and to back up the claim of some that God had given all the land to the Jews. Although the word "settlements" conjures up the image of temporary dwellings, even tents, the reality was often quite different. Some indeed were a few trailers, but others could be mistaken for American suburbs, complete with country club–style recreation centers and homes on cul-de-sacs. Within the gated settlement walls were people with money living well. Outside were shacks and Palestinians living miserable, impoverished lives. The more provocative Israeli settlers—and this group included dual citizens of the United States—seemed to invite resentment. With these extremists in mind, I had sometimes thought, "What a brilliant story Israel is, a desert that is now green; an innovative high tech economy; and a vibrant democracy. But where is the security when your neighbors hate you?"

The Oslo Declaration of Principles, signed in that memorable ceremony on the White House lawn, was intended to transform the Israelis and Palestinians from bitter enemies into partners. It set out a series of mutual steps designed to build confidence in preparation for talks between the two sides about the paramount "final status" issues.[1] It required the PLO to reaffirm its renunciation of terror and recognize Israel's right to exist. Israel agreed to begin transferring territory on the West Bank and in the Gaza Strip to Palestinian control. Chairman Arafat returned from exile in Tunis to establish the headquarters of the Palestinian Authority in the West Bank city of Ramallah. With international assistance, the Palestinians started to build self-governing institutions. Regional tensions eased. In 1994, Jordan joined Egypt as the only Arab countries formally to make peace with Israel. Israel also established new ties with dozens of other countries, including liaison offices with several Arab states. Foreign investment poured in and Israel's economy boomed.

None of this could have happened without the leadership of Yitzhak Rabin. The Israeli prime minister was a military hero who had developed the Israeli fighting doctrine based on movement and surprise that proved so successful in the 1967 war. Israelis who questioned the vigilance of other Labor Party leaders had confidence in Rabin's toughness and strength. Unlike some of his successors, Rabin believed that incidents of anti-Israeli violence should not be allowed to sidetrack negotiations, because he believed that terrorists should not be empowered to prevent peace. He said often it was common sense to fight terror as if there were no negotiations and to negotiate as if there were no terror. He distrusted the Palestinians, and especially Arafat, but argued that a carefully designed peace was the only pragmatic path for either side, given their destiny to live together as neighbors sharing the same land.

I first met Rabin and his wife, Leah, in the early 1970s when he served as ambassador to the United States. The couple enjoyed Washington and meshed well with the diplomatic community. Two decades later, when I was at the UN, they sometimes came to New York for meetings of the General Assembly. One night, at a dinner at the Israeli mission, I toasted Rabin, quoting Leah's recollection that the first time she had met Yitzhak, he had looked like King David with his curly hair and piercing blue eyes. Rabin "may have lost some of that hair," I said, "but he still has the eyes of David."

On November 4, 1995, I was in my Georgetown house when I received a call from the State Department Operations Center. "Madam

---

1. The final or permanent status issues included security, borders, settlements, refugees, and Jerusalem.

Ambassador, we have terrible news. Prime Minister Rabin has been assassinated." I felt as if I had been punched, knowing in an instant that the globe had changed for the worse. Rarely has one bullet, this one from a right-wing Israeli fanatic, destroyed so much. As this is written, the space Rabin once filled remains empty.

The whole world watched—and much of it attended—Rabin's funeral. For Jordan's King Hussein, this was his first public visit to Israel, and for Egypt's President Mubarak, his first trip ever to the Jewish state. The ceremony itself was memorable for Leah Rabin's bravery, President Clinton's warmth, King Hussein's rousing call for peace, and the heartbreaking testimony of Rabin's seventeen-year-old granddaughter, Noa Ben Artzi-Pelossof. "Others greater than I have already eulogized you," she told us, "but none of them ever had the pleasure I had to feel the caresses of your warm, soft hands, to merit your warm embrace that was reserved only for us, to see your half smile that always told me so much, that same smile which is no longer, frozen in the grave with you."

THE CHALLENGE OF implementing Oslo had been daunting even with Rabin alive. The Palestinians wanted land; the Israelis security. The question was how much land Israel would return and what kind of security assurances the Palestinians would provide. Earlier in 1995, the parties had signed a follow-on Interim Agreement, known as Oslo II, which provided for Israeli withdrawal from seven Palestinian population centers in three phases over a period of eighteen months. Left unspecified was how much land was to be transferred, a major source of dispute. The Palestinians believed they had been promised, before final status talks began, all of the West Bank and Gaza except for Jerusalem, settlements, and security outposts. This could amount to as much as 90 percent of the contested territory. The Israelis disagreed emphatically, saying that the matter was entirely within their discretion, and pointed out that Rabin's foreign minister, Shimon Peres, had convinced Arafat to accept a pact without any precise percentage.

It was Peres who had initially launched the Oslo negotiations and who had always been more optimistic about peace than Rabin. A former prime minister and Labor Party leader, Peres truly believed Israel might one day live surrounded by friends. In a country of talkers, he was among the most inventive and stirring, and his succession to Rabin's office upon the latter's death was widely welcomed. Unfortunately, he lacked Rabin's military credentials and charismatic bluntness. If Rabin were the Israeli equivalent of George Marshall, Peres was more like Adlai Stevenson, a leader admired for his faith in human nature by a population doubting whether that quality alone would keep them safe.

In May 1996, Israelis went to the polls. Peres had been favored to win a full term, but a series of terrorist bombings late in the campaign killed dozens of Israelis, placing his election in jeopardy. The attacks embarrassed Arafat, who responded by cracking down vigorously on Palestinian extremist groups. In Egypt, Mubarak hosted an international conference, during which President Clinton and more than a dozen Arab leaders stood shoulder to shoulder with Peres in condemning terrorism. It was an unprecedented show of support, but not enough to save Peres' candidacy. Benjamin Netanyahu, leader of the opposition Likud Party, took full advantage of Israeli fears, accused Peres of weakness, and pledged to end terrorist attacks.

Upon taking office, Netanyahu—called Bibi by friends and foes alike—inherited a peace process he had condemned and Israeli commitments he didn't like but couldn't explicitly deny. He began by taking a hard line, appointing ultraconservatives to his cabinet and refusing to meet with Arafat. In September, Israel opened an archeological tunnel near a major Islamic holy site in Jerusalem's Old City, setting off clashes that killed eighty Palestinians and fifteen Israelis. For the first time, Palestinian security forces fired on Israeli troops. In March 1997, two months after I became Secretary of State, Israeli bulldozers began a controversial construction project in the East Jerusalem neighborhood of Har Homa (known by the Palestinians as Jebel Abu Ghneim). To the Palestinians, the construction seemed intended to destroy contiguity between Arab neighborhoods in East Jerusalem and Palestinian populations to the south and east. This mattered greatly, because Arafat had insisted that Jerusalem be the capital of a future Palestinian state, while Israeli leaders were determined that Jerusalem not be divided. On March 21, a suicide bomb at a café in Tel Aviv killed three Israeli women. Netanyahu accused Arafat of having given a "green light" to terror. The peace process, on a respirator since Rabin's death, seemed about to become unplugged.

Early in my tenure, the President and I had talked about how much time Middle East negotiations consume. We agreed that I wouldn't travel to the region until it was clear specific gains could be achieved. Travel wasn't necessary in the first months, in any case, because so many Middle East leaders came to Washington. What we found in our discussions was that a clear crisis of confidence had arisen between the Oslo partners. Netanyahu argued that the central premise of the Declaration of Principles was being disproven: the Palestinians had received some land and responded with demands for more. With terrorism still a problem, Netanyahu said neither his cabinet nor his conscience would allow him to turn over additional land, except in return for real peace. He proposed that we forget about the further Israeli troop withdrawals required by the Interim Agreement and proceed directly to talks on the final status issues. He even suggested a Camp David setting, in which President Clinton could explain the facts of life to Arafat. Arafat meanwhile insisted that the Israelis were refusing to meet their commitments and making it harder for him to control extremists. He needed to show his people something more tangible in return for accepting Israel as a partner.

We wanted to find a way to restore trust but felt it would be fruitless at that point to propose our own plan. Instead we encouraged the two sides to work together out of the public's view to find a basis for resuming formal talks. After weeks of secret discussions, they announced their willingness to return to the bargaining table.

In the Middle East, however, there seems to be some rule that every good development is followed by fresh trouble. On July 30, 1997, two terrorist bombs exploded in Jerusalem's Mahane Yehuda market, killing 14 Israelis and injuring 170 more. Flying back from a trip to Asia, I called Netanyahu to offer condolences and Arafat to demand that he arrest extremists, confiscate arms, and ban groups that advocated violence. Arafat condemned the killings but said he could not justify a crackdown after a year's stalemate in the peace process.

Upon landing in Washington, I went directly to the White House, where we decided on several steps. First, we would send Ambassador Dennis Ross[2] to the region to insist that the Palestinians resume security cooperation with the Israelis. Second, if Ross made progress, I would make my first trip as Secretary to the region and try to restart negotiations on political issues. Third, we would attempt to mobilize support for the peace process both in America and the Middle East.

On August 6, I appeared before the National Press Club to provide a public framework for our effort. Because of the sensitivities involved, I was careful to weigh every word to be sure it would not be misinterpreted or taken out of context. Since we had had little time to prepare the speech, my team kept making last-minute changes. As I headed to the podium, I wasn't even sure the pages were in the right order.

---

2. Ross, who served as Middle East advisor both to the President and me, comprises equal parts intelligence, dedication, and just plain decency. No hours were too long, no trip was too much, no possibility was too remote if it served the cause of peace. In contrast to some special envoys who seemed to carry their own klieg lights, Dennis was self-effacing. The same description applied to his colleagues Aaron Miller, Gamal Helal, and Nicholas Rasmussen. As this is written, Ambassador Ross is completing what will surely be the definitive book on the Middle East peace process.

Having hurried to get there, I felt flushed, and as I started speaking, the television lights were blinding. For a moment I thought I would faint. I continued reading with half my mind on the words and the other half warning me of the consequences if I passed out. A male member of the cabinet could faint—in fact, one of them had, right next to me as we were presented to the press at the start of the term—but I could imagine the headlines if I collapsed on stage.

I began to feel better when it was clear that the pages in front of me were in fact in the right order. It was an intentionally upbeat speech, but also frank in arguing that peace was possible only if both parties were prepared to make hard choices. Through Oslo, the Israelis and Palestinians had agreed on a road map for transforming what had been an irresolvable confrontation into a political negotiation. There could be no going back. I predicted that the current crisis would ease if the Palestinians made a 100 percent effort to fight terror and the Israelis refrained from taking unilateral steps such as the Har Homa construction. I also took pains to draw a distinction between terrorism and expanding settlements, saying, "There is no moral equivalency between suicide bombers and bulldozers, between killing innocent people and building houses."

More specifically, I agreed with Netanyahu's point that Oslo's incremental approach to peace was no longer sufficient; I hinted that the United States might support accelerated final status talks. I also spoke of the responsibility of the Arab world to accept Israel as a member of the international community, and of every country to lend its support to the peace process.

The first rule of public relations is not to raise expectations too high. As I prepared to leave for the Middle East, this wasn't a problem. In late August, Arafat was photographed embracing a leader of the terrorist group Hamas. On September 4, three suicide bombers struck simultaneously along Ben Yehuda promenade in West Jerusalem. Netanyahu imposed new closures on the West Bank and Gaza, arrested militants, and withheld millions of dollars in Palestinian tax revenue.

I DID NOT anticipate any breakthroughs on my first visit to the region, but I did seek to reassure Israel that America would stand by it in the fight against terror and to persuade Arafat that he must be a full participant in that fight. I also wanted to appeal directly to the Israeli and Palestinian people for their support and to look for a way to frame negotiations that each side could accept.

At dawn on September 10, I arrived at Israel's Ben Gurion Airport and made the forty-minute ride into Jerusalem. The city is a place of mesmerizing intensity, sacred even to atheists. It seems every stone has significance and is remembered in a different way. As one diplomat told me, "Jerusalem is so complicated, God had to send three separate messengers."

History is always present in the Middle East. So on the first day, I visited the Holocaust Memorial at Yad Vashem; the next morning I went with Leah Rabin to pay my respects at Yitzhak Rabin's grave. I brought with me a stone I had taken from Terezín, the Nazi concentration camp where three of my grandparents had been taken. In accordance with Jewish tradition, I placed the pebble on Rabin's gravestone and said a short prayer for them all. Earlier, in Washington, Leah had given me a pin shaped like a dove that I had worn as a silent greeting to her while delivering my speech on the Middle East in Washington. Now she gave me a matching necklace, with a note saying that sometimes even a dove needs reinforcements.

Bibi Netanyahu was the youngest Israeli prime minister. Pugnacious, partisan, and very smooth, he reminded me of Newt Gingrich. Netanyahu had spent years in the United States and could speak idiomatic English with no noticeable accent. I commented to President Clinton that I had to keep reminding myself that Netanyahu was not an American. In discussions with us, the Israeli leader could be both disarming and somewhat disingenuous. We would think we had reached an understanding and were moving toward an agreement, only to find that that wasn't his intention at all.

I had read a lot of psychobabble about Netanyahu. One theory was that he was trying to curry favor with his father, who had supposedly preferred his older brother, a hero slain while commanding the famous Raid on Entebbe. The senior Netanyahu was a devoted disciple of a hard-line ideology known as Revisionist Zionism, which his son also seemed to embrace.

In Jerusalem I asked Netanyahu if he considered the Oslo process dead. He replied, "Arrest militant Hamas leaders, seize all arms, shut bomb workshops, end all incitement to terror by anyone, including mosque teachers. If the Palestinians do that, we should go to final status talks, because the Interim Agreement with phased pullbacks just encourages conflict and terror."

The Israeli prime minister ridiculed the idea that Arafat was too weak politically to take such steps; he said that Arafat could smash Hamas in two months if he wished. I didn't disagree but pressed him to acknowledge Israel's own responsibilities. Terror would be easier to stop if the Palestinians could see concrete benefits from the peace process. Netanyahu insisted that terror was the only issue. "Israelis know that, without peace, they may have to fight. But they think they will have to fight anyway and would rather fight a weak Palestinian Authority than a stronger internationally recognized Palestinian state."

Arafat and Netanyahu lived about twenty miles and one universe apart. During my eight years in government, Israel had four prime ministers. For all those years, and the preceding twenty, the Palestinians had been represented by a single man, a fact that was testimony to Arafat's skill as a manipulator and survivor.

To a Western audience, the Palestinian leader began with some aesthetic handicaps, including his perpetual stubble and high-pitched voice. The aftereffects of a 1992 plane crash had decreased his stamina and shortened his attention span. Perhaps to compensate, he constantly made notes in a small notebook he pulled out of his breast pocket. In conversation he could be charming, but most of the time he was difficult.

My first telephone calls to him were particularly hard. Even though Arafat understood English, we used interpreters. I usually wanted to make a point or solicit a response about a specific issue. Arafat wanted to explain the history of the whole Palestinian struggle, so he made speeches into the phone at a volume sufficient to render the instrument almost unnecessary. Still, he was the only person empowered to negotiate on behalf of the Palestinian people. Optimists believed that, at Oslo, Arafat had made a strategic decision for peace. Pessimists feared that he was playing a cynical game, pocketing Israeli concessions while planning future violence. I wanted to decide for myself.

Oslo demanded that Arafat make a transition from leader of a nationalist movement that employed terror to leader of an autonomous government that would fight terror. It also required him actually to *administer* the West Bank and Gaza, instead of traveling around the world getting the red-carpet treatment. Suddenly Arafat had to worry about sewers, telephone bills, issuing drivers' licenses, and having to deal with a parliament and a relatively free press. It was soon evident that Arafat wasn't very good at the job. His autocratic style left no room for democratic development. His failure to implement economic reforms alienated prospective international donors, and his attempt to co-opt rather than eliminate terrorist elements within Hamas only heightened Israeli intransigence.

The combination of corruption, intermittent violence, and an exploding population caused the low standard of living in the West Bank and Gaza to plummet further. Since Oslo, per capita incomes had gone down and joblessness up. Young people were coming of age without hope—bad news for the Palestinians, and no better news for Israel.

On the occasion of my first trip, I met Arafat in his Ramallah headquarters, a stark, modestly furnished white building the Israeli military would reduce to rubble five years later. Sitting in front of a large picture of Jerusalem's Dome of the Rock, Arafat was in a relatively passive mode, complaining about the Israeli closures and the withholding of tax revenue. He said Netanyahu was to blame for failing to fulfill his promises under Oslo but didn't quibble this time when I pressed him bluntly to help on security. I said that we needed to see actions, not promises, and that terror was every bit as destructive to the Palestinian cause as it was to Israel. He responded by agreeing to develop a plan for dismantling the terrorist infrastructure of Hamas—a plan about which we would never stop haggling.

At that time, Hamas had tens of thousands of members, many of whom were engaged in solely civilian pursuits—running schools, mosques, summer camps, and social services. Within the body of Hamas, however, were cancerous networks that manufactured explosives, planned ambushes and kidnappings, and brainwashed young people into carrying out suicide attacks. There were terrorist cells in most of the Palestinian population centers.

In general, Palestinian authorities had been willing to act against Hamas when provided with specific information regarding a particular facility or planned attack, less willing when simply provided with lists of people to arrest. They had also been reluctant to initiate measures on their own. Arafat preferred that the extremists focus their anger on Israel, not him. As a result, his promises were less than credible. And the question of an effective response to terror was and would remain the central issue in pursuing Middle East peace.

In the midst of my whirlwind visit, I went to a school in Ramallah for a session with Palestinian students. The day before I had fielded questions from Israeli students concerned about terror, assuring them that America understood their worries and would stand by them. But the Israeli students were economically well off, lived in nice homes, and had many career options in front of them.

In Ramallah few of the young people lived in nice homes or felt in control of their lives. They saw themselves as victims and asked questions about their future that I had no hope of answering to their satisfaction. One student who had been born in Jerusalem asked why he hadn't been allowed even to visit that city for three years. Another asked why Jerusalem couldn't serve as the capital of both Israel and a Palestinian state. A third asked my feelings "about the terror resulting from the midnight arrests of innocent people, pointed weapons, humiliating remarks at roadblocks, attacks on our religion, and destruction of homes."

My answers reflected our policy, but our policy was to be silent about the future status of Jerusalem, leaving that issue to the negotiators. Because we needed to work with both Arafat and Netanyahu, I couldn't be explicit about the mutual failures of leadership responsible for Palestinian suffering. I also had to say what I believed, which is that Israeli security measures, however severe, didn't justify terrorism. Nothing I said eased the students' sense of helplessness, grievance, and uncertainty about the future. The meeting spurred me to find out more about the legitimate needs of the Palestinian people. I thought to myself, "The young Palestinians aren't responsible for the unfair hand history has dealt them; they'll never achieve what is fully fair in their eyes, but the peace process is the best path to the best deal they can get."[3]

Within a few days of my departure, both sides took small steps in the right direction. Arafat arrested militants and closed a TV station that was being used to incite hate. The Israelis released half the customs revenue they had withheld. Security closures gradually eased as security cooperation increased. And negotiators agreed to meet with me during the annual session of the UN General Assembly in New York in late September.

Almost simultaneously, Netanyahu suffered a costly embarrassment. On September 25, a Hamas official named Khaled Meshal was assaulted by two men as he got out of his car in Amman, Jordan. One assailant pressed a lead-colored instrument behind Meshal's ear, injecting poison that immobilized Meshal's spine. Within minutes, Meshal's bodyguard had subdued the two attackers in a bloody fistfight and turned them over to Jordanian police, who quickly realized that the men were Israeli agents.

The result was a major self-inflicted blow. King Hussein, probably Israel's best friend in the Arab world, almost broke relations. Netanyahu went personally to Amman to apologize, but the King refused to see him, sending word instead that, should Meshal die, the Israeli agents would be tried publicly and hanged. Ultimately Netanyahu provided the antidote to the poison, saving Meshal's life, and agreed to release seventy Palestinian prisoners being held as terrorists, including the spiritual leader of Hamas, Sheikh Ahmed Yassin. For months both the Israelis and I had been badgering Arafat to arrest terrorists, and now Netanyahu found himself with no choice but to release one of the biggest culprits—a fact Arafat would recall repeatedly in months to come.

---

3. In 2002, after I was out of office, I spoke at Guilford College in North Carolina. A young woman who was in the audience said she had also heard me speak that day in Ramallah. She reminded me of the meeting and reminded me that everything had since become much worse.

NEGOTIATIONS CONTINUED WITH little progress through the end of 1997. By the coming of the new year, we had concluded that neither side was likely to propose a package acceptable to the other. We had made gains on questions such as a Palestinian airport and safe passage for Palestinians between cities, but the issue of further Israeli troop withdrawals was at an impasse. The decisions we were asking the parties to make were extraordinarily difficult, but also urgent, so we decided to present our own proposals to Netanyahu and Arafat separately, hoping they would consent to a trilateral meeting with the President at which an agreement could be announced.

On January 19, 1998, Netanyahu arrived in Washington where he spoke at an event for evangelical Christians. Among his hosts was the Reverend Jerry Falwell, who was then promoting a ridiculous video purporting to implicate President Clinton in drug dealing and murder. Not surprisingly, the media portrayed Netanyahu's participation in the event as a direct slap at the President.

We met in the Oval Office the next day. We had nothing to gain from a spat with Netanyahu, so the President began by suggesting they "put the issue of snubs and slights behind us. We have to have a positive attitude." It quickly became clear, however, that Netanyahu was not ready to agree to our proposals, nor was he going to stick around for any three-way meeting. Instead he urged us to accept a plan for permanent security zones in the West Bank and Gaza in return for Israeli withdrawals. We couldn't do this, because the zones involved final status issues and so had to be dealt with in permanent status talks. Over and over again, Netanyahu stressed the difficult political situation he faced at home, saying that his cabinet wouldn't allow him to be more flexible.

Prior to the session in the Oval Office, I had had breakfast with Netanyahu at the Mayflower Hotel. After the White House meeting, I met with the prime minister again in his tenth-floor suite, then returned to the White House to brief the press, before going back to the Mayflower. At 9:40 P.M. we all returned to the White House to meet once more with the President; we stayed until after midnight. It was hard and intense work, though I did wonder how so many people who were so smart could talk so much without saying anything new.

FIVE HOURS LATER I was up with a cup of coffee skimming the *Washington Post*. But I wasn't reading about the Middle East. Instead, I was scanning a story headlined, "Clinton Accused of Urging Aide to Lie; Starr Probes Whether President Told Woman to Deny Alleged Affair to Jones' Lawyers." My first reaction was to groan. There had been so many stories about Special Prosecutor Kenneth Starr's endless investigation into Whitewater related (and unrelated) matters that I wanted to tune this story about some woman named Lewinsky completely out.

That evening, after hosting the just-arrived Arafat for dinner, I went to Andrews Air Force Base to bid good-bye to Netanyahu. Expressing concern about the increasingly sensational news reports, he told me he had also been through the experience of having his personal life raked over. He asked whether he should call Clinton to express sympathy, and I said I thought such a gesture would be appreciated.

The next morning we met with Arafat. Before we began, the White House allowed the press into the Oval Office for a photo opportunity. Sitting together, the President and the Palestinian leader responded to a few inquiries about the peace process. A White House press aide said, "Thank you, Mr. President," signaling an end to questions. This led to an uproar from the press, as if raw meat had suddenly been withdrawn from a pack of starving lions. Finally the President said, "Go ahead" and was asked about Monica Lewinsky. I couldn't help wondering what Arafat was thinking. He had come to discuss the fate of his people, just as Netanyahu had done two days before. The eyes of the world were on Washington, but they weren't seeing a debate on the great issues of war and peace. Instead they were witnessing the creation of a new era—entitled "All Monica, All the Time."

That day, as expected, Arafat rejected Netanyahu's offer of a small and rigorously conditioned further withdrawal of Israeli troops as "peanuts" and warned that continued lack of progress might spur an "explosion of violence." He didn't say yes or no to our proposals but produced a letter clarifying the elimination of anti-Israel statements from the Palestinian National Covenant. He also endorsed a plan for security arrangements that would include 1) a ban on the military wings of Hamas; 2) confiscation of weapons; and 3) consultations prior to the release of certain categories of prisoners. He agreed as well to our proposal that later Israeli withdrawals, called for in the Interim Agreement, could take place after the initiation of final status talks. All this was to the good, but when Arafat pressed for a larger initial withdrawal, the President replied, "I don't accept what Netanyahu is offering, but I also can't accept what you're demanding."

In the afternoon I again briefed the White House press. As usual, I said we were "narrowing the gaps." Although true, this description was wearing thin. That evening we met again with Arafat, except this time in the President's study in the White House residential quarters, where I had had my interview before being designated Secretary of State. After

Arafat and his delegation left, the President, switching subjects, told Sandy Berger and me that there was nothing to the allegations being made against him and that the trouble would soon be over.

The next morning, around 11 A.M., we assembled for a rare meeting of the full cabinet. I was sitting in my customary seat, immediately to the President's right. I could only see the side of the President's face, but there was nothing in his body language to indicate hesitation or uncertainty. He told us that the allegations against him were groundless and we should go on with our work. There was nothing to be concerned about. We fiddled with our briefing books, feeling bewildered and thinking it inappropriate to ask questions.

It did not occur to me at that moment to disbelieve the President. I didn't think he would lie because I thought he was smart enough to know he would be caught if he did, making things even worse. This was, after all, the central lesson of Watergate and virtually every subsequent White House scandal: the cover-up, more than the initial wrongdoing, is what is most likely to bring you down. I was convinced the President must realize this. I also had no respect for Starr and others obsessed with attacking the White House. It was obvious that some people had been trying to bury the President in mud for years.

There are times in Washington and in politics more generally when the battle lines are drawn and neutrality is untenable. This was one. The President had said the allegations were untrue, and that was the end of it. As the meeting broke up, a White House aide came over and explained that a few cabinet members were going out to say what had happened to the press. He asked if I would join them. I said yes. We went outside to where the media was set up by the West Wing's northern door. I said, "We have just come from a really terrific cabinet meeting, which the President started by saying we should stay focused on our jobs and he will be fine."

In answer to a question, I said, "I believe the allegations are completely untrue." Immediately I was joined by Commerce Secretary William Daley, who said, "I'll second that definitely." "Third it," chimed in Health and Human Services Secretary Donna Shalala and Education Secretary Dick Riley. The next day, before a foreign policy meeting on Iraq, the President said to me, "You were great yesterday. Thank you. I appreciate it."

THROUGHOUT THAT TURBULENT SPRING, while the Lewinsky scandal continued to make the headlines, we continued pressing on the Middle

East. The President's compartmentalizing skills would require a Homer to chronicle.[4] In late March, we achieved a breakthrough of sorts when Arafat expressed his agreement with our ideas "in principle" and urged us to go forward "with God's blessing." This reflected the weakness of his position, because our proposals were far closer to the original Israeli concepts than to his. For example, Arafat had asked that an additional thirty percent of West Bank territory be transferred to Palestinian control as final status talks got under way. The Israelis had agreed in January to offer about nine percent, and in March Netanyahu told the President privately that he might be able to go as high as eleven percent. We had suggested thirteen percent, over most of which Israel would retain ultimate security authority. Our plan required that the land transfers go forward in parallel with security measures designed to halt anti-Israeli terrorist activity. During a contentious series of meetings in London in May, I tried hard to persuade Netanyahu to move the extra two percent, but he wouldn't.

That summer the Israelis and Palestinians turned once again to secret meetings. Drawing on U.S. proposals, they narrowed their differences, even settling the spat about how much additional land Israel needed to return. The answer was thirteen percent, of which three percent would be nature preserves. This allowed the Palestinians to say that they had held firm to the number they had previously accepted, while Israel could say they were giving only ten percent to the Palestinians and the rest to Mother Nature.

The biggest issue remained security. The Palestinians had pledged months earlier to develop a plan to stop terrorists. At the request of the negotiators, CIA Director George Tenet began working with Palestinian authorities. Tenet had a well-earned reputation for frankness and fairness and was trusted by everyone. This mattered because the Israelis couldn't afford to rely on generalized commitments: they needed specific benchmarks against which to judge performance, and felt the CIA would make Palestinian security measures more credible. The Palestinians believed that their security efforts were more likely to satisfy Israeli and world opinion if they had CIA approval. The agency dreaded playing umpire in a deadly contest in one of the world's toughest neighborhoods, but no other institution had the same ability to work with both sides.

---

4. Of course the President was not the only one who could compartmentalize. While writing this section, I came across the following note of reminders to myself, dated January 28, 1998: "1) Call Senator Helms; 2) Call King Hussein; 3) Call Foreign Minister Moussa; 4) Make other congressional calls; 5) Prepare for China meeting; 6) Buy nonfat yogurt."

Another important issue concerned the Palestine National Council (PNC), an umbrella group that theoretically set policy for Palestinians everywhere. Under the Oslo Accords, the PNC's Covenant was to be amended to eliminate calls for the destruction of Israel. In Washington in January, Arafat had produced letters claiming that the PNC's Executive Committee had eliminated the offending language. Netanyahu argued that a vote by the entire PNC was required. The Israeli desire for clarity was legitimate, for it is hard to make peace with an adversary still formally committed to your destruction. Arafat resisted such a balloting because he was unsure he could control the outcome.

By early September, the outline of an agreement was in sight, but mutual mistrust remained too high for the parties to take the final steps on their own. The question we faced was whether to risk the prestige of the Presidency by inviting Arafat and Netanyahu to a summit reminiscent of the 1978 meetings at Camp David that produced Egyptian-Israeli peace.

I supported a summit, but with reservations. Although I was learning patience, the Middle East style of negotiating grated. Being partial to direct talk, I was eager to bring this round of the peace process to a climax. At the same time, I was unsure that even President Clinton could persuade Netanyahu and Arafat to reach a full accommodation. Neither wanted to be blamed for a breakdown in the process, but both seemed to fear the domestic political consequences of actually reaching an agreement. They therefore tended to respond to concessions by becoming more difficult rather than more forthcoming. That way the process continued, but accountability was put off to a future day. Both Netanyahu and Arafat had staked out hard-line public positions. Neither would want to be accused of caving in to U.S. pressure. If we convened a summit that failed, we would look impotent, and people would blame the Secretary of State for misjudging the odds. We didn't, however, have many alternatives. For the first time since Oslo had been signed in 1993, some polls showed a majority of Palestinians so frustrated that they favored using terror to force Israel to withdraw to 1967 borders. Israel had also uncovered evidence that the military wing of Hamas was planning a new round of attacks. So while we were talking, the clock was ticking.

At the UN General Assembly session that fall, I succeeded in bringing Arafat and Netanyahu into their first direct contact in eleven months. Because everyone's schedule was crazy, the meeting was set for around midnight in my old apartment in the Waldorf, then occupied by my very able successor, Ambassador Bill Richardson. While waiting, I doubted whether the Middle East's dyspeptic duo would even show up, but they did. I wanted to see them together to judge whether a face-to-face summit

ILLUSTRATION BY MICHELLE CHANG

might succeed. Initially they sat stiffly and looked at the interpreters, or at me, or at the plants, but not at each other. I urged them to begin a real dialogue aimed at decisions on the hard issues and invited them to join the President at the White House the following day. They agreed, and I left them alone to say whatever was on their minds. Sitting in the adjacent room, I was relieved not to hear shouting. The next day in Washington, the President announced plans for the summit, to be preceded by another trip to the region by me.

During that trip, Netanyahu, Arafat, and I met at a military outpost on the Israeli side of the checkpoint between the Jewish state and Palestinian Gaza. After talking for a couple of hours, Netanyahu suggested ordering sandwiches. Arafat said he had planned on having lunch with me at his guest house on the other side of the checkpoint. Graciously, he asked Netanyahu if he would like to join us. Bibi stunned us all by saying, "Sure." He thus became the first Israeli prime minister to enter Palestinian Gaza. We had lunch around a T-shaped table, sampling among other delicacies a *denise*, a local fish that Arafat laughingly referred to as "Dennis," after Dennis Ross. Netanyahu asked Arafat if he could light up a cigar, and the Palestinian leader presented him with an entire box of Cuban Cohibas. About a dozen men started smoking the things, and I felt like doing the same in self-defense. As the conversation warmed, I offered a toast to diplomacy, and Arafat, Netanyahu, and I joined hands in front of the world's cameras.

Present at one of our meetings was Ariel Sharon, who was about to be named Israeli foreign minister and coordinator for final status negotiations. The seventy-year-old Sharon was Netanyahu's most prominent competitor for the hearts and minds of Israel's right wing. He had called Oslo "national suicide" and argued that the best attainable outcome in negotiating with Palestinians would be a tense state of nonbelligerency. Sharon was despised by many, especially Arabs, for his role in Israel's invasion of Lebanon in 1982, during which allied Lebanese militia massacred hundreds of unarmed Palestinian refugees. The leading Hebrew-language biography of the prospective new foreign minister was entitled *He Doesn't Stop at Red Lights.*

For fifteen years the U.S. government had had little to do with Sharon. He was, however, a hero to some Israelis because of his membership in that country's founding generation. Like Moshe Dayan and Yitzhak Rabin, he had fought in Israel's wars and helped nurture the nation into a powerful modern state. Netanyahu's decision to make Sharon his foreign minister meant one of two things. Either he expected the upcoming summit to fail and would use Sharon's stubbornness as an excuse; or he expected the summit to succeed and wanted Sharon's presence to shield him from the vituperation of hard-liners at home.

The purpose of a summit is to intensify the pressure on both sides, making it easier for leaders to justify difficult decisions. There was nothing routine about such an event. To bring the parties along required thousands of hours and hundreds of meetings and phone calls on the part of the President, me, and our team. It was hard, painstaking work. But that is the only way progress toward peace in the Middle East had ever been achieved. As we made final preparations for the summit, we were well aware that our task had barely begun.

NINETEEN

"Palestinians and Israelis Coming Together"

A T THE REQUEST of the White House, the State Department developed a game plan for how we expected the summit to unfold. We warned the President that one or both sides would threaten to walk out and that a breakthrough wouldn't occur until the parties were convinced that the summit's end was at hand. Because Netanyahu was being asked to give up land—something he could not retrieve—he would demand the firmest possible security guarantees. It was important for him to be able to boast that he had bargained harder and obtained better results than his Labor Party predecessors. Arafat's interest was to achieve the transfer of land without acceding to what Palestinians would consider humiliating Israeli demands. President Clinton could relate to Netanyahu as someone who shared his passion for politics. Arafat responded well to the President because the President treated him with respect and understood Palestinian needs. The big question was whether Netanyahu and Arafat would acknowledge that each had a responsibility to the other. If not, we could reach an agreement on paper that would break down immediately in the streets.

The day the summit was supposed to begin, the President and the rest of our team met with the two leaders at the White House. Arafat, as was his custom, referred to himself as permanent vice-president of the Organization of the Islamic Conference. This prompted Vice-President Gore to ask what it was like to be a permanent vice-president and whether that was a good or a bad thing to be.

President Clinton then made a short statement to the press. When a reporter shouted a question, the President refused to respond, saying confidently, "All three of us have determined that we should not at this moment take questions. Instead, we should set about the business at hand." Moments later Netanyahu appeared on the White House lawn and invited questions from reporters in both English and Hebrew. As soon as he finished, Arafat moved to the mike. The summit hadn't even begun, and already the ground rules were being broken.

We had chosen the Wye River Conference Center in Maryland for the negotiations because it was close to Washington and spacious enough to allow us to meet in whatever groups made the most sense. We hoped the idyllic 1,100-acre setting would have a calming effect: Wye itself is a vast estate with meadows, cornfields, and a "world-renowned" herd of Black Angus cattle.

The accommodations we had arranged were separate but not equal, especially for us. The original estate mansion, known as Houghton House, was beautifully furnished with antiques. We put the Palestinians there. The Israelis we put in River House, a comfortable modern facility with a wooden deck and smaller surrounding buildings and gardens. As good hosts, we took more modest rooms.

The advantage of this arrangement was that it gave each side privacy. The disadvantage was that it left us a considerable distance apart. For me, this meant traveling to various sites in my official limo with flashing lights and a small motorcade. Out in the middle of nowhere, amidst songbirds and geese, it seemed ridiculous, but Diplomatic Security insisted on it. Later Arafat would create his own spectacle, riding a bicycle for the first time in decades, pedaling the bright red bike around the estate with his kaffiyeh blowing in the wind and his security detail jogging alongside.

The summit began with a plenary meeting at the main conference center. Entering, Netanyahu went over to the Palestinian side and shook the hands of each delegate. Arafat responded in kind. The mood was good—deceptively so. The summit would rapidly deteriorate into an exercise similar to the herding of cats.

Our timetable was conceived on the basis of hope, not experience. We began on a Thursday and planned to finish by Sunday night. We thought this deadline might prove realistic because Netanyahu was due in Jerusalem the following Tuesday to open the fall session of the Knesset, the Israeli parliament. Accordingly we tried to create a sense of urgency: the two delegations responded the next day by going shopping.

We decided that nothing would be agreed until everything was agreed. This meant that the parties could agree on lesser issues without being locked in later if the negotiation fell apart. Ordinarily, when the President was meeting with one side, I would meet with the other. When the President shuttled back to Washington, I would keep the negotiations moving. We established committees to handle specific issues. The United States would draft the accord, based on discussions with the two parties.

During the first day, the President and I each met separately with Netanyahu and Arafat for about an hour, followed by a cozy dinner with just the four of us in a private home just outside the conference center. Even though we were away from Washington, we had White House china and a dinner featuring yellowtail snapper and chicken followed by the ever-present gold-foiled White House mints. The President, characteristically empathetic, encouraged the two leaders to express their concerns frankly. Arafat spoke calmly about Palestinian aspirations, the security problems created for Palestinians by Israeli settlers with guns, and his own concern about extremists. He made a point of reminding us that it had been Netanyahu who had released Sheikh Yassin, the leader of Hamas. Netanyahu's response was statesmanlike and included a commitment to work with the Palestinians against terrorism. Good negotiators know it is essential to put yourself into the other person's shoes. President Clinton was a master at that, and now he tried to persuade Netanyahu and Arafat to think about how they might help each other cope with the reaction of radicals to any agreement they might reach. It was a farsighted approach, but it assumed that the leaders cared about each other's political standing.

Netanyahu and Arafat met alone the next morning, with the State Department's translator and Middle East expert Gamal Helal acting as interpreter. Netanyahu was the host, sitting on the back deck of his delegation's lodgings, overlooking the river. When Dennis Ross and I joined them for lunch, the atmosphere was as frosty as the October sun was bright. Netanyahu was pressing Arafat on the issue of the Palestinian Covenant and demanding the apprehension of Palestinians accused of terrorism, including thirteen members of the Palestinian security services. These were hard issues for Arafat, and he was grim. It didn't help when the Israeli prime minister referred to the West Bank as "Judea and Sameria," complained about Arab car thieves, and failed to accompany the protocol-sensitive Arafat to the door when the meal was finished.

During the day, the committees we had set up reported to the delegation heads. As I listened, I thought, "There are no simple issues. The Palestinians should have an airport, but the Israelis are right to worry about what is flown in. The Palestinians should be able to go freely from the West Bank to Gaza, but the Israelis are right to be concerned about the possible movement of criminals and terrorists." The parties were close to agreement on most issues, but getting them to travel the distance between close and there wouldn't be easy.

That evening the Israelis decided to have their Shabbat (Sabbath) dinner alone at River House, so I invited the Palestinian delegation to join us in the main dining room. Despite the toughness of the negotiations, we had many moments of laughter. This occasion particularly was marked by frequent toasts and relaxed talk. I had my photo taken with Arafat's deputies Abu Ala and Abu Mazen—a picture we later dubbed "Madeleine and the Abus."[1] I was pleased by our ability to break through cultural barriers, but language barriers aren't always so easily bridged. When I introduced my deputy chief of staff Suzy George to Arafat, she said in Arabic what she thought meant "My house is your house." In fact, she told the Palestinian leader, "You are part of my family and I am a very fertile valley." Suzy's Arabic had come courtesy of Gamal, who now burst into the room and laughingly explained the joke he had played to a smiling Arafat and a reddening Suzy.

After working all night, Dennis reported on Saturday morning that the Palestinians had agreed to the substance of the security provisions we had proposed but were determined to dilute specific references in the text. Their problem was political. Israeli demands on security were reasonable but highly intrusive. They included a list of specific people—whom Netanyahu referred to as the "thirty killers"—to be arrested, a weapons collection plan, and understandings about how to prevent civilian institutions, such as mosques, from being used by terrorists. Naturally the Israelis wanted to see these issues dealt with as explicitly as possible, while the Palestinians preferred to keep the language vague.

Sunday was supposed to be the summit's final day. Instead we spent it going backwards. In the afternoon Netanyahu told the President that he didn't believe a full agreement was possible. As an alternative, he pushed the idea of a partial pact that would include the thirteen percent Israeli withdrawal and Palestinian cooperation on security but leave most other issues unresolved. When the President asked us about this proposal, both Sandy Berger and I argued against it. We had struggled for more than a year to bring the leaders together: we needed to make the most of the opportunity we had.

Around midnight the President met alone with Ariel Sharon, who

---

1. In March 2003, Abu Mazen (also known as Mahmoud Abbas) became Palestinian prime minister, as part of an effort to reform the Palestinian Authority and give power to someone other than Arafat.

had just arrived at Wye. Swaying him was critical, because it was hard to believe that Netanyahu would reject an agreement Sharon accepted—and impossible to believe that the prime minister would say yes if Sharon were shaking his huge head back and forth, arguing the contrary. The meeting was not pleasant. Sharon stuck to the Israeli demand for only a partial agreement and lectured the President on his failure to release the convicted spy Jonathan Pollard.[2]

We ended Sunday frustrated. The Israelis were trying to take half the deal off the table, while their formidable foreign minister raised new complications. The next afternoon, however, President Clinton was both creative and upbeat. He told the two sides that he still thought a complete deal was possible. Knowledgeable about the details and deftly steering the discussion, he invited each team to defend its position and offered ideas for resolving differences over the issues he had listed, arranged from easiest to hardest. Referring to a yellow legal pad with all the points neatly arranged in his totally illegible handwriting, the President expressed optimism about the work that was being done on the security plan, drawing on examples from negotiations with the factions in Northern Ireland. When the Palestinians asked for the release of prisoners from Israeli jails, the President expressed sympathy for the families involved but also cited his anguish as governor of Arkansas when a prisoner he had released later committed murder.

At dinner that night, Sharon came in just as we were about to be seated—an awkward moment because he hadn't been expected. Also, Sharon prided himself publicly on his refusal to shake Arafat's hand. Well aware of this, Arafat gave Sharon a little semi-salute, which Sharon seemed to ignore. During the meal Sharon did much of the talking, trying to be gregarious. I considered it odd, however, that Sharon talked about Palestinians in the third person with Arafat and his delegation sitting there at the table. Sharon said he was a rancher who had always gotten along well with Palestinians and admired them for their productivity

2. Pollard was a former U.S. navy analyst who had been convicted in 1986 for selling highly sensitive data about America's intelligence infrastructure to Israel. The Israelis had lobbied for years for Pollard's release. The issue was unrelated to the Middle East peace process but intimately related to Israeli politics. Pollard would be a trophy Netanyahu could use to make an agreement more palatable to Israel's right wing. However, when I mentioned to George Tenet that the Israelis had raised the issue, the CIA Director was angry. He and his agency were resolutely opposed to letting Pollard go, because it would seem to suggest that treason was acceptable if you had the right friends. I agreed with Tenet.

as farmers. When Arafat complained that Palestinian farmers in Gaza were starving, Sharon replied, "Mr. Chairman, they are not."

After dinner President Clinton continued his sales job. I thought to myself, "He's like a psychiatrist trying to make his patients drop all their defense mechanisms and reveal honestly what they think and feel. It's impossible even for Netanyahu to outtalk him." For the first time, I felt an agreement was really possible. The President made both participants think hard about the stakes. To Netanyahu, he stressed the importance of strengthening Arafat's ability to deal with radical Palestinian elements. To Arafat, he returned yet again to the issue of security, but also stressed the importance of finding a way to accommodate Israel on the issue of formally revising the Palestinian Covenant.

We had been at Wye only a few days, but that was sufficient to develop a morning routine. Despite the late nights, I got up early and went for prebreakfast walks in my blue jogging suit. When I sat down to eat, I was joined by our negotiators, led by Dennis Ross, Wendy Sherman, Assistant Secretary of State Martin Indyk, deputy Assistant Secretary Toni Verstandig, Gamal Helal, and the estimable Aaron Miller. Aaron had nicknamed Wye River "Camp Albright—a camp for very, very bad boys."

King Hussein and Queen Noor had come to Wye River, so on Tuesday I went to visit them. The King, who had made peace with the Israel of Yitzhak Rabin in 1994, had left his sickbed at the Mayo Clinic in Minnesota to be with us. A few months previously he had been diagnosed with cancer. When he entered the room, he looked greatly changed from previous occasions I'd seen him. As a diplomat you are often compelled to mask your emotions. I needed all the control I had not to appear shocked at the sight of the formerly robust monarch. His color was terrible; chemotherapy had robbed him of his hair, beard, and eyebrows. I felt like crying—and praying. There was nothing different, however, about the King's mind or his commitment. I reviewed where we stood in the negotiations, and he offered to do all he could to help.

That night Dennis, Martin, and I met with Arafat's senior advisor, Saeb Erekat, and other Palestinian delegates to nail down an agreement on security, which was essentially a long list of things the Palestinians had to commit to do. We were making progress—although there were still sticking points—when by prearrangement the President dropped by and offered to pose for pictures. Suddenly the Palestinians were all smiles. The photographers took group pictures, then Saeb Erekat asked for a personal photo, and of course that meant everyone had to have one. All the while, the President was mixing his banter with a serious message, "Your people are counting on you. Ten years from now, from the positions you will then have, you will look back on this and know you did the right thing." On his way out, the President turned to me and said quietly, "Get me this agreement now so I can go to the Israelis."

Not long after the President left, we reached an understanding, which the Palestinians said they had to run by Arafat. I asked, "Can't you just call him?" They said, "No, we have to take it to him." I said, "Fine. Let's go together." So we drove to Houghton House, where Arafat was waiting. I met with him alone for about ten minutes, stressing how vital it was that I be able to tell the President that we had finally agreed on security. Then the delegation came in and explained the understanding we had reached; the chairman said yes. I told Arafat, "Mr. Chairman, if your actions match your commitments, you have taken an historic step toward peace and toward meeting the basic needs of your people."

After I had reported the good news to the President, we met with Netanyahu. We told him about the security approach the Palestinians would adopt. We also assured the prime minister that we would carefully consider any Israeli concerns as we developed a final text.

The President then left for the White House and I returned to my cabin. It was well after midnight, so now officially October 21. A perfect excuse, I thought, to call Netanyahu. When the prime minister picked up the phone, I said, "Please allow me to be the first to wish you a happy forty-ninth birthday." Bibi replied, "Thank you, Madam Secretary, but is that really why you called?" I said, "Yes, of course, and please take a very hard look at the Palestinian security plan and the draft agreement. We will try to get you the best possible answers on your concerns and on the text. Once we have taken your concerns into account, if you think a deal is doable, the President will return to discuss the remaining issues. If you think in the end it is not enough, so be it. We will say it has been nice. We would very much like to have your comments by noon tomorrow."

The Israelis evidently didn't like our draft, because the following day they decided to play games. First Sharon failed to show at a planned 11 A.M. meeting. When called, he said he needed to take a shower. Several hours later Arafat observed, "Sharon must have drowned in the tub." Then we received word from our administrative people that the Israelis had asked for help in getting to the airport; their suitcases were stacked on the lawn.

I called Netanyahu and asked to see him. As my motorcade headed toward River House, the Diplomatic Security agents stopped the car and said one of the Israeli delegates wanted to talk to me. They pointed to Israeli Defense Minister Yitzhak Mordechai, who was crossing a field. Mordechai said he had arranged to go for a walk in order to intercept me.

"I am not packed," he said. "We should stay and try to get this done." I agreed, "We can't let this opportunity slip away. If your team has concerns, we need to stick with it and work them out." As the "world-renowned" Black Angus cows looked on, we embraced diplomatically and went our separate ways.

River House, at that moment, was a peculiar scene. The delegation's suitcases were set out around the semicircular driveway, which is one reason we were convinced the Israelis were bluffing. If they had wanted to leave, they could have. I walked past the luggage, pretending not to notice, and greeted Netanyahu with "Let's go over the draft text." He said, "Fine." During the meeting there were no threats or posturing by the prime minister. We agreed that Dennis Ross would work with George Tenet and the parties to fine-tune the assurances on security. Netanyahu reiterated his views on the Palestinian Covenant. We both talked about the need for each side to live up to its obligations.

At this point Sharon broke in to say that he had come to Wye in order to get an agreement, despite the fact that Arafat had violated every agreement he had ever signed. The Palestinians didn't represent democracy, "They're a gang of thugs," he said. I replied, "We don't see the Palestinians either as democratic or as a gang but as a people living next to you. We are your best friends. If we fail here, your security will deteriorate. If you think of them as a gang, there's no hope: they will act like a gang." Sharon responded, "I have lived with Arabs all my life, and I don't have a problem with Arabs. I have a problem with these leaders, or at least some of them, who are murderers. It's a mistake to deal with them."

I decided that, with time growing short, I would camp out in a small office near River House and keep track of everything that was going on. I was there when Dennis rushed in with a copy of a press release announcing the Israeli delegation's intention to depart unless the Palestinians agreed immediately to fulfill their obligations on "the transfer of wanted terrorists and the revision of the Palestinian Covenant."

Netanyahu hadn't threatened to leave during our meeting. To do so now via a press release was unacceptable. As we were trying to figure out how to react, Israeli Ambassador Zalman Shoval came to apologize: Netanyahu, he said, hadn't known about the statement. Shoval seemed genuinely embarrassed; I told him I accepted his apology. At that moment Tenet arrived with news that the two sides had reached agreement on security. If anything was going to shift momentum in the right direction, this was it.

Back to Netanyahu. I told the Israeli leader that I knew he was under pressure but the time had come to make a decision: was he serious or not?

Tomorrow was absolutely the last day. We needed to get the full draft agreement to the Palestinians right away. Bibi nodded.

The final day of negotiations turned out to be the day with no end. We began with a trilateral at the main Wye conference center at 10:30 A.M. There followed meetings in virtually every imaginable permutation. President Clinton had returned from Washington patient but determined, willing to listen to real arguments but fed up with posturing. Dropping the threats of the previous day, Netanyahu began modifying Israeli positions. In the early afternoon the Israelis even proposed that the two sides meet alone. During their talks they agreed on a number of issues, including a clever idea for meeting Netanyahu's demand that Arafat convene the Palestine National Council. Under the plan, Arafat would invite the PNC and members of other organizations to an expanded meeting in Gaza. President Clinton would join Arafat in addressing the audience, which would be asked to affirm its support for revising the Covenant and for peace, whether by a show of hands, a stamping of feet, or applause. Sandy Berger immediately expressed doubts about putting the President in this position, which I agreed was risky. The President, however, was confident he could work even the toughest of crowds.

At 5 P.M. we all assembled to compare notes. One unresolved issue was Arafat's request for the release of certain categories of Palestinian prisoners. Netanyahu said he understood the importance of this to the Palestinians. He wouldn't, however, agree to set free members of Hamas or any individual with blood on his hands. He said he could release only common criminals, people detained for lack of proper paperwork, and those jailed for security offenses not involving murder—in all, several hundred people. Arafat argued at least a thousand prisoners should be eligible.

For five hours we worked through the issues. Dinner was brought in. We were clearly headed in the right direction, but not necessarily for an overall agreement. There was enough tension that a fight on almost any subject could have stopped us cold. Then I announced that we had a visitor.

I had been told that King Hussein had reached the stage in his illness where it was a risk for him to meet with a large group. Any infection would be life-threatening. I asked everyone to wash his or her hands with a disinfecting liquid we passed around. The King walked in, and everyone stood up. Although our hands were clean, we were almost afraid to touch him.

The President explained to King Hussein where the negotiations stood. The contrast between Clinton's heartiness and the monarch's frailness couldn't have been sharper. When the King began to speak, the room fell silent. He said that history would judge us all, and that the issues now separating the parties were small compared to the stakes. "After agreement," he continued, "both sides will look back and not even recall these issues. It is now time to finish, and to fulfill the responsibility you have to your peoples and especially to your children."

The King's condition added to the power of his words. As I listened, I thought again of the loss of Rabin, and of how much the death of another courageous leader would cost the Middle East. I also thought of how, nineteen months earlier, a Jordanian soldier had gone crazy and killed seven Israeli schoolgirls. Unlike other Middle Eastern officials, Hussein hadn't made excuses; he had gone personally to Israel, to the homes of the victims, knelt with their families, apologized on behalf of his nation, and expressed sorrow. There was profound substance in that gesture because it showed respect and caring about every human life, Arab or Israeli. It was only a gesture, but it contained within it the solution to all that bedeviled the Middle East.

Before the King left, he went around the table shaking hands. Arafat, who would ordinarily have kissed the King's cheek, instead kissed his shoulder, to avoid passing germs to the stricken man.

THE KING'S VISIT gave us all an emotional boost, but as the talks continued, fatigue set in. The large main dining room served as a background for many disparate scenes. Various members of all three delegations were sitting comatose or asleep in the chairs, while conversations took place at small tables. As one conversation ended, people carried on with a different group. The fire crackled in the fireplace and the hum of discussion continued. Everywhere there were coffee cups, baskets of candy, cookies, and discarded bottles of water.

The President alternated between going over the notes he had made on his yellow pad and meeting with one or both of the other leaders. Clad in a red sweater, glasses perched on the top of his nose, his face a mixture of fatigue and resolve, Bill Clinton was determined and focused. Around 2:30 A.M. I saw him huddled in intense conversation with Netanyahu and Arafat, with Gamal Helal interpreting feverishly. Abruptly Arafat rose, stalked to his own table, and just sat there. A few minutes later the President got up and stormed out, saying, "This is outrageous. This is despicable. This is just chicken shit; I am not going to put up with this kind of bullshit."

Gamal came over and told me what had occurred. The three leaders had been talking about the issue of the Palestinian prisoners. Netanyahu said he could release five hundred, but only if Arafat "took care of" one particularly prominent Palestinian and arrested the thirty "killers" during the first two weeks. Arafat asked how he was supposed to "take care of" the Palestinian, "Just execute him?" Netanyahu responded, "I won't ask, you won't tell." This caused Arafat to get up and the President to explode.

We were all taken aback by the President's outburst; he had been so patient. Netanyahu was also surprised. Seeming to sag physically, he asked if he could see the President alone. I urged President Clinton to ask Bibi if he would agree to a release of 750 prisoners, which was halfway between the two positions. The leaders met for forty-five minutes. When the President emerged, he said Netanyahu had acquiesced.

Several more sleepless hours lay ahead. As issues were agreed to in principle, the drafting teams struggled to finalize the text. This process often uncovered differences over detail that had to be resolved by the three leaders. Finally, as dawn was breaking around quarter to seven, the last issues were hashed out. We were all too fried to be sure how we felt, but there were at least a few minutes of handshaking and celebration. We began planning for a ceremony at the White House, then noticed Bibi sitting alone on a sofa, glowering. That couldn't be good. The President came up to say that Netanyahu was threatening to back out of the agreement unless the United States released Jonathan Pollard.

I told the President, "This is blackmail. It's also the wrong policy. We can't go along." Sitting down next to Netanyahu, I told him that he would be making a fatal mistake if he decided to scuttle the deal. He said that as far as he was concerned, there was no deal, because he would never have made the concessions he had if he had not counted on rebalancing the scale with the release of Pollard. Without that, he would never be able to get Israeli support for the agreement.

To this day I do not know what made Netanyahu believe that we were going to release Pollard. The President said he had never made any such commitment. It is possible, however, that Bibi somehow misread the President's instinctive empathy during their one-on-one meetings or that Sharon unintentionally misled the Israeli prime minister. The alternative is that Netanyahu just thought he could steamroll the President. In any case, the result was a mess.

Throughout the morning, we worked on a number of fronts to persuade Bibi that he had made a good deal even without Pollard. I asked King Hussein to weigh in, then met with Arafat—who wasn't aware of the problem—just to keep him calm. I spent more than an hour with Defense Minister Mordechai, who was again helpful. Jamie Rubin struggled to fend off the press, who had been told by the Israelis that the agreement was being held up because the President had reneged on a promise over Pollard. We had to deal with a few voices on our own team telling the President that releasing Pollard might not be such a bad idea. On top of all this, we had to deal with a time crunch, because this was Friday and if we were going to have a White House ceremony, we needed to end before the start of the Jewish Sabbath at sundown. It seemed all hope was gone; Sandy and I both felt we would be physically ill.

Then, meeting alone with Netanyahu yet again, the President finally persuaded him to back down, but at a price. The prime minister wanted to change the mix of Palestinian prisoners released so that more would be common criminals and fewer would be people arrested for security offenses. The President told us what had been agreed; the only task left was to persuade Arafat to accept this altered deal. That was to be my job. While preparations were made to decamp for Washington, Dennis and I boarded our last Wye-style motorcade to see Arafat. After we explained the proposed change and said it was the best the President could do, Arafat nodded his head. This is when we were able to cash in the goodwill the President and I had accumulated with the Palestinians. Now we finally did have an agreement.

I rushed to my cabin to change and leave for Washington. The only problem was I had eaten so much junk food in nine days at Wye, I had trouble fitting into my clothes. Fortunately I had a loose-fitting jacket that came with my navy blue dress. A good dose of makeup helped cover the circles under my eyes. There was no hope for my hair.

We flew by helicopter to a landing area near the reflecting pool and rushed to the White House. Gathering in the Red Room, still dazed from lack of sleep, I felt encouraged. Netanyahu had moved from opposing the Oslo Process to becoming part of it. Arafat seemed more comfortable in the role of negotiating partner. The previous day—actually earlier in that same sleepless day—the two sides had been able to reach agreement on important issues by sitting down and dealing directly with one another. That had not happened in three years.

The Palestinians would get more land, an airport, a seaport, safe passage between the West Bank and Gaza, a prisoner release, a commitment to restrain Israeli settlement activity, and a fresh influx of economic aid. The Israelis would get unprecedented security cooperation, the jailing of wanted Palestinians, repudiation of offensive language in the Palestinian Covenant, and a quick start to final status talks.

It had been thirteen months since my first visit to the Middle East as Secretary of State. At the outset there had existed a near total crisis of confidence between the two parties. Clearly levels of mistrust remained high, but Dennis Ross and his team had achieved the improbable through their unshakable dedication, patience, and tactical creativity. And President

Clinton had risen above a thicket of political and personal preoccupations to reaffirm his status as world leader.

As for my role, Sandy Berger used a sports analogy, which with me is always a risk. He said I had played the role of a starting pitcher in baseball; I had gotten the team into the eighth inning, then turned the ball over to the relief pitcher—President Clinton.

The signing ceremony at the White House for the Wye River Memorandum was among the most moving ever conducted by sleepwalkers. The President was his usual eloquent self. Prime Minister Netanyahu was gracious and statesmanlike. Chairman Arafat's remarks included a blunt renunciation of violence.

The dominating spiritual presence, however, was provided by the man with the least imposing physical presence. In his last public appearance at the White House, King Hussein spoke, with no notes but much passion, about the need to end the culture of death, destruction, and waste and to occupy a place "beyond ourselves, our peoples, that is worthy of them under the sun, the descendants of the children of Abraham— Palestinians and Israelis coming together." He warned that some would respond to this agreement with violence and urged the majorities on both sides to stand firm against the enemies of peace.

The Wye River Memorandum was designed to be a way station along the road to a comprehensive peace between Israelis and Palestinians. We were to learn in years to come how rocky and treacherous that road would be. But it also gave me hope that tough negotiations would be capped with agreements if we pushed long and hard enough—a hope that inspired both the President and me until our final days in office.

When I think of Wye now, the image that comes to mind is not of the squabbling delegations or the disappointing events to follow, but of King Hussein and Queen Noor, sitting in chaise longues overlooking the Wye River at sunset, bundled up in blankets, aware of the coming darkness but sharing and savoring the last moments of light.

TWENTY

Dueling with Dictators

T HE PURPOSE OF foreign policy is to influence the policies and actions of other nations in a way that serves your interests and values. The tools available include everything from kind words to cruise missiles. Mixing them properly and with sufficient patience is the art of diplomacy. The challenge is often greatest when the goal is to push or pull a country across the line separating international scofflaws from respectable members of the world community. I faced such challenges repeatedly as Secretary of State, especially when dealing with a turbulent Iran, a stubborn Libya, and a repressed Cuba.

FROM MY EARLIEST days as Secretary of State, President Clinton and I were intrigued by the possibility of better relations with Iran, whose strategic location, cultural influence, and size made it a pivotal state in one of the world's most combustible regions. There were obstacles to a new relationship, however, including history. In 1953, the Eisenhower administration orchestrated a coup that ousted Iran's elected prime minister and returned its shah, Reza Pahlavi, to power. During the next quarter-century, the shah maintained close relations with the United States and aggressively modernized Iran's economy, while also ruthlessly repressing domestic opposition. In 1979, massive street demonstrations forced him from power and installed what soon became—under Ayatollah Ruholla Khomeini—a radical and fiercely anti-American theocratic regime. That November, the Carter administration reluctantly permitted the exiled and dying monarch to enter the United States for medical treatment. In retaliation, extremists stormed our embassy in Tehran and seized more than four dozen hostages, holding them for over a year.

The negative images of that era shaped the American view of Iran and were reinforced when Iranian-backed terrorists in Lebanon kidnapped Americans and Europeans in the 1980s. During the first Clinton administration we pursued a policy of "dual containment," essentially equating Iran with Iraq. Both were considered "rogue regimes," repeat violators of international law, undemocratic and hostile to our interests. Our policy was to isolate them and deny them the capacity to develop advanced arms.

In May 1997, Iran's youthful electorate stunned observers by selecting a new president, Mohammad Khatami, an avowed reformer who sounded wholly unlike his conservative predecessors. At his postelection press conference, he said, "We are sorry that America's policies have always been hostile toward us." He installed a moderate cabinet and—mindful of his popularity with female voters—named a woman vice-president. In his public statements he spoke with hope, not bitterness, and emphasized freedom rather than orthodoxy. In a January 1998 interview with CNN, Khatami drew a parallel between the American Revolution and Iran's own struggle for independence, while advocating a "dialogue of civilizations," beginning with the exchange of scholars, artists, journalists, and tourists. He did, however, mix thorns with the olive branch, faulting America for its alleged Cold War perspective.[1]

That same month, Yasser Arafat showed us a letter he had received from Khatami. Reversing Iran's previous position, the letter backed Palestinian participation in the Middle East peace process, acknowledged Israel's legitimacy, and discussed the possibility of a regionwide peace if the Palestinians were allowed to establish a state on the West Bank and Gaza. I concluded that Iran no longer belonged in the same category as Iraq. The time was ripe to move beyond dual containment.

In June 1998, I gave a speech in which I welcomed Khatami's election and the growing popular pressure in Iran for greater freedom. I also endorsed Khatami's call for intercultural communications, saying that if Iranian officials were ready, we were prepared to sit down without preconditions and develop a road map to normal relations. Trying to spark such a dialogue, I spoke respectfully about Iran's history, culture, people, and president. I must admit, however, that it was awkward trying to couple expressions of friendship with criticisms of Iran's ongoing support for terrorism and other egregious policies.

The problem was that, under Iran's constitution, Khatami had lim-

---

1. This CNN interview wouldn't have escaped my attention in any event, but its impact was reinforced by the identity of the interviewer. Christiane Amanpour had recently become engaged to my spokesman, Jamie Rubin.

For Madeleine Albright!   PANCHO   Paris September 98

ited power. Iran's military, intelligence, police, and judicial institutions were still answerable to the Supreme Leader Ayatollah Ali Khamenei, who regularly incited his audiences to chant "Death to America." The forces under Khamenei's control were responsible for Iran's support for anti-Israeli terrorist groups, its pursuit of nuclear weapons, and the suppression of human rights.

Iran did not react to my speech immediately because it was too busy celebrating its World Cup soccer win over the United States, a victory Ayatollah Khamenei greeted with customary grace: "Once again, the arrogant enemy has suffered the bitter taste of defeat." More interesting was what happened in the streets. Amid the celebration, one youth started to torch an American flag, while others began passing out "Death to America" leaflets. The crowd responded by ripping the flag away, dousing the flames, and tearing up the leaflets.

President Khatami did not respond until several days later. "We believe there is a change in their tone," he said, "but we're always looking for action." This was clever, since it was the same mantra I had been using when asked about the evidence of change in Iran. Soon after, an Iranian diplomat asked a former State Department official whether the relatively friendly nature of my remarks had been a trick, saying there were doubts in Iran about our intentions. The Iranian said that his government thought the influence of American Jews was too strong to permit real flexibility in the U.S. position. He noted that President Bush, in his 1989 Inaugural Address, had said with reference to Iran, "good will begets good will." The hostages held in Lebanon had later been freed, yet U.S. hostility had continued unchanged. The American participant in this discussion passed along its substance with the conclusion that only direct government-to-government talks could clear the air. Having reached the same conclusion, we made efforts to contact Khatami privately, only to be rebuffed. We soon recognized that although President Khatami and Ayatollah Khamenei seemed far apart in their public pronouncements, we wouldn't be able to deal with one and not the other.

There was anticipation, nonetheless, when Khatami visited the United States for the UN General Assembly meetings that fall. While in New York, Khatami issued a ringing call for free expression and the rule of law, earning warm applause from an audience of influential Iranian-Americans. He won more points—even prompting the United Kingdom to restore diplomatic relations—by declaring, "We should consider the Salman Rushdie matter as completely finished."[2]

The United States and Iran shared an interest in Afghanistan, where civil war raged and nine Iranian diplomats had recently been murdered. For every crisis, it seemed, the international community formed a group; we had created the "six plus two" to discuss Afghanistan. Members included Afghanistan's half-dozen neighbors, among them Iran, plus Russia and the United States. Partly to facilitate a meeting between Iranian Foreign Minister Kamal Kharrazi and me, Kofi Annan scheduled a meeting of the "six plus two" at the ministerial level. This would have been the first high-level encounter between representatives of our two countries in more than a decade. I hoped the session might help thaw relations.

The meeting was held in the UN Secretariat building, in a room barely bigger than the hollow square table at its center. Iran's seat was across from mine, and as I walked in, the Iranian representative smiled and gave a bow, which I returned. At the same time, I was puzzled. Kharrazi had been Iran's UN ambassador when I had served in the same capacity for the United States, so I knew how he looked. Now I thought he must have put on weight. When it was my turn to speak, I said it was a special pleasure to see colleagues who had also used their UN experience to become foreign ministers. The Iranian smiled again. This was fine, but I remained uncertain. I wrote a note to the officials seated behind me,

---

2. Nine years earlier, Iranian authorities sentenced the British author Rushdie to death, in absentia, for disrespect toward Islam in his novel *The Satanic Verses*. Despite Khatami's words, some Iranian clerics insist the death sentence against Rushdie still stands.

"Are we sure this is Kharrazi?" I heard some whispering as members of my brain trust—our most knowledgeable experts on Iran—conferred. The answer came back, "We don't know."

The mystery was resolved when the chair addressed the Iranian as "Mr. Deputy Foreign Minister." Obviously, not Kharrazi. We learned later that the supreme leader had instructed both Khatami and his foreign minister to avoid any contact with U.S. officials during their visit. Kharrazi did give a speech at the Asia Society, the same location as my earlier speech, in which he addressed some of the points I had made. The diplomatic ballet continued.

Toward the end of 1998, Khatami's movement toward liberalization came under siege. A half-dozen leading Iranian dissidents, writers, and intellectuals were murdered, a number of independent newspapers were shut down, and allies of Khatami were charged with corruption. Meanwhile the president's coalition was badly divided between technocrats who wanted to modernize the economy and leftists who wanted to equalize social conditions. The result was paralysis while inflation rose and growth came to a virtual halt. We were in an awkward position because we could not help the reformers by siding openly with them. To the ayatollah and his cohorts, we were still the Great Satan, and it wouldn't benefit the forces of change to have the devil as their advocate.

It wasn't until early in 2000 that we decided to take a second run at improving relations. The time seemed right. Khatami's supporters had rebounded spectacularly in elections that February, winning control of the parliament. Iran had signed the Chemical Weapons Convention and become a regional leader in fighting narcotics. Its position on the need for a negotiated solution to Afghanistan's civil war paralleled our own. And Iran had intercepted vessels trying to smuggle Iraqi oil in violation of UN resolutions. Iran's policies on other issues, however, remained deeply troubling. Tehran continued to provide the Lebanon-based terrorist group Hezbollah with arms and to finance anti-Israeli violence by Palestinians. Iranian leaders, including Khatami, didn't deny these facts but argued that those fighting to "liberate" Muslim lands shouldn't be described as terrorists.

Despite its many denials, we also believed that Iran was still trying to acquire or build nuclear weapons. True, Israeli officials had been warning for nearly a decade that Iran would have nuclear arms within three years, predictions which had proved inaccurate. On the other hand, the lesson of Aesop's fable "The Boy Who Cried Wolf" is that the wolf ultimately shows up. Iran's nuclear ambitions date back to the shah, and it has continued to expand its nuclear power sector even though it is among the world's largest oil producers. It has its own uranium deposits, a uranium ore concentration facility, nuclear research centers, and two research reactors—in addition to clandestine sites where it may be trying to fashion the core of an atomic device.[3]

Another grave problem was the June 1996 attack on Khobar Towers, a housing complex used by U.S. military forces in Saudi Arabia. Nineteen Americans were killed in the truck bomb explosion. In late 1998, the FBI obtained information that appeared to implicate Iranian officials in directing the attack, using Hezbollah to carry it out. Five months after I left office, an indictment was issued that highlighted links between Hezbollah and Iran and indicted thirteen members of Saudi Hezbollah. The tragedy highlighted again the complexity of dealing with a divided Iran. We couldn't ignore the ayatollah's hard-line policies when reaching out to the Iran of Khatami, and we didn't want to ignore the promise of reform while trying to rein in the ayatollah. During the preceding two decades, we had had one policy for the Soviet Union under Communist rule, then another for Russia under democratic rule. In Iran both the totalitarians and the democrats were present at the same time.

In February 2000, I sent a memo to the President suggesting we acknowledge the positive steps Iran had taken, while retaining our best carrots and sticks. The President gave me the green light, so in March I announced the lifting of import restrictions on Iran's principal non-oil exports—carpets, pistachios, dried fruits, and caviar. While these are considered luxury items in the United States, their production and marketing in Iran were associated with the middle class, much of which had voted for Khatami. I hoped that by opening our market we could generate good will while forging new connections on the commercial level. In my speech I once again wove together statements of concern about Iran's security policies with expressions of respect and invited Iran to engage in an official dialogue.

The reaction was favorable at home and in Europe, but predictably divided in Iran. The ayatollah was reportedly outraged that I had referred to him—accurately—as "unelected." Khatami emphasized the more positive aspects of the speech but said again that our deeds were insufficient for a new relationship.

There was a further complicating factor. In the spring of 1999, Iran's Ministry of Intelligence arrested thirteen members of the country's Jewish community, along with seven Muslims. After detaining the group for

3. Our opposition to Russia's sale of nuclear technology to Iran was a major issue in our bilateral relations with Moscow throughout my term as Secretary of State.

several months, authorities charged them with spying for the United States and Israel. Working with Kofi Annan, the EU, and other friendly countries, we put diplomatic pressure on Iran to release the prisoners or at least grant them a fair trial. These efforts had some impact, although not enough to avoid an unsatisfactory outcome. Twelve of the accused were found guilty and sentenced to prison.[4]

The bitter clash between reformers and traditionalists in Iran continued through my last year in office. Reformers struggled in vain to keep newspapers open, place candidates on the ballot, and develop a coherent economic plan. Khatami, while remaining relatively popular, grew less bold in his statements. In the fall, he came to New York for the UN Millennium Summit and an event billed as the Dialogue of Civilizations, which he had initiated.

Kofi Annan suggested that I attend the Iranian president's speech to the Dialogue, which I did. In a mutual display of courtesy engineered by the Secretary General, both Presidents Clinton and Khatami remained to hear the speech of the other at the UN General Assembly the next day. At each event the Iranian's remarks, although erudite and idealistic, were vague. In response to questions, he exhibited as much impatience with his more militant followers as with his conservative opponents. In meeting with Iranian-Americans, he refused to take questions at all—a contrast to his open exchange with a similar group in 1998. I was disappointed. Khatami seemed to be settling uncomfortably into the role of survivor, a man who had figured out just how much he could push and was reluctant to pick any new fights. It remains to be seen what this pragmatism will accomplish in the long run.[5]

The Clinton administration policy toward Iran was calibrated appropriately. We could have achieved a breakthrough only by abandoning our principles and interests on nonproliferation, terrorism, and the Middle East, far too high a price. We could have avoided the charge that we were too soft on Iran by ignoring the reform movement entirely, but that would have left us isolated internationally and provided no incentive for Iran to change further. Instead we chose a course that, though incremental, helped to move our relationship in the right direction, while opening

4. Of those convicted, eight received pardons after serving a portion of their jail terms. By February 2003, all had been released from custody.

5. I attended a second meeting of the "six plus two" group on Afghanistan during the 2000 General Assembly. This time Foreign Minister Kharrazi did attend, although we didn't have any private conversation. This is one instance where gender did make a difference; we did not shake hands. At the same session in 2001, Secretary Colin Powell and Kharrazi were photographed with hands clasped.

the door to increased contacts. By offering an unconditional dialogue, we put the onus on Iran to explain why it was unwilling even to talk about our differences and laid the groundwork for formal discussions if and when they become possible. And by recognizing the popular desire for democracy in Iran, we encouraged its citizens to imagine a future free from the repression of the present and past.

As THIS IS WRITTEN in mid 2003, the struggle between liberalization and repression in Iran is intensifying. Who wins will matter greatly to our prospects for curbing terror, halting the spread of nuclear weapons, stabilizing the Middle East, and deepening understanding between nations with Muslim majorities and the West. This last point is crucial, because for decades the high birth rates in Muslim-majority nations in the Middle East and South Asia have generated more young people than their anemic and centralized economies can absorb. The average age in Iran, for example, is roughly fifteen.

A young person growing up poor in one of these countries can't be blamed for pessimism, even desperation. He (or she) may find twenty people in his community competing for every job, and a dozen mouths in his family hungry for every meal. He can't agitate for social or political change without risking jail and perhaps torture. He is likely to have little respect for his government, which may be unresponsive and corrupt. The petroleum wealth enjoyed by a small fraction of his fellow Muslims will not have trickled down to him. Despite his poverty, the world of the wealthy is all too visible in shop windows, on television, and among those who pass him by on the streets. In the mosque he is taught that he is the equal before God of any man and—if observant—will spend eternity in paradise. He may also be taught that he is poor because it serves the interests of Americans and Jews to keep him so and that the United States is waging war on Islam, which he has a sacred duty to defend.

The radicalism present in some parts of the Islamic world is relatively recent. It has grown as the sense of anger and helplessness has grown, and as the inequities within Arab and other Muslim countries have widened. It has been fueled by the myth and reality of Arab-Israeli strife and by the chronic failure of leaders in many Islamic countries to deliver on their promises. Those leaders have responded to the rise of radicalism in different ways. Some have cracked down on extremist groups. Some have outlawed even peaceful political opposition. Others have tried to co-opt extremist leaders with payoffs and favors. Some have tolerated incitement to terrorism provided it is directed toward America and Israel and not them. Iran, with its dueling leadership, is a unique case.

Overall, I believe America's official reaction through Democratic and Republican administrations alike has been awkward and ineffective. One problem is that we have been afraid to push too hard for democracy, especially in Arab countries. We worry, perhaps with reason, that if radical Islamists obtain power through an election, there would be no more elections—the "one person, one vote, one time" phenomenon. We also worry about the temporary instability that might be created. Whether or not our fears are justified, we're left looking hypocritical as we're stuck supporting regimes whose policies if practiced elsewhere in the world we would condemn. A second problem is that, because of the perceptions that have developed and hardened, we can do all the public diplomacy in the Muslim world we want, and not truly succeed unless there is a breakthrough in relations between the Palestinians and Israel. A third is the astonishing mutual ignorance that exists between much of America and most of Islam. In a world of twenty-four hour global television, we should know each other far better than we do. That is why, in 1999, I asked Counselor Wendy Sherman to review efforts within the State Department to improve our outreach to the Muslim world, an initiative covering everything from personnel recruitment and training to public diplomacy and foreign assistance. We also began a series of discussions with American Muslims that included the first Iftaar dinners ever to be hosted by a Secretary of State to mark the breaking of the fast during the Islamic holy month of Ramadan.[6]

Overcoming ignorance and misunderstanding is hard work not accomplished overnight. The best minds on both sides of the divide between Islam and the West will have to apply themselves. It helps that there are many voices of Islam already in the West and important examples of democratic openness in Muslim-majority countries. Few initiatives would be more important to the direction of the world in the twenty-first century than a true dialogue of civilizations of the type proposed by Iranian President Khatami but thus far only timidly and intermittently advanced.

6. These efforts were a learning experience. We found, for example, a reflexive tendency within the department to refer any issue related to Islam to our Bureau of Near Eastern Affairs—this despite the fact that far more Muslims live outside that region than in it. During one of Counselor Sherman's meetings, a respected career ambassador, who had served in South Asia, questioned the wisdom of recruiting Muslims to serve in U.S. diplomatic posts. "I'm just making an observation here," he said, "but you know those people pray five times a day. That can be pretty disruptive." When I learned of these comments, I was appalled.

BEFORE OSAMA BIN LADEN, there was Libyan leader Muammar Qadhafi. On December 21, 1988, a Pan American commercial airliner exploded in the skies over Lockerbie, Scotland, killing 259 passengers and crew, along with 11 villagers on the ground. About three-quarters of the victims were American, including college students returning home for the holidays. After a two-year investigation, American and British authorities indicted a Libyan intelligence officer and an employee of the Libyan national airlines, accusing them of placing a bomb in the airline baggage system.

The United States and United Kingdom demanded Qadhafi surrender the two men for trial in a U.S. or Scottish court. When he refused, the senior President Bush eschewed force in favor of law enforcement and diplomacy, turning to the tool of multilateral sanctions. With strong support from the British and French, the UN prohibited the sale of arms and oil production equipment to Libya and banned air travel to and from that country. The Security Council promised to suspend the restrictions if Libya turned the suspects over for trial and to lift them entirely if Libya renounced terrorism, accepted responsibility for the crime, and agreed to compensate the victims' families. A battle of wills began.

During my years at the UN, I succeeded first in strengthening the sanctions and later in preventing others from weakening them. My most valuable allies were the families of the victims who traveled to New York to observe the council. I will not forget our first meeting. We sat around a table in the UN mission. One after another, parents, siblings, and children talked about their lost loved ones and their frustration at our inability to force Qadhafi's hand.

As they talked, I thought of my daughter Katie, who had studied in Great Britain the same year Pan Am 103 had been destroyed. I shuddered, thinking how horrible it must have been to wait at the airport, hear a news report, or pick up the phone and learn that the loved one you were expecting was no more. It sickened me that I couldn't assure the families that the measures we had in place would be sufficient to achieve accountability. The council reviewed Libyan sanctions every four months. Sitting through more than a dozen such sessions, I could see impatience with sanctions growing among my colleagues. This was partly due to Qadhafi, who was doing his best to change his image from an irresponsible radical into something more respectable. Seeming to pull back from direct involvement in terrorism, he improved his relationships with Arabs and Africans. He gained sympathy among Muslims and some members of the Security Council by arguing that the UN's prohibition on air travel made it impossible for religious Libyans to visit holy sites in Saudi Arabia. And he claimed that the sanctions were hurting his economy, making it harder to obtain equipment for hospitals and agriculture.

In 1996, the Organization of African Unity (OAU) proposed that Libya turn over the two suspects for trial in a neutral country. We immediately said no, arguing that justice was only possible if the trial took place under the laws of the victims, either American or Scottish. As our prospects for maintaining sanctions dimmed, however, we began to consider other options.

My legal advisor, David Andrews, and David Welch, the acting assistant secretary of state for Near Eastern affairs—who had lost a friend and fellow Foreign Service officer on Pan Am 103—raised with me the idea of accepting a trial in the Netherlands before a Scottish judge and under Scottish law. No one was sure whether this unprecedented approach was realistic, but I was willing to explore anything that would help the families of the victims; the British, Welch said, were already thinking along the same lines. It happened that I spent Christmas in 1997 with my daughter Alice and her family in London. While there, I was invited by Robin Cook to the foreign secretary's official country house, where we had a long discussion about Libya. Nine years had passed: the Pan Am 103 families had already waited too long. We agreed that we wanted the suspects in custody before the tenth anniversary. We would push ahead with the third-country plan.

I was careful, at this point, to maintain secrecy. We didn't want Qadhafi establishing new conditions on cooperation or critics savaging the concept before it could be fully developed. We did, however, need the help of the Justice Department, so on January 15, 1998, I met with Attorney General Janet Reno. I admired Janet both for her accomplishments and her unpretentious nature, attributes in Washington that are rarely found together. Throughout her years in office, politicians and pundits tried to bait, manipulate, or intimidate Reno, all without success. During the first Clinton administration, I had a get-acquainted dinner with her in a D.C. restaurant. We were a funny-looking pair, given our disparity in height—a sort of Mutt and Jeff. While we were eating, a man came over and tried to give each of us a ring made up of an intricately wrapped dollar bill. He was perfectly pleasant, but Janet said imposingly, "As Attorney General, I cannot accept money, and as a lawyer I must advise Ambassador Albright it would be illegal for her to accept any as well."

On Libya, Reno had equally firm opinions. She didn't want to retreat from our earlier insistence on a trial in the United States or Scotland. "We will be accused of negotiating with terrorists," she told me. "And what if the suspects are turned over, and there is a mistrial, or an acquittal because of perjury or tainted evidence? Do the suspects just go free?" I assured her that we would present our proposal on a "take it or leave it" basis, without negotiation, and that our lawyers had persuasive answers to her other questions. I also said that the sanctions regime was fraying and that suggesting a third-country trial was a no-lose proposition. "If Qadhafi turns over the suspects, that's good. If he refuses, it should be easier for us to maintain or even strengthen sanctions." Reno was unconvinced but agreed to meet with Dave Andrews, who was directing our initiative, and to have Justice Department lawyers consult with their Scottish and later their Dutch counterparts. To my consternation, there followed months of legal and political thrashing about. Bill Clinton and Tony Blair wanted to proceed rapidly, and so did I. The lawyers on all sides, however, were behaving as lawyers do, responding to each answer with a new inquiry, thereby slowing things down but in the end preventing fatal mistakes.

Eventually the third-country plan took shape. We consulted the victims' families privately; the majority supported us, though some were bitterly opposed to what they saw as a concession, using blunt language to vent their feelings in our conference calls. Their criticisms hurt because we had worked so hard on this case, but I could not be angry since I didn't know what I would have said or done in their place.

On August 24, Robin Cook and I announced the new "take it or leave it" offer. The initial response from Tripoli was encouraging. Qadhafi told Arab diplomats he wanted a solution; Libyan and UN lawyers began discussing the details. One snag soon developed. Qadhafi demanded that the UN lift sanctions, not merely suspend them, when the suspects were handed over. This was essentially a symbolic issue; a new Security Council resolution would be required to reinstate sanctions whether they were lifted or suspended. Symbols, however, sometimes matter. "Suspension" meant there would still be a cloud over Libya. "Lifting" meant clear skies and a fresh start. We were not about to allow that until Libya accepted responsibility for the crime and paid compensation. The bombing of Pan Am 103 had not, after all, been an accident; it was premeditated mass murder.

Ultimately our persistence paid off. In March 1999, Qadhafi agreed to turn over the two men, with sanctions suspended, not lifted. The suspects arrived in the Netherlands on April 6. A little less than two years later, the Scottish court convicted the Libyan intelligence officer and sentenced him to life in prison. The second man was acquitted for lack of sufficient evidence. According to the judges, "the conception, planning, and execution of the plot which led to the planting of the explosive device was of Libyan origin."

In the case of Libya, multilateral sanctions—while slow and imperfect—did succeed in persuading Qadhafi to do something he hated doing. The result was the trial, conviction, and jailing of the man most directly responsible for the murder of 270 people and the grief of thousands more. That trial also fixed responsibility for this act of terrorism squarely on Libya and set the stage for discussions aimed at obtaining a direct admission of culpability and compensation, issues that would, unfortunately, drag on for some time. Like many foreign policy outcomes, this one was far from fully satisfactory, but it did show that we could use the tools of diplomacy to achieve a measure of accountability and respect for the rule of law.

ONE RESPONSIBILITY I HAD, both as ambassador and Secretary of State, was to answer questions from the American public, usually after giving a speech. Except for the Middle East, Cuba was the topic raised most often. Depending on where I was, the questioners tended to view Fidel Castro either through a red lens or through rose-colored glasses. One group wanted to know why we were not enforcing laws against Castro more rigidly, the other why it was logical to permit trade with China, Vietnam, and other Communist nations but not Cuba.

I did not like defending the Cuba trade embargo because it had been in place through eight presidential administrations without accomplishing anything decisive. The embargo had not, for example, deterred Castro from meddling in Central America and Africa during the Cold War, nor had it provided the leverage required for democratic change in Cuba itself. Instead Castro used the specter of "Yankee imperialism" to preserve his macho image.

However, when the Cold War ended, so did Castro's claims to international relevance. Leftist rebels in El Salvador and Guatemala put down their weapons and ran for office. Elected leaders replaced Communist regimes throughout Central and East Europe and in Russia itself. The loss of Soviet subsidies sank the Cuban economy. During my first years at the UN, Castro seemed a relic; I began talking quietly with other administration officials about the possibility of normalizing relations and easing or lifting the embargo, wondering whether the time might have come to deprive the dictator of his excuses.

I stopped wondering abruptly in 1996 when Castro's military shot down the two Brothers to the Rescue aircraft. One legacy of that tragedy was the enactment of legislation written by Senator Jesse Helms formally extending the embargo until Cuba becomes a full-fledged democracy. Previously the embargo was an executive order that could have been

lifted by a President without the approval of Congress. The new law applied to Cuba a standard that we set for no other nation, and seriously limited what any administration could do to prepare for the day when Castro, now in his seventies, finally departs the scene.

That day is inevitable, but we had no plan for dealing with the day after. Would the Cuban people take to the streets and demand their freedom? Would Castro's henchmen struggle to maintain power through a violent crackdown? Would thousands of Cubans try to flee to the United States by sea, as they had during past crises? Would U.S.-based adventurers seek to "liberate" the island? Or might there be a peaceful transition to democratic rule?

Obviously, from every perspective except the Communist, the last alternative was best. Yet, with Castro still there, it was not possible for Cubans to prepare for an orderly transition to democracy and a free market economy. I felt we should do all we could within the constraints of U.S. law to help Cubans have an early taste of free enterprise and build institutions independent of their government. I also wanted them to know we had not forgotten their plight.

On January 21, 1998, Pope John Paul II began a five-day visit to Cuba. I was intrigued by the prospect because two decades earlier the same pontiff's pilgrimage to his native Poland had electrified democratic forces and set in motion a chain of events that brought down the Berlin

Wall. In that case, the Communist government, not wanting to support the visit, made the mistake of turning the logistics over to local parishes. As Polish churches made arrangements for the Pope's appearances, they rediscovered their independent power. Polish citizens flooded into the streets to cheer their beloved countryman and revel in a sudden sense of "people power" and freedom. I had often described the phenomenon in a totally ungrammatical but accurate sentence: "They discovered how many of each other there were."

Despite the obvious differences of geography and culture, I hoped a similar process might be triggered by the Pope's trip to Cuba. During his visit the Pope presided at numerous services, met with the young, comforted the ill, and gave homilies and speeches to large, enthusiastic crowds. The majority of his remarks were aimed at inviting allegiance to Catholic doctrine, but he also made forceful statements in support of free expression, human rights, and the release of political prisoners.

Unlike the Polish regime, the Cuban government maintained tight control over events. Castro personally welcomed the pontiff and attended his climactic mass in Revolutionary Square. Although American attention was diverted (news of Monica Lewinsky had just broken), the Pope's journey lifted Cuban spirits and created a sense of anticipation about the future. It also shamed Castro into reinstating Christmas as a holiday for the first time in forty years.

President Clinton was as interested in Cuba as I was, and by the time the Pope had returned home, we had developed some ideas for helping the Cuban people without doing any favors for the government. In February, I went to Florida to gauge the potential reaction of the politically sensitive Cuban-American community to the measures we were considering. My guide in navigating the Miami scene was deputy Assistant Secretary of State for Public Affairs Lula Rodriguez, a Cuban-American who had grown up in the city, knew everyone, and combined toughness with an exuberant determination to get things done. Lula helped arrange meetings not only with the best-known community leaders but also with a range of businesspeople, church officials, younger citizens, and even entertainers such as pop diva Gloria Estefan and her husband, Emilio, who hosted a dinner for us in their home.

Most older Cuban-Americans had been driven from their homeland by Communist rule. I had, too, so we had something important in common. But I hadn't grown up within a large refugee community. My family hadn't been active in Czechoslovak-American politics. And Czechoslovakia didn't lie ninety miles off America's shores. Nevertheless, I felt I could understand the bond among Cuban-Americans and their sense of common identity. I could see how the new waves of immigrants would remind them of the land of their birth and kindle renewed anguish at its loss of liberty. There is a tendency in some circles to dismiss Cuban-Americans as politically extreme and monolithic, but I never found this to be the case.

What I found instead was a spectrum of opinions heavily influenced by individual experiences and age. Many older people still dreamed of their native country as it was, remembering the houses they grew up in and a population whose ethnic heritage was primarily European. Their anger toward Castro was personal, their support for the embargo absolute.

Members of the middle generation, in their forties and fifties, also despised Castro but were more pragmatic. Many I talked to were interested in helping Cuban dissidents and in working to nourish some sort of civil society. Most were enthusiastic about the Pope's visit and saw it as a potential turning point. One told me, "This is the first time in almost forty years the Cuban people have come together to hear someone other than Castro."

I also talked to some younger Cuban-Americans who wanted to lift the embargo and launch a "Sears invasion" of consumer goods that would deprive Castro of his ability to blame America for economic hardships.

I did find one area of general agreement, and that was support for remittances—money Cuban-Americans send to their families still in Cuba. After the aircraft shoot-downs, remittances were banned, but this didn't stop hundreds of millions of dollars from being sent; it just meant that the money flowed through secret channels. As one conservative Miamian told me, "We émigrés are the biggest advocates of the embargo. We're also the biggest breakers of the embargo." Unfortunately, much of this money was being sucked up en route by corrupt foreign officials. Although remittances helped the regime by bringing in hard currency, they also gave Cubans a means for surviving without depending on the government.

I returned from Miami thinking that at least a modest Cuba initiative was viable. However, before going ahead I wanted to hear the Pope's reflections on his trip to the island and discuss ways the United States and Vatican could work together. I also wanted to be able to say, at least generally, that the Pope supported the measures we were preparing. So I took advantage of a trip to Europe in March 1998 to stop in Rome.

Entering the Vatican is like walking into a Renaissance painting. The walls are high, the corridors long, the doorways arched, the atmosphere hushed. The guards wear ornate Swiss guard uniforms from a prior century, and the protocol is elaborate and precise. After arriving, I was escorted at exactly the prearranged time down a passageway by a man in white tie with silver chains around his neck. We proceeded deliberately through several rooms, each graced by beautiful sculptures or paintings. Finally I was ushered into the Pope's study.

His Holiness was seated at the near end of a long wooden table in the large room. Having been raised Catholic, I had grown up respecting the papacy in general, but because of his democratic credentials I had special respect for John Paul II. He rose to greet me, and we exchanged pleasantries in Polish. "But I thought you were Czech," he said before we switched to English. I told him I was a friend of Zbig Brzezinski, and the Pope nodded and said I should send his regards. He looked the way one would expect, all in white with a rosy complexion and an aura that made me feel I should bow my head, which I had covered with my black, big-brimmed hat.

As we talked, the Pope leaned forward on his elbows, so I spoke louder. I told him I had studied Communism my whole life and admired the part he had played in bringing freedom to Poland. I said his trip to Cuba had the potential to spark similar change and that we were watching the government's reaction closely. Some political prisoners had been released, but other dissidents had been arrested. The Pope assured me that he was also watching and remained in regular contact with the Cuban church.

I said we wanted to try to funnel some assistance to Caritas, the church's humanitarian relief organization in Cuba. We hoped to let the Cuban people know we wished to help them and make it easier for them to prepare for self-government. I said I understood that the church in Cuba was not like the church in Poland. He said, "Absolutely not." In Poland the Catholic Church is intimately identified with the nation.

As we talked briefly about the exile community in Miami, he mentioned his opposition to the embargo. It was, he said, harmful to ordinary people. However, he was pleased with the idea of trying to work with us to help Cubans, and urged me to stay in touch with Cardinal Angelo Sodano, the Vatican's secretary of state.

The half hour allotted for our meeting passed quickly, and I rose to go. But first the Pope walked into a larger reception room to greet the rest of my delegation; he expressed surprise at how many were women. Some reporters entered, and while saying good-bye I asked the Pope to pray for me. He said, "I will do as you asked." Reporters overheard the Pope's answer but not my request, and so were eager to know what His Holiness had agreed to do for the United States. I just smiled.

Returning to Washington, I announced that Cuban-Americans would be allowed to send remittances directly to relatives in Cuba. Charitable organizations would be permitted to charter flights, instead of paying much more to route them through some third country. We streamlined licensing procedures to make it easier for religious and other nonprofit organizations to ship drugs and medicine, and we promised to work with Capitol Hill to develop a proposal for donating food.

Early in 1999, we took four additional steps with the same general purpose: expanding exchanges, allowing remittances to be sent by any American, authorizing the sale of food to privately owned restaurants, and expanding direct flights to and from Cuba.

These measures made a difference. By the time I left office, more than a hundred thousand Americans were traveling to Cuba annually for a wide range of academic, cultural, and social purposes. The United States was approving the transfer of tens of millions of dollars in medical equipment each year, and an estimated $1 billion was being sent in remittances. Licenses for humanitarian assistance had risen sharply, and Congress had authorized direct sales of food to Cuba for the first time in almost four decades.

The initiatives are helping to do what they were intended to do—reduce Cuba's isolation. They will not, however, affect Castro's longevity. Obviously the Cuban dictator is less than eager to join his old buddies from the Warsaw Pact era as a toppled statue, and he does have some advantages. Despite his excesses, Castro is not a bland, foreign-imposed apparatchik of the type that governed Central and East Europe during the Cold War. He is the original charismatic leader. The fact that Cuba is an island makes it easier for the government to control the flow of information. And he was insulated from the effects of the papal visit because the Pope is Polish, not Cuban, and because of the Cuban church's reluctance to play a political role.

Castro was relentless, nevertheless, in trying to stamp out the tiny sparks of freedom that surfaced in the wake of the Pope's pilgrimage. In March 1999, four peaceful dissident leaders were convicted in a closed trial that was condemned in Europe and many parts of Latin America. I kept a list on my desk of the jailed dissidents and mentioned them often in public statements, trying to keep a spotlight on their treatment and generate pressure for their release.[7] In November 1999, Castro hosted the Ibero-American Summit in Havana. Instead of using the summit to embarrass Washington, Castro was embarrassed by the number of foreign

---

7. Efforts to focus attention on Cuba's human rights record were hindered in late 1999 and the first months of 2000 by the furor over the custody of Elián González, a little boy plucked by the Coast Guard from the waters off Florida. As for the dissidents, Marta Beatriz Roque, Félix Bonne, and René Gómez Manzano were freed in 2000, Vladimiro Roca in 2002.

dignitaries seeking to meet with embattled prodemocracy activists and by the summit declaration calling for freedom of political expression. More recently Castro has been embarrassed further by Oswaldo Payá's Varela Project, which has gathered thousands of signatures on behalf of a national referendum on political rights. Showing that champions of freedom stick together, Payá was nominated for the Nobel Peace Prize by Václav Havel.[8]

WHILE I WAS helping to shape our Cuba policy, there were plenty of people lobbying me, from both sides. Often this pressure irritated; in one case it fascinated. The Nobel Prize–winning author Gabriel García Márquez was not someone I expected ever to meet. In 1997, Mexican President Ernesto Zedillo hosted a state dinner for President Clinton, and García Márquez was there. I told him I had given his novel *Love in the Time of Cholera* to Havel as a present only to have the Czech president tell me that he had already read and loved it. This was the kind of thing authors liked to hear, and we had a good discussion.

When García Márquez came to Washington a year later for a state dinner for Colombia's President Andrés Pastrana, he asked if I could meet him and his wife for lunch and a longer conversation. I pretend to be a dignified person, but the truth is I have little shame, so I thought I would try to get the famous writer to autograph some books. I looked at home for my own copies of his works, but was unable to find them, my housekeeper having decided to arrange my library by size rather than author or subject. I rushed out to one bookstore, then another, finally showing up at lunch carrying a big bag and feeling like a groupie. García Márquez, a handsome man with silvery hair and an animated, intelligent face, grinned and consented to sign every volume.

As we ate, "Gabo" explained why he had wanted to see me again—Castro. García Márquez had met the Cuban leader in 1975 while writing a book on the revolution. The two had been friends ever since. He told me we were all wrong about Fidel; the Cuban dictator was looking for a reason to reconcile with the United States but couldn't do so with the embargo in place. He said Castro was a good man, even a religious one, and remained popular among his people despite the many economic hardships.

I replied that the law made it impossible for us to lift the embargo and that Castro could have ended it at almost any time during the previous

8. In the spring of 2003, Castro unleashed yet another round of repression, imprisoning dozens of dissidents, while the attention of many was distracted by the second Gulf War.

three decades simply by holding free elections. Since it soon became clear that García Márquez and I were not going to change each other's opinions, I told him I would much prefer to discuss his writing. He said people thought he had made up the stories in his books, but they were all true, just not in the right order. His memoirs, which he was then writing, would explain where everything came from.

I stayed in touch with Gabo during the remainder of my term, called him during his bout with lymphoma, and conferred with him about the terrible problems faced by his native Colombia. The best time we had was in Cartagena, where after a small dinner at the presidential residence we toured the city and he showed me landmarks from *Love in the Time of Cholera*. He also gave me some counsel that has stayed in my mind ever since. "When you write your memoirs," he said, "remember: do not be angry."

The supportive hands of Růžena Spieglová and Olga Körbelová keep me from falling. I found this photo, the only one I have of my grandmothers together, while looking through my mother's papers in preparation for writing this book. I will treasure it as long as I live.

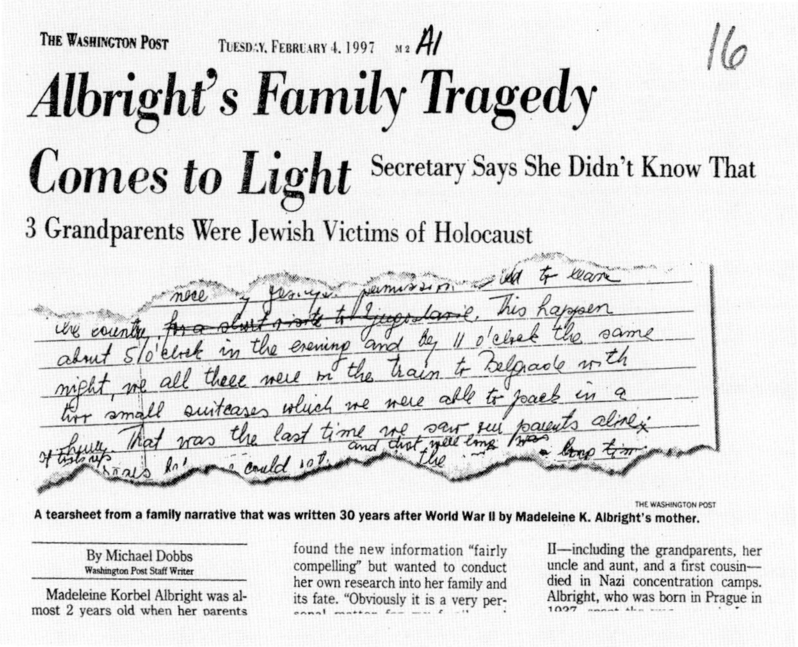

THE WASHINGTON POST TUESDAY, FEBRUARY 4, 1997 M 2 A1 *16*

Albright's Family Tragedy

Comes to Light   Secretary Says She Didn't Know That

3 Grandparents Were Jewish Victims of Holocaust

[handwritten family narrative, partially legible:]
were ... young... permission... old to leave
the country for a short visit to Yugoslavia. This happen
about 5 o'clock in the evening and by 11 o'clock the same
night, we all three were on the train to Belgrade with
her small suitcases which we were able to pack in a
hurry. That was the last time we saw our parents alive...

A tearsheet from a family narrative that was written 30 years after World War II by Madeleine K. Albright's mother.   THE WASHINGTON POST

By Michael Dobbs
Washington Post Staff Writer

Madeleine Korbel Albright was almost 2 years old when her parents

found the new information "fairly compelling" but wanted to conduct her own research into her family and its fate. "Obviously it is a very personal matter for my family and I

II—including the grandparents, her uncle and aunt, and a first cousin— died in Nazi concentration camps. Albright, who was born in Prague in 1937 spent the war...

Headline on the front page of the *Washington Post* on the day of
President Clinton's first State of the Union address of his second term.

President Clinton. One of the qualities in him that I always admired: he was a great listener.

THE WHITE HOUSE

THE WHITE HOUSE/ROBERT MCNEELY

If you want to share an umbrella I am holding, you have to be ready to duck. Sandy Berger and I had our tensions, but compared to most national security advisor/secretary of state pairings, we were very compatible. Walking ahead of us was another compatible duo, President Clinton and Vice-President Gore.

Dinner in New York with Israeli Prime Minister Yitzhak Rabin. His assassination in November 1995 left a void that has not yet been filled.

DAVID KARP

DEPARTMENT OF STATE/USIS/MATTY STERN

Answering questions at a joint press conference with Prime Minister Benjamin Netanyahu. The Israeli leader's skepticism about the peace process did not prevent him from reaching an agreement with the Palestinians at Wye River. In the center observing us is my spokesman and close advisor, Jamie Rubin. To his left, speaking into a cell phone, is the State Department's director of communications, Kitty Bartels.

Known by his people as Al-Malik Al-Insan ("the Humane King"), King Hussein ruled Jordan from 1953 until his death in February 1999, four months after this photo was taken. A fierce defender of the Arab people, he was also a champion of peace.

DEPARTMENT OF STATE

NATO Secretary General Javier Solana was as delightful as a dinner companion as he was accomplished as a world leader.

In Independence, Missouri, on March 12, 1999, the Czech, Polish, and Hungarian foreign ministers have just signed documents signifying the admission of their countries into NATO. I could not resist holding the documents up before the cheering crowd.

Comparing notes with Chairman of the Joint Chiefs of Staff General John Shalikashvili, at his retirement party in 1997. One day I was standing with General Shali outside the White House when a third official walked up and greeted us as "war and peace." Shali replied, "Yes, but which is which?" Behind us are Defense Secretary Bill Cohen and his wife Janet Langhart Cohen.

Russian Foreign Minister Igor Ivanov and I traded many diplomatic barbs; here, we traded hats. As the inscription implies, when we worked together, we were a mighty team.

We had a surprise visitor at my sixtieth birthday party. Senator Jesse Helms, possessing old-fashioned political views and old-fashioned manners, was proud of both. On policy, he often infuriated me. In person, we never exchanged a harsh word.

The foreign ministers of Southeast Asia made us all sing for our suppers. In 1997, I was Evita. The following year I teamed up with Russian Foreign Minister Yevgeny Primakov in a skit we entitled East-West Story. Batting my eyes, I sang, "I want to know what you think of me." Yevgeny crooned back, "Look in your file at the KGB!"

With Sean Connery at the Kennedy Center Awards dinner. Later, I was referred to jokingly as the 'new Bond girl.'

Actor Patrick Stewart is a good friend. In his capacity as Captain Jean-Luc Picard of the Starship *Enterprise*, he invited me to meet his crew. In this group, I am the one with the unusual looks.

My opening day throw for the Baltimore Orioles generated a *New York Times* photo of me with the caption, "Now Pitching for the United States."

The President at Camp David trying to improve my bowling form. I'm so easy to teach he didn't even have to put down his diet Coke.

TWENTY-ONE

As the World Turns

I AM OFTEN ASKED to describe what life was like as Secretary of State. The best one-word answer is "motion." The world never stopped revolving and neither did I. No matter how much I did, there was more to do. The most important nouns in my life were phone, plane, meeting, and memo. I found to my distress that it was impossible to maintain many of the personal friendships I had forged in Washington during the previous two decades. I made and had to break so many dates for dinner or a show that I finally stopped trying. I simply did not have time for a private life.

The exception was my grandchildren, with whom I spent absolutely as much time as I could. They didn't care what job I had, so long as I could fix a grilled cheese sandwich, read a Dr. Seuss book, or buy a toy train. They did, however, think it perfectly natural to see their grandmother on television or traveling around with a group of friendly ninja protectors. When I was younger, I couldn't understand why older women insisted on talking about their grandchildren. Now I understood: it's impossible not to.

But such personal moments were rare. The issues I dealt with did not start and stop conveniently so I could concentrate on one while the others stood still. In the middle of tense, high-stakes meetings I was often handed notes about phone calls I urgently needed to make in response to entirely different events that had just taken place half a world away. Little was certain except the uncertainty about what the next day might bring, whether developments in international affairs or events at home that threatened to impinge on our management of foreign policy. Through it all I concentrated on trying to do the best job I could, in a way that reflected my own style and personality. The first year especially was a time of learning a new role, and I was delighted with how smoothly events generally went. The second year was a different matter—a time of severe testing, policy set-backs, political controversy, and moments of self-doubt.

SHORTLY AFTER I was sworn in as Secretary of State, Henry Kissinger introduced me to an audience by formally welcoming me into the "frater-nity" of those who had held that position. Replying, I said, "Henry, I hate to tell you, but it's not a fraternity anymore."

President Clinton shattered the glass ceiling for women in foreign policy. During his eight years as President, seven of the top ten positions in the State Department were, at one time or another, filled by a woman. No area of responsibility was out of bounds. Women were put in charge of economic policy and arms control, management, public diplomacy, and relations with Capitol Hill. At the same time, I often looked around at meetings of the President's foreign policy team, which included repre-sentatives from the NSC and other major departments and agencies, and found myself the only woman in the room.

As Secretary I was determined to make efforts to improve the lives of women and girls part of the mainstream of U.S. foreign policy—a step long overdue. One of America's core goals was the promotion of democ-racy, but democracy wasn't possible if women were treated as second-class citizens or victimized by discrimination or abuse.

At the 1995 Women's Conference in Beijing, the United States had made a series of commitments aimed at advancing the status of women in our own country and supporting such efforts overseas. To implement these commitments, the President established the White House Inter-Agency Council on Women, chaired by Donna Shalala, our dynamic Sec-retary of Health and Human Services. When I became Secretary of State, the President asked me to take a turn as council chair.

We celebrated the transition on International Women's Day in March 1997. Both the First Lady and I spoke to a gathering at the State Depart-ment, and in subsequent months we built on our earlier friendship to forge an unprecedented partnership. Throughout my term, the First Lady was a major foreign policy asset. A self-taught diplomat, she was an enor-mously popular unofficial ambassador for the United States. I was once asked whether it was appropriate for the two of us to work together so closely. I agreed that it was a departure from tradition but pointed out that times had changed. "I'm not Thomas Jefferson," I said, "and Hillary sure isn't Martha Washington."

Our shared goal was to move beyond lip service and afterthoughts to convey the message to each State Department bureau and embassy that I cared about whether women were included in democracy-building projects, whether programs were underway to combat violence against women, whether microenterprise was being encouraged to give women access to credit, whether the special needs of women refugees were being met, and whether family planning programs were being given the priority they deserved. To dramatize this commitment, I insisted on meeting with groups of women activists whenever possible on my trips overseas.

While serving at the UN, I had brought together a group of women permanent representatives. Now I convened the world's women foreign ministers each year during the UN General Assembly sessions in New York. We always began with a serious discussion about how to focus global attention on problems such as the shocking rise in criminal trafficking in women and girls. We were still a small group—growing from a handful to more than a dozen—but we found quickly that our joint projects had more impact and weight than initiatives we undertook separately. We also compared notes about our personal lives and what it was like to operate in what was still largely a male environment. Whether we were from Africa, Europe, Latin America, or elsewhere, our experiences in many respects were the same. We had, it seemed, to work doubly hard to be taken seriously, and triply hard to actually push our agendas through.

ACCORDING TO DEAN ACHESON, "The first requirement of a statesman is that he be dull." Acheson said nothing about stateswomen, however, so I didn't feel bound by his prescription.

I saw my duty as Secretary to represent my country, help formulate policy, and manage the State Department. I tried to avoid doing anything inconsistent with the dignity of the office, but I was also determined to be myself, and my self did not match the conventional image of a Secretary of State. I could have chosen to submerge the differences as much as possible and done my best to imitate the men who preceded me. I could have shunned informal settings, dressed conservatively, and reined in my penchant for blunt speaking. But the job would not have been as enjoyable, and I would not have been able to accomplish as much as I did.

The novelty of my appointment attracted considerable interest. I decided to capitalize on that attention, hoping that if people saw me enjoying the challenges of the job, they might be more interested in world affairs. Beginning with the young, I often visited public schools to read to the smaller children and answer questions from their elder brothers and sisters. Frequently I used a globe to show where I was traveling and explain why Americans should care about events on the far side of the sphere. Of course it was the youngest students who always asked the hardest questions, such as wanting to know whether people in Australia had to walk upside down—and if not, why not. My educational efforts received a boost when I was featured in the *Mini-Page*, a Sunday supplement distributed to hundreds of newspapers. The headline read, "First Woman Secretary of State Talks to Kids." Inside there was a message from me, a word jumble featuring such terms as "treaties," "visas," and "cabinet," and a connect-the-dots puzzle that challenged children to draw my hair.

In April 1997, the Baltimore Orioles asked if I would take the place of the President—who had hurt his knee—and throw out the first ball of the baseball season in front of the huge opening day crowd. I called my daughter Anne, the softball player in the family. She told me bluntly, "Mom, you throw like a girl." So I agreed to pitch only after Anne and my Diplomatic Security detail agreed to coach me. I borrowed an old mitt and practiced pitching with the agents in the State Department basement, at a nearby park, and even on the tarmac at Andrews Air Force Base while wearing high heels just before flights.

The day of the game, I arrived early at the Orioles' stadium, Camden Yards, and practiced under the stands before venturing onto the field for the opening ceremonies. Wearing black slacks and an Orioles jacket, I stood next to Iron Man Cal Ripken Jr. and marveled at the greenness of the close-cut grass, the smallness of the diamond, the hugeness of the stadium, and the loudness of the 48,000 fans. I also worried, because many minutes passed before they gave me the ball and I strode to the pitcher's mound. Had my finely tuned throwing arm started to cool?

I stood there, peering toward the plate. As Orioles catcher Chris Hoiles sized me up, he began walking toward me, from sixty, then fifty, then forty, finally stopping about thirty feet away. He positioned his huge catcher's mitt to give me a good target, then held up two fingers, which meant curve. I shook my head. He held up one finger, which meant fastball. I nodded and went into my windup, drew my leg back, pivoted smartly, and brought my pitching arm forward, releasing the ball with a small Monica Seles grunt and a sharp snap of my wrist. The ball would have smacked forcefully into Hoiles' mitt had our planet lacked gravity. It might have gone further had I not forgotten to remove my gold bracelets. As it was, it made the journey with only one bounce. Hoiles trotted up and gave me the ball, a handshake, and a grin. I walked off, offering a silent prayer for the President's health during future springs.[1]

---

1. An editorial in the next day's *Wall Street Journal* was entitled, "Madeleine K. Clemens." Personally I found the editors' comments uncommonly perceptive: "Of critical impor-

WARREN CHRISTOPHER HAD his elegant neckties; I had my pins or brooches. Once while I was at the UN, the government-controlled Iraqi media—angered by my criticism of Saddam Hussein—published a poem calling me a variety of colorful names, including a "snake." About that time I was required to meet with a senior Iraqi official. I happened to have a pin of a coiled snake, so I wore it to the meeting. When I met with the press, the television cameras focused on the pin, and so did the journalists' questions.

Thereafter I enjoyed picking out a pin appropriate to the message of the day. For example, Mary Jo Myers, the wife of future Chairman of the Joint Chiefs of Staff General Richard Myers, presented me with a pin combining the insignia of America's five armed services, a pin I often wore when speaking to the military. I used a spider on those (rare) occasions when I was feeling devious, a balloon when I was up, the Capitol building to show bipartisanship, and a bee when I was looking for someone to sting. When I met with the Russian foreign minister on the subject of the Anti-Ballistic Missile Treaty, the pin I wore was shaped like a missile.[2] The Russian asked, "Is that one of your interceptor missiles?" I said, "Yes, and as you can see, we know how to make them very small. So you'd better be ready to negotiate."[3]

DESPITE THE INEVITABLE moments of irritation, my first year as Secretary felt like an extended honeymoon. The issues seemed fresh and the challenges surmountable. The press was friendly and the work endlessly interesting. Feeling that I had the best imaginable job, I was determined to

tance, her head appears to have remained steady and her eyes focused on the target throughout, unlike the average Presidential hurler, whose head usually flops from far right to far left in the short span of a single pitch."

2. The missile pin had been made by Lisa Vershbow, a professional jewelry designer whose husband was our ambassador to NATO.

3. Before long, I started telling reporters looking for news to "read my pins." I was surprised and flattered when Helen Drutt English, an authority on contemporary jewelry and the owner of an art gallery in Philadelphia, invited jewelers from around the world to create pins in a tribute to "Brooching It Diplomatically." More than sixty artists responded with an eclectic collection of pieces that were exhibited both domestically and overseas. Gijs Bakker of the Netherlands designed one that was superimposed on a photo of me on the catalogue cover. It shows the head of the Statue of Liberty, with two real watches for eyes. Bakker set one of the watches upside down so I would know how long an appointment had lasted and the other right side up so a visitor would know when it was time to leave. I am often asked about which of the artists' pins I wear the most, but the brooches belong to the artists, not to me, except for one designed by Helen Shirk of Buffalo, New York, that I received as a gift after I left office.

make the most of every minute. I was in the office early and stayed late—a schedule easier for me than for others because I had relatively few family responsibilities. I tried to nurture a strong sense of teamwork within the department and elsewhere in the administration. I attended diligently to the important relationships I was developing with other foreign ministers and on Capitol Hill.

One Sunday in 1997, during my first UN General Assembly session as Secretary, having a few hours free, I decided to take a long walk up Madison Avenue with my sister. It was a lovely fall morning, and my ego soared as people all along the way smiled and waved. A woman who said she was Israeli asked me to do something about her prime minister. A man hollered, "Hey, darlin', you've got to stand up to the Serbs." We found a place to eat lunch that was quiet until a Greek busboy discovered us and engaged me in conversation about Cyprus. Later we stopped for dinner at a place I thought was Italian but turned out to be Albanian; the owner came over and we began talking about the Balkans.

The next morning I was still smiling from all the recognition I had received. I felt like pretty hot stuff. Then I went to have my hair done. Because of all the traveling I was doing, hair had become a major problem. I was always going to different people, who either wanted to redo me or were too afraid to touch my hair. When I looked in the mirror, I never knew what I would see. That's why I wore so many hats.

This time I was trying a salon new to me, but highly recommended. I went armed with a photo, which I gave to the hairdresser, and said, "This is how I want to look. Now please just treat me like a normal person, pull, tease, do whatever you need to." After he finished, I thanked him, said he had done a great job, and promised to come back whenever I was in New York. Then I asked his name. "Anthony," he replied, before inquiring, "And you are . . . ?"

NOT UNEXPECTEDLY, I found during that first year that I enjoyed having my own plane. I remain grateful to the men and women of the U.S. Air Force who kept me aloft for more than one million miles over the full term and brought us down safely every time. I was also grateful to Dick Shinnick, the leader of my administrative staff, who made sure the thousand moving parts involved in every trip came together in the right way at the right time.

One of those parts was my luggage, which was always placed in the cabin for security reasons and for the quick changes I might need to make depending upon the temperature of our destination. Invariably we seemed to travel back and forth between the hottest and coldest climates.

Most of my predecessors had wives to pack for them. I didn't, so I developed my own crazy routine. I would arrive home late with a schedule of events, sit down in front of the TV, and fill in what I would wear, even figuring out which pin would work. Then the fun would begin as I tried to find out where the clothes I had selected were and if I could still fit into them since the last trip. If anyone had appeared at my house at such a time, they would have discovered a very un-Secretarylike person running around muttering to herself. At first I kept track of what I had worn in each country, so I wouldn't repeat, but after a while I gave that up.

Like many Americans, I tried a variety of exercise and diet programs. When I was on the plane, the crew did its best to accommodate whatever regimen I was on. They found room for a portable stair stepper and weights and always had tuna fish and the right kind of crackers. They heated my homemade cabbage soup when I was on a diet featuring that gourmet dish, and they obeyed my order that KitKat chocolate bars be banned from my cabin. No matter what, however, during each trip there was that special moment when exhaustion overcame discipline and my favorite taco salad smothered in everything arrived, along with smuggled-in KitKats.

Part way through my first around-the-world trip, I thought I would be traveling so much I would need a hobby to help fill the time. So when we stopped for refueling at an air base in Japan, Elaine Shocas and I went to the PX and each bought a Singer Tiny Tailor sewing machine. Our plan was to sew little flags of each country we visited and eventually make a large quilt with the American flag in the middle. At the first opportunity we bought material for our flags, and we took everything along with us on the next trip. Needless to say, in four years no Tiny Tailor ever emerged from its box. When I wasn't working, I was usually too tired to do anything except watch movies. I did have a policy of not watching international thrillers, as they reminded me too much of my day job.[4] I also slept when I could, and I started taking sleeping pills so I could rest on command and be ready for whatever was scheduled at the next stop.

IN MANY FOREIGN COUNTRIES there is a minister of culture. America has no such position, but cultural awareness is an essential part of our diplomacy. Our ambassadors and Foreign Service officers are schooled in the histories, traditions, and customs of the countries to which they are

---

4. However, I couldn't resist watching Harrison Ford in *Air Force One* while traveling with the President *on* Air Force One.

accredited. Because of America's global influence, we are particularly susceptible to the allegation that we do not respect the sensitivities of others. During my tenure I attempted to address the problem by helping to organize the first White House Conference on Culture and Diplomacy, hosting a reception annually in honor of the Thelonius Monk Jazz Competition, increasing funds for international student exchange programs, and supporting efforts to educate the world about America's cultural diversity.

On a more personal level, I had to meet a challenge none of my predecessors had to face, so to speak, in quite the same way. I had to master the art of diplomatic kissing. This was more complicated than it sounds because people from different places had different styles. In most cases when I was greeted by another foreign minister, I received a single peck on the cheek. However, in Latin America the maneuver was complicated by the fact that in some countries they kiss on the left and in some on the right. I could never remember which, so there were a lot of bumped noses. The French of course kiss on both cheeks. The Belgians and Dutch kiss three times. In Botswana, four times.

As for Yasser Arafat, he could only be described as dogged and unpredictable. Sometimes he would do one cheek, sometimes two, and at other times both cheeks, the forehead, and the hand. He also tried to kiss President Clinton, who towered above him, so Arafat ended up laying his head beneath the President's chin.

One of the more unusual displays of cultural diplomacy would occur at the annual meeting of the Association of Southeast Asian Nations (ASEAN). Perhaps for the same reason that karaoke started in Japan, the Asians loved to put on a show. In fact, they expected every delegation to perform a song or skit or dance routine—starring its foreign minister—as entertainment for the final dinner. Some countries took the event quite seriously and rehearsed for months. Others recruited professionals. Historically, American secretaries of state had been extremely reluctant participants. My initial reaction to the Asian tradition was "They must be out of their minds." However, I soon discovered that I was, at heart, a ham.

For the 1997 ASEAN meeting in Malaysia, our embassy had drafted lyrics to the tune of "Mary Had a Little Lamb." The words were witty but the song was just not me. So on the long plane ride to Kuala Lumpur I dumped a young woman for an older one: Evita replaced Mary. I made my stage entrance in a long black dress, with crimson lipstick, a shawl, and a large flower in my hair. With my diplomatic team backing me up, I serenaded the crowd with "Don't Cry for Me, ASEANies." The performance was received with great whoops and cheers. I would have become insufferable if one envoy had not told the press: "Madeleine was very sassy, the new Madonna, even though she can't sing to save her life."

The next year I was determined to top my own act, which meant I needed help. In Malaysia, Yevgeny Primakov had not sung, but rather used a whistle to direct his delegation, who sang dressed as sailors in the Russian Black Sea fleet. I praised his performance shamelessly and suggested we secretly join forces for the 1998 ASEAN meeting in Manila.

In between discussions on the Balkans and Iraq, we came up with a story about star-crossed lovers we called the East-West Story. The night before the performance, we held a raucous rehearsal in my room—the Douglas MacArthur suite—at the Manila Hotel. Primakov was the Tony character, backed by his gang, "the Russkies," while I had Natalie Wood's role, reinforced by my gang, "the Yankees." The next day, our staffs put out word there would be a "rumble" that night, but few got the reference until the Russkies and Yankees took the stage with snapping fingers and menacing looks. I entered from the left wearing an embroidered *barong* blouse, singing, "The most beautiful sound I ever heard—Yevgeny, Yevgeny, Yevgeny," to which Primakov replied in his thick Russian accent, "Madeleine Albright—I just met a girl named Madeleine Albright." This parody too was a hit and, more important, helped ease our relations with the Russians at a difficult time.

Culture was also at the heart of one my favorite perquisites as Secretary. Each year five performing artists were selected for the coveted Kennedy Center Honors. The awards were presented at a black-tie dinner held in the State Department's Diplomatic Reception Rooms. Invitations to the event were among the most sought-after in Washington; I had long since stopped trying to get one. However, as Secretary I was not only invited but had to host the dinner. Never was a responsibility more welcome.

From 1997 to 2000, the awardees included Bill Cosby, Willie Nelson, Clint Eastwood, Stevie Wonder, Lauren Bacall, Bob Dylan, Jessye Norman, Plácido Domingo, Chuck Berry, Judith Jamieson, Angela Lansbury, Mikhail Baryshnikov, and others. However, for reasons I swear were purely artistic, my favorite was Sean Connery. He had an impact on everyone. As one reporter put it, all the men in the room wanted to be James Bond and all the women wanted to be with Sean Connery.

During the photo session, Connery put his hands on my shoulders while I gazed up at him. The photo ran worldwide. When I visited Saudi Arabia a few days later, I was met by Prince Bandar, the Saudi ambassador to the United States. Bandar arrived flashing an Arabic newspaper with the Connery photo on the front page. As we walked through the airport, he kept shouting, "Make way for Madeleine Albright, the new Bond girl; please make room for the new Bond girl."

BY RANK, but also by force of personality and intellect, President Clinton was the undisputed head of his own foreign policy team. He was a first-class picker of brains, a voracious reader, an excellent listener, a constant learner, and a superb student of history. His energy was astounding, and his capacity to charm his counterparts both extraordinary and useful. During his two terms he grew steadily on the world stage and became, as other leaders retired, one of the globe's senior statesmen.

The President didn't schedule regular one-on-one meetings with any member of the cabinet. I couldn't complain, however, because I did see the Chief Executive frequently with others or alone. I often stayed behind after Oval Office meetings because the President had written me a note or signaled me with his eyes. He also had a disconcerting penchant for making phone calls at night, often quite late. I was glad to receive them but sometimes wondered how much sense I made after he woke me up.

Nothing is more vital to an effective foreign policy than a strong and engaged President, but it also helps if the secretary of state and national security advisor function effectively as a team. Historically this relationship has been tense. My relationship with Sandy Berger and his deputy James Steinberg[5] was far from trouble-free, but compared to some earlier NSC-State pairings we worked together well.

The President had often praised Sandy to me, saying he had a "fine mind" and had "helped hold things together" during the first term. I fully agreed and found Sandy to be very fair, but during my own four years, I sometimes became irritated by what I saw as the NSC's attempts to micromanage. At first I blamed myself, because my default drive is always to cooperate. Then I blamed the male dominance of the system. The truth is that problems arose when Sandy and I tried to occupy each other's space. Although the NSC's job was supposed to be limited to coordinating the actions and policies of the departments, proximity to the President sometimes tempted Sandy and his staff to assume an operational role. My objections were undercut by my past association with the very operational Brzezinski. During the Carter years, Zbig's NSC had driven the State Department crazy. So when I complained, Sandy—who had been in the State Department at that time—said he was only doing what Brzezinski had done.

Notwithstanding the occasional gripes, Sandy and I knew that, whatever happened, we were going to sink or swim together. Neither of us

---

5. I first worked closely with Jim Steinberg during the Dukakis campaign. At the NSC, no one worked harder, cared more passionately about matters of right and wrong, or did more to prevent interagency disputes. Berger and Steinberg made a strong team.

would emerge a hero if our foreign policy flopped. We both felt an obligation to submerge any personal irritations and work together. To facilitate this, we made frequent use of a direct phone link between Sandy's office and mine that, on some days, might be used a dozen times or more. Every Monday when in town, the two of us had lunch with Secretary of Defense Bill Cohen in Sandy's office. Dubbed the ABC lunches (A for Albright, B for Berger, C for Cohen), the sessions were useful in coordinating policy, breaking logjams, and clearing the air.[6]

I had first met Bill Cohen more than two decades previously when I was working for Senator Muskie and he was a U.S. Representative from Maine. Later, while monitoring Congress for the NSC, I had criticized Cohen in a written report to Brzezinski because of his opposition to the SALT II arms control treaty. I was embarrassed after I became Secretary when I learned that the long-forgotten memo was about to surface in the *Washington Post*.[7] Immediately I went out and bought some books on forgiveness and presented them to Cohen as a gift. "What are these for?" he asked, puzzled. I replied, "You may not understand now, but you soon will." I don't know if it was the books, but when the story broke, he forgave me. Although I did not always agree with the Secretary of Defense, we were usually able to work through problems caused by the differing perspectives of our two departments. I always found Bill honest in his approach and resolute in implementing policies once they had been agreed upon. He is also a very interesting man, an intellectual, poet, and novelist with boyish good looks that seem likely to last him all his life.

One reason our foreign policy team functioned well is that despite small problems we all actually liked one another and often got together socially. One Sunday night at Camp David in January 1998, I watched *Good Will Hunting* with the Clintons and many of my colleagues. Robin Williams, Matt Damon, and the rest of the movie's cast were also there. The film ends with the Damon character going off to California in search of his girl. This prompted the President to say that he had once given up a job in the McGovern campaign to go off and meet Hillary. After dinner we went bowling, which I had not done since high school. With the President

6. We also gathered on Wednesday mornings for breakfast with a larger group that included CIA Director George Tenet, the Vice-President's top advisor Leon Fuerth, General Henry "Hugh" Shelton, Chairman of the Joint Chiefs of Staff, and Bill Richardson and later Richard Holbrooke, our ambassadors to the UN.

7. The item on my memo ran in the *Post*'s "In the Loop" column, which became an instant institution in Washington when started in 1993 by Al Kamen, one of the capital's wittiest and most irreverent journalists.

serving as my personal instructor, I remembered how to release the ball without injuring myself or alarming the Secret Service. Those viewing the series of photographs have taken note that we were in perfect sync.

THROUGH 1998 AND BEYOND, the Monica Lewinsky story dominated the headlines. That didn't prevent us from doing our jobs, but the uproar was impossible to block out. Ordinarily, before the President held a press conference with a foreign leader, the foreign policy team helped him prepare. Now we had to leave the room early so the President could also review the investigation-related subjects about which he was sure to be asked.

With all that was going on in the world, our foreign policy team met almost constantly during the weeks after the scandal broke. We didn't talk much about what we were learning from the newspapers. We did discuss the fact that we were all being watched and had to steer a steady course. Although he didn't need to, I was glad Sandy said early on that we were not to take into consideration what was happening with the investigation as we deliberated policy issues. We had only one priority and that was to serve the best interests of the United States. As the weeks passed and more information came out, it was clear the atmosphere at the White House had grown exceptionally tense. The First Lady came to the State Department for lunch in mid February and, when I asked how she was doing, merely grimaced. In March, I was invited to Camp David again, I suspect at Hillary's instigation. There were also more invitations to watch movies at the White House. This was such a difficult time for the Clintons that it may have been easier to have other people around. The result was a kind of forced bonhomie, with tight smiles and small talk.

My colleagues from around the world couldn't understand why anyone would care what the President might or might not have done. As a leader, he was enormously popular; he received an enthusiastic and rare standing ovation when appearing before the UN General Assembly at the height of the controversy. I knew, however, that the matter did have serious political consequences in the United States. I still wanted to believe that the whole business had been cooked up to destroy the President and that this would become clear when the full truth came out.

It didn't help that if 1997 had been the year most things seemed to go right in foreign policy, 1998 was the year everything—at least for a time—seemed to go wrong. During that year's opening months, the Middle East peace process was stalled, we had repeated unresolved run-ins with Saddam Hussein, and there was an outbreak of violence in the

Yugoslav province of Kosovo. Then in May, the government of India conducted an underground nuclear test, its first since 1974. Although we worked hard to persuade the Pakistanis not to follow suit, two weeks later they did. During the previous fifty years, India and Pakistan had fought three hot wars and numerous skirmishes, while constantly exchanging hostile rhetoric. Now both countries had nuclear weapons and the world was a more dangerous place.

It was also becoming more chaotic. The economies of the famed Asian tigers had suddenly ceased to roar. First in Thailand, then in Indonesia, Malaysia, the Philippines, Hong Kong, and South Korea, economies accustomed to double-digit growth slowed, then headed into reverse. By early 1998, Asian financial institutions were taking the hit for hundreds of billions of dollars in faulty investments, several national currencies were in virtual free fall, local stock markets were plummeting, and tens of millions of people were facing a return trip to the wrong side of the poverty line. Contrary to the fulminations of Malaysia's xenophobic Prime Minister Mahathir Mohamad, the financial crisis had been caused not by too much economic liberalization but by cronyism, corruption, and greed. I knew at the time that the devastation would have extensive political and social consequences in Asia, but was not sure in what direction or how deep.

The answer came in Indonesia in May, when the thirty-two-year reign of Suharto came to a dismal end amid riots, rising unemployment, and political fragmentation. Although the United States and Suharto had always maintained cordial relations, the Indonesian leader was one of America's least distinguished partners. Like Ferdinand Marcos in the Philippines, he found ways to make government service pay extremely well—not only for himself but for his entire family. Also like Marcos, he blocked the development of democratic institutions. Forced by popular pressure to resign, Suharto left behind an impoverished treasury and a divided society.

In mid June, war broke out in the Horn of Africa between Ethiopia and Eritrea, two partially democratic countries with previously respected leaders and absolutely nothing to gain from the conflict. Meanwhile the mammoth and strategically important Democratic Republic of Congo, formerly Zaire, was being ripped apart by a struggle involving troops from five nations plus a number of armed guerrilla groups. In Sudan, the decades-long civil war continued to rage.

In late summer, I traveled to Capitol Hill to participate in a closed-door briefing for the House of Representatives on North Korea. It turned out to be a highly partisan and acrimonious session, during which some members wrongly accused me of lying about an important matter involving classified information. On the last day of August, North Korea added to the mix of problems by launching a three-stage Taepo Dong rocket that flew over Japanese territory before falling into the Pacific. The provocative missile test understandably rattled Japan and raised concerns that the North Koreans might eventually develop missiles capable of attacking the United States.

It seemed that wherever I looked, I saw either gridlock or peril. For all the power of the United States, we were not able to dictate events. The North Koreans, Serbs, Israelis and Palestinians, Indians and Pakistanis, Iraqis, Russians, African leaders, even our allies seemed indifferent or hostile to our requests. My personal confidence level was down. I saw myself as an activist Secretary but often felt like I was spinning my wheels. My honeymoon with the media had developed into at best a rocky marriage. My natural proclivity to discount praise and magnify criticism was kicking in.

Within a five-day period at the end of August and start of September, the *New York Times, Washington Post,* and *Wall Street Journal* published front-page stories describing me, essentially, as a failure. Numerous magazine articles echoed the theme. The primary charge was that my rhetoric so far outpaced America's capacity or willingness to act that our foreign policy was losing credibility. There were personal criticisms as well. *New York Times* columnist Maureen Dowd wrote that I had failed in my special responsibility as a betrayed woman to denounce the President publicly over Lewinsky. The *New Republic*'s Martin Peretz, mixing recent foreign policy revelations with my family's history, observed cattily, "Of course, concealing important truths is one of Albright's lifetime habits." Reporters began asking about rumors that I intended to resign, and I began telling friends that the reason I looked fatter was that I had grown a thicker skin.

In a way, all the criticism didn't surprise me. I had lived in Washington long enough to know that conventional wisdom about prominent officials often had a short shelf life. I knew I would get nowhere if I took the attacks personally. Sitting in the midst of this flack, I tried to examine what had happened.

Were we trying to do too much? Was I to blame for pledging actions the administration couldn't or wouldn't back up? Were the President's troubles a more substantial handicap than we were prepared to admit? Were we failing to explain our policies to the American people? Were hostile and partisan elements of Congress contributing to the problems by trying to undercut us at every point?

The answer, I concluded, was a little bit of all the above. At the same time, I thought our policies were the right ones. In the frenzy of the moment, our critics were ignoring our accomplishments while failing to credit the difficulty of our jobs. We were in a brand-new world. We had no manual to guide us in protecting American citizens, interests, and values in a rapidly changing environment. We were hampered by a lack of foreign policy resources, a highly charged political environment, a media demanding easy answers and fast results, divided allies, and a world that simultaneously demanded and resented American leadership.

As I worked through these issues, I found support from sources both naturally sympathetic and surprising. Tom Pickering sent me a memo saying, "What we are being pilloried for is the failure to bring to conclusion a number of works in progress. But diplomacy isn't instant coffee." He suggested we push ahead patiently, take one issue at a time, and spell out the rationale behind our policies as clearly as possible. Good advice, but it was becoming increasingly evident to me that our various foreign policy tools were not always capable of solving a problem; sometimes our only good option was to manage it.

During the first week of September, I called Senator Jesse Helms to inform him about recent developments. He said, "Fine, but first I want to say something to you that is personal. I hope all this stuff isn't bothering you. I take real offense at articles saying you have failed just because not everything is going right. You haven't failed. You have done the best you could, and at an appropriate time I will make that clear." I said that what bothered me were the accusations I hadn't told the truth. Helms said, "I may not always agree with you, but you always tell me the truth. You give it to me straight. I can't ask for better than that. So I hope you won't worry and remember, if anyone tries to take your job, they'll have to go through this committee." There were times Helms infuriated me. At that moment I was very glad we were friends.

I found solace, as well, in the biography of Dean Acheson by James Chace. I was usually too exhausted to read much, but making my way through the book a little at a time, I found some interesting parallels. One thinks now of Acheson and Truman presiding over a period of vigorous American leadership and creativity in world affairs. Their accomplishments were still revered in our era, and must, we might assume, have been recognized in their own. In truth, Acheson confronted a chorus of critics far fiercer than mine. His relations with Congress were often ugly; he was plagued by calls for his resignation; his patriotism was questioned; he argued constantly with the Secretaries of Treasury and Defense; he bemoaned the State Department's steady loss of influence; and he was criticized for exaggerating the threats our nation faced in order to mobilize popular support for effective international action. Through it all,

Acheson maintained a true course, relying on the mutually reinforcing tools of force and diplomacy, confident in the goodness of American leadership, and resolute in defense of democratic interests and values. His story reminded me that even the most historically respected Secretaries had had bad days.

On Wednesday morning, September 9, 1998, I woke up in New Orleans. I had been invited to address the annual convention of the U.S. veterans organization, the American Legion, and I felt nervous. This was a huge event, with thousands of people in the auditorium and a thousand more watching via video in a nearby room. I worried because I had been accused of lying, many of our policies were in a rut, I had never served in the military, and I had been spending all my time amid the bureaucratic and partisan warfare of Washington, D.C. I was afraid the Legionnaires would boo. I began to feel better during our prespeech breakfast when everyone was cordial and we had a practical discussion about the timely topics of terrorism and homeland defense.

As I got up to speak, I looked out warily over a sea of broad shoulders and medal-bedecked sport coats and women dressed in red, white, and blue. Gradually I realized just how much I had in common with this audience. As they responded to my speech, I felt better. I talked about how America's freedoms must always be protected. I talked about the threat posed by extremists, the dangers created by missiles, and the need to thwart the ambitions of tyrants like Saddam Hussein. I spoke of the importance of backing our diplomacy with force and using diplomacy to keep our fighting men and women out of harm's way. It was not yet 10A.M. in the night owl capital of the world, but the audience was awake and listening and applauding.

It dawned on me that these were not the kind of people who judged you based on what they might have heard or read the day before. They didn't care about gender or partisan advantage or who was up or down in Washington. What mattered was that I was there representing the United States. The concepts of opposing evil, defending liberty, and working hard on behalf of American ideals weren't theoretical to them, they were a reality, and nothing could be more real to me. After my recent interactions with Congress, the press, and sometimes even my own colleagues, it was liberating to talk about patriotism in front of people who did not roll their eyes. That audience reminded me that the right move in a tight spot is not to try to "spin" your way out. It's to stand up, speak plainly, and if necessary, shove back.

The next day, I referred to the American Legion speech during the most peculiar White House meeting I ever attended. Chief of Staff Erskine

Bowles had told me that the session's purpose was to allow President Clinton to apologize to the cabinet for not being truthful about Lewinsky. The press had a special interest in what the President would say to Donna Shalala and to me. We were the two women from the cabinet who had defended him in front of television cameras the last time the full cabinet had met, back in January. As a result, some women's groups were outraged that we hadn't quit.

Before the meeting, I called Donna to ask what she intended to say. She was furious; she told me she would use her opportunity to tell the President off. I factored that into my thinking as I headed to the White House. As the cabinet's senior member I would be expected to speak first after the President. I knew each of us would have to struggle with the question of how to react, and each would do so in accord with his or her own feelings and experience. My own feelings were torn; I hoped the President's words would help put my thoughts in better order.

The meeting was to be held in the residential part of the White House instead of the Cabinet Room. The setting was less formal and we would avoid the perpetual press stakeout on the executive mansion's front lawn. I welcomed this arrangement because I did not intend to go in front of the cameras again, no matter how the meeting went.

As we assembled, I again talked to Donna. She seemed to be working up a good head of steam. We moved upstairs to the third floor and into what is known as the Yellow Oval, a room facing the Ellipse and Washington Monument and more distantly the Jefferson Memorial. Gold banquet chairs were arranged in a semicircle in front of two armchairs in which the President and Vice-President would sit. I sat directly in front of the President's chair with Janet Reno to my left. Other cabinet officials were perched on various sofas and chairs. Senior members of the White House staff were present as well. When we were settled, the President came in. He began by saying that he owed us an explanation. He said he was really sorry for what he had done. He knew it was wrong and he had caused a lot of pain to his family, to the country, and to us. He said he would have to work to atone for it for the rest of his life. Then he said that the reason he had done it was that he had been in a rage for the past four and a half years. He had been a good actor and had put on a smile but had been angry throughout. He talked in that vein for some time, without making eye contact with me or anyone else—then stopped.

As he spoke, I felt lost. The President had started out in a way I had expected, but the rest was surprising and did not make much sense. I wasn't sure he had really apologized and if so, whether it was for what he had said or for what he had done. I also didn't understand the rage. Sure, the critics had unfairly and often maliciously piled on, but in the end he had been reelected handily. In any case, what kind of excuse was that?

When the President finished, I tried to summarize in just a few words the conflicting emotions I felt. I said that obviously this was a difficult and sad time. It was hard for the President, for his family, and for us all. What the President did was wrong, and he had admitted that. Now we all had jobs to do. I said I had been proud to represent the administration at the American Legion Convention the previous day, and I had seen in that audience plain American people who were generous and forgiving. I then looked at the President and said, "The sad thing is we had all expected you to be Mike McGwire and hit seventy home runs. It is so rare to have a Democrat reelected and able to serve two terms. You have given us all a great opportunity and now we all have to prove ourselves worthy of the people's trust through our work."

Donna Shalala spoke soon after. She said bluntly that the President had behaved inexcusably and that it was more important for a leader to have the right morals than to have the right policies. The President didn't quarrel with Donna's characterization and agreed that it was just as vital to be a good person as it was to be a good President, but he added a little testily that, if her logic prevailed, the nation would have been better off if Richard Nixon had been elected in 1960 instead of John Kennedy. After Shalala spoke, the atmosphere in the room began to change. James Lee Witt, head of the Federal Emergency Management Agency, started talking about redemption and quoting from scripture. Like the President, he was from Arkansas and could sound like a revivalist preacher. Transportation Secretary Rodney Slater, Labor Secretary Alexis Herman, and Housing Secretary Andrew Cuomo also cited passages from the Bible. Interior Secretary Bruce Babbitt talked about going to confession as a child. EPA Administrator Carol Browner was one of the few to strike a more down-to-earth note when she said that the President's actions had forced her to have conversations with her ten-year-old son she never imagined she would be required to have. Vice-President Gore, speaking last, reminded us somewhat cryptically that King David had had a broken spirit and a brave heart.

As we prepared to leave, each shaking hands or in some cases hugging the President, White House aide Douglas Sosnick said to me that what we had witnessed was "a southern thing." It was part religious meeting, part encounter session, and part revival. To me it had felt simultaneously uncomfortable and warm, inadequate and cathartic, weird and typical. With the world in turmoil, elections coming, and an impeachment trial expected by year's end, the administration's team needed to get back together. At the same time, without questioning anyone's sincerity or doubting the importance of personal redemption, I did not think it was the cabinet's role to play pastor. I was angry with the President for risking so much for less than nothing, but I had learned from my own experience not to be surprised when a man lies about sex. In any case I felt no sense of personal grievance. The President had not betrayed me; he had betrayed the First Lady and it was up to Hillary, not the cabinet, to deal with that. Our job was to help this admittedly imperfect but richly talented and well-intentioned man do the job he had been elected to do for the country we all had pledged to serve and defend.

As for me, I learned again the danger of wandering rhetorically into the alien world of male sports. As Erskine Bowles smilingly reminded me, McGwire's first name was Mark, not Mike.

ON A NUMBER of occasions when times were difficult, Hillary Clinton and I got together, along with our chiefs of staff Elaine Shocas and Melanne Verveer, for informal meetings of the "Frank Group," so dubbed because we were comfortable enough with each other to speak our minds. Sometimes we met at the White House and sometimes at the State Department. On most subjects Hillary was franker than I, saying I should place less stock in collegiality and more on saying what I thought.

We did discuss the injustice of the Whitewater accusations and how they diverted attention from important work. This, more than anything else, caused the First Lady to become angry. Given my own experience with Joe, I thought she might want to share her feelings about the business with Lewinsky, but she never raised the subject and I did not feel it my place to pry. She obviously had a greater capacity than I did to keep private matters contained. When I was upset with Joe, half the city of Washington had known how I felt. My heart was on my sleeve. Hillary's was better protected. She is a person fully in charge of herself and in any case didn't want anyone feeling sorry for her. I could identify with that.

There is no way an outsider can understand the relationship of a married couple, certainly not the Clintons. My assessment from watching them over the years is that they are great friends who love each other deeply, worry about each other, and talk all the time. They also complement each other, because their work habits and modes of thinking are so different. Their finest achievement: Chelsea. Most of us first noticed her when she was a pre-teen with braces and curly hair. She grew up at the White House, becoming a graceful, well-educated, and unspoiled young woman. She was a wonderful addition to every foreign trip she joined.

She read a lot and wandered the aisles of Air Force One joking with all. For me, her most notable appearance would come near the end—during the Middle East peace negotiations at Camp David in 2000. She stayed in the background, absorbed what she was seeing, and kept us all, including her father, in good humor.

One occasion with the First Lady I found particularly memorable, although I don't know if she saw it the same way. Hillary had invited me to dinner at the White House with Queen Noor. I had met the Queen a number of times, both in Jordan and in the United States. When she first married King Hussein, there were hundreds of articles about her. I felt I knew her because I had met her parents and because she had attended the National Cathedral School, as had my own daughters. This extraordinary American beauty had become a serene Jordanian queen, devoted to her husband, family, and new country. As the King was dying, she maintained her strength and dignity. Now she was alone, a woman in her forties with children, trying to figure out the next phase of her life while preserving the legacy of her husband. The three of us had dinner in the private dining room in the residence. We nibbled on the first two courses, but when it was announced that we had a choice of three desserts, we simultaneously asked for samples of them all—rich chocolate, fruit pie, and heaps of ice cream.

The three of us talked about everything from global problems and people we knew in common to the question of writing our memoirs. Hillary was the experienced author, having already written the best-selling *It Takes a Village*; she gave practical advice about timetables and editors. She hadn't yet decided how she would approach writing about her life in the White House. Queen Noor was determined to write, not so much to share things about herself but to make sure the world understood and fully appreciated her late husband and to express her own love for Jordan and the Arab people. I listened and asked questions, wondering how I would ever be able to blend the personal with all that I wanted to say about policy.

When I got home I reflected on what had been a remarkable evening. We were three women of disparate backgrounds who had been given extraordinary opportunities to participate directly in the highest level of world affairs. We were each passionate in our beliefs, had experienced severe tests at certain stages in our lives, and were now very much in the public eye. It struck me as well that we had in common a personal connection related to the men we had married. In different ways and at various times, we had each been left to explore the boundaries of our own inner strength by a husband who had deceived, deserted, or died.

PART FOUR

Waging War, Pursuing Peace

TWENTY-TWO

A Special Kind of Evil

"**O**UR EMBASSIES HAVE been bombed." Those words slowly penetrated the thick fog of sleep as I awoke in Rome on August 7, 1998—my worst day as Secretary of State. On that day our embassies in Kenya and Tanzania were bombed: more than 220 people died, including 12 Americans and 40 Foreign Service nationals—local citizens employed by our embassies—and almost 5,000 Africans and Americans were injured.

The day was supposed to have been a joyous one. Jamie Rubin was getting married outside of Rome to Christiane Amanpour, CNN's international correspondent. I had arranged my schedule so I could make the wedding and was looking forward to a few days off in Italy. Elaine Shocas was also going to the wedding; my daughter Alice, who was in London, was to meet up with us in Rome.

We had booked a suite at the Excelsior, a fine old hotel on the Via Veneto, not far from the U.S. embassy. We landed in mid-morning and planned to sleep for a few hours and take in a leisurely lunch and do some shopping before meeting up with Alice for the pre-wedding party that evening.

Shortly after going to sleep, Elaine was roused by one of my security agents telling her that the State Department Operations Center was desperately trying to reach us. She called the department, then woke me to deliver the horrifying news. The explosions that tore into our embassies were all but simultaneous, and from the beginning the prime suspect was a renegade Saudi national—Osama bin Laden.

I was soon on the phone to Washington, to Kenya, and to Tanzania, and the next few hours were spent making sure that as much help as possible was being provided to both embassies and governments, as well as trying to gather information about those responsible. In between calls I sat mesmerized as TV pictures showed our embassies shrouded in smoke.

Rescue workers pulled feverishly at slabs of metal and stone, drawing cheers when victims were found alive. The strikes had come at mid-morning, when offices were busy and visa lines long. I felt numb and out-raged—I wanted to go to Africa immediately—but was persuaded my presence at that point would not help. There would be too many logisti-cal and security issues connected with such a visit; we couldn't afford to divert any resources from the urgent task of rescue.

I made a brief statement to the press from our embassy in Rome and was greeted by loud applause from the crowd that had formed outside, a reminder that America had many good friends around the world. Soon we were on our way to Shannon, Ireland, where we waited for the air force to bring us home. The airport was closed but the staff came in any-way, bringing us Irish coffee and smoked salmon. A man with a thick Irish brogue said, "When America is injured, every country aches."

Shock, when sufficient, can unite a nation and a generation. Most Amer-icans a decade or two older than I am could never forget where they had been when they first heard that the United States was under attack at Pearl Harbor. Americans of my age recall when John Kennedy was killed and, five years later, Martin Luther King Jr. and Robert Kennedy. The bombings of our embassies in Africa had a devastating impact, but obviously, there were other tragedies to come—the bombing of the USS *Cole* and the greatest shock of the new century, the attacks of September 11, 2001. Together these outrages framed a new threat to world peace, a special kind of evil.

MANY OF THE roots of the Africa embassy bombings—like those of the crimes on September 11—can be traced back to the Soviet Union's 1979 invasion of Afghanistan, an assault that sharply intensified the Cold War. The United States responded by giving money, stinger missiles, and other weapons to the Afghan resistance, the Mujahedeen. This strategy worked; the hated Soviets were eventually driven out. It was a great vic-tory but with unintended consequences. After the Soviets withdrew from Afghanistan in 1989, the United States lost interest in the region, leaving behind thousands of militant people with few jobs but many guns.

During the first half of the 1990s, local warlords exploited this vacuum, carving Afghanistan into pieces until 1996, when most were defeated or co-opted by a fiercely conservative group, the Taliban. Observers hoped the Taliban's narrow but disciplined vision of Islam might produce more stabil-ity than clashing warlords. Indeed, incidents of rape, looting, and extortion declined under its rule. Leaders in neighboring Pakistan openly supported the new group, in part because the more secure conditions enabled them to resume exporting goods through Afghanistan to points further north.

In those years, Taliban leaders didn't express hostility toward America; in fact they thanked the United States for its role in ousting the Soviets. They had, however, inherited a problem. The terrorist financier Osama bin Laden had been expelled from his native Saudi Arabia and was then back in Afghanistan. With him was a multinational collection of organizers and trainees known as al-Qaeda. Like bin Laden, many members of this network had joined America in helping the Afghan resistance but had turned hostile after U.S. involvement in the 1991 Gulf War. Bin Laden demanded an end to America's military presence in Saudi Arabia. In February 1998, he vowed to kill Americans anywhere in the world, prompting me to issue an official worldwide alert drawing attention to his threats.

The Taliban had another problem, this one of their own creation. They were cultural imperialists, determined to impose their primitive precepts upon their countrymen—and women. They deprived their citizens of basic freedoms, prevented a generation of Afghan girls from attending school, and drove a significant fraction of Afghan women into clinical depression, physical breakdown, even suicide. Late in my first year as Secretary I visited Pakistan and privately warned its leaders, "Your country is in danger of being isolated because of its support for the Taliban." Publicly I said with accuracy, if not diplomacy, "We are opposed to the Taliban because of... their despicable treatment of women and children and their general lack of respect for human dignity."

During that trip I visited a refugee camp near Peshawar, about twenty-five miles from the Afghan border, not far from the Khyber Pass. Waiting for me in a classroom were about fifteen women, who recounted haltingly how the Taliban had prevented them from attending school, forbidden them from holding jobs, and prohibited them from leaving their houses unaccompanied by a male. The refugees spoke of their longing to return to Afghanistan but said they couldn't go back so long as the Taliban held power. As they spoke, I sensed their nervousness. The press had cameras and the refugees did not want their faces photographed. Many still had relatives in Afghanistan and feared that their willingness to meet with me, if known, would have severe repercussions.

Words at such a time are rarely adequate. I told them that I would never forget my visit with them and that America would do everything it could to help. A few moments later I addressed a gathering of local dignitaries and refugees of both genders and all ages sitting on rugs in a makeshift courtyard. The sun was getting low, and I was startled to see the shadows of the Pakistani marksmen guarding us inflated by the angle to a height of twenty feet or more.

I told my audience that it was part of my job to care about issues of war and peace, development and human rights. I added that no country could modernize or become prosperous without the contributions of all its citizens, and no society could move forward unless women had access to schools and health care and were protected from physical exploitation and abuse.

When I finished, I walked forward to shake hands with the crowd. The youngest children were in front, sitting cross-legged. I extended my hand, but the children were so small, they couldn't reach. I was afraid if I bent over any further I would tip over, so I got down on my knees and greeted them that way. Their hands were thin and wiry, their eyes haunting, their faces beautiful, their smiles unforgettable. For a moment the rest of the world's turbulence became background noise and I felt less like a diplomat than like a mother.

TERRORISM, BY DEFINITION, violates the law, and effective law enforcement is one of the best means of fighting it, but the judicial process is sometimes very slow. In extreme circumstances, bolder actions may also be required. That was the case following the Africa embassy bombings.[1]

A week after those tragedies, CIA Director George Tenet told us at a White House meeting that the evidence of Osama bin Laden's involvement was conclusive and that we were receiving threats of possible new attacks daily. Our security people had identified diplomatic posts in thirty-eight cities where al-Qaeda was active. We couldn't sit around and wait until the terrorists struck again.

President Clinton gave the green light for a retaliatory mission. We restricted our planning to the smallest possible group and continued with our routine schedules so as not to tip off bin Laden. We intended to hit three terrorist bases near Khost, about ninety miles south of Kabul. These camps, which included housing, storage, and training facilities, were run by Pakistanis and Arabs associated with bin Laden's network. The men trained there might be assigned to spread terror in Kashmir and Central Asia or deployed for longer-term missions in Europe and the United States. We needed to act immediately because we had information that terrorist leaders—possibly including bin Laden—were gathering at one of the camps to plan further attacks. We hoped to hit them when it would have the greatest impact.

1. At the same time law enforcement measures were also applied. In May 2001, four members of the al-Qaeda network were convicted in New York of involvement in the bombings and later sentenced to life in prison. Other suspects remain in custody.

We also reviewed sites in Sudan, where bin Laden had lived for a period prior to 1996, building up his terrorist network, and where he still had business interests. The target chosen was a pharmaceuticals factory. We were told by our intelligence people that bin Laden had invested in a military complex of which the factory was a part. They said a soil sample indicated the presence of a degraded form of the compound VX, one of earth's most poisonous substances.

Despite the imminence of air strikes, I wanted to travel to Kenya and Tanzania to express condolences and see what more we could do to help. In order to make the trip and return as rapidly as possible, I used one of the Doomsday planes equipped with midair refueling capability. I had never witnessed the refueling process, so when the time came during the long flight, I asked the pilot if I could sit behind him. With a mixture of dread and awe, I watched as two huge tanker planes filled with fuel approached us. The first aligned itself twenty to thirty feet in front of our plane, so close I could see the face of a crewmember lying on his stomach, using joystick-like controls to guide a long boom that attached itself to our plane and transferred the fuel. To keep the aircraft aligned, the tanker was on automatic pilot, while our plane switched to manual control. This required our pilot to use all his strength to steady the plane. The entire process was repeated with the second tanker. When it was over, I was exhausted, even though I hadn't done anything. I figured the pilot's shoulders must ache, so started rubbing them. He told me, "Ma'am, this is the first time in the history of the U.S. military that a pilot has gotten a back rub from the Secretary of State."

Later I marveled to Air Force Lieutenant General Robert "Doc" Foglesong, my military advisor from the Joint Chiefs, how extraordinary the refueling procedure had been. He agreed and mentioned that the President's plane, Air Force One, also had midair refueling capability, but that it wasn't used when the President was aboard. "Why not?" I asked. "Are you kidding?" he laughed. "Two huge planes filled with fuel traveling hundreds of miles an hour while only feet apart? Much too dangerous."

Upon landing in Tanzania, I went to our embassy in Dar es Salaam. The facility, located miles from downtown, had previously been owned by Israel, so it was better fortified than most. Still, we had been lucky: a water tanker had blocked the terrorists' truck from breaching the perimeter. Far fewer people had been killed in the attack there than in Kenya.

Our embassy in Nairobi, by contrast, was in the middle of a bustling city. This is the kind of location we used to prefer for our diplomatic posts, wanting to appear open and part of the capital. That era ended when suicide bombers attacked a marine barracks and the U.S. embassy in Beirut in

1983. Since then new embassies were supposed to meet rigorous standards and be located away from busy streets, with space for double walls, checkpoints, and vehicle inspection areas. These requirements made new embassies safer but also more expensive. In consequence, during the previous decade few had been built. Older embassies, such as that in Kenya, were less well-protected and had to compete with more than 200 other facilities worldwide for the limited money available for improvements.

A few months earlier, Ambassador Prudence Bushnell had written to me expressing concern about her embassy's vulnerability to terrorism. She urged me to use Kenya as an example when pressing for additional funds. The letter became news in the aftermath of the bombings. As Bushnell wrote, "Everyone is doing the right thing given resource constraints. The constraints are the problem. The solution is to address the security of chanceries around the world." I agreed. That's what I had been doing my best to accomplish, but it wasn't until the embassy bombings that I was able to get the full attention of those controlling the purse strings in Congress and the administration. Unfortunately, the only real solution in Kenya would have been to relocate the embassy to a less crowded site. That would have cost millions of dollars and could not even have been started before August 7.

From a distance, television pictures of the Nairobi bomb site had filled me with anger and sadness. Close up, the reality was even worse—a smaller version of what we would know later as Ground Zero. When I arrived at the site, the embassy's skeleton was still upright, but the interior had been wrecked by blown-out windows, blasted partitions, and flying office equipment. The explosion had turned these objects into instruments of death. The majority of fatalities resulted from the collapse of the building next door, which had been reduced to a pile of glass, bricks, and concrete. What stopped the heart were the personal objects still visible—a crumpled shoe, a scrap of shirt, a torn handkerchief, a crushed baby stroller.

I visited a nearby hospital to see some of the Kenyans who had been hurt. As I went from bed to bed, I told them how sorry I was. Like other victims of terror, these were just everyday people who had been going about their lives, only to find themselves in the wrong place at the wrong time. Many were heavily bandaged; others had cuts on their hands and faces. At Ambassador Bushnell's residence I met with members of our embassy team. Like their counterparts in Tanzania led by Chargé John Lange, they had done an outstanding job responding to the tragedy, dealing with local sensitivities, supporting the investigation, and restarting embassy operations. As they coped, they had also wondered about the twists of fate that had left them alive while taking their colleagues and loved ones away.

It had been my solemn privilege to accompany the bodies of ten of those colleagues across the Atlantic to a ceremony with President and Mrs. Clinton at Andrews Air Force Base, near Washington. The coffins were placed aboard a C-17 nicknamed the "Spirit of America's Veterans." While in the air, I studied the descriptions and photographs I had been given of the Americans who had died. Among them were a Foreign Service officer and his beloved son; a young marine corps sergeant from Tallahassee; an epidemiologist and mother of three who had been working to save children from malaria; an air force budget officer from South Bend, Indiana; a political officer who was also a jazz musician; a State Department administrative worker from Valdosta, Georgia; a Foreign Service officer with two daughters who had arrived in Kenya only eleven days before the bombing; an air force master sergeant following in her father's footsteps; an employee from the general services office; and two from the office of the defense attaché, including an army sergeant from Missouri with a boyish face, the father of a two-year-old.[2]

Emotionally drained, I tried to sleep on a cot along the side of the plane. The coffins lay behind a heavy khaki-colored canvas curtain. Sometime during the flight I awoke, parted the curtain, and sat with the caskets, whispering a prayer and thinking. The victims ranged in age from twenty to sixty and were of African, Asian, and European heritage. Some were military, some civilian; they were almost equally divided between women and men. Theirs were the faces of America, the kind of unpretentious but remarkable people who represent our country overseas, doing their jobs, solving problems, winning friends for democracy. I thought with some bitterness about the persistent stereotypes of embassy life, in which diplomats supposedly go about in striped pants, give fancy parties, and live in splendor. The reality is much more mundane, the work harder, the rewards fewer, the risks greater. America had confronted evil at other points in my life—Hitler, Stalin, racism, ethnic cleansing, and genocide—but now our country had been drawn into conflict against an enemy that was not clearly visible, on a battlefield that was undefined and in which we would all be on the front lines.

I experienced at that moment an almost crushing sense of responsibility. Like most people in public life, I had often talked about how government officials should be held accountable. It is easy enough when you are

2. The victims were Julian Bartley Sr., Julian Bartley Jr., Sergeant Jesse Aliganga Jr., Dr. Mary Louise Martin, Arlene Kirk, Uttamlal ("Tom") Shah, Molly Hardy, Prabhi Kavaler, Sergeant Sherry Lynn Olds, Ann Michelle O'Connor, Jean Dalizu, and Sergeant Kenneth R. Hobson.

pointing the finger at someone else. I felt now as if all eyes were on me. I knew I could not guarantee the safety of our people, but I had a responsibility to do everything within my power to try. This was no longer a matter of simply doing my job, but one of loyalty, honor, and trust.

A while before we were to land, I was told by the crew that I had to go back to my seat. I sat down and fell asleep, my seat facing the curtain. As we landed, I opened my eyes. The curtain had been pulled back. Nothing now separated me from the coffins. In the brief time I had slept, each had been covered with an American flag.

AT 11 A.M. on August 20, seventy-nine cruise missiles were launched from U.S. ships in the Red and Arabian Seas, hitting their targets in Afghanistan and Sudan a couple of hours later. The simultaneity of the strikes was meant to replicate the pattern of the two embassy bombings. As soon as we knew the missiles had reached their targets, the President—who proceeded with his vacation to maintain the element of surprise—startled reporters in Martha's Vineyard by announcing our decision to respond militarily. He immediately returned to Washington.

Operation Infinite Reach severely damaged al-Qaeda training camps and killed perhaps twenty members of bin Laden's network while injuring several dozen others. If, as we suspected, bin Laden himself had been there, he got away. The response showed nevertheless that we could hit the enemy on its home ground and that America could not be attacked with impunity. Most members of Congress applauded the mission, but public reaction was generally muted. Terrorists had hit American embassies but not yet attacked our homeland. There were even those who thought we had overreacted and questioned the President's motives. Citing the movie *Wag the Dog* (in which the White House fakes a war to distract attention from a sex scandal), partisan commentators suggested that we were trying to shift the spotlight from problems with the special prosecutor. These allegations were groundless and repugnant, but contributed to an atmosphere in which there were virtually no calls from Congress or the media to take further military action against al-Qaeda. We would, however, continuously explore the possibility of doing just that, while pressing ahead on the diplomatic front.

TWO DAYS AFTER the cruise missiles were launched, the phone rang in the office of Michael Malinowski, a senior member of the State Department's Bureau of South Asian Affairs. The Taliban's founder and leader, Mullah Omar, was on the line. This was unprecedented. Omar almost never spoke to westerners. Now he told Malinowski that our air strikes had been counterproductive, that President Clinton should resign, and that U.S. forces should vacate Saudi Arabia. Rejecting this malarkey, Malinowski pressed Omar to hand over bin Laden and proposed a formal dialogue. Omar agreed to talk.

Several weeks later, U.S. Ambassador to Pakistan William Milam initiated a series of meetings between U.S. officials and the Taliban that continued for the next two years. Throughout, the problems we had with the extremist movement weren't due to any failure on our part to communicate clearly. Indeed, our message was simple: "Bin Laden is a terrorist. He is a murderer of innocent people and implacably hostile to the United States. If you have any interest in better relations you must help bring him to justice." The Taliban leaders didn't say no; instead they offered a menu of lame excuses. They argued that it would violate cultural etiquette to mistreat the beneficiary of their hospitality and that bin Laden was a hero to Afghans because of his 1980s' anti-Soviet role. "We will be overthrown if we give him to you," they said. "Our people will assume we took money from you or the Saudis."

Late in 1998, I selected Lieutenant Colonel (ret.) Michael Sheehan, a former student of mine at Georgetown who was also a former Green Beret and advisor to me at the UN, for the position of State Department coordinator for counter-terrorism. With input from colleagues such as Assistant Secretary of State for South Asia Rick Inderfurth, Sheehan soon developed a strategy for increasing pressure on the Taliban. Although we did not have much leverage in Afghanistan, we decided to pull every lever we did have simultaneously. First, we sent a message to the Taliban that we would hold its leaders accountable for any future terrorist actions traceable to bin Laden and that we reserved the right to use military force either preemptively in self-defense or in response to further attacks. Second, we asked Pakistan, Saudi Arabia, and the United Arab Emirates (UAE), the only three countries maintaining diplomatic relations with the Afghan regime, to back our demand that bin Laden be turned over. If the Taliban still refused, we would press the three governments to deny landing rights to the Afghan airline, freeze financial assets, and prohibit Taliban leaders from traveling internationally. We also threatened to impose bilateral economic sanctions against the Taliban and ask the UN to enact global restrictions.

In succeeding months we implemented this strategy according to plan, only the plan did not work. Both the Saudis and UAE complied with our request to restrict landing rights, and the Saudis downgraded their diplomatic ties and denied visas to Afghans traveling for nonreligious reasons. We pressed the Pakistani leadership relentlessly to lean on the Taliban, saying that "bin Laden has killed Americans and plans to kill again. That makes him our enemy. And that makes those who support him our enemy. Don't put Pakistan in that position." We imposed sanctions against the Taliban in July 1999. The UN Security Council did the same in October on a unanimous vote that included several Muslim-majority nations. All this left the Taliban isolated, but it didn't make them give up bin Laden.

When first consolidating their power, Taliban leaders had focused exclusively on seizing territory and arms and had little apparent use for bin Laden. As the months passed, however, bin Laden and Mullah Omar developed a symbiotic relationship. The terrorists needed a safe haven in which to train. Omar needed bin Laden's money and muscle. By mid 1998, Omar may have felt his survival hinged on bin Laden's backing. Although we continued to meet with the Taliban, the dialogue became more sterile as Omar grew more hostile. In repeating our warning to the Taliban, Mike Sheehan was explicit: "If bin Laden or any of the organizations affiliated with him attacks the United States or U.S. interests, we will hold you personally responsible."

We felt it necessary to reiterate our threats because we were convinced that groups affiliated with bin Laden were still active and probably trying to develop or acquire chemical and biological weapons. Sheehan warned us repeatedly that bin Laden was preparing to strike again. So, despite the difficulty of holding the public's attention, the President, Secretary Cohen, and I raised the issue of terrorism repeatedly at home and overseas. And even as we applied diplomatic pressure, we played a worldwide game of defense, striving to prevent further attacks.

To this end we intensified law enforcement cooperation with other countries, resulting in the quiet arrest and prosecution of scores of suspects. We offered rewards, froze terrorist assets, tripled our counterterrorism budget, enhanced antiterrorism training, and accelerated research into antiterrorism technology. The President issued a series of directives to enhance our ability to disrupt terrorist operations abroad and prepare for the possibility of strikes on U.S. soil. He requested funds to improve disaster planning, create a national stockpile of drugs and vaccines, train state and city health response teams, and protect critical infrastructure such as power grids and computer networks from cyberattacks. At the Pentagon, Bill Cohen announced plans to create National Guard rapid reaction teams that would be prepared to aid communities victimized by chemical or biological attacks.[3] Tragically these initiatives didn't prevent September 11, but they prevented other attacks and laid the groundwork for what would come later—a concerted national program of homeland defense.

With U.S. embassies so clearly at risk, my preoccupation was with resources. From my first day as Secretary, I had pestered the President and the Office of Management and Budget (OMB) to increase funding for international affairs programs and operations. After the embassy bombings, I became truly and intentionally obnoxious. With help from Senator Ted Stevens, Representative David Obey, and others, we were able to muscle through an emergency appropriation of more than $1 billion for security upgrades that fall, including barriers around the State Department itself, but that was just a small start toward solving a large problem.

In the aftermath of the bombings, I had appointed accountability review boards, chaired by retired Admiral William Crowe, former Chairman of the Joint Chiefs of Staff and later U.S. ambassador to Great Britain, to investigate and make recommendations. In January 1999, Crowe proposed an appropriation of $1.4 billion a year for at least ten years for embassy construction and repair. Delighted, I promptly took the request to OMB, which was not so pleased. The White House budgeteers doubted our ability to spend so much money quickly and wisely. Instead they recommended $3 billion over five years, with an appropriation the first year of just $36 million. I said, "Congress will have my head if I go up and try to defend this budget and they will be right. It's ridiculous. We need more."

As I predicted, leaders in both parties were outraged. OMB soon agreed to a compromise, and its attitude mellowed further after its director, Jack Lew, inspected embassies in East Europe and the Balkans. By the time I left office, we had gained agreement for appropriations close to the level recommended by Admiral Crowe, an agreement that was critical because we had learned that the dangers to our personnel were no longer localized but global. There was no such thing as a low-risk post. If we had soft spots, we could expect our enemies to exploit them.

---

3. The White House also used the bully pulpit of the presidency to heighten awareness of the terrorist threat and rouse global support for defeating it. For example, President Clinton told the UN General Assembly that combating terrorism was at the top of the American agenda and should be at the top of the world's. He urged every nation to deny support and sanctuary to terrorist groups, cooperate in extraditing and prosecuting suspects, regulate more rigorously the manufacture and export of explosives, raise international airport security standards, and combat the conditions that spread violence and despair.

I welcomed the Crowe recommendations, but wanted to make sure that implementing them would not come at the expense of other State Department operations. The dollars we use to build and safeguard our embassies come out of the same pot of money we use to pay salaries, recruit staff, and meet other day-to-day needs. I warned both Congress and OMB, "If we raise spending on security without increasing the overall size of the pot, we will end up with buildings that are safer, but also empty, because we will not be able to afford any staff. You cannot leave me with this choice." I added that the State Department had been starved for resources for too long. Every year, we faced the need to shift funds from worthy programs in order to meet emergency requirements. We ended up robbing Peter to pay Paul, and then robbing Paul as well.

EARLY IN MY TENURE, I chose David Carpenter to serve as assistant secretary of state for diplomatic security. This was a job traditionally reserved for members of the Foreign Service; I decided to break precedent. David, who had served as head of the President's Secret Service detail, was the first law enforcement professional to hold the position, joining our team in March 1998 on a contract basis. Four days after the embassy bombings, he was officially sworn in. I liked him because he had the same determination I did—to prevent any more of our people from being killed.

The decision to close an embassy due to an imminent threat, whether for a day or a month, was one of the most sensitive we had to make. In this period we were receiving about a thousand threats a month against U.S. facilities or officials overseas. Had we responded to each by closing down the facility in question, we would have been paralyzed. If we had refused to order shutdowns when circumstances indicated caution, we might have paid with more lives. The only way to make an informed decision was to analyze each threat.

Together with Under Secretary for Management Bonnie Cohen, Carpenter pushed hard and successfully to have a Diplomatic Security officer stationed at the CIA, so we would know the moment a threat against one of our posts was received. We also had staff in the State Department Operations Center working literally every hour of every day to coordinate our response. In each case the embassy weighed in with its own assessment of whether a warning was credible. Many leads we received came from people who walked into one of our embassies and asked to see the ambassador or someone else in charge. Occasionally these informants provided vital information. More often they were motivated by hopes for a reward, whether in the form of money or a U.S. visa. Sometimes they were there to case the embassy, for purposes of intelligence gathering or possible terrorism. We had no more urgent task than to check each story.

The Crowe report recommended that a single high-ranking officer be accountable for all security matters. To accomplish that, I proposed creating the post of under secretary of state for security, terrorism and related affairs. Pending congressional action, I decided I had to be the one to make the final decisions, albeit with professional advice, so virtually every morning when I was in Washington, I sat in my office with Carpenter sifting through the latest information. In one case members of a separatist group, armed with a shoulder-fired missile, actually entered a building opposite our consulate in a European city. Because of good intelligence, local authorities stopped the terrorists before they could strike. The incident illustrated the value of a strong relationship with the host country. Fortunately, even nations indifferent or hostile to us don't want to see terrorist attacks on their home ground. In one instance where we were not getting cooperation, I called the country's ambassador in Washington and said that if we did not get the help we sought, we would close our embassy and tell the world why. Cooperation quickly followed.[4]

Our worries about the possibility of another major terrorist attack peaked toward the end of 1999, as the world prepared to celebrate the new millennium. The administration placed our law enforcement and intelligence apparatus on full alert. We warned Americans living or traveling abroad to exercise extreme care. To guard against the possibility of an assault with anthrax, we sent supplies of the antibiotic Cipro to all our posts and laid plans to procure masks that could be donned quickly in the event of a chemical or biological attack.

Back in Washington, we had an interagency team on duty around the clock. Over the course of a few days in mid December, three attacks were prevented and the potential perpetrators arrested. In the Middle East, a group of terrorists who had been schooled in Afghanistan were picked up while plotting to bomb the Radisson Hotel in Amman, Jordan. A plan to kill tourists visiting Mount Nebo, the peak Moses is said to have climbed

---

4. Terrorism was not our only concern. The Cold War was over but the practice of espionage was not. I was compelled to tighten security at the State Department following the 1998 penetration of a secure area by a mysterious man in a brown tweed suit, the 1999 discovery of a Russian listening device in a conference room, and the 2000 disappearance of a laptop containing highly classified information. The measures I ordered to dispel complacency, increase security patrols, restrict access to the department, and hold personnel accountable were resented by some colleagues and led to media reports of low morale. Given the seriousness of the lapses, however, I am convinced the critics were wrong and that my rigorous policies were both necessary and correct.

just before his death, was also foiled. The third plot—against Los Angeles International Airport—was stopped by an alert customs official who ordered thirty-three-year-old Ahmed Ressam to open his car trunk as he tried to enter the United States from Canada. More than a hundred pounds of explosives were found. Ressam subsequently provided a detailed account of his training in surveillance, assassination, and explosives and testified that a host of terrorist attacks had been planned around the world prior to the end of 1999. In each of these cases, there were links to al-Qaeda and Osama bin Laden. Although other threats concerned us, the Saudi terrorist remained the focus of our antiterrorism efforts.

THE DAY AFTER our retaliatory cruise missile strikes in August 1998, the White House convened a meeting to study further military options. Our prime target hadn't been hit, further hardening our resolve. In subsequent weeks the President specifically authorized the use of force to kill or capture bin Laden and his top aides. Initially we prepositioned B2 bombers that could reach Afghanistan within a day's notice. Later we shifted to submarines equipped with cruise missiles permanently on call in the Arabian Sea. The Pentagon, eventually wearying of this deployment, said that prolonging it was not justified in the absence of better information about bin Laden's whereabouts. However, President Clinton insisted, because it gave us the capability to hit bin Laden quickly if "actionable intelligence" did materialize. Obviously we couldn't strike unless we had a fair degree of certainty where bin Laden would be. The President pressed for intelligence about the caves near Afghanistan's border with Pakistan, but our military experts were not able to construct a sufficiently convincing scenario for an effective assault.

Anxious to explore every alternative, we studied the possibility of sending in a special forces team to snatch bin Laden. There were problems with this approach as well. Quality intelligence remained essential, because we couldn't send a team in on a hunch. Nor was it an easy mission to "right-size." The smaller the team, the more likely it might catch bin Laden by surprise, but the higher the risk that it would fail through lack of numbers or equipment breakdown. The larger the team, the more likely it could protect itself, but the less likely it would surprise. And if bin Laden were warned, there were many places he could hide. Besides, if we really had good intelligence, missiles could get the job done more rapidly and with less risk.

There was never any doubt that, if we thought we had a good chance to get bin Laden, we would go after him. We all felt the loss of those murdered in the embassy bombings—we had met with the families—and were determined to prevent additional attacks. At the same time, we were required by the circumstances to set a high standard for success. If we launched another high-profile mission that didn't capture or kill bin Laden, we would lose ground. The terrorist would surely take to the airwaves to crow about his survival and burnish his image among his radical followers.

Prior to Operation Infinite Reach, we had received word of a scheduled meeting of terrorist leaders, with bin Laden's presence a good possibility. Although we consumed every bit of intelligence we had, we never got a comparable break again. On several occasions I was notified that we were preparing a strike only to be told later that our information had proven unverifiable or wrong. We sometimes found out where bin Laden had been or where he could be going or where someone who looked like him might be, but the leads were always too late or too vague. It was maddening. I compared it to one of those arcade games where you manipulate a lever hooked to a clawlike hand that you think, once you put your quarter in, will easily scoop up a prize. But every time you try to pull the basket out, the prize falls away.

At the President's direction, the military continued to pursue ideas for improving our real-time information on bin Laden's whereabouts. In 2000, beginning in late summer, the Pentagon tried using the Predator, a slow-moving unmanned drone, to gather photographic data in Afghanistan. The results were encouraging, but then the aircraft crashed. The NSC proposed arming a new drone with a missile. Early in 2001, the air force tested a prototype, but the Bush administration chose not to deploy either armed or unarmed Predators in Afghanistan until after September 11.

One question that has since been raised is why we did not simply invade Afghanistan, depose the Taliban, and disperse al-Qaeda on its home ground. As far as I know, this option was not seriously proposed. There would have been reason to justify military action, but without the megashock of September 11, an invasion of Afghanistan would not have been supported by the majority of our citizens or our allies, and would have been condemned throughout the Arab and Islamic worlds.

President Clinton's second term ended without any additional successful terrorist attacks against U.S. diplomatic posts. As we know, however, diplomatic facilities are not the only targets. One reason terrorism is such a threat is that it can be directed almost anywhere. On October 12, 2000, a small boat pulled alongside the USS *Cole*, as it was refueling in Aden Harbor off the Yemeni coast. The boat exploded, ripping a sixty-by-forty-foot hole in the steel hull of the navy vessel, killing seventeen and wounding thirty-nine.

I immediately called President Ali Abdullah Saleh of Yemen, who had recently visited the United States and pledged his friendship. He promised a thorough investigation, and local authorities soon arrested suspects. Unfortunately, there was a breakdown in cooperation between Yemen and the FBI. Our ambassador, Barbara Bodine, worked with some success to get the two sides to cooperate by encouraging Yemen to be more forthcoming and the FBI to avoid trampling on local prerogatives. Although suspicion immediately fell on bin Laden, we did not have the kind of direct evidence developed after the embassy bombings. It wasn't until after I left office that the FBI conclusively established a link between al-Qaeda and the *Cole* attack.

THE OBVIOUS CONCERN following a catastrophe is whether it could have been prevented. Like Pearl Harbor and the assassination of JFK, the September 11 attacks have been and will continue to be the subject of scrutiny by official commissions, the media, and academic writers. Much attention has been paid to apparent failures of coordination between the CIA and FBI. I know from my own dealings with the two agencies that their cultures and missions are very different. At the same time, there is a tendency to look at the past through the prism of the present. The Twin Tower attacks were like a lightning bolt illuminating much that had previously been less obvious. Sadly I was not surprised that we were attacked or even shocked that an airplane hijacking was involved. I was startled, however, by the level of coordination and by the fact that the hijackers had spent so much time training in the United States.

The scale and nature of those attacks posed both immediate and extensive long-term challenges for our military, our diplomats, our law enforcement agencies, and those charged with homeland defense. They added a new dimension to long-standing fears about weapons of mass destruction falling into the wrong hands, and they inspired changes in U.S. military doctrine that would ignite worldwide controversy in future years.

The response by the Clinton administration to the Africa embassy bombings and other attacks on our watch resulted in the apprehension of many terrorist suspects and established a strong precedent for international cooperation in fighting terror. We used both force and diplomacy to attack bin Laden and disrupt al-Qaeda, accomplishing much but missing the clear victory we so ardently sought. That specific quest would continue, as would the larger battle of ideas.

During my years as a diplomat, I naturally thought in global terms. As an optimist, I hoped to strengthen international acceptance of the idea that terrorism is wrong, just as genocide, ethnic cleansing, slavery, apartheid, and racism are wrong. One challenge was to reach a common understanding of the term "terrorist." The label is a loaded one, especially controversial when applied to those struggling on behalf of a nationalist cause. I had many conversations with Arab leaders who argued that anti-Israeli groups like Hamas and Hezbollah shouldn't be considered terrorists because their struggle to recover lost Arab land had legitimacy. I was told, "They're only doing what American patriots did in their war for independence against Britain." I replied, "I don't remember George Washington and Paul Revere telling their sons to blow themselves up in order to kill British children."

There are many muddy situations around the world, where it is difficult for outsiders to make judgments. Often there is merit and fault on both sides, and the best one can hope for is a pragmatic solution, even if it leaves moral loose ends. There are also many autocratic governments that seek to establish clarity where there is none, smearing political opponents as "terrorists" whether or not that description applies.

But to admit that many situations are unclear is not to say that clarity of responsibility is impossible to sort out. When someone places a bomb in the federal building in Oklahoma City, or sends poison through the mail, or opens fire on people praying in a mosque, or turns a vegetable market into a scene of carnage, or flies an airplane into an office building, the moral issues are simple. It does not matter how angry, desperate, or demoralized a person might be. There is no political, historical, religious, economic, or ideological justification for willfully murdering innocent people. Such crimes must be opposed by each of us, in every country, on every continent, every day.

I made this point to an international audience that I was invited to address by Henry Kissinger in April 2000. I said that the security challenges facing America had changed and that the threat posed by conventional military forces had declined. Instead I suggested that unconventional threats such as terrorism "have created a battlefield populated by civilians. In response, we must reorient our strategies, understanding it is no longer enough to play geopolitical chess: the game board is not two-dimensional anymore." I argued that, in fighting terrorism, weapons proliferation, and crime in this new world, we would be dependent not simply on our own resources or on the help of traditional allies but on the contributions of "every willing nation" and every regional and global institution.

The message of that speech remains relevant today. But the reason it sticks in my mind is not so much what I said but where I said it. It was in a restaurant called Windows on the World, located atop the World Trade Center, in the city of New York.

TWENTY-THREE

"Milošević Is the Problem"

I REMEMBER LONG AGO seeing pictures of a brilliant chess master, perhaps Bobby Fischer at the age of twelve, playing a dozen games at once against different opponents. He would go from table to table, study the pieces, make his move, and proceed to the next opponent. This is how I felt as Secretary of State, except that I was no child prodigy and the faces I saw as I proceeded from one table to the next were those of Saddam Hussein, Muammar Qadhafi, Fidel Castro, and Ayatollah Khamenei. The games were complicated because a change in the momentum of one altered the dynamic of every other; our moves were decided by committee and leaked in advance by those who disagreed; new and contradictory strategies were being shouted out by a chorus from Capitol Hill; and the chessboard for the Middle East kept tipping over, requiring the contest to begin again. The game room was already crowded to overflowing early in 1998 when yet another familiar adversary—Slobodan Milošević —came crashing through the door.

IN LATE FEBRUARY and early March around the small town of Prekaz, in the Yugoslav province of Kosovo, Serb paramilitary units stormed through ethnic Albanian villages, killing scores of people. Whole families were burned alive in their homes. Women, children, and elderly were among the victims; thousands of people fled. It was the worst violence in the province since World War II. An angry crowd gathered in its capital city of Pristina to protest the killings, which were part of an operation to shut down ethnic Albanian guerrillas who had been ambushing Serb police.

If this had been an isolated incident, it would have been a tragedy without global impact, but the killings were laden with history and context. The province of Kosovo, about the size of Connecticut, is home to just over two million people. Fatefully, the province is located on the jagged dividing line roughly separating Europe's Muslims from its Christians, in this case ethnic Albanians from ethnic Serbs.[1] In such a neighborhood, the present is all too often defined by the past.

In 1389, Serb forces were defeated by the mobile cavalry of the Ottoman empire in an epic clash near Pristina. The Serb leader, Prince Lazar, was captured by the Turks, brought before the Turkish sultan, and beheaded. To this day many Serbs, while celebrating the bravery of their forces, are motivated by a desire to avenge the defeat. For centuries after the battle, the Ottomans ruled Kosovo and the rest of Serbia, but no empire lasts forever, and the Ottoman spent most of the 1800s getting smaller. Serbia regained its independence in 1878 and in 1912 briefly reasserted control over Kosovo. After World War I, Serbia (including Kosovo) was incorporated into the Kingdom of Serbs, Croats, and Slovenes, later known as Yugoslavia.

In 1974, under Tito, Yugoslavia's constitution was amended to grant Kosovo full autonomous status and allow its large Albanian population to establish its own parliament, schools, and other institutions. For the next fifteen years Kosovo's government was in the hands primarily of Albanian Communists. Serbs living in Kosovo complained of discrimination and mistreatment. This grievance created an opening for Milošević, when he came to power in Belgrade in 1989, to burnish his credentials as a Serb nationalist by adopting the cause of the Serb minority in Kosovo. Soon after taking office, he dispatched his police to close schools and began the systematic denial of the Albanians' political and economic rights.

The result was rising tension. Both the Serbs and Albanians had valid historic claims, but Kosovo, the place many Serbs considered their heart, had long since been lodged in a foreign body. More than 90 percent of Kosovo's people were Albanian. Surrounding the province were significant ethnic Albanian populations in neighboring Macedonia and Greece, as well as Albania itself. Violence between Serbs and Albanians in Kosovo could engulf the entire region.

The senior Bush administration, which had generally been passive in the Balkans, decided to make a bold commitment as it prepared to leave office. On Christmas Day 1992, U.S. diplomats informed Milošević that the United States would be prepared to respond militarily if the Serbs initiated an armed conflict in Kosovo. Three weeks after President Clinton took

---

1. For purposes of simplicity, the term "Albanians" will be used throughout the next three chapters to describe the ethnic Albanian component of Kosovo's population. Unless otherwise specified it does not refer to the citizens of the country of Albania.

office in 1993, Secretary Christopher reaffirmed this "Christmas warning."

To their credit, the Albanians chose to resist Serb repression peacefully, creating a parallel set of "shadow" institutions. Under the leadership of Ibrahim Rugova and the Democratic League of Kosovo (LDK), they pressed their case for independence, but in a nonviolent manner. As a result, while the war in Bosnia boiled, Kosovo simmered. The official institutions, controlled by Serbs, coexisted with unofficial bodies, controlled by Albanians. But the Yugoslav police maintained a stranglehold on the province and were widely hated for their tactics of intimidation. Kosovo was extremely tense but not at war.

After the 1995 Dayton Accords were signed, however, the situation began to heat up further. Kosovo's Albanians looked around and saw that the Bosnians, Croats, Slovenes, and Macedonians had all left Yugoslavia to form independent states. The Albanians shared the same ambition but the Dayton Accords did nothing for them. Many grew impatient with the denial of their rights and the appeals for patience from civilian leaders. Some turned to violence, joining a resistance movement known as the Kosovo Liberation Army (KLA). At the time we knew little about this loosely organized group, except that it had carried out small-scale attacks against Serbs in Kosovo. From sources in the region, we received word in January 1998 that Milošević was preparing to respond with a military crackdown.

Fearing a crisis, we pressed the Serb leader repeatedly not to initiate a new wave of repression, reminding him once more of the Christmas warning. We sought to strengthen Albanian moderates by encouraging a dialogue with Belgrade aimed at restoring Kosovo's autonomy, and we discouraged international support for the KLA. We also explored ways to help prodemocracy forces inside Yugoslavia, believing that the problems of Kosovo and the region would not be solved until Milošević was removed from power. These efforts reflected the vision—which President Clinton and I shared—of a free and undivided Europe encompassing the Balkans at peace. To fulfill that vision we had first to defeat, displace, or outlast the fiercely nationalist leaders who emerged when Yugoslavia broke up. With Franjo Tudjman's health failing in Croatia and Bosnia finally stable, Milošević was the last powerful obstacle to the integration of the Balkans into a democratic Europe.

Prior to the Prekaz massacre, Yugoslav authorities had assured our chief Balkans negotiator, Ambassador Robert Gelbard, that they would respond with restraint to any attacks. Obviously they had lied. The Serb rampage was sure to radicalize Albanians, weaken moderates, and bolster the KLA. Milošević had already started three wars in the Balkans (against Slovenia, Croatia, and Bosnia). He seemed ready to begin a fourth.

WHEN THE VIOLENCE in Bosnia first erupted, I had not yet entered government. Later, at the UN, I was one member of a team. Now I was Secretary of State. The killings at Prekaz filled me with foreboding matched by determination. I believed we had to stop Milošević immediately. In public, I laid down a marker: "We are not going to stand by and watch the Serbian authorities do in Kosovo what they can no longer get away with in Bosnia." Hoping to rally international support, I attended a meeting in London of what was known as the Contact Group, a trans-Atlantic Balkans task force consisting of the United States, Russia, the United Kingdom, France, Germany, and Italy.

Foreign Secretary Robin Cook, host for the meeting, began by circulating a draft statement listing sanctions to be imposed, steps Milošević could take to get those sanctions lifted, and the threat of further sanctions if he did not. It was a stick, carrot, stick approach. Robin and I were on the same wavelength. He reported that he had met with Milošević and found him utterly uninterested in a political solution. Our only route was to compel him to change his policies.

I spoke next and with as much intensity as I have ever mustered, pointing out that Lancaster House, the majestic building in which we were meeting, was the same structure in which Western foreign ministers had held so many fruitless sessions about Bosnia. We were even in the same room. Earlier in the decade the international community had ignored the first signs of ethnic cleansing in the Balkans. We had to learn from that mistake. The violence in Kosovo was recent, but the problem created by Milošević's ruthless ambition was not.

I warned that Kosovo had implications for the entire region. We could not allow the Serbs to define it as a purely internal matter. Milošević was claiming that the Kosovars were violent, but the violence began with him. The Albanians had had autonomy under Tito, but Milošević had taken it away. There would have been no KLA had the Kosovars not been deprived of their rights. We had to approve concrete measures that would expand our leverage over Belgrade. That was how Milošević had been brought to the table at Dayton, and that was the only language he would respond to now.

I thought I had been persuasive, but apparently not. French Foreign Minister Hubert Védrine asked for a delay in sanctions, a clearer condemnation of the KLA, and an explicit statement of opposition to independence for Kosovo. Italy's Lamberto Dini worried that sanctions on Milošević might result in less rather than more cooperative behavior and urged that we do more to halt arms smuggling to the KLA. Yevgeny Primakov, who hadn't wanted to have the meeting at all, had sent one of his deputies as a protest. Robin Cook and I took turns beating up on the Russian envoy, who had apparently decided his best tactic was to wear us out. When we pressed him to accept at least some sanctions, he said he was under instructions to oppose any punitive measures. Then he began to filibuster.

The debate grew heated, and as I listened I doodled on my writing pad with fierce energy. Having come into the meeting prepared to state my strong views clearly, I was determined not to betray the trust of those who looked to America for leadership. At one point the ordinarily hawkish Jamie Rubin urged me to compromise on a particular measure. I glared and said, "Jamie, do you think we're in Munich?"

After four hours we had achieved a consensus except for Russia. The rest of us joined in calling for a moratorium on export credits, a war crimes tribunal investigation, and the denial of travel visas for senior Serb officials. We agreed to send a high-level envoy (former Spanish Prime Minister Felipe González) to facilitate a dialogue between the Serbs and Albanians, and we warned Milošević of additional sanctions unless Serb security forces in Kosovo were reduced.

I had obtained most of what I'd hoped for, but the momentum did not last. As the days went by, my European colleagues gave Milošević higher marks for compliance than I did. They emphasized the withdrawal of some Serb security forces. I produced evidence that Serb special police were digging in, not pulling out. The Europeans mentioned Belgrade's invitation to reestablish an international presence in Kosovo. I pointed to Milošević's refusal to accept the mission headed by González. The Europeans didn't think it necessary to impose additional sanctions. I thought it essential.

A second Contact Group meeting was scheduled for March 25 in Bonn. I arrived the night before and had dinner with Primakov. Yeltsin had just fired almost everyone else in his cabinet. Primakov explained that he had survived because he had been an ally of Yeltsin since they had been in the Politburo together. Yeltsin was comfortable with him because he wasn't a potential rival.

On Kosovo, we agreed a civil war would have disastrous consequences but otherwise held sharply differing views. Primakov defended Milošević; he thought the Albanians, not the Serbs, were now the destabilizing force. He also said that Russia considered Kosovo a domestic matter and that sanctions against Milošević would only inflame Serb nationalists. My own feeling was that Russia's position was shaped less by solidarity with their fellow Slavs than by the possibility that international action there would serve as a precedent for outside intervention in Russia, where Chechen separatists regularly clashed with the army.

The Contact Group meeting, chaired by German Foreign Minister Klaus Kinkel, agreed on essentially nothing and convinced me that this group was not the right body to counter Milošević. Obviously, Russia would be difficult, and France and Germany were almost always reluctant to confront Moscow. The Italians did a lot of business with the Serbs and disliked sanctions. It was all too easy for Milošević to immobilize these countries with reassuring gestures and empty words.

I concluded that we should not be content to follow the consensus on Kosovo; we had to lead it. That would only be possible, however, if I were able to forge a consensus within my own government—not an easy task. The NSC and Pentagon were growing uncomfortable with my declarations of resolve. The administration was not anxious to get into another confrontation involving the threat of force. The Defense Department, which had yielded on the question of maintaining U.S. troops in Bosnia, was unwilling to contemplate further missions in the Balkans. As a result, to my dismay, the administration had stopped reaffirming the 1992 Christmas warning.

I felt it urgent that we again raise the possibility of bombing. Milošević would interpret the absence of an explicit warning as a green light for repression. We had to implant some spine into our policy. On the afternoon of April 23, Bob Gelbard, Strobe Talbott, and I sat down in the West Wing of the White House with Sandy Berger.

I warned that the steps we had been taking were not sufficient. Kosovo was headed for a major confrontation unless there were a political deal, which would not happen until Milošević felt threatened—which he would not so long as the use of force remained off the table. Our current position was "nothing has been ruled out." This sounded weak because it was weak. It was a clear step back from our earlier position and a reprise of our early timidity on Bosnia.

Gelbard echoed my comments, saying that we needed to use the threat of force to persuade Milošević to negotiate. To make that credible, it was vital for NATO to begin laying plans for a bombing campaign. At this point Sandy Berger broke in exasperated. "You can't just talk about bombing in the middle of Europe. What targets would you want to hit? What would you do the day after? It's irresponsible to keep making threatening statements outside of some coherent plan. The way you people at the State Department talk about bombing, you sound like lunatics."

I had always taught my female students at Georgetown to interrupt; now I did, saying, "I'm tired of this. Every time someone talks about using force, they're subject to ad hominem attacks. Five years ago, when I proposed using force in Bosnia, Tony Lake never let me finish my argument. Well, now I'm Secretary of State and I'm going to insist we at least have this discussion."

IN LATE SPRING, when Milošević stepped up helicopter strikes and ordered the burning of villages in Kosovo, we went not to the Contact Group but to NATO. At U.S. urging, the Alliance began planning for several possibilities, including preventive deployments in Albania and Macedonia to keep the conflict from spreading, air strikes in the event of a harsher Serb crackdown, and a peace implementation force in case a political settlement were reached.

The diplomacy became more complex when the British circulated a draft UN Security Council resolution authorizing the use of force. This was well intentioned but not well conceived. I called Robin Cook, who said his lawyers had told him a council mandate would be needed if NATO were to act. I told him he should get himself new lawyers. If a UN resolution passed, we would have set a precedent that NATO required Security Council authorization before it could act. This would give Russia, not to mention China, a veto over NATO. If the resolution failed, it would be seen as a victory for Milošević and make it that much harder for NATO to move. The third possibility was that the resolution would pass but only after having its teeth extracted to gain Russian acquiescence. Three possibilities: three bad outcomes; not a good plan.

Our goal was a negotiated settlement between Milošević and the Albanians that would grant a substantial measure of self-rule to the province. To achieve that, we first had to identify negotiators for the diverse and divided Albanian side. Ibrahim Rugova, the elected leader of their shadow government, was a slight, mild-mannered intellectual known for the scarves he always wore and his reputation for pacificism. But the KLA, which controlled the guns, would not accept Rugova as negotiating on its behalf. Neither would some other Albanian political leaders, who saw him as too passive toward the Serbs and too heavy-handed toward dissent within his own party.

Rugova had always refused to meet with Milošević, but in May 1998 he agreed to lead a small delegation to Belgrade to see if a political process could be launched. This proved a false step. The Serb press seized the opportunity to publish pictures of Milošević and Rugova sharing a laugh. Coming at a time when Serb police were pillaging Albanian villages, the photo further damaged Rugova's standing among his own people.

We tried to repair the damage by bringing his delegation to Washington, to show our respect and urge unity. During our meeting, I was discouraged by the body language of Rugova's colleagues, who sat stiffly and even gestured dismissively while he talked. Rugova was forthright, nevertheless. He said that conditions in Kosovo were worsening day by day and called for NATO to establish a no-fly zone that would stop Serb helicopter attacks. He said the goal of the Albanians was independence, but they might accept an interim status as an international protectorate or even, he joked, as the fifty-first American state. I told him we couldn't support independence but would do our best to help Kosovo achieve autonomy and security.[2]

As the meeting broke up, Rugova presented me with a small semi-precious stone from Kosovo. One of the Albanian leader's quirks was that he regularly handed out rocks. The previous day President Clinton had received a five-pound chunk of quartz. I have been around a lot of dissidents in my life, in Central Europe and elsewhere. Usually you can sense the fervor with which they approach their cause. Rugova was an anomaly. Although he often proved bewildering, I came to believe that one of his strengths was that he was constantly underestimated. People disregarded him but he didn't go away, and when Kosovars voted, they did so more often for him than for anyone else.

Throughout the Kosovo crisis, Milošević's diplomatic strategy was to blame everything on the KLA "terrorists." No one did more than the KLA to help this strategy. Almost every time we succeeded in restraining Milošević, the guerrillas exploited the opening and started a fight. Their ranks continued to grow, drawing strength internally from students and nationalists, externally from ethnic Albanian sympathizers as far away as the United States.

During the spring and early summer, Milošević was under pressure from Russia and the Contact Group to withdraw the extra security forces he had sent to Kosovo. He refused to do this or to make any move to restore political rights. For the most part, however, he did confine military and police actions to the border region and along major transit routes. The KLA took advantage by filtering into the countryside, establishing

---

2. Our reluctance to endorse independence was shaped less by principle than by a pragmatic assessment of attitudes in the region. Macedonia and Greece strongly opposed independence for Kosovo because they feared it might inflame separatist ambitions within their own ethnic Albanian populations. Other countries also had minorities with aspirations for independence, including Russia's Chechens, Georgia's Abkhaz, Turkey's Kurds, and Spain's Basques. More generally, some Europeans feared that an independent Kosovo would become a hotbed of Islamic extremism and organized crime. We couldn't achieve our goals in Kosovo without support from Europe, and we wouldn't have Europe's support if we backed independence for Kosovo.

checkpoints on secondary roads, and boasting to the media about "liberated zones." KLA members promised to protect Kosovars in these zones and even began producing license plates and holding KLA beauty contests.

By mid June, it had become obvious that no political settlement would be possible without the rebels, so our diplomats began meeting with KLA representatives. This infuriated Milošević and nettled the Europeans, but it was the only way to make progress. In our initial contacts, KLA officials were straightforward about their goal, which was liberation. Their agenda, they said, was strictly military, and they were confident of success. Consequently, they had no interest in a cease-fire or negotiations.

My own view of the fighters was mixed. I sympathized with their opposition to Milošević, understood their desire for independence, and accepted that force was sometimes necessary for a just cause to prevail. On the other hand, there did not appear to be much Jeffersonian thinking within the KLA. Often indiscriminate in their attacks, they seemed intent on provoking a massive Serb response so that international intervention would be unavoidable. I wanted to stop Milošević from marauding through Kosovo, but I didn't want that determination exploited by the KLA for purposes we opposed. We therefore took pains to insist that we would not operate as the KLA's air force or rescue the KLA if it got into trouble as a result of its own actions. We condemned violence by either side.

The KLA was Milošević's worst enemy, but its attacks helped him diplomatically. If he had been smart, he could have turned world opinion against the guerrillas by accommodating the aspirations of Kosovars for control of their own governing institutions while carrying out disciplined security missions aimed at cutting KLA supply lines, arresting KLA members, protecting civilians, and responding to attacks. The international community couldn't have opposed this course; indeed, we would have applauded a settlement that established provincial autonomy while safeguarding human rights. Tragically, Milošević was not capable of seeing Kosovo as a political and diplomatic problem to be solved. He saw only an opposition to be crushed. Because he did not care about the rights of Albanians, he thought we would not care either. Many painful months would pass before we would prove him wrong.

IN JULY 1998, the KLA made good on its earlier boasts and launched a "summer offensive." It was a disaster. The Serb counteroffensive was overwhelming and sustained. Their strategy was to cut the guerrillas' supply lines by seizing control of areas along the province's border with Albania, then expelling the insurgent force from literally every village.

The result was a campaign of intimidation that drove hundreds of thousands of civilians along with KLA fighters into the mountains and woods. Milošević thought this was his opportunity to destroy the guerrillas while terrorizing the independence-minded Kosovars into abandoning their dreams. But his assault had two very different consequences.

First, by weakening the guerrillas, the offensive actually increased pressure on Milošević to negotiate a political solution. When the KLA was strong, the Albanians couldn't negotiate coherently because Rugova was too weak and the KLA too dogmatic. The guerrillas were promising to liberate Kosovo from Serbia without negotiations or compromise. They also pledged to protect civilians in the zones they had "liberated." But when the Serbs attacked, the KLA left. Villagers were brutalized by the Serbs and disillusioned with their so-called protectors. As a result, Rugova regained enough standing to put together a negotiating team without being labeled a traitor. Even the KLA accepted the need for talks.

This meant that our negotiators were finally able to begin discussions with the two sides about what autonomy for Kosovo might look like. The second consequence of the Serb offensive was less benign. Thousands of displaced Kosovars faced the prospect of freezing to death during the approaching winter. Many families who had fled from Serb guns were afraid to return home as long as Milošević's forces were on the attack. Although Milošević felt sufficient pressure to talk to Rugova about autonomy, it was not likely to be enough to make him agree on specific terms. He was, after all, winning the war.

Clearly, economic sanctions alone were not going to stop Milošević from killing Albanians. As I had believed from the outset, we needed to back our diplomacy with force. I made this case yet again to my administration colleagues, arguing that if we did not act, the crisis would spread, more people would die, we would look weak, pressure would build, and we would end up resorting to force anyway under even more difficult and tragic circumstances.

I also argued that we should initiate a concerted strategy aimed at ending Milošević's rule in Belgrade. I understood that pragmatism dictated at Dayton that we deal with Milošević to end the Bosnian war, but I never trusted him. His ambitions were not the kind that could be satisfied except at great cost to others. Our interests in Kosovo, moreover, stemmed from our interests in a peaceful Europe, and Yugoslavia would never find its way into such a Europe with Milošević at its helm. We needed to send the message to Serb businesspeople that he was bad for business, to the Serb military that he invited the destruction of their institutions, and to the Serb middle class that he was wrecking their hopes for a peaceful and prosperous future. My arguments, combined with daily news of disasters from Kosovo, ultimately prevailed. The President approved a strategy for supporting alternatives to Milošević through overt, public means; we also decided to push for a clear-cut Alliance decision on Kosovo.

Our plan was for NATO to compel Milošević to halt his offensive and reduce the number of Serb security forces in Kosovo to the level that existed before the violence began. Milošević also had to agree to negotiate seriously with the Albanians to develop interim arrangements on autonomy. If he did not take these steps, NATO would launch a sustained campaign of strikes against Serb positions in Kosovo and Serbia itself. Although we could not count on the UN Security Council for an explicit authorization of force, we did work through the council to gain an endorsement of our political objectives. On September 23, the council adopted a resolution declaring the situation in Kosovo a threat to peace and security and listing a series of actions Milošević had to take. The following day, NATO issued a formal warning that air strikes would be authorized if the Serb offensive continued.

On September 30, we held a meeting of the Principals Committee in the White House Situation Room. On the table in front of us was a photograph from that morning's *New York Times*. In the center of the photo was the image of a dead body, skeletal in appearance, mouth open, seeming to issue a last silent cry. The body was one of eighteen women, children, and elderly awaiting burial in the Kosovo town of Gornje Obrinje. Several days earlier Serb police had found fifteen of the victims hiding in a gorge and murdered them. Three men, including a ninety-five-year-old paralytic, were burned to death in their homes. Another sixteen civilians were found shot or hacked to death in nearby villages. This was Milošević's answer to the United Nations and NATO.

That morning, as I looked at the photo and read the accompanying story, I thought again of my vow not to allow a repeat of the carnage we had witnessed in Bosnia. There, several hundred thousand people had been killed. In Kosovo the current toll was several hundred. For most, it was not too late, but we had to summon our resolve.

The Principals Committee recommended to President Clinton that he send Richard Holbrooke—then a private citizen—to Belgrade to deliver NATO's terms. During the year, Holbrooke had accompanied Bob Gelbard on several trips, trying to make use of the relationship he had established with Milošević during the Dayton negotiations. We were sending him now to show our willingness to explore every reasonable alternative to force. Arriving in Belgrade, Holbrooke was unable to make progress, because we still lacked sufficient leverage.

Milošević remained unconvinced that NATO would move beyond its repeated warnings. He knew some European leaders were pushing for a second and more explicit UN Security Council resolution, one that Russia would surely veto. A new coalition government—including the semi-pacifist Green Party—was preparing to take office in Germany. Italy had assured us it would stand firm, but the Prodi government was about to fall amid parliamentary concern about the prospect of air strikes being launched from Italian bases. Milošević, in one of his periodic charm offensives, had ostentatiously withdrawn a small number of troops from Kosovo. He seemed intent on drawing out his negotiations with Holbrooke in hopes that NATO would become divided. In response, we had to get the softness out of NATO's position.

On October 8, Holbrooke and I met in Brussels with representatives from the Alliance. Together we argued that an agreement with Milošević was possible only if NATO authorized the use of force. We then went together to a meeting of the Contact Group in London to make the same assertion and assure the Europeans that we were doing everything possible to get the Russians on board. This meant dealing with a new personality. Boris Yeltsin, beset by economic woes, had fired yet another prime minister, this time replacing him with my friend Yevgeny Primakov. The new foreign minister was a career diplomat, Igor Ivanov, whom I would also come to know fondly and well.

For purposes of convenience, the meeting was convened in the VIP lounge of Heathrow Airport. Half a dozen foreign ministers were present, each with a retinue of aides. The small room was impossibly crowded; there were even airport staff walking around offering tea and biscuits. I asked Robin Cook if we could limit the meeting to principals. He agreed. There followed a tense discussion in which German Foreign Minister Kinkel repeatedly pressed Foreign Minister Ivanov to support a UN Security Council resolution authorizing military action. Ivanov said Russia would veto such a resolution, asserting that Milošević had already promised to withdraw troops. I responded by saying, "Milošević is a congenital liar." The meeting failed to alter the Russian position, but it did serve to convince the Europeans that, in this case, the UN Security Council was not going to act decisively. If nations wanted to avoid a catastrophe in Kosovo that winter, they would have to move forward with the justification we already had.

Following the meeting, Holbrooke headed back to Belgrade with dramatically increased leverage. While we had not agreed on everything with our NATO allies, we had done a lot of consulting and cajoling in the preceding months, which now paid off. The French had announced that they would support NATO action on humanitarian grounds, despite their preference, in principle, for a Security Council resolution. The incoming German Chancellor, Gerhard Schröder, assured President Clinton his government would vote yes. Next the Italians too came fully on board. Early on the morning of October 13, NATO formally authorized the use of force, allowing four days for compliance. A few hours later, Holbrooke announced that he and Milošević had a deal.

Under the agreement, Milošević had ten days to reduce the number of Serb troops and police in Kosovo. Refugees and displaced persons would be allowed to return to their homes. Up to two thousand international observers would be deployed under the auspices of the Organization for Security and Cooperation in Europe (OSCE). NATO was given authority to overfly Kosovo to verify Serb actions. Elections would be held within nine months and a new multiethnic police force would be trained. Yugoslavia would have to cooperate with war crimes tribunal investigations. Finally, Belgrade pledged to negotiate with leaders in Kosovo to achieve a settlement that would return autonomy to the province.

The October agreement was more Band-Aid than cure. The commitments Milošević made could and would be reversed, but for the time being the agreement allowed hundreds of thousands of people to come down from the hills to spend winter in their homes. It reinforced the truth that Kosovo's fate was of international concern, and it established a set of formal obligations Milošević had accepted, and against which he could be held accountable. Perhaps most important, the NATO authorization of force was suspended, not withdrawn.

IN A MATTER OF WEEKS, the Band-Aid began to peel away. Unlike Bosnia, where years of fighting had sapped the will of all sides, Yugoslav and Albanian extremists were neither exhausted nor satisfied. In November, Milošević replaced the leaders of his security forces with hard-liners who bragged that they could wipe out the guerrillas in days. Meanwhile the KLA prepared for war by recruiting new fighters and bringing in weapons from Albania. Despite the winter snows, sporadic ambushes and shootings kept Kosovo tense.

In Washington, I read the reports filed each day by the international verification team, headed by U.S. Ambassador William Walker. Walker had served in war zones before; he had done a first-rate job leading a UN peacekeeping mission in Croatia, during which he had often dealt with Milošević. Now he was supervising a team whose job was to drive around Kosovo in bright orange vehicles and report what they saw. Since this was perilous duty for unarmed personnel, the monitors restricted their operations to daylight hours, a constraint not shared by either Serb forces or by the KLA.

We knew the return of warmer weather would make the transportation of warriors and weapons easier and violence more likely, so we had to move quickly if we were to avoid a bloody spring. I had asked one of my closest advisors, James O'Brien, an architect of the Dayton Accords, to join Ambassador Christopher Hill in leading the negotiation. The two had proposed a creative settlement under which Kosovo would remain within Yugoslavia while fashioning a new civilian police force and other institutions of self-government. Without closing the door to eventual independence, the proposal called for an interim period of at least three years before that explosive question would be addressed.

The Serbs were telling us privately that Milošević was open to a deal, but we questioned on what terms. We needed to test him, but first we had to persuade the Albanians to unify their negotiating team and agree on a set of achievable goals. This still proved difficult. The KLA was regaining strength and with it a reluctance to compromise. The various Albanian leaders spoke of each other with disdain, sometimes threatened each other with violence, and couldn't agree on a negotiating agenda. Precious weeks slipped by as, to our frustration, they would not even consent to meet.

As the winter passed, my fears grew. With the Albanians in disarray, Milošević couldn't be blamed for not negotiating. Because the KLA was on the move, our allies were not willing to blame, let alone bomb, the Serbs. Because Milošević couldn't be trusted, it was impossible to persuade the KLA to rely for Kosovo's protection on the small, unarmed team of OSCE monitors. The result was that negotiations went nowhere, while violence spread.

In mid December, Serb forces killed thirty-one members of a KLA unit seeking to cross the border from Albania. A few hours later ethnic Albanians machine-gunned six Serb teenagers in a Kosovo bar. Two days later, a local Serb official was found dead on the road to Pristina airport. Within a week, Serb forces were once again attacking Albanian villages.

I felt we had to try something new. The situation was emerging as a key test of American leadership and of the relevance and effectiveness of NATO. The Alliance was due to celebrate its fiftieth anniversary in April. If my fears proved correct, that event would coincide with the spectacle of another humanitarian disaster in the Balkans. And we would look like fools proclaiming the Alliance's readiness for the twenty-first century when we were unable to cope with a conflict that began in the fourteenth.

On January 15, 1999, the Principals Committee met to consider a "new" strategy. The accompanying papers were rich in detail and superficially comprehensive. With lengthy sections on "revitalizing negotiations" and "increasing leverage" over the two sides, the proposal set out a list of goals. The problem was that it was all rhetoric. The so-called "decisive steps" were muddled. There was no clear path to a solution.

During the meeting, I said that the proposed strategy was not enough and we had to begin looking at Kosovo with a wider lens. "The cease-fire negotiated in October," I said, "is balanced on the edge of a knife. We're already beginning to see the violence we didn't expect until spring. We must go back to our allies and renew the threat of air strikes. We must tell Milošević bluntly that we will use force if he doesn't meet his commitments. We must go to the public and highlight his failures. We must emphasize over and over again that Milošević is the problem."

My remarks weren't received with much enthusiasm. As I looked around the table, I saw "There goes Madeleine again" glances being exchanged. The "new strategy" for Kosovo was approved, but I feared it would produce only the same old results. Afterwards I raged to my staff that we were acting like "gerbils running on a wheel," in constant motion but getting nowhere. Unless something dramatic happened, the Serbs were going to launch a new offensive and Bosnia's past would become Kosovo's future.

TWENTY-FOUR

Kosovo: Diplomacy
and the Threat of Force

SOME PEOPLE WAKE to the sound of roosters crowing or alarm bells ringing or coffee cups rattling. As a Washingtonian, I wake to all-news radio. Since it was a Saturday—January 16, 1999—the radio switched itself on a little later than usual but still well before dawn. As I lay there in the midwinter dark, I heard an announcer reporting on a massacre five thousand miles away. The details wouldn't be long in coming. "There are a lot of bodies up there," Ambassador Bill Walker told reporters, "men who have been shot in various ways, but mostly very close up." Forty-five people were dead in the town of Racak, in Kosovo. Walker had seen the bodies himself, many scattered about a snowy ravine, others thrown together in a pile, each with horrible wounds, all wearing civilian clothes, one decapitated. When asked who was responsible, Walker did not equivocate. "It was the Serbian police."

Walker's team of international verifiers had not been able to stop the Racak massacre, but they were able to prevent it from occurring in secret. According to witnesses they interviewed, the Serbs had begun shelling the day before. Then paramilitary forces entered the town, herded women and children into a mosque, rounded up adult males, and led them away. Later, villagers found the bodies.

Much of that Saturday I spent at home talking to half the world on the phone. We had worried that Kosovo would explode once the winter snows melted. Now I called Sandy Berger and said sadly, "It looks like spring has come to Kosovo early this year." We asked that General Wesley Clark, NATO's supreme commander, and General Klaus Naumann, chairman of the Alliance's Military Committee, be dispatched to Belgrade to warn Milošević against further abuses, demand that the war crimes tribunal be permitted to investigate Racak, and remind him that NATO's threat to use force remained in effect. I called NATO foreign ministers to propose that the Alliance review and update plans to launch military strikes. And I called my top advisors, seeking a strategy that would combine force and diplomacy to stop Milošević without turning Kosovo over to KLA guerrillas.

At the earliest opportunity, I convened a group in my office that included Strobe Talbott, Jamie Rubin, and Morton Halperin, a brainy and iconoclastic survivor of Washington battles who had recently replaced Greg Craig as director of our Office of Policy Planning.[1] Together we developed an approach linking the threat of air strikes to the goal of achieving a political settlement. After all, the Albanians deserved more than the right to have their deaths publicized by international inspectors. If the Serbs refused to negotiate in good faith, NATO would employ air strikes to compel them to do so.[2]

If our plan were implemented, I could foresee three possible outcomes, two of which were preferable to the status quo. Ideally, NATO threats and the international spotlight would cause both sides to agree to a settlement. The result would be self-government for the Kosovars with security guaranteed by a NATO-led peacekeeping force. If the Serbs said no and the Albanians yes, the settlement would be preceded by a period of bombing that would last as long as necessary to bring Milošević to the table. If both sides said no, the result would be a mess for which both sides would bear responsibility.

That evening of January 19, I began a debate with the other national security principals that would continue almost without pause for the next four days. I was convinced that we were at a watershed, and said so. Initially Defense Secretary Cohen and General Hugh Shelton, who had replaced John Shalikashvili as Chairman of the Joint Chiefs, expressed

---

1. Craig left to become one of the lawyers defending the President during the impeachment trial. I was sorry to see him go, but I knew the President had made a wise choice recruiting him.

2. This proposal was not conceived solely in my office. Our ambassador to NATO, Alexander Vershbow, had insisted for months that NATO would ultimately have to use force to prevent Milošević from terrorizing Kosovo. If that happened and air strikes drove Serb forces from the province, Hubert Védrine and Robin Cook wanted to be sure a NATO-led peacekeeping force would be authorized to take their place. Otherwise the Europeans feared that power in Kosovo would be seized by the KLA.

doubts about my approach and argued vigorously against a peacekeeping force. They didn't want to have to support a second major long-term mission in the Balkans, and they worried about getting caught in the middle of a civil war. They doubted our ability to rouse public support for the obscure cause of Kosovar autonomy. And they wondered whether Congress would come up with our share of peacekeeping costs. Their preference, therefore, was to preserve the verification team rather than insert an effective armed presence. If there were to be a NATO force, they argued, it should not include Americans.

I understood why Pentagon officials felt this way, but their alternative made no sense. The verifiers wouldn't be able to maintain order. Without NATO protection, the guerrillas would never disarm. Without U.S. participation, there would be no NATO protection, and without NATO to stop him, Milošević would continue attacking. With both sides fighting, disaster was inevitable. The way to avoid disaster was to use diplomacy backed by the threat of NATO force to achieve and implement a political solution.

I respected Secretary Cohen and General Shelton but thought that, in this case, they were wrong. I had learned from Bosnia not to take disagreements personally, so I kept my voice flat and tried to keep everyone focused on the realities. Slowly and steadily during the hours of high-level meetings, my arguments gained ground. Ironically, Milošević helped me to make my case by insisting to Generals Clark and Naumann that the only people killed at Racak had been terrorists. He said the war crimes tribunal had no jurisdiction and claimed Bill Walker was biased. When Clark mentioned the possibility of NATO air strikes, Milošević called him a "war criminal."

We also received intelligence indicating that the Serbs were planning an assault on large KLA units and command centers during a two-week period in March, followed by a months-long operation to wipe out pockets of resistance. Such an offensive would result in many deaths and the displacement of hundreds of thousands of people. By January 23, I had pushed our team to agree on a plan to encourage negotiations by threatening air strikes and to support a NATO-led peacekeeping force, with U.S. participation "possible." The Pentagon stressed, however, that such a force would be available only in a "permissive environment," which meant with the consent of Belgrade. Pocketing my gains, I did not argue that point—then.

With my own government more or less on board, I now had to worry about the rest of the players. I knew that the concept of a NATO force would be supported by Europe and that the idea of linking air strikes to a high-profile peace conference would be attractive to our friends in Paris, provided of course the talks were held in France. I still needed to clarify who would guide this initiative. My preference was NATO, which was strong and cohesive and had succeeded in Bosnia. The Europeans, especially the French, preferred the six-member Contact Group, where their voices would not be diluted by so many other countries. I thought it might be possible to use both, but only if Russia—a Contact Group member—did not obstruct. That meant I had to determine how hard Moscow would push and in which direction. Fortuitously I was scheduled to visit Russia that very week.

I had first met Igor Ivanov when he was a deputy to Yevgeny Primakov and found him somewhat formal. As we got to know each other after he succeeded Primakov as foreign minister, I found him intelligent and charming. Like Primakov, however, he could also be tough, and my discussions with him on Kosovo tended to be circular. I would tell Igor that Milošević was the problem because his repression had created the KLA. Ivanov would concede the point but argue that the guerrillas had since become the biggest threat. We both favored a political settlement but could not agree on how to achieve one. I said Milošević wouldn't negotiate without the threat of strikes. Ivanov said Russia couldn't tolerate the use of force against fellow Slavs. Then I would point out that Milošević was the source of the problem, and we were back at square one.

I seized the chance to break out of this cycle in an extracurricular setting—the Bolshoi Theater, where Ivanov had invited me to attend a performance of *La Traviata*. The two of us sat together in the president's box, which had been built for the czars and was encased in plush red velvet. The production was superb, but although my eyes and ears were focused on the stage, my mind was on Kosovo. During the intermission, Ivanov and I went into an anteroom, where champagne and caviar were laid out. I didn't waste words.

"Look, Igor," I said, "I'll tell it to you straight. If Kosovo explodes, we'll face huge obstacles in working together on a whole range of issues. We can't let that happen. There has to be a political settlement. But the Albanians won't lay down their arms unless NATO is there to protect them. And Milošević will never allow NATO in unless we threaten force. The Europeans are worried about your reaction if NATO tries to act without going to the Security Council, but I can't entrust this to the council, because Milošević knows you will veto force, which means our threats won't be credible, which means there will be no political settlement, which means war in Kosovo. This is a real Catch-22."

For a minute Ivanov studied me carefully. Then he said, "Madeleine, if you do not mind, what exactly is a 'Catch-22'?"

I explained as best I could, then continued, "Igor, this is serious. I need to be able to tell the Europeans that NATO can threaten force in order to get a political settlement and that you will find a way to live with this."

He again thought for a moment before responding. "Russia will never agree to air strikes against the Serbs," he began. "That would be totally unacceptable. NATO has no right to attack a sovereign state." Then his tone softened, and he added, "We do, however, share your desire for a political settlement, and perhaps the threat of force is needed to achieve that. I do not see why we cannot try to work together."

It was the middle of the night, but after the opera I returned to the hotel and called the other Contact Group foreign ministers, knowing every word I said would be recorded for Russian authorities. If I were misrepresenting Moscow's position, I expected to find out in short order. I told my colleagues that Ivanov would not prevent us from moving ahead and that we must all join in presenting an ultimatum to Milošević.

For once, everything went according to plan. In London on January 29, I joined the Contact Group in announcing that peace talks would commence in Rambouillet, France, on February 6. Both sides would be asked to accept a plan that would give autonomy to the people of Kosovo and that would be implemented by a NATO peacekeeping force of roughly twenty-eight thousand. Kosovo's status would be reconsidered after three years, with the "will of the people" among the factors taken into account. With help from the international community, elections would be held and democratic institutions established. Our goal was to persuade both sides to say yes. Ivanov joined us in announcing the plan.

RAMBOUILLET IS A summer resort town of about twenty-five thousand people located amid forests southwest of Paris and famed for breeding world-class merino sheep. This distinction invited media speculation about whether negotiators would be able to guide the two delegations into a single pasture. The French had chosen to conduct the talks in a fourteenth-century château surrounded by manicured gardens and approached by a long, tree-lined gravel driveway. The castle itself is labyrinthine, with elaborate hallways, myriad staircases, and eclectically furnished rooms. Among its treasures is Marie Antoinette's bathtub, tucked away in a small room just off the kitchen on the ground floor.

Although Robin Cook and Hubert Védrine were the official cohosts, the day-to-day negotiations were to be coordinated by the troika of U.S. Ambassador Chris Hill, EU Representative Wolfgang Petritsch, and Russian Ambassador Boris Mayorski.

The sixteen-member Albanian delegation included the moderate political leader Ibrahim Rugova, respected newspaper editor Veton Surroi, the scholarly Rexhep Qosja, and representatives of other political parties, independents, and the KLA. Unexpectedly, the delegates chose as their head a lanky twenty-nine-year-old KLA commander, Hashim Thaçi, with whom we had had little contact. Thaçi's designation appeared to reflect the continued decline in the standing of Rugova, who responded to the affront by saying almost nothing. When one of our diplomats asked Rugova why he was so inert, he replied, "That's my style."

The Serb delegation, meanwhile, included some well-regarded lawyers along with a number of Muslim Slavs, Turks, and Roma chosen to show Milošević's supposed commitment to ethnic diversity. By the end of the first week our diplomats were reporting that the Serb delegation was not treating the negotiation seriously, while the Albanians—insisting on the right to hold an explicitly binding referendum on independence—were as "stubborn as dead mules." Chris Hill said it might help if I joined them earlier than originally planned.

I agreed and arrived at the talks with two main goals. The first was to convince the Serbs that a deal would be in their best interests, which I believed. The second was to persuade the Albanians to accept the framework agreement the Contact Group had proposed.

I began by sitting down in Paris with Milan Milutinović, the president of Serbia, acting as Milošević's surrogate. Milutinović had slicked-back silver hair, a beautifully tailored suit, and polished English. I told him the political settlement we had put forward would be good for his country. It would disarm the KLA, maintain Kosovo within Yugoslavia, and allow the army to continue patrolling the border. The presence of the NATO-led peacekeeping force would help, not hurt, by safeguarding the human rights of Kosovo's ethnic Serb minority. "The alternative," I argued, "would result in the equivalent of Chechnya within your borders. You will find yourselves at even greater odds with the international community and NATO. It doesn't have to be that way. You can move into Europe and the West by seizing this opportunity for peace."

Milutinović replied, "I agree with sixty to seventy percent of what you have said. We should focus on the future and try to solve the problems in Kosovo by political means. We have accepted the idea of autonomy and democracy, but we are stuck on your proposal to insert an outside military force. That would be a disaster. Instead, you should work with us to dissolve the KLA. You should put your troops in Albania to keep weapons from reaching the extremists." Milutinović acknowledged that Belgrade had made a mistake by denying autonomy to Kosovo for so many years.

"This approach may well have undermined moderate voices, but the U.S. is on the wrong track. You should work with us to combat terror and violence."

I replied, "The Serb army is the best recruiting weapon the KLA has." Milutinović corrected me with a frankness I didn't expect. "No," he said, "I believe that distinction belongs to the paramilitary police."

Moving to Rambouillet, I began the first of many meetings with the Albanian delegation. The term "motley" could have been invented for this group, which ranged from the enigmatic Rugova to the pragmatic Surroi and the problematic Thaçi. None had previously participated in a complex negotiation, certainly not on the world stage, and they still had many disagreements among themselves. I was pleased that they had accepted the help of a small team of outside advisors, including former U.S. Ambassador Morton Abramowitz, one of my longtime friends and a formidable human rights advocate.

My message to the Albanians was the mirror image of my arguments to the Serbs. "You are leaders. You have been chosen to represent your people. Think carefully before you condemn them to a future of fighting. The agreement we have proposed will give you self-government, NATO protection, economic help, the right to educate children in your own language, and the ability to exercise control over your lives. If you accept it, you will move toward a future of prosperity, democracy, and integration with Europe. Reject it, and the outcome will be a war you will lose, along with international support."

Several delegates sought my reassurance that the United States would indeed participate in a peace implementation force, that they would not have to rely solely on Europe. Rugova emphasized that the Kosovars had always equated security with independence and that their willingness to delay any move for independence during an interim period was a concession. All agreed on the eventual need for a referendum on independence. Otherwise, one said, "We will find ourselves locked inside Serbia forever."

After the general meeting, I met with Thaçi privately in a drafty basement room. Then and in subsequent meetings, I was struck by his youth and inexperience, which seemed to make him alternately stubborn and eager to please. With Rugova, I had felt I was addressing an eccentric academic colleague. Thaçi was more like a student with brilliant potential and a penchant for turning in his assignments late.

Under our agreement, the KLA would be forced to disarm and shun any independent military role. I knew this would not be easy for Thaçi to accept, even with NATO promising to fill the security vacuum. That first afternoon, I urged him to think of other military organizations that had transformed themselves into political parties. Thaçi replied that he expected the Albanian delegation to sign the agreement but it would take time for the guerrillas to adjust. Trying to lock in Thaçi's prediction, I said, "I am pleased by your commitment to sign." He said, "I believe an agreement can be reached, but it's not just up to me, or to the KLA, or even to the delegation. There might be difficulties."

As the second week of negotiations began and I returned to Washington, there remained two major obstacles. The first was the Albanians' desire for an explicit referendum on independence, which I felt we would be able to soften. The second was the Serb opposition to an international military presence in Kosovo, which we would have to confront. Obviously the Serb position would not change unless Milošević decided to change it. So I called Belgrade.

During our twenty-minute conversation, I told Milošević the negotiations were making progress and that a settlement would improve relations between our two countries and help Serbia move ahead economically. However, this would only happen if he acceded to the peacekeeping force.

The Serb dictator assured me of his desire for peace, and of his commitment to a "multiethnic, multinational, multireligious Kosovo." He pointed out that the Serb delegation in Rambouillet included people from seven different nationalities. "It is," he said, "the Albanians who want a separatist state. That should not be the solution at the end of the twentieth century."

I replied, "Mr. President, I am pleased to hear you embrace the multiethnic ideal. It's about time. The agreement we have proposed includes protections for minority rights and for the Albanians who make up ninety percent of the population of Kosovo. I can assure you the agreement is very modern."

But Milošević apparently had conducted his own census. "With due respect, Madam Secretary, ethnic Albanians are only about eight hundred thousand of the one and a half million people in Kosovo. There are hundreds of thousands of Serbs and Montenegrins and gypsies and Turks. In Croatia the United States supported the ethnic cleansing of Serbs. I hope you're not trying to chase Serbs out of Kosovo."

"Mr. President," I said, "I know there are non-Albanians in Kosovo, and you know I have tried to help Serbs return to their homes in Croatia. But I don't want to argue. Time is short. I understand it might be hard for you to explain letting a NATO force into Kosovo, but we will do all we can to make it easier. I would like you to talk to Chris Hill, who can fully explain our proposal. After that, we can negotiate your specific concerns."

Milošević agreed to see Hill, and the call ended. I looked at the phone in disbelief. Milošević's assertions had sparked in me a childhood memory. At school in England when I was six or seven years old, we had played games in which the whole student body had been divided Harry Potter–like into teams that earned points doing various activities. When I first earned points for my team, I reported it to my father, who was extremely pleased. Wanting to elicit the reaction again, I began to make up exploits for which I was awarded more points, including, as I remember, pulling the teacher out of the rosebushes. Pretty soon I had racked up so many imaginary points, I decided to invent a special award. I came home saying I had won the "Egyptian Cup." My parents wanted me to bring it home, which I obviously couldn't do. Instead I invented a whole new set of lies about how awful everyone was to me. "They even make me sit on needles!" I exclaimed. My ever-protective mother insisted on going to my school to find out what was happening to her poor child. The whole truth came out and I was quite properly punished. In later years, whenever a story I was telling seemed at odds with the truth, my parents only had to say "Egyptian Cup" and I stopped.

I could have said "Egyptian Cup" to Milošević. According to him, the number of Albanians in Kosovo was being exaggerated by over 50 percent, and he himself was both a champion of ethnic tolerance and a twenty-first-century thinker. Our effort to budge him out of his parallel universe continued through the week. When I phoned him again on Thursday, he told me, "The critical issue for us is that we cannot have a solution that causes non-Albanians to flee. Kosovo has been the bulwark of the Christian West against Islam for five hundred years." So much for twenty-first-century thought.

Although I got little from Milošević directly, the Serb delegation did finally reply to the political sections of the draft. This encouraged us, but not the Albanians, who watched nervously as Contact Group lawyers began spending long hours with the Serbs.

During the week I called Thaçi, who said he wished more of the Albanian suggestions were being accepted. Overall, however, he remained optimistic. Returning to France, on Saturday morning I met briefly with the Albanian delegation both individually and collectively. The Kosovars said they would endorse the framework agreement when the two sides met with Contact Group foreign ministers that afternoon. Since the Serbs had still not addressed the security issues, the Kosovars had a golden opportunity to isolate Milošević. I fully expected them to seize it. Then the meeting took place.

The room was crowded and small. The foreign ministers sat together like a panel of judges, on one side of a long wooden table. From the start the session had an inquisitional feeling. By the end, it definitely did. The leaders of the Albanian delegation settled across from us. Thaçi, looking ill at ease, occupied the center chair.

The atmosphere was tense as we sat adjusting our headphones. There was really only one question to ask, and that is whether the Albanians would accept the framework. They had promised to answer affirmatively, but when the moment came, Thaçi did not give a direct reply. This created an opening for Italian Foreign Minister Lamberto Dini, who had always been highly critical of the KLA. He pressed Thaçi not only to accept the framework but also to renounce support for a referendum on independence. This was unfair. The proposal we had developed required the Kosovars to delay, but not abandon, their aspirations for independence. Again and again Dini pushed Thaçi to answer yes or no to what for Thaçi was a no-win proposition. As a result, Thaçi hemmed and hawed, failing to embrace the framework or give a straight answer. His fellow delegates—Surroi, Rugova, and Qosja—sat there like stumps, Surroi because he didn't think it his place to speak, Rugova because it was his "style," and Qosja because he thought Thaçi was doing the right thing.

I took off my headphones and slammed them on the table. The Albanians had told us that they would agree to the framework, and in response to my questions later, they did. But the damage had been done. The position of the Kosovars was murky at best. For the moment Milošević was off the hook.

Saturday was supposed to have been the last day of talks, but now we agreed to three more. The text was far from finished, and we needed time to change votes. Thaçi was not the only member of his delegation who had reservations. Because of the time we had spent during the week trying to engage the Serbs, a majority of the Albanians had become uncomfortable. They were listening to people from the outside who had told them not to trust the Europeans or us. They worried that the language they were being asked to accept would prove a permanent barrier to independence. They were also reluctant to disarm. It didn't help that the French unaccountably refused to let NATO officers into the château to brief them on the specifics of our military plan. Instead the briefing was conducted by a Contact Group lawyer, accompanied by a U.S. colonel who had managed to smuggle his uniform into the castle.

Making full use of the little time we had, we now made a concerted effort to reassure the Albanians, going over the full text with them so that they knew exactly what they were being asked to approve. We made clear the agreement would not prevent them from holding a referendum, although that wouldn't be the sole criterion in determining Kosovo's future status. Flying in from Brussels, General Clark met the Albanians at an air base outside Rambouillet to clarify NATO's commitment to protect Kosovars once an agreement was reached. We encouraged the government of Albania and prominent ethnic Albanians from around the world to communicate their support. And I beat the hell out of the delegation verbally.

The result was progress. When we started on Saturday night, nine members had voted no. By Monday, only Thaçi was still opposed. He presented a special problem because he was so difficult to engage on the specifics. It had become obvious that his indecisiveness wasn't the result of ideology or pressure from other delegates. He was watching his back. The KLA was not monolithic. A power struggle was going on involving other KLA commanders and the shadowy outside figures who provided the guerrilla army with money and guns. That explained the constant cell phone conversations engaged in by Thaçi and his aides. The KLA leader had seen Jamie Rubin denouncing Milošević on television, and the two had struck up a friendship. Now Thaçi told Jamie that he feared for his life.

After the fiasco on Saturday, I tried a variety of tactics. First I told Thaçi what a great potential leader he was. When that didn't work, I said we were disappointed in him, that if he thought we would bomb the Serbs even if the Albanians rejected the agreement, he was wrong. We could never get NATO support for that. "On the other hand," I said, "if you say yes and the Serbs say no, NATO will strike and go on striking until the Serb forces are out and NATO can go in. You will have security. And you will be able to govern yourselves."

Thaçi replied that the sole purpose of the KLA had been to fight for independence, and it was very hard to give that up. I said, "You don't have to, but you have to be realistic. This agreement is for three years. We know Milošević is the problem. But the situation could look a lot different in three years. This is your chance. Grab it, because you may never have another." Although clearly abashed and almost tearful, Thaçi would not say yes.

Monday was absolutely going to be the last full day. The Contact Group had set a drop-deadline of 3 P.M. Tuesday. Having had wall-to-wall meetings all weekend, I was hyper-irritated. Both delegations were being impossible. Everyone seemed to have become spoiled by the great French food. At one meal someone complained, "What happened to the cheese course?" I was ready to blow my stack.

All afternoon I thought about how we could persuade Thaçi. I had called everybody else I could think of who might influence the KLA leader, so finally, I decided to try Adem Demaçi. Demaçi was a longtime Kosovar nationalist who was among those pressuring Thaçi to take the hardest possible line. Reaching him in Slovenia, I asked him to encourage Thaçi to support our proposal.

Demaçi replied that he couldn't agree to anything without seeing me in person; he suggested I come to Slovenia for a talk. I said, "Look, the parties have been negotiating for two weeks. The deadline is hours away. I can meet you in the future, but now you should convey your agreement to Thaçi. Your failure will haunt you in days to come as ordinary Albanians lie dying."

Demaçi said, "We appreciate your efforts but will not be rushed. If it is necessary for thirty thousand Albanians to die, so be it, but we cannot give up our weapons in return for promises. We will never give up the dream to be free."

I said, "My proposal wouldn't make you give up your dream. Take this opportunity for peace. Tell Thaçi the agreement has your support."

Demaçi said, "It is not possible." I hung up in disgust. It was one of the more bloodcurdling conversations I ever had.

Notwithstanding Demaçi, our pressure ultimately paid off. We hadn't been the only ones frustrated by Thaçi. The rest of the Albanian delegation was becoming convinced that the agreement was favorable and would be supported by most Kosovars. For days we had been talking about the idea that the Albanians would not actually sign the agreement, just promise to do so. This approach had the advantage of enabling us to squeeze the Serbs while keeping the door open for them to sign. It also allowed the nervous Kosovar delegation time to be sure they had their constituents behind them.

As the Tuesday 3 P.M. deadline approached, Thaçi was still a problem, but then Veton Surroi, the "secretary" of the Albanian delegation, took matters into his own hands, proposing a short statement saying that the delegation had approved the agreement and would sign it in two weeks, after first explaining its terms to the people of Kosovo. As Surroi and others worked, there was intense wrangling with Thaçi over the statement's text, both in the English and Albanian versions. Finally Surroi said they could finish the job only if Thaçi were persuaded to leave the room for a few minutes. Our lawyer, Jim O'Brien, figured the best way to lure Thaçi away was to tell him Jamie Rubin needed to see him. So Jim and Thaçi went looking for Jamie, whom they couldn't find because he was briefing the press.

Finally Jamie arrived and went off with Thaçi, seeking to distract him with talk of movies and Hollywood. But after they had gone only a short way, Surroi said he had finished the statement and now needed Thaçi back. So Jim grabbed Thaçi and steered him toward the office, while Jamie complained, "Hey, I barely lit my cigarette." Once in the office, Thaçi tried again to modify the text, but Surroi would have none of it. The statement, signed by Surroi, was delivered to the Contact Group foreign ministers, and Jamie announced it publicly.

Despite the bumps and setbacks, we left Rambouillet with much of what we had sought. We now had a more or less united Albanian delegation and a clear vision of what a democratic Kosovo would look like. The Albanians had argued and hesitated, but they had chosen peace. Thaçi spent the next two weeks selling the Rambouillet agreement to KLA commanders and cadres. He resurfaced shortly before the negotiations were to resume in France on March 15 and accompanied the delegation to Paris. There they officially signed the eighty-two-page agreement in a five-minute ceremony boycotted both by the Yugoslav delegation and the Russian negotiator.

What would Milošević do now? We had told him that we were prepared to discuss specific Serb concerns. Although we could not compromise on the principle of a NATO-led peacekeeping force, we would work with him on how to describe the mission. We had proposed to negotiate an agreement to show that NATO would be in Yugoslavia by invitation, not invasion; we even suggested that the Serbs characterize the NATO troops as "anti-terrorist," since part of its job would be to make the KLA disarm.

Some revisionists have suggested that we missed signals from Belgrade that Milošević was willing to sign an agreement. That is nonsense. If the Serbs had been interested in negotiating seriously, they could have said so to any of the foreign visitors who poured through Belgrade in early March. But the message received by Russian, Greek, EU, American, and NATO officials alike was the same. "No," said the Serbs, "we will have nothing to do with an outside military force. We will deal with the terrorist threat in our own way. And it will not take long." In mid March, Ivanov went to Yugoslavia and found "only idiots who are ready to go to war."

For weeks, while conducting diplomacy in Europe, we had been working continuously on Capitol Hill. Although we had strong backing from such internationalist Senators as Joe Biden and Richard Lugar, there were many in both parties critical of the course we had set. Some questioned the legal basis for possible NATO air strikes. Others thought fighting over Kosovo would prove a quagmire, like Vietnam. A few said that Milošević hadn't yet been sufficiently vicious. Senator Donald Nickles of Oklahoma declared, "I don't think we should begin bombing unless and until the Serbs really begin a very significant massacre."

Through days of hearings, meetings, briefings, and phone calls, ultimately we prevailed. Shortly before the Rambouillet signing ceremony in mid March, the House of Representatives voted 219–191 to support the President's plan to send troops to implement a peace agreement, if one were reached. Although the vote was predictably partisan, we did receive support from Speaker Dennis Hastert and respected Republicans such as Illinois Representative Henry Hyde. As the time for diplomacy ran out, the Senate voted 58–41 to authorize the President to support NATO bombing. Few legislators were enthusiastic about the prospects, but the majority agreed that other options were even less acceptable.

We warned Milošević repeatedly not to launch an offensive, but we could see he was preparing one. Belgrade had assembled security forces in Kosovo that were approximately 50 percent larger than those used in the 1998 attacks. His negotiators turned up in Paris with a completely gutted version of the Contact Group agreement, beginning with the word "peace" crossed out. It is possible Milošević thought that we were bluffing or that the Russians would find a way to stymie NATO. Maybe he relied on bad advice about how quickly a fight for Kosovo could be won. Perhaps he thought his hold on power would be stronger if he stuck to the role of victim. In any event, he had made his choice. We would have to make ours.

On March 19, our foreign policy team met with the President to review our options. There were no good ones. George Tenet reported that the Serb offensive had already begun and had succeeded in forcing many KLA units to withdraw. The number of refugees and displaced persons was rising rapidly. The military's assessment was equally grim. Civilians in Kosovo were highly vulnerable to Serb attacks. At least at the outset, NATO air strikes could not help them. There was a risk that many innocent people would be hurt or killed. A NATO bombing campaign directed at Milošević's sources of power would weaken him, but we didn't know how long he would hold out.

As I listened, I watched the President. His eyes were as grim as I felt. On the eve of its fiftieth anniversary, NATO was on the verge of combat for only the second time in its history, the first having been in Bosnia. Our purpose was to win support for an agreement that didn't reflect the ultimate goals of either Albanians or Serbs. Victory would mean a long-term military commitment to maintain order in a very dangerous neighborhood, but backing down was unthinkable. Our decision was part of a much larger choice between autocracy and democracy and between bigotry and tolerance in the heart of Europe. I said, "Look, let's remember the purpose of using force is to stop Milošević-style thuggery once and for all. There's no guarantee it will succeed, but the alternatives are worse. If we don't respond now, we'll have to respond later, perhaps in Macedonia, maybe in Bosnia. Milošević has picked this fight. We can't allow him to win." The President agreed, saying publicly, "In dealing with aggressors in the Balkans, hesitation is a license to kill."

We sent Dick Holbrooke to Belgrade in one last effort to persuade Milošević to halt his offensive. Those talks yielded nothing except more delaying tactics, so I directed Holbrooke to come home. As the President's words reflected, we could not afford to wait any longer. By launching his offensive, Milošević had forced our hand; we had to act, even though the timing was awkward. Russian Prime Minister Primakov was en route to the United States for a visit. When Al Gore informed him by phone that NATO bombing was about to begin, a furious Primakov ordered his plane to reverse course and fly back to Moscow.

A few hours later, on the evening of March 23, NATO Secretary General Solana ordered General Wes Clark to initiate air operations.

It was after midnight. I had gone home exhausted, then stayed up late watching the television news reports; I was almost asleep when the phone rang. It was the President. He said, "We're doing the right thing here. We've got a long way to go, and this is not going to be over quickly, but I really think we explored every alternative." Together we recounted the efforts we had made to find a diplomatic solution, including the fifteen trips I had made to Europe to consult with allies during the previous year. We talked about our responsibilities to the Kosovars and especially to our own armed forces. Sending our young men and women into battle is the hardest decision any President can make. Whenever I visited American troops, I made it a point to try to establish eye contact, so that I would always be able to summon their faces to mind. No American leader should ever commit to military action before fully weighing the human costs. In this case, we had. The President said again, "I think we are doing the right thing." "Yes, Mr. President," I said, "we are."

TWENTY-FIVE

The Alliance Prevails

D URING THE FIRST DAYS of fighting, just about everything went wrong. Terrible weather interrupted and slowed the pace of our air strikes. NATO commanders had planned to demolish Yugoslav air defenses before sending aircraft against Serb armor and artillery pouring into Kosovo, but Milošević didn't activate his defenses in a way that would allow us to identify them. An American stealth fighter crashed. For almost a week, NATO's Operation Allied Force remained in first gear, while Milošević's security forces went on a calculated rampage.

The first night, CNN's Larry King asked me whether we were going to continue the strikes for "three, four days. . . . Is there a plan?" Wary of the criticism that Kosovo might turn out to be another Vietnam, I said I couldn't give details but "it's going to be a sustained attack, and it's not something that's going to go on for an overly long time." The next day, in response to a similar question from PBS' Jim Lehrer, I said we could expect the bombing to be over in a "relatively short period of time."

It was an extremely short time before I wished I had those words back. My answers—shorn of the modifier "relatively"—were cited on innumerable occasions as evidence that I was naïve about the risks inherent in NATO's use of force. That was a bum rap. It's true I had often argued that force was the only language Milošević understood, but I had not tried to convince anyone he was a fast learner. That's why I strongly objected to a French proposal, prior to the bombing, to schedule a pause in strikes after just a few days. I also phoned the UN high commissioner for refugees to suggest issuing a special appeal for help in advance of the flood of refugees from Kosovo that we anticipated, a suggestion that was turned down.

Before NATO bombing began, the Serb offensive had already driven a hundred thousand Kosovars from their homes. This figure grew rapidly in subsequent days. Milošević appeared to have four main goals: exterminate the KLA, reengineer Kosovo's ethnic balance on a permanent basis, frighten into submission the Albanians who remained in Kosovo, and create a destabilizing humanitarian crisis that would preoccupy the international community and divide the region.

These objectives were not unexpected, but we had underestimated the speed, scale, and ferocity of the Serbs' terror campaign. Homes in hundreds of villages were burned. Scholars, journalists, and political leaders who had advocated independence were tracked down and killed. Tens of thousands of people were made to board trains, which were then sealed from the outside and sent to the Albanian border. Thousands of others were herded along the same route by car or on foot. Serb security forces stripped the departing Kosovars of birth certificates, driver's licenses, car registrations, and other proof of identification. Their message to the Albanians was clear: "You must leave and we will not let you back."

On the fifth day I talked to Hashim Thaçi, who was still in Kosovo. He reported Pristina was like "a dead city" and listed half a dozen areas where the security forces were killing people. He said that sixty thousand Albanians had fled the northern city of Mitrovica and that, overall, half a million Kosovars were homeless. Thaçi appealed to us to begin airdrops of humanitarian supplies, but the Pentagon said this was not feasible because our planes, to avoid the risk of antiaircraft fire, had to fly too high.

At the worst point of the exodus, four thousand refugees—more accurately, deportees—were crossing the border into neighboring Albania or Macedonia every hour. The horrors we were witnessing spurred changes in both our military tactics and our diplomacy. General Clark requested more planes and an expanded target list that would take the war to Milošević and apply pressure to his security forces. I worked around the clock to make sure the application of force would be backed by a united Alliance.

As usual, my instrument of choice was the telephone. The question was how best to use it. There were nineteen members of NATO. I couldn't call the other eighteen every day, so I began with just a few, but even this took too much time. The alternative, though obvious, was still something new in international diplomacy—the conference call. I initiated many such calls among a group that came to be known as the "Quint"—and which also included Robin Cook, Hubert Védrine, Lamberto Dini, and German Foreign Minister Joschka Fischer. Fischer was an unlikely and therefore especially compelling ally. As the leader of his country's Green Party, he was a committed pacifist. As a modern German, he also took the lessons of history seriously, and his assessment of Milošević was especially telling. In a phone call on March 30, he told me, "For ten years Milošević has been acting like the Nazis in the 1930s. First he blew up Yugoslavia, then Croatia, then Bosnia, and now Kosovo. How many people has he killed? How many rapes and refugees is he responsible for?" Angrily, Fischer dismissed a proposal made by the Vatican and others for a bombing pause, "There can be no pause for Christians at Easter while the killing of Muslims continues."

Saying that it was vital for NATO to regain the political initiative, Fischer proposed that we issue a statement of war aims, the draft text of which he had already prepared. I liked the idea and also his statement but was troubled by one omission. Fischer's draft failed to specify that NATO must lead the peace force. The German foreign minister said he thought we should leave open the possibility of UN leadership in order to attract support from Russia. I said if we were going to soften our language at all, we first needed something tangible from the Russians or Milošević in return. This wasn't the time to start giving up bargaining chips. Fischer consented to the change. The statement, soon endorsed by all NATO, would hold up with little alteration throughout the war. Before allied bombing would stop, Serb security forces must withdraw from Kosovo, a NATO-led force must be allowed to deploy, and refugees must be allowed to return home safely. "Serbs out, NATO in, refugees back," became our mantra.

The scope and viciousness of the blitzkrieglike assault on the population of Kosovo sparked fierce criticism not only of Milošević but also of NATO, President Clinton, and me. Many in the media simply ignored the fact that the Serbs had struck first. They argued that Milošević was killing because NATO was bombing, instead of the other way around. Commentators who had blasted us earlier for failing to stand up to Milošević blasted us now for the apparent consequences of doing so. Pentagon officials were quoted anonymously as having warned me that the result of our policy would be disaster. Columnist Arianna Huffington's observation was typical: "It is now time to trace the lineage of the humanitarian and strategic catastrophe in Serbia to Secretary of State Madeleine K. Albright."

My intimate association with Kosovo policy was shown most dramatically when *Time* put me on its cover wearing an air force leather jacket and talking into a cell phone, with an expression that would have scared most children to death. Inside was a balanced article by Walter Isaacson, but bearing the title, "Madeleine's War." The President took me aside and said I shouldn't worry. "If I'd read everything they wrote last year," he said, referring to the impeachment ordeal, "I'd never have survived." Both at that time and later, I was struck that the Kosovars themselves universally applauded NATO's decision to act. The war brought many traumas to the Albanians but also hope of a future free from Milošević's heavy-handed rule.

Every day during this period I read stories about how badly we had miscalculated. President Clinton and I were determined to prove Milošević had made the error. The President said to me, "We can't blink. No second-guessing, just keep your eye on what it will take to win." I wrote notes to myself about the importance of staying focused. As grim as the news seemed and as horrible as I felt, I believed we had made the right decision. The imperative now was to persevere.

The conflict in Kosovo was won during the first ten days of April, when the administration could have made bad choices but did not. Dismayed by the early setbacks, we examined the idea of arming the KLA but rejected it as too likely to split the Alliance. We looked at proposals for partitioning Kosovo but rejected them as a legal and security nightmare and a poor precedent for resolving ethnic disputes. We revisited the possibility of a bombing pause but rejected it as a sign of weakness. We thought about declaring Milošević's removal from power an explicit war aim but rejected that because we had no short-term way to bring it about.

Instead we concluded that the air campaign would succeed if we continued to make it faster, harder, and smarter. Along with the British, we pushed the Alliance to intensify bombing and further expand the circle of targets. We increased humanitarian assistance to Yugoslavia's neighbors and warned Milošević not to extend the war into Albania or Macedonia. We agreed among ourselves that Kosovo would have to become an international protectorate after the war, with Yugoslav sovereignty retained in name only.

Within the State Department, we also put together a long-term reconstruction plan for the entire Balkans region.[1] Our goal was to show that the conflict was not an isolated skirmish but part of a broader struggle between the forces of virulent nationalism and the proponents of integration and democracy. If the latter were to prevail, we needed to stop drifting from crisis to crisis and engineer a decisive shift. As models, we cited the Marshall Plan that helped Western Europe recover from World War II and the Support for East European Democracy (SEED) program that helped Central Europe find its footing after the Cold War. We proposed that America join with others in providing generous long-term assistance to the Balkans' struggling democracies. This initiative would foster cooperation among countries throughout the region and, by

1. This strategy was the brainchild of Policy Planning director Mort Halperin and one of his top deputies, Daniel Hamilton. Richard Schifter, our special advisor for the Southeast European Cooperative Initiative, was instrumental in its formulation and implementation.

promising aid to Belgrade only if a change in government occurred, create an additional incentive to dump Milošević.

At a White House meeting in early April, I raised the State Department proposal and waited for a reaction. Receiving none, I was disappointed, until toward the end of the meeting the President himself said, "I want to go back to the point Madeleine raised earlier, because I think it's exactly right." He quickly became our initiative's strongest advocate, backing our ideas with resources, mentioning the proposal in all his speeches, and citing it when explaining our strategy to Congress.

Throughout this period the rest of the world didn't stop, so there was plenty of other business to conduct. Chinese Premier Zhu Rongji came to Washington with a proposal for bringing his country into the World Trade Organization. The President-elect of Nigeria, Olusegun Obasanjo, sought our help in restoring democracy and prosperity to Africa's most populous nation. Libya finally handed over for trial the two suspects in the Pan Am 103 case. And in Israel Prime Minister Netanyahu was in the middle of an election campaign battling for his political life. There were days when I was happy to focus on different parts of the world, even the Middle East, but for most of the next two months, the center of my universe was Kosovo.

My conference calls to allies, which took place almost daily in early April, reflected trans-Atlantic cooperation at its most urgent and real. This was hands-on diplomacy of a type never before practiced, because never before had there been such a combination of modern technology and political will. The calls proved an indispensable tool for brainstorming and coordinating the Alliance's political strategy. Sometimes I called Cook and Fischer in advance to suggest that a proposal might be better received coming from one of them than from me. The main point we all agreed upon was that we should speak with one voice on Kosovo, whether dealing with our own publics, Russia, or Milošević. We could not allow others to exploit even subtle differences among us. This principle applied not only to the Quint calls but also to those I regularly made to NATO Secretary General Solana and other Allied foreign ministers such as Lloyd Axworthy of Canada and Jozias van Aartsen of the Netherlands.[2]

---

2. These calls took place at all times of the day and night and on weekends. They were mostly business, but there were some lighter moments, especially during the few hours on a Saturday or Sunday when we had to be reached outside our offices. I might be called to the phone while standing in a dressing room trying on a new outfit. Robin Cook might be reached in Scotland while meeting with his constituents or between horse races at the local steeplechase course. With Védrine we never knew for sure because, whenever he spoke, his interpreter first got our attention by saying, "Paris wants to speak." Once we were startled

As the war entered its third week, the question on all our minds was, how can we bring this conflict to an end based on the objectives we have set? Certainly there was no shortage of proposals for settling on a lesser basis. Milošević began offering half-baked ideas almost as soon as the fighting began. Well-meaning members of Congress trooped across the Atlantic to meet with their Russian counterparts and came back with ill-conceived initiatives. Ukraine appointed a special envoy for Kosovo and announced its own peace plan. UN Secretary General Annan announced plans to appoint not one but two special envoys for Kosovo. The Czechs and Greeks were also floating ideas with Greek Foreign Minister George Papandreou making a creative behind-the-scenes effort to bring the violence on both sides to an end.

Seeing Russia as the key to an acceptable outcome, I favored a "double magnet" approach that first brought Russia closer to NATO's position, then Belgrade closer to Russia. Ideally, we could negotiate an arrangement based on the model used in Bosnia, with the Security Council authorizing, NATO leading, and Russia participating in a peacekeeping operation. This was a good concept but hard to act upon because the Russians were so angry.

We talked to them through many channels, but whether it was Clinton-Yeltsin, Gore-Primakov, or Ivanov and I, the Russian message to us was the same, even if the decibel levels varied: we had screwed up bigtime. Milošević, we were told, would never capitulate. The bombing had united the Serbs and made their leader a hero. It had also generated fiercely anti-American and anti-NATO feelings.

The Russians warned us that some of their military units were eager to fight on Serbia's side and that pressure was building for a pan-Slavic alliance among Russia, Yugoslavia, and Belarus. Russian nationalists and Communists were exploiting Kosovo for political purposes, at the same time that Yeltsin's opponents in the Duma were trying to impeach him on a grab bag of unrelated charges. Wary of appearing weak, Yeltsin threatened to retarget Russia's nuclear weapons toward NATO and accused the Alliance of bringing the world to the brink of global conflict.

In response, I began an almost continuous dialogue with Ivanov, telling him that I hoped our differences over Kosovo would not jeopardize cooperation on other matters. He said there was no avoiding it. "Russia cannot," he said, "sit around and watch NATO destroy a sovereign nation."

---

when Joschka Fischer began yelling in the midst of our call. "Joschka," we all said at once, "what's happening? Are you all right?" Fischer came back on the line. "No, I'm not all right. I'm watching the German-British football match and the English just scored."

The principle on which we had the sharpest differences concerned the need for an international peacekeeping force once the bombing stopped. Ivanov said he saw no point in considering the concept, because Milošević would not accept it and Yeltsin's government couldn't be seen as taking NATO's side. The Serbs, he said, could not be forced to accept foreign soldiers on their soil. I argued that Russia owed it to herself to do more than convey Milošević's positions. If Russia accepted the principle that refugees should be able to return, it should understand the reality that refugees would not dare to return without an effective international force to protect them. If the war dragged on and the refugees didn't go home, the Albanians would grow more extreme. It was not in Russia's interest to see a guerrilla army take root in Europe.

Throughout this dialogue, the Russians were frustrated by the weak hand they had to play. Their military options were few, their dependence on the West was growing, their domestic politics were toxic, and their putative client in Belgrade was a ruthless dictator. Every day of NATO bombing was a bad day for Yeltsin, whom hard-liners blamed for cozying up to America and getting nothing in return. Yeltsin knew that to stop the bombing he had to make a deal with us, but he did not like what we were offering. So the Russians approached our negotiations with pained ambivalence; their position would lurch toward ours, then settle in concrete for days or weeks, before lurching forward again.

By MID APRIL 1999, we had been fighting for four weeks. Thankfully, the weather had finally improved and so did the effectiveness of NATO air strikes; still, the conventional wisdom, peddled by armchair generals the world over, was that air strikes alone would not be enough. I disagreed but felt we should prepare for the possibility that the conventional wisdom might for once be right.

The previous year, NATO planners had estimated that a ground invasion of Kosovo would require more than a hundred thousand troops. As a civilian I did not feel I could challenge these estimates, but I did try to discuss with my administration colleagues the political assumptions that produced them. The British were raising the same issues. What if the air campaign succeeded in virtually immobilizing the Serb forces, but Milošević still refused to surrender? Would we allow the stalemate to go on indefinitely, or could we send in a moderately sized ground force? Our troops would hardly be entering hostile territory. The vast majority of Kosovars would cheer us on. The weeks of bombing had surely had an impact on the willingness of Milošević's troops to fight. We had already agreed that our forces could enter Kosovo in a "permissive" environment. British Prime Minister Tony Blair was suggesting that we should be prepared to move when the situation became "semi-permissive." This would allow us to avoid an endless bombing campaign and show Milošević that we intended to do whatever was necessary to win.

General Shelton responded by bluntly dismissing the idea that a military environment could be "semi-permissive." "You do not," he said, "get semi-shot." If hostile forces were present, the Pentagon must assume that they would act in a hostile manner. It would be irresponsible not to plan accordingly. That meant a huge force would be required and most of it, at the outset, would have to be American. Shelton said the Joint Chiefs could begin planning for a ground option, but it would take weeks and there was no chance of having troops in the field before mid July.

Secretary Cohen did not buy the "semi-permissive" concept either. He agreed nevertheless that both the Defense Department and NATO should draw up plans for a ground campaign. Referring to the criticism we were receiving from the press and on Capitol Hill, he said, "Our current position is untenable." The President also agreed, and he expressed regret at the wording of a statement included in his speech on the war's first day that had seemed to rule out the use of ground forces. The President was never convinced ground troops would be necessary, but he knew we could not continue to exclude the possibility. After all, if the future of Kosovo were important enough to fight for in the air, it was hard to say it was not worth defending on land.

The military logic of planning for a ground war was clear, but there was also diplomatic logic in deciding to do so before the NATO summit began in Washington on April 23. The Alliance must appear united on its fiftieth anniversary, but we were not united. As I knew from my Quint calls, the British favored the ground option, Germany and Italy were against, and the French would support it only in the unlikely event that it was authorized by the Security Council. We did not want to spend the summit squabbling about ground troops. What saved us in the end was largely the relationship between President Clinton and Prime Minister Blair.

On the eve of the summit, Blair came to the White House for a late-night meeting. The President hosted and I was there along with Sandy Berger and a small number of British officials. Blair was Churchillian in expressing determination to prevail on Kosovo, although that is where the resemblance ended. Blair's youthful demeanor and approachable manner made it hard not to call him "Tony," instead of the appropriate "Mr. Prime Minister." Blair had consciously carved out a role for himself as the leader who could explain America to Europe and the rest of Europe to America, bridging differences between the two. By age and disposition, he seemed the perfect match for President Clinton, with whom he could talk for hours about "Third Way" politics, world history, and their respective families. During our discussion that evening, the issue of Kosovo and ground forces hung in the air. Blair clearly had something he wanted to say to the President in private but was too polite to throw the rest of us out. Finally he asked the President where the W.C. was. Picking up on the signal, Clinton volunteered to show him. The two did not reappear for more than half an hour.

Whatever they discussed, the NATO summit was spared a split. Blair did not press his case for a firm commitment to a ground campaign. Both leaders emphasized unity in all their public statements. With U.S. support, NATO began planning for the possibility that air strikes would not be enough.

Originally, the Alliance summit was to have been a glitzy gala with a host of glamorous parties. Against the backdrop of a bleeding Kosovo there could be no such celebration. This was, however, still the largest gathering of heads of state ever held in Washington, D.C. Representatives were there not only from the Alliance itself but also from its partnership institutions, including every republic in the former Soviet Union except Russia.

On the summit's opening day, Generals Clark and Naumann argued that intensifying the air campaign and increasing economic pressure on Belgrade could cause Milošević to accede to our terms. There were no dissenters from the basic proposition that the Alliance had to stand together, turn up the heat on Milošević, and win. We also held a meeting with Ukraine and reached out to other non-NATO countries from Albania to Uzbekistan by holding special sessions on the Balkans and the Caucasus. NATO thereby demonstrated its intention to work closely with democratic forces everywhere. In return, the Alliance gained expressions of support from nations that once took instructions from Moscow but were now free to make their own judgments.

On the summit's last day, Boris Yeltsin called the President to suggest that Vice-President Gore and former Russian Prime Minister Viktor Chernomyrdin work together to find a solution to Kosovo. On May 3, Chernomyrdin arrived in Washington. He brought with him a letter from Yeltsin proposing a cease-fire, during which Kofi Annan and Chernomyrdin would journey to Belgrade to negotiate a settlement. That agreement would then be implemented by the UN. President Clinton replied that we would not allow the UN to negotiate on behalf of NATO.

The next morning, at a breakfast meeting in Vice-President Gore's residence, Chernomyrdin said that he was willing to keep pushing Belgrade but that Russia didn't want to do so too visibly or alone. Milošević, he said, was too stubborn and emotional ever to give in to NATO. We needed a third party involved, hence Moscow's proposal to send the UN Secretary General to Belgrade. It would be less humiliating for Milošević to negotiate with someone of stature who was also neutral. The idea made some sense but, as President Clinton had said, Milošević couldn't simply negotiate with the UN. We needed a different partner than Kofi Annan, so I suggested President Ahtisaari. Immediately Chernomyrdin rapped his hand on the table and smiled. "That is just the man."

President Martti Ahtisaari of Finland was indeed "just the man"—a widely respected diplomat, with UN experience, from a country that was historically neutral. The previous month we had proposed Ahtisaari as one of two UN envoys on Kosovo, but he had declined because he didn't want another full-time position. He did, however, agree to work with Chernomyrdin on what Ahtisaari presciently predicted would be a month-long effort to end the war.

On Friday, May 7, I had just finished a meeting with Kofi Annan when my executive assistant Alex Wolff told me that I had better sit down. "We don't know for sure," he said, "but CNN is reporting that NATO has bombed the Chinese embassy in Belgrade." We soon learned that B2 bombers really had dropped bombs on a building our pilots had thought was a Yugoslav weapons acquisition agency. Tragically, the targeters had confused the agency with a similarly shaped building nearby—the Chinese embassy. The fateful error caused the death of three Chinese and injured twenty. The fact that the embassy had been hit several times prompted Beijing to accuse us of a deliberate attack. In this case NATO's lofty military reputation worked against us, because the Chinese found it hard to believe we could make such a mistake.

The day after the bombing, I had just gotten into bed after attending the wedding of one of my top press aides, Kitty Bartels. Watching the news, I saw pictures of our ambassador in Beijing, James Sasser, peering from a shattered window at a mob of Chinese students throwing rocks and shouting. Especially after the tragedy in Kenya and Tanzania, I was extremely concerned about the safety of our people. Climbing out of bed, I tried urgently to call Foreign Minister Tang Jiaxun in China. "He is not available," I was told. So I decided I would do what I could from a distance to cool things down. I called the Vice-Chairman of the Joint Chiefs, General Joseph Ralston, and invited him to put on his uniform and join me in paying a midnight visit to the Chinese ambassador. Tom

Pickering and the NSC's Kenneth Lieberthal completed our delegation.

I had known Ambassador Li Zhaoxing from the days when we had both served at the UN. I told him the bombing had been a terrible accident and that we were extremely sorry. I said I knew what it was like to have colleagues killed and hoped he would convey my condolences to the families of those who had died or been injured. I also said I was worried about the safety of American diplomats in Beijing; it was vital the demonstrations not grow more violent.

Although Li and I had developed a good relationship, he was now very stern; he demanded I make a formal apology on Chinese television. Suddenly cameras materialized. I made a brief statement. When our delegation tried to leave, we ran into a group of Chinese "journalists" who blocked the hallway, asking us pointedly why we had killed their colleagues. My security detail hadn't been allowed inside, so we were alone and worried we would be trapped. Fortunately, General Ralston and Tom Pickering are good people to have with you in such circumstances—not only cool-headed but big. As they held our "journalist" friends back, we found our way to a side exit and into the street.

The bombing of the Chinese embassy temporarily shifted world attention away from Milošević's intentional cruelty and toward our unintentional mistakes. Milošević tried to exploit the moment diplomatically by announcing plans to pull a token number of his troops out of Kosovo. The Russians heightened the pressure by sending Chernomyrdin to China, where he labeled our bombing an "act of aggression." The wild card in all this was the political circus going on in Moscow. On the day Chernomyrdin went to Beijing, Yeltsin fired Primakov as prime minister. A week passed before Foreign Minister Ivanov was told he still had his job. When I called, he told me Yeltsin was berating the foreign ministry for failing to stop NATO bombing. Publicly, Yeltsin threatened to abandon diplomatic efforts if the air strikes did not halt soon.

The tragedy involving China and the political machinations in Moscow slowed the diplomatic momentum we had built up. We might have slid backward had the Russians been able to find a formula for dividing NATO, but in Germany Joschka Fischer stoutly defended the Alliance's policies in front of a Green Party convention—despite taking a red paint bomb to the head. Italy's prime minister called for a bombing pause but at the same time allowed his nation's aircraft to continue participating in NATO missions. I urged my colleagues to have patience and let the Chernomyrdin-Ahtisaari channel work. As long as the allies stayed together, time was on our side. We had reports that significant numbers of Serb soldiers were deserting. There were antiwar demonstrations in

Belgrade. Air strikes were not uniting people behind Milošević as it had appeared earlier they might; instead they had increased the desire of average Serbs for peace.

We also knew that the KLA was beginning to mount a modest comeback. NATO bombing had made it hard for Yugoslav forces to move about with heavy equipment or in large numbers. Now the guerrilla fighters adopted new military tactics aimed at seizing arms and ammunition from isolated posts. They also took advantage of sagging Serb morale to purchase arms directly from their adversaries, some Serbs apparently concluding that, even if they couldn't win the war, they could at least make a profit.

As the stalemate continued, I felt we were in a race in which both runners were tiring; the question was whose legs would buckle first. Surely there was a limit to the damage the Yugoslav government could endure without yielding, but it was unclear whether that limit would be reached before the center of gravity within NATO shifted toward compromise. The winning side would inevitably be the one showing the greatest will. Thus we began debating with renewed energy the need for a ground invasion. There were obvious risks, but it was sobering to sit through meetings in May in which "winterizing refugee camps" headed the agenda.

NATO never had to execute a ground campaign, but we did decide to double the number of troops in Macedonia and Albania. Ostensibly these troops would prepare to serve in the Kosovo peacekeeping mission, which would only be deployed after the war. However, as we wanted Milošević to realize, the troops could also form the core of a ground combat force if that were needed.

On May 27, the war crimes tribunal announced the indictment of Milošević, Milutinović, and three other Serb leaders for crimes against humanity. There were those who were nervous about Milošević's indictment, feeling that it would mean we couldn't negotiate with him. I was not in that camp. I was gratified by the indictments, because their message was the same one NATO had been sending for two months: those who perpetrate ethnic cleansing will end up failing to gain what they seek and losing what they have. The immediate question was whether the indictments would make Milošević less or more likely to accept NATO's terms.

The day after the tribunal's action, Chernomyrdin and Milošević, meeting in Belgrade for ten hours, produced a tantalizing joint statement declaring that the UN Security Council should pass a resolution regarding Kosovo "in line with the UN Charter." What did that mean? I called Ivanov, who refused to explain what, if anything, had changed. Instead he said that Russia was requesting that Chancellor Schröder, as head of the EU, invite Chernomyrdin, Ahtisaari, and a U.S. representative to Bonn for a decisive meeting. We sent Strobe Talbott.

On June 1, Talbott reported that after several meetings the Russian position was still not satisfactory. They hadn't yet accepted the need for all Yugoslav security forces to withdraw, and they wanted Russian peacekeepers to have their own sector inside postwar Kosovo. Sandy and I told Strobe to hold the line on the first point, and overnight Moscow yielded. On the second we agreed that this was an issue for the Alliance and Russia to work out; it didn't involve Milošević.

At last NATO and Russia had a common view. The resulting document, listing the conditions Milošević would have to meet to end the bombing, was relayed to Belgrade. This was the magnet we had wanted and Milošević feared. Convinced by Chernomyrdin and Ahtisaari that he would not get a better offer, and that the Russians would no longer back him, the Serb leader accepted the deal and asked his parliament to approve it. Around dawn on June 3, phones began ringing all over Washington and at varying times of the day in NATO capitals from Ottawa to Athens. The combatants had reached the finish line.

In the Quint calls during the war, I had summarized how the United States saw the various dimensions of international activity fitting together. Now we had to choreograph the next steps. Once the fighting stopped, a NATO-led force would maintain order in Kosovo as the Serbs withdrew. The UN would authorize the peacekeeping mission and take charge of civilian administration. The EU would coordinate reconstruction. The OSCE, under the leadership of stalwart Norwegian Foreign Minister Knut Volleback, would help organize elections and train civilian police.

To put all these elements in motion, and in the proper order, required a complicated diplomatic dance. First we had to draft a Security Council resolution that would provide the framework for a military agreement between NATO and Yugoslavia. This would spell out the timing of the withdrawal of Serb forces. The next step was to verify that withdrawal had begun, thereby triggering a halt to NATO bombing. Once that happened, Russia would agree to vote on a Security Council resolution authorizing the peacekeeping force, which would then deploy. After that, the refugees would feel safe enough to return and the KLA secure enough to disarm.

In the end all these steps were taken, and in the right order, but not without headaches. The language of the Security Council resolution was hashed out in twelve hours of negotiations by G8 foreign ministers in

Germany on June 7 and 8. All the first day, Ivanov tried to delete references to cooperation with the war crimes tribunal and suggested allowing some Serb security forces to remain in Kosovo. As we argued, I thought to myself, I'm the only one around this table who's done this work at the Security Council. I know I have to do what I did before—break the subjects down and deal with each of my colleagues separately until we had the consensus I sought. At the same time I knew I would have been furious, had I still been UN ambassador, that the foreign ministers were doing our job. I pushed back on every issue. Finding himself isolated, Ivanov finally gave way.

That agreement broke a deadlock between NATO and Yugoslav military leaders, who were conducting their own negotiations in nearby Macedonia. At last, on June 9, Yugoslav forces began to withdraw from Kosovo. The next day NATO air strikes were officially suspended and the Security Council resolution approved. The peacekeepers prepared to deploy. The only major issue remaining was how to define Russia's role in the NATO-led peacekeeping force.

Although there was still diplomatic work to do, I felt I could breathe normally for the first time in months. Despite all the doubters, the Alliance had held together, and through the creative mixing of diplomacy and force, we had won. It was a heady moment. Walking down the streets in Cologne, I received a round of applause. During the G8 meeting, Foreign Minister Fischer had said, "Well, if it was Madeleine's war, it is now Madeleine's victory." I replied that it was NATO's victory, but I did wonder how those who had named it my war as a pejorative felt now. At the G8 dinner, which was held in—of all places—a chocolate museum, I was the subject of chivalrous and wonderfully exaggerated toasts. After dinner President Clinton called and his opening line was, "So you're a happy girl." He was certainly a happy boy. He told me about a column he had just read by John Keegan in which the British historian had written, "There are certain dates in the history of warfare that mark real turning points.... Now there is a new turning point to fix on the calendar: June 3, 1999, when the capitulation of President Milošević proved that a war can be won by airpower alone."[3]

3. Three figures in the Kosovo story deserve special mention: As head of the international verification team, Bill Walker told the truth about the Racak massacre and galvanized NATO. James Dobbins, replacing Bob Gelbard as our special Balkans representative, proved a workhorse from Rambouillet onward. Acting UN Permanent Representative Peter Burleigh made sure the war-ending Security Council resolution was approved. Sadly, the three had something else in common. Each had his career curtailed by U.S. Senators, or

BEFORE RETURNING TO Washington, I stopped in Macedonia to meet with the government there and greet American troops who were preparing to enter Kosovo. I also visited a camp for Kosovar refugees—a dusty, sweltering city of twenty thousand deportees, most very young or very old, living in tents tethered to Macedonia's rocky soil. The only natural color came from tiny purple cactus blossoms, which like the camp's human residents were hardy survivors in a harsh environment. There were flags flying over the city, but they weren't the flags of any country. They belonged to the UN, the UN high commissioner for refugees, USAID, and Catholic Relief Services. Around the city was a fence, with sides tall enough and wire sharp enough to keep in the people supposed to be there and keep out those who did not belong.[4]

The city itself was furnished like a yard sale in a coastal town. In front of the crowded-in tents were cracked lawn chairs, crooked beach umbrellas, and plastic sandals, most often children's size. Despite the difficult conditions, the living spaces were kept spotless, showing the pride people had in their homes, even if those homes were tiny and temporary.

Approaching the camp, I could see figures gathering ahead on both sides of the path. Their shouting was indistinct at first, but then I couldn't help smiling. They were chanting "USA, USA" and "Albright, Albright." I began shaking hands and telling people over and over again, "You will be going back. Before long, you will be able to go home." A little boy carried a hand-lettered sign reading "I Love America" at the top and, at the bottom, "I want to return to Kosovo." I stopped and spoke to his mother, who told me the boy's grandfather had died on the way out of Kosovo and that his grandmother, if she had survived, was still in Pristina.

I was invited into a tent, where a small group of women and a few children had assembled. They spoke of their eagerness to go back. I urged

their overly empowered staff, who placed indefinite "holds" on their nominations to other positions. Walker was prevented from serving as ambassador to Argentina and later Pakistan. Dobbins was also denied a chance to serve in Buenos Aires. And no action was taken on the President's designation of Burleigh to be ambassador to the Philippines. The Senators who blocked these nominations never had to justify their actions, because Senate "courtesies" don't require them to do so. This practice is deeply demoralizing to members of the Foreign Service, harms our foreign policy, and is fundamentally at odds with democratic principles. Senators from both political parties are guilty of this abuse and I hope reformers end it.

4. After a hesitant start, the international effort to assist Kosovar refugees saved thousands of lives. Special credit belongs to Sadako Ogata, the indomitable UN high commissioner for refugees, and a team led by Julia Taft, assistant secretary of state for population, refugees and migration. Governments in the region also played a vital role, particularly Albania, Macedonia, and Italy.

them to be patient. "The Yugoslavs have planted land mines, and it will take time to clear them. I hope you will wait until we have told you it is safe and there is enough food for people to eat." I also told them that when they went back, NATO would be there to help them to lead normal lives.

The refugees reminded me how powerful the pull of home can be—especially in this part of the world, where there is less mobility than in the United States and families have lived for centuries tilling the same fields, walking the same roads, watching the sun rise above the same familiar hills. That is why ethnic cleansing—whether directed at Albanians, Serbs, or some other group—is so destructive. It doesn't mean simply moving people from one place to another, but ripping whole communities out by their roots and populating their villages with strangers who don't know the history or the local gossip or the names inscribed on headstones in cemeteries nearby.

Leaving Macedonia, I looked forward to sleeping on the long trip home. We were barely airborne, however, before the NSC called to say that Russian troops had entered Kosovo and were being hailed as heroes by Serbs in Pristina. Together, Sandy and I got on the phone with Strobe, who was en route home from Moscow. We advised him to "pull a Primakov," by turning his plane around and going back to the Russian capital. Later Strobe called to say that he had spoken to Ivanov, who assured him that the deployment was "a mistake" and the troops would be ordered to leave.

When I talked to Ivanov the next day, he said there had been a "misunderstanding" about whether the troops would be leaving. The Russians would remain at the Pristina airport, and if NATO deployed before there was agreement on the Russian role, more Russian troops would move in and occupy northern Kosovo. I thought to myself, "Either I am dreaming or this is the worst movie I have ever seen. In one day we had gone from celebrating victory to a farcical Cold War encore." I also worried that Ivanov no longer knew what was going on in his own government. There had clearly been some breakdown between civilian and military authority, although no one could be sure what Yeltsin might or might not have authorized. The potential for dangerous miscalculations, especially on the part of Russian officers, was extraordinarily high.

Even now, I believe it is possible that Milošević cooked up a deal with the Russian military—perhaps through his brother, Yugoslavia's ambassador in Moscow—to achieve a virtual partition of Kosovo. If so, the Russians were stopped from the further pursuit of this folly by the constraints of international diplomacy and law. The Russian military had prepared six transport aircraft to ferry thousands of troops to reinforce the small contingent at the Pristina airport. The flights never took off because the Russians were denied permission to cross the airspace of Hungary, Romania, and Bulgaria. Each of these countries had been a charter member of the Warsaw Pact. Now one was a NATO ally and the other two were leading candidates for admission. Their decision to stand up to Moscow at this moment of tension validated our strategy of NATO enlargement. It showed the important role Central European countries could play in strengthening regional security and quieted a crisis that could have produced something the Cold War never did—direct combat between NATO and Russian troops.

As it was, the NATO-led force deployed and ended up feeding the lightly supplied Russians at the airport, while negotiations continued on the appropriate Russian role. President Yeltsin called President Clinton and suggested they go off together to a "boat, a submarine, or some island so not a single person will disturb us," to solve the problem. Clinton suggested instead that the defense and foreign ministers of the two countries meet to resolve the matter, which—after a few days of spirited give-and-take—we did.[5]

I knew there would be no real break from work, but I needed a breather. I joined Anne, pregnant with my future granddaughter Maddie, and three-year-old Jack in Austria where her husband, Geoff, was teaching law that summer. I couldn't get too far away from Kosovo, however. With the war over, the Alliance had turned to the UN for help in an area where that organization had proven expertise—civilian reconstruction. Kofi Annan was about to choose the head of the UN's civilian mission in Kosovo, and I had told him I thought he was making a mistake. His choice was Bernard Kouchner, the French health minister and someone who years earlier had helped found Doctors Without Borders. I had heard Kouchner was difficult, but then he set up an appointment with me for lunch at a hotel not far from where I was staying. He brought a bunch of edelweiss, and as soon as we sat down he said, "I hear you don't like me." I tried to resist, but within minutes he was telling me all about his hopes for Kosovo. I was impressed by his deep convictions, humanity, knowledge, and dedication; I later called the Secretary General to tell him he was right after all.

Near the end of July, I visited Kosovo for the first time. The war had been over for about six weeks. Despite our cautions, most refugees hadn't waited to make the journey back. There were joyous family reunions and

---

5. These negotiations, conducted in Helsinki, resulted in Russia's placing battalions within the German-, French-, and American-patrolled sectors of Kosovo. Russia wasn't given its own sector, for fear that that would lead to the de facto splitting of the province.

somber discoveries of makeshift graves. To the surprise of many, the KLA signed a demobilization agreement Jamie Rubin had helped broker, but much uncertainty remained about the group's intentions. As expected, there were some instances of retaliation directed by ethnic Albanians against Serbs, many of whom retreated into Serbia proper. The old Kosovo lay shattered, and the process of rebuilding had barely begun.

While in Pristina, I spoke to an enormous crowd gathered in the city's central square. Because of all the roofs and windows, it was a difficult space to patrol, and while I was waiting in the UN headquarters before the speech, we heard a gunshot, but no one knew from where. To reduce the risk, I was driven the fifty yards or so between the door of the building and the small platform that had been erected in front of the crowd. As I got up, the van maneuvered so that one of its doors was open directly behind me: if something happened, I could just fall back in.

The crowd, swollen by returned refugees, was dressed in a mixture of Albanian national costumes and Chicago Bulls jerseys. As I acknowledged the applause, I studied the people in front of me. I thought of those I had seen so recently in the refugee camp, and of others in newspapers and on TV—faces strained by hardship, contorted with fear, or filled with anxiety as families searched for loved ones who had disappeared. Now these same faces were smiling.[6]

I told the crowd, "I have been thinking about you for a long time, and about the suffering you have gone through. Today, we must pledge that never again will people with guns come in the night, and never again will there be massacres in Kosovo." This was met with loud cheers.

I said, "We must support the war crimes tribunal, because those indicted for ethnic cleansing and murder should be held accountable, and Slobodan Milošević must answer for his crimes." The crowd yelled even louder.

Then I said, "Democracy cannot be built on revenge. If we are to have a true victory in Kosovo, it cannot be a victory of Albanians over Serbs or NATO over Serbs. It must be a victory of those who believe in the rights of the individual over those who do not. Otherwise it is not victory. It is merely changing one kind of repression for another."

The audience became silent. You could have heard a pin drop.

Obviously, I did not expect the wounds of body and mind in Kosovo to heal quickly. The passions of war burn too hot. But I did want to

---

6. I was later sent a photograph of a graffiti-covered wall in Pristina that reflected ethnic Albanian sentiment at this time: Its message: "Thank you NATO, Toni Bler, Shroder, Sollana, Klinton, Shirak, Robin Kuk, Prodi, Klark and Olbright."

deliver a tough message. In my conversations with Europeans, even during the war, I had detected deep skepticism toward Albanians. I told the crowd bluntly, "There are those who believe Kosovo will never escape its past. They say that you will act towards the Serbs as the Serb military and police acted towards you; that you will make it impossible for Serbs to live in Kosovo. These critics point to tragedies such as the cowardly murder this past week of fourteen Serbs in Gracko, and they say, 'See, we are right. The Kosovo Albanians are no better than Milošević.' Today I want to make a prediction that you will prove those critics wrong."

This was a direct and necessary challenge. I feared that a few more cases of Albanians killing Serbs would squelch European enthusiasm for financing reconstruction in Kosovo. If that happened, Congress wouldn't pick up the slack. We had just fought a war; I was determined not to lose the peace.

After the speech, I was driven six miles south to what seemed a different world. In Pristina the Albanian majority had been relieved, celebratory, and triumphant. Outside the Serb Orthodox monastery of Gracanica, the mood was fearful and bitter. I was visiting the monastery to meet with Bishop Artemije Radosavljević and other local Serb religious leaders. The bishop had strongly opposed the NATO bombing, but he had also called for Milošević to resign because of the evils the tyrant had committed against Serbs and non-Serbs alike.

We were greeted by monks wearing traditional black robes with ropes for belts. We climbed a dark, curved stairway and entered a large common room with big wooden tables and benches. On the wall was a tapestry commemorating the Serb defeat in the Battle of Kosovo in 1389. Nuns brought in bowls of peaches and plums, cups of bitter coffee, glasses of apple juice and wine, and sweets dripping with honey and a thick vanilla paste served on a spoon. The bishop carried a scepter with a silver knob. The whole scene was out of the Middle Ages, except for the monks who sat along the far wall busily typing at computers or surfing the Web. Another monk cruised the room with a Minicam.

When I had met the bishop in Washington before the war, he had warned that a military confrontation would be a disaster. Now he showed me pictures of destroyed churches, recounted attacks that had been made on Serbs, and expressed his fear that all Serbs might have to leave Kosovo. I told him that outcome was the opposite of what I wanted; NATO peace-keepers and the UN would do everything possible to help his people feel secure. The bishop said that if Serbs were driven out, Milošević would be proven right. I agreed and said it was important for Kosovo Serbs to participate in the UN's effort to create self-governing institutions.

As we concluded our meeting, the bishop walked with me through the monastery gardens to our motorcade. Outside a crowd had gathered, their faces taut with hate as they spat and shouted pro-Milošević slogans. The prelate told me that these were not local people but hard-liners sent down from Belgrade. We got into our cars as the crowd surged toward us, some of the men exposing themselves, just to make clear what they thought of me. As soon as our motorcade left, the crowd stormed the monastery and got into an angry confrontation with the bishop. Fortunately, British troops were there to prevent anyone from getting hurt.

From Kosovo I flew to Sarajevo, where President Clinton and leaders from throughout Europe had convened to launch the Southeast Europe Stability Pact. This was the strategy we had developed to bring the Balkans into the continent's democratic mainstream. The choice of Sarajevo was a milestone in itself. During the war in Kosovo, the foreign minister of Bosnia had offered his country as a model for how different ethnic groups could work together. Given his nation's recent history, this was an astonishing claim, yet it had enough truth to inspire confidence that miracles could be accomplished.

The gathering in Sarajevo was held in the stadium that had been used for figure skating during the 1984 Olympics. As I listened to the speakers in English, French, German, and the various Balkan languages, I felt strongly the desire of leaders in the region to close the door on the past and embrace a democratic future. We had, I thought, a real chance to transform the patterns of history and replace the whirlpools of violence with a steady forward current.

Milošević had gambled that Kosovo would split the Alliance and open an unbridgeable gap between Russia and the West. Thanks to the determination of President Clinton, Prime Minister Blair, Secretary General Solana, and other NATO leaders, coupled with pragmatism at key moments from Yeltsin and Ivanov, we proved Milošević wrong. We also validated my own belief that America can use force legitimately and wisely in support of important diplomatic goals short of all-out war. We didn't have to flatten Yugoslavia or mass hundreds of thousands of troops in order to achieve our objectives.

As for the Alliance, the conflict demonstrated the vast disparity between America's capacity to conduct modern warfare and Europe's, but it also showed the value of the political support solidarity can bring. Notwithstanding the views of some skeptics, we won in Kosovo because of the Alliance, not in spite of it. In one way or another, every NATO member contributed to our success.

Certainly we were called upon to answer hard questions during the war, but we were sustained by the knowledge that, as difficult as those questions were, they were far easier than the inquiries we would have faced had we done nothing. If NATO had not acted, the Serb offensive would have permanently displaced more than half a million Kosovars, radicalizing many and creating a new source of long-term tension within Europe. Milošević would have been strengthened, perhaps tempting others to enhance their own power through similar methods. And NATO would have been left divided and questioning its own relevance as the twenty-first century dawned.

TWENTY-SIX

Freedom and Order
in the Global Era

T HE MILLENNIUM'S FINAL DECADE was commonly referred to
as the post–Cold War era, but that only told us what it was not. A
better description was the global era, a time characterized by
heightened interdependence, overlapping national interests, and borders
permeable to everything from terrorists and technology to disease and
democratic ideals.

For the leaders of countries not fully integrated into the international
system, this era presented a choice with sharp edges on either side. Such
regimes could either plug into the world economy and vastly increase the
flow of information and ideas into their societies, or try to remain aloof,
thereby risking economic stagnation in order to maintain firm political
control—at least in the short run.

For the United States, the choice posed by globalization was both
simple and complex. We had a clear stake in developing an inclusive
international system that would provide stability, uphold justice, spur
beneficial trade and respond to the universal desire for freedom. But this
was not a goal that could be achieved through some grand diplomatic
bargain. Rather it was a global objective requiring local steps, a process
comprised of hundreds of specific but widely varied projects. These
included the management of vital bilateral relationships such as those
between the United States and China and Russia; the promotion of democratic values worldwide; and working with leaders in Africa to end conflict and spur growth. Each was a separate subject, with its own list of key
issues and players. But each was also part of a larger struggle that would

determine whether the world began the new century coming closer together or falling further apart.

AMERICA'S MOST IMPORTANT relationship in Asia is with Japan. If anyone doubts that, they should think about what the region would be like if our two countries were adversaries instead of allies. We have been there and done that. While our trade relations have had their trying moments, Japan is America's trusted friend, a nation that has earned our affection and respect on every level and in every field. Our most complex relationship in Asia, however, and the one that demands the most constant tending, is with China.

Two decades previously, I had been in the White House when President Carter decided the time was right to normalize relations with Beijing. I remembered listening to Chinese leader Deng Xiaoping outline his plan for transforming his country's centralized economy to make room for private enterprise, foreign investment, and more choices for workers and budding entrepreneurs. The result of those plans had been to create thriving areas of growth alongside the country's stagnant state sector, lift millions out of poverty, and lay the basis for a market economy.

The economic opening had not, however, been matched by a political opening. The other part of Deng's legacy was the massacre at Tiananmen Square, jailed dissidents, secretive decision making, and the continuation of rigid one-party rule. During his 1992 presidential campaign, candidate Bill Clinton criticized the senior Bush administration for being soft on China's leadership. Once in office, initiating his own policy of "constructive engagement" with Beijing, he found himself exposed to the same criticism. For any U.S. administration, China is in its own category—too big to ignore, too repressive to embrace, difficult to influence, and very, very proud.

President Clinton hoped his exchange of elaborate state visits in 1997 and 1998 with Deng's successor, Jiang Zemin, would open at least a crack in China's wall of political repression. Good personal dynamics between the two leaders had been established at the first summit in Washington. In preparation for the second, I met with President Jiang in a walled-off compound near the ancient Forbidden City in Beijing. Jiang proudly showed me around the lakeside house that he had ordered refurbished in anticipation of the summit. He said that he planned to sit with the President on the veranda where, in addition to their serious discussions, they could indulge in their shared passion for appreciating music. During our meeting, the Chinese leader was gracious and worked hard at appearing cosmopolitan. He sprinkled his conversation with comments in Russian and quotations in English.[1] On other occasions, he quoted poetry, which caused his translator to furrow his brow. When Jiang smiled, which was often, he reminded me of the Cheshire Cat.

The summit itself was marred at the outset by China's insistence that the welcoming ceremony occur in Tiananmen Square, with all the unfortunate symbolism that entailed. For protocol reasons we had to agree, but I decided to make my own statement by wearing a white hat, the Chinese color of mourning.

We had the normal huge banquets and concerts. The First Lady and I visited with legal aid groups and religious leaders, even touring a refurbished synagogue in Shanghai. The highlight of the summit, however, was a joint Jiang-Clinton press conference in Beijing. The authorities surprised us by allowing the conference to be broadcast live over government television to hundreds of millions of Chinese, and President Jiang startled us by actually answering a question about repression in Tibet. President Clinton took advantage of the opportunity to speak eloquently about the need for freedom of expression and religion. Later, while addressing Chinese students, he made the essential point that political freedom is not the enemy of stability as some (including Chinese leaders) suggest, but rather the foundation of stability, helping nations to achieve change gradually and in keeping with the popular will.

Personal diplomacy is not enough, however, to reshape a government's basic philosophy. Only a few months after the summit, Beijing cracked down on the fledgling China Democracy Party and criminalized membership in an unthreatening but rapidly growing spiritual health movement known as the Falun Gong. Leaders were imprisoned, while followers were rounded up, lectured, and harassed. In addition, China continued to practice forced labor, limit freedom of religion, and abuse the rights of minority groups.

Obviously, the end of the Cold War had sent one message to the West, another to Beijing. Where we saw the promise of democratic change, Chinese leaders saw a threat. They realized that they could not prosper without integrating their country more fully into the world economy, yet they didn't feel they could survive without holding themselves apart from the worldwide trend toward more open political systems. The result was a balancing act that continues to this day.

The most delicate issue in U.S.-China relations was and remains Taiwan. It is long-standing U.S. policy not to challenge Beijing's view that

1. When shown the Lincoln bedroom during the first summit, Jiang began reciting the Gettysburg Address.

there is only one China, of which Taiwan is a part. It is also both U.S. policy and law to sell arms to Taiwan to minimize the chance that Beijing will try to regain control of the island by force. Our desire is that the two sides work out their differences peacefully. Our fear is that they will not. The Chinese would like us to pressure Taiwan into accepting reunification on Beijing's terms—roughly analogous to those now in effect in Hong Kong. We say it is not our place to pressure Taiwan except to refrain from provocative actions and words.

The relationship between Beijing and Taipei excites deep passions on both sides. Hit the right button in any conversation with a Chinese official and you will get a long history lesson. Because of these passions, no leader in Beijing can afford to compromise on the issue of reunification, while no leader in Taipei can afford to compromise on security. Although the status quo has not changed in years, it remains tense and unstable—one of those problems not always in the world spotlight but capable of erupting at any time. In recent years China has built up missile forces that could be used to intimidate Taiwan and purchased submarines that could blockade it. In response, Taiwan has received U.S. help in modernizing its air defense capabilities.

As Secretary of State, I visited China five times, accompanied by Stanley Roth, our witty and knowledgeable assistant secretary of state for East Asia and Pacific affairs. During our many official meetings, we had an agenda that included nonproliferation, terrorism, human rights, market access, Tibet, religious freedom, the environment, and international crime, as well as Taiwan. I had the impression, however, that the Chinese idea of a perfect meeting would have consisted of a single statement on my part reiterating America's acceptance of Beijing's one China policy. For them, Taiwan was by far the paramount issue.

The most tangible success of the administration's engagement strategy was the 1999 agreement, negotiated by our tenacious U.S. Trade Representative Charlene Barshefsky, clearing the way for China's entry into the World Trade Organization (WTO). This pact reflected a leap of faith on Beijing's part that China would be able to compete in the global marketplace while abiding by international rules. In order to qualify for the WTO, China needed to negotiate bilateral agreements that would dramatically reduce barriers to its markets in everything from computers and cars to crackers and corn. In return, China would be assured of equal treatment from other WTO members. For the United States, this meant extending to China the same trade status we normally accord other nations. Unless we did, our competitors would gain easier access to China's markets while we would not. Economically, this was a simple choice for the administration, but the approach had to be approved by Congress and politically it was a hot potato.

The President's announcement on January 10, 2000, that he planned to extend permanent normal trade relations status (PNTR) to China triggered a months-long debate set against a swirling backdrop of security fears, business interests, human rights concerns, and election year politics.[2] Many members of Congress, including the most liberal and conservative, believed that trade with China should be linked to human rights. They saw PNTR as a reward the Chinese hadn't earned and felt that withholding it might somehow cause the Chinese to become more democratic.

I realized that we wouldn't win the vote on PNTR if it were viewed as a trade-off between our economic interest in opening China's market and our concerns about human rights. Presented with an explicit choice between money and values, the majority of Americans would choose values every time. The administration had to show that it was possible to support PNTR and human rights simultaneously. To this end, I did something geographically insane.

Most years in recent times, the United States has sponsored or cosponsored a resolution critical of China during the annual meeting of the UN Commission on Human Rights (UNCHR). Whether we have lobbied for those resolutions intensely or belatedly, we have always lost, usually by a few votes. We have nevertheless considered it important to stick by our principles.

Ordinarily we are represented at the meeting by a special ambassador designated for that purpose. In 2000, with the PNTR debate raging and interest in China high, I decided to deliver our message personally. However, the President was scheduled to visit South Asia at the same time, and I didn't want to miss that. Seemingly I had to choose one or the other. Stubbornly I chose both.

On the evening of March 22, following a full day accompanying the President in India, I flew through the night to Geneva, where I would become the first U.S. Secretary of State to address the UNCHR. After nine hours aloft, we refueled in Crete at 2 A.M. The press and my advisors, having chosen during the flight to watch a half-dozen episodes of *The Sopranos*, wandered about the military terminal like zombies.

---

2. The administration's campaign to gain congressional approval of PNTR was led by Secretary of Commerce William Daley, Charlene Barshefsky, Treasury Secretary Lawrence Summers, and National Economic Council Director Gene Sperling. My job, in partnership with Sandy Berger, was to help explain the significance of the issue from the point of view of national security and foreign policy.

In Geneva the UN auditorium was packed with diplomats from fifty-four nations, representatives of nongovernmental organizations, and the media. In my remarks, I pushed back on an issue the Chinese frequently raised with us. They were proud of their country's status as one of five permanent members of the Security Council and frequently berated us for sidestepping that body. I pointed out that China's membership was not only a right but a responsibility. China was bound by the UN Charter; it had recently reaffirmed its commitment to the Universal Declaration of Human Rights; and it had signed the International Covenant on Civil and Political Rights. Unless it began to take those obligations seriously, it could not expect to be treated as a world leader.

As I told delegates the climate for human rights in China was getting worse instead of better, most of the Chinese delegation walked out. When I finished, Beijing's ambassador rose to assert without blushing that China was a democracy and fully respected human rights. If nothing else, my presence had forced the Chinese to defend the indefensible in front of the world. I returned to my airplane and, after many more hours hurtling through the sky, met up with the President again in South Asia. Although our resolution once again failed, I had made my point as dramatically as I could. It was possible to be vigorously pro-PNTR and pro–human rights at the same time.

On May 24, 2000, the House voted 237–197 to grant PNTR to China. In September, the Senate approved the measure by a wide margin.

Laying a wreath in memory of the victims of the August 7, 1998 terrorist bombing in Nairobi. Walking with me is Prudence Bushnell, our ambassador to Kenya. Holding a second wreath is Kenyan Foreign Minister Bonaya Godana. The tall blond man watching over me is the head of my security detail, Larry Hartnett.

In Vietnam in 1999, with U.S. Ambassador Peter Peterson, and Brigadier General Harry B. Axson, Jr. (right), and Lt. Colonel John M. Peppers (left), leaders of the U.S. military's Joint Task Force-Full Accounting. The occasion was a moving ceremony prior to the repatriation of four sets of remains of American servicemen killed during the Vietnam War. More than a quarter century after that conflict, the search for information concerning the fate of those unaccounted for goes on.

During NATO's fiftieth anniversary summit, I sat between President Clinton
and Great Britain's charismatic Prime Minister Tony Blair. Behind the
President is Deputy National Security Advisor Jim Steinberg.

I have a pin set showing three monkeys in the "hear no evil, speak no evil, see
no evil" mode. Otherwise, I have no comment on this picture, except to say
that Sandy Berger is saying, "That must mean I'm evil."

Exchanging views with American servicemen and women on duty overseas. Critics say members of our armed forces hate to serve in peacekeeping operations. That may be true for some of our troops, but most with whom I talked appreciated the opportunity to help wounded societies find their footing.

The article accompanying this photo was entitled, "Madeleine's War."

The G8 foreign ministers. Clockwise from lower left is France's Hubert
Védrine (seated), Italy's Under-Secretary of State for Foreign Affairs Umberto
Ranieri, Canada's Lloyd Axworthy, Germany's Joschka Fischer, Japan's
Masahiko Komura, Russia's Igor Ivanov, and facing me, Great Britain's Robin
Cook (seated).

The first gathering of the women foreign ministers (1997); we later grew into
the "fearsome fourteen." Pictured seated (l to r) are Tarja Halonen (Finland),
Andrea Willi (Lichtenstein), me, Lena Hjelm-Wallén (Sweden), and María
Emma Mejía (Colombia). Standing (also l to r) are Shirley Gbujama (Sierra
Leone), Nadezhda Mihailova (Bulgaria), and Zdenka Kramplová (Slovakia).

Following my icy meeting with Slobodan Milošević, I wanted to avoid any suggestion of warmth between us. I succeeded.

Standing beside North Korean leader Kim Jong Il and in front of a mural aptly depicting stormy seas. We were in the process of testing North Korean intentions when the Clinton administration's time ran out.

I had many serious and friendly talks with Crown Prince Abdullah, the de facto leader of Saudi Arabia.

In Saudi Arabia in 1997 with foreign ministers of the Gulf Consultative Council (GCC). I was always treated with respect, even when I told them I wanted to talk about women's rights. From the left are GCC General Secretary Jamil Ibrahim Al-Hujailan and foreign ministers Sheikh Hamdan bin Zayid Al-Nuhayyan (UAE), Sheikh Hamad Bin Jasim bin Jabir Al-Thani (Qatar), Sheikh Sabah al-Ahmad al-Jabir al-Sabah (Kuwait), Sheikh Muhammad bin Mubarak al-Khalifa (Bahrain), HRH Prince Saud Al-Faisal (Saudi Arabia), and Yusif Bin Alawi Bin Abdullah (Oman).

President Clinton and Vice-President Gore meet with the Middle East team in the Oval Office. Sharing the couch and studying his notebook is Ambassador Dennis Ross. Next to him is Assistant Secretary of State Martin Indyk. Across the room with his back half-turned is Sandy Berger.

Discussions with Israeli Prime Minister Ehud Barak were always intense. His manner could be abrupt, but his willingness to risk his political career and even his life in pursuit of a just and secure Middle East peace was beyond question.

PLO Chairman Arafat cheering my grandson Jack during his visit to my Virginia farm. There was a warm personal side to Arafat, but his politics were inflexible and, in the end, very costly to his people and to the entire Middle East.

China officially joined the WTO in December 2001; PNTR legally took effect that same month. This was an historic development the precise dimensions of which will only become clear over time. By entering the WTO, China committed to free itself from the "House That Mao Built," including state-run enterprises, central planning institutes, massive agricultural communes, and parasitic bureaucracies. The result should lead to more technological innovation, more use of the Internet, more frequent contact with foreigners, and more institutions and associations free from Communist Party control. There is no automatic connection between trade and democracy, but people can't help being shaped by their own experiences and observations. The millions of Chinese young people who are now learning to think for themselves economically will almost certainly be more likely than their parents to think for themselves politically. At an Internet café in Beijing, I saw young customers ordering how-to books on almost every conceivable subject. Knowledge, once it begins to be disseminated freely, is hard to fence back in.

Equally important, if China and the United States can achieve economic growth through participation in a global system governing trade, we may be able to find comparable benefits in cooperating on terror and proliferation. Indeed we have already made considerable progress. Several decades ago, Mao Tse-Tung encouraged Third World nations to obtain nuclear weapons as a means of equalizing power. Under his successors China has joined the Nuclear Nonproliferation Treaty, ratified the Chemical Weapons Convention, signed the Nuclear Test Ban Treaty, discouraged North Korea's pursuit of nuclear arms, and tightened controls on exports of sensitive technologies, although not to the extent we wished.

It would be a mistake to base U.S. policy toward China on any fixed assumptions, positive or negative, about the future. The Chinese measure their history not in years or even decades but in dynasties. Until shortly before the twentieth century, they had little reason not to see their land as the center of the world. However, since Western gunboats forcibly broke through China's imperial isolation, the nation has faced the trauma of exploitation, occupation, civil war, Communist insurgency, and the Cultural Revolution. Now that Communist ideology is in serious decline, nationalism is resurgent and China's regional and global role is rising.

The country nevertheless faces daunting problems, including high unemployment, a relentlessly growing population, pollution, corruption, disease, and a steady migration of peasants from the countryside to overcrowded cities. These challenges could cause Beijing's leaders to seek a stable international environment so that they can concentrate on addressing their domestic needs, or they may go looking for international distractions that will enable them to blame outsiders for whatever hardships their people face.

The question for the future is, how will the deep pride of the Chinese be manifested? Although Americans instinctively look to see how stories end, the answer will not come soon. Deng Xiaoping once said that Beijing would pursue reunification with Taiwan for however long it took, "even a hundred or a thousand years." President Jiang expressed the patient hope that, with sustained growth, China could become a moderately developed country in half a century.

In managing our relations with Beijing, we too need to think long-term. With all the other perils in the world, we should be in no hurry to cast China in the role of enemy. We should hope that China's economic reforms succeed, while welcoming contacts at all levels. But engagement with China is not the same as endorsement. We must keep our commitments to Taiwan and persist in pressing our concerns about such matters as weapons proliferation and human rights. We can't bully Beijing into acting against its own perceived self-interest. We can, however, appeal to the pragmatism of a new generation of leaders to find areas where our interests coincide.[3]

More than 150 years ago, Alexis de Tocqueville famously predicted that the relationship between Russia and America would shape the destiny of the world. I suspect, if he had returned to earth as the new millennium dawned, he wouldn't ignore Russia, but he would write first about China.

AT NOON ON December 31, 1999, Boris Yeltsin resigned, saying, "Russia must enter the new millennium with new politicians, new faces, new intelligent, strong, and energetic people." His successor as president was Vladimir Putin, who had been appointed four months earlier as Yeltsin's fifth prime minister since March 1998. The revolving door in the prime minister's office reflected a downward spiral in the Russian economy. Few societies have crashed harder without war. During the Great Depression America's economic output declined by one-third. During the 1990s, Russia's shrank by 55 percent to roughly the level of the Netherlands'. By

---

3. In March 2003, the Chinese National People's Congress selected sixty-year-old Hu Jintao to succeed Jiang Zemin as China's President and Communist Party chief. Former Ambassador to Washington Li Zhaoxing, to whom I had extended condolences after the accidental bombing of the Chinese embassy in Belgrade during the Kosovo war, was promoted to foreign minister.

decade's end, Moscow was barely collecting taxes, foreign investment had dried up, and 70 percent of Russians lived at subsistence level. People were eating less, getting sick more, dying sooner. A coterie of corrupt officials and businesspeople had robbed the country of many of its assets, lodging the profits in offshore accounts. On top of this, the Asian financial crisis drove down the price of oil, Russia's primary source of hard currency, thereby ruining a fistful of banks. By the time Putin became prime minister, the Russian media were referring to their country as "Upper Volta with rockets."

What was bad news in Russia was also bad news in Washington. For decades we had worried about the threat posed by a strong Russia; now we worried about the dangers posed by Russia's weakness. We feared that an angry populace would turn to extreme nationalists and that the underpaid Russian military might seek to profit by illegally selling nuclear technologies and arms. Russia's economic problems could depress prospects for growth from the Baltics and Central Europe to the Caucasus and Central Asia, and the spectacle of Russia imploding might tarnish the image of democracy worldwide. Poverty and deprivation were not what people had signed up for when the Iron Curtain lifted.

As we had with China, we tried to shape our policies with history in mind. In the eighteenth century, Peter the Great had begun opening Russia to the West, but on two occasions Western armies had invaded, led first by Napoleon, then Hitler. After World War II, the Soviet Union forcibly established a new security perimeter, stringing barbed wire across the heart of Europe. Now the barbed wire was gone and the question was how the new relationship between Russia and Europe would be defined. With support from our allies, the President had promoted the idea of partnership, bringing Moscow into the G8 and establishing the NATO-Russia Permanent Joint Council. Russia belonged, we felt, at the table of nations working to promote international stability and law. This premise was sorely tested in Kosovo, where Yeltsin appeared to ignore Milošević's crimes. It was tested again in a rugged region of the Caucasus—Chechnya.

When the Soviet Union dissolved in 1991, Chechen nationalists launched a struggle for independence. Several years of fierce fighting resulted in a settlement giving Chechnya considerable autonomy, but still within Russia. The conflict resumed in August 1999, only a few days after Putin became prime minister, when Chechen fighters announced plans to foment a regionwide Islamic revolution. The next month Russia was rocked by a series of terrorist bombings that killed almost three hundred people. Although lacking proof, Russia accused Chechens of the attacks and vowed to strike back. Under Putin's direction, the Russian military bombed Chechen cities and villages, before moving in on the ground. There were reports of indiscriminate violence and massacres, and tens of thousands of people fled their homes, prompting an international outcry.

At meeting after meeting, I told Foreign Minister Ivanov that Russia couldn't act as if all Chechens were terrorists; I pressed him to permit an independent investigation of the alleged atrocities, allow access for humanitarian organizations, and negotiate a political settlement. President Clinton confronted Yeltsin over the same issues at the November 1999 OSCE summit in Istanbul. In an emotional speech, Yeltsin accused us of meddling. Russian resistance was reinforced by the war's popularity at home. According to surveys when the conflict began, only 2 percent of Russians thought Putin the right man to replace Yeltsin. By New Year's Eve, the figure had risen to 56 percent.

In Moscow in January 2000, I became the first senior American official to meet with Putin since he became acting president. His first comment when I arrived at the Kremlin focused on the pins I was wearing, showing two hot air balloons. I said they were to show how hopes in Russia were rising. He smiled, then looked stern and turned to the cameras saying, "The U.S. is conducting a policy of pressure against us in Chechnya." As soon as the media left, he smiled thinly once more, telling me, "I said that so your domestic critics will not attack you for being soft."

Putin began by holding up his stack of talking points, then tossing them aside. We agreed that 1999 had been a hard year. "Russia has become controversial in my country," I said, "and the U.S. is controversial in yours. This is partly due to real differences and partly to the elections in each country. The only answer we can give to those who criticize us for working together is to prove we can get things done."

We sparred over the administration's proposal to negotiate changes in the Anti-Ballistic Missile (ABM) Treaty to accommodate a limited system of national missile defense, our concerns about the transfer of Russian nuclear technology to Iran, and Russia's manifold economic problems. On this last point, Putin clearly understood what his predecessor had refused to acknowledge: Russia desperately needed help but its leaders wouldn't get it by becoming angry or making empty promises. Putin said he was fully committed to cooperating with the International Monetary Fund (IMF), finding ways to lure foreign investors back to Russia, and reforming the tax code.

He spoke with a cool urgency but became passionate when the subject turned to Chechnya. That region, he declared, had been taken over by criminals who were stealing, kidnapping, peddling drugs, counterfeiting money, and plotting to establish a terrorist state. With help from the Tal-

GARNER, THE WASHINGTON TIMES

iban and other extremists, he said, radicals had gained footholds through-out Central Asia. "Do not try to squeeze Russia out of this region," he said, "or you will end up with another Iran or Afghanistan." Obviously aware of my own history, he said that Russia was acting the way I would have wished Europe had acted against the Nazis. "Instead of another Munich, we are fighting them now before they grow stronger. And we will smash them."

I responded that, in the long run, military pressure without a political option wasn't going to solve anything. "Are you prepared to seek a political settlement?" Putin replied that there was no one with whom to negotiate. "The legitimate leaders are petrified; the rest are thugs and murderers."

Throughout, I was trying both to listen to Putin and to size him up. I knew from his own writing and interviews that he was proud of his father's service in the military during World War II and had grown up wanting to work for the KGB, which he did. He loved Russia and was clearly embarrassed by the depths to which it had fallen. Putin was younger and more modern in his outlook than either Yeltsin or Primakov. He spoke confidently and, when I talked, took notes as if organizing his thoughts, looking up at the translator with expressionless blue-gray eyes.

On the question of Russia's basic political orientation—and his—Putin said bluntly, "Sure, I like Chinese food, it's fun to use chopsticks, and

I've been doing judo for a long time, but this is just exotic stuff. It's not our mentality, which is European. Russia has to be firmly part of the West."

In subsequent months Putin set out to restore respect for the Russian state. He reduced the prerogatives of regional governors and dispatched federal representatives to look out for Moscow's interests. Although the brutal fighting in Chechnya continued, he declared victory and officially restored Moscow's rule. He persuaded the new Duma to enact legislation that enabled Russia to resume paying pensions and salaries. He imposed budgetary discipline and allowed the ruble to rise, so that Russian-made products and food could compete in domestic markets.

Observing all this, our embassy in Moscow reported, "There is a new bounce in the national step." Putin's popularity transcended specific programs; he was filling a role no one could have predicted—the complete anti-Yeltsin but also chosen and blessed by Yeltsin. Whether performing athletic feats, piloting an aircraft, or congratulating Russian military officers, Putin seemed in control. He may have been aided by rebounding oil prices, but the shift in mood and momentum was startling.

There was, however, a problem. Beneath Putin's nationalism and pragmatism, democratic instincts were hard to detect. He clashed frequently with the independent media, apparently determined to see them either shut up or shut down. He didn't even give lip service to the value of a free press, and his attitude toward Chechnya showed little concern about the rights of those not ethnically Russian. While China had been able to fend off criticism by the UN Commission on Human Rights, Russia's Chechnya policy was condemned.

Clearly Russians wanted a leader who had a strong hand and would restore a sense of order and direction. The question was whether the new President had in mind the kind of "order" that would allow Russia to function as a successful democracy or the kind that translated into autocracy. America's role, I believed, was to encourage his citizens to maintain their faith in freedom and a market economy, understanding that the development of democratic habits takes time. Fortunately those habits, which are among the world's most benign addictions, had already begun to take hold in Russia. The country's early experience with freedom had been an economic disaster, but many Russians were wise enough to blame corrupt individuals, not democratic institutions, and to recall that corruption had also been widespread under Communism. As a result, they were eager for the modest help we provided in training entrepreneurs, aiding trade unions, and assisting advocates of human rights.

Although I had qualms about aspects of Putin's leadership, I was encouraged by his repeated commitment to find a home for Russia in the

West. Our job was to make him understand that the West would welcome Russia only if it retained its commitment to democracy, respected its neighbors' independence, and met global standards on weapons proliferation.

In June 2000, President Clinton flew to Moscow for his only formal summit with the new Russian president. When our delegation arrived, we found the Kremlin spruced up. Drab colors had been banished, the rooms painted in coral and teal. The old czarist thrones with ermine draperies were in place, albeit behind ropes. In the receiving line, Putin was curious once again about my pins, which this time consisted of three monkeys posed in the posture of "Hear no evil, see no evil, and speak no evil." I told him they were a reminder to myself to speak to him about Chechnya.

When talking to Bill Clinton, Boris Yeltsin had been bombastic, enthusiastic, erratic, hot-tempered, and warm. He spoke as if everything were personal and could be solved by the two Presidents sitting alone. Putin, by contrast, was clear-minded, cordial, and cool. Where Yeltsin gloried in his personal friendship with Clinton, Putin was primarily interested in conducting business.

The first day of the summit, President Clinton tried out his full bag of arguments in support of our ideas on national missile defense, the ABM Treaty, and further arms reductions. The Pentagon had briefed the Russians in detail about our concerns on Iranian and North Korean missile programs, and Putin acknowledged the potential threat. He argued, however, that there were less risky and more effective ways than national missile defense to cope with the new dangers. Although the two Presidents couldn't complete a deal on missile defense, they did agree on a plan to dispose of excess plutonium; they also agreed to create a joint military operation to provide early warning of space and missile launches.

That evening, after dinner, we had entertainment. Putin and Clinton sat in large chairs in the center with the rest of us clustered around. Usually at events like this the music reflects the culture of the host country. In this case the Russians had decided to please their guest of honor by selecting jazz. The program consisted of a band conducted by a rather elderly man, followed by a band of young people, followed by a saxophone player. They all sounded great, and President Clinton tapped his feet, as he always did during such performances, absorbing the music with his body. Putin meanwhile sat rigid and stony-faced. This reminded me, unfairly, of Lenin's complaint: "I can't listen to music too often. It affects your nerves, and makes you want to say stupid naïve things."

For Russia the twentieth century had been an epic drama featuring revolution, repression, and war, a drama in which a profound ideological struggle was played out and the cherished title of "superpower" was gained and lost. Putin had inherited the task of leading his country's quest for renewed greatness. Unlike China, which enjoyed two decades of sustained growth prior to the millennium's end, Russia entered the new era in a deep hole. Both countries now have leaders who understand the need to modernize and who are trying to sort out—though from vastly different starting points—the relationship between economic progress and political freedom, and the implications of cooperation versus confrontation with the West.

As the twenty-first century began, the world was fascinated by breakthroughs in engineering and research—among them the cloning of sheep, the mapping of DNA, the development of new medicines, and digital technology. I have no quarrel with better living through science, but I do not believe it is the best gauge for measuring progress. A more meaningful yardstick is the spread of democracy. As Secretary of State I found that if I ran down the list of challenges faced by the world—from terrorism and war to poverty and pollution—democracy was the surest path to progress.

Ever since I was a schoolgirl, I had liked forming clubs. Now, at the suggestion of our director of policy planning, Mort Halperin, I decided to propose gathering all the world's democracies. The timing for such a project seemed apt: more than two-thirds of the world's people lived under elected leaders, including a majority of Christians, Hindus, Jews, and Muslims. In three decades the number of electoral democracies had quadrupled from 30 to about 120, but this meant that there were also more places where democratic governments were threatened. This danger was especially present where democracies were fragile and new.

Throughout the Western Hemisphere, dictators were out and democrats in. When I visited the region, I carried with me two maps showing countries governed by authoritarian regimes in red and democracies in green. The map from a quarter century earlier was mostly red. The present-day map, aside from the scarlet scar shape of Cuba, was entirely green. This welcome transformation had begun in the 1970s, spurred in part by President Carter's human rights policies and accompanied by the realization that political reform trumped repression as a means of preventing Castro-style revolution. One by one, military dictatorships from Chile and Argentina to El Salvador and Guatemala were replaced by leaders chosen by the people. In several countries, armed guerrilla movements disbanded, disarmed, and continued to fight for their ideas as civilian political parties. The Summit of the Americas process, conceived during the first Clinton administration, ratified a new hemispheric consensus in support of free markets, open trade, and democratic institutions.

The late 1990s should therefore have been the best of times in Latin America and the Caribbean. Almost two decades had passed since the last successful military coup. In most countries, public debate was vigorous and conducted with little fear of official retribution. The new global economy had lifted overall growth rates and helped millions to achieve higher standards of living. The sad reality, however, was that millions more were being left behind. The gap between rich and poor was extremely wide; more than a third of Latin Americans were forced to live on two dollars or less a day. The peoples of Venezuela, Nicaragua, and other countries that had welcomed the onset of democracy were becoming frustrated: they felt exploited and betrayed by their elected officials, and they worried that corruption and crime were so ingrained that they could never be rooted out. Surveys indicated the majority of Latin Americans were dissatisfied with democracy and saw it as a means for a manipulative elite to legitimize repression of the poor. There were similar problems in Central Europe, Asia, and Africa, where newly democratic regimes struggled under inherited burdens and their own uncertainty about democratic ways.

A decade earlier, when the Berlin Wall had come down, there was dancing in the streets. Now the euphoria was gone and we were in a new phase. There was danger, in some quarters, that optimism would give way to defeatism and open the door to failed approaches from the past. In some countries there was even a growing nostalgia for the order and discipline of Communist rule.

As a warning, in 1999 veterans of Czechoslovakia's Velvet Revolution actually sponsored an Open Air Museum of Totalitarianism. Visitors were able to walk past half-empty fruit stands stocked with rotten oranges, negotiate with a cheating butcher selling steaks under the counter, argue with a government clerk who just could not seem to find the right stamp, and purchase books published in the 1950s about socialism's inevitable triumph.

I wanted to do all I could while Secretary of State to help struggling democracies succeed. We could accomplish much on a bilateral basis, so I singled out Nigeria, Indonesia, Ukraine, and Colombia as priorities for our assistance and attention because of their regional importance and the scale of the challenges they faced. Nothing would do more for the health of democracy in Latin America, for example, than the restoration of stability in Colombia, a country ravaged by ruthless guerrillas and drug traffickers. But I also wanted to try a global approach.

Working with Mort Halperin and Assistant Secretary of State for Democracy, Human Rights and Labor Harold Koh, I put together a proposal the President approved. Our plan was at once ambitious and modest. We wanted to bring democracies from around the world together, but we didn't propose creating a new institution with its own bureaucracy, building, and letterhead. We made clear that our goal was to strengthen democracy where it existed, not extend it elsewhere. I favored doing both, but if we had said our goal was to spark democratic revolutions, we would have scared other countries away.

Our plan was to identify a core group of countries that would then invite a larger group to a global forum. At the larger meeting, nations would pledge to adhere to democratic standards and discuss how to help each other restore, defend, and strengthen democratic institutions.

For diplomatic reasons we didn't want the project to appear "made in America." Our thesis, after all, was that democracy wasn't just a Western invention; it had roots in virtually every culture. We wanted this belief reflected in the conference's sponsorship, participation, and location. Thinking about which country might best play host, we decided to ask Poland, whose Solidarity movement had led the way in freeing Central Europe from Communist control. One of Solidarity's leaders, Bronisław Geremek, was now foreign minister. He was a true democratic hero, and I had known him for nearly twenty years.

At the NATO summit in April 1999, I asked Geremek if he would host the Community of Democracies conference. Immediately he said yes. In succeeding months, he and I contacted the foreign ministers of likely nations to see if they would join in sponsoring the event. We ended up with a list of eight: Chile, the Czech Republic, India, Mali, Portugal, and the Republic of Korea, in addition to Poland and the United States.

Even though we had President Clinton's support, there were many in the U.S. government, including quite a few in the State Department, who were unenthusiastic. The cynical thought our proposal naïve, the wary worried about a backlash from countries that would be left out, and legalists thought we would tie ourselves in knots trying to agree on whom to invite and how to define "democracy."

Systematically, we worked our way around these objections. At one juncture Halperin told me the bureaucracy was evenly split. "One half will go along only if we assure them the conference is just a one-shot deal. The other half will support us only if we tell them it will lead to something permanent. We're telling both sides what they want to hear and advising them not to believe what they're told by anyone else. So far it's working."

With the conference set for June 2000, we began considering whom to invite. Harold Koh compared the process to planning a wedding with eight sets of parents. Each of the cosponsoring countries weighed in with their opinions, most often wanting to give nations in their region the benefit of the doubt. We agreed not to limit attendance to established democracies. The whole point was to strengthen democratic forces in places they were weak or in danger. Ultimately, we settled on a standard that a government must have made a public commitment to the democratic path, including elections.[4]

In the end 107 countries sent representatives. The centerpiece of our deliberations was a draft declaration that the cosponsoring governments had circulated, through which participants could reaffirm their commitment to democracy and outline their shared concept of what democracy requires. The Warsaw Declaration set standards to which each participating government could be held accountable by its own citizens. This would be especially valuable if follow-up meetings of the conference were held. Initially the question of whether there would be any follow-up was in doubt, but in Warsaw governments lined up for the chance to host the second meeting, and the third and the fourth. By the time we left, a schedule of biennial meetings was set through at least 2008.[5] There is reason to hope that the prospect of being invited or not invited to those events will motivate some governments to do more to live up to the Warsaw Declaration than they otherwise would have. That possibility alone made the initiative worthwhile, but its long-term significance depends on how fully the concept is embraced by future leaders in America and worldwide.

A final reason for the Warsaw Declaration was personal. For half a century the name Warsaw had been linked to the Warsaw Pact. Bronisław Geremek told me he had wanted the chance, through the Community of Democracies, to link the name of the city he loved with a cause truly in keeping with the history and spirit of the Polish people.

As I talked to colleagues during the conference, I was excited by the feeling that we had begun something that might truly flourish. Certainly there was much support for the idea that democracies should work together. The conference also provided a rebuttal to those who believe that democratic

---

4. The conference was for governments, but nongovernmental organizations (NGOs) play a key role in democratic development. Recognizing this, we asked two leading NGOs, Freedom House and Poland's Stefan Batory Foundation, to organize a World Forum on Democracy to be held in Warsaw at the same time. This allowed us to invite activists who were struggling for freedom in countries not eligible for the official conference.

5. The second conference was held in Seoul, Korea in November 2002. The third is scheduled for Santiago, Chile in February 2005. The fourth will probably take place in Africa.

values have no place outside the West. Speakers from every part of the world proclaimed their commitment to democratic ideals and their determination to fight for democratic values. Among them was UN Secretary General Kofi Annan, who said his profoundest aspiration for the UN was that it too might one day become a "community of democracies." President Oumar Konare of Mali said the conference proved that democracy was a "universal value," a purposeful statement made even more impressive by the president's ability to express it in Polish.

Amid all this cheering for democracy, there was a single discordant note sounding from a horn that was French. Hubert Védrine hadn't wanted to come to Warsaw, and told me early on that he didn't see the point of talking to democracies about the merits of democracy. I told him I thought it vital for France to attend because it was one of the world's oldest democracies, and the conference would benefit from his ideas. Finally, Védrine agreed to come for a couple of hours and make a speech. He then announced on the eve of the event that France, alone among the governments represented, would not sign the Warsaw Declaration.

Although in Warsaw only briefly, Védrine found time to summon reporters and vent the reasons for his disdain. He said, "Democracy is not like a religion that lends itself to converts but rather a process of evolution that involves long maturing processes within nations on such matters as economics, the collective state of mind, and in the end, politics." He said he was uncomfortable with the idea that democracies were qualified to lecture others. "Let's not be self-congratulatory," he said. "Our democracies still have room for improvement."

Védrine did not say so, but I had a feeling that his problem was not with the conference or the declaration but with America. I had had many private discussions with Hubert, always in French and sometimes over meals at the grand Quai D'Orsay, the French foreign ministry, or in the winter beside a fireplace at the ministry's villa outside Paris. Although—or perhaps because—we disagreed so often, I enjoyed these encounters and genuinely liked Védrine. He was a true intellectual who had spent his career championing French interests and ideas. I respected that.

When not consumed by some urgent problem, our conversations dealt primarily with the complex relationship between our two countries. While I argued the cause of democratic integration and stressed the extent of our nations' shared interests, Hubert made plain his distress that the trend toward globalization was being driven by Anglo-Saxons. Already in 2000, President Chirac had labeled U.S. "unilateralism" a major threat to the world, while Védrine described America as a "hyperpower"—a status beyond superpower. I had two reactions to this. First, I asked Hubert whether the French were jealous, and he confessed they were. Second, I agreed with him that America couldn't lead effectively without working closely with its allies. I also maintained that France—which had sent Lafayette to assist in America's quest for freedom—should be at the forefront of efforts to achieve solidarity among democracies. Védrine smiled, "Ah, but you see, *chère* Madeleine, Lafayette did not go to help the Americans; he went to defeat the British."

As much as I welcomed sparring with Védrine, on the democracies conference he was simply wrong. The Polish have a slogan, "For our freedom, and for yours": the freedom of one country is linked to that of others. The truth of that statement had been illustrated in the period preceding the Second World War when first Manchuria, then Ethiopia, then Czechoslovakia, then Poland were in turn attacked, their invasions serving as the prelude to others. Free nations are helped by strong democratic neighbors and hampered by weak or unstable ones. The Community of Democracies is based on the conviction that nothing is more powerful or positive than free people working together.

A TALL, HANDSOME MAN in an African print shirt walked up to me and put out his hand. "Hello," he said. "I'm Nelson Mandela." It was like having George Washington introduce himself. I put out my own hand and he shook it. At the time I was still serving as UN ambassador in New York; Mandela was perhaps the globe's most famous and respected man. He was the embodiment of his nation's liberation from apartheid and a leader who had taught the world a profound lesson about choosing reconciliation over revenge. Mandela in the mid 1990s also embodied a growing sense of optimism about all of Africa. Predictions were widespread of a "new African Renaissance" to replace the legacy of colonialism and postcolonial failures. There was substance behind those hopes.

By the time I became Secretary of State, half of sub-Saharan Africa's forty-eight countries had qualified as electoral democracies, many with new leaders determined to follow the model of Asian "tigers" by embracing economic reform, opening markets, privatizing industries, and stabilizing currencies. Economic growth rates had tripled since 1990; countries such as Senegal, Ghana, Mozambique, and Côte d'Ivoire were expanding economically at rates of up to 7 percent a year. Uganda, scene to hellish violence under Idi Amin, had become a magnet for investment under President Yoweri Museveni. Ethiopia, once notorious for famine, was enjoying double-digit growth. And South Africa, of course, had Mandela.

Traditionally, Africa had played only a marginal role in U.S. foreign policy. I had a different conception. Just as I saw the health of Europe affected by stability and democracy in the Balkans, so I saw global prospects for security and prosperity influenced by progress in Africa. The President, who shared my sense of Africa's importance, had welcomed many leaders from the continent to the White House. He soon undertook an extended trip to Africa, which the First Lady had already visited twice.

Tragically, in many parts of Africa the millennium ended in disaster. Susan Rice, our dedicated assistant secretary of state for African affairs, had more countries in conflict to cope with than any of her colleagues. Although we developed a host of strong relationships with African leaders, we could not halt or prevent a series of debilitating conflicts.

On my first trip to Africa as Secretary, I visited a hospital in the remote town of Gulu in northern Uganda. The health care facility doubled as a nighttime safe haven for villagers from the surrounding countryside, who were being terrorized by a group known as the Lord's Resistance Army (LRA). The LRA's professed goal was to overthrow the Ugandan government and set up its own rule based on the Ten Commandments, whose meaning the group obviously didn't comprehend. Operating from across the border in Sudan, the LRA raided villages in Uganda, kidnapping boys to become soldiers and girls for concubines. Local residents became settlers on an untamed frontier, tending crops or flocks by day and retreating into a fort, or in this case a hospital, when darkness came.

Because it was daylight when I visited the camp, there were only about a hundred or so people milling around the large central courtyard of the facility. The number swelled to ten times that amount at dusk. I met a group of boys who had either escaped from the LRA or been ransomed. Some were so young when they had been taken that they had little memory of home. One was ten-year-old Geoffrey, who had been held for four years. His gaunt body was covered with welts and scars. Another boy, about six, said people from his village had been attacked two weeks earlier. His mother had shielded his baby sister and him with her body. When it was quiet, he rolled out from under her and found she was dead. He had taken his sister in his arms and walked for a day to the hospital.

I went to see a group of teenage girls who were sitting on mattresses, braiding each other's hair. They rose as I entered, looking as if they belonged in junior high school, yet several were already mothers, their babies the result of rapes perpetrated by the LRA. "Even if you are a very young girl," one of them told me, "you would be given to a man the age of my father."

As I started to leave, a young man came up holding an infant. "This is the sister of that boy you were talking to," he said. "Her name is Charity." I held the tiny orphan, seeing her eyes and feeling the need to provide some reassurance. "It's going to be all right," I said to the baby. But suddenly I was the one who needed reassurance. Turning to one of the hospital workers, I said, "It *is* going to be all right, isn't it?"

The LRA's activities were localized but symptomatic of a larger problem. Many of Africa's borders don't make demographic sense. Drawn by European colonizers, they don't necessarily reflect geographic or ethnic realities. The result is that everyone seems to get involved in everyone else's business. Sudan's radical Islamist government supported the LRA because the LRA harassed Uganda, which backed rebels fighting in southern Sudan. In Central Africa, the virulent rivalry between the Hutus and Tutsis helped ensnare the massive Democratic Republic of Congo (DROC) in war.

In May 1997, a Congolese guerrilla leader, Laurent Kabila, overthrew Mobutu Sese Seko, a corrupt dictator. Mobutu's departure was welcome, but Kabila's arrival set off a deadly chain reaction. In overthrowing Mobutu, Kabila had received help from neighboring Rwanda and Uganda, who then asked Kabila for help in eradicating Hutu militias based in the DROC.[6] When Kabila refused, the Rwandans took matters into their own hands in August 1998, sending forces into the DROC to fight Hutus and back Congolese rebels opposed to Kabila. The Ugandans also invaded and sponsored yet another rebel group. Kabila appealed to Zimbabwe, which provided troops in return for a share of the DROC's mining revenues. Several other countries also sent contingents, and the hated Hutu militia lined up with Kabila. Since the DROC countryside has few roads, the conflict rapidly became a struggle for control of airstrips and river transport points. Because supply lines were tenuous, people with guns took food from those without guns, and huge numbers of noncombatants died.

Ordinarily Kabila might have had a legitimate claim on international sympathy. He had overthrown a widely despised dictator, his country had been invaded, and a stable and peaceful DROC would be a boon to all Central Africa. Unforgivably, Kabila blew the opportunity by alienating other Africans, trying to extort money from foreign investors, refusing to cooperate with a UN human rights investigation, reneging on a promise

6. These Hutu militias included fighters who had participated in the 1994 Rwandan genocide directed primarily against Tutsis. The governments of Uganda and Rwanda, both controlled by Tutsis, wanted to punish the Hutu and prevent further attacks.

to hold elections, and failing to approve a constitution protecting political rights. During a press conference with me in Kinshasa, he exploded in anger when asked why an opposition leader had been detained. His policies—grimly reminiscent of Mobutu's—produced economic disaster and contributed to the widest and perhaps deadliest cross-border war in African history.

The hope that a new generation of African leaders would propel the continent forward rested on a group that included Isaias Afwerki of Eritrea and Meles Zenawi of Ethiopia. Although both had taken power by force, each knew how to speak the language of economic reform, and each had democratic pretensions, but by the middle of 1998, they had led their nations into a bloody war against each other in which neither side could hope to win anything worth winning. Tens of thousands of lives were lost in World War I–style trench warfare—except with more lethal weapons.

Just as heartbreaking was the conflict in the tiny West African nation of Sierra Leone. There a group known as the Revolutionary United Front (RUF) waged a brutal struggle for power against a democratically elected government. The rebels showed their contempt for the electoral process by slicing off the hands and arms of those thought to have voted "wrong" (that is, for the government) as well as the limbs of the voters' children. Since ballots in Sierra Leone are marked by thumbprints, the tactic had a perverse, sadistic rationale.

In 1999, I saw the horrifying results firsthand during a visit to the Murray Town Amputee Camp near Freetown, Sierra Leone. David Evans of the Vietnam Veterans of America Foundation showed me where the prosthetics were made and how children were trained to use them. He discussed the different challenges faced by those who are missing a leg, as opposed to a hand or an arm or both hands or both arms. These were not wounds that could be made whole, but if there was self-pity in that sun-baked camp, I did not sense it—just sadness and courage. I saw a baby with no arms being held by a mother with one arm. I hugged a three-year-old girl named Mamuna who was wearing a red jumper and happily playing with a toy car using the only arm she had. How could any human being have taken a machete to this girl? According to UN officials, much of the maiming was done by child soldiers forcibly recruited and given drugs. To discourage these "soldiers" from escaping, some were forced to kill members of their own families so they could never return home.

These and other outrages created a dilemma. In colonial times, conflicts in Africa were settled through negotiations among the European powers. During the Cold War, outcomes were influenced by military assistance and proxy troops provided by one bloc or another. In the new era, there were no similarly potent external forces seeking to maintain order. Consider, for example, the United Nations. The lesson of Somalia was that the organization invited disaster when it took sides in a conflict. The lesson of Rwanda was that the UN invited disaster when it heeded the lesson of Somalia. Despite a U.S.-led training initiative, Africa's own peacekeeping capabilities were not yet sufficient to intervene effectively in a major war. The solution to these conflicts had therefore to be found through diplomacy, with outside force introduced rarely and selectively.

During my years as Secretary, I worked with African and European diplomats to develop a model for negotiations that encouraged African leaders to design solutions with international support. In the Horn of Africa, Susan Rice, Special Envoy Tony Lake, and the NSC's Gayle Smith joined the Organization of African Unity in persuading Ethiopia and Eritrea to end their conflict. In the DROC, Zambia and other African nations, backed by the United States, EU, and UN, brokered a series of partial agreements that were partially implemented. It was not until December 2002 that a settlement was reached and even that has since slid into reverse.[7] In Sierra Leone the Economic Community of West African States (ECOWAS) forged an agreement in 1999 between the government and rebels that halted the slaughter for a time but didn't last. After a nearly disastrous start, a UN peacekeeping force heavily assisted by the British brought about a second cease-fire agreement in November 2000, paving the way to disarmament and relative peace. The seemingly endless civil war in Sudan resisted all diplomatic efforts despite countless time-devouring strategy sessions I had with Tom Pickering, Susan Rice, and Special Envoy Harry Johnston, often in consultation with concerned members of Congress.

Overall, the results of these initiatives have been mixed. True security will not come until there is a decisive political shift, which will not occur until the leaders driving the violence conclude that their tactics won't work.

As in the Balkans, there was a tendency in the less stable parts of Africa to view the struggle for power as a war where the winner gets everything and the loser nothing. This view was not limited to actual battlefields. In many countries, the idea of legitimate political opposition was novel and the space for true public debate narrowly restricted. This was why we made the promotion of democracy a centerpiece of Clinton administration policy toward Africa. In addition to the assistance we gave to civil

---

7. Laurent Kabila was assassinated in January 2001 by one of his own bodyguards. He was replaced by his more moderate son, Joseph, which helped to make a negotiated settlement possible.

society, our two primary economic initiatives gave preference to countries engaged in economic and political reform. The Africa Growth and Opportunity Act, which became law in May 2000 after a multi-year struggle, lowered many U.S. trade barriers to countries in sub-Saharan Africa. And our support for large-scale debt relief for Africa was designed to free up funds for investment in education, health care, and other social needs.

In all my efforts to exercise constructive American leadership, there was one recurring frustration, and that was money. Whether the specific need was debt relief for Nigeria or peacekeepers for Sierra Leone or judicial training for Rwanda, we were always left scraping for nickels and dimes. With the President's help, and that of congressional allies, I succeeded in adding about 25 percent to our budget for Africa from the record low level I inherited. But even when added to funds from other donors, this wasn't nearly enough. I found this situation especially difficult to explain to African leaders, because at the time our economy was booming and we had a large budget surplus.

Probably the most striking example of where we did much more (but still not nearly enough) was in the fight against HIV/AIDS. At the start of my term I expected AIDS to be a significant threat to democracy, prosperity, and security in Africa. I soon realized it was the dominant one.

Statistics are not adequate to describe the destruction being caused by this disease. Africa has 10 percent of the world's population and 70 percent of the people infected by the HIV virus. In some countries, the infection rate is above 20 percent. In Botswana, one of Africa's richest and freest countries, the average teenager is as likely to die from AIDS as from all other causes of death combined.

The only sure way to beat AIDS is to prevent it. This requires international financing, national leaders brave enough to confront the issue, and educators spreading the word at the local level. Uganda was among the first nations to be devastated by AIDS and also the first in Africa to fight back effectively. President Museveni urged every cabinet minister, school, church, and business to promote AIDS awareness, prevention, and treatment. Ugandans called this "the big noise," and it cut HIV infection rates by 50 percent.

In Kenya, by contrast, AIDS activists had to work around the fixed ideas of Daniel Arap Moi, the country's septuagenarian president, who opposed the use of condoms and sex education in schools. To make a point, while in Nairobi in 1999, I attended a presentation entitled "One Book, One Pen." It was given by a youth-oriented dance and acting troupe in a poor neighborhood on the outskirts of the city. The strong sun didn't bother the hundreds of colorfully dressed teenagers and their younger brothers and sisters who gathered, attracted by the music. I too found the drumming irresistible and when invited to get up and dance, I did.

The moral of the story the performers acted out was that if you try to write in more than one book, your pen will run dry, as it will if it's left without a cap—a clever if suitably unsubtle lesson encouraging abstinence, fidelity, and caution. The associated discussion also dealt with the vital issues of sexual coercion and the stigma attached to HIV infection. Later, in Botswana, I visited a clinic for women living with AIDS. The doctors there said that half the women who learned they were infected didn't tell their husbands for fear of being shunned. Because of the stigma, many at-risk Africans—and non-Africans, for that matter—refused to get tested. And when people who are infected don't acknowledge their condition, they are more likely to infect others and to fail to take the steps required to prevent the disease from being transmitted to babies.

In January 2000, Vice-President Gore chaired a special UN Security Council session on HIV/AIDS, the first time a disease has been so clearly recognized as a danger not just to public health, but also to world security.

During the UN General Assembly in September of that year, I joined with the world's twelve other women foreign ministers in calling upon all national leaders to join the public fight against AIDS and to recognize the increased need to protect women and girls. In Africa in recent years, for the first time anywhere, the majority of persons newly infected by the HIV virus were female. I am proud that, during the Clinton administration, the United States was the largest single donor to international HIV/AIDS prevention and treatment efforts. There is, however, no sensible upper limit to our contributions.

I had hoped when entering office to open a new chapter in U.S. relations with Africa and to help transform American perceptions of Africa as a place of poverty and strife into one of modernization and progress. I visited Africa seven times while in government and every year as Secretary. We also hosted an unprecedented conference of African cabinet members, and took steps to stimulate trade and investment with Africa through increased access to credit and insurance.

For all its problems, there is nothing African countries need to do that some have not already done. It's just a question of learning the right lessons. Tanzania's longtime President Julius Nyerere emphasized the importance of national identity, and shaped a country whose people think of themselves as Tanzanians, not as members of separate ethnic groups. Ghana's Jerry Rawlings and Mali's Oumar Konare are two of many African leaders who tolerated political opposition and established democratic precedents by turning power over to elected successors. In two decades, the ethnically diverse leadership of Mauritius has transformed a backwater economy based almost entirely on sugar into a modern one with the highest average income in Africa.

Overall, however, the persistence of conflict, poverty, and disease have put on hold realistic talk about a renaissance in Africa. It is hard to be optimistic, but there is a deep determination in Africa not to be left behind. On the day he was inaugurated as Nelson Mandela's successor, South African President Thabo Mbeki quoted a tribal proverb about "the dawning of the dawn, when only the tips of the horns of the cattle can be seen etched against the morning sky." As one millennium stood aside to make way for another, those with hopeful eyes could see in Africa at least the dawning of the dawn.

TWENTY-SEVEN

Inside the Hermit Kingdom

THOSE WRITING ABOUT the distant past can proceed without worrying that their subject will be transformed between the time they write and the time their work is published. For me, that is a peril with every chapter, and most particularly this one. I am writing in May 2003 about events that occurred primarily during my years as UN ambassador and Secretary of State. Much of what the Clinton administration attempted in its Korea policy has unraveled since I left office, opening scenarios for the future ranging from the restoration of stability to a nuclear-armed North Korea to war. Wherever matters now stand, what follows is intended to shed light on the nature of opportunities lost or seized.

ON JUNE 25, 1950, North Korean troops, backed by China and the Soviet Union, invaded South Korea, setting off a bloody three-year war. My father was teaching that summer at the University of Washington in Seattle, and I—having just become a teenager—read my way through a vast collection of comic books found in our rented house. It was not a television war, but my family followed the seesawing fortunes of the two sides closely as the United States and other nations fought under the UN flag to repel the invaders. I cared about the outcome, because my father had made clear to me that the allied effort was part of the worldwide struggle against Communism. Unfortunately, the war ended not with peace but stalemate. A demilitarized zone (DMZ) was created to separate the two sides, and U.S. troops were deployed in South Korea as a deterrent to further aggression from the North. They have been there ever since.

Four decades passed between the war and the day I became UN ambassador, but my view of North Korea, or the Democratic People's Republic of

Korea (DPRK), did not change because the fundamental nature of the regime did not change. North Korean President Kim Il Sung was among the world's most destructive dictators, cruel to his people, hostile toward the South, and heedless of international law. He also grew obsessed, near the end of his life, with developing a nuclear arsenal. This ambition may have been hastened by his country's rapid economic decline resulting from the Cold War's end. For decades after its creation in 1948, North Korea had been more prosperous than its southern neighbor due to the preferential ties it enjoyed with the Soviet Union and East Europe. The loss of those relationships, coupled with a series of natural disasters, crippled its economy.

In 1993 and 1994, the DPRK became the first country to announce plans to withdraw from the Nuclear Nonproliferation Treaty and from the nuclear safeguards regime administered by the International Atomic Energy Agency (IAEA). The government indicated its intention to remove fuel rods from its nuclear reactor and extract the weapons-grade plutonium they contained—enough to make half a dozen nuclear weapons. This precipitated a crisis between Washington and Pyongyang. Tensions were at the boiling point; the possibility of a real war lay beneath the escalating war of words. At the UN one day, I had to sit through a particularly vituperative speech from the North Korean representative. I knew I was being baited and so bit my lip: the North Korean would have liked nothing better than a fight. Instead I said, "Saturday is my birthday, and although I am sure this was not the intention, I would like to thank the DPRK representative for making me feel forty years younger with his rhetoric from the deepest depths of the Cold War."

The Clinton administration, determined to stop Pyongyang from developing nuclear weapons, was considering options up to and including military strikes aimed at the North Korean reactor. Fortunately, the North Koreans did not push their luck that far. Ambassador Robert Gallucci, one of our ablest diplomats, had engaged in lengthy negotiations with Pyongyang. In 1994, he seized an opening created by former President Jimmy Carter to conclude an accord known as the Agreed Framework. This required the North to shut down its reactor, seal eight thousand fuel rods containing reprocessed plutonium, and freeze its plutonium production facilities under IAEA inspection. In return, the United States and its allies agreed to help North Korea cope with its immediate fuel shortages and pay for the construction of two civilian nuclear power plants.[1] Although criti-

1. Under the Agreed Framework, the DPRK wouldn't receive the final components necessary to operate the light-water nuclear reactors until it disclosed the full history of its nuclear weapons programs.

cized by some for not resolving every issue on the Korean Peninsula, the Agreed Framework ended the immediate crisis and prevented the North from realizing its potential to develop dozens of nuclear bombs. The Korean Peninsula nevertheless remained one of the world's most dangerous places. When I became Secretary, I wanted to explore every opportunity for reducing the risk of a military confrontation. Three factors caused me to conclude that a high-profile effort was both needed and timely.

The first was North Korea's weakness. Kim Il Sung had prided himself on the concept of *juche*, or self-reliance. But when he died in 1994, he bequeathed to his son, Kim Jong Il, a society dependent on the charity of the outside world for food, fertilizer, and fuel. The question we faced was whether the DPRK's plight would prompt it to act responsibly to reduce its isolation, or rashly. We had good reason to try to influence its choice.

A second factor was the election, in December 1997, of Kim Dae-jung as president of South Korea. During the Cold War, South Korea's rulers had used the Communist threat to justify governing with an iron hand. Kim Dae-jung, by contrast, was a lifelong democratic activist who had spent years in prison for his outspoken views. I first met Kim in 1986 when I was in South Korea as part of a delegation from the National Democratic Institute. Even though he was under house arrest, he expressed his ideas without fear and eagerly shared a bold vision for South Korean democracy. Before we left, he wrote a message to each of us on a small white board using Korea's distinctive calligraphy brushes. His advice to me was, "If you seek real, practical solutions, then you will achieve them." When I returned to Seoul in 1998 to visit the newly inaugurated President Kim, I brought along the board he had given me, and he reautographed it.

Meeting Kim Dae-jung as president, I saw a parallel to Václav Havel and Nelson Mandela, both of whom had also journeyed improbably from prison to the presidency of their respective countries. Each had used the time in confinement to develop a distinctive philosophy about politics and life. No one could argue with greater credibility than Kim that democracy and respect for human rights were compatible with Asian values. During our official meeting, the seventy-two-year-old leader explained his plans for a new "sunshine policy" toward North Korea. Other South Korean presidents had given lip service to the idea of reconciliation with the North, but Kim Dae-jung was determined to pursue peaceful coexistence. He saw great danger in North Korea's almost paranoid sense of insecurity.

A third factor driving events was North Korea's military prowess. Few governments have ever made such a clear choice between butter and guns. Despite the starvation of its people, the DPRK has built a million-man army and developed the ability to manufacture and sell sophisticated weapons to foreign buyers. Missiles and dangerous technology are its leading cash crops. In August 1998, Pyongyang tested a three-stage Taepo Dong missile of a type potentially able—with further development and testing—to reach U.S. territory. The combination of long-range missiles and North Korea's capacity to produce nuclear bombs that could be delivered by those missiles was obviously an extremely grave concern.

Taking into account each of these factors, the President and I asked former Defense Secretary William Perry, who was uniformly respected for his judgment and toughness, to head an interagency review of our Korea policy. Perry was reluctant to take the assignment but finally agreed to do so because he knew the stakes were so high: a miscalculation leading to war on the Korean Peninsula would produce massive casualties. The stability of East Asia and the safety of thirty-seven thousand American troops deployed in South Korea depended on diplomats doing their jobs.[2]

Perry was assisted and later succeeded by State Department Counselor Wendy Sherman; both were helped by Ambassador Charles Kartman, our Special Envoy for Korean Peace Talks. Together they consulted widely at home and in Asia and Europe. Dr. Perry made clear the status quo was unacceptable and recommended a diplomatic initiative that was both comprehensive and step-by-step. He rejected the theory of some that North Korea was on the verge of collapse; saying we had to deal with the DPRK as it was, not as we might wish it to be. He suggested a systematic testing of North Korean intentions by offering Kim Jong Il a choice between confrontation and the chance to improve relations by agreeing to refrain from unsupervised nuclear activities and to end destabilizing missile development programs and exports. In May, Perry and Sherman met directly with top North Korean officials in Pyongyang to lay out our proposals. The North Koreans did not provide a clear response until four months later, but when they did, it was positive. Instead of going ahead as planned with another missile test, they declared a moratorium on such

---

2. The dangers in the region had been dramatized for me by a helicopter trip to the demilitarized zone in 1997. The armistice line is less than forty miles north of Seoul, leaving the city well within the range of North Korean rockets and vulnerable to attack by the hundreds of thousands of DPRK troops massed close to the DMZ. On the near side of the line is Camp Bonifas, named for an American company commander who had been murdered by the North Koreans in 1976. I was transported by Humvee to an observation post, directed to what must have been the world's biggest binoculars, and pointed in the right direction. What I observed was a landscape that seemed about as lush and livable as the moon—and a North Korean military officer peering back at me.

tests as long as talks with the United States about improved relations were under way. To lend momentum to the diplomatic process, President Clinton announced plans to suspend restrictions on nonmilitary trade, financial transactions, travel, and official contacts.

Meanwhile Kim Dae-jung's sunshine policy also appeared to be bearing fruit. In June 2000, Kim Jong Il welcomed him to Pyongyang for an unprecedented summit between the two leaders. Their meetings were cordial, and in the summit's afterglow, groups of separated Korean families were allowed to visit each other for the first time in five decades. North and South Korean athletes marched as one during opening ceremonies of the 2000 Olympic Games, and Kim Dae-jung was awarded the Nobel Peace Prize for his efforts at reconciliation.

Meanwhile North Korean diplomats, so accustomed to the role of wallflower, were now in the spotlight. That July, the annual convening of the ASEAN Regional Forum in Bangkok featured the first meeting ever between the North Korean foreign minister and the U.S. Secretary of State. When Foreign Minister Paek Nam-Sun and I shook hands prior to our scheduled fifteen-minute talk, three successive waves of photographers recorded the moment. I had been told not to expect much of Paek, but he was smoothly professional. Our discussion lasted more than an hour; I described it afterwards as "substantively modest, but symbolically important." One matter we talked about was whether Kim Jong Il would send a high-level envoy to the United States, just as President Clinton had sent Bill Perry to Pyongyang. Once again, the North Koreans were deliberate—which is to say, slow—in responding. Unused to consulting with a democracy, they had the habit of doing nothing for months, then making a decision and expecting an immediate response.

In October 2000, Kim Jong Il finally did decide to send a high-level emissary—Vice Marshal Jo Myong Rok, the number two man in the military. This was an important sign that, whatever choices North Korea made, its army would be part of the decision. Jo wore a gray suit to his meeting at the State Department with me, but less than half an hour later arrived at the White House in full military uniform, complete with epaulets, medals (including at least one for fighting against America in Vietnam), and ribbons. With a flourish, he presented a letter from Kim Jong Il and invited the President to come to Pyongyang. The President said he would study the proposal, but that arrangements would have to be made in advance to assure the success of any trip. Jo pressed for a more definitive response. The President suggested I go first to prepare the ground. Jo said if the President and Secretary came together, "We will be able to find the solution to all problems."

It seemed that the whole point of Jo's mission was to secure a Clinton visit, but clearly North Korea's top-down decision-making style didn't fit well with our practice of trying to "pre-cook" arrangements as much as possible before committing the President. More positively, Jo's delegation had come with some unexpectedly constructive proposals related to their missile programs. It appeared to us that a summit might well produce an agreement in principle that, if fleshed out, could make East Asia less dangerous. So I was intrigued when Vice-Marshal Jo accepted our insistence on a preparatory visit and invited me to Pyongyang.

The two delegations also issued a joint communiqué making clear our countries' desire to move beyond the hostilities of the past. Each side pledged "no hostile intent" toward the other. This potentially historic step, requiring no sacrifice on our part, was designed to ease North Korea's insecurity and make it more willing to accept restrictions on its weapons programs. That night the Vice-Marshal hosted a dinner that was quite relaxed, perhaps overly so. I spent much of the evening trying to fend off the North Korean delegation's aggressive style of drinking, which appeared to require the constant refilling of glasses and near-continuous toasts.

Diplomacy with North Korea is not just a bilateral affair. Our East Asian allies are always there either in body or spirit. The South Koreans have an agenda with the DPRK that overlaps ours but isn't always ordered the same way and is obviously influenced by the national identity they share with those north of the DMZ. The Japanese were less concerned with North Korea's efforts to develop long-range missiles than with their own vulnerability to the dozens of mobile mid-range missiles the DPRK had already deployed. Tokyo also insisted, understandably, that North Koreans account for the Japanese citizens they had kidnapped during the 1970s and '80s to serve as language teachers.[3] As a result, our diplomacy with North Korea resembled a sack race, with us trying to be sure our partners were comfortable with what we were doing, and Australia, China, Russia, and Europe also consulted about every major step we took.

THERE WERE LOGISTICS ISSUES on all my trips, but North Korea offered unique challenges. Since we had no diplomatic presence in Pyongyang, we had to create a miniature embassy from scratch. The technicians we sent ahead found six different types of electrical outlets, sometimes

3. Not until September 2002, did Chairman Kim admit that the Japanese allegations were accurate. He confessed that North Korea had abducted thirteen men and women, of whom only five were still alive.

several different kinds in the same room. Negotiating a schedule was also complicated. The North Koreans insisted I visit the tomb of Kim Il Sung. Ordinarily this would have been a simple enough courtesy, but Kim Il Sung had started the Korean War, in which fifty-four thousand Americans and hundreds of thousands of Koreans had died. He had then instituted a cradle-to-grave propaganda system that blamed America for the war and brainwashed his countrymen into worshipping him as a god. There may be places more impoverished than North Korea, but nowhere had the spontaneity of the human spirit been more determinedly crushed. Because it seemed a diplomatic necessity, I would visit the tomb of the man responsible for all this, but I couldn't pay his memory any respect.

The other scheduling complication was that no specific time was set for my meeting with Kim Jong Il. We assumed that such an encounter would take place on the second day of the two-day visit, but the North Koreans wouldn't tell us for certain, nor would they fix a time. In the highly structured world of international diplomacy, such uncertainty is unusual, but no American secretary of state had ever visited Pyongyang, and North Korea is not like anywhere else.

In other countries we saw police or military holding traffic back while our motorcade traveled from airport to hotel. In Pyongyang there was no traffic to hold back. Ours were the only cars on the road. Even so, the pedestrians we passed did not even glance up as we drove by. After passing some drought-stricken rice and cabbage fields, we saw paint-deprived apartment houses ranging from three or four stories high outside the city to twenty or more stories in town. I hated to think of slogging to the upper floors of those buildings when the power was out, with no electric lights or elevators—if they had elevators.

Inside the city, neat and healthy-looking children brightened the scene as they made their way to school in red-and-blue uniforms. A few rode bicycles but most were on foot. On the plane trip in, I had watched a documentary on children in the rural parts of the country. Those children were decidedly unhealthy: two-thirds of all North Korean children suffered from chronic malnutrition; many had been abandoned by their parents and left to scavenge. I knew the sights I would see would be contrived to leave us with an impression far different from the reality.

After freshening up at our guest house, we headed into the heart of Pyongyang, a city with wide boulevards, clean parks, and views of the beautiful Tae-dong River. In contrast to other Asian cities, there were practically no neon lights or even advertising. I could see no evidence of a restaurant, grocery store, department store, or bank. Instead the cityscape was dominated by empty streets and vast vacant squares of stone leading to structures such as the Grand People's Study House, the Juche Tower, and May Day Stadium.

My car pulled up at Kim Il Sung Memorial Palace, where I was greeted briskly by Vice-Marshal Jo and escorted on slippery marble floors past a long line of guards to the bier where the late dictator's embalmed body lay under glass. I paused briefly and moved on. During our short meeting, I gave Jo a letter from President Clinton extending his greetings and outlining the administration's hopes for my trip. Like every other North Korean I would meet, Jo wore a pin bearing the face of Kim Il Sung. I wore my largest American flag pin.

From the mausoleum I went to a kindergarten near a large apartment complex, where I danced briefly with a group of highly disciplined five-year-olds, swaying to a song I learned later was about the glories of fighting imperialism. I also met with the local head of the World Food Program, which was feeding about eight million North Koreans—including those kindergarteners—with help predominantly from the "imperialist" United States.

During our break for lunch, we learned that my schedule of meetings with various officials had been scrapped and that in midafternoon I would instead meet with Chairman Kim, also known as the "Dear Leader." I looked forward to the encounter with curiosity. We knew little about Kim, who was reputed to be an unworldly recluse, more interested in making and watching movies than in governing. However, according to Kim Dae-jung and Chinese and Russian officials who had recently met the DPRK leader, he was knowledgeable, good-humored, and relatively normal. Personally I was not sure how normal I would be if I had grown up being fed on Marxism in a sealed-off world, surrounded by heroic images of my father and myself. So I was uncertain what to expect.

Upon arriving at the chairman's guest house, I was directed to stand on a bilious green carpet in front of a large mural of a storm at sea. The press began snapping as soon as Chairman Kim walked in wearing his customary khaki leisure suit. He greeted me holding out both hands and smiling broadly. I was wearing heels, but so was he, which made us about the same height, and for a while we just stood there, letting the media do their work. I could not help but notice one movie camera operated by the North Koreans that must have been vintage 1950s.

At our meeting across a highly polished wooden table, Kim—who had a round face, wore large eyeglasses, and sported amazing puffed-up hair—began by congratulating me on my energy. He knew I had arrived in the morning after a marathon flight and was impressed that I was ready to go to work despite my age (only five more years than his). He thanked me for my visit to the mausoleum and expressed gratitude that, when his father had died, the North Koreans had received a message of condolence from President Clinton. He also expressed appreciation for the humanitarian assistance we had been sending and said he hoped President Clinton would come to Pyongyang. "If both sides are genuine and serious," he said, "there is nothing we will not be able to do."

I had been told that the best way to get results in diplomacy with North Korea was to take my time and try to build a relationship slowly. This approach was fine for careerists, but I would be out of Pyongyang in two days and out of office in three months. So I cut to the chase. After offering some reassurances about U.S. intentions in East Asia, I told Kim that I hadn't yet decided what to tell President Clinton but that I couldn't recommend a summit without a satisfactory agreement on missiles.

Kim said he took the issue seriously because America did, even though we were wrong to believe that his country would ever attack anyone. He said his nation had begun the program solely out of a desire to launch peaceful communications satellites, perhaps three a year. But if another nation would agree to send the satellites into orbit on North Korea's behalf, he would have no use for missiles.

As for their exports, which I said were a major problem, Kim said that North Korea was selling missiles to Syria and Iran to get desperately needed foreign currency. "So it's clear, since we export to get money, if you guarantee compensation, it will be suspended."

I replied, "Mr. Chairman, we've been concerned about your intentions for fifty years, and so we have been concerned about your production of missiles. And now you say it is just to earn foreign currency."

"Well, it's not just foreign currency," he said. "We also arm our own military as part of our self-reliance program."

He added that his armed forces were worried about South Korean capabilities, but "if there is an assurance that South Korea will not develop five-hundred-kilometer-range missiles, we won't either. As for the missiles already deployed, I don't think we can do much about them. You can't go inside the units and inspect them, but it's possible to stop production. It's been ten years since the collapse of the USSR, the opening of China, and the disappearance of our military alliance with either country. The military wants to update its equipment, but we won't give them new equipment. If there's no confrontation, there's no significance to weapons. Missiles are now insignificant."

Kim said I could make his comments public, but I replied that I needed to report to the President before talking to the press. At the end of our conversation he indicated we would meet again the following day. He then said he had a special surprise. "I have changed the entertainment. We have prepared a spectacular program in May Day Stadium that will help you understand North Korean culture and arts. The Western world thinks we are belligerent, and the U.S. has a lot of misunderstanding about us. It is important to know us directly. You can relax and enjoy it."

When I reached the stadium that evening, everyone was already seated. As I walked in with Kim, the huge crowd gave forth a volcano of rapturous sound—which I knew was not for me. The arena was enormous and every seat taken. The contrast to the almost empty streets was startling; where had all the people come from?

The exhibition itself resembled an Olympics opening ceremony on steroids and, as I soon realized, was far more political than cultural. It was a repeat of a spectacle prepared in honor of the fiftieth anniversary of the Korean Communist party—no cause for joy in my book. It began with a giant image of a hammer for workers, a brush for intellectuals, and a sickle for farmers. Then suddenly, everywhere, there were children dancing, gymnasts cartwheeling, sequined costumes swirling, and people flying about on little rockets. There were youngsters dressed up as flowers, soldiers thrusting their bayonets, fireworks, and people shot from cannons into a net. There was a human card section rapidly and precisely flashing tens of thousands of placards showing detailed murals and illustrated slogans accompanied by thunderous patriotic chants. And there was a full orchestra playing songs such as "The Leader Will Always Be with Us" and "Let Us Hold High the Red Flag." More than a hundred thousand people performed; perhaps two hundred thousand watched.

In the midst of all this the card section showed a Taepo Dong missile being launched into the East Asian sky—exhibiting North Korean pride at the controversial 1998 test. Even before the robotic applause began to fade, Chairman Kim leaned over to me and said through his interpreter, "That was our first missile launch—and our last." Overall it was an evening of mixed messages. I was encouraged by Kim's apparent promise, even though made in such a peculiar setting, and hoped to make it stick. At the same time the gaudy ceremony—which the chairman told me he helped design—left me almost speechless. I had certainly been impressed by the young acrobats but appalled by the energy and money wasted celebrating the very philosophy that produced the country's destitution. As Kim and I emerged, U.S. reporters yelled out, "What did you think?" I responded, "It was amazing," adding later, "I have never seen a hundred thousand people dance in step. I guess it takes a dictator to make that happen."

That night our delegations met for dinner. Kim and I exchanged toasts, followed by one with Jo. I was relieved when Kim discouraged attempts by other North Korean officials to keep my glass filled and challenge me to more toasts. Kim himself drank considerably less than his companions, though he did take pride in serving French wine.

During our conversation, when I asked how many computers his country had, he said a hundred thousand, three of which he used himself. He later requested the address of the State Department website. He also brought up the question of language and asked me what I thought of his interpreter. "Is he as good as Kim Dae-jung's?" This threw me because I didn't want to get the poor interpreter in trouble. "Kim Dae-jung has one of the best interpreters I have ever heard, a woman. Your interpreter is equally impressive." At this, Chairman Kim beamed; so did his interpreter.

Kim said he wished more of his people spoke English and would be pleased if Korean-Americans came to teach the language. As the evening wore on, I asked whether it was true that he was a movie buff. He smiled and said, "Yes. I try to catch up on the latest movies every ten days or so, and I like the Oscars."

I met with Chairman Kim again the next afternoon. I said we had given his delegation a list of questions and that it would be helpful if his experts could provide at least some answers before the end of the day. To my surprise, Kim asked for the list and began answering the questions himself, not even consulting the expert by his side. Yes, he said, the proposed ban on missile exports would apply to existing as well as new contracts, provided there was compensation. Yes, the ban would be comprehensive and apply to all missile-related materials, training, and technology. Yes, North Korea intended to accede to the multinational Missile Technology Control regime, provided South Korea did as well. Verification issues, he said, would require further discussion. I suggested we have our respective experts meet the following week and he agreed, proposing Malaysia as a site.

I asked him about his attitude toward the presence of American troops on the Korean Peninsula. He said his government's view had changed since the Cold War: American troops now played a stabilizing role. He added, however, that there was a fifty-fifty split within his military on whether or not to improve relations with the United States and that there were people in the foreign ministry who had opposed even his decision to talk to us. He said, "As in the U.S., there are people here with views different from mine, although they don't amount to the level of opposition you have. There are still some here who think U.S. troops should leave. And there are many in South Korea who are opposed to the U.S. presence as well." Kim said the solution rested with the normalization of relations.

I asked if I could make public the commitment he made to me after the depiction of the missile launch at the stadium, and he said I could make all of our discussions public, with the exception of one issue involving the sensitivities of a third country. I told him I thought our discussions had increased understanding on both sides.

Kim replied, "When the South Koreans came, I asked whether they were looking for horns on my head. They said no. Yes, there were a lot of misunderstandings between us. For example, we did not educate our children right. Our children were taught to call your countrymen 'American bastards' instead of just 'Americans.'"

That night we had another joint dinner, this time in a place called Magnolia Hall. In accordance with protocol, we were hosting—which meant a bicultural menu featuring American roast turkey with kimchi and Korean baked pigeon (head on) accompanied by strawberry shortcake, Californian and Korean wines, and thankfully, water. Kim and I gave each other gifts and talked about economic issues. He admitted that his country was in dire straits, trapped in a vicious circle, because the drought had made it impossible to generate hydroelectric power, thermal plants were hurt by a lack of coal, and they couldn't mine coal without electricity.

I asked him whether he would consider opening his economy and he responded, "What do you mean by 'opening'? We will have to define the term first, because opening means different things to different countries. We do not accept the Western version of opening. Opening should not harm our traditions." He added that he was not interested in the Chinese model of mixing free markets and socialism. Instead he was intrigued by the Swedish model, which he said was basically socialist. Pondering the idea of North Korea as Sweden, I asked him if there were any other models.

He said, "Thailand maintains a strong traditional royal system and has preserved its independence through a long, turbulent history, yet has a market economy. I am also interested in the Thai model." I wondered to myself whether it was Thailand's economic system or its preservation of royalty that most attracted him.

As our plates were taken away, one end of the room abruptly rose and became a stage lined by blinking red, yellow, green, and white lights. Music began to blare and twelve young women skipped on stage dressed in knee-length silver outfits, which apparently represented spring. They did a Vegas-style production number—although decidedly PG-rated—then huddled in the middle of the stage. When they dehuddled a few seconds later, they were dressed in summery green. We all wondered how they had done it, when a few minutes later, after another dance, there was another huddle during which their dresses turned blue for fall, another dance, and a final huddle from which they emerged in Christmassy red and green. The quick-change trick soon became apparent when one unlucky dancer failed to make the Velcro-assisted change from fall to winter colors on time, and moved about for the rest of the night with a look of agony on her face. Kim told me he had choreographed the whole show. I wondered whether the hapless dancer would ever perform again.

The next morning, my aircraft flew east, then south, then west, avoiding the unpredictable airspace over the demilitarized zone before landing in Seoul, where I consulted with Kim Dae-jung and the Japanese foreign minister. Then I headed home, bearing with me three sets of impressions.

The first concerned the prospects for a summit. Certainly North Korea's response to my visit showed its leader was serious. The DPRK seemed willing to accept more significant restraints on its missile programs than we had expected. I had avoided any specific discussion of compensation, but the costs of what the North Koreans were seeking in food, fertilizer, and help in launching satellites would be minimal compared to the expense of defending against the threats its missile programs posed.

My second impression was of Kim Jong Il himself. I could confirm Kim Dae-jung's view that his DPRK counterpart was an intelligent man who knew what he wanted. He was isolated, not uninformed. Despite his country's wretched condition, he didn't seem a desperate or even a worried man. He seemed confident. What did he want? Above all, normal relations with the United States; that would shield his country from the threat he saw posed by American power and help him to be taken seriously in the eyes of the world.

On a personal level, I had to assume that Kim sincerely believed in the blarney he had been taught and saw himself as the protector and benefactor of his nation. The core problem with Communism is that it subsumes the rights of the individual to the supposed interests of society, and once you have discounted individual rights, it is a short step to discounting human suffering. Ideological brainwashing might be easier to swallow as an excuse if the people at the top shared in the sacrifices. In North Korea, as in the old Soviet Union, the upper echelons wallow in privilege. Chairman Kim's gymnastic extravaganza probably used enough electricity to light Pyongyang for a week. And he was personally responsible for increasing the wealth and prerogatives of senior military officers, presumably to ward off threats from the only group capable of challenging him. One could not preside over a system as cruel as the DPRK's without being cruel oneself, but I did not think we had the luxury of simply ignoring him. He was not going to go away and his country, though weak, was not about to fall apart. My conclusion was that we should approach Kim in a businesslike way, not hesitate to engage in direct talks, and take advantage of North Korea's economic plight to drive a bargain that would make the region and world safer.

Finally, I had tried to form an overall impression of North Korea itself. I had been in the country only two days and spent much of that time closeted with the country's least typical citizen. I was, however, interested in the country's psychology. If what was visible reflected what was real, North Korea's entire political, economic, and social life continued to revolve around the teachings of a single human being, Kim Il Sung, and his only slightly less celebrated son. Driving around Pyongyang, I didn't see any statues of Marx or Lenin. There were only the Korean father and son, gazing jovially down on their people.

Seeing average North Koreans on the streets, I was tempted to imagine budding Thomas Jeffersons (or Kim Dae-jungs) striding by, nursing their thirst for freedom, waiting only for an opening to express their desire for democratic rule. This was, however, surely a fantasy. Most North Koreans entered government-run nurseries at the age of three months. The tots I met at the World Food Program were as well drilled as an army drum and bugle corps. North Korea had never experienced anything resembling a Solidarity movement or a Prague Spring.

Whether most of its citizens accepted the propaganda they were being fed, or half-believed it, or were sick to death of it was impossible to tell. Most likely they were so preoccupied with survival that they didn't spend much time questioning what they had no reason to believe they could change. It was clear they had little accurate knowledge of the outside world.

Back in Washington we had to decide whether President Clinton should go to Pyongyang. Sandy Berger and I both felt that he should if it would lead to an acceptable deal on missiles. The President himself was more than willing to make the trip, but we still had to navigate our way through some rapids that included North Korea's diplomatic style, our allies, domestic politics, and the press of other business.

When American and North Korean experts met in Malaysia during the first week of November, members of our team spelled out exactly what we were hoping a summit might achieve. They told the DPRK representatives that we envisioned a joint statement of mutual obligations, coupled with the exchange of confidential letters spelling out the details. There would not be time, under President Clinton, to negotiate a detailed, comprehensive agreement.

As I had discussed with Chairman Kim, we wanted the DPRK to refrain from the production, testing, deployment, and export of whole classes of missiles (including those threatening Japan) in return for our agreement to arrange for civilian North Korean satellite launches under safeguards outside the country. We wanted the North to phase out missiles already deployed. We wanted an agreement on verification principles coupled with a commitment to work out the means of implementation. And we wanted North Korea publicly to accept the presence of U.S. troops on the Korean Peninsula. We also expected the DPRK to adhere fully to the Agreed Framework and refrain from unauthorized nuclear activities. The best leverage we had was North Korea's desire for full normalization of relations. We would not gratify that desire unless and until all our conditions were met.

We knew that we would have to accept some degree of uncertainty if the President did, in fact, go to Pyongyang. The toughest issues involved already deployed missiles, which we would insist be part of the negotiation, and the overall question of verification. I had found Chairman Kim prickly and unreceptive to any questioning of North Korea's trustworthiness or any perceived violation of its sovereignty. He would fight the idea of on-site inspections, yet we had no faith in his word. No agreement was possible unless we had the ability to make sure the DPRK was complying.

Based on our discussions, we were reasonably confident that North Korea would agree to a deal ending the potential threat posed to us by long-range missiles and nuclear arms. We thought they would agree to export restrictions that would make it harder for Iran and the DPRK's other customers to acquire weapons that threaten our allies. We thought North Korea would also agree not to deploy new missiles that could strike Japan and South Korea.

Kim Dae-jung strongly urged the President to go to Pyongyang, saying he was sure Kim Jong Il would want the trip to be a success, and under ordinary circumstances the deal whose outline we thought we had in hand would have justified a trip by the President. We were, however, operating under extraordinary circumstances because we had so little time. Many in Congress and within the punditocracy opposed a summit because they feared a deal with North Korea would weaken the case for national missile defense. Others argued that a summit would "legitimize" North Korea's evil leaders, ignoring the precedent set by President Nixon's 1972 visit to China and the many Cold War summits between Washington and Moscow. Still others suggested that it was too late and the President should leave further negotiations to his successor. After George W. Bush was declared the winner of the 2000 campaign, President Clinton asked him if he would object to a summit in Pyongyang. The President-elect answered quite properly that this was Bill Clinton's decision. We can only have one chief executive at a time.

Ultimately neither the critics, nor the transition, nor our potential differences with North Korea stopped President Clinton from going to the DPRK. Wendy Sherman spent much of December waiting to fly to Pyongyang to seek further concessions with a suggested date for the summit in her pocket if the talks went well. However, day by day, week by week, the White House delayed making a final decision because of the scheduling chaos created by crisis-driven negotiations on the Middle East.

As the holidays neared, the President felt he had to choose between a trip to North Korea—which would also require stops in Seoul and Tokyo—and a crash effort to reach closure with the Israelis and Palestinians. In a final effort to sidestep this choice, we invited Chairman Kim to come to Washington. The North Koreans replied that they could not accept the invitation. Given the public character of Kim's invitation to us, the lateness of our invitation to him, and the importance of "face" in East Asian diplomacy, this response was unsurprising but also unfortunate. We had tried, but unlike Chairman Kim we lived in a democracy, and democracy dictated that our team depart the stage.

IN THE KOREAN LANGUAGE there are many possible endings for each verb. Leaving office, I felt there were also many possible directions in which events on the Korean Peninsula might run. I thought we had created a diplomatic opening the incoming Bush administration would surely explore. During the transition, Secretary-designate Powell encouraged me to believe that the new group would pick up roughly where we left off. As he and the world soon learned, this wasn't to be the case. In March 2001, Kim Dae-jung, in Washington to meet with the President, was informed that the administration would not continue negotiations with the North until it had completed its own policy review. In the summer of 2002, the administration was finally ready to resume serious talks, but by then it had come across new and troubling information. The DPRK had acquired the means and apparently was preparing to begin or had begun a clandestine program of enriching uranium. If true, this would be a clear violation of the Agreed Framework. When confronted with the allegation by Assistant Secretary of States James Kelly, North Korean representatives reportedly admitted it.

In subsequent weeks, matters took repeated turns for the worse. The administration refused to satisfy the North's desire for direct talks or reiterate the 2000 joint declaration of "no hostile intent." It also joined the North in declaring the Agreed Framework dead. The DPRK then upped the ante by kicking out international inspectors and stating its intention to unseal the fuel rods at its nuclear reactor and resume the production of plutonium. This development, in turn, brought events full circle, raising the same specter President Clinton had faced at the start of his administration—a North Korea armed with enough nuclear bombs to threaten its neighbors while deterring attacks on itself, all the while searching for customers willing to pay cash for fissile materials or bombs. All in all, a dangerous mess and a wholly unacceptable status quo.

The way out in 2003, however, does not differ much from the way out in 1994. A serious policy toward North Korea would encompass four principles. First, it must result in a verifiably nuclear-free Korean Peninsula. We cannot accept North Korea as a nuclear power. Second, it must include a willingness to engage in direct talks with North Korea, not as some reward to Pyongyang but as a means of doing what is necessary to prevent proliferation and the risk of war. Third, it must be carried out in full coordination with our allies. Finally, it must be implemented with urgency.

For the inside story on what happened next, we must await the memoirs of those serving at the time, for it is beyond the scope of my own.

IN NOVEMBER 2002, I returned to Seoul for the second conference of the Community of Democracies, except this time I was a participant in the nongovernmental part of the festivities. While there, I met for perhaps the last time with Kim Dae-jung. When I had first seen him as president, he was a refreshing change from his predecessor, in part because his predecessor's son had been accused of bribery. Now, with only a few months left in office, Kim's popularity had plunged, in part because his own sons had been involved in a corruption scandal. I went to the Blue House (equivalent to the U.S. White House), where I was ushered into a small back room. Kim was still in fair health, though walking with considerable difficulty. We talked about what we had tried to do together to reach out to the North. Although many had labeled Kim's sunshine policy a failure, he disagreed.

"I never expected everything to change quickly," he told me. "But we have laid the groundwork. The leaders of the North and South have met. Families have reunited. It is no longer big news to go back and forth."

"What about the North's nuclear program?" I asked.

Kim said, "It is deeply troubling. The North will not change until it believes it can do so safely. They don't trust anyone. They saw what the U.S. did against Serbia, which has no nuclear weapons. They work closely with Pakistan, which acquired nuclear weapons despite international warnings and is now a U.S. ally. They think they may need such weapons to deter attack. Without making threats, we must convince them that threats do not work. But they keep making the same mistakes over and over again. We had our best chance for a breakthrough in the last days of your administration. You understood the situation here and how much was at stake. You devoted your full energy. I will always be grateful to you and President Clinton for the support you gave."

As I talked with Kim, one of the great democratic heroes of the twentieth century, I reflected that history does not divide itself conveniently into four-year chunks, like presidential administrations. It flows constantly, in this case sweeping aside our efforts to test Pyongyang and blocking Kim Dae-jung from realizing his hopes. When I rose to leave, Kim started to extend his hand, then put out both his arms and we embraced.

In Oscar Wilde's epigram, "The good ended happily and the bad unhappily. That's what fiction means." In the reality of the Korean Peninsula, the fate of good and bad are bound together by geographical proximity and by technologies with the potential to end us all.

TWENTY-EIGHT

The Fruitless Quest

T HE MILLENNIUM was drawing to a close and in the Middle East all eyes were drawn to calendars and clocks. In May 1999, Israeli voters elected Labor Party leader Ehud Barak, defeating Bibi Netanyahu. Barak took office with an ambitious agenda for completing comprehensive peace negotiations with Syria, Lebanon, and the Palestinians by the fall of 2000, so he could then concentrate on Israel's extensive economic and social needs.

In Syria, President Hafiz Asad had long vowed to regain the Golan Heights, seized by Israel in the 1967 war. But the ailing Asad was running out of time if he wished to recover the Golan on the right terms.

Six years after the Oslo Accords, the Palestinians still did not have their country. Striving to lead a frustrated, divided, and impoverished people, Yasser Arafat warned that before long he would unilaterally declare a Palestinian state.

And in Washington our foreign policy team was acutely conscious that its months in office were dwindling, and with them the chance to build a bulwark against potentially catastrophic violence in the Middle East.

We were all in a race against time.

IN OCTOBER 1998, at Wye, Israeli and Palestinian negotiators had agreed on the path to a comprehensive peace. For a short while it seemed that momentum toward reconciliation might build, but problems soon arose. Deadlines were missed. The Israelis did not return all the land they promised. The Palestinians lagged in confiscating arms. The Israelis were supposed to release Palestinian prisoners, and so they did—but from the Palestinian perspective not the right ones. The Palestinians arrested terrorist suspects but, Israel claimed, not the guiltiest ones. Driven by political extremists on both sides, the language of peace was supplanted by vitriol.

Publicly and privately, I told Arab leaders that "peace is not a spectator sport," but with the exception of Jordan, the Arab world didn't respond. However reluctantly, Netanyahu had risked his career for peace, but his gamble did nothing to soften Arab attitudes. Finding himself trapped, he called for new elections and, in May 1999, was voted out of office.

Netanyahu's conqueror, Ehud Barak, entered office like a rooster at dawn. Similar to his mentor, Yitzhak Rabin, he had the credentials of a warrior; in fact he was the most decorated soldier in his nation's history. While in the military, he had his name changed from Brog to Barak, which means "lightning." Again like Rabin, Barak felt it essential for Israel to make peace with its neighbors, in part as protection against the powerful threats posed by Iran and Iraq. He also believed that peace was possible because of Israel's strength. Arabs would negotiate not because they had ceased to hate Israel but because it was the only way to recover lost lands.

Although the administration had been officially neutral, Barak's election was greeted with smiles from the Oval Office to the corridors of Foggy Bottom. The new prime minister was fifty-seven, with a compact build, a round, boyish face, and intense brown eyes so dark they reminded me of coal. I first met Barak in his capacity as opposition leader in 1997, during my initial Middle East tour. As we left that meeting, I said to Dennis Ross, "Wouldn't it be terrific if we could deal with him as prime minister?" Now we had that chance.

Part of the urgency that drove Barak stemmed from the debacle in southern Lebanon, where Israeli troops had been deployed since the early 1980s against attacks by the Iranian-backed Hezbollah militia. Although justified, the Israeli presence gave Hezbollah the chance to portray itself as a patriotic force fighting to recover Lebanese land. By the late 1990s, the deployment was domestically unpopular in Israel because of casualties to its soldiers. Barak pledged to withdraw within a year. Seeing himself as a different kind of leader than Netanyahu, he was confident that he could negotiate a peace with Syria and Syrian-controlled Lebanon in a matter of months. To him the incentives were clear: Syria was the last hostile state on Israel's border with a significant military, and Asad was powerful enough to deliver on his promises and rein in Hezbollah. A deal would leave Israel with greater security and Syria with the land—or at least most of the land—it had lost.

I first met Asad in Damascus in 1997. Riding into the city, I was surprised by the number of satellite dishes on roofs and balconies. They were everywhere. My sense was that Syria would change overnight if the

Asad regime's boot were lifted from its neck. Syria possesses a literate population, a relatively enlightened attitude toward women, and an ancient, cosmopolitan, trading culture. It could be a key to bringing the Middle East fully into the twenty-first century if its people were not living under what amounts to a police state.

I was determined, upon reaching Asad's palace, to make a strong impression. This was complicated by the impression the setting of our meeting made on me. The palace was hard to believe. There was more marble than you could imagine and, of course, in that part of the world, the carpets were splendid. There were sweeping stairways and you could envision James Bond exiting right, pursued by scimitars. Asad received me in a huge, sparsely furnished room with sofas, and two carved wooden chairs with cushions. Before sitting down, he drew back the curtains to reveal a spectacular view of his capital, one of the world's oldest cities.

After proclaiming his respect for President Clinton and me, Asad gave his version of past negotiations, recalling his own commitments with far less clarity than the promises made to him. He said that Rabin had pledged in 1995 to return the entire Golan Heights if Israeli security and water concerns were met. "I cannot settle for anything less," Asad told me. "No person or child in Syria would agree to make peace with any party that kept even one inch of our land. In any place in the world, any-one who concedes his own land is seen as a traitor."

Polite, straightforward, and stubborn, Asad's position in 1997 was still his position two years later. He said he would resume negotiations only on the basis of his understanding of the commitments made by Rabin. Barak wanted the President to go to Damascus and "stun" Asad into resuming talks. The President said I should go instead, and no one was more surprised than Barak when I succeeded in persuading Asad to agree to negotiate "without conditions." The result was two days of pro-ductive discussions in Washington between Barak and Syrian Foreign Minister Farouk Shara. They agreed to return for a round of intensive negotiations in January. The site chosen was a conference center in Shep-herdstown, West Virginia, a quaint village just across the state line from my farm.

Although both sides seemed eager, the Shepherdstown talks were unlikely to be a diplomatic slam dunk. To achieve peace, the parties would have to reconcile apparently irreconcilable needs and find a common def-inition of what returning the Golan Heights actually meant. The central question was, where was the boundary? Where was the line that existed before the June 1967 war?

Asad, who never tired of telling us that he had swum in the Sea of

Galilee as a youth, insisted that Syrian territory extended to the eastern banks of that body of water and also the Jordan River. For him, refusal to compromise on land was a matter of honor, or perhaps wounded machismo; he had been defense minister when Syria lost the Golan Heights. If he were to allow Israel the use of land east of the river and sea, it would have to be as a Syrian gift, not an Israeli right. Because Israel depended on the Sea of Galilee for 40 percent of its freshwater needs, Barak sought to retain enough territory to ensure full and secure sovereignty over the two bodies of water. The amount of land in question was small, but both sides were dug in.

The first day in Shepherdstown was consumed by a fight over the order of issues to be negotiated. After hours of squabbling, Barak and Shara agreed to discuss all issues simultaneously. During the next couple of days, we worked to narrow differences on such matters as the timetable for Israeli withdrawal, security assurances for Israel, and the means of normalizing diplomatic relations. As at Wye, the U.S. delegation set to work preparing a draft agreement.

I noticed quickly that the two sides, and especially the Syrians, were far more direct with me than with President Clinton. When Shara was with the President, he was formal in his statements and generally aiming to please. With me he complained all the time, especially about Barak's failure to reiterate Rabin's commitment to full withdrawal if Israel's security needs were met. The Syrians had agreed to begin talks with only an indirect commitment from Barak on this point but had expected something explicit as soon as talks began. We had expected it too. Instead, Barak backed away.

Prior to Shepherdstown, the Israeli leader had been full of confidence about his capacity to persuade his people to share his vision of peace. This confidence seemed to waver as the reality began to sink in of what a deal with Asad would entail. Like Netanyahu before him, Barak was feeling political pressures from home. Those pressures, in turn, were grounded in some long-standing truths.

First, a generation of Israelis had grown up believing that the Golan Heights were essential to defending Israel. Until 1967, Syrian guns had been trained on Israel's narrow territory from the Golan's high ground. After that year, Israeli guns were pointed at Damascus, completely altering the strategic relationship between the two countries.

Second, there were now about seventeen thousand Israeli settlers on the Golan who would strongly—perhaps violently—oppose efforts to remove them.

Third, there were more than a million recent immigrants to Israel from the former Soviet Union and elsewhere who didn't necessarily know the full history and saw no reason why Israel should give up any land.

Fourth, Israel's opposition politicians didn't hesitate to challenge the prime minister's tactics even if they could not credibly question his courage. Likud Party chairman Ariel Sharon accused Barak of "total surrender" just for going to Shepherdstown.

Finally, the Israelis were understandably put off by Syria's attitude. Both former Egyptian President Anwar Sadat and Jordan's King Hussein had made magnanimous gestures to relieve Israeli anxieties. Even Arafat had spoken about the need to end mutual suffering. Asad, however, refused to negotiate personally with the Israelis and seemed to want them to be as anxious as possible. Although he claimed to have made a "strategic decision" to seek a settlement, his manner was unrelentingly hostile. He had a reputation as a man of his word, but many Israelis found it hard to believe that he would ever make peace.

One purpose of a closed off-site negotiation is to nurture a sense of common purpose and camaraderie. At Wye relations between the top Israeli and Palestinian leaders had been cold, but negotiators at the working level didn't hesitate to mix during meals and fresh-air walks. At Shepherdstown they never even shared a table.

By the time the weekend arrived, everyone was cranky, so on Saturday, while the Israelis observed Shabbat, I invited Shara to join me in playing tourist. First stop was Harpers Ferry. I have taken many visitors there and most, whether homegrown or foreign, are captivated. Thomas Jefferson had looked out upon the place where the Potomac and Shenandoah merge and declared that the view alone was worth a trip over the Atlantic. My guests were also fascinated by the story of John Brown's ill-fated effort to spark a slave rebellion shortly before the Civil War. Brown's story has always exemplified for me the danger of noble intentions not tied to common sense. Shara was enjoying himself so much, he actually removed his tie.

After the scenery and history lesson, we headed for my farm, where the State Department's Office of Protocol had preceded us. This added to the incongruity of the venture because the Protocol Office knows fancy, while the farm is homey. What is more, my son-in-law Greg was there with my grandson David. To be helpful, Greg had built a blazing fire. The only problem was that the chimney had just been fixed and the flue was closed, so when Farouk Shara and I arrived at what was supposed to be a relaxed setting, we found the doors and windows open and everyone running around trying to get the smoke out. Shara shook hands with David and Greg before venturing with me into the house, where we sat and talked about the history of Syria, occasionally rubbing our eyes while waiters served tea.

The next day I accompanied Barak and his wife, Nava, to Antietam, site of the single bloodiest day in American history. On September 17, 1862, more than twenty-two thousand Union and Confederate soldiers were killed or wounded. As a military man, Barak listened carefully to the details of the battle from Bruce Riedel, an NSC expert on the Middle East and a Civil War buff. We went from there to Harpers Ferry and later to my farm for lunch. While we ate, I carried on with the Civil War theme, saying the mountain behind my property had been part of the underground railroad; freedom-seeking slaves had hidden behind the wide stone walls and fireplaces of local houses.

When we were outside, Barak noticed that I had a large clock on my barn with the wrong time on it. I told him it had been on a French tower; I had bought it at an antique show but had never been able to make it work. I knew Barak liked to take timepieces apart, so I wasn't surprised when he said, "Next time I come, I will fix the clock."[1]

Back at Shepherdstown, the negotiations continued. Progress was made around the edges, but the core issues were unresolved. When President Clinton had presented our draft agreement, the increasingly hesitant Barak stalled. Slow-walking the process, the Israeli prime minister proposed that the delegations take a few days to study the paper, make some preliminary comments, then adjourn before returning for a second round. President Clinton said it was okay with him if we all took a break but warned that half-finished peace agreements were not like cheeses that grow better with age; they were more like bananas that rot.

In recapping, Shara compared the talks to a stalled car the Syrians and Americans were pushing because the Israelis hadn't turned on the ignition. I said, "No, I think the car engine is starting to catch, but right now it's still going *grrr, grrr*." Dennis Ross then said, "If you don't like the car analogy, let's talk about bicycles." Shara said, "No, bikes are for Palestinians." Dennis replied, "Well, maybe we have to hot-wire the car." Shara said that he had done that as a teenager.

Later I reminded Shara of our trip to Harpers Ferry, where we had seen rocks in the river. I said that some of the rocks were slippery, but we had to stay in the river and try to cross. He said, "We are not even in the river."

The outer limit to such comparisons, however, was reached in yet a third conversation with Shara, one I cannot imagine he would have had with a man. We were talking about the extent to which a leap of faith was

---

1. If former Prime Minister Barak finds time now to read this, I hope he knows he has a standing invitation—and that I have a clock that still needs mending.

required in any peace negotiation when Shara said, "Well, suppose we were to get married. That is a commitment we would only make if we knew it would work."

I replied, "Right, but what if we got married and I wanted to travel and you didn't want me to go?"

"That's not a problem," said Shara, "because I believe in equality."

"Fine," I said, "but what if our definitions of equality aren't the same?"

"Still no problem," said Shara, "because we are both intelligent and want to get along."

"Yes, but suppose you had been with the Taliban and your history distorted your judgment so that, no matter how hard you tried, you couldn't see my views as reasonable. Could the marriage still work? I hope so, because Israel and Syria have quite a history." I finally concluded there was little point in resorting to metaphors at all.

To allay my doubts, I asked both Shara and Barak privately if they seriously believed an agreement would be reached. They each said yes, which I found encouraging until I probed for the reason. They each believed that in the end President Clinton would intervene to force concessions upon the other. I did not doubt the President's skills, but I didn't see how even he could perform magic tricks. We left Shepherdstown without any kind of closing ceremony or press conference, expecting to be back in nine days' time.

Returning home, the negotiators from both sides were put under a microscope. In such circumstances there is a strong temptation to put out a version of events that places your own team in the best light and casts a shadow over the other. That is why secret negotiations have their place, and why President Clinton warned about the short shelf life of a draft peace plan. Even before Shepherdstown had adjourned, a story appeared in an Arab journal published in London outlining the draft U.S. peace paper and emphasizing Asad's demand for complete Israeli withdrawal from the Golan. On January 13, an Israeli newspaper published the entire draft text, with a report detailing a list of concessions Syria had made.

Both delegations had vowed to preserve the confidentiality of the negotiations. Even with the future of the region and potentially many lives at stake, neither kept that vow. The consequences were predictable. The Syrians publicly disavowed the concessions they had made on lesser issues, while restating their determination that Israel yield on returning all of the Golan. The scheduled second round of talks was canceled.

It might have been logical at this point to put further Syrian negotiations on hold and refocus on the potentially explosive Palestinian track. This was our preference and that of many members of Barak's own government. However, Barak, having pledged to withdraw Israeli troops from Lebanon by summer, wanted to have an agreement with Syria in place to ensure an orderly withdrawal and secure aftermath.

He believed firmly that Asad would take the deal he was preparing: the return to Syria of all the Golan Heights except for a strip five hundred meters wide along the Sea of Galilee and eighty yards wide along the east bank of the Jordan River. In compensation, the Israelis would exchange a parcel of inland territory that had not previously been in Syrian hands. Barak's idea was to package this proposed map with detailed Israeli positions on other issues and have the President present them in a one-on-one meeting with Asad. In his view, he was offering the Syrian leader the chance to recover 99 percent of the Golan; no reasonable man could possibly refuse.

Far less confident, I offered to test the waters in Damascus first, thereby shielding President Clinton from what might well be a very public failure. Barak had no such concern. Perhaps it was his military background, his personality, or the peculiarities of the Israeli political system—in which foreign and defense ministers often came from different political parties than the prime minister—but he saw diplomacy as the province of heads of government. Unlike Netanyahu, he didn't feel it appropriate to meet or talk regularly with anyone except the President whom he phoned constantly. He did not believe anyone except the President should be negotiating with Asad. He told us that only President Clinton would be able to "shake" the Syrian leader and, in so doing, jar loose some flexibility.

Always the micromanager, Barak produced a complete script for the President's use with Asad. In a manner I thought patronizing, he said it would be fine for the President to improvise the opening generalities, but the description of Israel's needs had to be recited word for word.

President Clinton went along with this process for several reasons. He had more hope than the rest of us that the initiative would succeed, and certainly Barak's offer was more forthcoming than any other the Syrians were likely to receive. The President had also promised to support those in the Middle East who were willing to run risks for peace; astute diplomatic strategist or not, Barak led the region in this category. Finally, the President's inherent optimism encouraged him to believe that a concentrated push couldn't help but produce movement.

The President and I met with Asad and Shara in a ballroom of the Intercontinental Hotel in Geneva on March 26, 2000. Since there were only two Syrians present, we had to keep our delegation small. We sat around a coffee table in armchairs, with the President and Asad next to each other. I was on the President's other side and Dennis Ross was beside me. The NSC's Robert Malley took notes. At the far end of the room was a wooden screen, behind which several other American officials sat eavesdropping, suppressing coughs so that they would not be discovered.

President Clinton began by thanking Asad for coming and acknowledging the physical difficulties the obviously ill leader faced. Asad replied, "I never get tired of seeing you."

The President gave an abbreviated version of his "our children will thank us" speech, outlined the historic opportunity before us, and said he was gratified that he had been able to earn the trust of Syria without losing the trust of Israel. Then he said that he wanted to make a formal presentation of what the Israelis were prepared to do. Asad replied, "Fine, I will not respond until you finish, but what about territory?"

"The Israelis," said the President, "are prepared to withdraw fully to a commonly agreed border."

Asad said, "What do you mean by 'commonly agreed?'"

President Clinton started to explain and Dennis pulled out a map based on Barak's ideas, which showed a line running down the east bank of the Jordan and the Sea of Galilee, with the Israeli strip of land clearly delineated.

"Then he doesn't want peace," said Asad, not even bothering to study the map. "It is finished."

And so it was. For the next two hours, the President, Dennis, and I struggled to save the situation, but the fundamental problem sat in the room like a boulder. The Israelis would not yield on the need for land around the water. Asad would not admit to Israeli sovereignty over an inch of what he considered to be Syrian land. The President tried a couple of times to go through Barak's full list of talking points, but the Syrians were dismissive.

I reminded Asad that President Clinton had come to this meeting only because of his commitment to peace and that Syria was not likely to get a better Israeli offer. I urged him not to throw away the chance to recover 99 percent of the Golan Heights in a dispute over a narrow strip of land.

Shara intervened: "The problem is not a matter of kilometers. It is one of dignity and honor. The Israelis don't lose if they return our territory. No one can do more than President Asad to see that Israel is accepted in the region once an agreement is reached."

As we prepared to leave, the Syrians urged President Clinton not to say they were to blame for the failure of the negotiations. The President said only, "The world will judge."

In pushing the Syrian track so urgently, Barak had sought to forge an historic agreement with a bitter Israeli foe while securing Israel's northern border, preserving access to water, and clearing the way for climactic talks with the Palestinians. He had, however, misread Asad. What seemed logical to Barak did not seem logical to the Syrian president. Asad had staked out a position from which he did not think he could retreat even marginally without tarnishing his own carefully burnished image.

Meanwhile the sands of the hourglass continued to slip away. President Clinton did not have much time left. Asad had none. On June 10, 2000, the Syrian president died of a heart attack, having failed to recover an inch of his country's land.

In THE 1993 FILM *Groundhog Day*, the main character, played by Bill Murray, is condemned to relive one particular day over and over again, until finally he works out how to make the personal and professional choices that will have the best results for everybody. Each morning he wakes to find he is back where he was the day before, with the same events and same conversations in store until he can discover his way through. The film could just as easily have been about the Middle East.

LIKE MOST CABINET MEMBERS, I looked forward to visits to Camp David, the historic presidential retreat in Maryland. In July 2000, I spent fifteen days there, locked in with Israeli and Palestinian leaders. We worked day and night; and night and day the lovely countryside was enshrouded in a suffocating fog like a Biblical plague. After arguing so long with men from three cultures about the Middle East, when I left at last, I didn't care if I ever went back. But if the Middle East is ever to know peace, that peace will grow from ideas first explored during those two stormy weeks.

Yasser Arafat had initially welcomed Barak's election as prime minister, and in fact claimed some credit for it, but his enthusiasm soon waned. He had capitalized on Netanyahu's blunt language and right-wing politics to capture sympathy for his cause. Barak, with his bold positions and ardent pursuit of peace, threatened to undermine Arafat's status as professional victim. Barak also took away the spotlight from the Palestinian leader by negotiating with Syria.

After Asad's refusal to deal, Barak turned his attention to withdrawing Israeli troops from the security zone they had occupied at great cost in Lebanon for seventeen years. Although most Israelis were relieved by the withdrawal, Arafat's partisans were angry. They pointed out that the

Palestinians had decided in 1993 to recover their land through negotiations with Israel. Seven years later, all they had to show for their efforts was a small slice of territory and a life subject to daily humiliations. Lebanese Hezbollah, which had chosen the path of armed confrontation, had succeeded in recovering land. The Syrians refused even to shake hands with the Israelis, yet Barak had offered to return more than 99 percent of the Golan Heights. The Israelis, said the Palestinians, were sending precisely the wrong message—that Hamas was right and a hard line was the only way to liberate Arab territory.

I told Arafat he was interpreting Barak's efforts to negotiate with Syria in the wrong way. They were not signs of weakness but reflections of Israel's desire for peace. Barak did not want Israel to spend another generation as an occupying power and so was prepared to negotiate seriously. The Israeli prime minister said a settlement would be possible only if Israelis took into account Palestinian aspirations. "If we don't succeed," he said, "a new round of violence will begin, and we will bury our victims and they will bury their victims, and a generation later we will sit down once more to the same geography, the same demography, and the same problems."

Although his approach was far bolder, Barak shared his predecessor's distaste for the piecemeal approach of the Oslo Accords. Each of the steps required by Oslo stirred furious debate within Israel, extracting a political price. Believing that it would be easier for him to present a single conclusive package than to keep trying to sell pieces of peace, Barak pushed for an all-encompassing agreement. To spur progress, he hinted at negotiating positions surprisingly favorable to the Palestinians. These outraged his opponents but helped Israelis understand that peace would require painful concessions. Netanyahu had sought to dampen Palestinian expectations. Barak tried to give Israelis a more realistic understanding of what they would have to give up.

As for Arafat, Barry Schweid, dean of the State Department press corps, asked me if the Palestinian leader were doing anything to prepare his people to make hard choices. I had to say he was not. In Arafat's view, those choices had all been made in 1993, when Palestinians accepted the Oslo process. Since then his long-range demands had been consistent. He was for a Palestinian state with its territory based on the 1967 borders and its capital—like Israel's—in Jerusalem. In his Arabic speeches he did not cite the importance of addressing Israeli concerns or the need for compromise. He acknowledged Israel's existence but not its moral legitimacy. Instead of trying to forge a new Palestinian consensus, he reinforced the old one.

In June 2000, I traveled to the Middle East twice. Barak wanted President Clinton to convene a Camp David–style summit. Arafat didn't. The Palestinian leader was angry at Barak for postponing Israel's Wye commitments and for trying to mollify his country's right wing by allowing settlements to expand even faster than they had under Netanyahu. He was also upset that after sidetracking Palestinian talks for months, Barak was now demanding that Arafat speed up. The Palestinian leader told me a summit was too important a card to play without some expectation of success, and he didn't want to be blamed for its likely failure.

Barak meanwhile was pushing us hard. He predicted that, in the "pressure cooker" environment of a summit, President Clinton would be able to "shake" Arafat into an agreement. We were skeptical; Barak had made the same prediction about the President's ability to sway Asad. Moreover, the Pandora's box labeled "permanent status issues" had never before been unlocked. Those issues were laden with emotion and dauntingly complex. The two sides were publicly committed to widely disparate positions. Success would require a mutual commitment of creativity and political will that was far from likely, given Arafat's presummit mood. At the same time, the President—concerned about more violence and deeply committed to peace—was reluctant to substitute his judgment for that of an Israeli prime minister so determined to make history. Arafat, while asking for more time, couldn't specify what would be gained by waiting. On July 3, 2000, President Clinton invited both leaders to Camp David for a summit to begin the following week.

CAMP DAVID IS perched on what easterners call a mountain and those of us who have lived in Colorado call a hill. It's a fenced-off corral of trees, paths, flowers, cabins, and recreational facilities most efficiently traversed by golf carts. From the front steps of his cabin President Clinton could see Barak's quarters to his right and Arafat's to his left. Mine nestled a few yards from Barak's in the nearby woods.

Because the President was due to leave eight days after the summit began for a meeting of G8 leaders in Japan, we didn't have much time. We decided to spend the first two days soliciting proposals, then present a paper on the third that would include both Israeli and Palestinian positions and our own ideas. Meanwhile the President's first task was to change Arafat's psychology. If the negotiations were to succeed, we had to convince the Palestinian leader that he hadn't made a mistake by coming. "Just tell him," Sandy Berger told the President, "it will be the proudest moment of your life to stand next to him in Palestine when the Palestinian national flag is being raised." The Chief Executive gave Sandy a "you must be crazy" glance. "Proudest moment of my life? What about Chelsea's birth?"

The Arafat meeting did not achieve its purpose. The President was inspiring and eloquent. The PLO chairman was attentive, polite, and mute. The first meeting with Barak was equally frustrating. The Israeli prime minister had arrived late because he had barely survived a vote of no confidence in the Israeli parliament. He was in a prickly mood and preferred that nothing happen for a few days because if success were achieved too soon, it would look as if he had not negotiated hard enough. So the leader who had been in such a rush now wanted to slow things down, like an orchestra conductor flitting between adagio and allegro, inviting dissonance. He thought we should let the pressure build on Arafat until there was a crisis, then move to our endgame. This was the reverse of our approach. We thought Arafat needed something at the outset that would draw him in and cause him to negotiate constructively. And we didn't know what Barak's endgame was because he would not tell us.

On the third day I met with Barak in his cabin, which was called Dogwood but rapidly renamed Doghouse by his own staff. The prime minister was dressed completely in black, which matched his outlook. He complained about the Palestinian style of negotiation. He said Israel was constantly moving its position by jumping forward but that when Arafat jumped, he always landed in the same place—a point hard to dispute. Barak asked to see the paper we were drafting. I said Dennis was in the process of briefing the Israeli negotiators. Barak said, "I must see it. Maybe my negotiators will make a mistake. I have to let you know whether I can accept or reject it."

Shortly after, we learned the answer. Barak's thumb pointed down. Not wanting to "corner" the Israeli leader at the outset, the President asked Dennis to draft a new paper simply listing Israeli and Palestinian positions. That suited Barak fine. Arafat, however, was furious when he received the new paper because it made reference to Israel's plan to expand Jerusalem so that Palestinians could establish their capital in an outlying neighborhood instead of within the city's traditional boundaries. He would never accept this "Israeli trick." Around 2:30 A.M., the Palestinian negotiators Saeb Erekat and Abu Ala came to my cabin, where Dennis and I tried to calm them down. Finally Dennis said, "If you don't like our paper, fine. Just negotiate directly with the Israelis." Saeb said, "You mean we can ignore the paper?" "Yes."

So after three days we had drafted one paper rejected by Barak and a second rejected by the Palestinians. Meanwhile members of Barak's team were telling us that their leader had been misunderstood and we should have stuck with the first paper. In any event, we were left with no paper and no progress, an outcome that caused tensions within our own team. The NSC was impatient, the State Department was concerned by the constantly shifting signals, and we were all exasperated. John Podesta, the smart and fair-minded new White House chief of staff, helped to mediate and get us back on track. Meanwhile President Clinton encouraged each of the two leaders to walk in the shoes of the other, just as he had at Wye. But Arafat was sick of hearing about Barak's domestic political troubles, which he said the Israeli leader had simply made up; for his part, Barak dismissed the idea that Arafat needed help controlling Palestinian extremists.

To try to focus the parties, we encouraged them to sit down in small teams and work through the main issues together. These included borders (and settlements), security, refugees, and Jerusalem.

On borders, the Palestinians began with the demand that Israel return all lands occupied during the 1967 war to make up the territory of their new state. This was what Anwar Sadat had obtained for Egypt and the Sinai in 1978 and what Asad was demanding for Syria, but by the year 2000 there were more than 180,000 Israeli settlers living in the West Bank and Gaza, the majority concentrated in areas close to Israel proper. Barak wanted to annex enough of the West Bank to allow 80 percent of the settlers to remain under Israeli rule. He also wanted to control strips of territory in the Jordan Valley and Gaza to prevent attacks and the movement of arms and terrorists. The Palestinians, while willing to accept some early warning stations, opposed any permanent Israeli military presence in the Jordan Valley. They also wanted to be compensated for land annexed for settlements by receiving territory of equal size and quality elsewhere.

The issue of refugees was both legalistic and deeply emotional. According to the UN's registry, there were about four million Palestinians who had been or were descended from those made homeless by the 1948 and 1967 wars. The Palestinians asserted the right under international law to return to their homes. This quest had been the core objective of the PLO throughout its history. But if this right were exercised, Israel would lose its status as a predominantly Jewish state. And if Israel accepted legal and moral responsibility for the refugees' fate, the very legitimacy of the country's creation would be undermined in the eyes of its enemies. Such concessions were obviously not acceptable. A deal still seemed possible, however, because some Palestinian negotiators were willing to discuss privately the idea of a limit on the number of refugees who would be allowed to return to Israel, while the Israelis had agreed that an international system could be set up to compensate refugees and the governments that had hosted them.

The border and refugee issues, although almost impossible to resolve, were easy compared to the problem of Jerusalem. Barak, like virtually every other major Israeli politician, had pledged his commitment to an undivided city. The Palestinians demanded the return of East Jerusalem, which had been occupied during the 1967 war. In our negotiations the political geography of Jerusalem would be discussed in four concentric circles. In the outer circle were suburban neighborhoods that had also been occupied in 1967. In the second were neighborhoods extending into the center of the city. The third circle consisted of the ancient walled city of Old Jerusalem, with its Jewish, Armenian, Christian, and Moslem quarters. And in Jerusalem's heart was a thirty-five-acre area of fountains, gardens, buildings, and domes that Jews refer to as the Temple Mount and Muslims as Haram al-Sharif, or Noble Sanctuary. This tiny area has more places sacred to Christians, Jews, and Muslims than anywhere else in the world.

The compound is believed by Jews to be located on the site of the ancient temple built by King Solomon and restored after the Jewish exile in Babylonia. Below the Temple Mount is the Western Wall, which includes the Wailing Wall, the holiest site in Judaism. Jews go to the Wailing Wall to pray and leave prayers on pieces of paper between its ancient stones. The platform of the Haram al-Sharif is identified by Muslims as the sanctuary from which the Prophet Muhammad is said to have ascended through the heavens following his night journey from Mecca to Jerusalem. It also encloses the Dome of the Rock, the third holiest site in Islam, and also the historic al-Aqsa Mosque.

The question for negotiators was how to sort all this out. Jonathan Schwartz, an inventive lawyer on our team, created a menu of ways to modify and describe the concepts of political, legal, and administrative authority or sovereignty. If a solution to the Jerusalem conundrum were to be found, we believed it would have to be through a formula that allowed both sides to say that they were in control of what mattered to them most.

In search of common ground on all issues, we met in small groups with each side individually and both sides together. We arranged meetings in which the Israelis and Palestinians met without us. We scheduled gatherings in cabins that were close-in and others in relatively remote locations. We encouraged the two sides to exchange ideas informally at meals, during breaks in basketball, while communing with nature, and in secret. We planned for the President to look in on sessions. We asked that negotiators report to him or me at the end of the day.[2] We even once locked two nego-

<hr>

2. The person responsible for coordinating all this was the resourceful Elizabeth Jones, deputy assistant secretary for Near Eastern affairs.

tiators from each side in the President's office from midnight until ten A.M.

All the while, our team did everything possible to create the right mood. At times members of the delegations helped. After all, these were people who had come to know each other well over the years and who had formed likes and dislikes that crossed national lines. The first Friday the Israelis invited the Palestinians and Americans to share the Shabbat dinner. Arafat was in a gracious mood, blessed everyone, and even spoke a few words of Hebrew.

At other times, tension broke through. Early on, the President blew up at Palestinian negotiator Abu Ala for not showing any flexibility on the question of borders. Having made his point, he motioned to me and we strode dramatically out—at precisely the moment a downpour began. It was either get wet or forfeit the drama of our exit, so we went and got drenched.

Barak was clearly drained by the hours he spent on the telephone tending political fences at home. During the first days the only real progress being made was through back-channel discussions. That halted when Barak forbade the other Israelis to talk about Jerusalem. It was impossible not to admire Barak. I personally found him to be a remarkable person with courageous ideas, a dedication to peace, and complex strategies. His people-to-people skills, however, left something to be desired. He tended to let others know immediately that he thought he was smarter than they, which even if true, was not a smart tactic. He had his own sense of what was logical and didn't seem to understand that listeners would be more receptive if he leavened his explanations with humor and tact. He was also very aloof toward the Palestinians.

On several occasions, I went to Arafat's cabin just to take his temperature, which I found constantly rising. Convinced we were conspiring with the Israelis against him, he went on at length about the promises Barak had broken. Thrusting his arm upwards, he proclaimed as if to a big crowd, "I am not a slave, I am Yasser Arafat." When I pushed the chairman to be more forthcoming, he gazed back fiercely and said, "The next time you see me will be when you are walking behind my coffin." Most of the conversations were less theatrical but no more productive. Arafat was not proposing anything. He seemed a tired and isolated old man.

His personal intentions aside, the dilemma he faced with his constituency was as real as the problems Barak faced with his. At Arafat's suggestion, I briefly left Camp David to meet with a group of Palestinian leaders who had gathered in the nearby town of Emmitsburg. They were upset that they hadn't been allowed to meet with Arafat because of the rules we had established to prevent leaks. I tried to give the group a sense of what was going on at the talks without revealing anything that would harm the negotiations. I told them any agreement would require painful compromises on both sides and urged them to help prepare the Palestinian people for an agreement. They said they fully understood the need for compromises and would of course support Arafat, provided he did not accept anything violating the "Palestinian consensus" on refugees, borders, or Jerusalem. In other words, an agreement would be fine as long as all the concessions were Israel's.

It was the eighth day and we had made few gains. President Clinton told Barak we either had to end the summit or go for a limited agreement. Barak asked for time to think, then requested a meeting with the Chief Executive alone. When the President returned, he was smiling. He said the Israelis would agree to return 91 percent of the West Bank and—while not accepting a one-for-one exchange—would accept the principle of a swap for some of the land to be annexed for settlements. They would accept Palestinian sovereignty over both the Moslem and Christian quarters of the Old City in Jerusalem, as well as most of the outer suburbs. The Palestinians would be given planning, zoning, and law enforcement powers over the Arab neighborhoods closer in, and "custodianship" over the Haram al-Sharif. Barak suggested that the President say to Arafat that if the Palestinians agreed to these ideas, the United States would also try to persuade Barak to adopt reasonable positions on security and refugees. We finally had Barak's bottom line, and it was both far-reaching and brave.

He had moved much further than his predecessors. Most dramatically, he had agreed to an arrangement that would allow Arafat to establish a capital for Palestine within Jerusalem. This was a breakthrough that could change the whole future of the Middle East. Of course there was no guarantee the Palestinians would accept, and we didn't expect them to do so unconditionally. The Israeli proposal wasn't complete, and we were still operating on the principle that "nothing is agreed until everything is agreed." However, the President finally had some new cards to play. He promptly invited the Palestinian leader to his cabin. The two talked until around midnight, after which President Clinton walked Arafat back to his quarters. The President reported that the Palestinian leader had initially dismissed the proposals. He then began listening carefully and at last agreed to come back with an answer. His reply arrived in the middle of the night—no.

We asked ourselves whether Arafat was simply waiting until the last minute to show a new bottom line. Dennis Ross said he often waited until it was one minute to midnight. The problem, Dennis added, was that sometimes Arafat's watch was set wrong. Hoping for the best, the President delayed his Asia trip by a day, and we made a series of fruitless calls in search of support from Arab leaders.[3] Although we didn't have the basis for an agreement, I didn't want to give up because I feared what the results of our failure might be. Barak was reacting to Arafat's rejection with the fury of a failed suitor, while Arafat was hinting darkly that the Palestinians had alternatives to negotiation. We couldn't allow them to return home in a confrontational state of mind.

Negotiations inevitably lead to some playacting. Sometimes it's useful to pretend that you have a warmer relationship than you actually do. At other times, a show of anger or walking out is useful. I believe it's unacceptable, however, for leaders to let tantrums obstruct important initiatives. If women leaders had acted the way Arafat and Barak did during Camp David, they would have been dismissed as menopausal.

THE NIGHT THE President left for Asia reflected the confusion, tiredness, and determination we all felt. The rains were torrential; it was dark well before night. Preparing to leave, members of both delegations were anxious and depressed. The White House Communications Office announced that the summit was over. I met with the Palestinians, who blamed the Israelis, then with Barak, who blamed Arafat. The President showed up, dressed for a closing press conference, and joined me in urging the Israeli prime minister to stay. Barak called the President soon thereafter and said that he wouldn't leave if Arafat agreed to negotiate on the basis of the ideas they had discussed the night before. Clinton then went to Arafat and said he had persuaded Barak to stay. Because he thought it obvious, he did not specify that the discussion would have to be on the basis of the ideas presented the previous evening. Happy to talk when under the impression nothing else was required, Arafat agreed to remain. The President proceeded to give a fairly upbeat press briefing before departing for Washington and Asia. I went to bed pleased that the summit was still on. I had no idea the two leaders had precisely opposite conceptions of what would happen next.

The following morning the entire Palestinian delegation showed up for breakfast with big smiles, ready to discuss "all issues." But because the Palestinians said they hadn't accepted the new ideas, the Israelis refused

3. One side effect of Barak's secrecy was that we had been unable to prepare the way with friendly Arab governments. We couldn't sell them on the advantages of a deal in advance because we didn't know in advance what the deal might be. When we called, they wouldn't agree to put pressure on Arafat because they were unsure of the full context of the negotiations.

to talk. Barak thought Arafat had lied. Obviously, I had inherited a serious misunderstanding. I sat with my team and pieced together what had happened. In the end I went to Barak and explained that the misunderstanding had been our fault but that I didn't want everyone just sitting around until the President returned. Barak agreed to have informal talks, so I said I would announce them at dinner. He said, "Fine." But when he arrived for the meal, he told me he had changed his mind. I said it was too late and we went ahead.

Informal meetings began that night and continued for the next three days. The negotiators engaged in a relatively freewheeling exchange of ideas. It was clear that at least the younger Palestinian delegates wanted to make progress. To promote a cooperative mood, we arranged joint basketball games, and in the evening I hosted a "boy" movie, *U-571*, about the capture of a World War II German submarine. After the film one of the Israelis joked that a submarine would make a good addition to the military aid his government was requesting from the United States.

Although the informal talks went well, I ended up paying a high price for insisting that Barak let his people participate. The Israeli leader became morose, barely left his cabin, and sent word that he was not to be disturbed even by his own delegation. I suspected he was putting on an act, since he had often accused Arafat of manipulating us with his moods, but Barak's staff was so embarrassed I discarded the idea.

I felt it was my responsibility to lighten Barak's mood. He was, among his many accomplishments, a gifted classical pianist, so I thought we might arrange for a piano to be moved into his cabin, allowing him to practice. I asked our administrative people whether they would be able to locate a good piano that would fit through the door of Barak's quarters. After much checking, the answer came back that this could be done. Since I didn't want to send a piano without asking Barak, and since Barak wasn't taking phone calls, I decided to "bump into" him during his afternoon walk. In the woods I strode toward him and he toward me. His eyes were on the ground and I think he would have passed without saying a word if I hadn't stopped and said, "Hello." "Hello," he replied. I said, "How are you doing?" "Fine." I said, "With the President away, we thought you might want a diversion. Would you like us to have a piano moved into your cabin? It would be no trouble." He answered, "No." I inquired, "No?" Again, he said, "No."

I don't give up easily. At Barak's request, we had insisted the negotiators from the two sides not leave Camp David. With the President gone, however, the Israeli leader decided he wanted to go to Gettysburg. Left to enforce the rules, I had at first said no, but then thought, "This is ridiculous, I'm not a jailer." So I said to Barak, "Well, you said you were interested in Gettysburg. Today's Friday, tomorrow is the Sabbath. How about we visit the battlefield on Sunday?" At this he perked up. It was settled. We would go to Gettysburg.

Having offered to take Barak on an outing, I had to think up something for Arafat, so I suggested a Saturday excursion either to Harpers Ferry or my farm. He chose the latter—even though I had told him my children, grandchildren, and their friends would be there. "That will make it even better," he replied.

All the way to the farm I thought I must have been crazy to suggest the visit. After we arrived, I thought I truly had a disaster on my hands when my two-year-old grandson, Daniel, waking from his nap, took one look at Arafat with his stubble and kaffiyeh and let out a piercing scream. As the day progressed, however, it was hard to believe that the man who was so intractable at Camp David was the same person who cheered my other grandson, Jack, as he dove off the diving board, kissed my baby granddaughter Maddie, and happily posed for pictures with people in their bathing suits.

Passing time during the forty-minute ride back to Camp David, I encouraged Arafat to talk about himself. He chose to recount how he had come to the Palestinian cause. He said he had dedicated his life to that mission and spoke of his success in having his Fatah movement recognized as the embodiment of Palestinian dreams and in bringing the PLO back from exile to the West Bank and Gaza. Listening to him, I couldn't question his commitment, but there were still no words of compromise, and no sign that his vision extended to anything more forward-looking than victory over Israel.

At Gettysburg the next day Barak was also in an amiable mood. I pushed the theme of leadership as we stopped at Little Round Top and High Water Mark, where Confederate General George Pickett's desperate charge had met its disastrous end. Barak had a good time and posed happily for the Israeli photographer he had brought along. We had gone early so that the pictures could be broadcast on the nightly news in Jerusalem and Tel Aviv. During the return trip, Barak told me that he wanted the President to force Arafat to accept his ideas before negotiations resumed. He said we should tell the Palestinians that the United States would sever contacts with them if they did not yield. I said I wasn't sure that Arafat would respond to threats, and besides, Israel benefited as much as America did from our contacts with the Palestinians. Barak disagreed.

We hoped the President's return would force some decisions. To sharpen the focus, we decided he should meet with representatives from each side together on each of the major issues, beginning with security. As the President sat down with the two sides at 11:30 P.M. on July 24, yellow pad in hand, I was reminded of the all-night session that climaxed Wye. Maybe there was hope: breakthroughs in the Middle East always seemed to occur under cover of dark. The first hours of discussion this night dealt with such matters as early warning stations, Palestinian demilitarization, and the nature of an Israeli presence in the Jordan Valley. It was encouraging because both sides were engaged and the differences didn't seem insurmountable, but also discouraging because neither side was offering anything new. When the session broke at 5:30 A.M., many issues remained on the table.

The meetings resumed five hours later. What little momentum there was dissipated rapidly. The Israelis had given all they could. The Palestinians still refused to move, producing a map that showed no new ideas. The President finally asked Palestinian negotiator Saeb Erekat to see if his boss would accept a plan that mirrored Barak's but used the term "sovereignty," albeit heavily modified, in connection with more of what Arafat had sought within Arab sectors of Jerusalem. Two hours later, Erekat returned and read a note from Arafat in which he thanked the United States for its efforts, expressed a willingness to continue negotiations, and said that the Palestinians couldn't accept any arrangement that left the Israelis with even the most limited kind of sovereignty over Haram al-Sharif.

Camp David was over.

Sighing audibly, the President turned to us and said, "I don't like to fail, particularly at this." He then called Barak, who predicted that the summit's outcome might well mark the end of twenty years of efforts to achieve an Israeli-Palestinian peace. In his statement to the press, President Clinton tried to praise Barak without burying Arafat. He lauded the Israeli for his vision and courage while crediting Arafat for little more than showing up. In a literal way, this kept a commitment we had made not to blame Arafat for scuttling the summit, but such statements are usually exquisitely balanced, and with Israeli and American negotiators now free to provide background to the press, the imbalance in the President's words gained added weight.

ALTHOUGH WE LEFT Camp David disappointed, we were able to find traces of silver lining. Barak's political opponents were railing against the proposals he had made, but the determined prime minister had once again moved the debate's center of gravity. Israelis were now conditioned to yield significantly more than they had previously contemplated in return for a definitive end to the conflict. The Palestinian negotiators talked publicly about how much had been accomplished and spoke hopefully about the future. Arafat had shown the Arab and Muslim worlds that he could stand up to American and Israeli pressure. If he decided to use that added credibility to consult with Arab leaders and achieve a new and more realistic consensus, there was still a chance a settlement could be reached.

Private discussions were held between Israeli and Palestinian representatives throughout August and September. I was on the phone regularly with Arab leaders, stressing the risks Barak was taking and urging them to tell Arafat to do something more than just sit there with his hand out. During the General Assembly session in New York, I met again with the Palestinian chairman and probed to see whether he had moderated his position. Arafat rose from his seat, shaking his fist, and stormed out of the room. He returned for his meeting with the President, during which he crossed the room to smother me with kisses. Talk about mood swings.

Despite Arafat's intransigence, the Palestinians were urging us to get directly involved and make "bridging proposals." Toward the end of September the negotiators came to Washington and met for three days at the Pentagon City Ritz-Carlton. Dennis Ross, who attended some of the talks, reported that the two sides felt they were making progress. Meanwhile, on September 25 in Israel, Barak invited Arafat to his home, where they shared a convivial dinner and took turns speaking on the phone to President Clinton. Before leaving that night, Arafat said he took Barak aside and urged him to prevent opposition leader Ariel Sharon from carrying out his plan to walk on the esplanade of the Temple Mount/Haram al-Sharif. The request was ignored.

On September 28 Sharon, accompanied by a thousand armed police and soldiers and a coterie of Likud Party politicians, marched across the plaza containing the al-Aqsa Mosque and the Dome of the Rock. Palestinians responded the next day with large demonstrations and stone throwing near the Western Wall. Israeli police reacted by opening fire with rubber bullets, killing four and wounding two hundred. A new round of violence had begun.

Why did Sharon do it? Presumably he went to assert Israel's claims to sovereignty and establish a political advantage over Barak. Did he have a right to visit the Temple Mount? Yes, but for him to exercise that right at that particular time was like throwing a lighted match into a gasoline can with all the children in the neighborhood standing by. There will always be those who applaud such gestures. History, however, does not.

History will also show that Arafat made the worst of yet another opportunity. Instead of using the incident to demonstrate Palestinian maturity in the face of Sharon's provocative act, he reminded the world why even the most open-minded Israelis have misgivings about a Palestinian state.

Whether violence was already planned or Arafat ordered it now or merely failed to restrain it, the results were the same. Palestinians began heaving stones, bottles, pipe bombs, and gasoline bombs at Israeli soldiers. The soldiers fought back with tear gas and gunfire. Palestinian television showed footage of the 1989 intifada and played patriotic songs. Arafat closed the schools and students rushed into the streets. A twelve-year-old Palestinian boy was caught in a cross fire and killed, and the image of his frightened face was shown over and over again on televisions around the globe. Palestinian funerals stirred emotions that overflowed into violence, prompting reprisals that led to more funerals. Whatever Arafat's role, Palestinian rage was genuine. Barak, who had made no move to prevent Sharon's visit, now was inviting the Likud leader to join him in a national emergency government. When Israeli Arabs, who were certainly not controlled by Arafat, engaged in unruly demonstrations, the police fired on them too, killing five one day and more the next.

The Israelis felt that they were acting with restraint because they were using a fraction of their firepower. Barak was personally involved in trying to calibrate the response in ways that would minimize loss of life. To Palestinians, however, the issue of fairness was revealed in the statistics. During the first week, at least forty-nine Palestinians were killed, nine Israeli Arabs, and two other Israelis. Day by day, the horror escalated. In Nablus, the Tomb of Joseph was desecrated by a Palestinian mob. Two Israeli reservists were pulled out of a building, stabbed and stomped to death, and their bodies paraded through the streets. Israeli helicopters fired rockets into Ramallah and Gaza City.

From Washington, we watched with sadness and shock. Within a few weeks we had gone from discussing coexistence to wondering whether we could stop a return to all-out war. Each side could see now only what was worst in the other. In early October, I hosted a meeting at the residence of U.S. Ambassador Félix Rohatyn in Paris at which Barak and Arafat pledged to halt the violence. After a few quiet days, fighting resumed. Two weeks later, President Clinton cochaired a similar exercise in Egypt, with similar results.

Both despite and because of the violence, President Clinton was determined to continue pushing for a solution. Before the fighting had started, the two sides seemed to think they were making progress. Two days after the November election, we met with Arafat in the White House. The President was blunt. "I've got ten weeks left in office and want to use that time to produce a comprehensive agreement, a historical agreement, a real reconciliation. I want you to have your own state. I know the complexity of the issues, but I think you can do it. I want to know from you, Chairman Arafat, if you are with me. Can you commit yourself to me in this endeavor?" Arafat said to him, "I count on you, Mr. President. I think we can do it together, and we will follow any move you want to take."

In meetings later that month, Arafat convinced at least some Israelis that he was making a real effort to curtail violence and wanted to reach an agreement before our team left office. Barak's staff took this progress seriously enough to begin talking about which Arab leaders might be persuaded to attend the signing ceremony. The Israelis wanted to be optimistic because Barak had decided he had no choice but to call elections, to be held in early February. His opponent would be Ariel Sharon. The Israelis hoped Arafat would be more flexible now that the prospect of another Likud prime minister loomed. At first the Israelis insisted the talks be bilateral, with no U.S. presence. By mid December that had changed: now the Israelis wanted us to be involved. We invited negotiators from the two sides for a round of "now or never" talks revolving around the written peace documents we had prepared. The talks began on December 20.

After the negotiators had met for three days, the President summoned them to the Oval Office. "We know you're working hard," he told them, "but at the rate you're going, you won't make it. What I'm going to give you is not a U.S. proposal, but rather our idea of what will be needed on core issues to reach an agreement. If either side refuses to accept these parameters, they're off the table. We can talk about refinements, but these ideas are not to be negotiated. I would like answers from your leaders in four days."

The key to the parameters was a trade-off. The Palestinians would get sovereignty over the Haram al-Sharif/Temple Mount, but they would have to accept that Palestinian refugees wouldn't be guaranteed a right to return to Israel. In both cases the trade-off would be tempered. Israel would have sovereignty over the Western Wall. Palestinian refugees not settling in Israel would be guaranteed the right to return to Palestine, or to resettle elsewhere with compensation. The new Palestinian state would consist of 94 to 96 percent of the West Bank, plus 1 to 3 percent of Israeli territory as a swap. Its capital would be in Arab East Jerusalem.

Israeli troops would withdraw from the Jordan Valley over a period of three years, while an international force was gradually introduced. At the end of that time, the Palestinian territory in the West Bank would be contiguous, but a small Israeli presence would remain in fixed locations under the authority of the international force. During the following week, we solicited support from Arab leaders, who termed the President's proposals "historic" and pledged to back them. On December 25, Barak said on Israeli television that he would accept our ideas if Arafat did. But instead of an answer, the Palestinian chairman sent us a letter arguing against Israeli sovereignty over the Western Wall, against any Israeli military presence in the Jordan Valley, against any compromise on the right of return, and in favor of complete Israeli withdrawal within months, not years. The Palestinians had not moved a centimeter. The typewritten letter was signed by Arafat with a handwritten note wishing us all a Merry Christmas and a Happy New Year.

Still the show went on. Arafat returned once more to the White House. Meetings between Israeli and Palestinian negotiators continued even after President Clinton left office. The two sides suspended talks shortly before the Israeli elections, saying an agreement was "closer than ever." The Palestinians' failure to accept the best peace offer they would ever get contributed to the election of Ariel Sharon, a man with little sympathy for their cause. With the hour of terror at hand, the peace process lapsed into a coma.

People ask about my greatest disappointment as Secretary. This was it. Obviously the issues and history were achingly complex; nothing about the Middle East is simple. Leaders have a responsibility to their constituencies; if they do not meet it, they are usually not leaders for long. But true leadership requires the capacity to shape public opinion, not merely reflect it.

Certainly the Israelis could be faulted for the extremism of some and more generally for their policy on settlements. But the core failure was the Palestinians' obsessive focus not on how much could be gained but on the relatively little they would be required to give up. They wouldn't yield a dime to make a dollar. Arafat feared that if he said yes, he would be killed. He didn't want to share the fate of Anwar Sadat and, on a personal level, I couldn't blame him. Yet Barak walked willingly into the crosshairs of the Israeli extremists who still revere the assassin of Yitzhak Rabin. Thus the difference between a survivor and a leader.

If Arafat had chosen differently, Palestine would now be a member of the United Nations, its capital in East Jerusalem. Its people would be able to travel freely between the West Bank and Gaza. Its airport and seaport would be operating. Palestinian refugees would be receiving compensation and help in resettling. Instead the Palestinians have their legalisms, their misery, and their terror.

As this is written, a settlement of the type envisioned at Camp David does not seem realistic. The Oslo process has been pronounced dead and the search for a replacement is still in its early stages. The logic underlying the need for peace, however, has never been clearer; it is written in the blood of Palestinians and Israelis alike. Israel must have secure borders, but as its leaders have said, it cannot be secure as an occupying power. Palestinian misery will continue until a new consensus is forged that accepts compromise and excludes terror. Even then, as Barak prophesied, the two sides, having buried their victims, will "sit down once more to the same geography, the same demography, the same problems."

TWENTY-NINE

Had We But World Enough, and Time

I DID NOT WANT IT TO END, but from the first day of course I knew it would. Working each day with the portraits of my predecessors staring down from the walls, I was ever conscious of the passage of time. But I didn't want to become a portrait myself until I had poured absolutely everything I had into the job. With half a year remaining, I joked of my intention to take permanently to the air, crisscrossing the international dateline so every day would last thirty-six hours and I would have nine months left to work, not six.

As it was, my last months as Secretary were a blur in which the full range of normal business and travel had to be squeezed in and around our search for breakthroughs in North Korea and the Middle East and responding to the terrorist bombing of the USS *Cole*. We didn't sleep much. Amid the turmoil good news arrived, and from an unlikely direction. The final pieces of a democratic Balkans were being pushed into place.

Late in 1999, Croatian president Franjo Tudjman died and was succeeded by leaders who were anticorruption, prodemocracy, and committed to supporting the Dayton Accords. This was a crucial development to which the United States, Canada, and Europe responded rapidly with technical assistance and a warm welcome into such institutions as the Partnership for Peace. I traveled to Croatia twice in three weeks, first to meet with the presidential candidates, then to attend the inauguration of President Stjepan Mesić. Our show of prompt support was intended to bolster democratic forces in Croatia and to send a message to neighboring Serbia, which remained isolated and held back by its president, Slobodan

Milošević. Few believed, however, that Milošević could be dislodged.

Well before the war in Kosovo, I gained administration support for a policy of trying to replace Milošević. For two years we moved both behind the scenes and in public toward that end.[1] With colleague Joschka Fischer and others, I urged Serb opposition leaders to build a real political organization and focus on pushing Milošević out. In the spring of 2000, we decided to shift focus and "follow the money," placing new sanctions on the regime and making efforts to track Milošević's assets so he would feel impoverished and under threat. I met with prodemocracy mayors and found ways they could secure aid for their people without it being siphoned off by the federal government. In public remarks I said repeatedly that the United States wanted Milošević "out of power, out of Serbia, and in the custody of the war crimes tribunal." I was confident that when given a fair chance, the people of Serbia would reject Milošević. Critics dismissed this as wishful thinking, but they underestimated Serb courage. A political earthquake was under way.

As if tempting fate, Milošević overreached, calling for presidential elections on September 24, 2000, the first time in eight years that his name would appear on a general election ballot. Perhaps because he had surrounded himself with advisors afraid to tell him the truth, he was confident he could portray himself as the champion of Serb nationalism against an array of outside meddlers such as the U.S. Secretary of State. He was equally confident that, if the voters deserted him, he could use his authority over state institutions to rig the results. He proved mistaken on both counts.

It helped that the Serb opposition came together effectively in support of a scholarly anti-Communist named Vojislav Koštunica, who also had the advantage of strong nationalist credentials. The opposition organizers were now far more adept than they had been during earlier anti-Milošević initiatives. With monitors at every polling station, they obtained and quickly announced certified vote counts at the local level, so subsequent manipulations by Belgrade were transparent. Within hours Koštunica claimed victory, pointing to results showing that he had received more than the 50 percent needed. During the next twelve days Milošević struggled to save himself. First denying then grudgingly acknowledging Koštunica's lead, he claimed that his opponent had nevertheless fallen short of a majority and that a runoff was required. As anti-Milošević demonstrators swarmed into

---

1. Within the U.S. government this effort was spearheaded initially by ambassador Bob Gelbard, then by Jim Dobbins, acting assistant secretary of state for European affairs. The final successful push was led by Jim O'Brien, special advisor to the President and Secretary of State for democracy in the Balkans, whose powers of persuasion in Washington and Serbia were key.

Belgrade, many coming from the democratic municipalities we had helped, I worked nonstop to intensify diplomatic pressure. The British, French, and Germans all called upon Milošević to acknowledge his defeat.

The Russians, typically, were behind the curve. With Milošević's brother sitting in Moscow as Yugoslavia's ambassador, they were unwilling to switch to a new horse, notwithstanding the evidence of Serb popular will. I called Foreign Minister Ivanov frequently, but we were both traveling and our cell phones mysteriously seemed to lose their connection whenever I mentioned Serbia. "You have got to tell Milošević to give up," I told him. "Your own credibility with the Serbs depends on it." More than once Igor responded, "Madeleine, Madeleine, I can't hear you, Mad-el-eine." On October 5, the Serb people took matters into their own hands by seizing the parliament building and state-controlled media. Validating Tennyson's observation that "authority forgets a dying king," the police did nothing to preserve Milošević's empire. Many in the army switched sides. The pillars of Milošević's power vaporized almost overnight. Only then did Ivanov travel to Belgrade to congratulate Koštunica on his victory.

The democratic uprising in Serbia recalled for me the 1989 Velvet Revolution in Czechoslovakia. The old leadership, once challenged, crumbled rapidly. There was relatively little violence. The mass of people, led by students, got fed up with a regime that had failed economically, politically, and diplomatically. Milošević had led his people into four wars and lost every one, he had been indicted as a war criminal, and now the Yugoslav majority decided to stop obeying him. Within nine months he was not only out of power but at The Hague, awaiting trial for crimes committed in Croatia, Bosnia, and Kosovo.

While coordinating support for a democratic transition in Serbia, I learned how necessary it can be to remain in the background. Many Serbs resented the West because of NATO's actions. (I was even sent a roll of toilet paper of a type on sale in Belgrade featuring pictures of Robin Cook, Joschka Fischer, and me.) After Koštunica's victory, the United States was careful to assign full credit to the Serb opposition, while giving the new president the space he needed and Zoran Djindjić, the new prime minister, time to consolidate his government and ensure the backing of Yugoslav security forces.

I was proud on January 4, 2001, to welcome Yugoslav Foreign Minister Goran Svilanović to the State Department. Although the meeting itself was unremarkable, it was a personal coda for me. Only a few months earlier the prospect of a cordial discussion between the Yugoslav and American foreign ministers would have been unthinkable. The Serb people, whom my father had so respected and who had aided my family's flight from Hitler, had at long last overthrown their own dictator, and here was Svilanović expressing confidence that the era of conflict in the Balkans had come to an end. We all knew that Yugoslavia still faced an array of challenges, but the naysayers had been proven wrong and my faith in the Serb people justified.[2]

There were many who thought the Balkans were not an area of importance, but they were mistaken. During my time in government the Balkans provided the context for a debate about the global role of the United States, the relevance of NATO, the evolution of Russia, the limits of sovereignty, and the possibility of extending democracy to lands lacking a democratic tradition. In the Balkans we faced a series of choices about whether to yield passively to humanitarian crimes or act to stop them, whether to accept the likes of Tudjman and Milošević or oppose them. We had to decide whether it was appropriate to use American power to halt large-scale humanitarian crimes, and whether to join in peacekeeping missions designed to prevent a recurrence of such atrocities. Finally, we had to decide whether to exercise diplomatic leadership in the region or defer to the Europeans, who lived closer and claimed to understand better than we the dynamics created by the past.

The Balkans constituted a testing ground for Clinton administration foreign policy, a place where failure was constantly predicted and our goals derided as unrealistic and naïve. Certainly the region remains deeply troubled, but in every part of it the criteria for success have changed. The appetite for conflict has waned, and the drive for ethnic dominance has been muted by desires for integration with the West, modernization, education, and the strengthening of democratic institutions. Even as emotional an issue as the legal status of Kosovo seems likely to be resolved through peaceful means, and the Balkans are moving toward their rightful place within a Europe whole and free.

THROUGHOUT MY YEARS in government, democracy was my theme. It was, after all, thanks to democracy that I had become Secretary of State—and would soon become an ex-Secretary of State. In Serbia I had wit-

---

2. The Serb people would be tested again in March 2003, when Prime Minister Djindjić was assassinated by powerful members of the criminal underworld, a murder that demonstrated the ongoing threat posed by organized crime. Despite the tragic circumstances, the transition to new leadership was smooth, and the forces of reform have made clear their intention to fight to establish the rule of law. The new Prime Minister, Zoran Živković, was one of the democratic mayors with whom I met prior to the defeat of Milošević.

nessed one kind of democratic transition. On the first of December 2000, I witnessed another, traveling to Mexico for the inauguration of that country's new president, Vicente Fox. This was no ordinary inauguration. Fox's election marked the end of seventy-one years of rule by Mexico's once all-powerful Institutional Revolutionary Party (PRI). Popular reaction was joyful, but the prospect of such a change after more than seven decades put members of the PRI, still in control of their Congress, in a sour mood.

Vicente Fox seemed perfectly cast for the role of president—six foot four, handsome, outgoing, wearing cowboy boots; he combined dignified looks with an informal style. He began his inaugural speech to the Mexican congress and a roomful of foreign dignitaries by saying "*Buenos días*" to each of his four adopted children. In his remarks he vowed to reduce corruption and increase education, to give more attention to human rights and the environment and—speaking with particular passion—to promote a more dignified life for Mexico's indigenous populations. He had even added words of his own about protecting the poor when taking the oath of office.

The outgoing cabinet, including my colleague Foreign Minister Rosario Green, sat on one side of the podium, looking distinctly uncomfortable. The elected representatives sat in front of them on either side of the aisle. There was considerable tension, and PRI members didn't hesitate to voice their dissatisfaction by booing when Fox criticized the old "authoritarian regime." In reality both parties had cause for pride. Fox had run a strong campaign focused on the problems created by decades of PRI rule, while the outgoing President, Ernesto Zedillo, seated next to Fox, had supported the democratic reforms that made a fair election possible, and was turning over to his successor a strong economy and warm relations with the United States.

As I watched the proceedings, I felt I was fast-forwarding to my own future. Each year members of our cabinet had met with our Mexican counterparts to discuss issues that ranged from controlling cross-border pollution to coordinating immigration policy. The next time those meetings were held, they would be held without me. Although Washington's inaugural pomp and circumstance would have a different rhythm, the result would be identical. One President would be out and another in. And the American Secretary of State, like Rosario Green, would have to find new challenges to pursue.

PART OF THE PROCESS of leaving office is trying to sum up. This is especially complicated in foreign policy, where almost everything is subjective, few victories are permanent, and there is no scoreboard to record wins and losses. As I made my last official round of interviews, however, I felt we had a good story to tell.

When Bill Clinton was elected, the key question internationally was whether in the absence of a superpower rival, America would withdraw from the world. President Clinton himself had entered office determined to focus on the domestic economy. While in power, however, he quickly assumed the stature of world leader. As a result, President Clinton left behind an America more prosperous than ever in a world freer than ever.

Fully conscious of the persistent threats posed by terrorism and weapons proliferation, the President had built the foundation of a global antiterrorist network that his successor at first partly neglected, then augmented dramatically after September 11. The nightmare of "loose nukes" from the former Soviet Union had been addressed, although coping with it remained a work in progress. We had maintained sanctions against Saddam Hussein while severely limiting his military options and weakening his capabilities. Working with our allies, we had blocked North Korea's quickest route to nuclear weapons and gained the suspension of advanced missile tests. We had stabilized and democratized the Balkans.

In the Middle East, we had given Yasser Arafat every opportunity to realize the basic aspirations of his people. We had tended our alliances in Europe and Asia with care, and as a result they were cohesive and strong. We were on good terms, but had held to our principles, in relations with Moscow and Beijing. We had strengthened our security guidelines with Japan, opened a new chapter in our relations with India, increased cooperation in our own hemisphere through the Summit of the Americas, and worked to integrate Africa into world markets. The President, who had inherited a sluggish U.S. economy burdened with high deficits, bequeathed to his successor sound fiscal policies, a record surplus, and a country whose international economic leadership was undisputed. Around the world America was recognized as a driving force in support of peace, democracy, economic opportunity, a more open trading system, and the rule of law.[3]

We had also led on less traditional foreign policy issues, including efforts to improve the lives of women and increase respect for human rights generally. We organized our foreign policy institutions to prepare them for a new era and helped reform the United Nations. We participated in efforts

---

3. I also took pride in dedicating the State Department building to Harry S Truman, who had been President when I arrived in the United States and was for me the embodiment of the principled use of American power. As Missouri Congressman Ike Skelton told me, "Some of your accomplishments may erode with time, but the Truman Building will remain, etched in concrete."

to establish a permanent international criminal tribunal and to curb the threats posed by land mines and global warming. And we had worked to increase the use of the Internet and other advanced technologies as tools for development. This is a diverse list, but each item on it was connected to the goal of building a more integrated, stable, and democratic world, with increased security for all who respect the interests and rights of others.

While summarizing our record, I shared with interviewers some of the more specific lessons I had learned. The first is that I hoped never again to hear foreign policy described as a debate between Wilsonian idealists and geopolitical realists. In our era, no President or Secretary of State could manage events without combining the two. Under President Clinton we were determined to do the right thing but in a tough-minded way. We tried to strengthen multilateral institutions but recognized the need for America to take the lead in such areas as the Balkans and Middle East. We promoted democracy but also worked when necessary with nondemocratic states. We defended human rights but understood that other urgent issues, such as nonproliferation, sometimes had first claim. We were willing to take on hard jobs, but diligent about enlisting the aid of others and careful not to make commitments we could not keep.

Some argued that we were inconsistent, but it is not possible to conduct foreign policy within a rigid framework where every stimulus is matched by a preordained response. A policy maker must leave room for flexibility and innovation. Every situation is different, and when problems arise, our leaders need the fullest possible range of options. These include everything from the art of verbal persuasion to sanctions to participation in peace operations to various gradations in the use of force. Choices must be based on such factors as the gravity of our interests, the likelihood of success, the willingness of others to do their share, the degree of popular support, and the consequences of inaction. Military force must be used selectively, sometimes in a limited manner and at other times with fewer constraints.

A second lesson is that we need to obtain adequate resources for our international operations and programs. I support generous funding for our armed forces, but even most U.S. military leaders agree that there is a gross mismatch between what we allocate for military purposes and what we spend to advance our overseas interests by other means. It takes money to stop terrorists, forge peace, prevent proliferation, defeat drug cartels, promote exports, strengthen democracy, fight pollution, combat AIDS, save lives through family planning, and otherwise defend our interests and values. Today the United States spends barely more than a penny out of every federal dollar for these and other international purposes combined. I am proud that during my four years as Secretary we were able to increase appropriations by 17 percent. The fact remains, however, that we are spending only about one-tenth as much for these purposes, in real terms, as we did when George Marshall was Secretary of State half a century ago.

Third, I do not believe any foreign policy can fairly represent the American people if it does not support democratic practices overseas. During the Cold War we had an excuse to view almost every challenge through the prism of our rivalry with the Soviet Union; our wisest leaders understood even then that American leadership must be based not only on what we are against but also on what we are *for*. And from Central America to Central Asia, our interests dictate that we should be *for* a world in which the democratic tide continues to rise. More countries have elected governments than ever before, but many democratic transitions are fragile and further progress cannot be assumed. Free nations must help one another. That is why the Community of Democracies initiative is so important.

Fourth, it is vital for America to find the right role for itself—not an easy proposition. While I was at the United Nations, President Clinton referred to America as "the indispensable nation." I liked the phrase and borrowed it so often that it became associated with me. Some thought the term arrogant, but I didn't intend it that way. Rather, I felt it captured the reality that most large-scale initiatives required at least some input from the United States if they were to succeed. I did not mean to suggest we could simply go it alone. My purpose was not to put down others, but rather to stir a sense of pride and responsibility among Americans, so that we would be less reluctant to take on problems.

Although the United States has much in common with other nations, it is also unique in power and global reach. This uniqueness creates enormous opportunities but also dangerous temptations. For better or worse, American actions and policies serve as an example. This means, in the absence of a balancing power, that the United States must have the discipline to limit its own actions in accordance with the standards it applies to others. If we attempt to put ourselves above or outside the international system, we invite everyone else to do so as well. Then moral clarity is lost, the foundation of our leadership becomes suspect, the cohesive pull of law is weakened, and those who do not share our values find openings to exploit. I have always believed America to be an exceptional country, but that is because we have led in creating standards that work for everyone, not because we are an exception to the rules.

Part of leaving office is regretting the things that might have been done better. As I have said, my biggest regret came while I was still at the

UN, when we failed to comprehend rapidly enough the evolving genocide in Rwanda. As Secretary of State, because I was interested in so
much, I was insufficiently ruthless in setting priorities. I did not want any
part of the world to feel that America was indifferent. I also felt, at times,
that I had not done enough to restore the foreign policy primacy of the
State Department, but the travails of my successor lead me to think I did
as well as others would. The globe is so interdependent that nearly every
cabinet department now has a legitimate international role. Finally, our
administration should have had the vision to risk upsetting traditional
friends in the Middle East by pressing for democratization within the
Arab world—including a direct challenge to the indoctrination of young
people in tenets advocating violence and hatred. We should also have
pushed Israel harder to halt the expansion of settlements, a policy so
harmful to negotiations.

One thing I had mixed feelings about but couldn't really regret was
saying no to Václav Havel when he suggested that I try to succeed him as
president of the Czech Republic. I was incredibly honored, and the idea of
living in Prague Castle certainly has a fairy-tale appeal. But I told Havel the
Czech people should be led by someone who has lived among them these
past decades, and that of course, I had long since become an American.

As in any leave-taking, the hardest part is saying good-bye. Some relationships are strictly professional, but others blossomed into true friendships, even unlikely ones, and weren't so easy to dismiss. Although Yevgeny
Primakov left office in 1999, he still called me, jointly with Ivanov, to
express greetings at Christmas. It was obvious, even over the phone, that
each was in a holiday mood.

I was particularly touched when Hubert Védrine, with whom I had
both collaborated and sparred so often, organized a going-away dinner
for me in Paris. Robin Cook, Joschka Fischer, Lamberto Dini, Igor
Ivanov, and Javier Solana were there at the Château de la Celle-Saint-
Cloud. I only wish I had had a tape recorder to capture the many toasts,
which were bilingual and extremely flattering. No doubt the tributes
were exaggerated, as they always are at such events, but the warmth and
feelings of partnership were very real. Through the years we had faced
down Milošević, grappled with Saddam Hussein, adapted NATO, and
helped Europe's new democracies to find their place inside a secure and
united continent. It was a job on the whole well done. I had to struggle to
keep my emotions in check: Igor had gone to so much trouble with his
present—a Russian tea set with the pictures of each of the foreign ministers on a cup and an accompanying platter that read, "Madeleine's Dream
Team." Védrine hugged me and presented me with a magnificently

bound two-volume set of de Tocqueville's *Democracy in America*. His wink told me that our differences over the United States as a "hyperpower" and over the Community of Democracies had never been personal.

ON JANUARY 19, 2001, I signed my pro forma letter of resignation as Secretary of State and called President Clinton to thank him for his kind words on a video shown during an appearance I had just made on the *Oprah Winfrey Show*. We had one day left in office, and the President was thinking—as was I—about opportunities missed. Fuming about all the time we had invested in Arafat, he said he wished he had taken the chance of going to North Korea instead of staying in Washington to make a final push on the Middle East.

My last day I made the traditional farewell address to the State Department. In Dean Acheson's memoir, he includes a picture of his audience on this occasion, almost exclusively white men in hats. The group that greeted me was much more diverse and, I suspect, demonstrative. The loudspeaker was blaring Aretha Franklin as I threaded my way through a wall of friends and colleagues to a podium set up on the steps near the department's main entrance. There I recounted some of the highs and lows of the previous four years and thanked those around me for their efforts on behalf of our country. I also said to cheers that "it says something very good about America that the first female Secretary of State is about to be succeeded by our first African-American Secretary of State."

The last day ended as last days do—with the packing. Since I had been through the process before, I knew the drill. Most of those who had worked in my office and helped me now to fill my boxes were career people. They would stay after I left to help the new team, which already had offices on the ground floor and was champing to move up. The names on the doors and pictures on the walls would be changed by the following sunset. Democracy is fair but a trifle brutal. History will record, nevertheless, that the sixty-fourth Secretary of State did not have to be dragged out by her heels. I simply took one last look around, checked the placement of my farewell note to Colin Powell, and left.

Shortly after the Inauguration ceremonies I received a phone call from Harold Koh, who had headed our bureau on human rights. Harold said that when Colin Powell's face had appeared on television his nine-year-old son Willie had yelped in surprise. "How could they give Madeleine's job to that person?" the boy asked. Sternly Harold lectured his son about equal opportunity. "It's not that," Willie said, bewildered. "It's just I never thought the secretary of state could be a man."

I opened a new office in downtown Washington where I could work on this book and other projects. It was lovely but not quite the same. From my old office I had been able to see the Lincoln Memorial. From my new one I could see Loeb's Delicatessen. Travel was different too. After eight years, I was on my own. I went to California for a speech, flying commercial, and decided to take the red-eye back. That evening I was sitting in the Admiral's Club reading the newspaper, waiting for the plane. A man came in and looked around. There were rows of empty seats, but he sat down next to me and put his briefcase on my foot.

After a minute he said, "You're Madeleine Albright."

"Yes, I am."

He said, "I just saw a documentary about you."

"Oh."

He said, "According to Michael Douglas, you like to flirt."

"Not everybody is Michael Douglas."

He said, "You've lost your job and all your power; you must feel awful."

"This is America, it's how the system works. I feel fine."

He said, "No, I used to work for Marilyn Quayle, and when she lost *her* job, *she* felt awful. So you must feel awful."

This almost stumped me. But then I said, "You know what? I don't feel awful, I feel proud."

MY REPLY CONTAINED THE TRUTH, but not the whole truth. I did feel more proud than awful, but leaving public office after so long a period of intense activity in the spotlight is not easy. The daily cycle of stimulation stops abruptly. It's no simple thing to give up a job you love, which has allowed you to feel that you are making a difference. I don't believe anyone in a comparable position who says, "I'm glad it's over." Reading the daily newspaper becomes a passive rather than an active experience—the difference between watching a play and performing in one. During the first months, when something important happened in the world, my physical and mental reflexes were still conditioned—prompting a rush of adrenaline and sparking thoughts of what should be done and who should be called; this was followed by a quieting realization that the doing and calling were being done by others. I was also irritated by the disdain shown by some in the incoming administration toward the accomplishments, efforts, and diplomatic hard work of the previous eight years.

There were, of course, some welcome sides to resuming a normal life. I was able to spend more time with my sister, Kathy, and brother, John, and his family. I was thrilled that my daughters Anne and Alice and their families lived nearby and that Katie came often for visits with her children, Benjamin and Eleanor. I soon found that managing foreign policy and baby-sitting grandchildren require many of the same diplomatic skills. I went to the farm often, driving my own car for the first time in years and learning how to pump gas. But some adjustments were easier than others. I couldn't just pick up every old friendship. Some people had moved away or become so involved in other activities that they were now unavailable—just as for years, because of my job, I had been. My circle of acquaintances was now enormous, but my circle of close friends much smaller than I would have wished. I still had Wini, Mary Jane, and Susan from Wellesley days, but Emily had died.

One of the hardest parts of writing a memoir is facing the implication that when you reach the end, your life—or at least the interesting part—is over. I don't feel that. While in government, I learned the strength of my voice. Back now on the outside, I am finding a new voice, grounded in the depth of my experience and my continuing sense of responsibility to contribute what I can to the students I teach and to the larger debate about the direction of U.S. foreign policy. In a variety of ways that fit together well, I am still working to promote democracy, open markets and the rule of the law. To those ends, I have established The Albright Group, a global strategy firm helping businesses and organizations grow and encouraging democratic market economies. I am also chairman of the National Democratic Institute; teaching once again at Georgetown; serving as president of the Truman Scholarship Foundation; directing projects for the Pew Foundation and the William Davidson Institute of the University of Michigan Business School; and giving speeches across the globe. In the midst of all this, I slow-ran the Winter Olympics torch through the streets of Washington in 2002.

Almost everywhere I go, I am recognized—although not always accurately. One woman mixed me up with Florida's ex-Secretary of State Katherine Harris. A group in Colorado was thrilled to bump into "Margaret Thatcher." A traveler in line at one airport stared at me for a while before asking, "Are you?" I replied, "Yes." He turned to his friend. "See, I told you. That's the person who does commercials for Northwest Airlines." I felt better when a man in Boston came up to me and inquired, "Are you Madeleine Albright?" When I said yes, his face fell. "Rats," he said, "I just lost a twenty-dollar bet."

But the encounters that mean the most to me are with women of various ages who recognize the real me and come up to say thank you. I especially treasure the young women who say that my example has inspired them to raise their sights so that they now feel that serving as secretary of state or in even higher office is a realistic goal.

When Secretary of State Cordell Hull was nearing his departure from office in 1944, he confided to a friend that he was "tired of intrigue... tired of being bypassed... tired of being relied upon in public and ignored in private... tired of fighting battles which were not appreciated... tired of making speeches and holding press interviews—tired of talking and tired of service."[4] There were times during my years in government when I, like probably every other cabinet member, would have subscribed to his complaints. The job was inexorable. Every day there was something new, but the old problems never went away. There were times I felt stymied by my own government, treated unfairly by Congress and the press, and frustrated by my inability to wave a wand and magically reshape events.

On the whole, however, my view of the job is the opposite of Hull's. (In fairness, he was ill by the time he left.) Whatever my day-to-day complaints, I was always conscious of the privilege I had been given to serve at all. I never viewed the job as a burden—or as something to which I had a permanent claim or entitlement. As someone who had leapt from slippery rock to slippery rock throughout her career, I loved the constant stimulation of being Secretary, of being able to say a dozen times every day after a phone call or meeting, "What's next?"—knowing the answer would involve ever-changing issues of importance to people around the globe.

The America I have always loved is changing too. The threat of terrorism after September 11 has made our society less open. Revered precepts of due process are being reexamined. A growing divide is evident between the United States and longtime allies. The future relevance of the United Nations is being questioned. These trends should prompt not passive acceptance but vigorous debate. The welcome promised by the Statue of Liberty is very real to me, as it is to millions of American immigrants. The protections afforded by the Bill of Rights have stood for more than two centuries as our country's great gift to the world and its most powerful and productive force for change. The great institutions forged by the trans-Atlantic partnership that saved freedom in the twentieth century are in jeopardy. I believe firmly that they must be rescued and revitalized if that blessing is to survive the twenty-first.

I look to the future, nevertheless, with confidence not so much because of what has changed but because of what has not. The principles in which I have believed since childhood are as reliable as they have ever been.

---

4. *The War Diary of Breckinridge Long*; selections from the years 1938–1944. Selected and edited by Fred L. Israel. Lincoln, University of Nebraska Press [1966] pp. 386–88.

These are the self-evident truths of equality and of the irreducible value of every individual that were articulated by Jefferson and interpreted memorably by Lincoln through his Emancipation Proclamation and Gettysburg Address. There is much in life that is complicated and beyond our understanding, but the basic principles of human liberty are not so complicated, and if we hold to them, we will find a way to correct our mistakes and set a true course.

That is one reason I am so grateful to President Clinton for giving me the opportunity to represent the United States of America to the world. It offended some people and bemused others, but I could not help wearing my patriotism on my sleeve and, for that matter, my chest. I am aware that the American experiment has blemishes, but I still find it a miraculous success, forging unity out of an extraordinary diversity of backgrounds and cultures. And I remain proud of the difference America has made in the lives of those everywhere who cherish government of, by, and for the people.

In his novel *One Hundred Years of Solitude*, my friend Gabriel García Márquez writes of individuals ensnared, as we all are, by the inescapable cycles of life. The sun rises and sets, the seasons pass, the years go by, the wheels turn, and the axle irremediably wears down. We are not given a choice of whether to participate in this process. If we live, that is our lot. But this does not leave us without meaningful choices. I have always believed, because I learned it from my parents, that you have to fight to achieve all you can, not literally but with the gifts you have. At first to me that meant doing well in school. Later it meant being a good wife and mother and so on through all the stages of my life up to and including Secretary of State and beyond. I was taught to strive not because there were any guarantees of success but because the act of striving is in itself the only way to keep faith with life.

People sometimes ask me how I want to be remembered. I reply that I don't want to be remembered; I am still here. But when the day comes, I hope people will say that I did the best with what I was given, tried to make my parents proud, served my country with all the energy I had, and took a strong stand on the side of freedom. Perhaps some will also say that I helped teach a generation of older women to stand tall and young women not to be afraid to interrupt.

September 20, 1909:	Josef Körbel (father) born.
May 11, 1910:	Anna Spieglová (mother) born.
October 28, 1918:	Czechoslovakia established.
April 20, 1935:	Josef Körbel and Anna "Mandula" Spieglová marry.
May 15, 1937:	Marie Jana (Madeleine) born in Prague.
September 29, 1938:	Munich Agreement.
March 15, 1939:	Nazis occupy Prague.
March 25, 1939:	Josef, Mandula, and Madeleine Körbel escape Czechoslovakia.
September 1, 1939:	Nazis invade Poland; WWII begins.
1939–1945:	Korbel family in England.
October 7, 1942:	Kathy Korbel (sister) born.
May 7, 1945:	Germany surrenders.
May 1945:	Korbel family returns to liberated Czechoslovakia.
September 1945–1948:	Josef Korbel serves as Czechoslovakia's ambassador to Yugoslavia and Albania.
January 15, 1947:	John Korbel (brother) born.
September 1947:	Madeleine Korbel sent to boarding school in Switzerland.
Early 1948:	In early February, Czechoslovakia becomes member of new UN Commission for India and Pakistan (Kashmir). Josef Korbel assigned to Commission.
February 25, 1948:	Communist coup in Czechoslovakia.
March 10, 1948:	Jan Masaryk found dead.
May 1948:	Josef Korbel begins work for Kashmir Commission. Family goes to London.
November 11, 1948:	Madeleine Korbel, with mother, sister, and brother arrive in U.S. Father follows in December.
April 4, 1949:	NATO Alliance created.

June 7, 1949:	Korbel family granted political asylum by the U.S.
Summer 1949:	Korbel family moves to Denver.
1955–1959:	Madeleine Korbel at Wellesley College.
August 14, 1957:	Madeleine Korbel granted American citizenship.
June 11, 1959:	Madeleine Korbel and Joseph Albright marry.
July 1959:	Joe Albright serves in Army at Fort Leonard Wood, Missouri; Madeleine Korbel Albright (MKA) works for *Rolla Daily News*.
1960–1961:	Joe Albright works at *Chicago Sun-Times*; MKA works at *Encyclopaedia Britannica*.
Spring 1961:	Joe Albright begins at *Newsday* in Long Island, New York.
June 17, 1961:	Anne Korbel Albright and Alice Patterson Albright (daughters) born.
Summer 1962:	Joe Albright at *Newsday's* Washington bureau. MKA begins graduate work at SAIS, Johns Hopkins.
July 2, 1963:	Alicia Patterson Guggenheim dies. Albright family returns to Long Island.
March 5, 1967:	Katharine Medill Albright (daughter) born.
Spring 1968:	MKA earns certificate from Russian Institute and Master of Arts degree at Columbia University.
August 21, 1968:	Prague Spring ends with Soviet invasion.
September 1968:	Joe Albright becomes *Newsday's* Washington Bureau Chief.
Spring 1970:	Harry Guggenheim sells *Newsday* to Times Mirror Company.
May 1976:	Ph.D. degree granted by Columbia University.
August 1976:	MKA becomes chief legislative assistant to Senator Edmund Muskie.
November 2, 1976:	Jimmy Carter elected President.
July 18, 1977:	Josef Korbel dies.
1978–1981:	MKA works on staff of National Security Council.
September 1981:	MKA begins Woodrow Wilson Center fellowship on Poland.
January 13, 1982:	Joe Albright announces he wants a divorce.
January 31, 1983:	Divorce final.
1982–1992:	MKA on faculty at Georgetown University School of Foreign Service.

1980s:	MKA serves as foreign policy advisor to Democratic presidential nominee Walter Mondale and vice-presidential nominee Geraldine Ferraro in 1984 and presidential candidate Michael Dukakis in 1987–88.
October 4, 1989:	Mandula Korbel dies.
1989–1992:	MKA president, Center for National Policy.
1989–1990:	Fall of Berlin Wall; Velvet Revolution, Václav Havel becomes president of Czechoslovakia.
1991–1992:	War breaks out in the Balkans.
November 4, 1992:	Bill Clinton elected President.
December 1992:	U.S. troops begin humanitarian relief mission in Somalia.
December 21, 1992:	President Clinton designates MKA as U.S. Permanent Representative to the UN.
February 1, 1993:	MKA begins as U.S. ambassador to the UN.
May 25, 1993:	UN Security Council (UNSC) establishes the International Criminal Tribunal for the former Yugoslavia.
June 26, 1993:	U.S. bombs Iraqi intelligence headquarters in retaliation for assassination attempt against former President George Bush.
September 13, 1993:	Israeli and Palestinian leaders sign Oslo Declaration of Principles.
October 3, 1993:	18 U.S. soldiers killed in Somalia, prompting U.S. withdrawal.
October 5, 1993:	UNSC authorizes peacekeeping mission in Rwanda.
October 8, 1993:	U.S. deploys USS *Harlan County* to Haiti.
January, 1994:	MKA and Chairman of the Joint Chiefs General Shalikashvili travel to "Partnership for Peace" candidate countries.
April 6, 1994:	Plane crash kills Rwandan president; genocide begins.
May 3, 1994:	President Clinton signs PDD 25 establishing criteria for participation in UN peacekeeping operations.
July 31, 1994:	UNSC authorizes restoration of democratically-elected government in Haiti, by use of force if necessary.
September 19, 1994:	U.S. troops enter Haiti to ensure restoration of democratically-elected government.
October 21, 1994:	U.S. and North Korea sign Agreed Framework.

December 9–11, 1994: President Clinton hosts first Summit of the Americas in Miami, Florida.

Mid July, 1995: Massacre in Srebrenica, Bosnia-Herzegovina.

September, 1995: UN's Fourth World Conference on Women in Beijing; MKA meets with Aung San Suu Kyi in Burma.

November 21, 1995: Dayton talks conclude a peace agreement on Bosnia.

February 24, 1996: Two civilian planes shot down by Cuban fighter pilots.

December 5, 1996: President Clinton designates Ambassador Albright to serve as secretary of state during his second term.

December 17, 1996: Kofi Annan elected 7th UN secretary general.

January 23, 1997: MKA sworn in as 64th secretary of state.

January 30, 1997: Michael Dobbs of the *Washington Post* interviews MKA on her family's heritage.

April 18, 1997: President Clinton and MKA announce reorganization of the State Department and other foreign affairs agencies: incorporating ACDA and USIA, and assuming authority over the AID budget.

April 24, 1997: Senate approves Chemical Weapons Convention.

May, 1997: Guerilla leader Kabila overthrows Zaire's President Mobutu setting off a regional conflict drawing in neighboring Rwanda, Uganda, and Zimbabwe.

May 27, 1997: Presidents Clinton and Yeltsin sign NATO-Russia Founding Act.

July 8–9, 1997: NATO Summit in Madrid: Czech Republic, Hungary, and Poland invited to become members.

November 21–24, 1997: APEC Summit in Vancouver, Canada, focuses on the escalating Asian financial crisis.

January 7, 1998: In a CNN interview, Iran's newly elected President Mohammad Khatami hints at possibility of improved relations with the U.S.

January 20–23, 1998: Israeli Prime Minister Netanyahu and PLO Chairman Arafat in Washington for Middle East peace talks.

January 21, 1998: Monica Lewinsky scandal becomes public.

February 23, 1998: UN brokers agreement with Iraq temporarily ending crisis over weapons inspections that had erupted the previous October.

February–March, 1998: Violence breaks out in the Yugoslav province of Kosovo. MKA warns Milošević to withdraw excess forces.

March 20, 1998:	MKA announces initiatives to improve people-to-people relations with Cuba.
April 30, 1998:	U.S. Senate votes to admit Poland, Hungary, and the Czech Republic into NATO.
May, 1998:	India and Pakistan conduct nuclear tests.
May 21, 1998:	Indonesian President Suharto resigns amidst protests following nearly a year of economic crisis.
May 25, 1998:	Irish citizens accept the Good Friday Peace Accords.
June 17, 1998:	MKA in speech offers to work with Iran to develop road map leading to normal relations.
June 24–July 3, 1998:	MKA accompanies the President on visit to China.
August, 1998:	Iraq again suspends cooperation with UN arms inspections.
August 7, 1998:	Terrorists linked to Osama bin Laden bomb U.S. embassies in Nairobi, Kenya and Dar es Salaam, Tanzania.
August 20, 1998:	U.S. launches cruise missile attacks on suspected terrorist camps in Afghanistan and a pharmaceutical factory in Sudan tied to bin Laden.
August 24, 1998:	U.S. and UK propose conditions for Pan Am 103 trial.
August 31, 1998:	North Korea test fires a three-stage Taepo Dong missile. Former Defense Secretary William Perry soon begins interagency review of U.S. policy on North Korea.
Mid-October, 1998:	Yugoslav authorities agree to a cease-fire in Kosovo.
October 15–23, 1998:	Middle East talks resulting in Wye River Memorandum.
December 16–19, 1998:	U.S. and U.K. conduct Operation Desert Fox against Iraq.
January 8, 1999:	Crowe report recommends increased funding for embassy security worldwide.
January 15, 1999:	Massacre in Racak, Kosovo.
January–February, 1999:	Senate trial of President Clinton results in acquittal on all articles of impeachment.
February 7, 1999:	King Hussein of Jordan dies.
February–March, 1999:	Talks in Rambouillet, France on Kosovo. Albanians agree to draft settlement; Serbs do not.
March 12, 1999:	Poland, Hungary, and Czech Republic officially join NATO Alliance.

March 16–18, 1999: U.S. hosts U.S.-African Ministerial Conference for Partnership in the 21st Century.

March 24–
  June 12, 1999: Following a renewed Serb offensive in Kosovo, NATO conducts air war against Yugoslavia.

April 5, 1999: Libya turns over Pan Am 103 suspects.

April 7–10, 1999: Chinese Premier Zhu visits Washington for PNTR talks.

April 23–25, 1999: NATO 50th Anniversary Summit in Washington.

May 17, 1999: Israel elects Ehud Barak prime minister, defeating Benjamin Netanyahu.

June 9–12, 1999: End of Kosovo conflict.

August–
  September, 1999: Conflict in Chechnya resumes.

October 13, 1999: Senate rejects Comprehensive Test Ban Treaty.

October 18, 1999: Indonesian parliament declares 1976 annexation of East Timor null and void.

November 15, 1999: U.S. and China reach agreement on trade relations, laying groundwork for China's entry into the WTO.

December, 1999: U.S. and international efforts foil a series of terrorist plots timed to coincide with Millennium celebrations.

December 31, 1999: Boris Yeltsin resigns as Russian president, designates Vladimir Putin successor. Putin elected March 2000.

December 31, 1999: U.S. cedes back control of the Panama Canal.

January 3–10, 2000: U.S. hosts Israeli-Syrian peace talks in Shepherdstown, West Virginia.

March 17, 2000: MKA announces lifting of restrictions on selected Iranian non-oil exports.

March 26, 2000: President Clinton and Syrian President Asad meet in Geneva.

May 18, 2000: Africa Growth and Opportunity Act becomes law, lowering U.S. trade barriers to countries in sub-Saharan Africa.

May 24, 2000: Israel completes withdrawal from the security zone in southern Lebanon.

June 8, 2000: MKA attends special UN session: "Women 2000: Gender Equality, Development, and Peace for the 21st Century."

June 25–27, 2000: Poland hosts initial "Towards a Community of Democracies" conference.

July 11–25, 2000: Camp David Middle East summit.

September 19, 2000:   Senate grants final approval for PNTR with China.

September 22, 2000:   MKA dedicates main State Department building as the "Harry S Truman Building."

September 24–
   October 5, 2000:   Yugoslav President Milošević defeated in election by Koštunica.

September 28, 2000:   Israeli politician Ariel Sharon visits the Temple Mount/Haram al-Sharif; violence breaks out.

October 10–12, 2000:   North Korea's Vice Marshal Jo Myong Rok in Washington, visit results in a Joint Communique pledging no hostile intent between U.S and N. Korea.

October 12, 2000:   Terrorists bomb USS *Cole* in Yemen.

October 22–25, 2000:   MKA visits Pyongyang, North Korea.

November 2000–
   January 2001:   Last efforts to negotiate Middle East settlement fail.

January 20, 2001:   MKA's last day as Secretary of State.

AS UN AMBASSADOR

June 30–July 3, 1993:	Switzerland, Somalia, Maldives, Thailand, Cambodia
July 18–21, 1993:	Mexico and El Salvador
December 16, 1993:	Hungary
January 4–13, 1994:	Germany, Croatia, Poland, Hungary, Slovakia, Czech Republic, Belgium, Bulgaria, Slovenia, Albania, Romania, Netherlands
March 25– April 5, 1994:	South Africa, Mozambique, Croatia, Bosnia-Herzegovina, Sudan, Italy, Brazil, Argentina
May 8–9, 1994:	Canada
August 26– September 6, 1994:	Germany, Slovakia, Czech Republic, Austria, Moldova, Georgia, Armenia, Azerbaijan, Russia
November 24, 1994:	Haiti
December 14–16, 1994:	Belgium
February 23– March 2, 1995:	United Kingdom, Oman, Kuwait, Czech Republic, Italy, Switzerland, Honduras
March 31, 1995:	Haiti
May 1–6, 1995:	Israel, Jordan, Egypt, Czech Republic
September 3–12, 1995:	China, Burma, Philippines, Thailand, Indonesia
November 16–17, 1995:	Israel
December 8–9, 1995:	United Kingdom
January 12–13, 1996:	Hungary, Croatia, Bosnia-Herzegovina
January 17–22, 1996:	Liberia, Angola, Burundi, Rwanda, Egypt
February 6, 1996:	Haiti
March 19–23, 1996:	United Kingdom, Switzerland, Croatia, Bosnia-Herzegovina, Macedonia

April 25–30, 1996:   Belgium, Norway, Sweden, France

July 2–7, 1996:   Czech Republic, Poland, Slovakia, Austria

July 16–20, 1996:   Greece, Cyprus, Turkey

August 28–
   September 4, 1996:   Uruguay, Chile, Bolivia

AS SECRETARY OF STATE

Based on the U.S. Department of State website "Travels with the Secretary" at:
http://secretary.state.gov/www/travels/index.html

February 15–25, 1997:   Italy, Germany, France, Belgium, United Kingdom, Russia, Republic of Korea, Japan, China

March 19–22, 1997:   Finland

April 30–May 2, 1997:   Russia

May 4–10, 1997:   Guatemala, Mexico, Costa Rica, Barbados

May 25–June 1, 1997:   France, Netherlands, Portugal, Croatia, Serbia-Montenegro, Bosnia-Herzegovina

June 25–July 1, 1997:   Vietnam, Hong Kong

July 6–14, 1997:   Spain, Poland, Romania, Slovenia, Russia, Lithuania, Czech Republic

July 25–30, 1997:   Malaysia, Singapore

September 9–15, 1997:   Israel, Palestinian Authority, Egypt, Saudi Arabia, Jordan, Syria, Lebanon

October 12–17, 1997:   Venezuela, Brazil, Argentina, Haiti

November 13–24, 1997: United Kingdom, Switzerland, Qatar, Bahrain, Kuwait, Saudi Arabia, Pakistan, India, Egypt, Canada

December 4–18, 1997:   United Kingdom, Switzerland, Ethiopia, Uganda, Rwanda, Angola, Democratic Republic of Congo, South Africa, Zimbabwe, Belgium, France

December 21–23, 1997: Bosnia-Herzegovina, Italy

January 28–
   February 3, 1998:   France, Spain, United Kingdom, Kuwait, Saudi Arabia, Bahrain, Egypt, Israel, Palestinian Authority

March 5–10, 1998:   Ukraine, Italy, Germany, France, Spain, United Kingdom, Canada

March 23–25, 1998:   Italy, Germany

April 4–6, 1998:   Haiti, Trinidad and Tobago

April 15–20, 1998:   Chile

April 26–May 9, 1998:	Russia, Japan, China, Republic of Korea, Mongolia, United Kingdom
May 16–18, 1998:	United Kingdom
May 27–29, 1998:	Luxembourg
June 1–2, 1998:	Venezuela
June 3–5, 1998:	Switzerland
June 11–12, 1998:	United Kingdom
June 24–July 4, 1998:	China, Japan
July 24–August 2, 1998:	Philippines, Papua New Guinea, Australia, New Zealand
August 12–13, 1998:	Germany
August 17–19, 1998:	Kenya, Tanzania
August 29–September 3, 1998:	Croatia, Bosnia-Herzegovina, Russia, Austria
October 5–8, 1998:	Israel, Palestinian Authority, United Kingdom, Belgium
November 13–16, 1998:	Malaysia
December 7–10, 1998:	Belgium, France
December 12–15, 1998:	Israel, Palestinian Authority, Jordan
January 24–29, 1999:	Russia, Egypt, Jordan, Saudi Arabia, United Kingdom
February 13–15, 1999:	France, Mexico
February 19–23, 1999:	France
February 27–March 7, 1999:	China, Thailand, Indonesia, United Kingdom
March 10–11, 1999:	Guatemala
April 11–13, 1999:	Belgium, Norway
May 4–6, 1999:	Belgium, Germany
June 6–11, 1999:	Germany, Belgium, Macedonia
June 15–22, 1999:	Switzerland, France, Finland, Germany, Slovenia, Romania, Bulgaria
July 23–30, 1999:	Singapore, Italy, Kosovo, Bosnia-Herzegovina
September 1–13, 1999:	Morocco, Egypt, Israel, Palestinian Authority, Syria, Lebanon, Turkey, Vietnam, New Zealand
October 17–24, 1999:	Guinea, Sierra Leone, Mali, Nigeria, Kenya, Tanzania
October 31–November 2, 1999:	Norway
November 14–23, 1999:	Turkey, Greece, Italy, Slovakia, Bulgaria, Kosovo

December 5–9, 1999:	Saudi Arabia, Syria, Israel, Egypt
December 16–18, 1999:	Germany, France
January 14–16, 2000:	Colombia, Panama, Mexico
January 27– February 3, 2000:	Switzerland, Russia, Croatia
February 17–19, 2000:	Croatia, Albania
March 2–11, 2000:	Portugal, Czech Republic, Bosnia-Herzegovina, Belgium
March 17–26, 2000:	Italy, India, Bangladesh, Switzerland, Pakistan, Oman
April 13–19, 2000:	Ukraine, Kazakhstan, Kyrgyzstan, Uzbekistan
May 23–26, 2000:	Italy, United Kingdom
May 29–June 5, 2000:	Portugal, Germany, Russia, Israel, Egypt
June 5–7, 2000:	Israel, Palestinian Authority, Egypt
June 12–13, 2000:	Syria
June 21–29, 2000:	China, Republic of Korea, Poland, Israel, Palestinian Authority, Germany
July 26–August 2, 2000:	Thailand, Japan, Italy, Russia
August 14–19, 2000:	Brazil, Argentina, Chile, Ecuador, Bolivia
August 30–31, 2000:	Colombia
September 29– October 5, 2000:	Iceland, France, Germany, Egypt
October 15–18, 2000:	Egypt, Saudi Arabia
October 22–26, 2000:	Democratic People's Republic of Korea, Republic of Korea
November 13–18, 2000:	Brunei
November 25–27, 2000:	Austria
November 30– December 2, 2000:	Mexico
December 6–12, 2000:	South Africa, Mauritius, Botswana, Algeria
December 12–16, 2000:	Hungary, Belgium
January 10–12, 2001:	Spain, France

ACKNOWLEDGMENTS

A FEW DAYS AFTER I LEFT OFFICE, I went with friends from my college days to a health spa, Rancho La Puerta, in Mexico. It proved to be a perfect choice, although it had a stern rule forbidding phone calls from anyone during certain times. Anyone except Harvey Weinstein. I won't try to speculate how he managed it, but Harvey got through at least three times to talk about my book and his hope that I would choose Miramax Books as its publisher. Harvey's powers of persuasion are legendary, but it was his, Tina Brown's, and Jonathan Burnham's enthusiasm and appreciation for the historical context in which I hoped to write my autobiography that made my decision an easy one.

In many ways, writing my memoirs has been a solitary experience. I alone can reflect on my life, recall pleasant and unpleasant moments, and describe my feelings. But as with diplomacy, I didn't do it alone. For the views and recollections contained in this volume, I accept full responsibility. For the book's existence, I have many people to thank and am pleased to do so.

Bill Woodward is rightfully considered one of the most gifted speechwriters in the country, and I was fortunate that he worked for me through the UN and Secretary of State days. He knew the issues so well that I could not imagine writing about those years without him. He was my collaborator and we learned that working on a book is a special ordeal. We joke that it is a miracle our friendship survived almost three years of searching for the right words, tone, and substance for each part of the story I had to tell. My chief researcher, Laurie Dundon, has been extraordinary. She has reviewed thousands of official documents, verified facts with lightning speed, asked probing questions, and shared her particular expertise on the Balkans. Elaine Shocas has played a unique role in my life and in every aspect of this book. With uncommon insights and a remarkable memory, she has added color, depth, and warmth to the tale.

Richard Cohen, a superb editor as well as an accomplished author, helped me transform what would have been a massive tome into a manageable text. He taught me, often under protest, that "less is more." He survived my endless questions and I survived his sometimes very British edits to my American words. Sarah Crichton helped me find my voice early on and continued to provide invaluable advice—as well as wonderfully irreverent emails. It was not essential but certainly is a bonus that both my editors are now my friends.

Jonathan Burnham, president and editor-in-chief of Miramax Books, offered wise counsel and a steady hand, as well as graciously extending my deadline on more than one occasion. He is that rarity, a man both elegant and modest. My thanks also go to the entire Miramax team for its hard work, professionalism and good company: Publisher Kathy Schneider, Susan Mercandetti, Hilary Bass, Dev Chatillon, Jennifer Sanger, Bruce Mason, Jaime Horn, JillEllyn Riley, Jennifer Besser, and Andrew Bevan. Kristin Powers, director of production, did a remarkable job in overseeing every detail of this book. I am grateful for the work of my international literary agent Linda Michaels and her associates Teresa Cavanaugh and Daniela Rapp and my skilled attorneys Robert Barnett and Deneen Howell of Williams and Connolly LLP.

Among those who shared their perspective and provided guidance concerning what to include were Gabriel García Márquez, Michael Beschloss, Tom Oliphant, Lissa Muscatine, and Bradley Graham. Tina Brown was present at the inception of this project and never wavered in her support; I am delighted that she remains a part of my life.

The help of my Czech and Slovak friends has been invaluable. Many were dissidents during Czechoslovakia's darkest days and in the forefront of events described in this volume. Their assistance has both enriched the material and made it more accurate: Michael Žantovský, Tomáš Kraus, Martin Palouš, Alexandr Vondra, Martin Butora, Zora Buterová, Pavol Demeš, and Jaroslav Šedivý.

Many gave generously of their time and expertise, sharing memories or reading all or parts of the manuscript: David Andrews, Ralph Alswang, Carol Browner, Marcia Burick, David Carpenter, Pat Carter, Bonnie Cohen, Kitty Bartels DiMartino, Wini and Mike Freund, Bob Gallucci, Suzy George, Marcia Greenberger, David Hale, Janet Howard, Cameron Hume, Rick Inderfurth, Stu Jones, Barbara Larkin, Mary Jane Lewis, Judy Lichtman, Evelyn Lieberman, Frank and Dale Loy, Rod and Larissa MacFarquhar, Millie Meyers, Aaron Miller, Jim O'Brien, Susan Rice, Sharon Robinson, Lula Rodriguez, Dennis Ross, Jamie Rubin, David Scheffer, Debi Schiff, Rika and Carl Schmidt, Marie Šedivá, Stu Seldowitz, John Shattuck, Wendy Sherman, Dick Shinnick, Mo Steinbruner, Lisa Švejdová, Mark Talisman, Susan and David Terris, Toni Verstanding, Melanne Verveer, Jenonne Walker, Nichole Tucker Walton, Meridith Webster, David Welch, Maggie Williams, and Alex Wolff.

Among the colleagues and staff who helped sustain me in a million ways through their daily support were Diana Sierra, Margo Morris, and Zina Brown. Nate Tibbits, my technology guru, honed my computer skills and retrieved countless pages I would otherwise have lost. Martha Fuenzalida, Lucia Rente, Dorothy Burgess, and Margo Carper kept my body and soul together over many years. My interns never ceased to amaze me with their ingenuity and enthusiasm for every task: Tuck Evans, Bailey Hand, Erin Lanahan, Nell McGarity, Jane Rhee, Sonja Renander, Ryan Rippel, Rachel Shields, and especially Kris Hamel, Kerryann Locey, Trey Street, and Julia Voelker. Sergeant Louis Rinaldi and his team of New York City's Amtrak Police Department have assured my safe passage for many years.

The material in this book is based in large part on official government documents from my years in office. The State Department has reviewed this text to ensure that issues of national security are not compromised. I am required by law to say what is true, which is that the opinions and characterization in this book are my own and do not necessarily represent official positions of the United States government. My appreciation goes to Secretary of State Colin Powell for offering the complete cooperation of the department, including the assistance of Under Secretary of State for Management Grant Green, Assistant Secretary for Administration Bill Eaton, Deputy Legal Advisor Jim Thessin, Paul Claussen and Evan Duncan of the office of the Historian, Maryann Alt, chief of the research section, U.S. mission to the United Nations, and the entire Secretariat Staff—S/S and S/S–EX, especially George Rowland. I would like to acknowledge and thank the team headed by Margaret Grafeld and Alice Ritchie for its extensive work; in particular, Mark Ramee for carefully reviewing the manuscript and managing the clearance process and Mitzi Hardrick for supporting our many research requests. I also thank the officials of Georgetown University's Edmund A. Walsh School of Foreign Service and the Mortara Center for International Studies for their assistance; the officials and staff of the Kent Denver School, the University of Denver's Graduate School of International Studies and Penrose Library, *The Denver Post* and the Rockefeller Foundation Archives for providing me with documents, news articles, and photographs.

The production of any book is a major undertaking and I appreciate the diligence and creativity of those involved in this effort: Peg Haller, Susan Groarke, Rachel Smith, Brenda Horrigan, Nancy Wolff, Pat Fogarty, Carrie Smith, Ink, Inc., and Doyle Partners. I am very grateful to Diana Walker and all the photographers and the cartoonists for allowing me to reproduce their work. On many occasions over many years, I have told photographer Timothy Greenfield-Sanders that he has done as well as anyone could with the material before him.

It isn't easy having an older sister or mother become a public figure. While it has some advantages—meeting the President and attending a few state dinners—it is also intrusive. So I want to thank my family. They were not only great sports: my sister Kathy, brother John, and his wife Pam were crucial in reconstructing our family's history. Our parents always encouraged "family solidarity" and would be delighted that we have achieved it and also enjoy it.

I especially want to recognize and thank two of my cousins. Alena Korbel provided recollections about our years in London during the war. Dáša Šimová filled in many blanks in our family's story and I regret that she had to relive some painful times in doing so. We are now catching up for the many years we missed.

My daughters Alice, Anne, and Katie, my sons-in-law and grandchildren kept me simultaneously buoyed and grounded with love and humor. What more could I ask?

I HAVE ALWAYS BELIEVED there is a special place in Hell reserved for those who receive recognition and do not share credit. If so, there may already be a very warm seat set aside for me. Nearly every chapter of the early drafts of parts two through four of this book included sections devoted to the people who worked with me on the various issues involved. My editor called these the "Academy Award thank-you" sections and marked them with a red pen (or more accurately, the delete button). I insisted that many names go back in, but had to admit that a fully accurate description of the teamwork involved in our diplomacy made for slow reading. As a result, I regret to say that the hard work and creativity of State Department colleagues are often not recounted with the specificity I originally intended or the detail warranted by reality. I am very sorry for that and have appended the list below as an act of partial expiation. I was and remain extremely grateful to those cited below and many others not mentioned, including our ambassadors, embassy staffs, civil servants, Foreign Service officers, Foreign Service nationals, special advisors, and envoys who helped and supported me—and the foreign policy of the United States—with their energy, advice, ideas, and day-to-day professionalism. Please accept my thanks for your assistance and friendship, and for greatly enriching the substance of the material contained in this volume.

UNITED STATES MISSION TO THE UNITED NATIONS (1994–1997)
Ambassadors Edward "Ned" Walker, Jr., Edward "Skip" Gnehm, Jr., Karl "Rick" Inderfurth, Victor Marrero, Irvin Hicks, David Birenbaum, Richard Sklar, Herbert Donald Gelber.

Officers and Staff
Patsy Agee, Maryann Alt, Luiz Amaral, Paul Aronsohn, Joan Baldridge, Jonathan Barrett, Kitty Bartels, Elmira Bayrasli, John Blaney, John Boardman, Dorothy Burgess, Nancy Buss, Graham Cannon, Frantzy Charlemagne, William Clontz, Douglas Coffman, Thomas Countryman, John Cuddihy, Jeffrey De Laurentis, Thomas Donlon, Walter Douglas, Hugh Dugan, Caroline Dulin-Shaw, Jordana Dym, David Ettinger, Angel Escobar, Ivan Ferber, Jean Fiorie, George Ford, Warren Forrest, Peter Fromuth, Adele Gilliam,

Sandra Grandison, Russell Graham, Rebecca Gaghen, Jeffrey Glassman, William Grant, Robert Grey, Joan Grippe, John Guerra, David Hale, Margaret "Nini" Hawthorne, Fiona Higgins, Cameron Hume, Frank Kirchoff, Patricia Kuffler, Stanley Jakubowski, Barbara Jones, Stuart Jones, Thomas Kearney, Holly Kenworthy, Craig Kuehl, Ellen Laipson, Harvey Langholtz, Leslie Lebl, Wayne Logsdon, Vivienne Manber, Edward Marks, Robert McCarthy, Daphne Martinez, Millie Meyers, John Menzies, Kara McGuire Minar, Robert Moller, Suzanne McPartland, Richard Naughton, Debra Nelson, Hong Ngo Nguyen, James O'Brien, Theodore Osius, Matthew Palmer, Leroy Parham, Wayne Rosen, Robert Rosenstock, Dorothy Sampas, David Scheffer, Rosalinda Seldowitz, Stuart Seldowitz, Scott Shaw, Susan Shearouse, Michael Sheehan, Laurie Shestack, John Singler, Jane Stich, Anne Stoddard, Krissy Sudano, Eugene Tadie, Michael Viggiano, William Wallace, Erin Walsh, Fanny Weisblatt, Dennis Welch, John Wiecks, Bisa Williams-Manigault, Carolyn Willson, Seth Winnick, William Wood, Frances Zwenig, and the men and women of the Diplomatic Security Service, New York Field Office.

I thank Secretary Warren Christopher and his entire team for their support and assistance during my years as U.S. permanent representative to the United Nations, especially Strobe Talbott, Peter Tarnoff, Thomas Donilon, Molly Raiser, Joan Spero, Lynn Davis, Richard Moose, Brian Atwood, Marc Grossman, Kenneth Brill, William Burns, Patrick Kennedy, Wendy Sherman, Genta Hawkins-Holmes, James Thessin, Maura Harty, Ertharin Cousin, and George Rowland, as well as Douglas Bennett, George Ward, Melinda Kimble and the entire Bureau of International Organization Affairs.

DEPARTMENT OF STATE (1997–2001)

Assistant and acting assistant secretaries of state and their bureaus and other department officials and their staffs

Administration: Patrick Kennedy.

African Affairs: Johnnie Carson, George Moose, Susan Rice.

Arms Control: Avis Bohlen, Lucas Fisher.

Coordinator for Counterterrorism: Christopher Ross, Michael Sheehan, Philip Wilcox.

Consular Affairs: Mary Ryan.

Democracy, Human Rights, and Labor: Harold Koh, John Shattuck.

Diplomatic Security and Office of Foreign Missions: Eric Boswell, David Carpenter, Patrick Kennedy.

East Asian and Pacific Affairs: Charles Kartman, Stanley Roth.

Economic and Business Affairs: Alan Larson, Brian Samuel,
Earl Anthony Wayne.

Educational and Cultural Affairs: William Bader.

Executive Secretary: William Burns, Kristie Kenney.

European Affairs: James Dobbins, Marc Grossman, John Kornblum.

Finance and Management Policy/CFO: Kathleen Charles, Bert Edwards,
Richard Greene.

Foreign Service Institute: Ruth Davis, Teresita Schaffer, Ruth Whiteside.

Human Resources/DG: Edward Gnehm, Jr., Marc Grossman,
Anthony Quainton.

Information Resource Management/CIO: Fernando Burbano,
Andrew Winter.

Inspector General: Jacquelyn Williams-Bridgers.

Intelligence and Research: Edward Abington, Thomas Fingar, Toby Gati,
Donald Keyser, Daniel Kurtzer, Phyllis Oakley, J. Stapleton Roy.

International Narcotics and Law Enforcement Affairs: Jane Becker,
J. Rand Beers, Robert Gelbard.

International Organization Affairs: Princeton Lyman, C. David Welch.

Legal Adviser: David Andrews, Michael Matheson, James Thessin.

Legislative Affairs: Barbara Larkin.

Near Eastern Affairs: Martin Indyk, Elizabeth Jones, Edward Walker, Jr.,
C. David Welch.

Nonproliferation: John Barker, Robert Einhorn.

Oceans and International Environmental and Scientific Affairs:
Eileen Claussen, Melinda Kimble, David Sandalow.

Policy Planning: Gregory Craig, Morton Halperin, Alan Romberg.

Political-Military Affairs: Thomas McNamara, Eric Newsom.

Population, Refugees, and Migration: Phyllis Oakley, Julia Taft.

Public Affairs: Richard Boucher, Nicholas Burns, James Rubin.

Protocol: Mary Mel French, Molly Raiser.

Resources, Plans, and Policy: Craig Johnstone, Anne Richard.

Science and Technology: Norman Neureiter.

South Asian Affairs: Karl Inderfurth, E. Gipson Lanpher, Robin Raphel.

Verification and Compliance: Edward Lacey, Owen Sheaks.

Western Hemisphere Affairs: Jeffrey Davidow, Peter Romero.

Ambassador-at-Large for International Religious Freedom: Robert Seiple.

Ambassador-at-Large for Newly Independent States: James Collins, Stephen Sestanovich.

Ambassador-at-Large for War Crimes Issues: David Scheffer.

Other principal officers, staff, and programs

Art in Embassies Program and Friends of Art and Preservation in Embassies (FAPE).

Blair House: Benedicte Valentiner, Randall Bumgardner.

Diplomatic Reception Rooms: Gail Serfaty, Wileva Johnston, Candida Pulupa.

Equal Employment Opportunity and Civil Rights: Deidre Davis.

Executive Secretariat: Gregory Berry, Robert Blake, John Campbell, Rose Likins, Stephen Mull, Carol Perez, Peter Petrihos, Maureen Quinn, Neal Walsh, Gretchen Welch, Alejandro Wolff.

Historian: William Slany, Marc Susser.

International Information Programs: John Dwyer, Jonathan Spalter.

Legal Advisers: Jamison Borek, Jonathan Schwartz, Melinda Chandler.

Legislative Affairs: Shirley Cooks, Meg Donovan, Michael Guest, Susan Jacobs, Kay King, Michael Klosson, Valerie Mims, Peter Yeo.

Medical Services: Cedric Dumont.

Operations Center: Karl Hofmann, Rose Likins, Harry Thomas, Sharon Weiner.

Policy Planning: Lee Feinstein, James O'Brien. Speechwriters: Taras Bazyluk, Durriya Ghadiali, Lukas Haynes, Heather Hurlburt, Justin Leites, Thomas Malinowski. Open Forum officials.

Protocol: David Pryor, Larry Dunham, Charles Kinn, Debra Schiff, Laura Wills.

President's Interagency Council on Women: Theresa Loar, Kathy Hendrix, Lidia Soto-Harmon.

Public Affairs: Deputy Spokesmen Glynn Davis, James Foley, Lee McLeeny, Philip Reeker.

Secretariat Line: James Bean, Paul Jones, Richard Mills, Carol Perez.

Secretary's Executive Assistants: David Hale, Alejandro Wolff.

Secretary's Executive Director: Richard Shinnick.

Secretary's Executive Office: Colombia Barrosse, Elmira Bayrasli, Jennifer Bonner, Ben Chang, John Crawley, Marie Damour, Kelly Degnan, Richard Denniston, Linda Dewan, Sheila Dyson, Price Floyd, Patrice Frey, Thomas Kelsey, Elizabeth Lineberry, Laurie Major, Heather McCullough,

Suzanne McPartland, David Pressman, Todd Robinson, Jane Stich, Nichole Tucker, Bisa Williams-Manigault, Diana Zicklin.

Unions and Professional Associations:
American Foreign Service Association (AFSA): Marshall Adair, Daniel Geisler, F.A."Tex" Harris, Alphonse LaPorta, John Naland and the members of the American Federation of Government Employees (AFGE).

Unsung Heroes: Sergeant Major Bruce and all the unsung heroes of the State Department.

White House Liaison: Charles Duncan.

I would like to extend my appreciation to all my colleagues at the Agency for International Development (AID), especially Brady Anderson, Brian Atwood, Harriet Babbitt, and Richard McCall. I salute the many dedicated public servants—current and former—from the United States Information Agency (USIA) and the Arms Control and Disarmament Agency (ACDA), who are now part of the State Department family, especially Joseph Duffey, Penn Kemble, and John Holum.

My thanks go to my military advisors and their aides from the Joint Chiefs of Staff for their assistance and for circumnavigating the globe with me many times: General Richard Meyers, General Robert "Doc" Foglesong, Lt. General Donald Kerrick, and Admiral Walter Doran.